W9-ARX-818

Personal Finance

A Lifetime Responsibility

Grady Kimbrell

Nathan Dungan

ST. PAUL • LOS ANGELES • INDIANAPOLIS

Developmental Editors: Cheryl Drivdahl, Trudy Muller, Susan Scott
Production Editor: Donna Mears
Copy Editor: Michele Gitlin
Assistant Editor: Hilary Finley
Editorial and Production Assistant: Amanda Tristano
Proofreader: Carol Rogers
Indexer: Ina Gravitz
Design and Production: Hespenheide Design
Production: Laurie Miller, Patti Zeman
Proofreader: Bridget Neumayr
Illustrator: Randy Miyake
Photo Researcher: Gabe Manchego

Cover Image: Scott Hirko Photography
Photo Credits and Acknowledgments: Credits and acknowledgments are listed on pages 466–467.

We have made every effort to trace the ownership of all copyrighted material and to secure permission from copyright holders. In the event of any question arising as to the use of any material, we will be pleased to make the necessary corrections in future printings. Thanks are due to the aforementioned authors, publishers, and agents for permission to use the materials indicated.

ISBN 978-0-82194-254-3

875 Montreal Way
St. Paul, MN 55102
E-mail: educate@emcp.com
Web site: www.emcp.com

Printed in the United States of America

17 16 15 14 13 12 11 4 5 6 7 8 9 10

About the Authors

Grady Kimbrell is a nationally recognized author and educator in business education. His teaching career includes instruction at the secondary, college, and adult education levels. His students have received numerous state awards in a variety of specialties. Visitors from throughout the United States have traveled to consult with him and study the cooperative education programs he has developed.

Kimbrell has served on numerous state instructional program committees and writing teams, designed educational computer programs, and produced educational films. He has been a presenter at educational conferences and conventions and has also planned major education conferences. As a way of providing assistance to other educators, Kimbrell has written many magazine and newspaper articles as well as more than a dozen textbooks.

As a pioneer in the use of computer technology for educational research, Kimbrell has assisted school districts with a variety of research and evaluation activities. His contributions in the field of education led to his inclusion in the Educators' Hall of Fame at his alma mater, Southwestern College, and in Who's Who in America.

Kimbrell holds degrees in business administration, educational psychology, and business education, and he has completed additional advanced course work in professional education.

Nathan Dungan is the founder and president of Share Save Spend®, an organization that helps youth and adults achieve financial sanity by developing and maintaining healthy financial habits. He has been widely quoted in numerous national newspapers and news magazines; has been a featured guest on CBS, CNN, PBS, and public radio; and created and hosted a Twin Cities public television special called *Money 'n' Sanity.* His book *Prodigal Sons and Material Girls: How Not to Be Your Child's ATM* was released in 2003.

Before founding Share Save Spend, Nathan was a top-performing financial adviser and vice president of marketing for a Fortune™ 500 financial services company. He earned his bachelor's degree from St. Olaf College, Northfield, Minnesota, and is a graduate of the University of Minnesota's Carlson School of Management Executive Development Program.

Content Reviewers and Program Contributors

Jenny Birkmeier
Anoka High School
Coon Rapids, Minnesota

Cheryl Burns
Bald Knob High School
Bald Knob, Arkansas

Terri Burton
Van Buren High School
Van Buren, Arkansas

Tim Casper
Hillsboro High School
Hillsboro, Oregon

Linda Lodgaard
Mounds View High School
St. Paul, Minnesota

Judy Martin
South Western High School
York, Pennsylvania

Renatta Meddick
Delsea Regional High School
Franklinville, New Jersey

Matthew Siers
Foley High School
Foley, Minnesota

Melissa Smith
Rogers High School
Rogers, Arkansas

Heidi Stirm
Melba High School
Melba, Idaho

Eileen Tims
Memorial Senior High School
Houston, Texas

Ruth Wilson-Phillips
Charles D. Owen High School
Black Mountain, North Carolina

Contents in Brief

Table of Contents

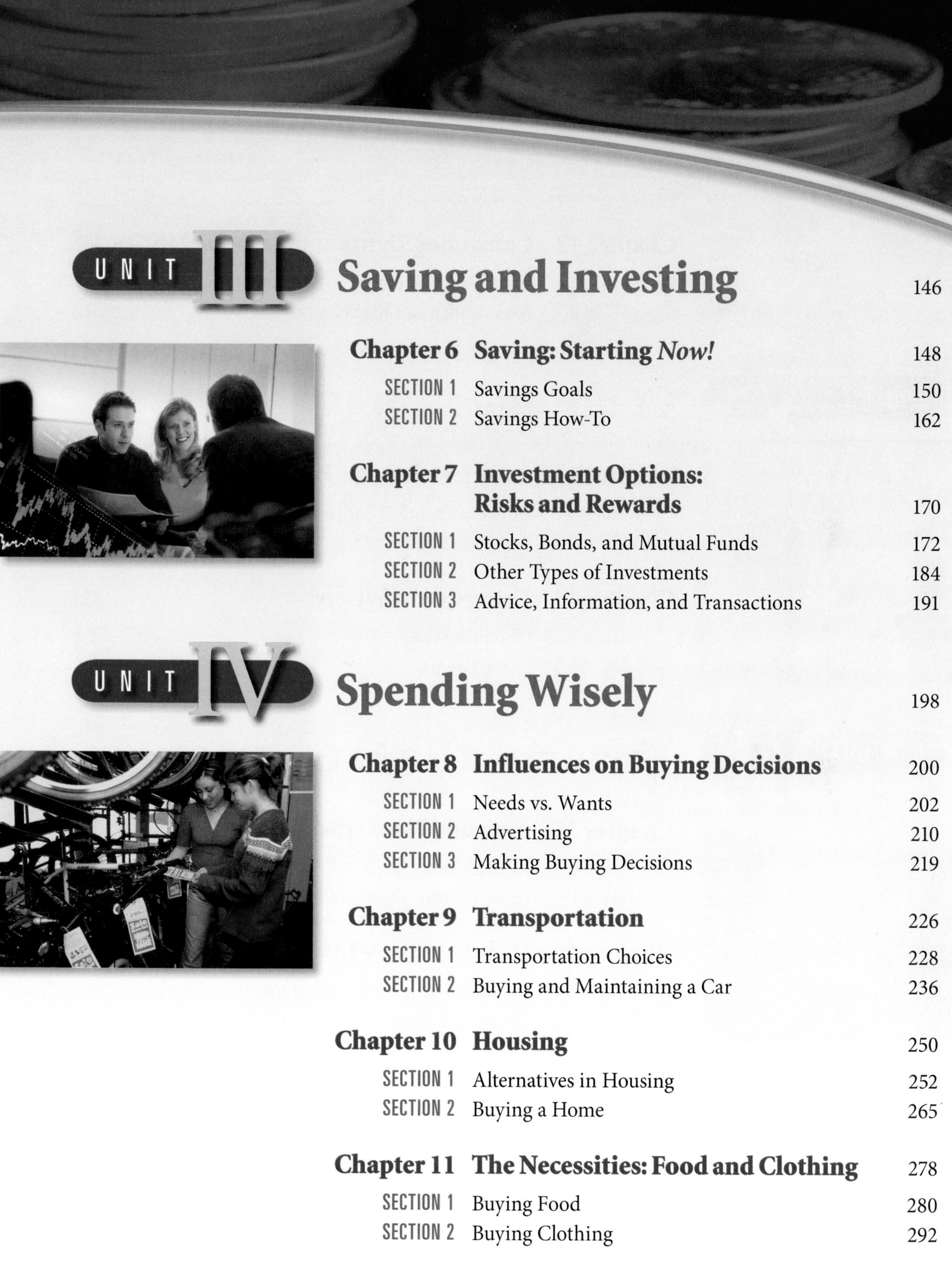

Studying Personal Finance

Chances are, *Personal Finance: A Lifetime Responsibility* is only one of several classes you are taking right now. You are probably going full speed from early in the morning until late in the evening, trying to fit in family, friends, school, work, recreation—and on and on and on. Being so busy, you would probably agree that you need to make the most of your study time. The following suggestions can help you become a more efficient learner, and perhaps increase your grade point average, while at the same time reducing your stress level.

A Study Technique That Works

Have you ever been reading for a while and suddenly realized that you have no idea what you just read? It happens to everyone. Maybe you were distracted or have other things on your mind, or maybe you are just tired.

A simple study technique can help you overcome these obstacles and improve your reading comprehension. You can use this method while studying *Personal Finance*, as well as for your other courses. This strategy is called SQ3R.

The acronym **SQ3R** stands for *Survey, Question, Read, Recite, and Review.* The following descriptions tell how to use SQ3R to learn more in less time. Each explanation includes specific directions for using SQ3R with *Personal Finance.*

S = Survey The first step in studying a book is to look it over, or survey it. Do not simply open your book and begin reading. Instead, scan the table of contents to get a feel for what the book will cover. Flip through the pages to get an idea of how the text is laid out, how much writing is on each page, and what kinds of features you will see.

Before you read a chapter, try to get a broad picture of it—to prepare your mind for what you are about to learn. Read the chapter and section titles, headings, subheadings, captions, and boldfaced key words. Look at the photos and figures. Try to identify the main ideas.

At the beginning of each chapter, *Personal Finance* has a focus feature called "Fact or Fiction." This gives true-or-false sentences about the most important topics covered. See how many you can answer. In addition, the front of each section presents a "Key Terms" list. See how many of these you can define before you begin your reading.

Fact or Fiction

What do you think? Are the following statements true or false? If you think they are false, then say what is true.

1. Most donors to charity are very wealthy.
2. Financial planning takes a lot of time and effort to do correctly.
3. It is best not to involve others in your financial planning, which is a private, personal matter.
4. When developing a financial plan, you have to consider your current financial situation—even if you plan to change everything.
5. Volunteering your time is just as important as sharing your money.

Q = Question After you survey a chapter, ask yourself some questions about what you have seen: What is the chapter about? What do I already know about the topic? (You will probably know more about some topics than others.) What do I hope to learn?

After you have formed a few questions about a chapter in *Personal Finance*, turn to the start of each section and read the "Focus Questions." These straightforward questions indicate what is to come. Try answering as many as possible before you begin reading the section.

> **Focus Questions**
>
> **1.** Why is it important to think about sharing your resources (money and time) with a cause or causes you believe in?
>
> **2.** What causes do you feel most strongly about? If you could do one thing to make the world a better place, what would it be?
>
> **3.** What are at least three ways you can share your time or money with a cause you believe in?

R(1) = Read The first *R* in SQ3R refers to *read*. You are now ready to read the chapter. Try to discover the things you hoped to learn during the Question step of SQ3R. As an active reader, you will think of new questions while you read. Write them down and look for the answers, or talk with your teacher about them.

While reading *Personal Finance*, try answering the "Fact or Fiction" questions from the beginning of the chapter and the "Focus Questions" from the beginning of the section. Also notice the boldfaced key terms and their definitions in the text and in the margin. Studying these terms can help you focus on the main points of the text. These terms also appear in the Glossary at the back of the book.

Each chapter of *Personal Finance* has a number of boxed features that tell stories, present examples, give facts, and show you how to find out more. These features can help you make connections between what you are reading and the real world—your world.

LOOK Before You Leap

Danielle is an advertising layout artist at the local newspaper. She wants to study psychology and eventually design advertising campaigns for a major ad agency. College will be necessary. She has visited three campuses of her state's public university, as well as a nearby private university.

All the colleges she is considering have strong art and psychology departments. They each have good relationships with businesses and public agencies that offer student internships. Any of them would be a good choice. Danielle decides she will attend whichever one accepts her first.

Danielle knows her education would cost more at the private college than at a state university, but she is shocked to learn it would actually cost *four times* as much. She is ready to cross the private school off her list—but then her boss convinces her that she should check in financial aid. He says she will need to contact the private school's aid office. He also points her to helpful Web sites.

A U.S. government site (http://fin.emcp.net/studentaid) has information about federal loans and grants. She can even calculate the amount she would be eligible for. The College Board site (http://fin.emcp.net/collegeboard) can help identify more than 2,000 other sources of funding, including scholarships offered by specific industries—such as advertising, Danielle's choice. She thinks maybe she can find a way to attend the more expensive college.

Before Enrolling

1. Why might it be worth it to spend the extra money to attend a private college?
2. Why would specific industries offer scholarships to college students?
3. Why is it a good idea to explore your financing options before applying for admission to a college?

Did You Know?

The average American experiences more than 5,000 advertising impressions every day. That is 1 advertising impression every 17 seconds! What are advertising impressions? They include TV commercials, online ads, commercial text messages, logos on clothing, billboards pushing products, and much, much more. How do you think those messages affect an individual's expenses?

Going Global

What is the number one life expectation of teens around the world? In the 2006 GenWorld Teen Study conducted by the public relations firm Energy BBDO, 70 percent of teens surveyed in thirteen countries said that financial security was most important.

In fact, teens in eight of the thirteen countries ranked their top life expectation as either "being better off financially than my parents," "being financially secure," or "being rich." A whopping 50 percent expect to own their own business someday.

Interestingly, in response to a different question, 70 percent also answered that they would "fight for a cause I believe in." So although teens around the world value financial security, they also value helping others.

Thinking Globally

1. Ask five or six of your classmates what their number one life expectation is. How do their answers compare with the percentages in the GenWorld Teen Study?
2. How could a goal of financial security also enable you to effectively work for a cause you believe in?

You Can Succeed Financially

In 2006, the only grocery store in rural Truman, Minnesota, closed—and then reopened. The Main Street Market's new lease on life came from 17-year-old Nick Graham, a high school student and a member of the school's football team.

After hearing that the grocery store had closed, Nick made a business plan. He used his life savings to invest in the store. A $10,000 down payment—saved mostly from years of working on his uncle's turkey farm—clinched the deal. Nick bought the store and now runs it.

His hard work is paying off. Most of Truman's residents choose to shop at Main Street Market rather than drive the 24-mile round trip to shop in the larger town of Fairmont, Minnesota. And Nick's optimism and work ethic are rubbing off on Truman. People see his store as an inspiration. They have continued rebuilding Main Street by reopening other shuttered storefronts.

What Would You Do?

1. Do you know of a neighborhood where a lot of businesses are closing? If you owned a business in that area would you move—or stay? Why? Explain your answer.
2. How can your values influence your decision in the situation described above (#1)?
3. In what other ways can teens help in the revitalization of their town or neighborhood?

R(2) = Recite The second *R* stands for *recite.* It does not do any good to read a long passage and then simply go on to another. Instead, restate the main idea of each passage in your own words—out loud, if possible. Write down your summary in your notes, as described on the next page. This will help you think about what you have just read, to make sure that you understand and remember the most important points.

As you read *Personal Finance,* stop at the end of each paragraph or before each subhead, and summarize what you just read. Then, write your summary in your notes. At the end of each chapter is a "Chapter Review and Assessment." The first part of this is a "Chapter Summary" that contains a summary of the main points. Recite these and then restate them in your own words.

R(3) = Review The third *R* stands for *review.* After reading a section or a chapter, check to find out what you remember. Try to answer the questions you thought of before you began reading.

At the end of each section of *Personal Finance* is a "Section Assessment" that includes "Factual Recall" questions and "Critical Thinking" questions. Answering these can help you hold on to all of the information you are taking in. In addition, the "Chapter Review and Assessment" is full of exercises to help you review and remember the important points from the sections. You could also make flash cards of the key terms to help you review. Finally, you will find even more review materials, including study guides and practice tests, at the Web site for *Personal Finance: A Lifetime Responsibility*—www.emcp.net/finance/URL.

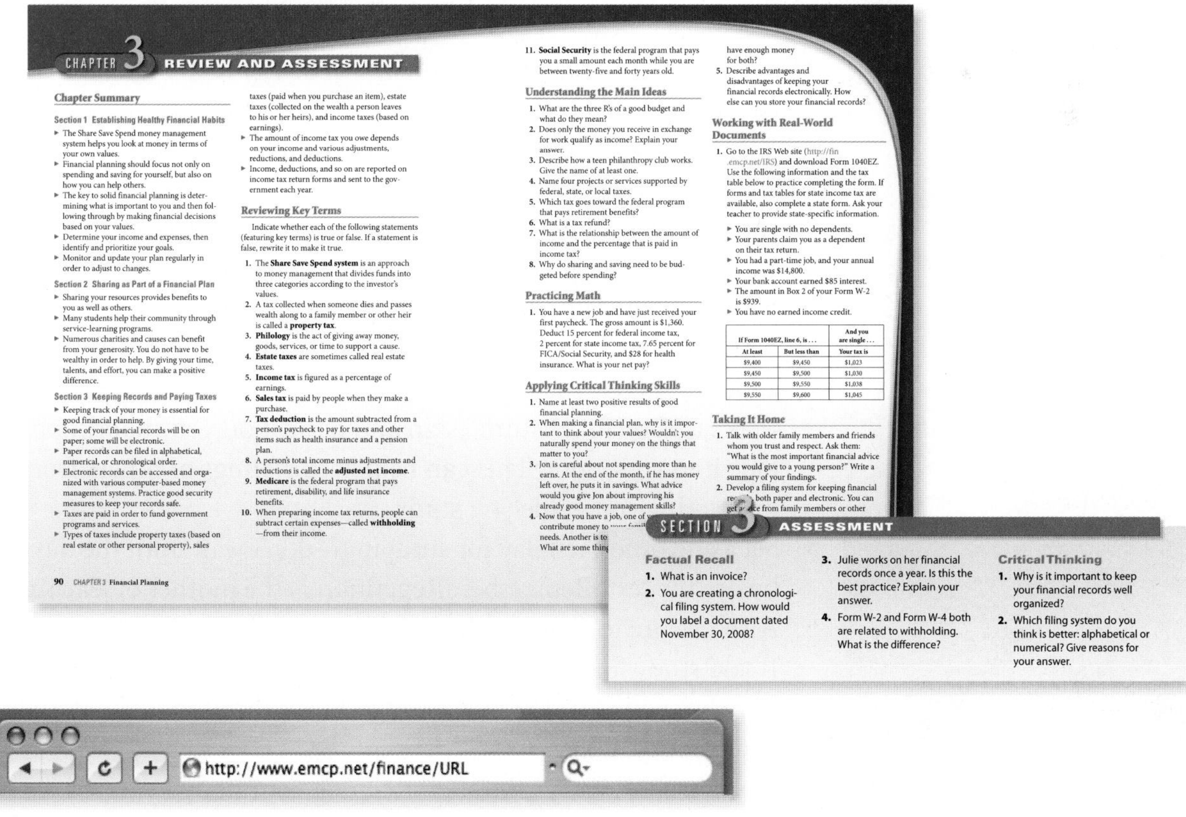

CHAPTER 3 REVIEW AND ASSESSMENT

Chapter Summary

Section 1 Establishing Healthy Financial Habits

- The Share Save Spend money management system helps you look at money in terms of your own values.
- Financial planning should focus not only on spending and saving for yourself, but also on how you can help others.
- The key to solid financial planning is determining what is important to you and then following through by making financial decisions based on your values.
- Determine your income and expenses, then identify and prioritize your goals.
- Monitor and update your plan regularly in order to adjust to changes.

Section 2 Sharing as Part of a Financial Plan

- Sharing your resources provides benefits to you as well as others.
- Many students help their community through service-learning programs.
- Numerous charities and causes can benefit from your generosity. You do not have to be wealthy in order to help. By giving your time, talents, and effort, you can make a positive difference.

Section 3 Keeping Records and Paying Taxes

- Keeping track of your money is essential for good financial planning.
- Some of your financial records will be on paper; some will be electronic.
- Paper records can be filed in alphabetical, numerical, or chronological order.
- Electronic records can be accessed and organized with various computer-based money management systems. Practice good security measures to keep your records safe.
- Taxes are paid in order to fund government programs and services.
- Types of taxes include property taxes (based on real estate or other personal property), sales taxes (paid when you purchase an item), estate taxes (collected on the wealth a person leaves to his or her heirs), and income taxes (based on earnings).
- The amount of income tax you owe depends on your income and various adjustments, reductions, and deductions.
- Income, deductions, and so on are reported on income tax return forms and sent to the government each year.

Reviewing Key Terms

Indicate whether each of the following statements (featuring key terms) is true or false. If a statement is false, rewrite it to make it true.

1. The **Share Save Spend system** is an approach to money management that divides funds into three categories according to the investor's values.
2. A tax collected when someone dies and passes wealth along to a family member or other heir is called a **property tax**.
3. **Philology** is the act of giving away money, goods, services, or time to support a cause.
4. **Estate taxes** are sometimes called real estate taxes.
5. **Income tax** is figured as a percentage of earnings.
6. **Sales tax** is paid by people when they make a purchase.
7. **Tax deduction** is the amount subtracted from a person's paycheck to pay for taxes and other items such as health insurance and a pension plan.
8. A person's total income minus adjustments and reductions is called the **adjusted net income**.
9. **Medicare** is the federal program that pays retirement, disability, and life insurance benefits.
10. When preparing income tax returns, people can subtract certain expenses—called **withholding** —from their income.
11. **Social Security** is the federal program that pays you a small amount each month while you are between twenty-five and forty years old.

Understanding the Main Ideas

1. What are the three R's of a good budget and what do they mean?
2. Does only the money you receive in exchange for work qualify as income? Explain your answer.
3. Describe how a teen philanthropy club works. Give the name of at least one.
4. Name four projects or services supported by federal, state, or local taxes.
5. Which tax goes toward the federal program that pays retirement benefits?
6. What is a tax refund?
7. What is the relationship between the amount of income and the percentage that is paid in income tax?
8. Why do sharing and saving need to be budgeted before spending?

Practicing Math

1. You have a new job and have just received your first paycheck. The gross amount is $1,360. Deduct 15 percent for federal income tax, 2 percent for state income tax, 7.65 percent for FICA/Social Security, and $28 for health insurance. What is your net pay?

Applying Critical Thinking Skills

1. Name at least two positive results of good financial planning.
2. When making a financial plan, why is it important to think about your values? Wouldn't you naturally spend your money on the things that matter to you?
3. Jon is careful about not spending more than he earns. At the end of the month, if he has money left over, he puts it in savings. What advice would you give Jon about improving his already good money management skills?
4. Now that you have a job, one of ... contribute money to ... needs. Another is to ... What are some thin... have enough money for both?
5. Describe advantages and disadvantages of keeping your financial records electronically. How else can you store your financial records?

Working with Real-World Documents

1. Go to the IRS Web site (http://fin.emcp.net/IRS) and download Form 1040EZ. Use the following information and the tax table below to practice completing the form. If forms and tax tables for state income tax are available, also complete a state form. Ask your teacher to provide state-specific information.
   - You are single with no dependents.
   - Your parents claim you as a dependent on their tax return.
   - You had a part-time job, and your annual income was $14,800.
   - Your bank account earned $85 interest.
   - The amount in Box 2 of your Form W-2 is $939.
   - You have no earned income credit.

If Form 1040EZ, line 6, is . . .		And you are single . . .
At least	But less than	Your tax is
$9,400	$9,450	$1,023
$9,450	$9,500	$1,030
$9,500	$9,550	$1,038
$9,550	$9,600	$1,045

Taking It Home

1. Talk with older family members and friends whom you trust and respect. Ask them: "What is the most important financial advice you would give to a young person?" Write a summary of your findings.
2. Develop a filing system for keeping financial re... both paper and electronic. You can get ...ce from family members or other

90 CHAPTER 3 Financial Planning

SECTION 3 ASSESSMENT

Factual Recall

1. What is an invoice?
2. You are creating a chronological filing system. How would you label a document dated November 30, 2008?
3. Julie works on her financial records once a year. Is this the best practice? Explain your answer.
4. Form W-2 and Form W-4 both are related to withholding. What is the difference?

Critical Thinking

1. Why is it important to keep your financial records well organized?
2. Which filing system do you think is better: alphabetical or numerical? Give reasons for your answer.

Creating a Good Study Space

If your chair squeaks, if your room is too dark, or if too much noise is coming from the family room, it's no wonder that you have trouble studying! Many conditions may keep you from studying productively. Use the helpful hints below to create a study space where you can concentrate on your work.

- Find a space that is free from interruptions and available when you need it—perhaps a corner of your bedroom.
- Use a flat surface, such as a desk, for writing and reading. You can read just about anywhere—say, lying on the floor—but the most productive studying occurs when you sit at a desk with your feet flat on the floor. This upright position opens your esophagus to allow oxygen into your lungs and eventually to your brain, and it allows blood to flow easily throughout your body. In addition, you're less likely to doze off or lose your concentration.
- Have a comfortable chair. If the chair is too soft, you may fall asleep—but if it's too hard, you will be distracted.
- Keep your study tools well-stocked and nearby, including pencils, paper, a calculator, a stapler, note cards, and a laptop, if you have one. If your desk has drawers, you can store these tools inside to keep the surface clear.

- Have reference materials available, such as a dictionary, a thesaurus, and an encyclopedia.
- Work near a window—there is no substitute for sunlight! If you study in the evening, you will also need a good reading light. Be sure the light-bulb does not flicker, or it could distract you.
- Keep the study space at a reasonable temperature. Warm air makes people fall asleep, so cooler temperatures are usually better for studying—but not too cold, or you will only think about how cold you are!
- Make a "Do Not Disturb" sign and hang it on your doorknob or tape it to your door. This can help keep siblings or others from distracting you while you study.
- Set aside time each day for studying—don't wait until the day before the test! Remember: Repetition is the mother of learning. Also be sure to give yourself a realistic amount of time to study. If you study for too long, you are likely to lose your concentration, but you need to study enough to get through the material and understand it.
- Drink water to stay hydrated. Keeping your body hydrated can help you stay alert and on task.

Tips for Taking Notes

As you read *Personal Finance: A Lifetime Responsibility*, you will cover a lot of material—how can you remember it all? Taking notes can help. It may seem like a waste of time to stop reading in order to write notes down, but in the long run, taking notes can actually save you time—and help you remember what you read!

Your notes should be a summary of the information you read. As mentioned in the SQ3R section, pausing throughout your reading to restate the material in your own words is a good way to remember and understand the information. Now all you need to do is write these summaries down. If you do, you will have great study notes for your tests.

Some people prefer to take notes on loose-leaf paper, while others prefer to write in a notebook or sketch pad. Still others might prefer writing on index cards, typing notes into a computer, or something else entirely. Use whatever method works best for you.

The first step to good note taking is: Do not write. Surprised? You're probably wondering, "How can I take notes without writing?" You will eventually need to write your notes down, but first, read a little. Use the SQ3R method: Survey the material and ask questions about it, and *then* begin reading and note taking. Note taking is part of the reading process.

As you read, you will see that each unit of *Personal Finance: A Lifetime Responsibility* is divided into chapters, which are divided into sections. Each section contains related information, with color-coded headings, that allow you to recognize specific topics more easily.

Use the color-coded headings as the basis for your note taking. For example, Chapter 1 is titled "Career Planning," and it is divided into three sections, as you can see on page 5. Let's say you begin taking notes on Section 1, "Your Income and Your Career."

The first thing you'll want to do is write down (or type in) the chapter title and then the section title. Make these clear on the page (or screen, or note card) so that when you use these notes to review for your test, you will be able to keep each chapter and each section in the right order—and find the one you need.

Next, flip through the section in your book and read the smaller headings, which are printed in red and purple ink.

Headings that appear in red indicate a large topic to be discussed, and purple headings indicate more specific aspects of that topic. If a topic being discussed under a purple heading needs even further division, those divisions are printed in blue.

While taking notes, it will be helpful to copy down these headings. They are clear markers of the points being made. After writing down both the chapter and section titles of Chapter 1, for example, you would next write down the first red heading, "Sources of Income" as seen on page 6. However, before writing down the first purple heading, you would summarize the two main introductory paragraphs that follow the introductory heading. (See the example summaries in Figure 1 on the next page.)

Now you will be ready to copy down the first purple title, "Wages, Salaries, Tips, and Commissions," also on page 6. You will read four paragraphs of text that follow. Summarize each paragraph in a brief sentence, and write it down. Then copy down the next purple title, "Entrepreneurship, or Business Earnings," and jot down a main idea for each of the two paragraphs that follow it. Continue this process section by section, chapter by chapter, throughout the book.

Some people like to use outlines to organize the material, and others like cluster charts, for example. There are many formats for laying out your notes, and you should use whichever one you prefer—if you are not sure, try several. For all formats, the material you put in them will be the same. (Again, see Figure 1 and check out two examples of note-taking formats.)

The idea is to create a list or chart of main ideas for each paragraph, division, and section within each chapter. Writing these down—taking notes—will help you remember the important ideas from *Personal Finance: A Lifetime Responsibility.* Read your notes once right after you have finished reading a section of the book, going over the ideas one more time to refresh your memory.

Usually you cannot write in textbooks, but on your notes you can use a highlighter or a different color pen to mark important points or make corrections and additions. Maybe you want to star a difficult section so that you can come back to it. Maybe you want to make a note next to an idea that you would like to remember for your own financial success. Maybe you decide to cross out something that isn't really that important. On your own notes, you can make whatever marks you need.

When it is time to study for your chapter test, you will have a ready-made study guide. Read your notes, think about the main points, and refer back to the book for more information. You will be amazed at how easy test preparation can be!

Figure 1 **SAMPLE FORMATS FOR TAKING NOTES**

When taking notes for *Personal Finance: A Lifetime Responsibility*, you could use a variety of methods. The format you use is up to you. Below are examples of two note-taking formats, based on the beginning of Chapter 1, that you might find useful.

Outline

An outline is a summary that shows the logical development of ideas. If you like to remember the ideas in the order in which you read them, use this format.

Cluster Chart

A cluster chart is a summary of thoughts organized together so that the entire idea is visible all at once. If you like to see the "big picture," use this format.

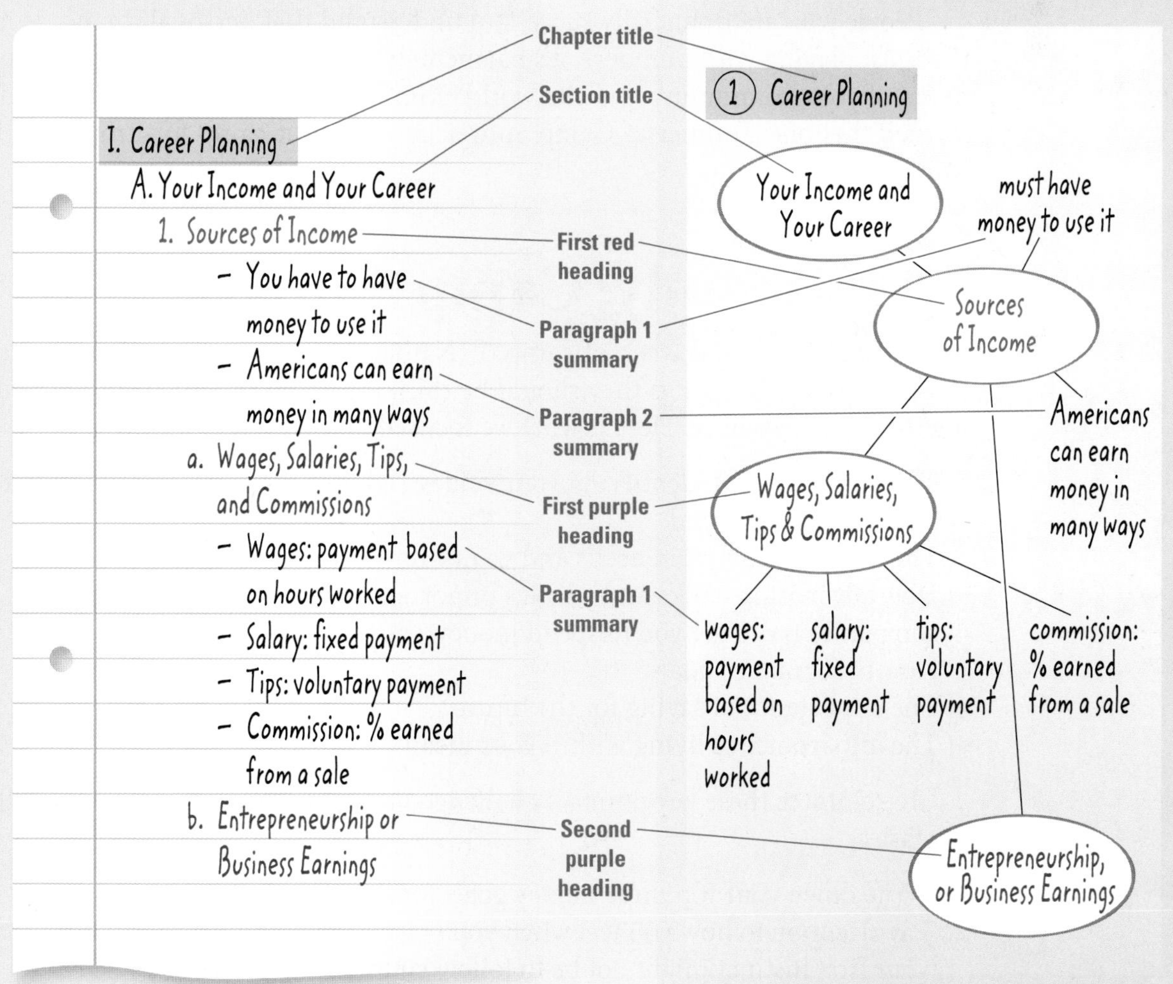

Introduction

Albert Einstein said, "The most powerful force in the universe is compound interest." But that was pre-MTV and shows like *My Super Sweet 16*, not to mention cell phones, text messaging, and credit cards.

When it comes to money in today's hyperconsumer culture, it's all about spending. In fact, the average high school student sees or hears some 5,000 ads every single day. That's a stunning number of invitations to spend your money! Rarely do you hear or see messages encouraging you to develop balanced and healthy money habits—particularly when it comes to saving and sharing.

The issue of financial literacy is a hot topic. So much so that in January 2008, then President George W. Bush created the Financial Literacy Advisory Council. According to the White House, this new agency was launched to "help keep America competitive and assist the American people in understanding and addressing financial matters."

People who are financially successful understand that personal finance is more than just playing with numbers; it's balancing your own needs and wants with the needs of your community and the world. Nine junior counselors (ages 15 and 16) learned this one summer at Camp Sunrise, a nonprofit camp for urban youth in Minnesota.

A Case Study: Camp Sunrise

During the second week of camp, I (Nathan) met with the junior counselors (JCs) to discuss the things they should be thinking about in anticipation of receiving their first paycheck. Here is what we focused on that warm morning:

- The importance of identifying your values and how they affect your ability to share, save, and spend
- The difference between needs and wants
- How advertising works and why it's important to be aware of all the ways companies try to get you to spend money
- How to set money goals
- The importance of saving for the future
- The importance of living within your means

To reinforce these key points, I challenged the nine JCs to complete the following tasks:

1. Write down your top three money goals for the summer.
2. Pay attention to how you feel when you receive your first paycheck. Note that your first instinct might not be to follow your money plan.
3. Open a checking or savings account, and use it to manage the money you earn.
4. As a group, pool some of your money and make a contribution back to Camp Sunrise as an expression of gratitude for the experience of working there.

During the last week of camp, community leaders, campers, and staff gathered to celebrate. At the party, the nine JCs stepped forward and gave the camp $135! Several of the adults in the crowd offered to match the contribution. By the end of the day, the camp had received almost $1,000.

Over the summer, several of the JCs had opened bank accounts, and all of them had set financial goals. Probably best of all, they had talked about money—for instance, on payday, they discussed what they were going to do with their earnings. Many of the JCs had also shared their money lessons with friends, family, and other counselors.

Making It Personal

Our goal in *Personal Finance: A Lifetime Responsibility* is to help you develop healthy money habits, like those learned by the JCs at Camp Sunrise. Regardless of what you hope to be someday—an engineer, an artist, a dental hygienist, an entrepreneur—making wise money decisions will benefit you. Good money habits can help you do things like save for college or trade school, use credit wisely, accomplish financial goals, choose the best options from a benefit plan at work, and contribute to a cause that means a lot to you.

As you embark on this new learning experience, remember that you can apply the many lessons from this book directly to your life. The following features were written specifically to help you do that:

- **You Decide** uses case studies and stories to engage you in a dialogue about real-life financial situations and challenge you to make personal choices.
- **Look Before You Leap** describes financial decisions you are likely to encounter, and the steps you can take to make the best decisions.
- **You Can Succeed Financially** discusses the exciting possibilities open to people who set personal financial goals and work to accomplish them.
- **Going Global** shows how key personal finance topics are treated in other countries.
- **Do Your Research** offers suggestions for using the Internet, libraries, and other sources to investigate personal financial topics of particular interest to you.
- **Get Good Advice** explains how mentors can help you learn about personal finance, how to identify and interview mentors, and how to share the results of your interviews.
- **Did You Know?** presents fascinating facts and figures that dispel myths, warn, inform, spark ideas, and encourage exploration.

Bottom line: You can use the information in this book to help you develop healthy money habits. *Payback:* A lifetime of successful sharing, saving, and spending!

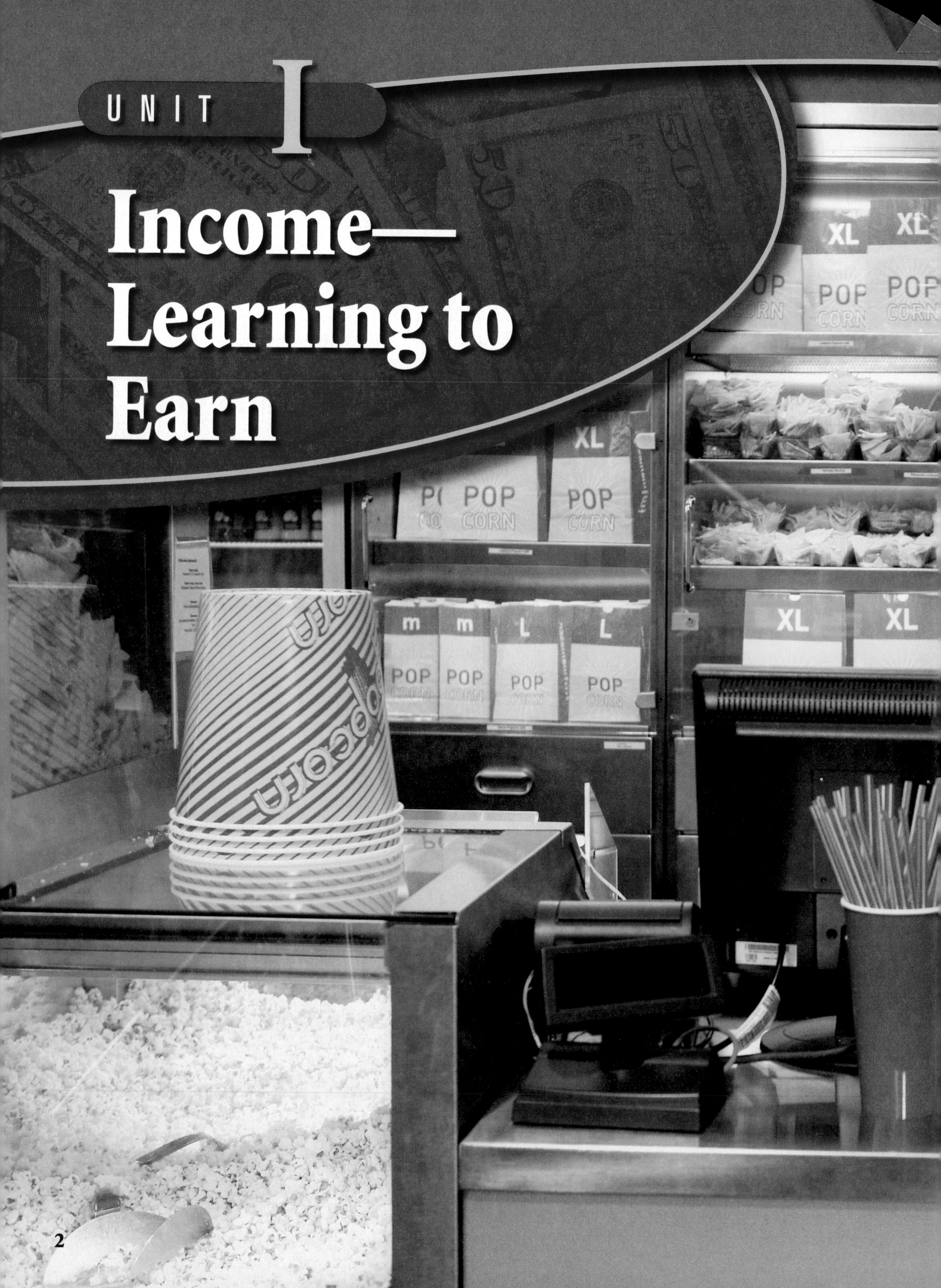

UNIT I

Income—Learning to Earn

CHAPTER 1 Career Planning

CHAPTER 2 Job and Career Success

CHAPTER 1

Career Planning

In the winter of 2004, pop star Michael Jackson was facing a cash crunch. A $70 million Bank of America loan would soon be due, and according to an article in the *New York Times*, Jackson might have difficulty repaying it.

When granting the loan, the bank must have been concerned about Jackson's spending habits. It had limited Jackson's spending to $1.5 million—per month! But Jackson was not too worried. He had earned a *lot* of money over the years and had invested it wisely in numerous assets—*before* he took out the loan. You too must put money into your bank accounts before you can take money out of them.

▲ **Even successful performers who earn millions of dollars, such as Michael Jackson, need to learn financial management skills.**

SECTION 1 Your Income and Your Career

SECTION 2 Finding and Applying for Jobs

SECTION 3 Interviewing and Pre-employment Testing

Fact or Fiction

What do you think? Are the following statements true or false? If you think they are false, then say what is true.

1. Most Americans work at jobs that pay them a wage or a salary.
2. When you leave school and begin working in your chosen career, you will take on a new identity.
3. Your first step in choosing a career is to do some daydreaming.
4. Career planning is not important, because most adult Americans will fall into their line of work by chance or by accident.
5. Newspaper classified ads are generally the best source of job leads.
6. Contacting employers directly can uncover jobs that you might not find through other sources.
7. Most businesses advertise their best jobs.

Answers on page 27.

Study Reminder

Knowing how to study can increase your knowledge, improve your grades, and cut down on your study time. See the ***Studying Personal Finance*** *pages at the front of the book for some tips to help you study this chapter.*

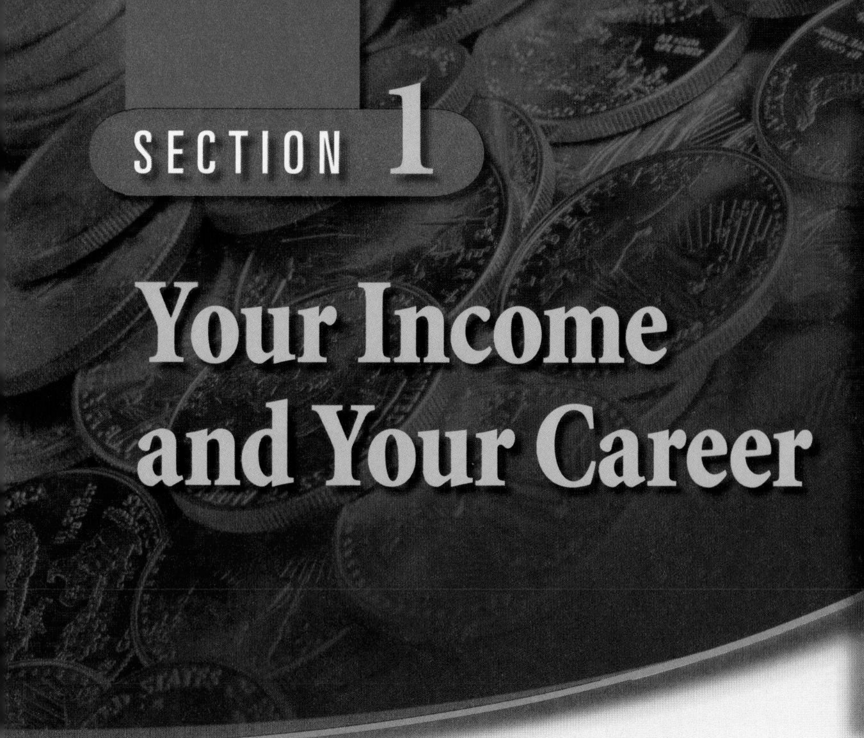

SECTION 1

Your Income and Your Career

Focus Questions

1. What are two ways of learning about financial aid for students?
2. What is the most important lesson to learn about handling personal finances?
3. How will your work affect your family and your choice of friends?

Key Terms

wages
salary
tip
commission
entrepreneur
sole proprietorship
partnership
corporation
investing
grants
royalties
inheritance
plan of action

Sources of Income

wages pay that is figured at an hourly rate

salary pay that is a fixed amount, regardless of the hours worked

▼ **The basic rule of personal finance: You must put money in before you can take it out.**

The most important lesson you can learn about handling personal finances is that, with few exceptions, *you must put money in before you can take it out.* That is, you must earn or acquire some money before you can begin sharing, saving, and spending it. A good starting point for learning about personal finance, therefore, is figuring out your best sources of income.

You can accumulate money in many different ways. Some common sources of income in the United States are listed below. More sources could be added to this list, but these categories provide the income for the vast majority of Americans:

- Wages, salaries, tips, and commissions
- Entrepreneurship, or business earnings
- Investment earnings
- Government payments
- Grants, royalties, and inheritances

Wages, Salaries, Tips, and Commissions

Most Americans work at a job that pays them either a wage or a salary. **Wages** are figured at an hourly rate. The employees are usually paid weekly or every other week. Overtime rates apply for hours worked beyond forty hours in a week. Generally, people working in so-called "trades"—occupations such as carpenters, electricians, masons, and other construction workers—are paid an hourly rate.

If someone is paid a **salary**, that person receives a set amount each month,

◀ What are the different ways in which the woman working in this lighting shop might be paid?

regardless of the number of hours worked. Employees who are paid a salary are not entitled to extra pay if they work more than forty hours in a week. People in professional occupations—such as attorneys, engineers, and accountants—are usually paid a salary.

You have probably received or given a **tip**, which is a voluntary payment that a customer makes to the employee, figured as a percentage of the bill. Workers such as waiters and hair stylists depend on tips for a major part of their income.

People working in sales are often paid a wage or salary *plus* a **commission**, which is a percentage of the total dollar amount that the employee sold during the pay period. Some salespersons are paid only a commission and do not receive either wages or a salary. Many real estate agents, for example, receive only a commission on the price of the property they sell.

Entrepreneurship, or Business Earnings

If you start your own business, join a family business, or buy someone else's business, you will be known as an **entrepreneur**. If the money coming into the business is greater than the money going out, the business makes a profit. Profit is how entrepreneurs get paid. Of course, if the business spends more money than it takes in, there are no profits—and no earnings for the business owner.

There are three basic types of business ownership. If you are the only owner, your business will be organized as a **sole proprietorship**. If you are a co-owner, you will be a partner in a **partnership** organization. Or you might form a **corporation**, which is a business owned by a group of stockholders. If you are the sole owner of a business, then all the after-tax profits are yours. In a partnership or corporation, you will get a share of the profits. You will learn more about entrepreneurship in Chapter 2.

Investment Earnings

As soon as possible after you begin earning and saving money, you will want to begin investing your money. **Investing** means committing your money for a period of time to an enterprise that (you hope) will earn more money. You can invest your money in stocks, bonds, or real estate, for example.

tip a voluntary payment that a customer makes to an employee, often based on the quality of service provided

commission a percentage of the total sale, paid to an employee instead of, or in addition to, salary or wages

entrepreneur someone who organizes, manages, and assumes the risks of owning a business

sole proprietorship a business owned by one person

partnership a business with co-owners, in which both parties are legally joined together

corporation a business owned by a group of stockholders

investing committing money to an enterprise in order to earn a financial return

You Can Succeed Financially

Tom Szaky and Jon Beyer were 19-year-old Princeton University students in 2001 when they had the inspiration to create a useful product from waste. Beyer's father was an expert on worms, and their idea was to feed garbage to worms and use the worm droppings as fertilizer. They entered and won a business plan contest sponsored by the university. The prize was $2,000 seed money. They borrowed another $18,000 from friends and family to build the equipment they would need to house and feed the worms.

The next year they began collecting the university's dining hall food waste (which they admit was the messiest part of the operation). Then they began turning out their product, which they named TerraCycle.

Finding Investors

The young entrepreneurs knew they needed to invest more to make the company viable as a business venture. Szaky entered and won several more contests, winning small amounts in prize money. Then in 2003 their plan won the $1 million Carrot Capital contest. Szaky actually ended up refusing the prize money in that contest because the rules said he would have to change the company in ways Szaky couldn't accept. But the publicity they received attracted other investors, and the company was off the ground.

Solving Problems

Once Szaky and Beyer had developed the process for making TerraCycle (an odorless liquid), they needed bottles to sell it in. They couldn't afford new bottles—but Szaky says their original intention had been to sell a product made completely from trash anyway. They decided to package TerraCycle in used soda bottles.

Next question: Where to get bottles? They started out by going through residential recycling bins, until they discovered that wasn't allowed. Then they began collecting bottles wherever they could, and buying them from recycling centers. They also developed a successful program with schools, churches, and other community organizations, buying their used bottles for 5 cents each. Even though 5 cents is more than they pay recyclers for the bottles, Szaky and Beyer say they are glad to support community groups, and the program increases consumer goodwill toward the company.

▲ **What personal qualities helped Tom Szaky (*left*) and Jon Beyer (*right*) become successful entrepreneurs?**

The Big Break

A huge break for the company came in May 2004, when Szaky convinced Home Depot that they should sell TerraCycle. Customers took to the product immediately. They liked its environmental friendliness, its cost, and its effectiveness—TerraCycle worked as well as top-brand chemical fertilizers. By 2006, TerraCycle was also sold at Wal-Mart, Whole Foods, and Wild Oats, and it did $1 million in sales in the first quarter that year.

What Would You Do?

1. Knowing that most new businesses fail, would you be willing to work for a small start-up company like TerraCycle? Explain your answer.
2. What are some reasons someone would be willing to take a low salary to work at TerraCycle?

You can't really begin investing until you have some "extra" money—money you can do without for months or even years. This means that you must have enough money to pay your bills and buy what you need, as well as enough saved for emergencies, before you can begin investing. You should, however, start *thinking* about investing as soon as possible. Because there are questions about the long-term stability of Social Security, and because fewer traditional types of pension plans exist today, you will want to earn as much money as you can through investments to pay for your retirement. You will learn much more about investing in Chapter 7.

Government Payments

Many people depend on checks from federal, state, or local governments to pay some or all of their bills. These payments come from many different funds and are paid out for a variety of reasons. Following are a few examples:

- Financial aid for students
- Social Security
- Medicare
- Medicaid
- Unemployment benefits
- Aid to dependent children

How is the government able to pay out all of this money? It comes primarily from taxes on employers and workers. In some cases (Social Security), both employers and employees pay into a fund from which the employees receive benefits when they retire. In other cases (unemployment benefits) the money is paid into the government fund by employers. Some of the funds (Medicare) operate like insurance policies. And in other cases (Medicaid, financial aid for students, and aid to dependent children), taxpayers provide the money.

One of the rare exceptions to the rule that you must put money in before you can take it out occurs with student financial aid. Education is so important that many individuals and institutions are willing to give money to students who need help paying for college. If you need some financial support while attending a college or university and you qualify for student aid, then you should certainly apply for it. Your school counselor can provide general information on the student aid that will be available when you begin college. In addition, most colleges and universities have a designated office to provide up-to-date information on student aid. You can also find a great deal of information on the Internet.

Grants, Royalties, and Inheritances

Grants, royalties, and inheritances are a few of the additional ways that people receive income.

Grants are payments that are given to people and institutions that do not have to be paid back. The U.S. government, state governments, and corporations all use grants to support certain types of work, including research in a variety of fields.

grants payments or property given to people or institutions, which do not have to be paid back

royalties a percentage of the sales in dollars paid to an author, songwriter, or inventor when copies of his or her creation are sold

If you write a book, the publisher will probably pay you in the form of **royalties**—a percentage of the sales in dollars when people buy your book. Royalties are also paid to songwriters for songs

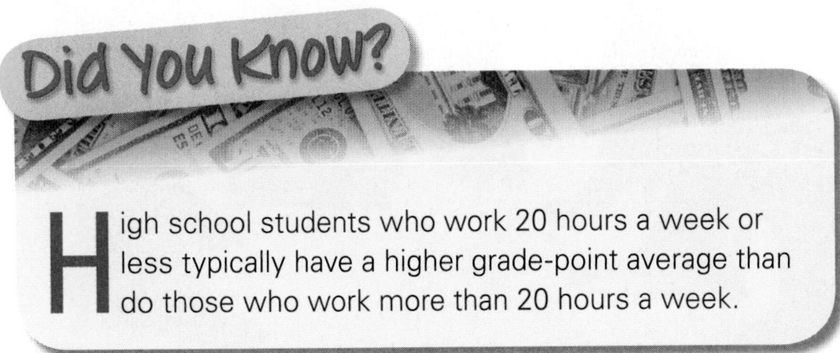

High school students who work 20 hours a week or less typically have a higher grade-point average than do those who work more than 20 hours a week.

inheritance an amount of money, property, or an object of value, given by someone who has died

they have written, usually based on the number of copies of CDs or albums sold. Actors may be paid a royalty in addition to a salary for their work in motion pictures, or they may accept no salary but receive a higher royalty rate. Money paid to property owners by a company that takes minerals, gas, or oil from their land is also classified as royalty income.

An **inheritance** is an amount of money, property, or an object of value that you receive from someone who has died, usually a parent or other relative. If you've inherited some money or assets, such as a house, rental property, or a business, then—with proper management—this can become a source of continuing income. You could also sell some of these inherited assets and reinvest the money in something that will provide an even greater income.

▼ Your career will probably be an important part of your identity throughout your adult years.

Your Work and Your Identity

The money you earn by working pays for the necessities of life: food and water, housing, safety, clothing, health care, and education. But your work does much more for you than simply provide an income.

During your years in school, all through high school and college, you are known to others primarily as a student. Your whole world revolves around your role as a student. This role provides your identity.

When you begin working in your chosen career, you will take on a new identity. To many, you will be known mainly by the work you do to earn a living. For instance, when we introduce people in a social setting, we might say, "This is Polly Baxter. Polly's an engineer." Our work becomes the central activity around which we plan our daily lives.

During our working years, the time devoted to work and related activities accounts for half of our waking hours. Students in high school today can expect to work for thirty to forty years. Many women (and some men) will interrupt careers while their children are young and then, after several years, return to jobs outside the home. Only a small percentage will never enter the job market at all.

Choosing Your Career

Many adult Americans did not specifically choose their career but "fell" into their line of work by chance or by accident. Because the work you do to

YOU DECIDE

Sophia has wanted to be a fashion designer for as long as she can remember. She has taken sewing classes since middle school—she even designed and made her own prom dress. She feels strongly that she can succeed in the world of style.

Answering an ad on her local Craigslist page, Sophia applies for a job at a small company that designs and makes women's sports clothes. The clothing line consists of simple styles in linen and rayon only. She makes it through the interview and is offered the job. Her initial duties would be as a seamstress, but the business owner is impressed by Sophia's drawings of her own designs. She tells Sophia that after she has sewed skillfully for six months or so, she would get a chance to create some samples of her own designs.

At home, Sophia learns that a family friend has left a message for her. There is another job opening—at a boutique in town that sells high-end designer clothes, the kind of clothes Sophia wants to design herself one day. The friend says he can put in a word for Sophia if she wants, and he is sure she will get the job.

Sophia is torn between the two. The clothes at the boutique are at the cutting edge of fashion. Even though she would only be selling, Sophia thinks she could study their cut and fabrics and learn a lot about design. On the other hand, at the sportswear company she would actually be sewing, and then maybe designing. But the clothes there are simple, classic designs, and the fabrics are all similar in weight and texture. She wonders if she would learn more by handling the high-fashion clothes she'd be selling at the boutique. At the same time, a job in sales does not seem to fit her career plan.

Should she . . .

1. ...take the seamstress job or the boutique job? Explain the reasons for your decision.
2. ...ask more questions about both jobs to help her make her decision? What questions could Sophia ask the sportswear company owner? The boutique manager?
3. ...base her decision primarily on salary? Explain your answer.

earn a living affects nearly every other aspect of your life, it is extremely important that you devote considerable time and energy to choosing your career. The best approach to choosing your career is to take it one step at a time, as follows:

1. *Daydream.* Visualize your life in the future. What activities and relationships would be most satisfying? What kind of a lifestyle do you want as an adult?
2. *Make a thorough self-assessment.* Evaluate your values, interests, skills, aptitudes, and personality characteristics.
3. *Gather career information.* Look over the definitions of the sixteen career clusters that were developed by the U.S. Department of Education and are available online with the Career Clusters Initiative (http://fin.emcp.net/careerclusters). One helpful Web site is O*NET (http://fin.emcp.net/onet), which provides information about skills, abilities, and work activities associated with various occupations. Other useful Internet resources are the *Occupational Outlook Handbook* (OOH), available online from the U.S. Bureau of Labor Statistics

Get Good Advice

Jennifer's sister is home from college for the weekend, and she is full of advice. Most of the time Jennifer just smiles and nods, but one suggestion hits home. Kalie says that applying for a job and working part-time are excellent practice for the future. In fact, she says, more and more colleges look for students who have held part-time jobs.

Jennifer already knows that about one out of five 16-year-olds has a part-time or summer job. She really wants to work, but she isn't sure how to fit a job in with homework and soccer practice and everything else. She decides to ask her parents and grandparents what they did about working when they were her age.

Do you know what kinds of jobs your parents and grandparents had as young adults? Ask them—or other older people—to describe their early work experiences. Use questions like these to help them remember:

1. Did you have a part-time or summer job while you were in high school?
2. If so, what steps did you take in finding and applying for the job?
3. Did you have a formal interview for the job? If so, how did it go?
4. What kinds of things did you do on the job?
5. What did you do with the money you earned?
6. How did you balance work and school?
7. How did having the job help you later in life?

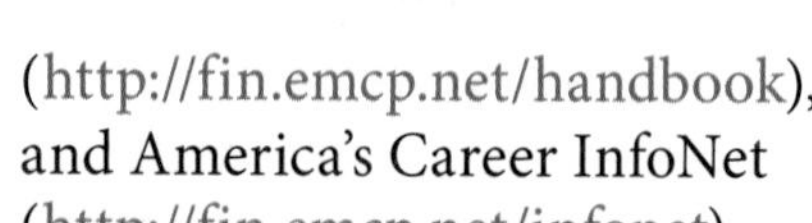

Summarize the answers you get, and share them with your class. Note the variety of work experiences, and summarize the lessons shared by the interviewees. Compile all the responses into a single list of suggestions for teens who want to work while in school.

(http://fin.emcp.net/handbook), and America's Career InfoNet (http://fin.emcp.net/infonet).

4. *Set a realistic career goal.* You will need to match your unique set of needs and traits with the requirements and rewards of a career.
5. *Make a decision.* After comparing your own characteristics with the requirements and rewards of various careers, you will choose your career—the work that will affect nearly everything you do.
6. *Outline a plan of action.* A **plan of action** is a list of the steps you will take to reach your career goal. It includes specific subgoals that chart the way to your chosen career.

plan of action a list of the steps needed to reach a career goal

SECTION 1 ASSESSMENT

Factual Recall

1. Name five common sources of income for Americans.
2. In what occupation do workers typically receive a commission?
3. Name two sources of information about financial aid for college.
4. Name three types of investments.
5. List the six steps for choosing a career.

Critical Thinking

1. Why is it important to earn money before spending it?
2. What is the risk of using loans and credit cards to buy whatever you want?
3. Salaried jobs do not pay overtime. Does someone earning an hourly wage make more money than someone earning a salary? Why or why not?

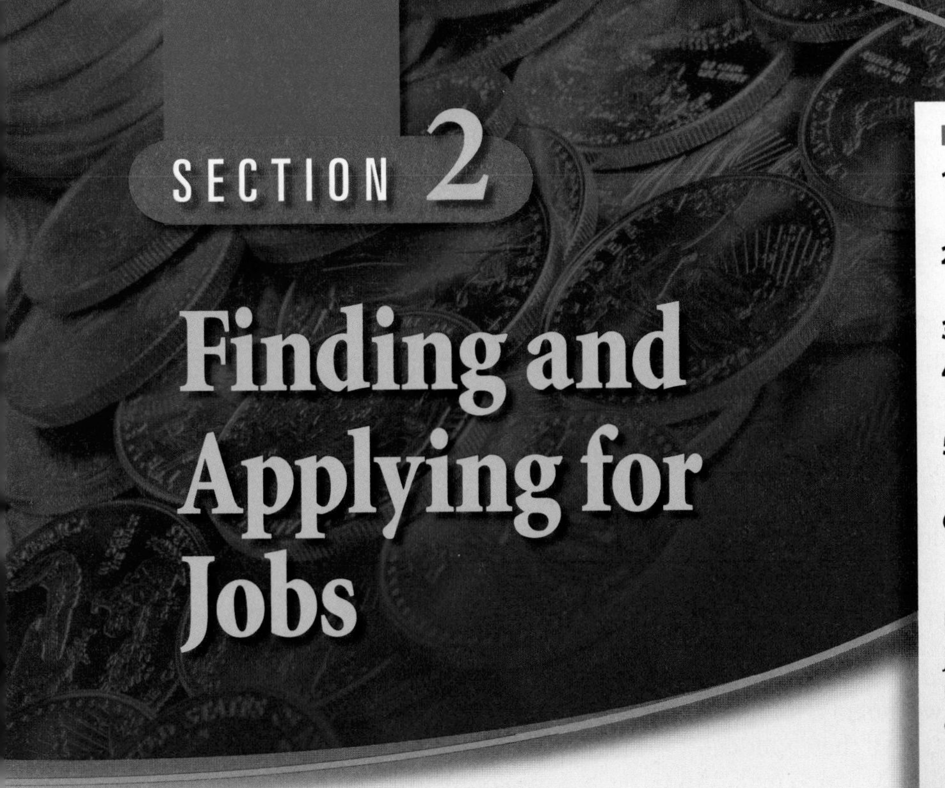

SECTION 2

Finding and Applying for Jobs

Focus Questions

1. What are the best sources of job leads?
2. What are three traditional sources of job leads?
3. What are three online job sites?
4. What information is usually asked for on an application form?
5. What legal document is required before you can be employed?
6. How can keywords help you get a job interview?

Key Terms

job leads
networking
employment agencies
portal site
application form
personal data sheet
work permit
résumé
keywords
cover letter

Obtaining Job Leads

Some people look for work by going from door to door in the business district, asking if there are any jobs available. This is not an efficient way to find a job. In this section, you will learn some proven methods that will make your job hunt both efficient and effective. You will learn where to look for **job leads** (information about jobs that are available) and how to follow up a lead with an application.

Networking

The best source of job leads for most people is through **networking**—the process of building professional relationships that assist both parties in reaching their goals. In recent years people have been putting more effort than ever into building networks with professional friends and friends of friends.

As a student, think of your network as all the people you know who could be sources of information on job leads. This includes your family, friends, and neighbors, in addition to your counselor, teachers, coaches, former employers, and business and professional people you know.

Begin your job hunt by talking with everyone you know who might produce a job lead. If your contacts don't know of any jobs available, they may be able to refer you to someone who does. About 80 percent of all jobs are found by networking. Many of the best jobs are never advertised because businesses fill them with friends of company employees.

job leads information about possible job openings

networking the process of building professional relationships that will assist both parties in reaching their goals

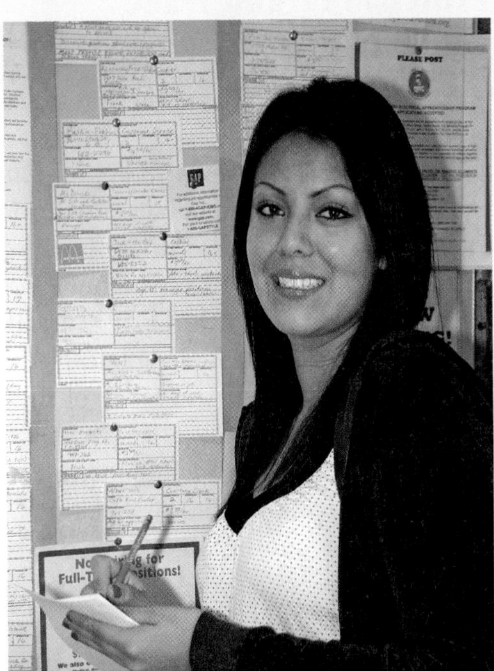

◀ Networking is the best bet for finding the job you want. Do not, however, overlook the job openings posted at state and school career centers.

Going Global

When you hear that a company has "gone global," it usually means that the company is expanding its market to other countries. But a company's workforce can also go global.

When U.S. firms hire employees outside the United States, the practice is known as *outsourcing*. Many manufacturing companies, as well as service industries such as telephone and computer tech support, outsource work. For instance, Contract Counsel is a company that provides temporary legal services. David Galbenski, its cofounder and CEO, is expanding his company by contracting with attorneys in India to prepare and code documents for his legal service.

There are 500 law schools in India, and more than 500,000 law students there graduate each year. All these graduates speak English, which makes India a natural choice for Contract Counsel's outsourcing. The Indian attorneys have lower salary expectations than their U.S. counterparts. Galbenski can bill their time to clients at a much lower rate and still make a larger profit for his company.

Whether clients will accept having their legal work done abroad by people who did not graduate from U.S. law schools is yet to be seen. Some have suggested that Galbenski should bring Indian attorneys to the United States for training before setting them to work. Galbenski's global gamble may or may not pay off. It's important to recognize, though, that in the search for a job, you may be competing with candidates all over the globe.

Thinking Globally

1. What are three jobs that could not be outsourced easily? Explain your reasons for listing each.
2. What is the likely effect of outsourcing on the salaries of employees who do those same jobs within the United States?

Professional and Trade Organizations

All career fields have one or more professional organizations. Most of these organizations have some type of job posting or résumé exchange program. Find out how the process works in your chosen career field, and learn about the most recent job postings. Then respond as soon as you learn about a job lead.

You may not be a member of any such group now, but you can learn about them by keying in "general professional organizations and associations" on Google or another Internet search engine. This may be an excellent source of job leads in the future, especially if you become a member of such an organization. Professional and trade organizations are also an excellent place for networking.

Job/Career Fairs

Career and job fairs are held regularly in most cities and communities. Businesses typically send one or two of their employees to these fairs to meet and talk with young people about jobs in their companies. If you plan to attend one of these fairs, try to identify ahead of time the companies that interest you the most. When you arrive, develop a strategy for breaking through the clutter and the crowds to talk with company representatives. Even if the companies at the fair don't have any jobs that match your interests and skills, this is still a way to meet some people who may become part of your network.

Did You Know?

Did you know that you can post a "position-wanted ad" on the Internet, describing the type of job you are seeking and your relevant skills? The ad should be brief and simple, and it should include your basic contact information.

On the positive side, these ads let you tell employers exactly what you want them to know about you, and you can update the information anytime. On the negative side, you never know whether recruiters and hiring managers are actually seeing your ad.

Traditional Sources of Job Leads

Some of the more traditional ways of locating job leads, such as reading the classified ads in your local newspaper and registering with public and private employment agencies, are not relied on as much as they once were. Even so, they are still worth checking because you never know for sure—you might find the almost-perfect job through one of the following sources:

- *Newspaper ads.* Some employers still use classified newspaper ads as their main source of recruiting job applicants. So, unless you have all the job leads you can possibly follow up, scan through the ads in your local newspaper.
- *Employment agencies.* **Employment agencies** match workers with jobs. Most cities have a tax-supported public employment agency whose services are free. Private employment agencies also provide assistance in finding lobs, but the job seeker usually has to pay a fee. In some cases, however, the employer will pay the fees.
- *Cold contact/direct mail.* Contacting employers directly when you don't know whether a job even exists may sound like a waste of time. This process is not as popular as it was in the past, but it sometimes uncovers jobs that you won't find through other sources. In these cases, contact the *director of human resources* or the *personnel manager.*

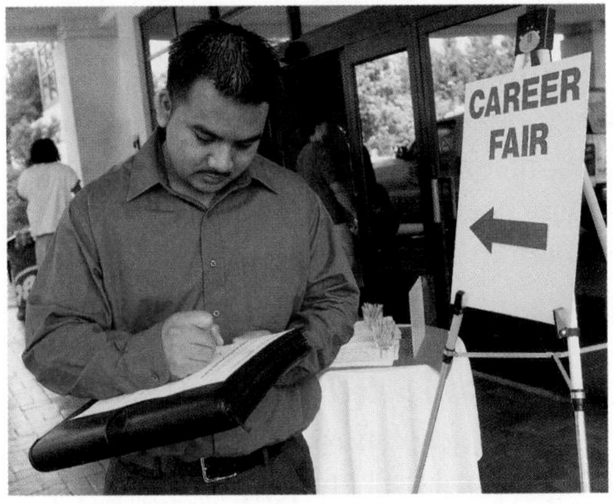

▲ Be on the lookout for job and career fairs in your area. Even if you do not find the job you want, you will acquire valuable information and make helpful contacts.

Searching the Internet

You can access online job listings and information about jobs any hour of the day or night. However, using the Internet to search for job leads is not necessarily an easy task. There is such an abundance of information that making your way through the maze can be a problem.

A good way to begin your online search is to use a portal site. A **portal site** is a Web site you can use as an entrance

employment agencies companies and institutions that help people find jobs or that find people to fill jobs

portal site a Web site that serves as an entrance to other related sites on the Internet

Do Your RESEARCH

Have you ever thought about living or studying abroad? An online service called iAgora (http://fin.emcp.net/iagora) targets young people interested in living, studying, and working abroad, mostly in Europe. It lists internships and jobs in thirty countries, including a brief description of the job and the company, as well as contact information. There are both free listings and "premium" offerings, which only those who have paid a small membership fee can see in detail.

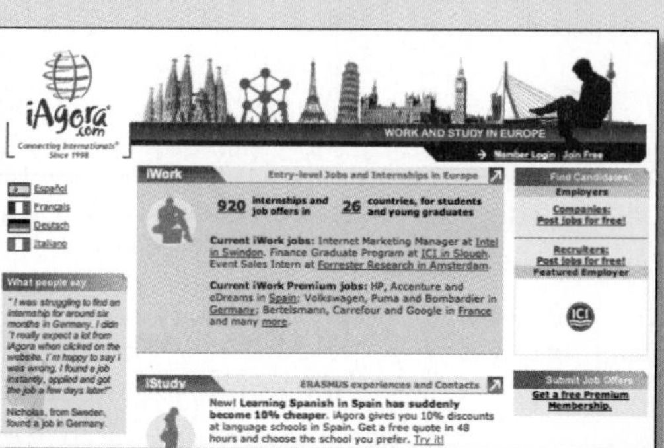

Anyone can sign on to iAgora. First you fill out a form detailing your skills and qualifications. Then the site matches you to appropriate jobs or internships, and you can browse those. You will find pages about living and studying in many countries. The Web site hosts forums where members share information about overseas work and school experiences and adventures. It also has pages of information on opportunities for studying abroad, with reviews of colleges and schools by current and former students.

Another useful site for international job seekers is Going Global (http://fin.emcp.net/goingglobal). This site is not a listing service. Instead, it has detailed information about each country it covers. It points out differences from the United States in culture, legal issues, and working conditions. The information is collected and updated by expert researchers in each country, not extracted from other Web sites. It also has links to employment services in other countries. Although much of the Going Global information must be purchased as PDF downloads, free pages are well worth browsing. While iAgora is directed to students and recent graduates, Going Global's target audience includes seasoned professionals as well as new job seekers.

Your Assignment

1. Sign onto iAgora and use its job-match feature to find the offerings you might be qualified for.
2. Go to the Going Global site and click on the country where you would most like to work. Browse the free pages about interviewing, résumés, and salaries.

to other related sites on the Internet. For instance, one good portal site for online job hunting is The Riley Guide (http://fin.emcp.net/riley). As you search the Internet, you will explore corporate career centers and online job sites.

Corporate Career Centers Online corporate career (human resource) centers are posted on the Internet by the hiring companies themselves. They are becoming an important source of job leads for both large and small firms. Many of these sites list not only job openings but also information about the company and guidelines for submitting résumés and applications. A sample home page of a corporate career center is shown in Figure 1.1.

Online Job Sites Online job sites provide listings of available jobs at a variety of companies. There are literally thousands of online job sites, and you should avoid most of them. The following sites, recommended by *U.S. News and World Report*, are among the most popular:

Figure 1.1 ONLINE CORPORATE CAREER CENTERS

If you are looking for a job in a particular industry, check out the Web sites for companies in that industry. You will learn more about the industry, and you will be able to identify any job openings for which you are qualified.

Most businesses have a section on their Web site, under which you will find a "Careers" or "Job Opportunities" category. On this page are listings of various kinds of career-related information.

Under a heading such as "Current Openings" you will find more detailed descriptions of the jobs currently available with the company. You decide which job is right for you.

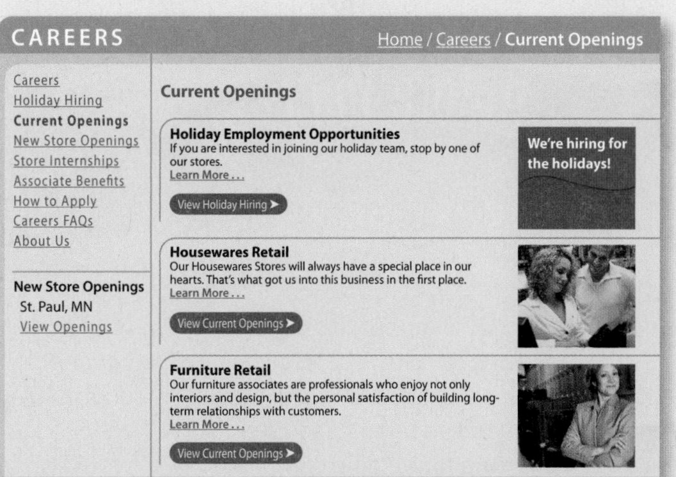

- CareerOneStop (http://fin.emcp.net/onestop): This is a portal to career resources and workforce information, sponsored by the U.S. Department of Labor.
- USAJOBS (http://fin.emcp.net/usajobs): This is the federal government's official job site, which lists more than 20,000 job openings.
- The Riley Guide (http://fin.emcp.net/riley): This site, written by a professional career consultant, is considered the best for anyone trying to choose a career. It provides links to job opportunities and also offers advice for job seekers on how to use the Internet to their best advantage.
- Job-Hunt (http://fin.emcp.net/jobhunt): This site claims to offer links to the most useful Internet-accessible job-search resources. It is a good site for those who already have a career goal and are now trying to find a job.
- Monster.com, CareerBuilder.com, HotJobs.com, and Craigslist.org: Thousands of jobs are listed on these popular sites—but they are visited by

millions of job seekers, so competition is strong.

- Indeed.com and SimplyHired.com: These sites are not as well known but list jobs from thousands of employment sites. You can view more than 4 million job listings on one site.

When you apply online, you will be asked to provide some personal information. Some sites share your information with various other companies and organizations. You should find out about each site's policy on sharing information. For instance, you may not want your current employer to know you are looking for another job. Another reason to be careful about giving out personal information is that some Internet sites disguise themselves as job sites when they are actually trying to sell you their products.

Organizing Your Job Search

Computers are great for organizing information, but it's a bit awkward to carry even a lightweight laptop computer everywhere you go, just in case you hear about a job lead. A better idea is to carry a small notebook for recording information on job leads. Or you might use a stack of index cards, usually the 3-by-5-inch size, as shown in Figure 1.2.

Graciela found what looked like a great job on an online job site. The application process took place by e-mail, and within a week she was told she had been hired. She would work for a shipping forwarding company. Her position was described as a "broker's agent"—which Graciela thought meant she would be on her way to becoming a loan broker, her career goal.

The company would send her a number of certified checks, which she would deposit in her checking account. Then she would send a smaller amount via money order to an overseas bank, keeping the difference as her commission. It sounded exotic and exciting, and she could do it from home while she continued to study finance.

Graciela told her career counselor about the job. They did some research together and could not find any proof of the company's existence. The counselor told Graciela that reputable businesses do not hire people through e-mail applications. The checks that Graciela received from the company would be fake. She would lose the money that she sent to the overseas bank. Graciela was shocked to learn that she had been the victim of a job scam.

Graciela decided to do an online search on "job scams" before using the Internet to find another job. She found useful information at Privacy Rights Clearinghouse (http://fin.emcp.net/privacyrights) and The Riley Guide (http://fin.emcp.net/riley), which had a page with links to many good sources of information. *A job that looks too good to be true probably is.*

Before Taking the Job

1. What questions might Graciela have asked to help her determine if the company was legitimate?
2. Would you trust an online job site's "guarantee" that the jobs they list actually exist, or would you do further research? Why or why not?

When you hear about a job opening, write down the name of the person to whom you should apply, as well as the company's name, address, and telephone number. Write the source of your lead in the lower-left corner. Use the back of the card to record what you do to follow up on the lead—such as the date you call to request an interview, as well as the time and date of the interview. You would also write down the name of the person you are to see, and, if necessary, directions to the company's office. Use a second card to write down information about the company.

Follow up each lead as quickly as possible. If you don't, someone else may already have that job by the time you get around to calling for an interview. Between times, when you are not following up on job leads, continue to look for new job leads as well. Every new lead increases your chances of finding just the right job.

Applying for a Job

When you apply for a job, you will usually have to fill out some paperwork and provide other documents to your prospective employer.

Job Application Forms

An **application form** consists of one or two pages of questions about you and your job qualifications (see Figure 1.3). An employer uses the information you provide to decide whether or not to have you come in for an interview.

Most application forms ask the same or similar questions. One good way to prepare for the job application process is to fill out a **personal data sheet**. This sheet is simply the detailed information about yourself that you need when you fill out the job application form. A listing of the kinds of information that you should include in your personal data sheet is provided in Figure 1.4 on the next page. Be sure to take this sheet with you when you apply for jobs.

Social Security Cards

Except for occasional work, such as gardening or babysitting, you will need a Social Security card. It is illegal for an employer to pay you until you have provided your Social Security number. Congress passed a law in 1988 that requires every person aged 5 or older who is claimed as a dependent on federal tax form 1040 to have a Social Security number. So you probably have one.

If you don't have a Social Security card, you can get an application form online, at your local Social Security office, or from your school work experience office. Write down your Social

application form a questionnaire that helps an employer determine whether or not an applicant is qualified for a job and should come in for an interview

personal data sheet a detailed list of personal information, which you bring to a job interview, that makes filling out the application easier

Figure 1.2 **SAMPLE JOB-LEAD CARD**

Front

Contact Person	Tess Martinez (Office manager)	**ADMINISTRATIVE ASSISTANT**
Business	Television and Radio, INC. 1234 South Main Street 888/888.8888	*Television and Radio, Inc.* has Admin. Asst. position open. Duties incl.: Vista, Excel, and PowerPoint©, Data entry, Phones, Copy/fax. Good salary.
Source	www.craigslist.com	Call Tess at 888.888.8888 or email tess@televisionradio.com. Attach an electronic copy of your resume.

Back

Interview Information	Called for interview on 5/16 Interview on 5/20 at 10:30 AM (ask for Mrs. Fitzgerald at the main desk)
Interview Results	Interview was positive. They will call with a decision next week.

Figure 1.3 SAMPLE JOB APPLICATION FORM

Gabriels *The Hobby Store*

APPLICATION FOR EMPLOYMENT

Various Federal, State, and Local Laws prohibit discrimination based on race, color, sex, religion, national origin, ancestry, age, disability, or marital status. Gabriels is an equal opportunity employer. Applicants for all job openings are welcome and will be considered without regard to race, color, religion, national origin, sex, age, sexual orientation, physical or mental abilities, or any other basis protected by State, Federal, or Local law. **Gabriels will verify Social Security numbers.** Employees will be subject to immediate termination if the Social Security Administration is unable to confirm the validity of the social security

PERSONAL INFORMATION

LAST NAME	FIRST	MIDDLE	
ADDRESS	CITY	STATE	ZIP
HOME TELEPHONE ( )	BUSINESS TELEPHONE ( )	MAY WE CONTACT YOU AT WORK? ☐ YES ☐ NO	
POSITION APPLYING FOR	DATE AVAILABLE	ARE YOU INTERESTED IN (CHECK ALL THAT APPLY)? ☐ FULL-TIME ☐ PART-TIME ☐ TEMPORARY ☐ SEASONAL	
IF YOU ARE UNDER 18 YEARS OF AGE, PLEASE STATE YOUR DATE OF BIRTH	ARE YOU WILLING TO RELOCATE? ☐ YES ☐ NO	ARE YOU WILLING TO TRAVEL? ☐ YES ☐ NO	WHAT PERCENT? %
HOW WERE YOU REFERRED TO GABRIELS?			

DAYS AND HOURS AVAILABLE

MONDAY		TUESDAY		WEDNESDAY		THURSDAY		FRIDAY		SATURDAY		SUNDAY	
FROM	TO	FROM	TO	FROM	TO	FROM	TO	FROM	TO	FROM	TO	FROM	TO

EDUCATION

	NAME	LOCATION (City, State, Zip)	DEGREE / AREA OF STUDY	TOTAL YEARS COMPLETED	GRADUATED	
					YES	NO
High School						
College						
Graduate School						
Other						

LEGAL

IDENTITY AND EMPLOYMENT ELIGIBILITY OF ALL NEW HIRES WILL BE VERIFIED AS REQUIRED BY THE IMMIGRATION REFORM AND CONTROL ACT OF 1986.	
DO YOU HAVE A LEGAL RIGHT AND NECESSARY DOCUMENTS TO WORK IN THE U.S.? ☐ YES ☐ NO	
WERE YOU EVER DISCHARGED BY ANY COMPANY? ☐ YES ☐ NO	IF YES, GIVE NAME OF COMPANY(IES)
REASON FOR DISCHARGES	

EMPLOYMENT HISTORY

List employment for the past ten years starting with your most recent position. Account for any time during this period that you were unemployed by stating the nature of your activities. Please indicate if you were employed under a different name.					MAY WE CONTACT YOUR PRESENT EMPLOYER? ☐ YES ☐ NO
DATES	NAME AND ADDRESS OF EMPLOYER	POSITION AND SUPERVISOR	WAGES OR SALARY	MAJOR DUTIES	REASON FOR LEAVING
FROM / MO. YR.	NAME ADDRESS	YOUR JOB TITLE	STARTING		
TO / MO. YR.	CITY STATE PHONE	SUPERVISOR	FINAL		
FROM / MO. YR.	NAME ADDRESS	YOUR JOB TITLE	STARTING		
TO / MO. YR.	CITY STATE PHONE	SUPERVISOR	FINAL		
FROM / MO. YR.	NAME ADDRESS	YOUR JOB TITLE	STARTING		

SPECIAL SKILLS

☐ TYPING ☐ LOTUS ☐ WORD PROCESSING ☐ 10 KEYS (BY TOUCH) APPLICABLE SKILLS OR EQUIPMENT OPERATED:

________ WPM ________ KEYSTROKES

MISCELLANEOUS

IS THERE ANY ADDITIONAL INFORMATION INVOLVING A CHANGE OF YOUR NAME OR ASSUMED NAME THAT WILL PERMIT US TO CHECK YOUR RECORD? IF YES, PLEASE EXPLAIN.

HAVE YOU EVER BEEN EMPLOYED BY THIS COMPANY OR ANY OF ITS DIVISIONS? ☐ YES ☐ NO	DATES EMPLOYED	WHICH DIVISION	SUPERVISOR	POSITION
LIST NAMES OF FRIENDS OR RELATIVES NOW EMPLOYED BY THIS COMPANY.				
HAVE YOU EVER BEEN CONVICTED OF A CRIME? ☐ YES ☐ NO (CONVICTION OF A CRIME DOES NOT AUTOMATICALLY DISQUALIFY AN APPLICATION FROM CONSIDERATION) IF YES, PLEASE EXPLAIN.				
ARE THERE ANY JOBS FOR WHICH YOU DO NOT WISH TO BE CONSIDERED? PLEASE EXPLAIN.				

PERSON TO CONTACT IN CASE OF EMERGENCY

THIS INFORMATION IS TO FACILITATE CONTACT IN THE EVENT OF AN EMERGENCY AND IS NOT USED IN THE SELECTION PROCESS.

FULL NAME	ADDRESS	PHONE	RELATIONSHIP TO YOU
PLACE OF EMPLOYMENT	ADDRESS	PHONE	

APPLICANT'S SIGNATURE

(COMPLETE BOTH SIDES OF APPLICATION)

Figure 1.4 PERSONAL DATA SHEET INFORMATION

Create a durable, easy-to-carry card or sheet with the following pieces of information about *you*. You will then have all the information you need to fill out application forms.

- **Your whole name**
- **Local (current) address**
- **Permanent address**
- **Telephone number**
- **Alternate telephone number** (cell phone, work number)
- **Emergency contact information** (name, address, telephone number)
- **Social Security Number**
- **Education History** (name of school, address, years attended, degree or certificate earned, year it was awarded, major and minor concentrations)
- **Work History** (name of business, address, telephone number, supervisor's name, start and end dates for employment, job title, brief description of job duties, starting and ending salary, reason for leaving). Have this information available from all of your past jobs, beginning with the most recent and working backwards.
- **Special Skills** (typing speed, foreign languages, computer programs)
- **Honors and Awards**
- **References** (name, address, telephone number, relationship to you). Always get permission from the person before you list him or her as a reference. Usually, employers will ask for three references, and often they specify that the person may not be a relative and you must have known the person for at least a year.

Security number and take it with you when you are applying for a job. Keep the card at home in a safe place.

Work Permits

Federal and state laws regulate the work conditions and the working hours of employees under age 16 or age 18. If you are under age 16, you will need a **work permit**—an official document that verifies your age and usually outlines the specific duties you are allowed to perform. Some states require work permits for employees younger than 18.

Your Résumé

Some employers get the information they need to make a hiring decision from an application form. Others accept applications in the form of résumés. A **résumé** (pronounced *REZ-oo-MAY*) is a summary of the job applicant's personal information, education, skills, work experience, and special interests.

A good résumé presents this information in a well-organized form that an employer can review in just minutes. After you have prepared one good résumé, you can customize it to relate directly to a specific job.

Résumés are prepared in a variety of formats, usually in an outline limited to one or two pages. In most cases, your résumé should include the following information in separate sections:

- *Job title:* State the name of the job or position for which you are applying. If you use the same basic résumé for different jobs, then you can change the job title accordingly.
- *Contact information:* State your name, address, phone numbers, and e-mail address.
- *Education:* List the schools you have attended and the courses you have completed that will help you perform this particular job. List any certificates, college degrees, and honors.
- *Special skills:* List any skills you have developed that show you are especially qualified for this job.
- *Experience:* List all of the jobs you have had, including volunteer jobs, and briefly describe your duties for each job.
- *School activities and awards:* List any that relate to the job for which you are applying.
- *References:* List several people who will give you good recommendations. Don't list your school friends. List professional people, teachers, or your school counselor. If you prefer, simply state that references are available on request. In any case, ask for permission before providing names of references.

Creating a résumé is often a nerve-racking experience, especially for those just entering the job market. Many services are available to help you craft your résumé. For entry-level jobs, it is probably sensible to use a free service such as the ones at Monster.com or Job-Star.org. The library will have books to help you, too.

A well-prepared, polished résumé can give you an advantage over other applicants. A résumé lets you describe your qualifications with wording similar to the employer's job description. An example of a good printed résumé is shown in Figure 1.5.

Electronic Résumés When you apply for a job listed on the Internet, you may be able to mail or fax a copy of your résumé to the employer. Sometimes,

work permit an official document that verifies an employee's age and usually outlines the duties that he or she is allowed to perform

résumé a summary of a job applicant's personal information, education, skills, work experience, and special interests

however, you are asked to send an e-mail message with your résumé attached. An electronic version of your résumé is known, simply, as an *electronic résumé*. It is an electronic file prepared using a word processing program. You may be asked to create a résumé using the Web site's own résumé builder.

You will want to prepare the document so that it will be easy to transmit and easy to read. Save your résumé file as a text-only file. Do not use any bold type, underlining, or italics. Use a traditional font, such as Times New Roman, and 12-point type.

Keywords Many companies that accept electronic résumés use a computer program rather than a person to scan résumés. A person will look it over only after the computer program determines that you are qualified. The program will search for keywords that indicate your qualifications.

Figure 1.5 **SAMPLE PRINTED RÉSUMÉ**

Gwendolyn DeSilva
1234 Forest Drive
Woodbridge, TN 31785
888.888.8888
gdes@myemailaddress.com

OBJECTIVE

An administrative assistant position.

SUMMARY OF SKILLS

Organizational
- Worked at local business to compile data and enter information onto computer server for easy access by all employees; implemented improvements for streamlining data entry without losing necessary information.
- Assisted in managing customer requests regarding product location; answered phones.

Secretarial
- Skilled in Vista, Word, Excel, Lotus 1-2-3, and PowerPoint.
- Experienced in document formatting and proofreading.
- Ability to type 68 words per minute with no errors.

Communication
- Wrote article for local and state newspapers about the importance of ergonomic furniture in the workplace.
- Delivered a speech to local woodcarvers association about the importance of maintaining regular dialogue between board members and furniture store employees, resulting in a monthly conference call between board members and hospital employees.

EDUCATION

- *Jefferson High School*, Woodbridge, TN (3.8 GPA).
- Graduated 12th in class of 425 students.

EXPERIENCE

- *Furnish Your Home*, Administrative assistant, Summer 2007, 2008.
- *Wood Is Beautiful*, Stock assistant, Summer 2006.

◀ What three things can you do to ensure that the information you post in an online résumé does not get into the wrong hands?

Keywords are verbs, nouns, and phrases that highlight previous job duties, job titles, industry names, technical areas of expertise, achievements, and names of personal traits. Good keywords include verbs such as *managed, supervised, analyzed, repaired, planned,* and *constructed.* Some experienced job hunters place a grouping of keywords in a "Summary of Qualifications" section near the top of the résumé.

The best source of appropriate keywords is the actual job listing that describes the job you want. The job description will likely contain most—perhaps all—of the keywords that the employer's computer will search for to select qualified applicants. However, expand your use of keywords by reading a number of job descriptions that are similar to the job you want—and then include them in your résumé, too. An example of an online job listing and an electronic résumé that uses keywords from that listing is shown in Figure 1.6 on the next page.

Electronic Résumé Banks An electronic résumé bank is a place where a large number of résumés are stored and available to employers who wish to review the qualifications of job applicants. The résumé banks you will find on the Internet are known as the "computer dating agencies" of the job search. Hundreds of employers all over the country subscribe to these matching services and list their job descriptions. This process may work better for applicants with extensive experience than it will for those just getting started.

Problems in Providing Personal Information

Be careful about how much and what kind of personal information you provide on your résumé. For example, if you are presently working, you may not want your employer to know that you are looking for another job. In addition, you do not want your identity stolen by criminals who troll cyberspace. (Identity theft will be discussed in Unit IV.)

Online résumé banks offer varying degrees of confidentiality. Some require passwords so that only employers who are authorized can search the database. Others are basically open to the world.

Do not use a job search site or a résumé bank that does not post a privacy policy on its Web site. Some sites allow you to mask your contact information. Before posting your résumé, make sure you will be able to delete it later.

Cover Letters

A **cover letter** is a short letter in which you introduce yourself and say

keywords the words and phrases in a résumé that a computer program will search for to determine whether an applicant is qualified for a job

cover letter a short letter to accompany a résumé, introducing the applicant to an employer and explaining why the applicant would do a good job for the company

Figure 1.6 ONLINE JOB LISTING AND ELECTRONIC RÉSUMÉ

Tailor your résumé to reflect the language used in the job description. If you do not have certain experiences, you cannot list them, but you can put down every skill and experience you have that is relevant to the job you are applying for.

Sample Online Job Listing

Skilled Trade Professionals Needed

Make a difference in the lives of customers by joining the world's largest home improvement retailer. Every day, customers of The House Store rely on our associates to make their home improvement dreams come true! They will depend on your expertise as a skilled trades professional to answer questions, provide guidance and recommend the best products for the job. Plus, with the increased security and benefits a career at The House Store can provide, you will be sure to make an impact every day.

Key Accountabilities

- Seek and provide customer service to all customers within department, with emphasis on residential, repair and remodel, and other professional customers
- Maintain expert knowledge on all products and services offered in department
- Remain up-to-date on all industry guidelines and practices
- Assist customers by explaining steps required to complete projects
- Conduct customer clinics and seminars
- Train, coach, and develop other associates
- Maintain a safe working and shopping environment

Minimum Qualifications

- 18 years or older
- Pass the drug test
- Pass the background check
- Pass the validated selection test
- Possess an active state/agency license within the last six years OR successful completion of Department of Labor approved 4-year apprenticeship program
- Minimum 5 years of experience working as an electrician or plumber

Preferred Qualifications

- 8 to 10 years of experience
- Knowledge of state and local electrical or plumbing codes

Sample Electronic Résumé

ALEXANDER WATT
6789 Main Street, Hillsboro, FL 34567
888.888.8888
alexwatt@myemailaddress.com

OBJECTIVE

A challenging career at The House Store utilizing more than five years of progressive, skilled professional electrical and general repair experience.

QUALIFICATIONS

- Self-motivated; able to work independently and as team member .
- Expert knowledge on related products and services, industry guidelines, and electrical codes allows the ability to answer customer questions, provide guidance, and recommend products.
- Profound ability to isolate defects in wiring, switches, and motors.
- Developed customer service skills, having dealt with a diversity of professionals and clients in residential repair and remodel jobs.
- Function well in high-pressure atmosphere.
- Adapt easily to new concepts and responsibilities.

PROFESSIONAL EXPERIENCE

The Lighting Store
Summer 2007-Present Electrical Contractor/Electrician
Write proposals/estimates for residential and commercial wiring, then perform work as requested. Handle electrical and general repairs (including washers, boilers, burners, and lock repair). Oversee assistants as required. Conduct customer clinics and seminars.

The Electric Company
Summer 2005-2006 Electrical Assistant
Dealt with electrical, heating, and assembly needs of residential customers.

Kite and Key Electricians
Summer 2004 Electrical Assistant

RELEVANT TRAINING

Sweels Windmill High School, Franklin, MN (3.6 GPA)
Relevant classes include:

- Electronic Circuits I and II
- Machine and Assembly Language
- Microprocessor Systems and Design

REFERENCES

Available upon request

why you think you can do a good job for the company. It is your first opportunity to tell the employer about yourself.

When you submit an electronic résumé, you may not have an opportunity to include a cover letter. However, when you send a printed résumé to an employer, you should always include one. An example is shown in Figure 1.7.

Prepare a custom cover letter to accompany each résumé that you mail to an employer. Address the letter to a specific person, usually the hiring manager, by his or her name. Your letter should speak to the needs of the company and how you can help fulfill those needs. Check the company's Web site, and incorporate what you learn about the company into your letter.

Employers receive letters, résumés, and applications by the hundreds and do not have time to read long letters. Get to the point. Introduce yourself in the first paragraph and give the title of the job for which your are applying. In the next one or two paragraphs, state your interests and qualifications and why you think you can do an especially good job for this company. In the closing paragraph, take the initiative by stating that you will call next week to arrange a time when you can meet to discuss the position.

Even one misspelled word or incorrect piece of information will tell the employer that you will probably be careless in your work. Make certain that you correctly spell the company name and the name of the person to whom your letter is addressed.

Figure 1.7 SAMPLE COVER LETTER

Ronaldi Asmeldo
2345 Main Street
Suburbia, MN 55412
888.888.8888
asmeldo1@myemailaddress.com

August 15, 20—

Ms. Soo Yin Cheung
Human Resources Manager
1-2-3 Accounting, Inc.
400 Division Street
Minneapolis, MN 55402

Dear Ms. Cheung:

I was excited to read about the Accounting position opening at 1-2-3 Accounting, Inc. I have several years of experience in a variety of fields, including accounting, business, and marketing.

In addition to my extensive office experience, I have strong communication and organizational skills, proven customer service ability, and well-rounded administrative skills. My broad background makes me an excellent candidate for this position.

Your company Web site says that you provide services for a wide range of small businesses. My father owns his own business, and I do the accounting for it. I understand many of the challenges your clients face, and I would enjoy helping them solve their unique problems.

Thank you for your consideration. I will call early next week to arrange an interview time.

Sincerely,

Ronaldi Asmeldo
Ronaldi Asmeldo

SECTION 2 ASSESSMENT

Factual Recall

1. What is the best source of job leads for most people?
2. Why is it necessary to have a Social Security number before you apply for a job?
3. How can you know which keywords are important to include in an electronic résumé?
4. If you have prepared a good résumé, is there still a need for a cover letter? Why or why not?
5. Why should you check your résumé and cover letter for errors?

Critical Thinking

1. How should you prepare for a job fair?

SECTION 3

Interviewing and Pre-employment Testing

Focus Questions

1. In what setting do employers usually make hiring decisions?
2. What are three things you should do to get ready for a job interview?
3. What are six things you can do to make a good impression in an interview?

Key Terms

interview
credit score

Your sole purpose in filling out an application form or preparing a résumé and cover letter is to convince an employer to interview you. An **interview** is the formal meeting in which you and the employer discuss the job and your qualifications. This meeting usually takes place in person, but it may occur over the phone or Internet. It is nearly always during the interview that an employer decides whether to hire you.

Prepare for the interview. This will boost your confidence and help make sure that the interviewer's first impression of you is favorable. Learn as much as you can about the company, practice what you will say, and dress appropriately.

interview a formal meeting between an employer and a job applicant

Did You Know?

People with visible tattoos are often eliminated as candidates for a job even if they are highly qualified. One tattoo shop owner says that if someone wants a tattoo on the wrists, hands, or face, "we give them a 15-minute lecture on how it will be there for the rest of their life." Many of his customers switch to a tattoo that will not be visible on the job.

Making a Good Impression

An old saying is certainly true of the job interview: "First impressions are lasting impressions." The first minute of your meeting with an interviewer is the most critical. Make a good impression in the first minute, and the interviewer will have positive feelings about you throughout the interview.

Jennifer Scott, manager of recruitment at the Petro Company in Stamford, Connecticut, had this to say about what makes for a good versus a bad interview:

"The worst mistake someone can make for an interview is being late. It doesn't matter how bad the traffic was. There's no excuse for being late—ever." What makes for a good impression? "Someone who's well-prepared all around. They've dressed appropriately, arrived on time or even a few minutes early, and they have a list of good questions they want to ask."

Here are some practical suggestions for making a good impression at a job interview:

- *Go alone.* Some young people take along a friend for support, but this is unprofessional and always makes a bad impression on employers.
- *Smile and make eye contact.* When you meet the person who will interview you, smile and look the person in the eye.
- *Answer questions thoughtfully.* Give yourself time to compose thoughtful answers. Speak with confidence and enthusiasm and use standard English. It is called *standard* English because it is consistent, and it is understood by all English speakers.
- *Handle illegal questions intelligently.* An employer's questions must be related to the job you are seeking. In the United States, it is illegal to deny employment solely on the basis of a person's age, color, disability, gender, sexual orientation, national origin, race, religion, or creed. If you are asked an illegal question, you will have to decide whether or not to answer. You may answer such a question if you wish. However, if you give the "wrong" answer, you might be harming your chances of being hired.
- *Ask good questions.* Usually you will be invited to ask some questions. Use your first question or two to show a sincere interest in the company and the job. Money may or may not be discussed by the interviewer. If not, it is all right to ask how much the job pays—but wait until near the end of the interview.
- *When it's over, go!* Try to sense when the interview is almost over. Most interviewers will say something like, "Well, I believe I have all the information I need." Don't linger, and be sure to thank the interviewer for his or her time before you leave.
- *Write a thank-you letter.* Write a letter thanking the interviewer for his or her time and saying how interested you are in the job. A sample thank-you letter is shown in Figure 1.8 on the next page.

Answers to Fact or Fiction

1. True; **2.** True; **3.** True; **4.** False—Although many adult Americans fell into their line of work by chance, it is good to take a step-by-step approach to choosing a career since it will affect most aspects of your life; **5.** False—Some of the more traditional ways of locating job leads, such as reading the classified ads in the paper, are not relied on as much as in the past; **6.** True; **7.** False—Many great jobs are never advertised because businesses fill them with friends of employees.

▼ Bring a personal data sheet with you to your interviews to make the application process easier.

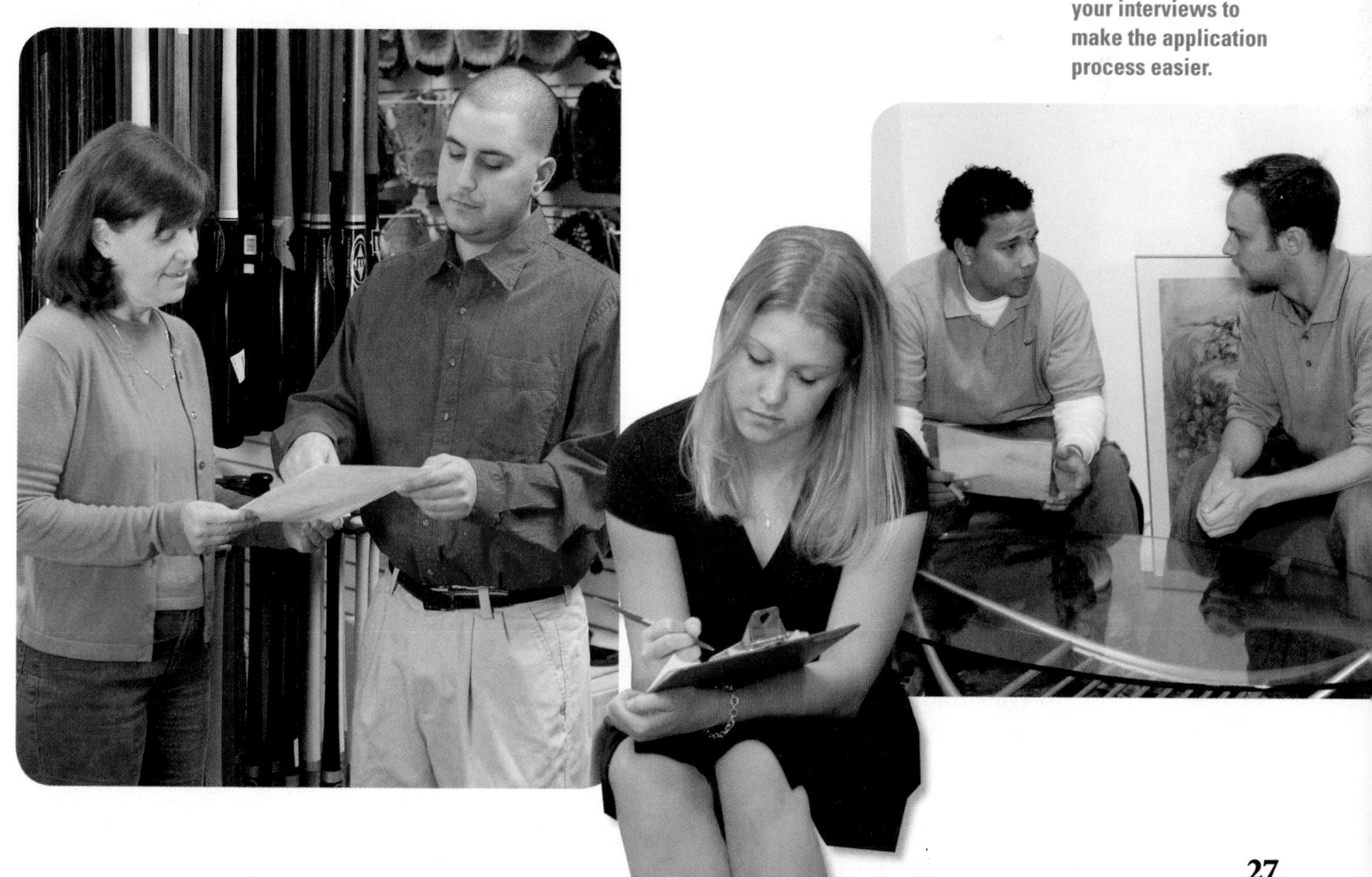

Figure 1.8 **SAMPLE THANK-YOU LETTER**

Start with your name, street address, telephone number, and e-mail address.

Howard Hammond
1234 Main Street
Santa Paula, CA 93060
888/888.8888
hoha@myemailaddress.com

Include the date.

May 12, 20–

Write the name and title of the interviewer, then the company name and address.

Mrs. Christine Jones
Editor
Best Publisher in America, Inc.
1010 Moneymaking Avenue, Suite 789
Portland, OR 97225

Use a greeting and the formal title of the interviewer (Dr., Mr., Mrs., Ms, Miss).

Dear Mrs. Jones:

Tell the interviewer you enjoyed the interview, and remind him or her of the position you interviewed for. Include a detail of what he or she said to show you were paying attention.

I enjoyed speaking with you about the Assistant Editor position at Best Publisher in America, Inc. The job you described is an excellent match for my skills and interests. I am especially excited about the opportunities for working on manuscripts at different stages in the development and production processes.

Remind the interviewer of all your good skills specific to the job. The interviewer may have talked to a lot of candidates. The thank-you letter can help him or her connect your name with your skills.

The duties the job will entail fit well with my work experience. I have edited articles and advertisements. Additionally, I worked in a writing lab and helped develop content in essays written by my peers. Not only did this train me to think about ideas and grammar, but it also taught me how to work well with others.

The third paragraph is your opportunity to list your other skills and interests. Remind the interviewer how qualified you are and that you are the best person for the job.

As we discussed in the interview, I am proficient in Vista, Word, Excel, and PowerPoint. I type 65 words per minute, and I can operate fax and copy machines. I speak Spanish fluently, and I had the opportunity to practice it when studying in Mexico on a school mission trip.

Thank the interviewer for taking the time to meet with you. Politeness makes a good impression.

Remind the interviewer of your interest in working for *this* company at *this* job, and that you are eagerly waiting to find out when you start!

I appreciate your taking the time to interview me. I am very interested in working with you at Best Publisher in America, Inc., as an Assistant Editor, and I look forward to hearing from you.

Use a respectful closing.

Sincerely,

Sign your name.

Howard Hammond

Type your name below your signature.

Howard Hammond

Pre-employment Testing

On most jobs, it takes awhile before new employees are productive enough to be profitable for the company. Many jobs require at least some on-the-job training, and the company pays for this training. Hiring employees who don't work out is not profitable and leads to a high turnover rate. To ease this problem, more and more companies have turned to pre-employment testing to screen out applicants who are not suitable for particular jobs. Among the tests most often used are those that measure aptitude, skills, and honesty. Psychological tests, personality tests, medical tests, and drug tests are also used for screening. Note the sample questions in Figure 1.9.

These tests are used only to see whether you would be a good fit for the job, so do your best but try not to worry. If you don't score well on a test for that job, then you probably wouldn't want the job anyway. Anyone who fails a test for illegal drugs, of course, would not be hired for any job.

Checking Your Credit Score

Many employers today look for another score, one they don't get from pre-employment testing—your credit score. A **credit score** is a number based on information in your credit report, and it indicates your credit risk. The credit report information comes from your credit accounts and loans, late payments, bankruptcies, and recent inquiries. There are several types of credit scores, but FICO (Fair Isaac Corporation) scores are most often used in the United States and Canada. Credit scores range between 300 and 850. The average credit score in the United States is about 680.

In the past, only banks and financial service companies checked credit scores on job applicants. Now employers in other business sectors are checking the credit records of potential employees. They view the credit score as a measure of responsibility and organization. Credit scores, however, were not designed to be a predictor of employability, and using them in this way can put young people at a disadvantage. Students and young workers do not have a long credit history—*so it is all the more important for your credit record to be squeaky clean.* Your credit record and credit score will be discussed more fully in later chapters.

credit score a number based on information in a credit report, indicating the person's credit risk

Figure 1.9 SAMPLE PRE-EMPLOYMENT TEST QUESTIONS

Shown below are just a few of the many types of questions you might be asked as part of a pre-employment test.

An example of a "Clerical Skills" test question:

Compare the numbers in Column A to those in Column B. Then answer the question below.

Column A		Column B	
75823	85537	87537	73358
82537	87537	85537	82357
73358		75823	

Which number in Column A has no match?

(A) 82537 (B) 85537 (C) 87537 (D) None

An example of a "Number Skills" test question:

Multiply the numbers below:

1.5 x 6.3

(A) .945 (B) 9.45 (C) 94.5 (D) 945

An example of a "Reading" test question:

Choose the one answer that BEST fits the meaning of the word in capital letters.

TRANSCRIBE

(A) to transport (B) to copy (C) to repeat (D) to exchange

ASSESSMENT

Factual Recall

1. What is the purpose of completing a job application form or sending a résumé and a cover letter?
2. Name three things you should do to prepare for a job interview.
3. How can a good credit score help you obtain the job you want?
4. At what point during a job interview should you ask how much the job pays?
5. What should you do after a job interview?

Critical Thinking

1. Being late for a job interview makes a bad impression. How can you avoid being late?
2. During a job interview, you are asked about your religion. What are some ways you could respond?

CHAPTER 1 REVIEW AND ASSESSMENT

Chapter Summary

Section 1 Your Income and Your Career

- Before you can spend money, you need to earn or acquire it.
- The five major sources of income for people in the United States are income from jobs; business profits; investment earnings; government payments; and grants, royalties, and inheritances.
- Your career will be a major factor in shaping your identity.
- Because your career affects every other aspect of your life, it is important to choose carefully.

Section 2 Finding and Applying for Jobs

- Networking is the best source of job leads.
- Professional and trade organizations are an excellent place for networking.
- Job/career fairs are another networking opportunity.
- Job leads can come from traditional sources, such as newspaper ads, as well as newer sources, such as the Internet.
- The Internet can be a good source of job leads, but you have to be careful. Select reputable sites and check their privacy policies.
- It is important to keep your job search well organized and to follow up quickly on job leads.
- Applying for a job usually involves an application form, a résumé, and a cover letter. You may also need other documentation.

Section 3 Interviewing and Pre-employment Testing

- Because hiring decisions are usually made during an interview, it is critical to make a good impression.
- Many employers require pre-employment testing.
- Many employers check a job candidate's credit score.

Reviewing Key Terms

Match the following terms with their definitions.

a. **wage**
b. **salary**
c. **tip**
d. **commission**
e. **entrepreneur**
f. **sole proprietorship**
g. **partnership**
h. **corporation**
i. **plan of action**
j. **networking**
k. **application form**
l. **personal data sheet**
m. **résumé**
n. **cover letter**
o. **grants**
p. **royalties**

1. The process of building professional relationships that assist both parties in reaching their goals.
2. Someone who organizes, manages, and assumes the risks of owning a business.
3. Pay that is figured at an hourly rate.
4. A questionnaire in which a job seeker answers questions about personal information and job qualifications.
5. A summary of a job applicant's personal information, education, skills, work experience, and special interests.
6. Pay that is the same each month, regardless of the number of hours worked.
7. A business with co-owners.
8. A list of the steps needed to reach a career goal.
9. A voluntary payment that a customer makes to an employee, figured as a percentage of the bill.
10. A short document introducing a job applicant to the employer and explaining why he or she would do a good job for the company.
11. A percentage of the total sale, paid instead of, or in addition to, salary or wages.
12. A business owned by one person.
13. A business owned by a group of stockholders.
14. An outline of the information usually requested on a job application form.
15. Payments given to people or institutions, which do not have to be paid back.
16. Percentage of sales in dollars paid to the creators of a work, such as a song, when copies of the work are sold.

Understanding the Main Ideas

1. What is the difference between a wage and a salary?
2. Why is it important to start thinking about investing even before you start doing it?
3. Describe the step that is missing from this procedure for choosing a career: daydream; make a self-assessment; gather information; set a realistic goal; make a decision.
4. If a business is not advertising its job openings, how might you find out about them?
5. Name three traditional sources of job leads.
6. Name three online job sites.
7. When you are doing an online job search, why is it a good idea to use a portal site?
8. Why should you follow up a job lead as soon as possible?
9. When preparing an electronic résumé, why should you save it as a text-only file?
10. List two reasons you should be careful about posting personal information on a job search site or résumé bank.
11. What is a work permit? Why might you need one?
12. What is the difference between a job application and a résumé?
13. List six things you can do to make a good impression during a job interview.
14. Why do some employers do pre-employment testing?

Practicing Math

1. Find out the minimum hourly wage in your state. At that wage, how long would it take to earn $500?
2. You have two job offers. Job A pays $33,500 per year and is in a state with 3 percent state income tax. Job B pays $32,500 and is in a state with no income tax. In which job would you receive more money?

Applying Critical Thinking Skills

1. Why is it important to examine your values, interests, and personality when thinking about a career? What influence do these have on what you do and how you feel about it?
2. Most people change careers several times during their working lives. Why is it still important to give careful thought to choosing your first career?
3. The government provides financial aid to help students pay for a college education. The benefit to the students is obvious, but what is the benefit to the nation?
4. Bigjobsite.com promises "thousands and thousands" of job listings. Is this site likely to help you locate a job? Why or why not?
5. When searching for a job, is it better to focus on finding just the right job or just the right company? Give reasons for your answer.
6. Your interviewer asks you a question and you do not know the answer. How should you respond?

Working with Real-World Documents

1. Obtain a job application form. What questions does it ask? Why are these answers important to the company?
2. Download several résumé forms from the Internet and compare them. Which do you think would be appropriate for someone just entering the job market? Explain your answer.

Taking It Home

1. Interview three people to find out how they came to be in their current careers. What role did planning play? What role did chance play?

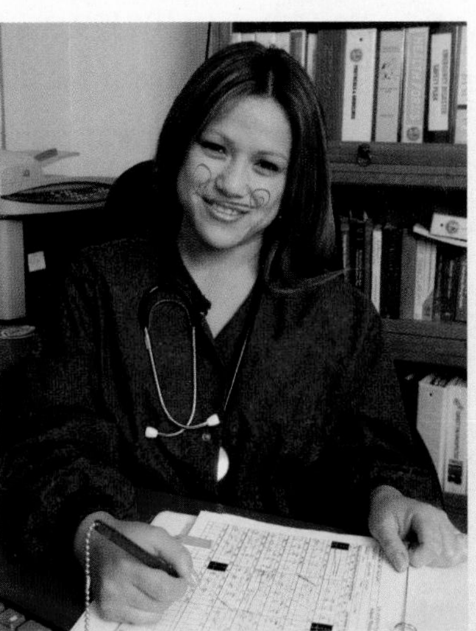

CHAPTER 2

Job and Career Success

You found the best job leads, and you filled out application forms. You wrote résumés and cover letters. You survived an interview—perhaps several—and you just accepted a job offer. Now what?

Starting a new job is always a little stressful. You don't yet know what will be expected of you. Do not forget, however, that you were hired because your new employer was convinced that you were the best person for the job— a good team member and a productive worker. There are plenty of reasons to expect that you will adapt quickly and soon be winning promotions and raises.

▲ **Congratulations—you got the job! Now you have a real opportunity to earn money and become a successful employee.**

SECTION 1 Success from the Start

SECTION 2 Promotions and Lifelong Learning

SECTION 3 Entrepreneurship: Owning Your Own Business

Fact or Fiction

What do you think? Are the following statements true or false? If you think they are false, then say what is true.

1. If you are clean and well groomed, your supervisor will probably assume that your work is reliable.
2. Every new employee must fill out and sign a Form W-4.
3. Legal immigrants do not need a Social Security card to work in the United States.
4. People get fired for using their computers at work for personal use.
5. Generally, state-supported colleges and universities are less expensive to attend than private schools.
6. Most entrepreneurs hold other jobs while they are starting up their own new businesses.
7. A sole proprietorship is so easy to set up that you may already own one without knowing it.

Answers on page 57.

Study Reminder

*Knowing how to study can increase your knowledge, improve your grades, and cut down on your study time. See the **Studying Personal Finance** pages at the front of the book for some tips to help you study this chapter.*

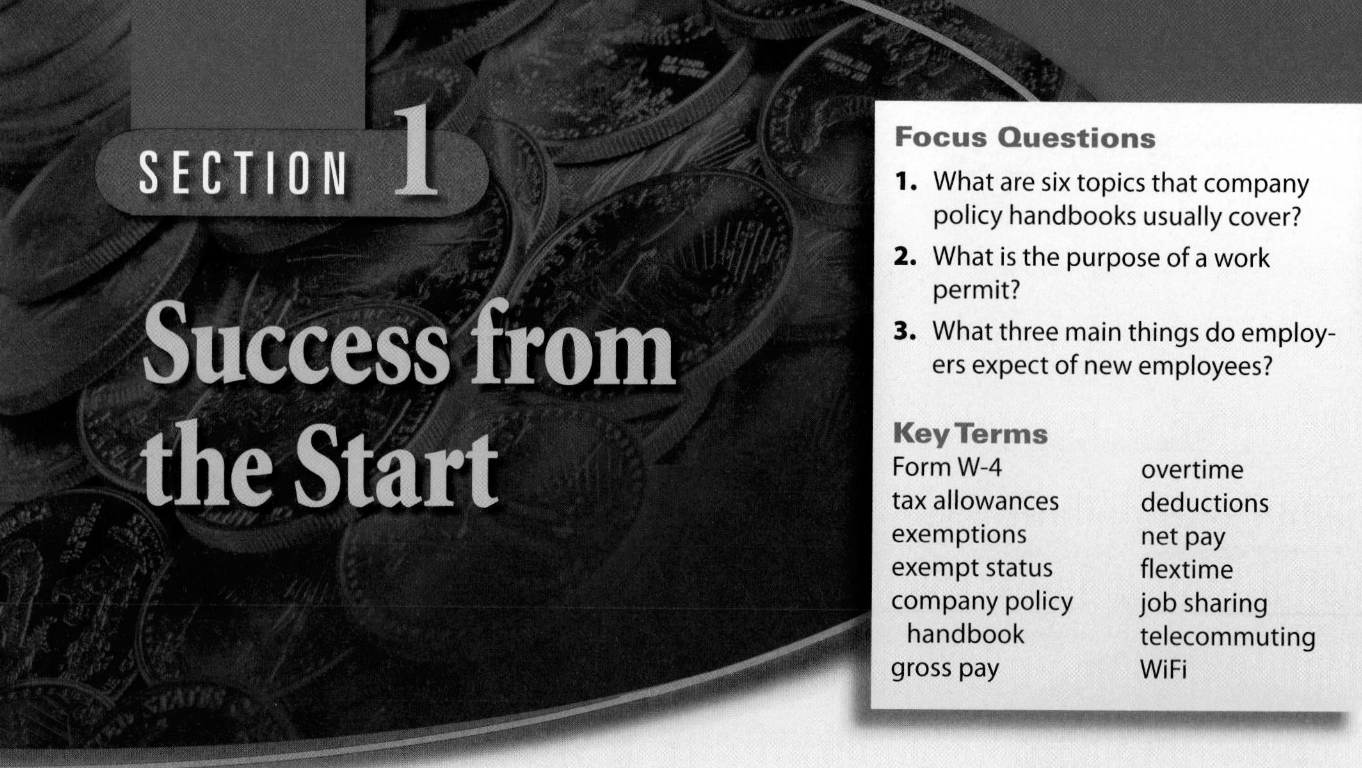

SECTION 1

Success from the Start

Focus Questions

1. What are six topics that company policy handbooks usually cover?
2. What is the purpose of a work permit?
3. What three main things do employers expect of new employees?

Key Terms

Form W-4
tax allowances
exemptions
exempt status
company policy handbook
gross pay
overtime
deductions
net pay
flextime
job sharing
telecommuting
WiFi

When you start a new job, it may take awhile to feel that you are really part of the team. Most employers understand this and will give you time to adjust to your new work environment. You will have some legal paperwork to read and sign. You may be given a company policy handbook.

You know that first impressions tend to be lasting impressions. On your first day, and at least for the first week or so of a new job, make your appearance count. Dress a little nicer, a little neater, than most of the other workers. "Dress how you want people to perceive you because it plays a huge role in how you are initially treated," advises GE Capital Credit analyst Desiree Devaney. "Perfectly groomed means efficient and reliable in your work; unkempt means disorganized and perhaps untrustworthy with difficult assignments. After awhile, people realize these things do not necessarily correspond, but initially, your looks and dress represent who you are."

According to AmeriCorps program coordinator Ann Marie Russell, your boss and coworkers form a lasting impression about you in the first days they know you. Right from the start, they form opinions about your typical behavior and the type of person you are. If you miss work or come in late during the first few days or weeks, you will already have lost their confidence in you. People will take you seriously if you seem to take yourself and your work seriously. Knowing how to handle yourself during the first few days on the job can give you a big advantage over other new employees.

▶ **First impressions count. Which of these people do you think will be taken seriously and trusted in the first days of a new job? Explain your choice.**

Legal Forms, Documents, and Company Rules

On your first day at work, you will probably be asked to go to the human resources office—sometimes called the personnel office—to read and sign some legal forms and documents. One of these forms specifies the amount of income tax to be withheld from your earnings. You will also need your Social Security number and perhaps a photo ID. If you are under age 18 (or 16 in some states) you will need a work permit, as noted in Chapter 1.

Many companies give new employees a handbook that explains company rules and general expectations. You will probably need to read and sign other papers as well, including health insurance forms.

Form W-4

Every new employee must fill out and sign a **Form W-4**, like the one in Figure 2.1. The W-4, titled the *Employee's Withholding Allowance Certificate*, comes

Form W-4 an IRS form indicating how much should be withheld from an employee's earnings to pay federal income taxes

Figure 2.1 **SAMPLE PORTION OF THE FORM W-4**

You use the Form W-4 to tell an employer how many tax allowances you have. The more allowances you claim, the less your employer will withhold from your paycheck to pay your federal income taxes. You can download the Form W-4 (and other tax forms) from http://fin.emcp.net/IRSpublications.

Personal Allowances Worksheet (Keep for your records.)

A Enter "1" for **yourself** if no one else can claim you as a dependent . . . . A ______

B Enter "1" if: { • You are single and have only one job; or • You are married, have only one job, and your spouse does not work; or • Your wages from a second job or your spouse's wages (or the total of both) are $1,000 or less. } . . B ______

C Enter "1" for your **spouse.** But, you may choose to enter "-0-" if you are married and have either a working spouse or more than one job. (Entering "-0-" may help you avoid having too little tax withheld.) . . . . C ______

D Enter number of **dependents** (other than your spouse or yourself) you will claim on your tax return . . . . . D ______

E Enter "1" if you will file as **head of household** on your tax return (see conditions under **Head of household** above) . E ______

F Enter "1" if you have at least $1,500 of **child or dependent care expenses** for which you plan to claim a credit . . F ______
(**Note.** Do **not** include child support payments. See Pub. 503, Child and Dependent Care Expenses, for details.)

G **Child Tax Credit** (including additional child tax credit). See Pub 972, Child Tax Credit, for more information.
• If your total income will be less than $57,000 ($85,000 if married), enter "2" for each eligible child.
• If your total income will be between $57,000 and $84,000 ($85,000 and $119,000 if married), enter "1" for each eligible child plus "1" **additional** if you have 4 or more eligible children. G ______

H Add lines A through G and enter total here. (**Note.** This may be different from the number of exemptions you claim on your tax return.) ▶ H ______

For accuracy, **complete all worksheets that apply.** { • If you plan to **itemize or claim adjustments to income** and want to reduce your withholding, see the **Deductions and Adjustments Worksheet** on page 2. • If you have **more than one job** or are **married and you and your spouse both work** and the combined earnings from all jobs exceed $40,000 ($25,000 if married) see the **Two-Earners/Multiple Jobs Worksheet** on page 2 to avoid having too little tax withheld. • If **neither** of the above situations applies, **stop here** and enter the number from line H on line 5 of Form W-4 below. }

Cut here and give Form W-4 to your employer. Keep the top part for your records.

Form **W-4** Department of the Treasury Internal Revenue Service | **Employee's Withholding Allowance Certificate** ▶ **Whether you are entitled to claim a certain number of allowances or exemption from withholding is subject to review by the IRS. Your employer may be required to send a copy of this form to the IRS.** | OMB No. 1545-0074 20–

1 Type or print your first name and middle initial. | Last name | 2 Your social security number

Home address (number and street or rural route) | 3 ☐ Single ☐ Married ☐ Married, but withhold at higher Single rate. **Note.** If married, but legally separated, or spouse is a nonresident alien, check the "Single" box.

City or town, state, and ZIP code | 4 **If your last name differs from that shown on your social security card, check here. You must call 1-800-772-1213 for a replacement card.** ▶ ☐

5 Total number of allowances you are claiming (from line **H** above **or** from the applicable worksheet on page 2) | 5 |

6 Additional amount, if any, you want withheld from each paycheck . . . . | 6 | $

7 I claim exemption from withholding for 20–, and I certify that I meet **both** of the following conditions for exemption.
• Last year I had a right to a refund of **all** federal income tax withheld because I had **no** tax liability **and**
• This year I expect a refund of **all** federal income tax withheld because I expect to have **no** tax liability.
If you meet both conditions, write "Exempt" here . . . . ▶ | 7 |

Under penalties of perjury, I declare that I have examined this certificate and to the best of my knowledge and belief, it is true, correct, and complete.
Employee's signature
(Form is not valid unless you sign it.) ▶ **Date** ▶

8 Employer's name and address (Employer: Complete lines 8 and 10 only if sending to the IRS.) | 9 Office code (optional) | 10 Employer identification number (EIN)

For Privacy Act and Paperwork Reduction Act Notice, see page 2. Cat. No. 10220Q Form **W-4** (20–)

from the Internal Revenue Service (IRS), a division of the U.S. Department of the Treasury. The W-4 indicates how much should be withheld from your earnings to pay your federal income tax. Whenever your tax situation changes, you will need to adjust your withholding by filling out and signing a new Form W-4.

The W-4 includes a worksheet to help you calculate your **tax allowances**. These allowances (or **exemptions**) reduce the amount of federal tax withheld from your paycheck. The more allowances you claim, the less your employer will withhold. However, if you do not withhold enough, you will owe more federal income tax at year's end. That means you will have to pay all the rest of your tax bill by April 15 of the following year. If the amount you owe is large, you might have a problem coming up with the money. In addition, you may have to pay a penalty if you fail to withhold enough. On the other hand, if your federal income tax for the year is actually less than the total amount withheld, the IRS will send you a *tax refund*.

tax allowances amounts calculated on the Form W-4 that reduce the federal tax withheld from a person's paycheck

exemptions another word for *tax allowances*

exempt status a release from paying taxes because of insufficient income

If you did not have to pay taxes last year and you expect to earn less than a certain amount this year ($900 in 2008), you may claim **exempt status**. In that case, write the word "Exempt" on line 7 of the W-4, and your employer will not withhold any tax. However, if your earnings increase during the year, you may no longer be tax exempt. It is important to keep accurate records and update your Form W-4 as necessary.

In addition to completing a Form W-4 for federal tax withholding, you may be asked to complete and sign a similar form for withholding state income tax in the state where you live or work.

▶ All new employees must fill out a W-4 form to indicate how much should be withheld from their earnings to pay their federal income tax.

Social Security Cards and Numbers

In Chapter 1, you learned that all workers must have a Social Security number before they can be legally employed in the United States. If you were born in the United States, you most likely have had a Social Security number and card since you were a child. If you did not get a Social Security number as a child, you will have to get one before you begin working. To obtain a Social Security number, you must prove your age and identity, as well as your U.S. citizenship or immigration status, by supplying documents such as the following:

- U.S. birth certificate
- U.S. passport
- Certificate of naturalization
- Certificate of citizenship
- U.S. driver's license
- State-issued non-driver identity card
- U.S. military identity card

The Social Security tax rate is 6.2 percent. Your yearly Social Security tax, then, is 6.2 percent of your total annual earnings—but only up to a certain amount ($102,000 for 2008); the amount can increase slightly each year. Any earned income above that amount is not subject to the tax. Your employer will contribute an equal amount on your behalf. If you own your own business, you pay both the employer's and employee's shares—totaling 12.4 percent of your earnings.

In addition to Social Security contributions, 1.45 percent of all earnings must be paid into the Medicare fund. If you are self-employed, the Medicare tax is 2.9 percent—which makes your total withholding 15.3 percent of gross earnings. Social Security benefits and the future of this government program will be discussed in a later chapter.

Work Permits

U.S. employers must check to make sure all employees, regardless of citizenship or national origin, can legally work in the United States. If you are not a citizen or a lawful permanent resident, you may need to apply for a type of work permit called an Employment Authorization Document (EAD). An EAD is issued by the U.S. Citizenship and Immigration Service (USCIS) and proves that you are allowed to work in the United States.

Beyond that, the *federal* government does not require work permits or proof-of-age certificates for a minor (under age 18). Most *states*, however, do require permits for workers under age 18—or under 16 in some states. Your school counselor will know whether you need a work permit. These permits are intended to protect young workers—from working long hours or from performing jobs that are considered too dangerous. The numbers of hours young people can work per day and per week are limited according to age. Special work permits are issued for those under age 14, permitting them to work as models, actors, or performers (singers, dancers).

Company Policy Handbook

The federal government and the Equal Employment Opportunity Commission (EEOC) require every business to have a formal **company policy handbook**. Handbooks outline the general rules and regulations of the company. Having these rules, policies, and procedures in a formal, written form provides a comfort level for all workers. Everyone will know what the company expects at the workplace and how the company will handle problems when they do occur. Figure 2.2 shows excerpts from a company policy handbook.

A policy handbook helps new employees in particular. It provides answers to basic questions and outlines what the company expects in terms of employee conduct and performance. You will want to read and understand everything in your company's policy handbook. Among

company policy handbook a booklet outlining a company's rules, policies, and procedures

Figure 2.2 **SAMPLE EMPLOYEE HANDBOOK EXCERPTS**

You can expect to find these and other topics covered in a company policy handbook.

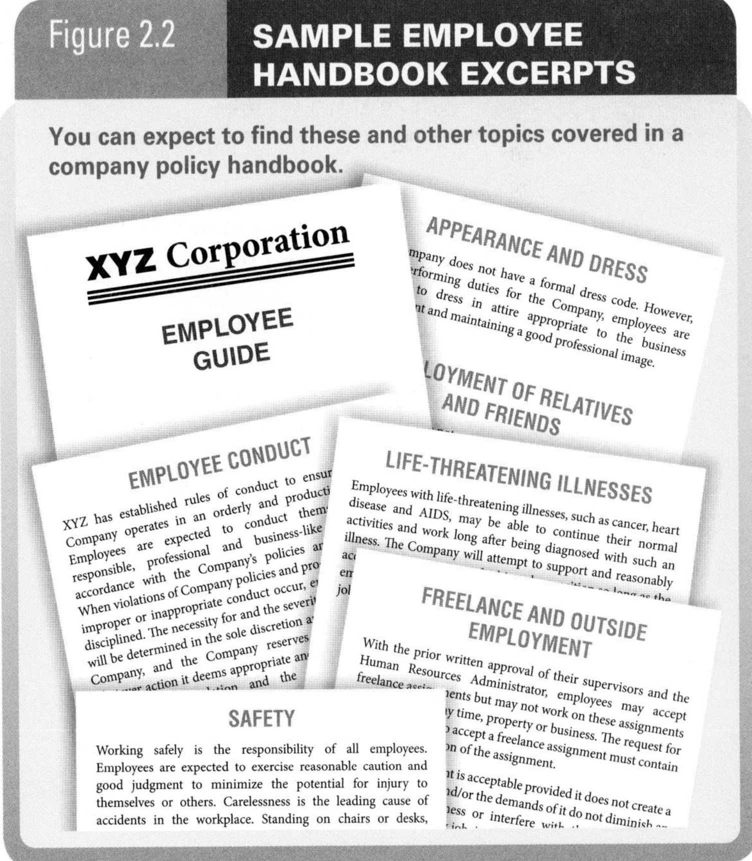

YOU DECIDE

Shavaun has been working with computers at home and at school since kindergarten. He recently started full-time work stocking shelves and cashiering at Mel's Electronics, which sells everything from oven timers to computers. Shavaun has also enrolled in night school at the local community college to study computer engineering.

Shavaun hopes to join the tech staff in Mel's repair department as soon as he can show Mel that he is qualified. His long-term goal is to own his own computer repair and support service, and he knows he needs on-the-job experience before going out on his own.

The Mel's Electronics company policy handbook clearly states that overtime is voluntary—that is, employees can refuse to work overtime. Mel is impressed with Shavaun's work and asks him to work overtime several days a week. Shavaun agrees at first, but after a few weeks he is too tired to study for his computer engineering classes. He even misses a couple of classes because he's working.

Shavaun tells Mel that he doesn't think he should work overtime during the college terms—though he is happy to work more during the holiday season and summer. Mel makes it clear that he is unhappy with Shavaun's decision. He implies that Shavaun may not have what it takes to run his own business.

Shavaun does not want to disappoint Mel and does not know where else he could get experience repairing computers. But he also knows that he needs to take college courses to learn more about how computers work and what can go wrong with them. He knows that he will have to work long hours if he wants his own business, but he isn't sure if he needs to start now.

Should he . . .

1. ...cut back on his night school course load? Quit night school entirely? Explain.
2. ...work as many hours in his job at Mel's as he would starting his own business? Why or why not?

other topics, most handbooks include information about the following:

- Personal appearance
- Working hours and overtime
- Break policy
- Standards of conduct
- Absenteeism and punctuality
- Salary and wage increases
- Performance reviews
- Insurance
- Holidays and vacations
- Medical and family leave
- Safety on the job
- Personal telephone calls
- E-mail policies
- Prohibited computer uses
- Substance abuse
- Termination procedures

Develop Good Working Relationships

You will want to do everything you can to promote smooth working relationships with your coworkers, your supervisor, and your managers within the company. Promoting good working relationships depends on learning what others need and want, both on the job and in their lives. By doing what you can to make others' work easier and their lives happier, you will be making your own job and life easier, too.

Do what you can to reduce the chances for conflict, and deal with conflict constructively when it does occur.

The following guidelines can help you promote good working relationships on the job:

- Always treat others with respect.
- Honor your commitments.
- Support others in achieving their work objectives.
- Provide clear, realistic, and timely proposals to management.
- Provide your supervisor/manager with timely and accurate reports on your activities and achievements.
- Provide your supervisor/manager with clear and accurate information on problems you encounter in doing your work or achieving company objectives.

Employer Expectations

Employers know it takes time to learn a job, and most are willing to allow you that time. You will probably have a lot of questions. If you cannot figure out how to do something right away, be quick to ask your supervisor or an experienced coworker, so that you can get on with the job. If their answers or instructions are complicated, take notes so that you can refer to them later. Your employer and your supervisor will see that you are trying to grasp the details of your job, and they will appreciate your effort.

Beyond that, employers have certain expectations of their workers—particularly that workers will follow company rules, have a good work ethic, and accept criticism with maturity.

Follow the Rules Your employer will expect you to follow the rules, beginning with those listed in the company policy handbook. And whether or not it is discussed in the handbook, keep your personal business on company time to a minimum. You may, on occasion, have to make or answer a personal phone call during working hours—but make such calls brief and infrequent. If your coworkers or supervisor see or hear you making too many personal calls, they may think you don't take your job seriously. Even if your supervisor never observes you making a personal call, the word will get around if you do it very often.

Work equipment—including your computer—is not for personal use. It is legal for employers to install software that tracks everything you do on office computers. Most employers today use this type of software. Your employer can read any personal e-mail that you send out from a computer in the workplace. Any Web sites that you visit using a computer on the job can be easily tracked as well. People *do get fired* for using computers at work for personal use. Don't risk it.

Develop a Work Ethic and a Positive Attitude Your employer will expect you to arrive on time, or even a few minutes early, so that you will be ready to

▼ Start establishing a positive working relationship from the minute you are introduced to a new coworker. Shake hands firmly, make eye contact, repeat the person's name and position, and express your interest in the person and his or her job.

begin work on time. You will be expected to work a full day for a day's pay, and to show up for work every day. Of course, you may encounter emergencies or you may get sick, but you must always call to let your employer know what is going on. Keep absences to a minimum.

When you arrive at work, greet everyone with a smile and a positive attitude to show that you are happy to be a part of the team. Be accepting and friendly toward everyone, and let your enthusiasm for your job show—even when you have problems outside of work.

Figure 2.3 **SAMPLE EVALUATION FORM**

Employee Performance Evaluation Instrument

Employee Name: ______________________ **Job Title:** ______________

Name of Evaluator: ______________________ **Date:** ______________

I. Organization and Planning

Evaluation of Performance	Outstanding	Satisfactory	Needs Improvement	Does Not Meet Expectations
A. Is punctual and regular in attendance	☐	☐	☐	☐
B. Utilizes work time efficiently	☐	☐	☐	☐
C. Performs all assigned duties promptly, accurately, and effectively	☐	☐	☐	☐
D. Demonstrates initiative and good judgment	☐	☐	☐	☐
E. Performs other duties as appropriate and/or directed	☐	☐	☐	☐

Comments:

II. Interpersonal Relations and Communication

Evaluation of Performance	Outstanding	Satisfactory	Needs Improvement	Does Not Meet Expectations
A. Creates an inviting and professional atmosphere	☐	☐	☐	☐
B. Maintains a cordial and effective relationship in meeting the public	☐	☐	☐	☐
C. Demonstrates courtesy and professionalism in all communications	☐	☐	☐	☐
D. Appropriately and effectively communicates with coworkers and the general public	☐	☐	☐	☐

Comments:

Accept Criticism and Admit Your Mistakes No one does every job perfectly. Your supervisor or a more experienced coworker may, on occasion, criticize some aspect of your work. In most cases, that's part of *their* job. Usually, their criticism is meant to be constructive, to help you improve on the job. Although it is never pleasant to receive criticism, try your best to accept their suggestions as being constructive. Thank the person—even if you suspect that the correction might not have been meant as constructive. That way, you can turn it into something positive.

Everyone makes mistakes. When you make a mistake, admit it immediately. Few employers will fire an employee simply for making a mistake. Admitting your errors shows that you can take responsibility for your actions, and it makes you look stronger.

Employee Expectations

As an employee, you can reasonably expect certain things from the company where you work. You already know that you can expect your employer to introduce you to other employees and explain company policies, rules, and regulations. You can also expect your employer to do the following:

- Pay your salary
- Provide certain *fringe benefits*—such as sick days, vacation days, health insurance, and possibly a pension fund for retirement
- Provide some training to help you perform your job
- Provide reasonable accommodations if you have a disability
- Tell you about changes in your duties, working relationships, pay rate, schedule, or vacation time
- Evaluate your work, providing both constructive criticism and praise when appropriate (see Figure 2.3)

Your Take-Home Pay: Where Did All the Money Go?

Charlene wanted to become a veterinarian. Assuming that she would gain useful experience, she accepted a twelve-week summer job at a riding academy in California. She fed, groomed, and exercised the horses. She helped with repairs to the barns and riding area. She was to work forty hours per week and would be paid $10 an hour. Charlene did not make precise calculations, but in round numbers she was counting on about $400 a week, or $4,800 for the twelve weeks.

After working two weeks, Charlene got her first paycheck. She was surprised to see that it was for only $675.72—not $800—and she had even worked a couple of hours of overtime! (**Overtime** hours are those worked beyond forty in one week; normally overtime pay is 1½ times the usual rate.) What happened to her money?

For that two-week period, Charlene's **gross pay**—the total amount earned before any deductions are subtracted—was based on working forty hours a week at $10 per hour, plus two hours of overtime:

80 hours × $10	=	$800
+ 2 hours × $15	=	30
Total gross pay	=	$830

Look at the paycheck stub in Figure 2.4, below. The amounts subtracted from the gross pay are called **deductions**. These include amounts taken out for Social Security tax, federal income tax withholding, and Medicare tax. Charlene also had deductions for California's state income tax withholding and state disability insurance (SDI) withholding. California law requires every one of these deductions.

The check for $675.72 represents Charlene's **net pay**—also called *take-home pay*—and is the amount she receives after all deductions have been subtracted. When Charlene reaches her goal and begins working as a veterinarian, she will likely have even more deductions taken from her gross pay, such as health insurance, dental insurance, retirement savings, and perhaps several others.

overtime hours worked in addition to the legal limit of forty hours per week

gross pay the total amount of wages or salary earned before any deductions are subtracted

deductions amounts subtracted from gross pay, such as Social Security tax, federal and state income tax withholding, health insurance, retirement, and so forth; also refers to expenses that are subtracted from income on a tax return

net pay the amount received after all deductions have been subtracted from a paycheck; also called *take-home pay*

Figure 2.4 **CHARLENE'S PAYCHECK STUB**

The paycheck stub below represents Charlene's first two weeks of work. The right-hand column under YTD, or Year-to-Date, is a cumulative record of all of her earnings and will increase with each paycheck. With this column, she always knows how much she has earned for the year.

PERSONAL AND CHECK INFORMATION
Charlene Jones
10000 A Avenue
Santa Paula, CA 95060

Soc. Sec. #: XXX–XXX–XXXX **Employee ID:** 4321
Hire Date: 06/22/08
Status:
Filing Status:
Federal: Single, 1
State: CA, Single, 1
Dept: 065

Pay Period: 06/22/08 to 07/04/08
Check Date: 07/09/08 Check #: 431000

EARNINGS	*DESCRIPTION*	*HOURS*	*RATE*	*CURRENT ($)*	*YTD HOURS*	*YTD ($)*
	REGULAR EARNING	80.00	10.00	800.00	80.00	800.00
	OVERTIME	2.00	15.00	30.00	2.00	30.00
	GROSS	82.00		830.00		830.00

WITHHOLDINGS	*DESCRIPTION*	*CURRENT ($)*	*YTD ($)*
	FEDERAL W/H	74.31	74.31
	MEDICARE	12.04	12.04
	STATE W/H CA	9.83	9.83
	SOCIAL SECURITY	51.46	51.46
	SDI W/H	6.64	6.64
	TOTAL	154.28	154.28

NET PAY		*CURRENT ($)*	*YTD ($)*
	$675.72	**675.72**	**675.72**

▶ Telecommuters work outside the office, usually at home. High speed internet service allows them to communicate with employers, coworkers, clients, and others.

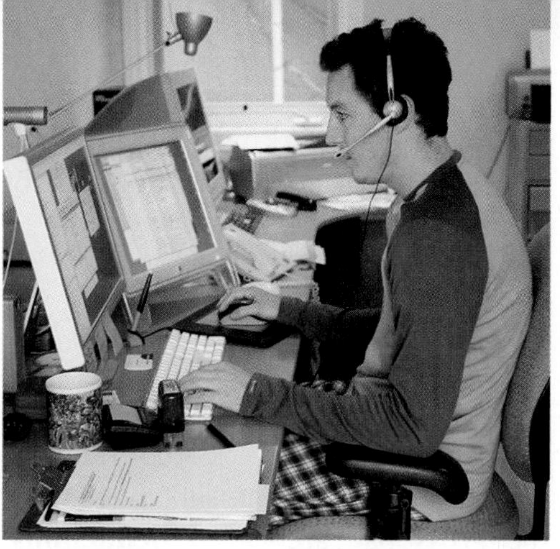

Alternative Work Arrangements

A study by Spherion Corporation, an international staffing and recruiting firm, found that 96 percent of employees preferred to work for an employer who helped them meet family obligations by offering work options like flextime, job sharing, or telecommuting. These alternatives to traditional work situations have become more common in recent years.

flextime a work schedule with flexible hours

job sharing a situation in which two or more employees share the same job

telecommuting working outside the office, usually from home, using a computer

WiFi short for *wireless fidelity*, a high-speed Internet connection

Flextime simply refers to flexible work hours. Most flextime employees work a full eight-hour day—but they begin early and leave early, or they start later in the day and leave later, rather than following the typical 9-to-5 schedule. Some flextime employees may work four ten-hour days or other combinations that total forty hours per week.

Job sharing occurs when two employees share one job. The employees may each work four hours per day, or one may work two days a week and the other work three days. The employees and the employer may agree to some other work arrangement that allows the workers to meet multiple demands on their time—like college classes, the raising of young children, or some other business obligation unrelated to this job.

Telecommuting refers to working outside of the office, usually from home. Telecommuting also makes it possible for employees to work after hours or on the road. It also allows people with disabilities to participate in wider job markets. Telecommuting has become a practical arrangement through the use of high-speed Internet service. Most hotels now provide wireless high-speed Internet connections (**WiFi**, short for *wireless fidelity*). In some places, an entire city will provide WiFi service for anyone who wants a connection.

Overall, telecommuting tends to reduce overhead, the need for office space, and turnover. It usually increases productivity too. It seems to work especially well for professionals, such as engineers or computer programmers. The Gartner Group, a technology research firm, estimated that in 2008, some 41 million employees around the world would spend at least one day each week telecommuting. The largest portion of telecommuters is U.S. workers.

SECTION 1 ASSESSMENT

Factual Recall

1. True or False: The federal government requires work permits for those under age 18.
2. What is the purpose of a company policy handbook?
3. Name three things employers expect of their workers.
4. Name three things workers can expect of their employers.

Critical Thinking

1. You have just started a new job and have questions about the company's overtime policy. Should you ask a coworker? Why or why not?
2. A friend sends e-mails to you at work. Is it OK to reply on the company computer? Why or why not?
3. Suppose you and a coworker have a disagreement and then have to work together on a project. How might you resolve the conflict?

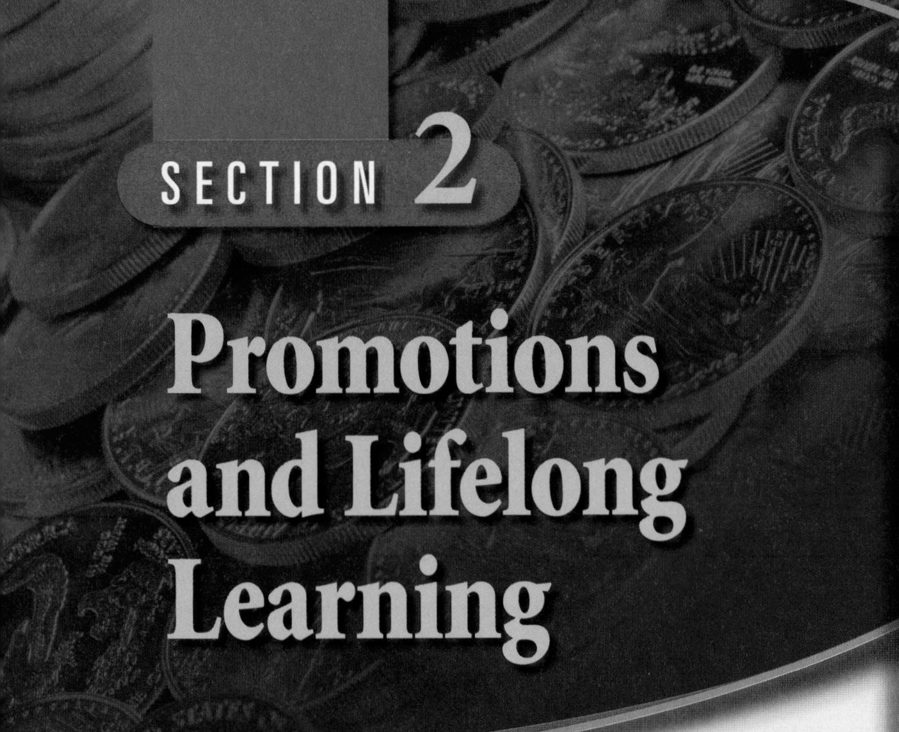

SECTION 2 Promotions and Lifelong Learning

Focus Questions

1. Why are many tasks formerly done by U.S. workers now performed overseas?
2. How do you go about selecting a college or university?
3. What are some alternatives to attending a four-year college or university?

Key Terms

mentor
in-service training
community college
trade school
apprenticeship program
learning networks

Summer jobs and the part-time jobs that you might take while you are in high school are usually temporary. They don't provide many chances for promotion to higher-level positions where you would have more responsibility and a bigger paycheck. But some exceptions come up. *Always perform your current job as if you are working toward a promotion.* If such an opportunity comes along, you will have a much better chance of being selected. Develop work habits now that make you stand out as *a candidate for promotion.* These skills will serve you well throughout your career.

The global economy of the twenty-first century has already brought changes. Many jobs formerly held by U.S. workers are now done overseas where labor costs are much lower. Even highly skilled workers in such countries as India and China will work for very low wages. When you begin full-time employment, you will be competing not just with other Americans but also with well-qualified workers worldwide.

Many entry-level jobs will require more than a high school education. Promotions in many companies already require a four-year college degree. After you become a full-time worker, continued success in your career will require that you commit to lifelong learning. Plan to take extra training seminars and evening classes to keep up-to-date. Many companies will set up the seminars or pay for classes to keep their employees educated.

Did You Know?

From 2001 to 2005, entry-level wages for both high school and college graduates dropped, even though the overall economy was growing. Much of the drop could be traced to job competition from overseas workers, and it did *not* affect the two groups of graduates equally.

Hourly wages for male high school graduates fell 3.3 percent, to $10.93. For female high school grads, the average was down 4.9 percent, to $9.08 per hour.

For college graduates, wages were down 7.3 percent for males and 3.5 percent for females. But entry-level wages were still almost twice as much for college grads as for high school grads: Men earned an average of $19.72 per hour, and women $17.08. Even in a tight job market, education paid!

Pay Raises and Promotions

Of course, do your best to perform on the job in a way that meets all of your employer's expectations, as discussed in Section 1. By doing so, you will meet the job's minimum requirements and you may qualify for an increase in pay after some period of time—usually after six months or a year. However, don't be satisfied with meeting just the minimum requirements. You will greatly increase your chances for promotion and continued advancement in your career if you actively pursue success. The following three tips for getting promoted will give you an advantage over most other young workers:

1. *Help your coworkers.* When you have finished with your own work, talk with your coworkers and supervisor to learn how you can help with additional tasks.
2. *Take the initiative.* Look for some unmet need and ask your supervisor if you may assume responsibility for fulfilling this need. Use your problem-solving skills. Look for better, more efficient, or less costly ways to approach tasks. Efficiency that leads to increased productivity will almost always win praise from management because it leads to increased company profits.
3. *Find a mentor.* A **mentor** is someone, usually an older person, who provides advice and support to guide your career. The best mentors are experienced workers who are especially knowledgeable, well-respected by other employees, and willing to share their experiences with you. A good mentor can provide valuable guidance that you couldn't get elsewhere. Your mentor may well be flattered to be approached, and a mutually beneficial friendship could result.

mentor a more experienced person who offers advice and support to guide someone's career decisions

Continuing Education and Training

Take advantage of every educational opportunity you can. The reality is that today and in the future your competition will not be limited to workers in your hometown, in your state, or even within the United States. The global

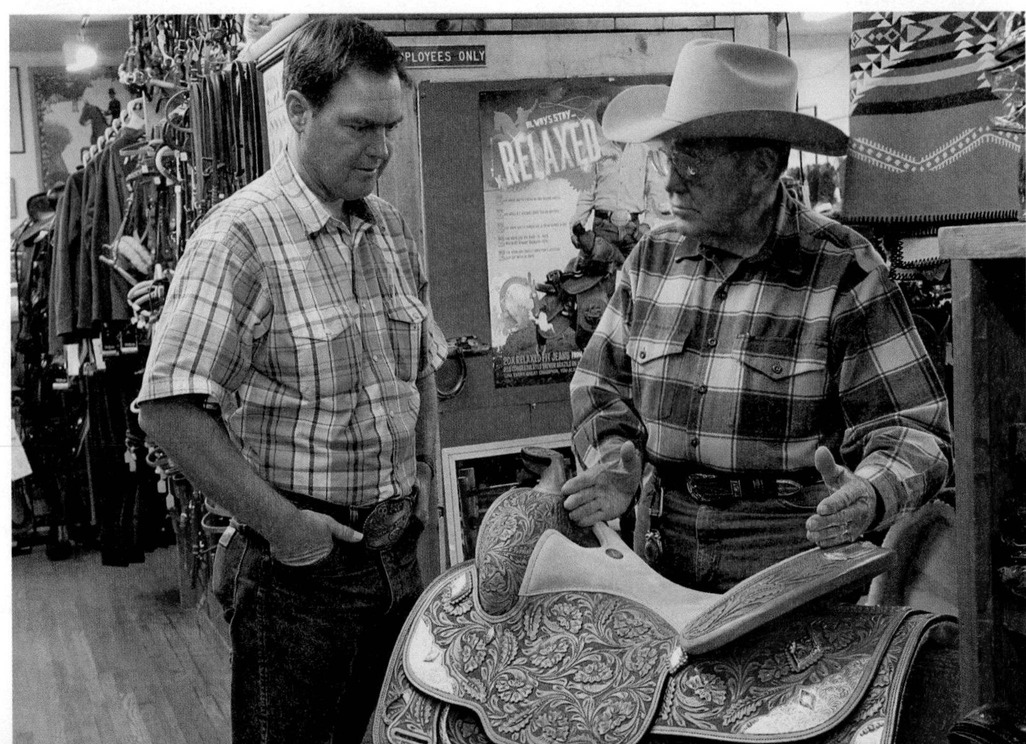

▶ **Whatever your age, you can probably find someone older and wiser and willing to help you learn. What kinds of things would you like to ask a mentor?**

economy is becoming more truly integrated. You will have to compete with workers all over the world. Because the labor costs of overseas workers are usually much lower, you can use advanced education to put yourself ahead of the competition. Be ready to learn new skills and new ideas—and to keep on learning. You will need to continue your education throughout your entire life.

Many companies provide **in-service training** for their employees. These in-service training sessions, sometimes called *professional development seminars*, seek to develop employee skills, provide information, and improve working relationships among current employees. Many companies also pay to send selected employees to professional conferences in other cities.

In-service training and conferences, of course, lie somewhere in your future when you work for a company full-time. For now, you need to consider what type of educational program will best prepare you to compete for a job in the career field you have chosen. You may decide, for example, that working part-time while also going to school part-time is the best plan for you. Or you may be better off attending school as a full-time student. If your goal is to prepare for a career in the trades or a skilled craft—such as electrician, carpenter, plumber, or technician—you might attend a trade school or you might decide to begin an apprenticeship. Your decisions will depend on your lifestyle, your career goals, and your finances.

Colleges and Universities

The United States has hundreds of colleges and universities. Whatever your lifestyle and career goals, probably a dozen or so schools could give you good chances for success. How do you know where to apply? Some helpful tips include the following:

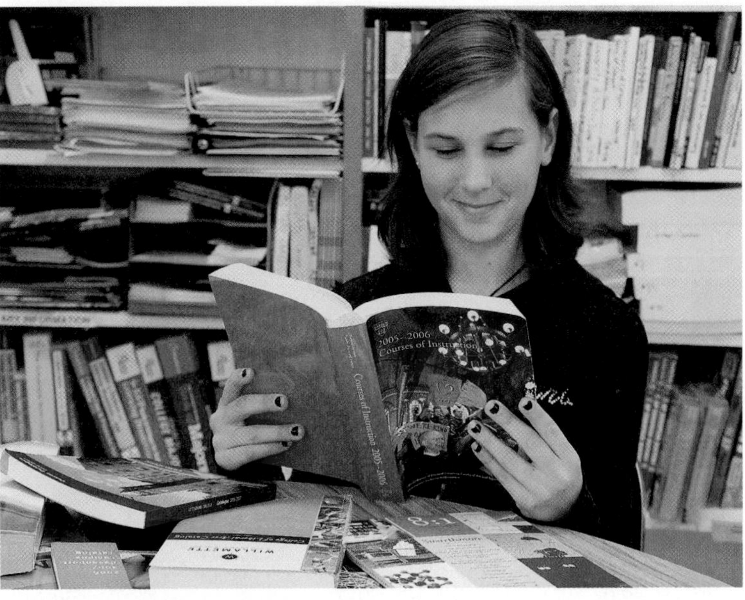

▲ College and university guides and catalogs tell you what different schools offer, what they require for admission, about how much they charge in tuition and fees, and much more.

- *Consider reputation.* Choose schools with good reputations for preparing students in the career you would like to pursue. Talk with your school counselor, look through college catalogs, research schools on the Internet, and talk with people already working in your chosen field.
- *Consider your financial resources.* Think about your financial resources—and your parents' willingness and ability to help you financially. Generally, state-supported colleges and universities are less expensive to attend than are private schools. For the 2004–2005 school year, the average cost for *tuition* (the price for instruction), fees, and books ranged from $5,491 to $21,235. The lower costs were at state-supported schools, and the higher costs were at private universities. Students who lived on campus spent, on average, another $6,222—or $690 per month—for room and board. These costs sound like a lot of money, but keep in mind that qualified students can apply for financial aid. In fact, for the 2005–2006 school year, 63 percent of students received some

in-service training employee classes for developing skills, providing information, and improving working relationships among employees; also called *professional development seminars*

LOOK Before You Leap

Danielle is an advertising layout artist at the local newspaper. She wants to study psychology and eventually design advertising campaigns for a major ad agency. College will be necessary. She has visited three campuses of her state's public university, as well as a nearby private university.

All the colleges she is considering have strong art and psychology departments. They each have good relationships with businesses and public agencies that offer student internships. Any of them would be a good choice. Danielle decides she will attend whichever one accepts her first.

Danielle knows her education would cost more at the private college than at a state university, but she is shocked to learn it would actually cost *four times* as much. She is ready to cross the private school off her list—but then her boss convinces her that she should check into getting financial aid. He says she will need to contact the private school's aid office. He also points her to helpful Web sites.

A U.S. government site (http://fin.emcp.net/studentaid) has information about federal loans and grants. She can even calculate the amount she would be eligible for. The College Board site (http://fin.emcp.net/collegeboard) can help identify more than 2,000 other sources of funding, including scholarships offered by specific industries—such as advertising, Danielle's choice. She thinks maybe she can find a way to attend the more expensive college.

Before Enrolling

1. Why might it be worth it to spend the extra money to attend a private college?
2. Why would specific industries offer scholarships to college students?
3. Why is it a good idea to explore your financing options before applying for admission to a college?

form of aid—either loans, grants, or both, according to the National Association of Student Financial Aid Administrators. Take some care if you choose to finance your studies with loans only: The average debt for graduating college seniors who borrow to finance their undergraduate degree is almost $20,000.

- *Read college guides and catalogs.* You can find out the approximate costs of attending most colleges and universities by reading college guides in your school or public library, or online. Each of these guides describes many colleges, their offerings, admission requirements, and other information. You will find more specific information in individual college catalogs.
- *Discuss your goals and plans.* Talk about your college plans and career goals with your school counselor, parents, and teachers. Discuss your ideas with someone who has already achieved success in your chosen field. Talk with friends who are now in college and ask them about the schools they attend.
- *Visit campuses.* Visit the campuses of schools that seem most promising and try to spend a few days on each campus. Take your time and ask questions. This is your chance to

evaluate the different schools to see how well they might fit your needs.

- *Apply to several schools.* When you decide you would like to attend a particular college, you will need to complete an application package. Many colleges and universities have four or five times as many applicants as they can accept—so it's wise to apply to several schools. Most students narrow their choices to about five or six schools—in part because the application fees themselves are high. If applicants are accepted by more than one school, they will have the final choice of where they will enroll.

Did You Know?

Surveys by industry and government agencies have estimated that between 79 percent and 99 percent of companies help their employees pay to attend college while they continue to work. The American Council of Education reports that roughly 20 percent of graduate students and 6 percent of undergraduate students get some form of tuition assistance from their employers.

One reason most companies help with college costs is to keep good employees on the payroll. It could take several years to get through a college education while working full-time. If the employer helps with college costs, the student is likely to stay with the company until graduation. Employees who are willing to take on the extra work necessary to get a degree are likely to be more ambitious and energetic than others. The employee develops company loyalty and also becomes a better-trained, more productive worker. Tuition assistance can help you at the same time it helps your employer.

Other Educational Opportunities

Your career goal may call for less than a four-year college program, or maybe your high school grades are not quite good enough to get you into the college of your choice right away. The thought of going to a four-year college or university may intimidate some students. If any of these situations describes you, don't worry. You have many educational alternatives.

▲ A two-year college may be a good option if you want to continue your education but don't feel that a four-year college is a good fit for you.

Community Colleges A **community college** (two-year college) is sometimes called a *junior college* or a *city college.* Attending a two-year college is less expensive than attending a four-year college or university. You probably have a community college nearby, perhaps in your home town. If so, you can live at home and save the cost of room and board while attending college.

When you enroll in a community college, you can even begin a four-year college program leading to a bachelor's degree. However, be sure you take courses that a four-year college or university will accept when you transfer after your first two years. Contact a counselor to help you plan your program if you wish to transfer.

Trade Schools A **trade school** is an institution of higher learning that teaches the skilled trades. It is not a college or university. If you attend a trade school, you will take courses only in your chosen

community college a two-year college that offers an associate's degree; also called a *junior college* or a *city college*

trade school an institution of higher learning that teaches the skilled trades

Do Your RESEARCH

Once you are engaged in full-time work, it may seem that you have no time to further your education. Perhaps there are not any colleges in your area. Or maybe you cannot find any degree programs that match your career needs. Getting a degree online can be a solution.

Many accredited land-based universities, colleges, and trade schools have online degree programs. You will also find "virtual" universities that have no physical campuses but exist only on the Web. Both types of online schools may be able to help you reach your educational goals. As with anything on the Web, though, it's important to do your research to avoid scams (false offers meant only to take your money). Your best choices will be schools with regional accreditation and professional accreditation.

U.S. News and World Report provides an online list of all regionally accredited universities offering online degrees (http://fin.emcp.net/elearning). It has information about cost as well as links to each university's Web site. Programs for different areas of study—business, education, public health, and so forth—are listed separately, so you can target the area you need.

Employers look for degrees from colleges with professional accreditation in their field. Here you may have to research a little deeper. For instance, the largest online institution is the University of Phoenix (UOP). It has 220,000 undergraduate and 60,000 graduate students. All programs at UOP are *regionally* accredited, but their most popular degree program, the MBA, is not *professionally* accredited. Would that make a difference to a potential employer? Consider factors like this before you enroll in an online degree program.

Your Assignment

1. Log on to the *U.S. News and World Report* site and browse the list of colleges in your area of interest. Compare costs and accreditations. Explore the Web sites of several land-based schools as well as some online offerings.
2. What advantages and disadvantages do you see with getting a college degree online instead of in person at a land-based university?

field. Many schools allow you to choose morning, afternoon, or evening classes. Class time is often spent in joblike settings solving real work problems.

Private trade schools charge tuition ranging from a few hundred dollars to several thousand dollars for a complete program. The length of time for instruction depends on the skills you wish to learn. For example, truck driving courses last from one to eight weeks, and medical technician courses last from forty-eight to seventy-two weeks. Most trade school courses can be completed in less than two years—so you can usually begin working full-time sooner than if you attend a two-year community college. If you are interested in learning more about trade schools, talk with your high school counselor.

apprenticeship program an education that combines on-the-job training with formal classroom instruction

Apprenticeships An **apprenticeship program** combines on-the-job training and formal classroom instruction. The teachers are experienced trade instructors. Training normally runs from two to five years, depending on the trade. Apprenticeship programs usually require you to graduate from high school. Apprentice learners work full-time, but

▲ Trade schools and apprenticeships provide training in technical skills like installing garage door openers and welding.

are paid only a percentage of what skilled workers earn. As apprentices increase their skills, their pay rate also rises.

Apprenticeships require cooperative effort by employers, schools, employee organizations, labor groups, and an apprenticeship agency. These training programs are flexible and can be established for training new workers in many careers. The most popular programs include training in machining, painting, plumbing, carpentry, and sheet metal/ HVAC systems.

Nontraditional Programs Successful people continue their education throughout their lives, either to learn new employment skills or for personal growth. They do this through a great many alternatives to traditional educational programs—or sometimes in traditional programs. Most lifelong students combine classes with full-time employment. Alternatives include adult evening classes and **learning networks**, in which individuals come together online to share their skills and knowledge.

Other educational alternatives include correspondence courses and courses on cassette tapes or DVDs. Some colleges even allow you to complete most of your studies for a bachelor's degree at home. Your public library can put you in touch with dozens of educational opportunities. Your local YMCA and YWCA probably sponsor a variety of classes for recreational education.

learning networks online discussions in which participants share skills and knowledge

SECTION 2 ASSESSMENT

Factual Recall

1. Why have many U.S. jobs moved overseas?
2. List six things to do when preparing to choose a college or university.
3. A four-year college or university is one place to obtain education for a career. Name three others.
4. Give two reasons why someone who already has a job should continue to pursue educational opportunities.

Critical Thinking

1. Your friend cannot decide whether to enroll in a four-year university now or attend a community college for two years and then transfer. List some pros and cons of each choice.

SECTION 3

Entrepreneurship: Owning Your Own Business

Focus Questions

1. What are four advantages of being an entrepreneur?
2. What are three forms of business organization?
3. What is a limited liability company (LLC)?

Key Terms

entrepreneurship
franchise
franchisor
franchisee
articles of incorporation
limited liability company (LLC)

Most Americans rely on salaries or wages that they earn by working for someone else. Most employees seem at least reasonably satisfied to perform their work according to the boss's wishes. Many say they love their jobs. Others, however, are not quite so satisfied with carrying out someone else's orders. Have you ever thought that you would like to be your own boss?

Since the mid-1990s, the number of people starting their own businesses has increased significantly. By 2007, more than 23 million people were managing businesses less than four years old. The downside: New businesses suffer a brutally high failure rate. Some surveys show that only one in five new businesses will operate longer than four years.

The Making of an Entrepreneur

entrepreneurship the skills related to organizing, managing, and taking on the risks of owning a business

Entrepreneurship (the skills related to organizing, managing, and taking on the risks of owning a business) is one of the four components of the American economy. The other three components are *land* (natural resources), *labor*, and *capital* (money used to purchase all of the equipment and materials to run a business). Entrepreneurs plan, organize, and manage their businesses, expecting to earn profits.

The number one reason Americans start a new business is to become their own boss. Most people have a vision that if they can be their own boss, they always get to decide what to do—and when, why, and how to do it. Of course, as a business owner, you still would have to consider other people's feelings and desires. For example, you would want to please your customers. If you had employees, you would have to consider their welfare. And if you had one or more partners, you would certainly need to agree with them about how to run things.

On the other hand, as an entrepreneur you would have freedoms that you might never have as an employee for another company. You would get to decide how big you wanted your business to be. You could be creative and incorporate your own ideas into your business.

You Can Succeed Financially

In early 2005, Chad Hurley and Steven Chen, two employees of PayPal, the Internet payment system, had an idea—a Web site where people could upload and share home videos. In May of that year, they launched YouTube.

The idea caught on with lightning speed. By the end of that first summer, viewers had added hundreds of new videos and thousands of viewers were joining each day.

What YouTube Is

YouTube is a way for everyone to have a chance at their fifteen minutes of fame—65,000 new videos are uploaded to the site every day. Home videos of unknown musicians playing guitar solos in their garages have led to major-label record deals. Some members produce video diaries, adding a new clip each day or so that others follow just like a TV soap opera. Some upload experimental films, hoping to attract the attention of film companies. With its video clips attracting 100 million views each day, YouTube is the world's busiest destination for video entertainment.

How YouTube Was Financed

Chen and Hurley financed the start-up with their credit cards. As the site got more visitors, they had to pay for more bandwidth. They didn't want to change the atmosphere of the site by selling ads, so they took the big risk of continuing to finance the site's growth themselves.

By the end of 2005, venture capitalists (professional investors who provide money to promising business ventures) realized the growth potential of YouTube. They invested $3.5 million in the site. Five months later, as YouTube became a cultural phenomenon with millions of visitors each month, they poured in another $8 million. By July of 2006, more than 30 million unique visitors a month were using the YouTube site. It was the thirteenth most-visited site on the entire Web.

In October 2006, while many financial analysts were still arguing about YouTube's long-term chances of success, Internet giant Google purchased the business for $1.65 billion in Google stock. Google kept YouTube as an independent subsidiary, hoping the Web site would continue its independent attitude and appeal to creative and spirited contributor-members. All forty YouTube employees, including the founders, continued in their jobs. Chad Hurley and Steve Chen's gamble on success paid off with one of the fastest and biggest Internet buyouts ever.

▲ **Entrepreneurs Steven Chen (*left*) and Chad Hurley (*right*) sold their YouTube business for $1.65 billion in Google stock less than a year and a half after they started it. Do you think this kind of success is typical for small businesses? Explain your answer.**

What Would You Do?

1. Hurley and Chen were early employees of PayPal and saw it go through many changes. How might that experience have helped them in starting YouTube? Can you see ways in which a current or former job might benefit you in the future?
2. Would you be willing to go into credit card debt to start a new business? Explain why or why not.

Get Good Advice

Small businesses make up 80 percent of all businesses in America. That's a staggering statistic.

Being an entrepreneur isn't for everyone, but it can be a wonderful way to pursue something about which you are passionate. Think of some famous people who started out as entrepreneurs: Bill Gates, Oprah Winfrey, and the Google Guys (Sergey Brin, Eric Schmidt, and Larry Page), to name a few. Imagine what your world would be like if those individuals had not pursued the ideas that captured their interest and imagination.

Most entrepreneurs have thick skins—in other words, they can handle rejection. Another common characteristic is that entrepreneurs surround themselves with really good people—people who have both different and complementary skills, including accounting, business planning, marketing, and public speaking. All these qualities can separate a good business from its competition.

Interview an entrepreneur in your community—someone who operates a small business, like a shoe repair shop or a plumbing service. Your local chamber of commerce or business association can help you find someone. Ask the owner questions like these:

1. What made you decide to start your own business?
2. What does it take to be successful?
3. How many hours do you work in a day? a week? a year?
4. What kinds of things do you give up to keep the business going?
5. Are the trade-offs worth it? Why or why not?
6. What is the best advice you can give someone interested in being an entrepreneur?

Check with your teacher about presenting the information you gather. You might invite the interviewee to speak with your class, or you could give a short talk abut what you learned.

A 2005 University of Michigan survey indicated that 80 percent of new entrepreneurs held full-time or part-time jobs when they started up their own new businesses. Most likely, they were holding on to their jobs until their own businesses could support them. Then they could afford to quit working for others.

Of new entrepreneurs in 2005, some 63 percent were men and 37 percent were women. Most—91 percent—were between 18 and 54 years old. Those under age 18 generally lack the resources and experience necessary to start a business. Adults in the early-career or mid-career stage often have both resources and experience—along with the optimism and drive to get a business going.

Advantages of Entrepreneurship

Working for yourself to create a new company has a number of advantages over working as an employee of another company. Besides fulfilling the desire to be your own boss, entrepreneurship has the following potential benefits:

- Being the boss and owning your own company can be very satisfying.
- Because you're the boss, you can set your own work hours—although some projects will demand a lot of your time.
- As the owner, you make all your own decisions.
- A successful business can bring financial security.

- You may create a successful business that you can leave to your children or others.

Disadvantages of Entrepreneurship

Entrepreneurship also brings with it a number of disadvantages. Although you'll have the freedom of being your own boss, you will also experience a great deal of struggle and stress.

Starting a business may be the most difficult experience of your life. You would need to do a great deal of research to determine whether you can develop a big enough market for your products or services. You would need to develop a business plan to guide every aspect of your business activities. You will experience no such thing as a 9-to-5 workday—your thoughts must be on your business regardless of the time of day or day of the week. Many successful entrepreneurs work sixty or seventy hours per week—sometimes even more. You also have to dedicate your heart and soul to developing a business that *might* succeed but has a greater chance of failure. Remember, only about 20 percent of new businesses last more than four years.

Do You Have What It Takes?

To help you decide whether entrepreneurship is for you, answer the following questions:

- *How well do you plan and organize?* Good understanding and organization of finances, inventory, schedules, and production are essential.
- *How good are you at making decisions?* Business owners must make decisions quickly and often under a lot of pressure.
- *How well do you get along with different personalities?* Business owners must develop good working relationships with customers, suppliers, employees, bankers, and other professionals such as accountants and attorneys.
- *Do you have the physical and emotional stamina required to run a business?* Planning, organizing, and managing a business take a lot of work and energy.
- *How will the business affect your family?* The very long workdays with few days off—if any—during the initial years of getting a business off the ground can take a toll on family life. You would need an understanding and supportive family.
- *Are you willing to keep an open mind and keep on learning?* Operating a business requires the ability to quickly research a problem and discover new solutions.
- *Do you have the passion to stick with it and make it work?* Do you want it badly enough to overcome all the obstacles that may well block your road to success?

▼ **Starting a business can be difficult. Create a plan to guide all aspects of your future business.**

Types of Business Opportunities

If you decide that the potential rewards are worth the risks, you may choose to become an entrepreneur. You may take any one of several avenues.

Perhaps your own family already owns a business. In this case, you might have an opportunity to take over or become part of that enterprise. This arrangement has some important advantages. First, the business is already established. Second, you may already have a lot of experience working in the business during your growing-up years. You would know a lot about the product or service, your customers, and your suppliers. Third, when you need help or when problems arise, you can seek guidance from members of your own family who have already worked in the business and have experience.

franchise a legal contract allowing an individual or group to operate a business in the name of a recognized company

franchisor the recognized company under which a franchise operates

franchisee the person who operates a franchise

A second way to get started is to purchase an existing business. This has some of the same advantages as taking over a family-owned business. You will want to review the financial records ("the books") and learn how successful the business has been in recent months and years. You may be able to keep the former owners as co-managers or employees, thus benefiting from their experience.

A third way to become a business owner is to purchase a franchise. A **franchise** is a legal contract that allows you to operate a business in the name of a recognized company. This company is known as the **franchisor**. Some examples are McDonald's and Subway restaurants, Meineke car care centers, and Supercuts hair salons. You would become the **franchisee**—the person who operates the business. Usually, this is an expensive way to get started. Franchise fees can run from about $15,000 to more than $300,000. The franchisor provides a great deal of help, however, including most of the planning, management training, and advertising.

A fourth way you might become an entrepreneur is simply to start your own business. This allows you the most control, but it takes a great deal of effort, research, and planning. Also, you will not have help getting started, as you would if you take over an existing business or purchase a franchise.

Did You Know?

Many successful entrepreneurs have shared the following advice so that you may learn from their experience:

- Love your work. You cannot be successful if you resent the job for the time spent away from your family.
- Treat your customers like they own you, because they do.
- If you think you can't, you're right.
- Do not do anything that you would not want to see in the newspaper the next day.
- Luck and skill should not be confused when judging others or when judging yourself.
- Simplify your communication.

Forms of Business Organization

Your business might be organized in one of three basic ways. Recall that these alternatives were introduced in Chapter 1. You might be the sole owner. You could take on one or more partners. Or you could form a corporation.

Sole Proprietorships

If you go it alone, your business will be a sole proprietorship. This means that you are the only owner. You will make all of the decisions, keep all of the profits, and pay for any losses.

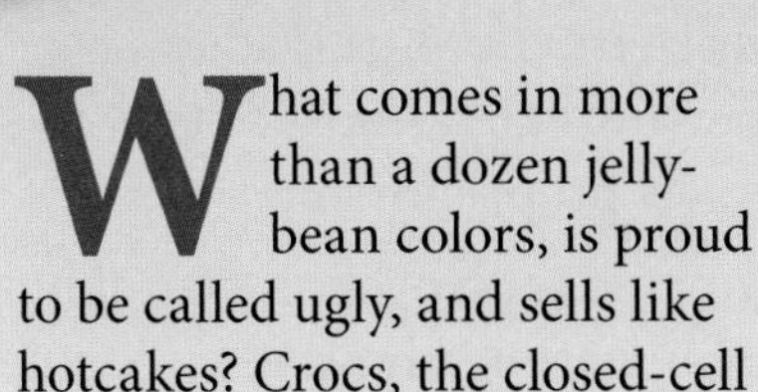

What comes in more than a dozen jelly-bean colors, is proud to be called ugly, and sells like hotcakes? Crocs, the closed-cell resin shoes.

Crocs were created in 2002 by three Colorado friends, who formed a corporation to produce a lightweight, slip-resistant boat shoe. The original model had ventilation holes on the top and sides and a movable heel strap. It was so comfortable and practical that gardeners, cooks, and hospital workers immediately demanded versions with special features for their professions.

Within two years, the shoes had a cult following all over the United States. For a time in 2005, the shoes sold so quickly that many retailers ran out. With no media campaign, information about the shoes spread by word of mouth.

Crocs are distinctive looking because of their bright colors, synthetic material, and tops full of holes. People wearing Crocs are often asked about them. They say they love them for their comfort and 2-ounce weight—and they recommend them freely. Americans traveling abroad were seen wearing them, and foreign visitors to the United States saw them here and searched for them in their home countries. Soon Crocs, Inc. began getting inquiries from overseas distributors.

The company's decision to go global was easy—the demand was already there. Fashion buffs on every continent have weighed in. They say they wouldn't be caught dead in a pair of Crocs—but that still leaves a big market for the clunky-looking clogs. Sales in the first half of 2006 were more than $130 million, with 23 percent coming from international sales.

Thinking Globally

1. If you worked for Crocs, would you expect to keep your job for your entire working career? Why or why not?
2. Crocs has expanded into other clothing lines and accessories. Why is that a good idea?

A sole proprietorship is so easy to set up that you may already own one without even knowing it. If you mow lawns on a verbal contract basis, charging a fixed price for each mowing, you are automatically a sole proprietor. Freelance writers, photographers, and salespeople who are paid only commissions or negotiated fees for each job all qualify as sole proprietors. Most small businesses start as sole proprietorships.

Sole proprietorships have the simplest form of filing taxes: Income and expenses are reported on a special page, called *Schedule C*, of the proprietor's federal income tax return. As described in Section 1, a sole proprietor will have to pay both the employee's and the employer's portion of Social Security taxes and Medicare. To save for retirement, you can put money into a Simplified Employee Pension (SEP), a Keogh plan, an individual retirement account (IRA), or a SIMPLE (Savings Incentive Match Plan for Employees) IRA. These savings programs will be discussed in a later chapter.

As a sole proprietor, you are personally liable for business-related obligations. In other words, if your business does not pay a vendor or loses a lawsuit, you could lose your car, your house, or other possessions to cover the debt.

Partnerships

A partnership is a business that is co-owned by two or more individuals.

Legally, there are three types of partners: general, limited, and silent. *General partners* share assets, profits, liabilities (the debts and other obligations of the business), voting rights, and management responsibilities. *Limited partners* do not have voting rights, and they are not held responsible for company liabilities beyond the amount of their investment. *Silent partners* invest in the company but have no say in its management. A partnership agreement defines the type of relationship and spells out the details of the relationship. See Figure 2.5 for a sample agreement.

Partnerships have several advantages over other forms of business organization, including the following:

- It is easier to raise start-up capital for a partnership than in a sole proprietorship.
- Several partners will provide more expertise and a greater range of knowledge and experience than a sole proprietor.
- Partners can share costs and risks, as well as share the workload.
- Partnerships are almost as easy to set up as sole proprietorships.

Compared with other forms of business organization, however, partnerships may have some of the following disadvantages:

- All general partners are liable for the debts and obligations of the partnership.
- Partners may disagree about management and operational procedures.
- Partners may have different business goals or time frames.
- Partnerships present a potential for personal disputes.

Figure 2.5 SAMPLE PARTNERSHIP AGREEMENT

These selections from a partnership agreement follow the standard format. An explanation is given first, followed by definitions of key terms and then the sections of the agreement. Sections may include—but are not limited to—the following:

- **Name**
- **Principal Place of Business**
- **Business and Purpose**
- **Term**
- **Capital Contribution**
- **Profit and Loss**
- **Distribution of Profits**

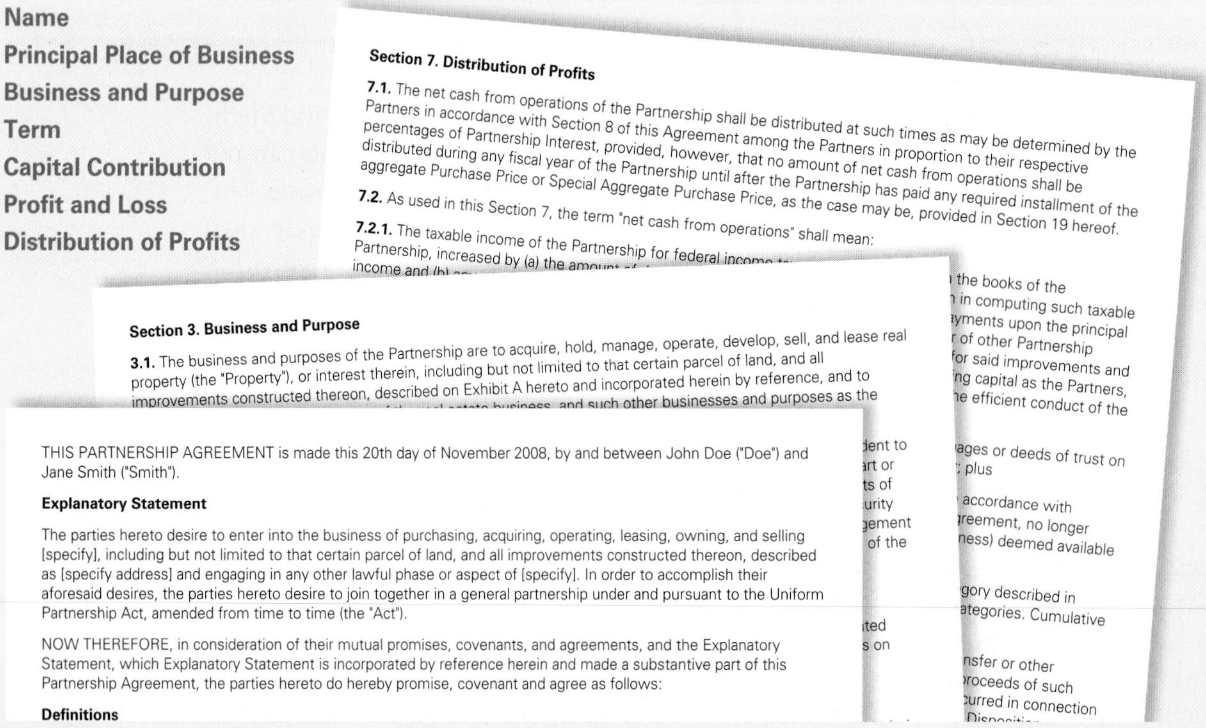

Section 7. Distribution of Profits

7.1. The net cash from operations of the Partnership shall be distributed at such times as may be determined by the Partners in accordance with Section 8 of this Agreement among the Partners in proportion to their respective percentages of Partnership Interest, provided, however, that no amount of net cash from operations shall be distributed during any fiscal year of the Partnership until after the Partnership has paid any required installment of the aggregate Purchase Price or Special Aggregate Purchase Price, as the case may be, provided in Section 19 hereof.

7.2. As used in this Section 7, the term "net cash from operations" shall mean:

7.2.1. The taxable income of the Partnership for federal income ... Partnership, increased by (a) the amount ... income and (b) ...

... the books of the ... in computing such taxable ... yments upon the principal ... of other Partnership ... for said improvements and ... ng capital as the Partners, ... e efficient conduct of the ... ages or deeds of trust on ... plus ... accordance with ... reement, no longer ... ness) deemed available ... gory described in ... ategories. Cumulative ... nsfer or other ... roceeds of such ... urred in connection ...

Section 3. Business and Purpose

3.1. The business and purposes of the Partnership are to acquire, hold, manage, operate, develop, sell, and lease real property (the "Property"), or interest therein, including but not limited to that certain parcel of land, and all improvements constructed thereon, described on Exhibit A hereto and incorporated herein by reference, and to ... business, and such other businesses and purposes as the ... dent to ... rt or ... ts of ... urity ... ement ... of the ... ted ... s on

THIS PARTNERSHIP AGREEMENT is made this 20th day of November 2008, by and between John Doe ("Doe") and Jane Smith ("Smith").

Explanatory Statement

The parties hereto desire to enter into the business of purchasing, acquiring, operating, leasing, owning, and selling [specify], including but not limited to that certain parcel of land, and all improvements constructed thereon, described as [specify address] and engaging in any other lawful phase or aspect of [specify]. In order to accomplish their aforesaid desires, the parties hereto desire to join together in a general partnership under and pursuant to the Uniform Partnership Act, amended from time to time (the "Act").

NOW THEREFORE, in consideration of their mutual promises, covenants, and agreements, and the Explanatory Statement, which Explanatory Statement is incorporated by reference herein and made a substantive part of this Partnership Agreement, the parties hereto do hereby promise, covenant and agree as follows:

Definitions

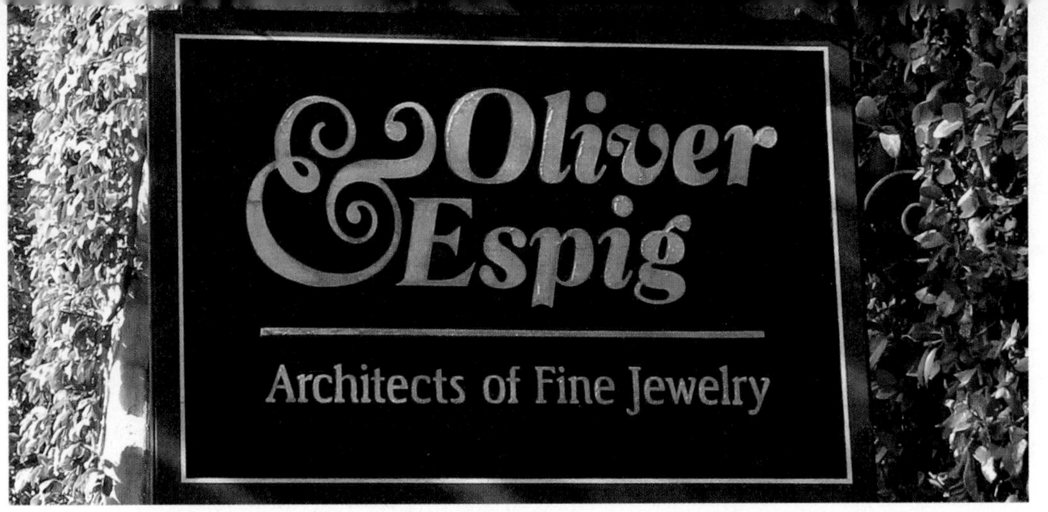

◀ Partnerships allow two or more people to combine their skills and talents in producing a unique product or service.

Corporations

A corporation is a legal entity—actually an "artificial person"—that can own property, acquire debt, sue, and be sued. Stockholders and a board of directors own the corporation and control its business, as noted in Chapter 1. Stockholders' liability is limited to the amount of their investment. Ownership is transferred by buying or selling stock. A corporation may enter into contracts, obtain loans, and continue to exist even after its stockholders die or transfer their shares to others. Unless limited by its **articles of incorporation** (the primary rules governing the management of a corporation) or by state law, a corporation continues indefinitely.

One relatively new type of corporate arrangement is called a **limited liability company (LLC)**. Technically, this is not a true corporation, although it has some of the same advantages. Owners have limited personal liability for the debts and actions of the company. Other features of LLCs are more like a partnership, providing management flexibility and tax advantages.

The first step in forming a corporation is to file articles of incorporation with the state where you wish to incorporate. In addition, new corporations must do the following:

- Write bylaws that govern its operation
- Hold a meeting of the board of directors
- Issue stock to stockholders

A corporation has to meet certain standards of bookkeeping, as well as maintain its own bank accounts, in addition to the other accounts of employees. Most corporations should consult an accountant when setting up accounting and record-keeping systems.

articles of incorporation the primary rules governing the management of a corporation

limited liability company (LLC) a relatively new type of corporate arrangement whose owners have limited personal liability for the debts and actions of the company, and with other features more like a partnership

Answers to Fact or Fiction

1. True; **2.** True; **3.** False—All workers must have a Social Security number before they can be legally employed in the United States; **4.** True; **5.** True; **6.** True; **7.** True.

SECTION 3 ASSESSMENT

Factual Recall

1. Name the four components of the U.S. economy.
2. Name four qualities of a successful entrepreneur.
3. What are four ways to become a business owner?
4. If you own a business, do you pay a higher or lower rate of Social Security tax than if you work for a company?

Critical Thinking

1. Do you think the advantages of entrepreneurship outweigh the disadvantages? Why or why not?
2. Which type of business do you think would be easiest to run: a sole proprietorship, a partnership, or a corporation? Give reasons for your answer.
3. Imagine that you have started up your own business. How can the Internet help you expand the business? What would be the pros and cons of doing business internationally?

CHAPTER 2 REVIEW AND ASSESSMENT

Chapter Summary

Section 1 Success from the Start

- When you start a new job, do your best to make a good impression from day one.
- On your first day at work, you will probably be asked to read and sign several legal forms and documents. You will also need your Social Security number and perhaps a photo ID. You may need a work permit.
- The federal government and the Equal Employment Opportunity Commission require every business to have a formal company policy handbook.
- Payroll deductions may be made for federal and state taxes, insurance premiums, retirement savings, and other items.
- Many employers now offer flextime, job sharing, or telecommuting to help employees meet personal or family obligations.

Section 2 Promotions and Lifelong Learning

- You can improve your chances of getting promoted by exceeding expectations and by actively pursuing success.
- As a worker, you will be competing not only with others in the United States but also with people overseas. You will need to continue acquiring new knowledge and skills throughout your working life.
- Education for a career can be obtained at four-year colleges and universities, community colleges, trade schools, and apprenticeship programs. There also are nontraditional programs, such as learning networks and correspondence courses.

Section 3 Entrepreneurship: Owning Your Own Business

- Entrepreneurs plan, organize, and manage their own businesses, expecting to earn profits.
- The number one reason Americans start a business is to become their own boss.
- Entrepreneurs have the freedom to make decisions and the potential to achieve success and financial security. They also must be willing to do research, work hard, and accept the risks that come with business ownership.
- Entrepreneurs may begin by entering a family business, buying an existing business or franchise, or starting from scratch.
- The basic forms of business organization are sole proprietorship, partnership, and corporation.

Reviewing Key Terms

For each of the following statements, refer to the Key Terms listed on pages 34, 43, and 50, and choose the one that best completes the sentence.

1. ______, or exemptions, reduce the amount of federal tax withheld from your paycheck.
2. ______ hours are those worked beyond the legal limit of forty per week.
3. Amounts subtracted from gross pay are called ______.
4. Most ______ schedules include a full eight-hour day, but the employee might start earlier or leave later than those who follow a typical 9-to-5 schedule.
5. When two employees work in the same job, the arrangement is called ______.
6. An employee who works at home and uses a computer to link to the central office is ______.
7. A(n) ______ is a more experienced person who provides advice and support to guide your career.
8. ______ programs combine on-the-job training with formal classroom instruction.
9. A legal contract that lets you operate a business in the name of a recognized company is called a(n) ______.
10. A(n) ______ combines some of the features of a corporation with some features of a partnership.

Understanding the Main Ideas

1. Give the two situations in which you need to fill out and sign a Form W-4.
2. If you are applying for a Social Security card,

what three things do you need to prove?

3. The Social Security tax rate is a percentage of earnings. Does everyone pay the same percentage? Explain your answer.
4. Whose responsibility is it to make sure an employee can legally work in the United States?
5. In what situation would you need an EAD (Employment Authorization Document)?
6. Why is net pay less than gross pay?
7. Name three alternative work arrangements.
8. Name three tips for improving your chances of getting promoted.
9. In which of the three types of partnerships do the members share assets, profits, liabilities, and management responsibilities?
10. Which type of partner has the least say in the management of a company?
11. Which type of business organization is the easiest to set up?
12. Who owns a corporation?

Practicing Math

1. You are an office manager with a yearly salary of $45,000. How much is left after deductions for Social Security and Medicare taxes? If you were in business for yourself, how much would you have to earn in order to end up with that same amount? (Ignore other deductions, such as income tax.)
2. Go to the IRS Web site (http://fin.emcp.net/IRS) and download Form W-4. Study the form to answer the following questions. Suppose you are single with no dependents, working one job, and are not a dependent yourself although you live with your parents. What is the maximum number of allowances you can claim? What is the minimum? If each allowance is worth $3,400, what is the maximum and minimum dollar value of the allowances you can claim?

Applying Critical Thinking Skills

1. You are an office assistant. Another assistant from a different department asks you to help with some photocopying. How should you respond?
2. Your boss has asked you to create and present a PowerPoint presentation for an important meeting. You want to make a good impression, and you are working hard. However, you don't think you will be able to finish on time. What should you do?
3. Do you think it is better to be a full-time student, or to be a part-time student so that you can work and earn money while you are in school? What situations may cause one option to be better than the other? Give reasons for your answer.
4. What might be the pros and cons of continuing your "day job" while starting up your own business? Explain your answer.

Working with Real-World Documents

1. The number of allowances you claim on your Form W-4 will affect the amount of income tax withheld from your paycheck. Suppose your gross income is $34,700. Use the table below to calculate how much federal income tax would be withheld if you claimed the maximum number of allowances. What if you claimed the minimum? (Use the Form W-4 that you downloaded in Math Practice activity 2, and refer to the lower portion of the form—the part labeled "Employee's Withholding Allowance Certificate.")

Wages (minus withholding allowances)		Federal income tax withheld		
More than	But not over		Plus	Of excess over
$0	$2,650	$0		
$2,650	$10,120	$0	10%	$2,650
$10,120	$33,520	$747	15%	$10,120
$33,520	$77,075	$4,257	25%	$35,520

Taking It Home

1. Identify a career that interests you. Work with your parents or guardians to gather information about the education or training requirements, the time involved, costs, and possible debt. Write a summary of your findings.

UNIT II

Managing Your Money

CHAPTER 3 Financial Planning

CHAPTER 4 Budgeting

CHAPTER 5 Checking Accounts

CHAPTER 3

Financial Planning

Money comes in, and money goes out, right? It's simple. What is there to plan?

The problem with that idea—which is shared by a lot of people—is that usually more money goes out than comes in. Even people who are super-wealthy can run into problems if the things they buy add up to more total dollars than the money they bring in.

▲ Use a financial plan to convert your pennies into dollars.

Financial planning means being aware of how much money is coming in—and then *planning* how to use it. It means never having to worry about bouncing a check or missing a payment. It means stability and peace of mind.

SECTION 1 Establishing Healthy Financial Habits

SECTION 2 Sharing as Part of a Financial Plan

SECTION 3 Keeping Records and Paying Taxes

Fact or Fiction

What do you think? Are the following statements true or false? If you think they are false, then say what is true.

1. Most donors to charity are very wealthy.
2. Financial planning takes a lot of time and effort to do correctly.
3. It is best not to involve others in your financial planning, which is a private, personal matter.
4. When developing a financial plan, you have to consider your current financial situation—even if you plan to change everything.
5. Volunteering your time is just as important as sharing your money.
6. You do not have to pay income taxes if you earn less than $5 per hour.
7. To file your income tax return, you are required to get help from a tax preparation service.

Answers on page 89.

Study Reminder

*Knowing how to study can increase your knowledge, improve your grades, and cut down on your study time. See the **Studying Personal Finance** pages at the front of the book for some tips to help you study this chapter.*

SECTION 1

Establishing Healthy Financial Habits

Focus Questions

1. Why do you think it is important to allot some money from each paycheck or allowance payment to savings?
2. In what ways should spending reflect a person's value system?
3. What are the steps in setting up a financial plan?
4. How can you tell if you are moving toward your goals? How do you know when you achieve them?

Key Terms

overdraft fee
Share Save Spend® system
income
expenses

When Darren started ninth grade, his mother took him to the bank to open up a teen checking account. He got a checkbook and a debit/ATM card and deposited his birthday money to get the account started. His mother added another $50 as a "cushion," so that if Darren accidentally spent more money than he deposited, he would not get an **overdraft fee** (penalty for having a negative balance in the account).

overdraft fee a penalty payment for having a negative balance in an account

Darren did pretty well that fall, checking his monthly statements to make sure everything was okay. But around the holidays, he used his checks and his debit card more than before. He bought a few presents and went out with friends during time off from school.

Then Darren received some mail from the bank late in December. He thought it was his statement—but it was an overdraft notice. He had written a check to the local pizza parlor for $14, but he did not have $14 in his account. The bank sent the check back to the pizza parlor, stamped "Insufficient Funds"—and charged Darren an overdraft fee. Not only had Darren used up his $50 cushion, but now he was in the hole by more than $20. And to make it worse, Darren would have to go to the pizza parlor to pay what he owed, plus the additional amount that the pizza parlor charged for a bounced check.

Being a smart money manager is not something that comes naturally—it takes a lot of thought. Good money managers take time to plan what to do with their money. They plan ahead about their spending. They make responsible short-term, medium-term, and long-term decisions. They avoid mistakes that could cost them even more money in the long run. How do they do it?

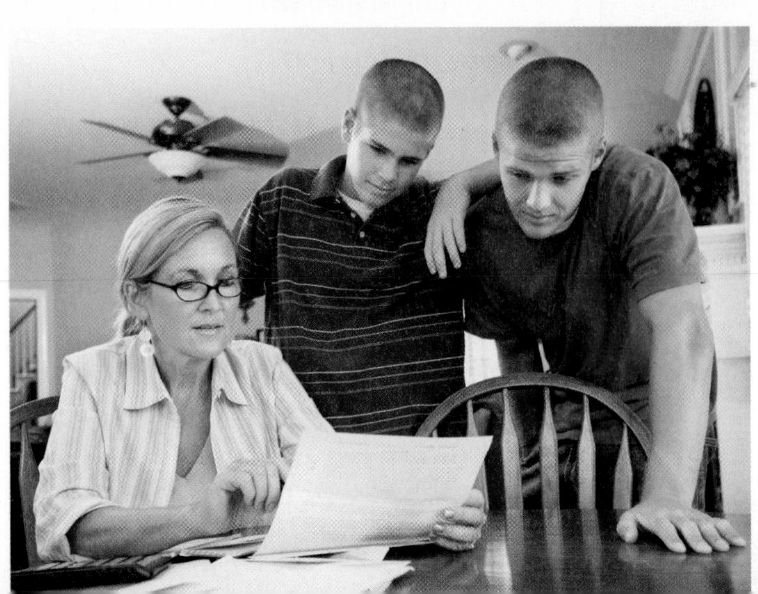

▼ Avoid overdraft fees by keeping track of your income and your expenses.

The Share Save Spend® System

Many good money managers use the **Share Save Spend system**, which involves dividing your funds into three categories: sharing, saving, and spending. It is a balanced approach to money management that helps you look at money in terms of your own personal value system.

Share Save Spend system an approach to money management that divides funds into three categories—sharing, saving, and spending—according to the individual's values

Sharing and Saving

Every day you are bombarded with messages about spending money on *things*—wanting, buying, having all sorts of products and services. One answer to this commercial aspect of life is to think

Tamara decided a year ago to follow the Share Save Spend financial planning system. She had a part-time job at a local ice cream shop, and her income was fairly stable. Her plan was to put half of each paycheck into her checking account, and the other half in her savings account. She planned to use half of her savings for her own benefit, and half for causes she believed in. Figure 3.1 shows her financial plan.

After a year's time, Tamara hoped to have about $1,600 in her savings account. Half—$800—she would use to buy a new mountain bike. The other $800 was to pay for a volunteer service trip with her church youth group to build houses in a village in Guatemala.

Now the year is coming to an end, and summer is about to begin. Tamara starts shopping around for mountain bikes, and finds one she just loves. The only problem is that it is $1,295. She could use some of the savings she set aside for the volunteer trip, but then she will not have enough money to go to Guatemala with her youth group. Tamara wonders whether she has to give up the volunteer trip, or give up the bike. Or is there another alternative?

Should she...

1. ...buy the bike she really wants and forgo the volunteer trip, or buy a less expensive bike and use her Share money as she had intended? Give reasons for your answer.
2. ...use her Share money for the trip, but continue saving until she has $1,295 for the bike she really likes—and go through the summer without a new mountain bike? Explain your answer.

Figure 3.1 TAMARA'S SHARE SAVE SPEND PLAN

	Income per week (after taxes)	Checking account	Saving for self	Saving for others (Sharing)
Week 1	$ 70.00	$ 35.00	$ 17.50	$ 17.50
Week 2	$ 65.00	$ 32.50	$ 16.25	$ 16.25
Week 3	$ 77.00	$ 38.50	$ 19.25	$ 19.25
Week 4	$ 60.00	$ 30.00	$ 15.00	$ 15.00
Month total	$272.00	$136.00	$68.00	$68.00

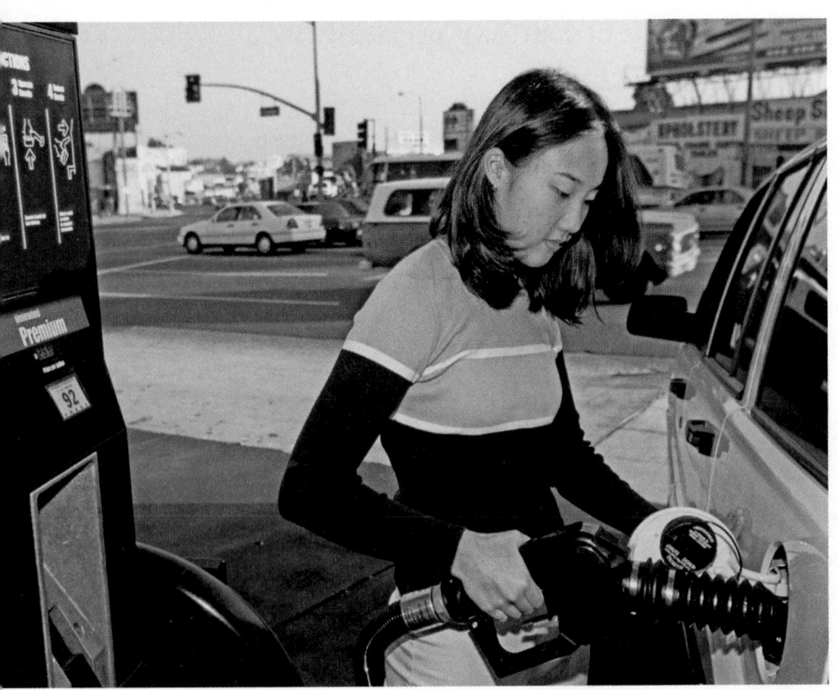

▲ After buying gas, write down the amount you spent in your budget records.

about your time and money in terms of what you can do for others—before you devote your life to acquiring and using all those *things*. Sharing can mean buying gifts for needy people at the holidays. It can mean making a donation to a cause you believe in. It can mean volunteering for an organization such as Habitat for Humanity. What you gain from these activities can far outweigh your costs—and you will be doing something important in a very personal way.

Saving involves putting away money for short-term, medium-term, and long-term goals. Short-term goals could include a new iPod or going to college. Long-term goals might be having a family, or even retiring from work. When you put sharing and saving ahead of spending, you are making a conscious decision to be responsible for your personal values and goals.

Spending

Of course you need a certain amount of money for everyday things like food, gas, and school supplies. But when you put spending last in the Share Save Spend system, you are putting less emphasis on your everyday wants. This allows you to resist the bombardment of media messages encouraging you to empty your wallet or your bank account as quickly as you can. Developing the ability to say "No, I don't need that" or "No, I can't afford that" will simplify your life—and it helps you develop good money management habits at the same time.

To keep track of spending, maintain good records. Always keep your checkbook up-to-date. Subtract every check as soon as you write it. Subtract debit card and ATM withdrawals right away, too. Go over your bank statement each month and be sure your checkbook and the bank's balance agree. That way, you will never have to worry about overdraft fees because you will always know exactly how much money you have to spend.

Your Values

Before you begin setting up your financial planning system, think about your own personal values: What is important to you? What parts of your life deserve the most attention? What charities and other causes do you support? After you have determined what your values are, think about how you can reflect those values in the way you use money.

A good way to get started is to talk to other people about their values and about their views on money. Think about people whose values you understand and respect. Perhaps a grandparent, parent, aunt, or uncle would be a good place to start. Talk to a variety of people. Try to gather different points of view. Someone who grew up during the Great Depression will have a unique perspective, and so will someone who grew up in a different country. Find out how the people you trust make financial

You Can Succeed Financially

In 2006, the only grocery store in rural Truman, Minnesota, closed—and then reopened. The Main Street Market's new lease on life came from 17-year-old Nick Graham, a high school student and a member of the school's football team.

After hearing that the grocery store had closed, Nick made a business plan. He used his life savings to invest in the store. A $10,000 down payment—saved mostly from years of working on his uncle's turkey farm—clinched the deal. Nick bought the store and now runs it.

After school and on weekends, he rings up and bags groceries. Sometimes he even makes home deliveries. Although Nick hopes to turn a profit in his new business, he says he opened the store mainly to help the town of Truman.

His hard work is paying off. Most of Truman's residents choose to shop at Main Street Market rather than drive the 24-mile round trip to shop in the larger town of Fairmont, Minnesota. And Nick's optimism and work ethic are rubbing off on Truman. People see his store as an inspiration. They have continued rebuilding Main Street by reopening other shuttered storefronts.

What Would You Do?

1. Do you know of a neighborhood where a lot of businesses are closing? If you owned a business in that area, would you move—or stay? Why? Explain your answer.
2. How can your values influence your decision in the situation described above (#1)?
3. In what other ways can teens help in the revitalization of their town or neighborhood?

decisions. Find out how their values influence those decisions.

How Values Influence Decisions

Think about how your financial decisions impact your own life and the lives of those around you. For example, what happens if you blow your whole paycheck on an evening out with friends? It might mean that you could not put any money into your savings account for awhile—and that means you have to wait even longer to get the car you are saving for. Maybe you would have to ask a parent for bus money. Perhaps you could not take your younger sibling to a movie like you promised. Or maybe you would have to work an extra shift next weekend instead of helping out at the food pantry as you had planned.

The key element in solid financial planning is determining what is important to you. You then need to follow through by making financial decisions based on your values. It is not very difficult to do, and it is not time-consuming. But it will help you clarify your own ideas and goals about money. This knowledge will give you a solid base on which to begin your financial planning.

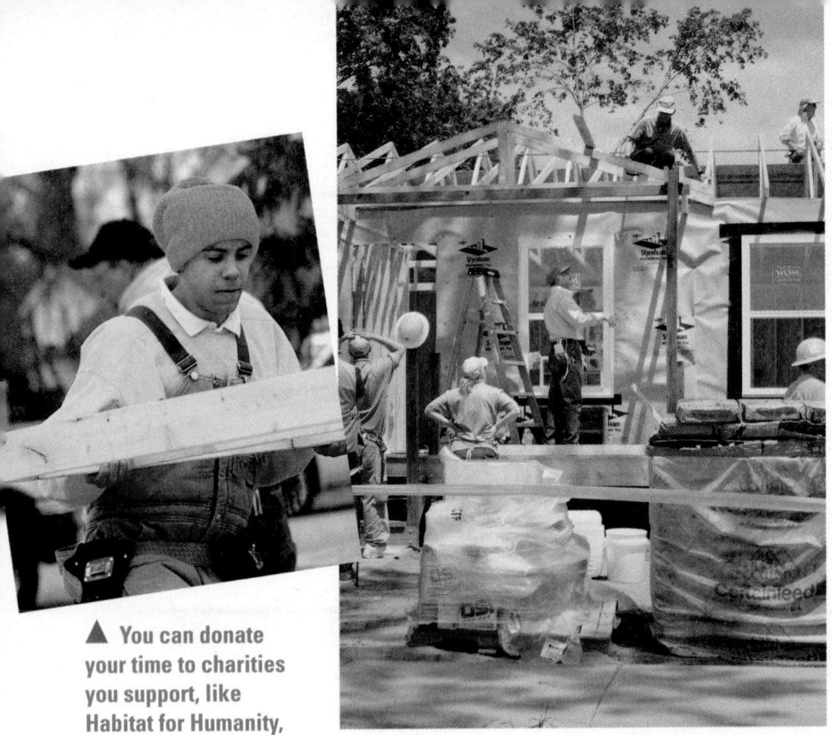

▲ You can donate your time to charities you support, like Habitat for Humanity, in addition to offering money.

Questions About Values and Money

You can learn a lot about money management from other people—friends and family members whom you trust and respect. Here are some questions to ask others about values and money:

- How do you save money? What do you do with the money you save?
- How do you share with causes you believe in? How did you decide to make those contributions?
- Do you avoid certain ways of spending money? Why, or why not?

After talking with several people, think about what they said. Then ask yourself the following questions about values and money:

- What charities and causes are important to me?
- How have I contributed time or money to causes I believe in? How could I contribute in the future?
- Whose values and actions do I admire? How could I mirror those philosophies and actions?
- What short-term goals do I have? What long-term goals do I have?
- What would I like to have money for that I currently do not?

Now you are ready to begin designing your own financial plan.

Your Financial Plan

Financial planning is a multistep process. The steps presented here will

▶ Amusement park tickets are expensive. In purchasing such tickets, what are these teens saying about their values?

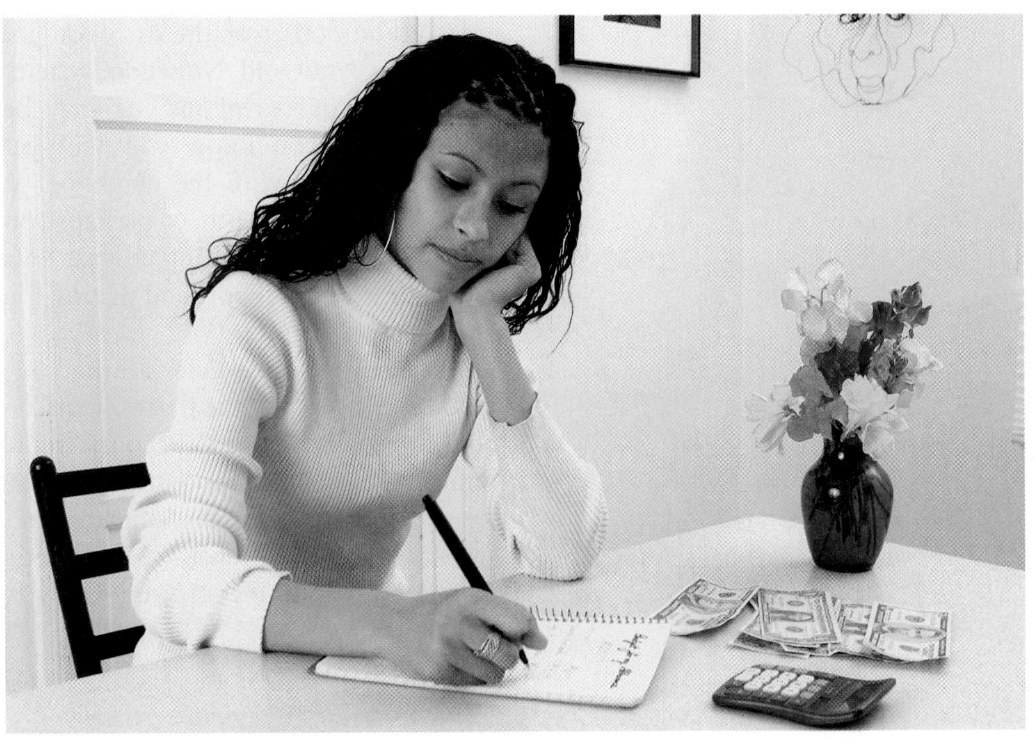

◀ **Good budgeting habits will help you save for all of your financial goals.**

enable you to start using a system like Share Save Spend to manage your money. To begin setting up your financial plan, here are the steps you should take:

1. *Determine your current situation.* Analyze how you use money now. Coming to terms with how you have spent (or *over*spent) money in the past can be a powerful lesson. Think about how to monitor your spending habits more carefully.
2. *Set and prioritize your goals.* Decide what goals you have for the short, medium, and long term. Your goals should be specific, measurable, and realistic. Determine which goals are most important to you.
3. *Develop a long-term plan.* Think about how you can work toward your goals. Make sure your plan is something you can do without a lot of trouble. If it involves working a lot more or spending a lot less, it may not be something you can do for very long.
4. *Organize your records.* Come up with a way to organize your bills, bank records, and other paperwork. You might do some of this on your computer with a program such as Excel, or you may use a spiral-bound notebook. You may also need to keep hard copies of important documents. The simpler your record-keeping system is though, the more likely you are to follow it. Financial record keeping is covered in Section 3 of this chapter.
5. *Set up a budget.* Your budget should reflect the three R's—reality, responsibility, and restraint. It should be doable, and it should express your values. As you begin using your budget, you will want to closely monitor how it is working for you and modify the plan if necessary. Budgeting is covered in Chapter 4.
6. *Keep it simple.* People who achieve their financial goals keep their plan relatively simple. In that way they can track their progress and follow through with their plan.

Figuring out where you are financially involves keeping track of two

▲ **Hang on to all of your receipts. You will need them to estimate your expenses and to make sure that you are not overcharged.**

things—money coming in and money going out. The money coming in is called your **income**. The money going out represents your **expenses**.

Determining Your Income

income money earned in exchange for work, or received from investments, allowance, or gifts

expenses the things people pay for with their money

You may get money through your allowance, from gifts, or in exchange for work. Some of this income may come on a regular schedule—a weekly allowance or a paycheck every other week, for example. Other income may be at irregular intervals—the birthday check from your grandmother or the cash you got for selling your old Nintendo system. Still other sources of income may be semiregular—you know you will get babysitting jobs with the neighbors at least five times a month, or perhaps you know you will be mowing at least four lawns in your neighborhood during the summer.

Be realistic when determining your income. Do not assume that you will be able to work a few more hours, mow another lawn, or sell more stuff on eBay to earn more money. The smartest and safest course of action is to base your plan only on the income you know is reliable.

Did You Know?

The average American experiences more than 5,000 advertising impressions every day. That is 1 advertising impression every 17 seconds! What are advertising impressions? They include TV commercials, online ads, commercial text messages, logos on clothing, billboards pushing products, and much, much more. How do you think those messages affect an individual's expenses?

Determining Your Expenses

Now, think about what you do with the money you have. Perhaps you save and share a little but spend most of it. Or maybe you spend it all—but you are not exactly sure what you spend it on.

A good way to evaluate your spending is to keep track of your expenses for a month. Then you can look back on the numbers and get a snapshot of your spending habits.

After you have made a detailed list (or *log*) of your spending for a month, put each item into a category. Categories might include things like Sports and Hobbies, Food (eating out, snacks), Clothing, Grooming (cosmetics, haircuts), Entertainment (movies, music, video games), Transportation (bus, car, gas), and Connectivity (cell phone, Internet).

After you have created your categories, determine how much money you spent in each category. Use a spending chart and spending log like those in Figure 3.2 to track and evaluate your spending.

You should now have a much better picture of how and where you spend

Figure 3.2 **KEEPING TRACK OF YOUR EXPENSES**

Write down everything you spend money on each day in your spending log, no matter how much or how little it costs.

Spending Log

Date	Item or service	Where purchased	Cost	Category
May 11	latte	Mug Shots	$ 4.25	Food
May 12	haircut	Barber Shop	$20.00	Grooming
May 12	movie	Cinema 16	$ 9.00	Entertainment
May 13	bus pass	City Bus	$35.00	Transportation

Your spending chart will show you how much you spend in each category. This person spends the most money on Sports/Hobbies and Food. If he needs to spend less, he could cut back in these areas. Of course, you may need to add other categories to your personal chart.

Spending Chart

	Week 1	Week 2	Week 3	Week 4	Total
Sports/Hobbies	$24.00	$32.00	$21.00	$27.00	$104.00
Food	$13.00	$20.45	$16.10	$18.00	$ 67.55
Clothing	$ 0	$ 0	$40.00	$ 8.00	$ 48.00
Grooming	$ 0	$20.00	$ 0	$ 0	$ 20.00
Entertainment	$ 9.00	$21.75	$ 9.00	$18.00	$ 57.75
Transportation	$ 0	$35.00	$ 0	$ 0	$ 35.00
				Grand Total	$332.30

your money. With this picture in mind, it is time to ask yourself the following questions:

- Did my spending reflect what is important to me?
- Two years from now, which of these purchases will still mean something to me?
- Would I be embarrassed if my family or friends saw my list?
- What percentage of my spending is for necessities?

Now that you know where your money comes from and where it goes, you are ready to think about your financial goals—what you want your money to do for you in the future.

Your Financial Goals

Consider this scenario. Henry's teacher recently asked him what his financial goals were. "Financial goals?" he repeated. "For what? I don't have any."

Henry's teacher explained that financial goals are just a subset of your bigger goals for yourself. She asked, "What do you want to do next week? Next year? In ten years?" Henry said that the following week he wanted to see the new horror movie coming out. He hoped to go to summer camp next year. And in ten years he hoped to be working as an interior designer. "Now, consider how you'll pay for all that," said his teacher.

After determining your income and expenses and examining your money-

Going Global

What is the number one life expectation of teens around the world? In the 2006 GenWorld Teen Study conducted by the public relations firm Energy BBDO, 70 percent of teens surveyed in thirteen countries said that financial security was most important.

In fact, teens in eight of the thirteen countries ranked their top life expectation as either "being better off financially than my parents," "being financially secure," or "being rich." A whopping 50 percent expect to own their own business someday.

Interestingly, in response to a different question, 70 percent also answered that they would "fight for a cause I believe in." So although teens around the world value financial security, they also value helping others.

Thinking Globally

1. Ask five or six of your classmates what their number one life expectation is. How do their answers compare with the percentages in the GenWorld Teen Study?
2. How could a goal of financial security also enable you to effectively work for a cause you believe in?

related values, you probably have some ideas about how you would like to change the way you use money. If you are planning to use the Share Save Spend system, you may be thinking about how you would divide your money among the three areas in that system. You need to come up with a list of goals for your use of money in the future. Then you need to prioritize those goals: Which are the most important? Which are things you need? Which are things you want? How do these goals match your values?

Identifying and Prioritizing Your Goals

The first step here is deciding what your goals include. A good way to start is to brainstorm a list of things you would like to accomplish with your income. Review your thoughts about money, and make sure your financial goals reflect your personal values. For example, do you feel strongly about nature and the environment? Your goals might include contributing to a conservation group and saving for a camping trip. Are animals your thing? You might include volunteering at an animal shelter and buying and caring for a new pet. If one of your high-priority values is participation in a sport, your list of goals could include new equipment you might need, contributions you can make to your team, and summer camps or clinics you might want to attend.

As you read through the list of goals you have brainstormed, consider whether each is a "want" or a "need." Needs are things you must have; wants are things you would like to have. Although clothing is a need, designer jeans are not. You might need transportation—but if the city bus is a reasonable option, then a car is a want, not a necessity.

Your financial goals should be *specific*, *measurable*, and *realistic*. A nonspecific goal such as "Save for a new skateboard" cannot be measured. Make it specific: "Save $5 a week for ten weeks until I have enough money to buy a skateboard." Now you can check to see if you are keeping up with your goal because there are measurements in place. Remember, though, that you cannot achieve any goal—even one that is specific and measurable—if it is not realistic. If you make $10 an hour and work only eight hours a week, you are not going to be able to buy a car in the foreseeable future.

It will also help to divide your goals into short-term, medium-term, and long-term goals. Your medium-term goals might include saving for a car, or finishing college. Your short-term goals might include having money to spend on a weekend trip with your family, making a contribution to the

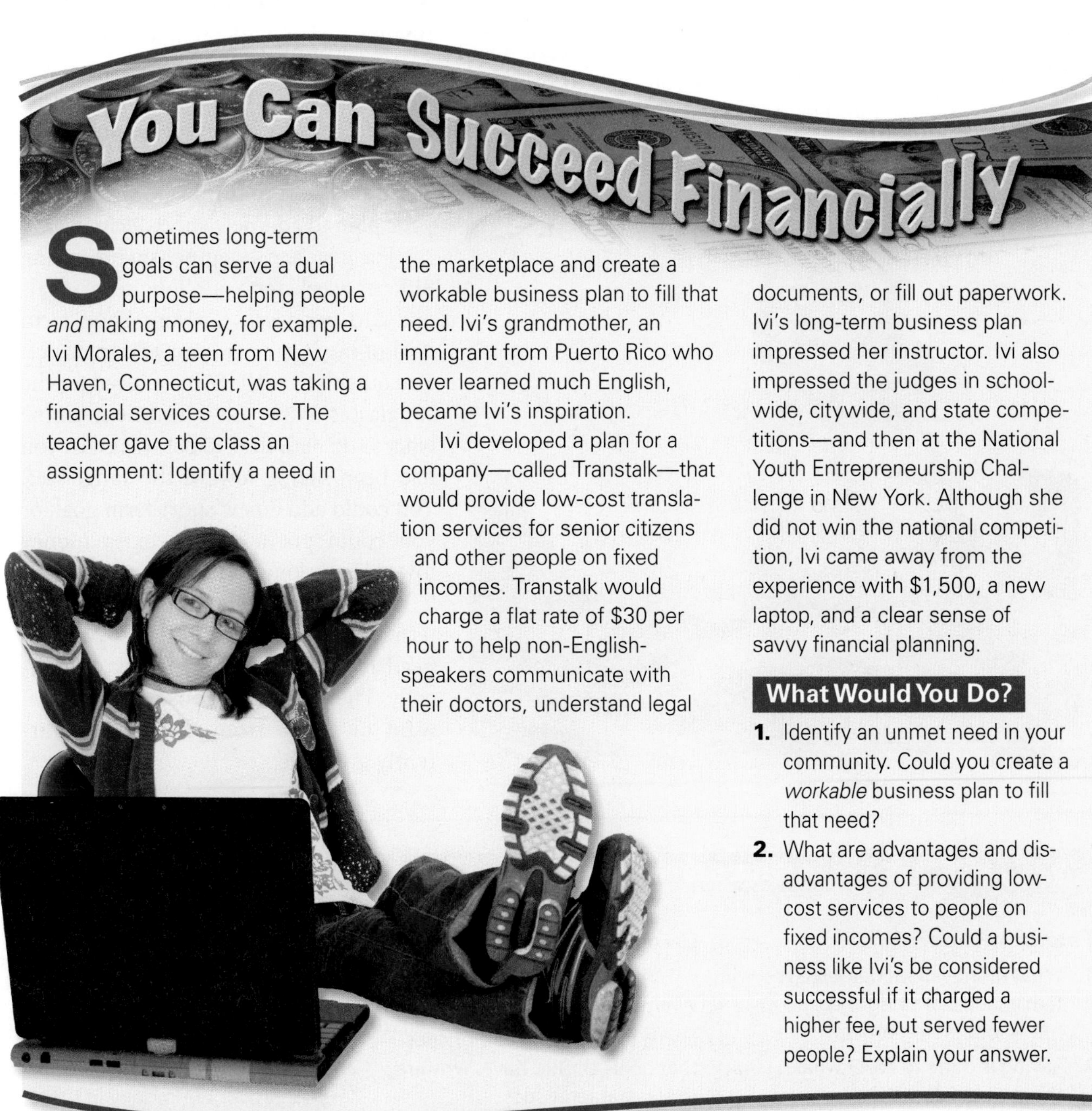

You Can Succeed Financially

Sometimes long-term goals can serve a dual purpose—helping people *and* making money, for example. Ivi Morales, a teen from New Haven, Connecticut, was taking a financial services course. The teacher gave the class an assignment: Identify a need in the marketplace and create a workable business plan to fill that need. Ivi's grandmother, an immigrant from Puerto Rico who never learned much English, became Ivi's inspiration.

Ivi developed a plan for a company—called Transtalk—that would provide low-cost translation services for senior citizens and other people on fixed incomes. Transtalk would charge a flat rate of $30 per hour to help non-English-speakers communicate with their doctors, understand legal documents, or fill out paperwork. Ivi's long-term business plan impressed her instructor. Ivi also impressed the judges in schoolwide, citywide, and state competitions—and then at the National Youth Entrepreneurship Challenge in New York. Although she did not win the national competition, Ivi came away from the experience with $1,500, a new laptop, and a clear sense of savvy financial planning.

What Would You Do?

1. Identify an unmet need in your community. Could you create a *workable* business plan to fill that need?
2. What are advantages and disadvantages of providing low-cost services to people on fixed incomes? Could a business like Ivi's be considered successful if it charged a higher fee, but served fewer people? Explain your answer.

school library fund, and buying a new pair of shoes. Decide on the total amount for each item. Then decide how much you should set aside each week for each item. Do the math, and you can determine how far into the future you can actually make each purchase.

Reaching Your Goals: Developing a Long-Term Plan

▼ Creating, implementing, and adjusting your financial plan will take time and effort. How will your efforts be rewarded?

So you have a list of financial goals you would like to reach, and you have prioritized them. They fit your value system—and they are specific, measurable, and realistic. Now you have to begin to move toward them.

Implementing Your Plan To move toward your goals, you will have to do two things: (1) continue to put the money away each week toward your goals, and (2) not use the money for something else. When you have money in the bank, you may be tempted to "borrow" from it to buy something you think you "must" have now. It is important to remember your initial goals and why you are putting the money away.

Adjusting Your Plan Your long-term financial plan will include your long-term goals—the big-ticket items you want to have in the future. Meanwhile, as time goes by you will be achieving your short-term and medium-term goals. It is time to think about adjusting your plan to add new short-term goals.

For instance, imagine you are saving $10 per week for your long-term goals and $10 per week for your short-term goal of buying a new pair of sunglasses. You quickly save the $50 you need for the sunglasses. Now you have to determine what to do with the $10 per week that you had been saving toward the sunglasses. You could add a new short-term goal, or you could put away the extra money toward your long-term goals.

When you are looking at your long-term plan—the "big picture"—you will need to evaluate your choices periodically. Then you can choose the path you want to follow from the options currently available.

SECTION 1 ASSESSMENT

Factual Recall

1. What money management system includes a category of funds for helping others?
2. Saving is done to meet what three kinds of goals?
3. List the six steps for setting up a financial plan.
4. What is a spending log?
5. Name the three characteristics that goals should have. Why are these characteristics important?

Critical Thinking

1. When you make a financial plan, why should sharing and saving come before spending?
2. Why is it useful to analyze how you have spent money in the past?

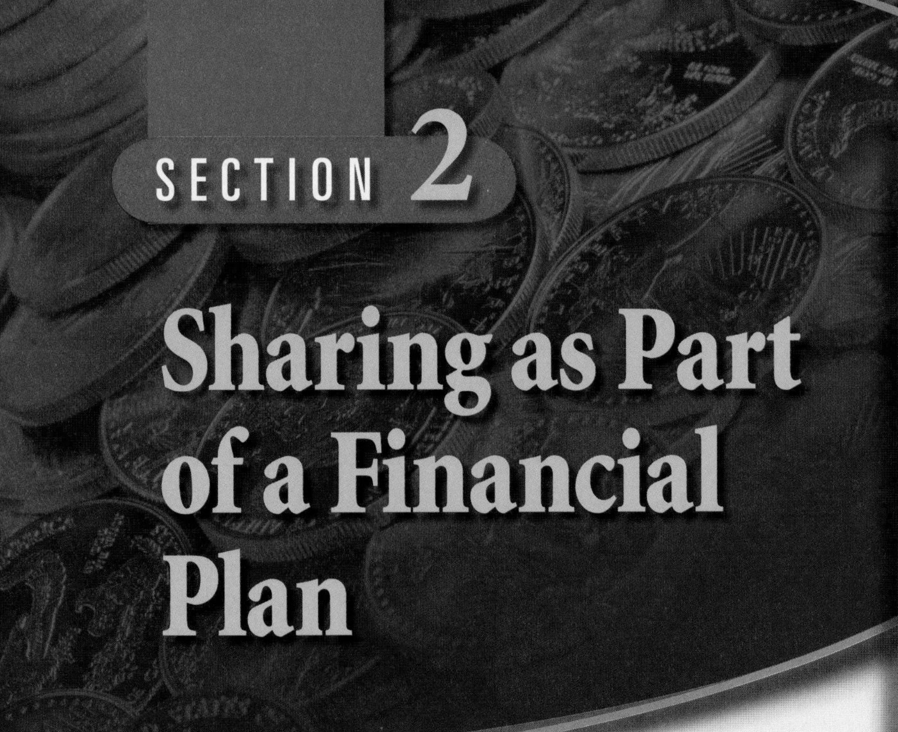

SECTION 2

Sharing as Part of a Financial Plan

Focus Questions

1. Why is it important to think about sharing your resources (money and time) with a cause or causes you believe in?
2. What causes do you feel most strongly about? If you could do one thing to make the world a better place, what would it be?
3. What are at least three ways you can share your time or money with a cause you believe in?

Key Terms

philanthropy
altruism
service-learning

As you know, financial plans such as the Share Save Spend system include sharing as a major component. Sharing sounds simple enough, but for many people it takes some self-reflection and consideration. Lupita, for example, grew up in the Latino barrio in Chicago. Her family is not wealthy. She works to make enough money to buy clothes for herself and transportation around town so that her parents will not have to pay for these things. She does not make a lot of money, though—and she figures that she deserves to keep her earnings for herself.

Did You Know?

Young people age 21 and under in America spend and influence the spending of more than $1 trillion a year. Imagine the result if 10 percent of that money were shared with charitable organizations at home and around the world.

Dori has always lived in a quiet neighborhood in a suburb of Boston. The houses in her neighborhood are spacious and the garages contain two or three luxury cars. There is no question that these families are well-off.

Dori knows that this lifestyle did not happen by accident. Her father, a heart surgeon, and her mother, a teacher, work hard. Because of her situation, Dori has never needed to work and has never had a regular job. She does babysit, however, and she sometimes takes care of neighborhood pets when their owners go on vacation. It seems to her that she really deserves to keep her money. Her family doesn't need it. Why should she give it to someone else?

Many young people might wonder why they should include sharing or giving in their financial planning. After all, students do not have a lot of money to begin with—how are they supposed to set some of it aside for others? Who would expect someone with a limited income to do that? What difference could the small amount that she would give do for anyone, anyway?

What Is Sharing, and Who Shares?

There are many reasons why it is important to consider sharing. When you share your resources with causes you are passionate about, you are more connected to your community and the world. Sharing earns you a sense of pride and well-being. Sharing allows you to discover what you believe in and to figure out a way to contribute to those causes.

philanthropy the act of giving away money, goods, services, or time to support a cause

altruism selfless concern for the welfare of others

Philanthropy is the act of giving away money, goods, services, or time to support a cause. Or you may call it *charitable giving*. Many people associate philanthropy with serving the poor or needy—but sharing what you have can also benefit other causes. You can help the environment, abandoned pets, organizations for the elderly, health-related causes, political or cultural activities, and educational programs. Another term that can be used to describe this kind of sharing is **altruism**—the selfless concern for the welfare of others.

Many people also associate philanthropy with wealthy individuals who are able to donate millions of dollars to causes they believe in. The fact is, however, that donors to charitable organizations are not all wealthy. According to a survey done by the Better Business Bureau, 86 percent of all adults in the United States identified themselves as donors. Even 73 percent of people whose annual household incomes were less than $30,000 regularly gave money to charitable causes. According to Freelanthropy, an organization that provides services to nonprofit companies, almost half of all households earning less than $25,000 per year gave at least $100.

▼ Melinda and Bill Gates visit the Manhica Health Research Center in Mozambique. The center was one of the beneficiaries of a $168 million grant from the Bill and Melinda Gates Foundation for malaria research projects.

Start Sharing Now

One generalization that surveys have shown about people who give is that most of them started giving early. If you make sharing a part of your life—and part of your financial plan—now, you will not have to wonder where to find the money or how to do it later. In fact, a large number of teens share their money, their time, and their talents with others. When asked why they do it, many answer that they are contributing to a cause they strongly believe in.

Get Involved Sharing with an organization you feel a bond with makes the gift more meaningful to you. You will feel like you are making a difference in something you believe in. Dog lover? Think about what you can give to your local animal shelter—financial gifts are always welcome, but you can also donate your time. Deforestation? Give gifts of money to reforestation efforts—and volunteer to plant some trees yourself. Become involved in the cause you support. Learn more about the organization's day-to-day efforts and long-term goals. You will find your place in a group that you will want to stay with for a long time.

Reap the Benefits Investing yourself in an organization you believe in can have benefits for you in other ways as well. Volunteering can provide you with valuable job experience and material for your college entrance applications. In addition, you will meet friends who share your interests and worldview. The people you work with may become future character references. Sharing your time and talents will also help you make the world a better place. You will feel better about yourself. If you choose to volunteer, you are in good company. According to a *USA Weekend* magazine poll, more than 65 percent of high school students today are volunteering in their communities—a greater percentage than ever before, going back half a century.

▲ An Americorps volunteer assists 4-H members making fossil mud cakes.

Find an Organization There are numerous charities and causes that stand to benefit from the talent and financial resources you can share. As a starting point, the following organizations are popular among young people:

- Kiva (http://fin.emcp.net/kiva) is an organization that helps you to "sponsor a business" by making a small loan—as little as $25—to one or more entrepreneurs in the developing world, empowering them to lift themselves out of poverty.
- New Global Citizens (http://fin.emcp.net/globalcitizens) is a campaign recently launched by Youth Philanthropy Worldwide. Its goal is to mobilize teens around the world to help solve the earth's biggest problems—poverty, access to education and health care, gender inequality, environmental degradation, war, and natural disasters.
- Facebook Causes (http://fin.emcp.net/facebookcauses), allows individuals to create Web pages that give visitors information about various causes as well as a chance to join the cause and, in some cases even donate to the cause.
- MySpace Impact (http://fin.emcp.net/myspaceimpact), provides information about nonprofit organizations, social causes, and politicians. It also encourages and awards social and political participation.
- Humane Teen (http://fin.emcp.net/humaneteen), a program of the Humane Society of the United States, offers a variety of opportunities for young people to help animals and make their voices heard on issues such as animal cruelty, factory farming, and animal experimentation.
- Do Something (http://fin.emcp.net/dosomething) is an online community where young people can learn about causes, get ideas for charitable projects, and take action to make the world a better place.
- Youth Volunteer Network (http://fin.emcp.net/youthvolunteers), a Web site sponsored jointly by Network for Good and YouthNOISE, helps teens find opportunities to share time and services close to home. It has message boards where young people can communicate about different causes and can also help you find the charitable organizations that best fit your values.

- Youth Venture (http://fin.emcp.net/venture) is a global network that inspires and invests in teams of young people who design and launch their own community-based charitable organizations.
- Student Conservation Association (http://fin.emcp.net/SCA) matches young people with internships and other conservation opportunities in a variety of environments—such as urban parks, national parks, and state forests.
- Landmark Volunteers (http://fin.emcp.net/landmarks) provides summer volunteer opportunities for students at more than fifty conservation landmarks around the country—from the Grand Canyon in Arizona, to the Morgan Horse Farm in Vermont, to Colonial Williamsburg in Virginia.

More Ways You Can Share

▼ Helping out in group activities benefits many students at once.

Some occasions seem to turn themselves into over-the-top spending fests. You can look at them in a new way, however. Birthdays and holidays provide opportunities for sharing. You can also share your time while you learn, through service-learning programs.

Birthdays Do your friends, parents, and siblings have plenty of "stuff"? As you seek out the perfect birthday gift, consider doing what Sheri did. She wanted to do something for her friend Tina, whose mother had recently died of cancer. Instead of buying Tina one more thing she didn't need, Sheri chose to participate in a cancer walkathon.

Sheri's friends and family pitched in and donated money for every mile she walked. When it was over, Sheri had raised more than $300 for a national cancer research fund—all to honor Tina's mother. Tina was overwhelmed with gratitude. At the end of the day, Tina probably would not have remembered if Sheri had given her a sweater or a CD for her birthday—but for the rest of her life Tina will remember that her friend was thoughtful enough to raise money for a cause that meant so much to her.

Holidays When the holidays roll around, why settle for the same old kind of gift? Be creative and search out something different. For instance, you can help hungry families around the world by purchasing a share of an animal from Heifer International (http://fin.emcp.net/heifer). Heifer gifts can be wool-producing sheep, milk-producing cows, chickens, rabbits, even honeybees. The simple yet powerful idea of this group is to give families a source of food rather than short-term relief. Millions of families in 128 countries have benefited. As the families share their animals' offspring with friends and neighbors—along with their knowledge, resources, and skills—they create an expanding network of hope, dignity, and self-reliance that reaches around the globe.

◀ Sharing your knowledge and skills with others can be a rewarding learning experience for both you and the student.

Service-Learning Have you ever heard the phrase "time is money"? It is commonly attributed to Benjamin Franklin—one of our country's early thinkers about philanthropy. In fact, Ben Franklin created the first all-volunteer fire department, a tradition that still exists in many communities today. For adults with busy schedules, it is often easier to give money than time. For young people, giving time has been formalized by the explosion of **service-learning**, a teaching method that combines service to the community with classroom studies. The National Youth Leadership Council offers this example:

> Picking up trash by a riverbank is *service.*
>
> Studying water samples under a microscope is *learning.*
>
> When students collect and analyze water samples and the local pollution control agency uses the findings to clean up a river . . . that is *service-learning.*

The concept is in full force around the country. In fact, many schools, colleges, and universities require students to complete a certain number of volunteer hours in order to graduate. The key is to maintain the habit after you finish with your formal education. One online resource that can help you match your interests with nonprofit organizations is VolunteerMatch (http://fin.emcp.net/volunteermatch).

An Example: Teens *Can* Make a Difference

You might think that a young person without much money really cannot do a lot to help others financially. But that assumption is not always true. In San Antonio, Texas, a teen group organized a philanthropy club to prove that young people can make a difference. They wanted to become better acquainted with issues and needs in their community and around the world. And they wanted to do something about those problems.

Here is how the club works: Each member donates $250 of his or her own money to a fund. Each teen's $250 is matched by private donors in the community. This idea is similar to an investment club, where people pool their money and make group decisions about how to invest it. The difference in this

service-learning a teaching method that combines service to the community with classroom studies

case is that the young people are making decisions about how to *share* the money in the fund—giving it away to causes and organizations that are important to them.

Everyone who participates in the philanthropy club has an equal voice and vote in the discussions and decisions. No single person is allowed to monopolize the conversation. Everyone can bring forward one idea each year. Those who do are required to make a brief presentation on why they believe it is a worthy cause. These presentations and discussions enable club members to become better informed about a variety of issues, and the presenters learn to speak in front of a group and defend their choices. After all the presentations have been made, the club then determines how best to allocate 5 percent of its total fund. The remaining money in the fund is left to grow, to be invested in future good works. In the fall of 2006, the group distributed $4,000 to various charities. These teens did indeed make a difference.

Why Do People Share?

Too often the act of sharing money takes a backseat to all of the spending choices that tempt us day in and day out. But throughout history there have been people whose sharing ultimately made a big impact on others. Let these individuals set an example of how you can share. Take Benjamin Franklin. It has been said that if someone needed money to start a business or help his or her family, Ben Franklin would share what he had and not ask for the money to be paid back. His instructions to the person he was helping: "If someone you know needs money someday, I hope you will pay it forward and help them out just as I have helped you." Now that is big-time generosity.

▼ These young men may not have extra money to give to worthy causes, but they can, and do, donate their time and skills to helping build new homes for others.

Interview Someone Who Shares

Who do you know who has a heart for helping others? Is it a family member, a friend, or perhaps a neighbor down the street? Interview one or more people you know who regularly share time and money with causes they believe in. Remember that the amount of money they share is not important (and it would not be appropriate to ask). What matters is the fact that they have built sharing into their routine.

Here are some questions to help you do the interview:

1. At what age did you start sharing with others?
2. Why is sharing important for you?
3. Did someone teach you how to share time and money when you were young?
4. How did you maintain a commitment to share while you were going to college?
5. What about when you were a young adult—did you stop sharing (especially money) while you were getting established (saving for a home, paying off student loans, buying a car)?

6. Which is easier for you to share—time or money?
7. Does sharing help you balance how you save and spend money?
8. [If the person has a spouse and/or children] How do you make decisions to share in your family? Is it hard to agree on how or where you will share?

As you will learn, people share for a variety of reasons. Hopefully your interview will give you a better idea of how and why people share. Sometimes the best money lessons are right in front of you—in the form of a parent, sibling, grandparent, friend, or neighbor. Ask the people you know to share their money stories. As you learned from Ben Franklin, you can share with others simply because it helps someone in need—and that in turn inspires others to give.

One Student's Story: Helping Orphans in Kenya

This section has explored the topic of sharing and how it can reflect your goals and values. Here is the story of a North Carolina high school student who put his goals into action.

As a young boy, Rob Stephens had spent time in Kenya while his father was a medical missionary there. Later, Rob's family adopted two children from Kenya—Rob's siblings. After his junior year in high school, Rob returned to Kenya for the summer to volunteer at an orphanage near Nairobi.

One thing that made a strong impression on Rob was the number of AIDS-affected orphans in Kenya. When he got home from his summer in Nairobi, he was determined to teach his peers about the plight of those children. He wanted not only to tell young people about the problem, but to get them involved in solving it.

He organized fund-raisers for the orphanage, including a statewide charity basketball tournament. He bought beads from a women's shelter in Kenya and brought them back for students to make into jewelry, which they sold to raise money for the orphanage. Later, he organized trips to the orphanage so his fellow students could witness firsthand how their contributions positively affected the lives of the children there.

In 2005, Rob received the Global Action Award from NetAid, a nonprofit organization that inspires young people to fight global poverty. You can learn more about NetAid and the opportunities it offers by visiting its Web site at http://fin.emcp.net/netaid. Meanwhile, Rob, now a student at the University of North Carolina, still makes trips to Kenya where he can visit the orphanage and see the impact of his work.

▼ Adoption is one way of providing charity to disadvantaged children.

SECTION 2 ASSESSMENT

Factual Recall

1. True or false: Seventy percent of households with less than $30,000 annual income give no money to charities.
2. Does philanthropy have to involve giving away money? Explain your answer.
3. If you want to help others but do not have much money, what can you do?
4. What is service-learning?

Critical Thinking

1. How do you benefit when you share resources with others?
2. Why do you think many schools require students to complete volunteer hours in order to graduate? Is this a priority at your school?
3. Respond to this statement: Only adults have the resources to help others.

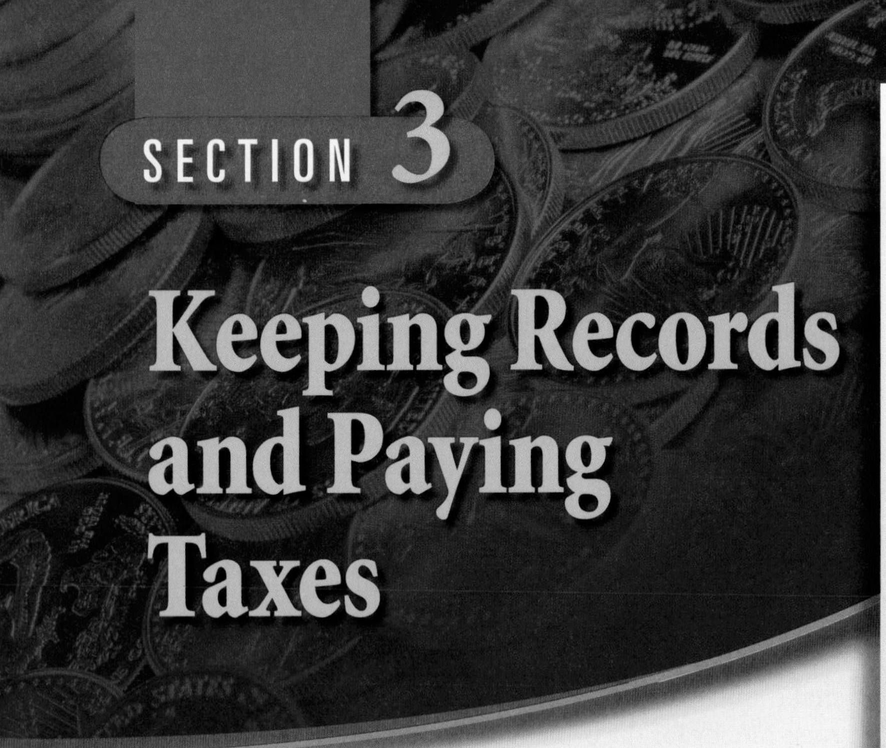

SECTION 3

Keeping Records and Paying Taxes

Focus Questions

1. Why do most financial record-keeping systems have various components? What might those components be?
2. How might a computer make financial record keeping easier?
3. What kinds of taxes are there? Which ones affect me?
4. How do I pay income taxes? Can I fill out the forms myself?

Key Terms

financial records	withholding
taxes	Social Security
sales tax	adjusted gross income
property tax	tax deductions
estate tax	Form W-2
income tax	

Mindy's father handed her the mail as he drove up the driveway from the mailbox. She flipped through the envelopes and saw her monthly statement from the bank. "Don't forget to file that," said her father. Mindy sighed.

Mindy and her father grabbed their things and went into the house. Mindy skipped up the stairs to her room and closed the door. She opened up her closet door and tossed aside the shirts and socks covering a dusty shoe box. She removed the lid and shoved in the bank statement. "Filed!" Mindy said to herself.

Keeping track of your money is essential for good financial planning. You want to avoid overdrafts and late fees. You want to measure how close you are to reaching your financial goals. And when tax season rolls around, you will need to locate the original copies of many financial records. Right now Mindy's "filing system" might seem easy—but if a check bounces or if she needs to find a receipt or canceled check, she will probably wish she had a better plan.

financial records documents such as bank statements, receipts, contracts, tax records, and bills, containing the history of how someone's money is spent

Organizing Your Financial Records

Financial records include a variety of documents such as bank statements, receipts, vehicle ownership papers, contracts, insurance papers, employment records, tax records, and bills (or *invoices*). Some of your financial records will be hard-copy pieces of paper. Other financial records are electronic and can be viewed and stored in your computer. Examples of computer records are online checking account registers, online bills and payment records, and financial plan spreadsheets.

Efficient record keepers understand the importance of a filing system that stores data logically and is also simple to use. You will probably need to design a slightly different filing system for paper documents than you do for your electronic records. The ultimate purpose is the same, however: a system that allows you to have fast and easy access to your financial information.

Filing Systems for Paper Documents

Paper documents are probably best kept in file folders. You can organize the file folders in a number of ways. Some documents are best arranged in alphabetical order, others in numerical order, and others in chronological order.

Alphabetical Order You can file your folders in alphabetical order according to the name of the business that each pertains to, or you can file them according to subject category. An example of folder labels in a name-based alphabetical system might be "Ford," "Geico," "IRS," "Jiffy Lube," and "Waco, TX." If you file by subject category, you might have a "Vehicle" folder, with subfolders for "Title," "Insurance," "Maintenance," and "Purchase agreement."

Numerical Order Sometimes it makes more sense to file items in numerical order. For example, if you send invoices to people for things like lawn care, musical performances, or babysitting, you might want to use a number-based system. You could give each invoice a number and then file them in numerical order to be able to find each one quickly. Your file folders might be labeled with spans of numbers like "001–299" or "1000–2000."

Chronological Order One type of number-based system uses chronological order. You can label each document with the date, and then file it in a folder that corresponds to the month or year. Typically, chronological filing systems use year-month-date order. So an invoice you send on May 10, 2009, might be labeled "20090510" or "090510."

Computer-Based Money Management Systems

Many banks and other financial institutions provide online access to your accounts. To use such a system, you usually must establish a *login* (username and password). For security purposes, the online system will also ask you for your account number and possibly some other personal information. Different banks offer different online services—but most allow customers to see their account balances, their account activity, and copies of checks they have written. Some also let you pay bills, transfer money from one account to another, or apply for a loan.

Other institutions also offer online services. Businesses such as cell phone companies, insurance companies, package delivery companies, public transportation systems, and schools and colleges commonly allow customers to make purchases and pay bills over the Internet. And of course you can make purchases from almost any company through the company's Web site. Services such as PayPal, for example, allow consumers to pay other individuals for purchases on online auction sites like eBay. When you pay a bill or make a purchase online, it is a good idea to print out (and file) the confirmation of your transaction. Another option is to request an e-mail confirmation and keep that in an electronic folder on your computer.

▲ A file cabinet with logically organized and clearly labeled file folders will give you peace of mind and make you a more efficient money manager.

Online Safety Most online financial service providers are safe to use. However, consumers have to be cautious. It is important to observe the following basic rules:

- Keep hard-copy records of your online transactions, and check them against statements from the bank or company you are doing business with.
- Do not give out personal or financial information unless you are absolutely sure you are at a secure site.
- Never click on links in e-mail messages that say you need to update your financial or personal information at a particular Web site—even if the message looks like it came from your bank or a company you know. Legitimate requests will not be sent by e-mail.
- Regularly update your operating system, firewalls, and antivirus and antispyware software and make sure you are using them.
- Read the privacy policies of companies you do business with before clicking "Okay," "Next," or "I agree" when filling out information.

Money Management Software Computer software for money management can help you maintain accurate electronic records. Programs like Quicken, QuickBooks, and Microsoft Money allow you to keep track of your bank account activity on your computer. You can also use these programs to download information from your online banking account—and then compare that information with your own figures to be sure they agree. Spreadsheet programs like Microsoft Excel, Microsoft Works Spreadsheet, and OpenOffice Calc enable you to create charts that log your income and spending. You can also use these charts to plan and monitor your financial goals.

Use Your System

Whatever tools you choose to keep your financial records in order, you will need to use them on a regular basis. Otherwise the system cannot be effective. Set aside an hour or so every other week or once a month. Use this time to file your paperwork, balance your checking account, and review other financial information. It might not be the most exciting highlight of the month, but it will keep you from worrying about money. By *using* your money management system, you will feel confident that your finances are in order—and that you are moving toward your financial goals.

Money management software and online financial services will help you achieve your financial goals—*if* you use these tools in a timely, consistent way.

Paying Taxes

Christopher had landed his first real job, after mowing lawns in the neighborhood for several years. Then he got his first paycheck. He was not happy: "If I'm making $7.75 an hour, and I worked twenty hours, how come my check is for only $127.64? It should be $155. I should have stuck with mowing lawns. At least I got to keep everything I earned then."

As you already know if you studied Chapter 2, not all of the money that you earn when you work for a company goes

Going Global

The British insurance company AXA found through research that in general, Brits are lazy about personal money management. In fact, a third of the people surveyed said they spend no time whatsoever going through their financial records. Not that the British are lazier than Americans or anybody else. In fact, most people around the world spend too little time and effort managing their money.

According to AXA's study, people who spend just one hour a month organizing and managing their financial paperwork are likely to save thousands of pounds (or dollars) each year. People who spend little or no time with their financial data are far less likely to have any savings at the end of the year.

The study concluded with seven tips for getting your financial information in order:

1. Spend an hour a month planning and reviewing your finances.
2. Each month, make a list with two columns: one for money coming in, the other for money going out. Make sure the second column totals *less* than the first column.
3. Talk about your finances with a trusted family member or friend. Ask for help, suggestions, or ideas about how to make changes.
4. Understand your debts, and realize how much interest you are paying on them. Know when they will be paid off. Explore ways to reduce your interest rates and pay off the debt as quickly as possible.
5. Pay off your debts before making new purchases or even before setting aside money for short-term savings. The amount you pay in interest on your debts is likely to outweigh any interest you might earn on your savings.
6. Think about your long-term financial future. It is never too early to think about your plans for college, living away from home, or buying your first car.
7. Take control. Do not be overwhelmed by your finances. Avoiding financial issues will not make them go away. Instead, monitor your money so you will not have to wonder if you have enough in your account or if you paid a bill on time.

Thinking Globally

1. If a similar study was conducted in the United States, do you think the results would be the same? Why or why not?
2. Do you think young people are more likely than older adults to avoid financial issues? Explain your answer.

into your paycheck. One thing you will have to budget into your financial plan is taxes. **Taxes** represent all the money that people pay to their local, state, and federal governments to fund government programs. Federal taxes are used for Medicare, Medicaid, education, the military, roads, and other public projects. Likewise, state taxes fund many of the same sorts of programs and projects. Local taxes often go toward police and fire departments, schools, parks, and community services.

taxes the money that people pay to their local, state, and federal governments to fund government programs and public services

Types of Taxes

One very common type of tax is the **sales tax**, which you pay when you make

sales tax a tax that people pay when they make a purchase

LOOK Before You Leap

Most states collect sales tax on purchases made within the state. The tax varies, but ranges from about 3 percent to about 7 percent. Some cities and other local governments add a sales tax of their own, commonly to help pay for a particular project that is supposed to be for the public good. For example, a city may charge an additional one-half of 1 percent to purchase undeveloped land for parks or to build a new library. The combined state and local sales taxes can add more than 8 percent to the cost of an item in some states.

The sales tax where Marcy lives is 6.5 percent. Marcy has been looking around at snowboards and is thinking about purchasing one. The one she likes has a price tag of $400. How much additional will she have to pay in sales tax?

Many consumers have been turning to the Internet for their purchases. When you buy online, you probably will not have to pay any sales tax. If you buy something from a company that has no stores within your state, the company does not have to collect sales tax for your state. If the company does have a store in your state, however, it will have to charge sales tax on your purchase.

So Marcy goes online to research snowboards. She finds the same board for the same price, from a company with no stores in her state. No sales tax will be added to the price. She should buy the snowboard online, right? Maybe.

Online consumers often avoid sales tax, but they usually cannot avoid shipping costs. So whatever Marcy saves in sales tax might be offset by the cost to have the board shipped to her home. Online shoppers need to determine the *entire* cost of their online purchases—including shipping—before deciding whether to buy on the Internet or at a local store down the road.

Before Buying

1. Marcy needs to determine how much she would pay in sales tax. How much extra will 6.5 percent add to the cost of her snowboard? Assume that shipping costs are $14.95. Should she buy online, or at the local store?
2. What if Marcy lived within an hour's drive of a state where the sales tax is only 3 percent? How might that influence her decision? Explain.

a purchase. People pay **property tax** (sometimes called *real estate tax*) on the land and homes that they own. Some states, counties, and cities also have a *personal property tax* on items such as automobiles and boats, and taxes on services such as hotel rooms and car rentals. The **estate tax** is collected when someone dies and passes wealth along to a family member. And of course there is the **income tax**, figured as a percentage of a person's earnings.

property tax a tax that owners pay on their land or homes; sometimes called *real estate tax*

estate tax a tax collected when someone dies and passes wealth along to a family member or other heir

income tax a tax figured as a percentage of someone's earnings

Everyone pays income taxes on the money they earn. As discussed in Chapter 2, state and federal income taxes are often automatically subtracted from your hourly wages, as you can see on your paycheck. If you earn $10 an hour, for example, you will probably notice that a twenty-hour workweek earns you *less* than $200. This is because of **withholding**—the money that has been taken out to pay taxes, Social Security, and perhaps additional fees like insurance and a pension plan.

The **Social Security** tax covers the federal program that people pay into while they are working. The money pays for disability, retirement, and life insurance benefits. This system has been under a lot of scrutiny in recent years. New laws may affect the amount of money you end up paying into the system and the amount you will collect when you retire decades from now.

Forms W-4, 1040, and 1040EZ

If you have an informal working arrangement, taxes may not be deducted from your pay. For example, maybe you have a successful moneymaking business mowing lawns, walking pets, or repairing bicycles. In those cases, you probably get paid directly by your clients. No taxes are taken out of those earnings. You will have to get the help of a friend, relative, or tax expert to see if you need to file with the IRS and pay taxes on your income.

When a company hires you for a job, however, taxes will be deducted from your paycheck. You will be asked to fill out a tax form called a W-4 (introduced in Chapter 2). This form helps you and your employer figure out how much money to withhold from each paycheck.

After the end of the year, you will fill out a Form 1040, the official government form used to report your income and calculate your federal income tax. Or you might fill out a simplified version used by most young people with part-time jobs, called a Form 1040EZ. If the amount withheld from your paycheck during the year is more than the amount of tax you owe, send in the form and you will get a refund. If not enough money was withheld, you will need to send in what you still owe along with your tax form. Income taxes are due by April 15 of the following year. Figure 3.3 on the next page shows samples of Form 1040A and Form 1040EZ.

Figuring How Much You Will Pay

Actual taxes are based on your **adjusted gross income**. This is your total income *minus* certain adjustments and reductions, such as contributions to

withholding the amount deducted from a person's paycheck to pay for taxes and other items such as health insurance and a pension plan

Social Security the federal program that people pay into while they are working, that pays disability, retirement, and life insurance benefits to eligible recipients

adjusted gross income total income *minus* certain adjustments and reductions such as contributions to a retirement account, interest on a student loan, and exemptions claimed on Form W-4

YOU DECIDE

Some people claim fewer exemptions than they are entitled to on their W-4 forms, so that more money is withheld from each paycheck. They figure they will get a bigger refund when they file their tax return next year because they overpaid.

Sam works part-time at a quick-service oil-change center. When he filled out his W-4 form, he decided to claim fewer exemptions. He calls it "forced savings"—money he is putting away to get back as a refund the following year. But then Sam starts thinking. If he puts part of each check into a savings account instead of handing it over to the IRS, he will be earning interest on the money. With his "forced savings" plan, on the other hand, the IRS is earning the interest on his money. So he wonders: It might be smart to withhold the right amount, so that he does not owe money to the IRS at the end of the year. But it might also be smart not to pay too much.

Should he...

1. ... claim zero exemptions and get a bigger tax refund? Or claim the exemptions he is entitled to and put more money into his savings account during the year?
2. ... also consider how much income tax he will have to pay on the added interest that his savings account earns? Why or why not?

Figure 3.3 SAMPLE INCOME TAX FORMS

Most people, when filing their first federal income tax forms, can use either the 1040A or the 1040EZ, which are much simpler than the standard 1040 form.

a retirement account or interest on a student loan. Another reduction would be the exemptions you claim on your Form W-4, as described in Chapter 2. Taxpayers can claim an exemption for themselves, as well as exemptions for their spouses and their dependents—usually children.

Certain other expenses can be used as **tax deductions**. These amounts are subtracted from your adjusted gross income before figuring your *taxable income*. Everyone gets a *standard deduction* of around $5,000 for a single person. However, if you had a lot of tax deductions that totaled more than the standard deduction, you would be better off making a list of *itemized deductions*. These may include doctor and dental bills, eyeglasses or contacts, prescription drugs, contributions to charities, and taxes paid to state and local governments during the year. To itemize your deductions, you need the financial records to prove that you actually had the expenses you claim.

tax deductions expenses subtracted from adjusted gross income before figuring a person's taxable income

As your income goes up, so does the percentage that you pay in income taxes. For example, as of 2007, if you are single and your taxable income is only $7,000 a year, you would pay about 10 percent in federal income taxes—or $700. If your taxable income is $32,000, you would pay a little more than $4,400—or about 14 percent. If your taxable income is $350,000, you would have to pay a little more than $100,000, or about 29 percent.

Figure 3.4 **SAMPLE FORM W-2**

22222 | Void ☐ | a Employee's social security number | For Official Use Only ► OMB No. 1545-0008

b Employer identification number (EIN)	1 Wages, tips, other compensation	2 Federal income tax withheld
c Employer's name, address, and ZIP code	3 Social security wages	4 Social security tax withheld
	5 Medicare wages and tips	6 Medicare tax withheld
	7 Social security tips	8 Allocated tips
d Control number	9 Advance EIC payment	10 Dependent care benefits
e Employee's first name and initial / Last name / Suff.	11 Nonqualified plans	12a See instructions for box 12
	13 Statutory employee / Retirement plan / Third-party sick pay	12b
	14 Other	12c
f Employee's address and ZIP code		12d

15 State	Employer's state ID number	16 State wages, tips, etc.	17 State income tax	18 Local wages, tips, etc.	19 Local income tax	20 Locality name

Form **W-2** Wage and Tax Statement **2008**

Department of the Treasury—Internal Revenue Service

For Privacy Act and Paperwork Reduction Act Notice, see back of Copy D.

Copy A For Social Security Administration — Send this entire page with Form W-3 to the Social Security Administration; photocopies are **not** acceptable.

Cat. No. 10134D

Do Not Cut, Fold, or Staple Forms on This Page — Do Not Cut, Fold, or Staple Forms on This Page

Filing an Income Tax Return

Everyone who is required to fill out a tax return is supposed to do it by April 15 of the following year. If a person earns less than a specified amount—$8,450 in 2007—then he or she does not need to file a return, unless that person had taxes withheld and might be eligible for a refund.

As a minor, you are probably claimed as a dependent on your parents' or guardians' tax return. In that case, you have to file if your earned taxable income is more than $5,150. If you do not file on time or if you are late paying your taxes, the federal government will tack on additional fees, penalties, and interest.

After the end of the year, your employer will send you a **Form W-2** (see Figure 3.4 above), a document that shows the total amount of money withheld from your paychecks throughout the year. Tax forms and instructions for filling them out can be found in public libraries, at post office branches, in banks, and on the Web site of the IRS (http://fin.emcp.net/IRS).

Answers to Fact or Fiction

1. False—According to a survey by the Better Business Bureau, 86 percent of all adults in the United States identified themselves as donors; **2.** True; **3.** False—You can learn a lot about money management from friends and family members whom you trust and respect; **4.** True; **5.** True; **6.** False—You do not have to file a return if you earn less than a specified total amount ($8,450 in 2007), not less than $5 an hour; **7.** False—Tax forms and instructions for filling them out can be found in public libraries, at post office branches, in banks, and on the Web site of the IRS.

Form W-2 an IRS document from an employer showing the total amount of money withheld from an employee's paychecks throughout the year

SECTION 3 ASSESSMENT

Factual Recall

1. What is an invoice?
2. You are creating a chronological filing system. How would you label a document dated November 30, 2008?
3. Julie works on her financial records once a year. Is this the best practice? Explain your answer.
4. Form W-2 and Form W-4 both are related to withholding. What is the difference?

Critical Thinking

1. Why is it important to keep your financial records well organized?
2. Which filing system do you think is better: alphabetical or numerical? Give reasons for your answer.

CHAPTER 3 REVIEW AND ASSESSMENT

Chapter Summary

Section 1 Establishing Healthy Financial Habits

- The Share Save Spend money management system helps you look at money in terms of your own values.
- Financial planning should focus not only on spending and saving for yourself, but also on how you can help others.
- The key to solid financial planning is determining what is important to you and then following through by making financial decisions based on your values.
- Determine your income and expenses, then identify and prioritize your goals.
- Monitor and update your plan regularly in order to adjust to changes.

Section 2 Sharing as Part of a Financial Plan

- Sharing your resources provides benefits to you as well as others.
- Many students help their community through service-learning programs.
- Numerous charities and causes can benefit from your generosity. You do not have to be wealthy in order to help. By giving your time, talents, and effort, you can make a positive difference.

Section 3 Keeping Records and Paying Taxes

- Keeping track of your money is essential for good financial planning.
- Some of your financial records will be on paper; some will be electronic.
- Paper records can be filed in alphabetical, numerical, or chronological order.
- Electronic records can be accessed and organized with various computer-based money management systems. Practice good security measures to keep your records safe.
- Taxes are paid in order to fund government programs and services.
- Types of taxes include property taxes (based on real estate or other personal property), sales taxes (paid when you purchase an item), estate taxes (collected on the wealth a person leaves to his or her heirs), and income taxes (based on earnings).
- The amount of income tax you owe depends on your income and various adjustments, reductions, and deductions.
- Income, deductions, and so on are reported on income tax return forms and sent to the government each year.

Reviewing Key Terms

Indicate whether each of the following statements (featuring key terms) is true or false. If a statement is false, rewrite it to make it true.

1. The **Share Save Spend system** is an approach to money management that divides funds into three categories according to the investor's values.
2. A tax collected when someone dies and passes wealth along to a family member or other heir is called a **property tax**.
3. **Philology** is the act of giving away money, goods, services, or time to support a cause.
4. **Estate taxes** are sometimes called real estate taxes.
5. **Income tax** is figured as a percentage of earnings.
6. **Sales tax** is paid by people when they make a purchase.
7. **Tax deduction** is the amount subtracted from a person's paycheck to pay for taxes and other items such as health insurance and a pension plan.
8. A person's total income minus adjustments and reductions is called the **adjusted net income**.
9. **Medicare** is the federal program that pays retirement, disability, and life insurance benefits.
10. When preparing income tax returns, people can subtract certain expenses—called **withholding**—from their income.

11. **Social Security** is the federal program that pays you a small amount each month while you are between twenty-five and forty years old.

Understanding the Main Ideas

1. What are the three R's of a good budget and what do they mean?
2. Does only the money you receive in exchange for work qualify as income? Explain your answer.
3. Describe how a teen philanthropy club works. Give the name of at least one.
4. Name four projects or services supported by federal, state, or local taxes.
5. Which tax goes toward the federal program that pays retirement benefits?
6. What is a tax refund?
7. What is the relationship between the amount of income and the percentage that is paid in income tax?
8. Why do sharing and saving need to be budgeted before spending?

Practicing Math

1. You have a new job and have just received your first paycheck. The gross amount is $1,360. Deduct 15 percent for federal income tax, 2 percent for state income tax, 7.65 percent for FICA/Social Security, and $28 for health insurance. What is your net pay?

Applying Critical Thinking Skills

1. Name at least two positive results of good financial planning.
2. When making a financial plan, why is it important to think about your values? Wouldn't you naturally spend your money on the things that matter to you?
3. Jon is careful about not spending more than he earns. At the end of the month, if he has money left over, he puts it in savings. What advice would you give Jon about improving his already good money management skills?
4. Now that you have a job, one of your goals is to contribute money to your family's household needs. Another is to save money for college. What are some things you can do if you do not have enough money for both?
5. Describe advantages and disadvantages of keeping your financial records electronically. How else can you store your financial records?

Working with Real-World Documents

1. Go to the IRS Web site (http://fin.emcp.net/IRS) and download Form 1040EZ. Use the following information and the tax table below to practice completing the form. If forms and tax tables for state income tax are available, also complete a state form. Ask your teacher to provide state-specific information.

- You are single with no dependents.
- Your parents claim you as a dependent on their tax return.
- You had a part-time job, and your annual income was $14,800.
- Your bank account earned $85 interest.
- The amount in Box 2 of your Form W-2 is $939.
- You have no earned income credit.

If Form 1040EZ, line 6, is . . .		And you are single . . .
At least	**But less than**	**Your tax is**
$9,400	$9,450	$1,023
$9,450	$9,500	$1,030
$9,500	$9,550	$1,038
$9,550	$9,600	$1,045

Taking It Home

1. Talk with older family members and friends whom you trust and respect. Ask them: "What is the most important financial advice you would give to a young person?" Write a summary of your findings.
2. Develop a filing system for keeping financial records, both paper and electronic. You can get advice from family members or other adults.

CHAPTER 4

Budgeting

Does the word *budget* make you flinch? Few people like to plan how much to spend on everything they might need or want.

That does not mean that people never worry about money. In fact, most people do. They wonder how to pay for things like unexpected car repairs—or even the gas to get to work.

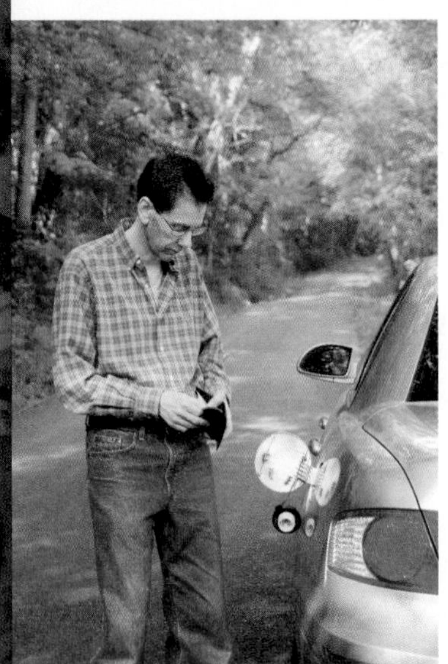

▲ It really can help to plan ahead!

Budgeting helps you plan ahead for emergencies and develop healthy money habits.

The key to budgeting is deciding how your values fit with your financial goals. It is important to decide how you will pay your bills (needs), save for future goals (wants), and share with others.

SECTION 1	Defining Your Goals
SECTION 2	Working Out Your Budget
SECTION 3	Using Your Budget

Fact or Fiction

What do you think? Are the following statements true or false? If you think they are false, then say what is true.

1. You do not need to consider long-term goals when you plan a budget because a budget is meant to cover only current expenses.
2. A budget should include estimates of the money you will receive as wages, allowance, interest on investments, gifts, and bonuses.
3. Budgets include all uses of money—savings, sharing and gifts to charities, and spending.
4. Most people who have healthy money habits as adults developed them when they were young.
5. If your budget is not working, you can adjust it or rework the numbers to try to make it work better.
6. You should review your budget once a year.

Answers on page 115.

Study Reminder

*Knowing how to study can increase your knowledge, improve your grades, and cut down on your study time. See the **Studying Personal Finance** pages at the front of the book for some tips to help you study this chapter.*

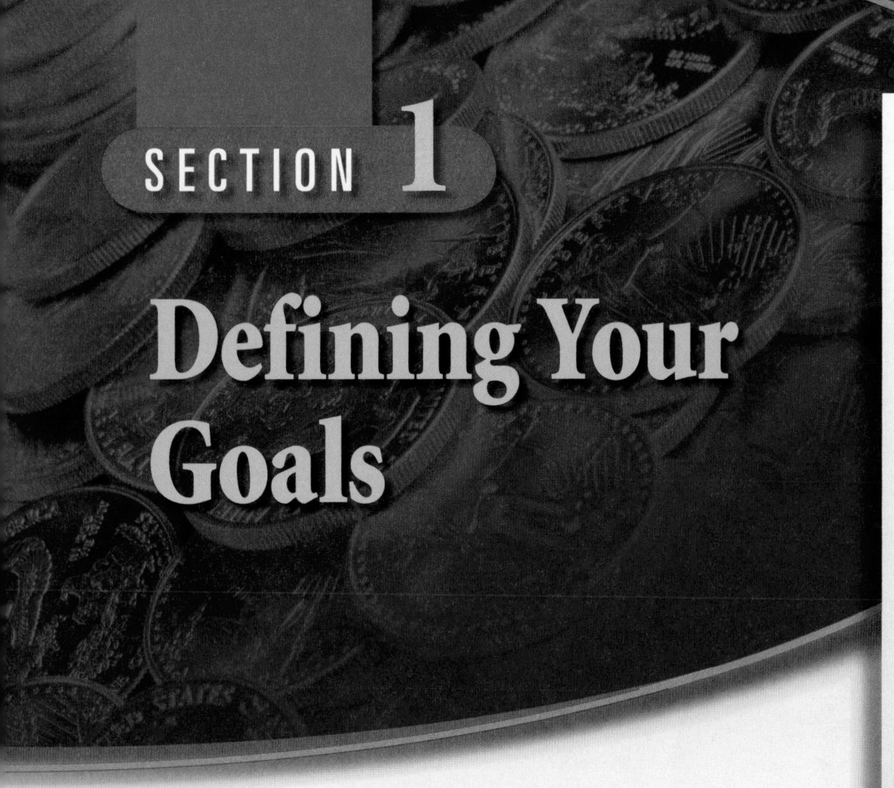

SECTION 1

Defining Your Goals

Focus Questions

1. Why is it important to set financial goals?
2. How important is it to link your values with your goals?
3. What is the difference between a short-term goal, a medium-term goal, and a long-term goal?
4. How can you plan for your sharing and savings goals?
5. What exactly *is* a budget?
6. What can you learn from adults who have achieved financial success?
7. Why should you include sharing and savings in your budget?

Key Terms

budget
short-term goals
medium-term goals
long-term goals

Goals and Values

budget a plan for how to use your money during a given time based on expected income

short-term goals things to be obtained or achieved in the next five years

medium-term goals things to be obtained or achieved in five to ten years

long-term goals things to be obtained or achieved in ten or more years

A **budget** is a plan for how to use your money. It usually covers a given period of time and is based on how much income you can expect during that time. It should also fit with your personal goals and values.

Where Do You Want Your Money to Take You?

The best way to start planning a budget is to look at your financial goals. In other words, consider what you hope to achieve in the next five years (your **short-term goals**), in five to ten years (your **medium-term goals**), and in ten or more years (your **long-term goals**). These goals represent where you want your money to take you. For a high school senior, short-term goals might include a CD player, a car, and a college degree. Medium-term goals might include earning an advanced degree, buying the first house, and studying or volunteering abroad. Long-term goals could be supporting a family, traveling around the world, remodeling a home,

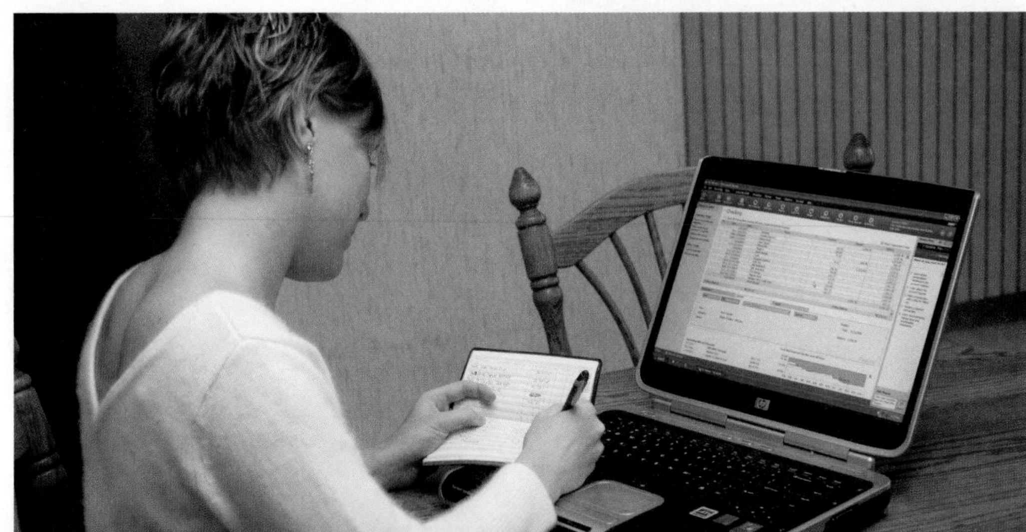

▶ Start planning a budget by creating short-, medium-, and long-term financial goals.

and retiring. Your budget will be your "road map" to these goals.

As you consider your goals, take some time to think about what is most important to you—in other words, your values. You might even want to make a short list of your values before you set off on the goal-setting exercise. Most people who link their goals to their values will find it much easier to stay motivated to achieve their goals.

Of course, everyone's goals will be different. Maybe yours include a liberal arts college, a teaching job, and lots of world travel. Perhaps you would like to have a log cabin in the wilderness, or you hope to raise cattle, or you want to have a family. At this point you want to review any work you did on your values and goals in Chapter 3.

Making a Goal Chart

As you think about the possibilities, clear your desk, except for a blank piece of paper and a pencil with an eraser. Make a grid with two columns and three rows, so the sheet of paper has six boxes. In the top-left box, describe how you see your life in five years. In the box underneath that, describe your life in ten years. In the bottom-left box, describe your life in twenty years. Now, in the right-hand column, list ideas for reaching your goals in each of those stages of your life. The ideas you list in this right-hand column are the basis for the short-, medium-, and long-term financial goals you set for your future.

Figure 4.1 shows how Alex, a high school junior, filled out his chart. When Alex looks at the second column, he sees

Figure 4.1 ALEX'S GOAL CHART

My life in 5 years: • Finishing school with a degree in library science • Having fun with friends • Taking lots of mountain biking trips	**How to get there:** • Planning financially for college; figuring out savings, work-study, financial aid • Saving money to spend on free-time activities
My life in 10 years: • Working at a university library • Buying a condo or townhome • Traveling to Asia and volunteering with a non-profit to teach English	**How to get there:** • Making sure to complete school in 4 years; getting good grades • Researching where I want to live • Saving money for home down payment and travel
My life in 20 years: • Working for the Smithsonian or other prestigious library • Having a family • Finding a vacation home	**How to get there:** • Making responsible career decisions • Planning for wife and children • Saving for vacation home

that he has several savings and planning goals for the short term, the medium term, and the long term. Alex's five-year financial goals involve putting money away toward college and for weekend bike trips. His ten-year goals involve saving for a home and teaching abroad. His twenty-year goals involve saving for family responsibilities and for a vacation home. He will want to keep all these goals in mind as he plans for the future and starts to think about a budget.

What short-, medium-, and long-term goals will you want to keep in mind as you formulate your budget plan?

Do Your Money Habits Fit Your Goals?

A good way to plan realistically is to look at your current money habits and consider how well they fit with your goals. Mateo filled out a worksheet (see Figure 4.2) to see how to modify his hab-

Going Global

Many people in developing countries have benefited from receiving microloans offered by organizations like Unitus, FINCA International, Women's World Banking, and SKS India. People who are self-employed or want to start a small business in developing countries often have no credit history, no collateral (possessions of value), and no source of money to invest. Microloans are small loans that they can use to start or expand a business.

Ester Gonzalez had a small sewing business in Buenos Aires, Argentina. She took out her first microloan as part of a group. After paying it back in full and on time, she took out several more loans. By budgeting carefully, she was able to expand her business, buy new equipment, hire employees, and pay back her loans.

Bayamma Neerudi, of Medak, India, bought a buffalo with her first microloan. With the money she got from selling milk, she was able to buy feed, pay off the loan, and save $2.75 each week. She has since taken out two more small loans—to buy a cart for the buffalo and to lease some land where she could grow rice—and paid them back successfully.

▼ These women are members of a micro-credit group on the island of Aralia in Bangladesh. The island is extremely poor and becoming more and more overcrowded. The microloans give them an opportunity to improve their living conditions.

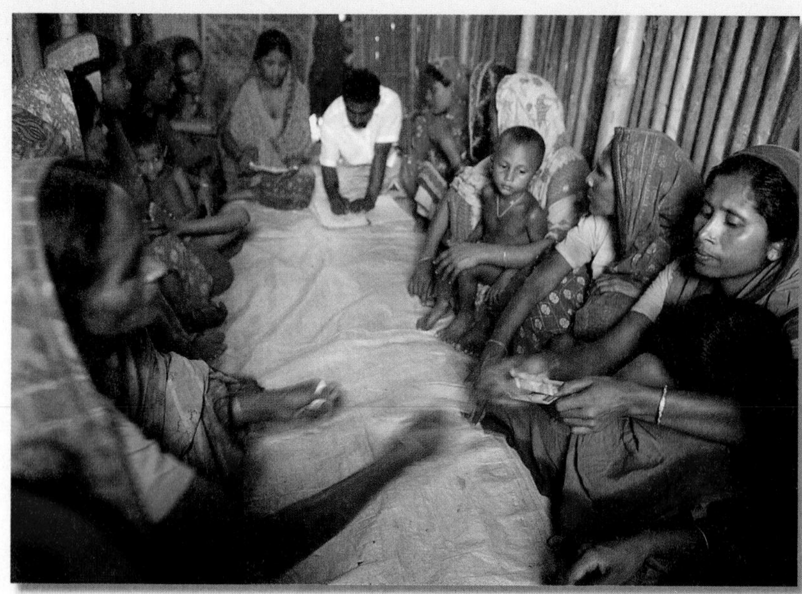

Thinking Globally

1. How do microloans benefit people in developing countries?
2. What benefit might you get from making a microloan of $25 to someone like Neerudi? What would you want to know before making such a loan?

its to meet his goals. A blank worksheet is in Figure 4.3. Take some time to make a copy of this worksheet and fill it out.

Planning for Your Sharing Goals

When planning for your sharing goals, think back to the discussion of sharing in Chapter 3. Also consider the dreams, goals, and values that you identified in your goal chart. These are the things in life that you think are important, that you want to support, and that would benefit the most from your support. Then think about what kind of support you could offer.

Chantille and her family live in a community where lots of the kids struggle with reading and writing. Her parents had to work full-time jobs and were not always around to help with her homework, but she considers herself lucky: Her grandmother helped

Figure 4.2 MATEO'S GOAL-PLANNING WORKSHEET

Mateo used this worksheet to outline his new sharing, saving, and spending goals.

Name: Mateo Gran de la Cruz		
My goals include sharing with: raptor center, food shelf		
My goals include saving for: vacation with cousin, snowboard		
My current monthly income: $420 (pizza parlor), $80 (from parents) = $500		
I now share $20 per month	I now save $40 per month	
I now share 4 % of my income	I now save 8 % of my income	
My goal is to share 10 % monthly	My goal is to save 20 % monthly	
That equals about: $50	That equals about: $100	
I plan to share 10 % monthly	I plan to save 20 % monthly	I plan to spend 70 % monthly
So I will have $350 to spend each month. I can do this!		

Divide amount shared by total income (I now share % of my income)

If you want to grow the amount you share, consider increasing the percentage (My goal is to share % monthly)

Divide amount saved by total income (I now save % of my income)

If you want to grow the amount you save, consider increasing the percentage (My goal is to save % monthly)

Figure 4.3 YOUR GOAL-PLANNING WORKSHEET

Like Mateo, you should create and fill out a goal-planning worksheet. The important thing is to strike a balance between sharing, saving, and spending. You can do it!

Name:		
My goals include sharing with:		
My goals include saving for:		
My current monthly income: $		
I now share $____ per month	I now save $____ per month	
I now share ____% of my income	I now save ____% of my income	
My goal is to share ____% monthly	My goal is to save ____% monthly	
That equals about: $	That equals about: $	
I plan to share ____% monthly	I plan to save ____% monthly	I plan to spend ____% monthly
So I will have $____ to spend each month.		

▶ **Get involved in something you believe in. Donating your time and money is rewarding and can make a big difference in the lives of others.**

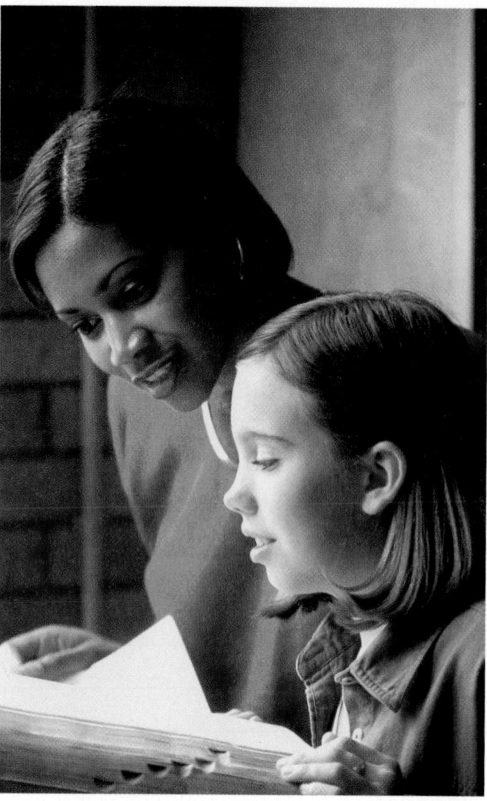

Chantille learn how to read when she was little and always encouraged her to do well in school. Chantille developed a love of reading.

The community center in Chantille's hometown offers free after-school care for young people. Chantille volunteers there two afternoons a week—helping to teach children to read. The center is always struggling financially, and there are not a lot of books for Chantille to use. She decides to commit 10 percent of her monthly income to buying children's books for the youth center.

Chantille has a part-time babysitting job, and she waits on customers at the deli that her father runs. She earns about $100 per week altogether. On average, she makes around $400 a month, so her sharing goal is to donate $40 each month to buy books for the community center.

Chantille's plan is a good one for many reasons. She is knowledgeable about the cause she supports—and she believes in its value. By combining her volunteer time and her sharing money toward this cause, she can make a bigger difference. Her self-esteem will also benefit as she invests more of herself in something she feels is important.

If you do not currently spend time doing something you believe in, think about how you can get involved. What one thing would you change in the world if you could? Then learn about the organizations that promote your cause. For instance, if you want to save the polar bears from extinction, investigate organizations that support your goal. You may not be directly involved in saving polar bears—but you could volunteer to promote the organization or you could oversee its fund-raising events. And of course, you could plan to donate some of your own money.

As you consider how much of your resources you want to share with others, think about how this sharing will affect your overall budget. Monetary contributions will certainly use part of your income. However, investing time, energy, and money in a cause you believe in can be more rewarding than spending money on "things." And if you spend time on your cause as well as money, you can have fun doing something that benefits others, something that does not require buying a ticket or paying an entrance fee.

Did You Know?

Did you know that people who focus less on spending and more on saving and sharing report being both happier and healthier? A professor studying the effects of materialism has found data to back up the old phrase "money can't buy happiness." Thanks to him we now know that finding balance in how we share, save, and spend can have a real impact on our emotional and physical health.

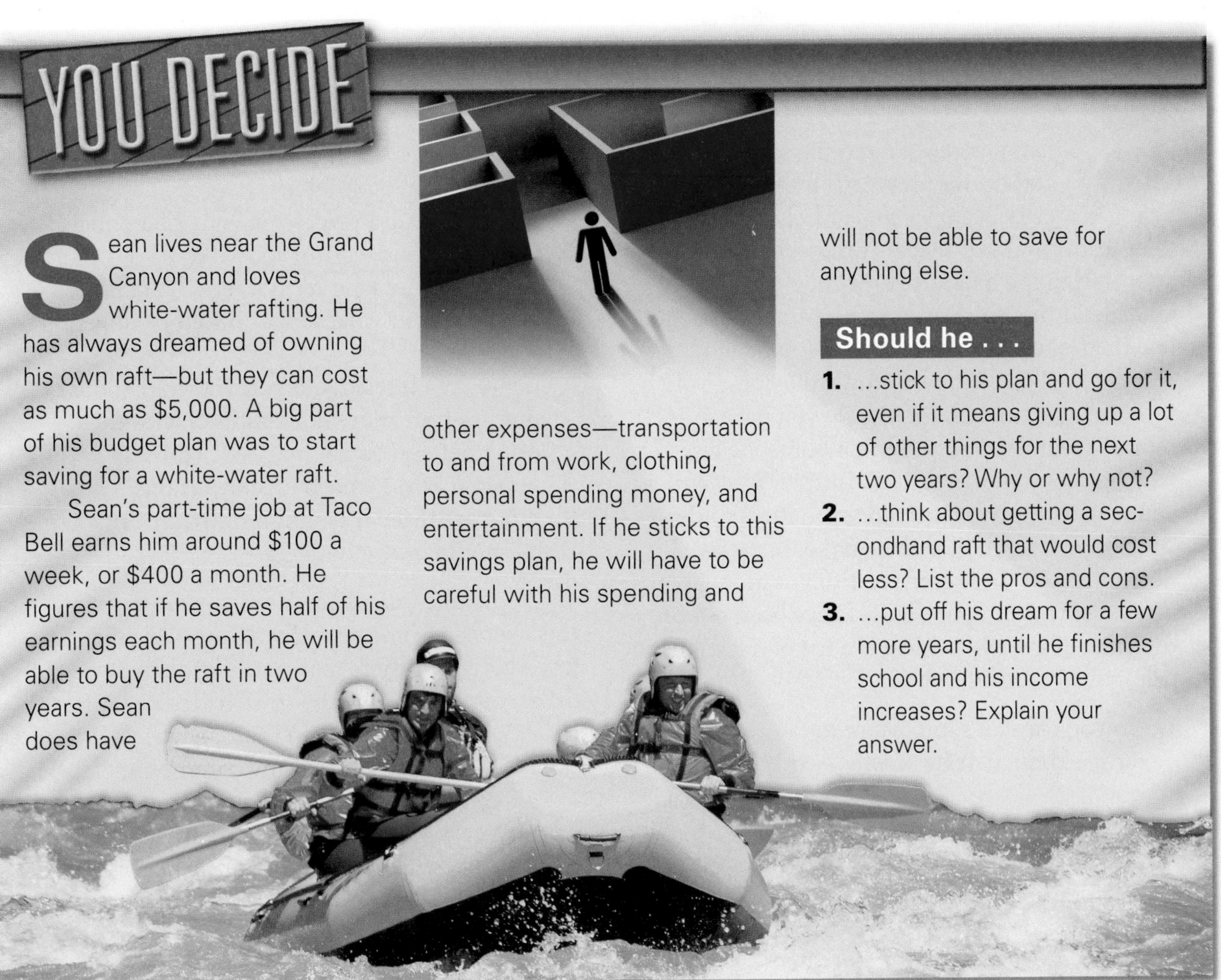

Sean lives near the Grand Canyon and loves white-water rafting. He has always dreamed of owning his own raft—but they can cost as much as $5,000. A big part of his budget plan was to start saving for a white-water raft.

Sean's part-time job at Taco Bell earns him around $100 a week, or $400 a month. He figures that if he saves half of his earnings each month, he will be able to buy the raft in two years. Sean does have other expenses—transportation to and from work, clothing, personal spending money, and entertainment. If he sticks to this savings plan, he will have to be careful with his spending and will not be able to save for anything else.

Should he . . .

1. ...stick to his plan and go for it, even if it means giving up a lot of other things for the next two years? Why or why not?
2. ...think about getting a secondhand raft that would cost less? List the pros and cons.
3. ...put off his dream for a few more years, until he finishes school and his income increases? Explain your answer.

Planning for Your Savings Goals

Once you have determined your short-, medium-, and long-term savings goals, think about how much money you need to set aside per month for each one. Remember that the more money you set aside toward a particular goal, the sooner you will reach that goal. If you have more than one savings goal—say you want a sound system *and* money for college—you will have to figure out how much to set aside for each item. Some goals, such as a college fund, are ongoing—that is, the amount you could set aside for them really has no end. Others, such as the sound system, are linked to a specific dollar amount.

To plan for a goal that has a specific dollar amount, you have to consider two things: the amount of time you are willing to wait before reaching the goal and the amount of money you are able to set aside each month. Say that in late January you decide to save for the sound system, which costs $1,000. You would love to have it by early summer, but that means you would have to put away $250 per month just for that one thing. You would have no extra money for anything else. If you waited until the end of summer to get the sound system, you would have seven months to save and would have to put away just $143 per month. If you waited a year to buy it, you would have to put away only about $83 per month. Once you know all this,

Get Good Advice

When it comes to making smart financial decisions, creating a budget is a critical step. People rarely achieve long-term financial success unless they pay attention to the details of how they share, save, and spend their money. A thoughtful budget—one that takes into account your financial values—will go a long way toward helping you achieve your financial goals. Do you have a money mentor, or do you know someone else who has good money habits? Interview several adults who seem to have money matters under control. Ask them how they make financial decisions. Use these conversations as an opportunity to learn from people who have been out on their own for a while. Here is a list of questions to help guide your interview:

1. Do you think it's important to have a budget? Why or why not?
2. Have you ever created a budget or money plan to guide your financial decisions? If so, how did it help you make better decisions with your money?
3. Did someone teach you how to budget, or did you learn on your own?
4. At what age did you create your first budget?
5. How can a budget help you achieve your short-, medium-, and long-term financial goals?
6. How did your values enter into the budgeting process?
7. If you are married, did you and your spouse discuss your individual budgets with each other before you got married? How did getting married affect your budget decisions?
8. What are three reasons an individual or a family should have a budget?

Remember, there are no wrong answers in this exercise. Some people you interview may follow a budget. Others may not. As you interview different people, note the similarities and differences in their answers. Do you notice any common themes? Do people in their twenties answer differently from people in their forties or fifties? If so, what is different about their answers? Do their responses influence your thoughts about using a budget?

you can choose the best option and start working toward your goal.

Planning for open-ended goals like a college education is a little trickier, but you can come up with certain benchmarks. For example, you might plan to save $1,000 by the end of your sophomore year in high school, another $1,000 by the end of your junior year, and an additional $1,000 by the end of your senior year. Of course, $3,000 is not going to cover the entire cost of a college education. For large open-ended goals like this, it is a good idea to ask others (such as parents or guardians) to help you figure out what the overall expenses might be and how to pay for them.

Perhaps you and your family discuss your college plans and determine that you will provide your own spending money and buy your own books and school materials. The rest will be paid for by student loans, help from your parents, and/or scholarships and grants. You will spend your summers at home, working during that time to earn money for the following year.

You calculate that you will need at least $70 per week in spending money. The average price for books each semester will be around $400. For your first year of college, therefore, you will need a little more than $3,000. If you were beginning your senior year in high school and wanted to save for that first year, you would have only twelve months to save $3,000—or $250 per month. If you were to start at the beginning of your junior year, you would need to save only half that amount each month. If you started saving at the beginning of your sophomore year, you would need to save only about $125 each month. If you decided that you could put away more than that each month, you might not have to work so hard during your summers off from college.

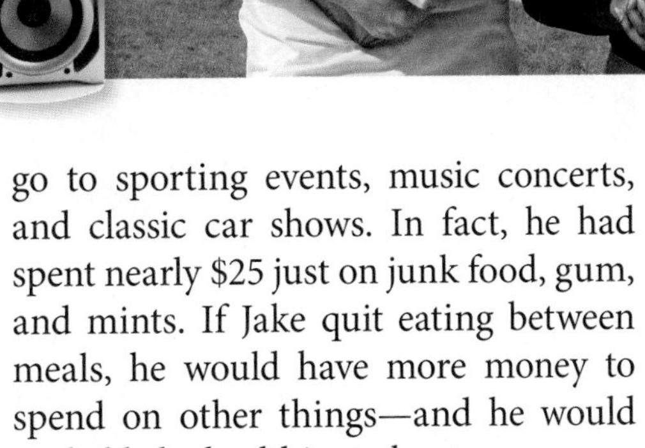

▲ The costs of college tuition, books, and room and board add up. Setting goals and starting to save early can give you a head start.

Weighing the costs and benefits of saving for a goal like college can be really eye-opening. It can also be a great life lesson in personal finance.

Planning for Your Spending Goals

Most people spend money without really thinking about it. But when you make *conscious* spending decisions, you will be spending your money on what you actually want rather than on whatever seems to come up.

Fifteen-year-old Jake was frustrated. He never had money to do what he wanted. He could not figure out what happened to the $300 he made each month working at the pizza parlor. He decided to track his spending for a week. He would write down every time he forked out money for something, no matter how small. Figure 4.4 shows what he came up with.

Jake's take-home pay averaged about $75 per week. During this particular week, $68 went toward miscellaneous unplanned spending.

Jake had never considered how a dollar here and a dollar there could add up so quickly. No wonder he had no money for other things he wanted to do—like go to sporting events, music concerts, and classic car shows. In fact, he had spent nearly $25 just on junk food, gum, and mints. If Jake quit eating between meals, he would have more money to spend on other things—and he would probably be healthier to boot.

Figure 4.4 JAKE'S DAILY SPENDING LOG

Day 1	Hot chocolate and doughnut	$ 3.50
	Soda	$ 1.00
	Gum and magazine	$ 4.00
	MP3 music downloads	$ 5.00
Day 2	Pizza and soda	$ 5.00
	T-shirt	$10.00
Day 3	Bus fare	$ 1.50
	Movie ticket, popcorn, and soda	$12.00
Day 4	Mints	$ 1.50
	Sports drink	$ 1.00
Day 5	Video games at arcade	$ 5.00
	Soda and candy	$ 2.50
Day 6	Chips and soda	$ 3.00
	MP3 music downloads	$ 5.00
Day 7	DVD rental	$ 8.00
Total		$68.00

▶ One way to stay within your budget is to pack your lunch at home—you can eat well and save money at the same time. In what other little ways can you save money?

Jake decided to use his money differently. He made a plan. Doing fun things with friends and with his brother was important to him, so Jake decided to set aside $40 per week for those activities. He would keep $10 cash for an occasional pack of gum or soda. He would put away the remaining $25 of his paycheck for sharing and saving.

Jake knew it would be easy to keep all his money in his wallet. But if he did that, he would waste it away. He decided to take two $20 bills each week and tuck them in his sock drawer. When he wanted to go to a concert or ballgame, the money would be there. The $25 for sharing and saving went straight into his savings account. He put only a $10 bill in his wallet, to make sure he did not spend any more than that on little extras.

Most people who have healthy money habits as adults developed them when they were young—probably in their teens, like Jake. They recognized the importance of establishing good money habits *before* they needed to make big decisions like buying a house, saving for retirement, or starting a business. Those big decisions may seem a long way off, but they will be here sooner than you think. You will have more options later in life if you plan now for your financial future and set thoughtful money goals linked to your values. Decisions like changing careers, moving to a different city, or investing in real estate will be easier if you develop healthy money habits now.

When it comes to making smart financial decisions, creating a budget is a critical step. People rarely achieve long-term financial success unless they pay attention to the details of how they share, save, and spend their money. A thoughtful budget—one that takes into account your financial values—is one key to achieving your financial goals.

SECTION 1 ASSESSMENT

Factual Recall

1. What is a budget?
2. What is a goal chart? What is its purpose?
3. Does a financial goal always have to include a specific dollar amount? Explain.
4. Why is it a good idea to start saving as soon as possible for your long-term goals?

Critical Thinking

1. What is the advantage of linking your financial goals to your values?
2. Describe three examples of short-term savings goals and three examples of long-term savings goals.
3. A friend complains that she is always running out of money even though she "never buys anything expensive." What advice would you give her?

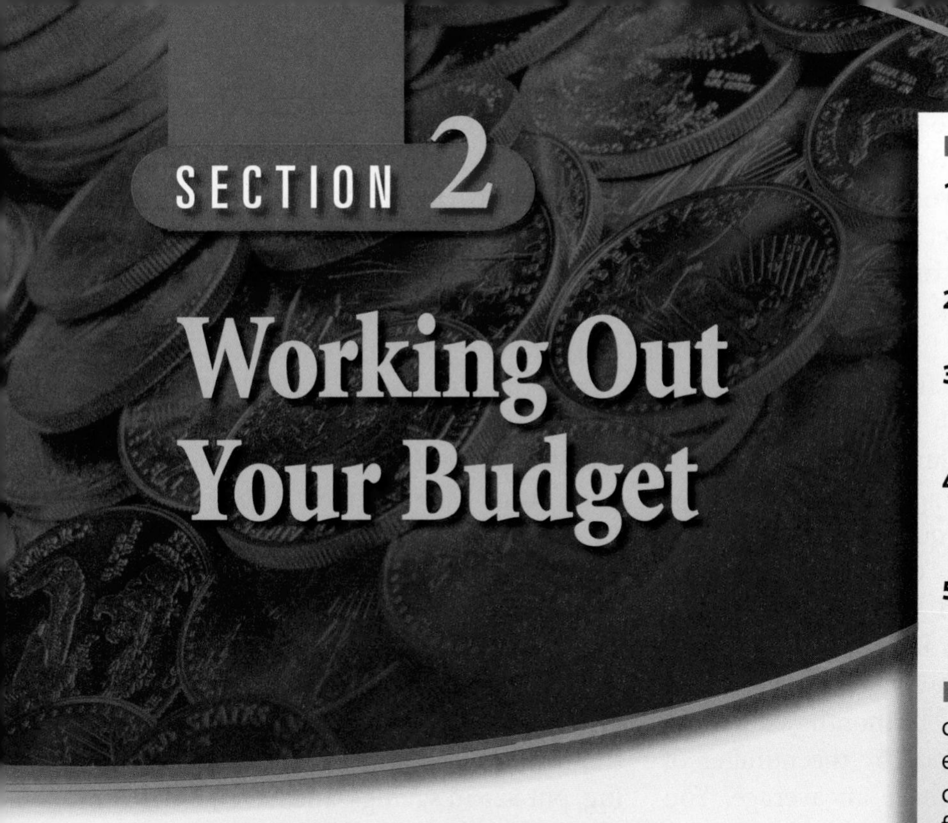

SECTION 2

Working Out Your Budget

Focus Questions

1. What is the difference between a fixed expense and a variable expense?
2. What income should you include in a budget?
3. Do unexpected gifts of money, say from a birthday present, go in your budget?
4. How can you come up with estimates for both income and expenses?
5. How can you protect yourself from large, unexpected expenses?

Key Terms

cash flow
estimate
cash flow statement
fixed expenses
variable expenses
emergency fund

Now that you have defined your financial goals and values, it is time to create your budget. The plan does not need to be complicated. In fact, people who do well at establishing and maintaining a budget tend to keep it simple. If it is too complicated or too time-consuming, there is a greater chance that you will lose interest or will just not have enough time to stay on top of your plan. But if you keep it simple—Share Save Spend—and set specific goals for each category, you will have a much better chance of staying on track.

Many training experts suggest that it takes thirty days of repeating an action to create a new habit. That goes for everything from trying to change your eating habits to developing healthy money habits. When you combine a little financial discipline (practicing healthy money habits over and over until they become routine) with thoughtful financial planning and goal setting, you can go a long way toward achieving a lifetime of financial balance, happiness, and success.

Estimating Income and Expenses

To put your budget plan into action, first look into the very near future—at either the upcoming week or the upcoming month. Estimate your **cash flow**—that is, how much money you will bring in (your income) and how much you will spend (your expenses)—during that time period.

cash flow the amount of money you take in (income) and give out (expenses)

▼ **Sticking to a budget is not easy. Keep it simple and set specific goals to create a healthy spending routine.**

Also consider the percentages that you want to share, save, and spend.

Estimating your income and expenses for budget purposes is not too difficult. An **estimate** is an educated guess or ballpark figure, based on the information you have. Estimating your income involves figuring out approximately how much money you expect to have coming in during the next week or month. Estimating your expenses involves figuring out what you will be using your money to pay for during that same time period.

estimate an educated guess or ballpark figure, based on the information you have

cash flow statement a summary of receipts and payments for a given period of time; also called an *income and expense statement*

The best way to estimate income is to look back at your paycheck stubs from the past three or four months. Add them together and divide by the number of stubs. Now you have an average. You can reasonably assume that this is close to what you will earn on a regular basis over time.

Estimate your expenses the same way. Review your spending for the past three or four months. If you have kept a spending log and a spending chart, as advised in Chapter 3 and earlier in this chapter, look at those. Which expenses come up on a regular basis? Which are less regular? Determine how much money you spent on average each week during those months. This will give you a good idea of how much you typically spend in a week.

Now go back and look at your Share Save Spend percentages. For example, perhaps you estimate your income as $50 per week. Your estimated expenses range from $15 to $25 weekly, averaging about $20. You want to share 10 percent of your income, save half, and spend the rest. So you will allot $5 for sharing, put $25 in savings, and have $20 left over for spending. This is a budget that can work.

As you get through the first few months of using a budget, review your estimates to see if you still think they are accurate. As you become more conscious of your spending, you might also become more careful—and will not be spending as much on unnecessary things. If that happens, you might want to tweak your budget.

Figure 4.5 **SAMPLE CASH FLOW STATEMENT**

Category	Week 1 Cash Flow
Income	
Job 1	$200
Job 2	$50
Total Income	$250
Expenses	
Auto insurance	$20
New sweater	$54
Haircut	$35
Cell phone	$13
Concert tickets	$75
Pizza	$18
Savings	
Deposit	$20
Sharing	
T-shirt for Darfur fund-raiser	$15
Total Expenses	$250

Preparing a Cash Flow Statement

Use a cash flow statement to record your budget estimates. A **cash flow statement** is a summary of your receipts and payments for a given period of time. It is also called an *income and expense statement.* An example is shown in Figure 4.5.

When you fill out a cash flow statement, list your income first, and then list all your expenses. Include fixed expenses, variable expenses, savings, and sharing, as described on the following pages.

Figuring Your Income

Your estimated income will include the money you expect to get from wages, allowance, and interest on your investments and savings. Do *not* include any unexpected or uncertain sources of money—such as birthday gifts, end-of-year bonuses, or cash you might get from selling things on eBay. Estimating your income is relatively simple if you always work the same number of hours each week and work for only one employer. If you have more than one job, if your hours change each week, or if other factors make your income less predictable, it will not be quite so easy to estimate your income.

Sara is a teen whose income is steady and predictable. She works at a candy shop every Tuesday, Thursday, and Saturday, for a total of fifteen hours a week. Her weekly take-home pay is $87. She can easily estimate an income of $348 per month.

Ali, another teen, has two part-time jobs. He works some days after school at a convenience store near his home. He also helps out his uncle on weekends at a family-owned restaurant. His hours vary from week to week, so he has to figure out the average amount of money he makes per month. The worksheet that he uses is shown in Figure 4.6. If he records his weekly income in this worksheet for several months, he can verify that his average income per month is around $435.

Some people's income is even more complicated than Ali's. A person may have a seasonal job (a job for just part of each year), such as mowing lawns, coaching a sport, or shoveling snow. Many teens have one job during the summer and a different job during the school year. They should base their budget on their lowest monthly income.

Janie works at a summer camp during the months that she is not in school. During the school year she works at a pet store. Her income during the summer is a lot higher than her income during the school year—so she bases her budget on her school-year income.

Figure 4.6 ALI'S MONTHLY INCOME WORKSHEET

Job 1 Convenience Store	Hours	Take-Home Pay
Week 1	12	$55
Week 2	10	$45
Week 3	16	$72
Week 4	8	$36
Job 2 Restaurant		
Week 1	8	$43
Week 2	16	$86
Week 3	4	$22
Week 4	14	$76
Monthly Totals	88	$435

▼ Whether you are working regular hours or get income from creative projects, seasonal jobs, or other sources, it is important to keep track of the money you are bringing in.

The extra money she earns during the summer goes into a mutual fund for college.

Figuring Your Expenses

After you estimate your income (the money coming in), you need to look at your expenses (the money going out). Some expenses are basically the same every month, but other expenses vary.

Fixed Expenses

Expenses that stay the same from month to month are **fixed expenses**. A typical adult's fixed expenses may include rent or mortgage, car payment, health insurance and auto insurance premiums, and student loan payments. These expenses are payments that you have to pay no matter what—they cannot go unpaid, and in most cases they cannot be paid on credit. They are the first expenses to list in your budget. They are easy to plan for, because they are always there and they do not change much. Your fixed expenses right now may be limited.

fixed expenses expenses—such as rent or mortgage, health insurance premiums, and student loan payments—that stay the same from month to month and must be paid no matter what

variable expenses expenses—such as auto repairs, clothing, and medical costs—that vary from month to month

Some fixed expenses may vary somewhat from month to month. However, they do not fluctuate too much, and they are always due at the same time each month. These include bills for electricity, water, cable TV service, and heating fuel.

Fixed expenses that vary from month to month can be a challenge when you are preparing a budget. You can estimate how much to allow for them by averaging, as described earlier. If you know what the range can be for a particular expense, you will be better off budgeting an amount near the high end of that range to be sure you have enough to cover your expenses. For example, Tina's electric bill has ranged between $80 and $100 for the past year. She can add up the total paid for the year, and then divide it by 12 to get an average monthly amount that she can budget for. If Tina paid $1,080 total for the year, she would divide that amount by 12 to get an average of $90 per month. She would then set her budget accordingly—or even a bit higher, to make sure she has enough to cover the bill each month.

Another category that can be considered a fixed expense is food. Of course everyone needs to eat—but this part of your budget can vary greatly depending on your lifestyle, your ability to create a grocery list and go shopping every week, and your willpower to limit eating out. Americans eat more than 50 percent of their meals away from home.

The bottom line is that your fixed expenses should be just that—fixed. For your budget to be successful, you must get a handle on your fixed expenses and then monitor them from month to month.

▶ **Keep track of how many times you go to the gas station each month and multiply that number by how much it costs you to fill up your gas tank. Use the result as an estimate for your fuel expenses each month.**

Variable Expenses

Variable expenses are those that change from month to month. Computer service bills, auto repairs, clothing, and out-of pocket medical and dental costs are all variable expenses. They can be more difficult to calculate than fixed expenses because of their changing nature. Still, you need to estimate how much you think you will spend on variable expenses when you plan your budget. Use the averaging technique described earlier—but be aware that the actual amount you spend each month will vary.

Among your variable expenses are *unexpected* expenses that can catch you off guard. Perhaps an auto repair is more expensive than anything you imagined. An out-of-town funeral, plumbing disaster, or car accident could leave you in a bad financial situation.

Many people plan for unexpected expenses by including an **emergency fund** in their budget. Setting aside about 5 percent of your monthly income can help ensure that you are prepared for any unexpected expense. If your average monthly income is $500, setting aside $25 per month for emergencies can give you peace of mind. You will be able to tackle almost any unexpected expense that might arise.

You might want to set up a separate savings account for your emergency money to be sure it doesn't get lost in your other savings. Resist the temptation to spend your hard-earned emergency savings on some other purchase. It is important to keep your emergency funds for their true purpose—an emergency!

▲ Unforeseen expenses such as car repairs can put a dent in your budget. Set aside extra money each month to prepare for these unexpected events.

Sharing and Savings

In addition to your income, your expenses, and your emergency fund, your budget should include sharing and savings. Now is the time to take another look at your goals and values. What do you want your money to do for you? What causes are important to you? Do you have a time frame for reaching your goals?

Determine how much you want to set aside each month for sharing. Remember that you can increase your participation in important causes by giving your time and talent as well as money. Also decide how much you will set aside each month for future expenses. When you save regularly, you can watch your savings grow as you get closer and closer to your goals.

emergency fund money set aside for unexpected expenses

SECTION 2 ASSESSMENT

Factual Recall

1. Why is it best to keep a budget plan simple?
2. How can you estimate your monthly income for the near future?
3. What income should *not* be included in your budget?
4. How can you estimate your expenses for the near future?
5. How can you protect yourself against large, unexpected expenses?

Critical Thinking

1. Would it be accurate to say that fixed expenses pay for needs and variable expenses pay for wants? Why or why not?
2. What could be done to decrease fixed expenses?

SECTION 3

Using Your Budget

Focus Questions

1. What features does a good budget have?
2. What is likely to happen if you do not stay on track with your budget?
3. What should you do if your budget does not seem to work?

Key Terms
budget surplus
budget deficit

budget surplus a situation in which money is left over after all expenses have been paid

budget deficit a situation in which there is not enough money to cover expenses

Do people really use budgets? Try asking several people you know whether or not they live on a budget. Pay attention to how many you have to ask before someone says, "Yes, I budget." Their financial paperwork might fit all on one page, or it might be more complicated. In any case, it is important to know how much you have—and to live within your means.

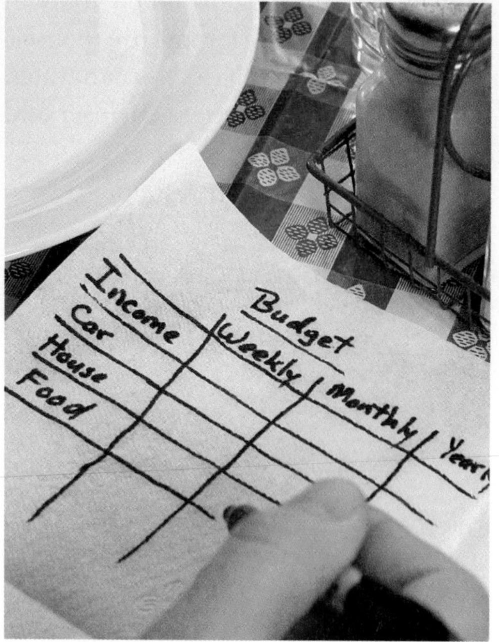

▶ Everyone has different income and expenses. Find a way to organize your budget to fit your lifestyle.

Setting Up a Budget: Two Examples

Now that you know what to include in your budget, you are ready to set it up. Here are two examples to show you how to do it. You can see that an unmarried young person's budget is typically much simpler than the budget of a married couple with children. The budgeting process gets even trickier if you are self-employed, if you have a lot of unusual expenses, or if you make large commitments to sharing or savings.

Shauna Jackson just graduated from high school and lives with her parents. She has two part-time jobs and works about 50 hours a week. She also house-sits for people when they go on vacation. Her budget is presented in Figure 4.7.

Yee and Sue Chen are a middle-aged couple with two school-aged children. They both work full-time, and on weekends they operate a small produce stand at the farmer's market. See Figure 4.8 for their budget.

Notice that both budgets reflect more incoming money than outgoing money. It is difficult to be precise to the penny when making a budget. The important thing is to make sure that the "income" number is always at least a little bigger than the "expenses/savings/sharing" number. When that is the case, the difference between the two numbers is the **budget surplus**—the money left over when everything is paid for. If the outgoing money number is bigger than the income number, you have a **budget deficit**—that is, you do not have enough money to cover your expenses.

Setting Up Your Own Budget

Now it is time for you to plan your own budget. Look back on your spending habits, and consider the goals you have set for your financial future. What are your spending priorities? How much do you plan to save? What are you saving for? With which causes do you want to share your money?

Recording the Actual Numbers

Use your cash flow statement to determine what your income is. Your sources may be wages from a job or from allowance. Or perhaps you earn money from babysitting, playing in a band, or tutoring. Figure out how much money you have coming in during an average month and then for the entire year. Do not include "windfall" money, such as money you might receive for your birthday. You cannot rely on such unexpected sources as part of your budget.

Next, refer to your cash flow statement to identify your expenses. List your fixed expenses—the ones that are the same every month no matter what, such as auto insurance or car payments. (You may not actually have any fixed expenses right now.)

Figure 4.7 SHAUNA'S BUDGET

		Monthly	Yearly
Income (after taxes)	Average pay from Job 1	$816	$9,792
	Average pay from Job 2	$884	$10,608
	Average pay from house sitting	$400	$4,800
Total Income		**$2,100**	**$25,200**
Fixed Expenses	Room/board paid to parents	$200	$2,400
	Auto insurance premium	$70	$840
	Cell phone	$50	$600
Variable Expenses	Clothing	$150	$1,800
	Personal care services/items	$100	$1,200
	Fuel/auto maintenance	$250	$3,000
	Entertainment/recreation	$200	$2,400
Savings	Emergency fund	$100	$1,200
	Medium-term for education/apartment	$400	$4,800
	Long-term for travel	$250	$3,000
	Short-term for car trade-up	$200	$2,400
Sharing	Animal rights organization	$50	$600
	Rain forest protection organization	$50	$600
Total Expenses/Savings/Sharing		**$2,070**	**$24,840**
Income Minus Expenses, or Surplus		**$30**	**$360**

Figure 4.8 THE CHENS' BUDGET

		Monthly	Yearly
Income (after taxes)	Yee's wages	$2,500	$30,000
	Sue's salary	$2,700	$32,400
	Income from produce stand	$750	$9,000
	Interest from investments	$60	$720
Total Income		**$6,010**	**$72,120**
Fixed Expenses	Mortgage	$1,600	$19,200
	Auto payment	$300	$3,600
	Utilities	$400	$4,800
	Health/life/auto insurance premiums	$200	$2,400
	Cell phone service	$60	$720
	Groceries	$500	$6,000
Variable Expenses	Clothing	$300	$3,600
	Personal care services/items	$200	$2,400
	Television/Internet/phone service	$90	$1,080
	Fuel/auto maintenance	$300	$3,600
	Entertainment/recreation	$250	$3,000
	Kids' lessons, sports, etc.	$500	$6,000
Savings	Emergency fund	$250	$3,000
	Medium-term for boat	$150	$1,800
	Long-term for kids' college	$200	$2,400
	Long-term for retirement	$200	$2,400
	Short-term for vacation	$150	$1,800
Sharing	Habitat for Humanity	$100	$1,200
	Local pet shelter	$100	$1,200
Total Expenses/Savings/Sharing		**$5,850**	**$70,200**
Income Minus Expenses, or Surplus		**$160**	**$1,920**

Do Your RESEARCH

A number of Web sites offer free tools and advice to help you with your budgeting. Most also have chat rooms where you can share ideas about money with other members of the online community. For example:

- Wesabe.com (http://fin.emcp.net/wesabe) provides easy-to-use, Web-based software to give you a better understanding of how you spend money. Members can chat, ask for or provide tips, and learn from articles and other resources. You can enter your financial information and organize it on the secure site. You can share your financial habits with other members, but your personal information is kept secret.
- Geezeo.com (http://fin.emcp.net/geezeo) has tools that let you enter all your banking information securely on its Web site and then check it whenever you want—either online or by phone. You can add a financial goal and track your progress toward reaching it. You can also discuss financial topics with other members.
- Zecco.com (http://fin.emcp.net/zecco) is an online service of the Zecco investment brokerage house. You can discuss investments with other members on the Web site.
- NetworthIQ.com (http://fin.emcp.net/networthiq) offers many features similar to those at Wesabe and Geezeo. In addition, you can set up a profile of people with whom you would like to discuss finances—by age, occupation, income, or location.
- Buxfer.com (http://fin.emcp.net/buxfer) is another site where you can track your account balances, spending, and other business. You can also keep track of to whom you owe money and people who owe you money. If you set up a group—say of family members or friends—you can monitor these debts together. This site also allows access using your cell phone.
- Billmonk.com (http://fin.emcp.net/billmonk) allows you to settle your debts instantly. You can keep your financial records here—and the site also helps you keep track of books, DVDs, or other items you have borrowed from the library or from friends. Popular with roommates and college students, it can also be used to split bills like rent, utilities, or meals.

If you decide to use one of these sites, remember that information you post is never 100 percent secure, and information you find is never 100 percent reliable. Be careful sharing your personal and financial information, and talk to a trusted adult about any information or advice you get.

Your Assignment

1. Visit one or two of these Web sites and try out the tools they offer. Do you think you would use these tools regularly? Why or why not?
2. Identity theft is always a concern, especially when you provide financial information online. Do these sites have security protection? How can you find out?

Now think about your variable expenses—clothing, personal care, entertainment, food, gasoline, bus fare, lessons, and so forth. Remember that some expenses can vary widely from week to week. For instance, you may go for weeks or even months without spending anything on car repairs, and then get hit with a $500 bill. Looking back over a year's time (or even two to three years' time) can help you come up with a good idea of how much you can expect to spend in a particular area. Then you can figure how much to put away each month toward your variable expenses. Figuring this amount into your budget will ensure that you have enough to cover automobile-related, entertainment, clothing, and other variable expenses that arise.

You will also need to decide how much to set aside for savings goals, including an emergency fund, and for sharing. How much money will you put away for each of your savings goals? For causes you have chosen to support? Use the same averaging techniques discussed earlier, and enter those amounts into your budget plan. Use Figure 4.9 to plan your budget.

Finally, look at the cash flow numbers. Is your incoming money greater than your outgoing money? Do you need to change any of the numbers? You might have to increase or decrease the amount you entered for a particular expense or savings or sharing goal. Keep working until the incoming and outgoing money figures are relatively close—with the income number greater than the expense number.

Figure 4.9 YOUR BUDGET

		Monthly	Yearly
Income (after taxes)			
Total Income			
Fixed Expenses			
Variable Expenses			
Savings			
Sharing			
Total Expenses/Savings/Sharing			
Income Minus Expenses, or Surplus			

Qualities of a Good Budget

Once you have roughed out your budget, you might be asking yourself: Is it workable? A good budget has the following qualities:

- *It is based on your values.* Use your money the same way you use your time and other assets. Make sure your use of money reflects who you are as a person.
- *It is geared toward your goals.* Make sure your budget fits with your current goals, as well as your short-, medium-, and long-term future. Set aside enough of your money toward future goals so that you can see progress toward those goals—but without making your present life financially difficult.
- *It is practical.* If you set aside too much of your money toward future goals, you will not have enough to live on right now. Also be sure that your goals are not too much of a stretch. Do not plan to save for items that are beyond your means financially. You will only be disappointed when you realize that a round-the-world vacation or a top-of-the-line car is an unrealistic goal for a teenager with a part-time job.
- *It is flexible.* You can modify your budget if it is not working or if your life circumstances change. A new job might prompt you to update your budget. A new goal or a new cause you want to support might mean you have to make some changes. Most likely, you will want to modify your

You Can Succeed Financially

Klaire and Trav Johnston, a young married couple in Australia, wanted to stick to their budget. They surfed the Net looking for an easy-to-use budgeting tool that they could access when they were away from home—actually "out there doing the spending," as Klaire put it.

Not finding what they were looking for, Klaire and Trav decided to develop the tool themselves. The result is their company, Mobibudget. Their software can be accessed on the Internet and is compatible with cell phones that have Internet access. It has a "what's left" feature that tells you exactly how much spending money you have available—making it easier to decide if you can afford to stop at a restaurant, or if buying a loaf of bread and some peanut butter would be a better option.

At first Mobibudget was available only in Australia, but the idea caught on quickly. People began to "Mobi" all over, and now the tool is available worldwide. In the United States, consumers can sign up for $5 per month or $50 per year—perhaps a small price to pay to avoid bank overdraft fees.

What Would You Do?

1. Klaire and Trav Johnston built a successful business by providing a service that helps people do something difficult—stick to their budget. Would you be willing to pay for a service like Mobibudget? Explain your answer.
2. Why would people *not* need a service like Mobibudget? What other tools can help people stay on budget?

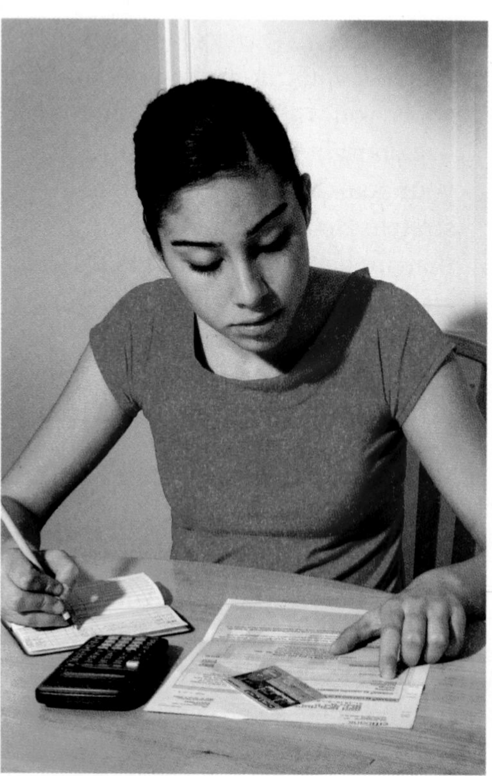

▶ Modify your budget when your lifestyle changes. You will probably need to rework your budget when you graduate from high school.

budget when you graduate from high school.

- *It is accessible and easy to use.* Keep your budget in a notebook or on your computer—where you can easily find it, check it, and modify it. Take a look at it every week, every two weeks, or every month and see whether your actual use of money is keeping in line with your budgeting plan.

Helpful Online Resources

When you plan your budget, you are not alone. Here are some Web sites that can help you calculate your personal budget goals:

- **CU Succeed** (http://fin.emcp.net/cusucceed) has a savings calculator, budget spreadsheets, and other tools you can use to plan a budget.

- **Money Instructor** (http://fin.emcp.net/moneyinstructor) has a number of budgeting worksheets you can use to plan a budget, determine fixed versus variable expenses, and lay out your savings goals.
- **Bank High School** (http://fin.emcp.net/bankhs) has a "managing your money" section with interactive features on budgeting, spending, withholding taxes, and more.

Trying Out Your Budget

After you have finalized a budget that you think will work for you, try it out for two weeks. See how well you stick to it. Monitor your progress by breaking it down into weekly numbers, and then spend some time at the end of each week to see if you are on track.

Keeping Track of Income and Expenses

Take a look at Shauna's budget broken down into weekly amounts, as shown in Figure 4.10. The numbers are rounded to whole dollar amounts. For payments that are made monthly, like room and board, Shauna has planned to set aside enough money each week so that she will have the full amount at the end of the month.

Shauna is monitoring her budget. After two weeks she records her spending to see if she is staying on course. The two-week results are shown in Figure 4.11.

The first week, Shauna managed to live within her budget and ended up with a $55 surplus. But the second week, she had a $65 deficit. This meant that after two weeks, she had a $10 deficit and would need to revise her budget. If she were to continue outspending her income, she could be in trouble.

Figure 4.10 SHAUNA'S WEEKLY BUDGET

		Weekly	Monthly
Income (after taxes)	Average pay from Job 1	$204	$816
	Average pay from Job 2	$221	$884
	Average pay from house sitting	$100	$400
Total Income		**$525**	**$2,100**
Fixed Expenses	Room/board paid to parents	$50	$200
	Auto insurance premium	$18	$70
	Cell phone	$13	$50
Variable Expenses	Clothing	$38	$150
	Personal care services/items	$25	$100
	Fuel/auto maintenance	$63	$250
	Entertainment/recreation	$50	$200
Savings	Emergency fund	$25	$100
	Medium-term for education/apartment	$100	$400
	Long-term for travel	$63	$250
	Short-term for car trade-up	$50	$200
Sharing	Animal rights organization	$13	$50
	Rain forest protection organization	$13	$50
Total Expenses/Savings/Sharing		**$521**	**$2,070**
Income Minus Expenses, or Surplus		**$4**	**$30**

Figure 4.11 SHAUNA'S TWO-WEEK BUDGET RESULTS

			Actual	
		Budgeted Weekly Average	**Week 1**	**Week 2**
Income (after taxes)	Average pay from Job 1	$204	$210	$190
	Average pay from Job 2	$221	$225	$200
	Average pay from house sitting	$100	$100	$50
Total Income		**$525**	**$535**	**$440**
Fixed Expenses	Room/board paid to parents	$50	$50	$50
	Auto insurance premium	$18	$18	$18
	Cell phone	$13	$13	$13
Variable Expenses	Clothing	$38	$25	$50
	Personal care services/items	$25	$25	$15
	Fuel/auto maintenance	$63	$50	$30
	Entertainment/recreation	$50	$35	$65
Savings	Emergency fund	$25	$25	$25
	Medium-term for education/apartment	$100	$100	$100
	Long-term for travel	$63	$63	$63
	Short-term for car trade-up	$50	$50	$50
Sharing	Animal rights organization	$13	$13	$13
	Rain forest protection organization	$13	$13	$13
Total Expenses/Savings/Sharing		**$521**	**$480**	**$505**
Income Minus Expenses, or Surplus		**$4**	**$55**	**–$65**

Figure 4.12 YOUR TWO-WEEK BUDGET RESULTS

Use this sample to create your own budget analysis worksheet. Add columns of weeks to keep a regular log. Eventually, you will see your spending and savings patterns, or habits, emerge. Discipline yourself to stay within your budget, and watch your surplus increase!

			Actual	
		Budgeted Weekly Average	Week 1	Week 2
Income (after taxes)				
Total Income				
Fixed Expenses				
Variable Expenses				
Savings				
Sharing				
Total Expenses/Savings/Sharing				
Income Minus Expenses, or Surplus				

Now monitor your own budget results. Use a chart like the one in Figure 4.12 to keep track of your weekly cash flow for two weeks. Do you end up with a surplus or a deficit at the end of each week?

Assessing and Revising the Plan

If a couple of weeks go by and you find you are having trouble ending with a small surplus each week, either you are spending more than you should or your budget plan is not going to work for you. If you fall behind on bills or if you are not able to set aside money for a savings goal or sharing cause, you may have to revise your budget.

Every so often, plan to review your budget to see if it needs revising. Do you have two or more deficit weeks in a row? If so, you may need to cut back on your spending. Is there one particular category where you are consistently spending more money than you had budgeted? Think about what is causing the problem. Maybe you could take the bus instead of driving, or take a lunch to school instead of buying in the cafeteria. Perhaps you can think of free or inexpensive activities to share with friends—biking, walking, going to a museum, attending free concerts.

Look at your fixed expenses. Are you making several small payments, perhaps for a car loan and a couple of credit card bills? Find out whether you can *consolidate*, or combine, those debts into one smaller payment. Your parents or bank might be able to help with this. (Loan consolidation is covered in more detail in Chapter 13.)

If you just cannot find a way to cut back your spending, consider modifying your budget in another way. Perhaps you should not plan to set aside as much money each week toward your big savings goal. Instead of saving $100 per month toward a new camera, for example, maybe you should try for only $50 or $75.

Changes in your savings goals or in your commitments to sharing are good reasons to revise your budget. You would also need to revise your budget if you got a new job or if there were major changes in your spending habits—such as becoming a car owner instead of a bus rider. Any major life changes should prompt you to take out your budget and rework it.

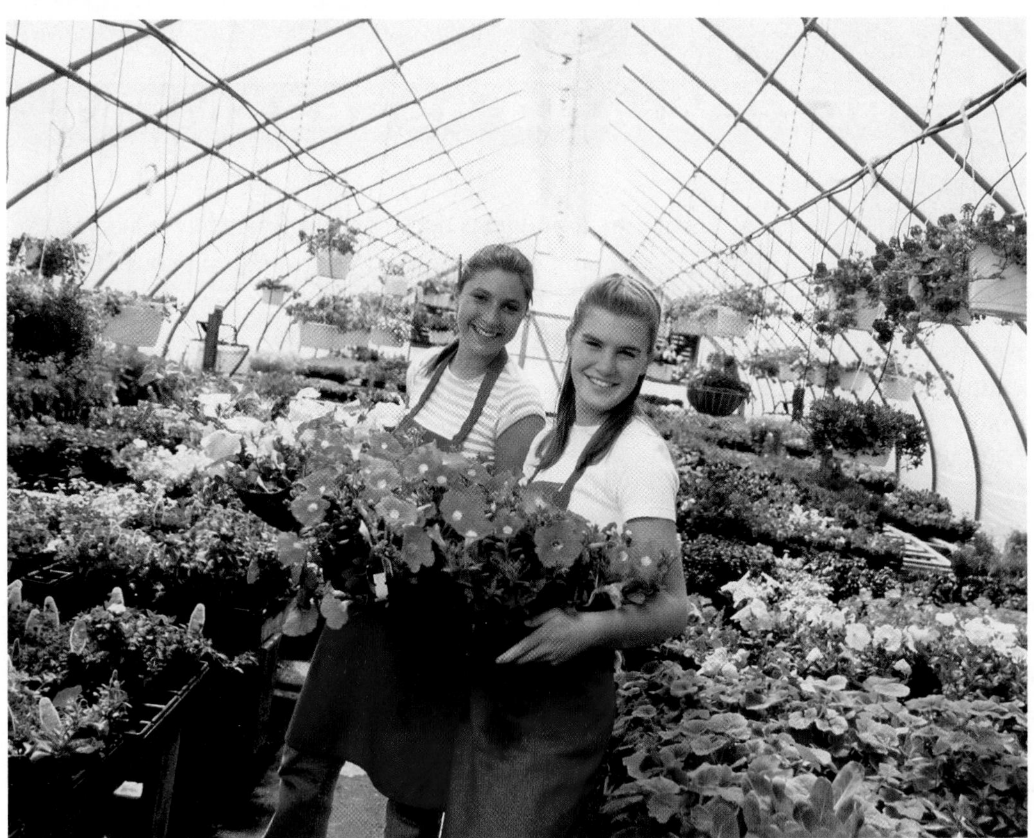

◀ **When you get a new job, you need to re-evaluate your budget. Suppose you get a summer job working in a greenhouse. How will that affect your budget?**

By creating and sticking to a budget, you make sure that you do not have to worry so much about money. But it is essential to review it periodically to see where you stand. To get started, plan a monthly budget. Monitor it for at least two weeks to see how it is working. Once you have a realistic budget, review it every couple of months to see if it is still working for you.

Remember—your budget is something you can take with you through life, modifying it along the way. It is not a set of unbending rules. It is a flexible plan that you develop for yourself—to help yourself share, save, and spend according to the goals and values you have identified. Working and living with a budget is not difficult, and it should not be a burden. For many people, it provides financial freedom. Just as you would not go to school without a pen, consider your budget a necessary tool for your financial well-being.

Answers to Fact or Fiction

1. False—You must consider all your goals because a good budget will include savings to reach your long-term goals; **2.** False—Your budget should include only expected sources of money like wages, allowance, and interest on investments; it should *not* include unexpected or uncertain sources of income like bonuses and gifts. **3.** True; **4.** True; **5.** True; **6.** False—If you have a monthly budget, you should review it every couple of months, or if you have a weekly budget, review it after a couple of weeks.

SECTION 3 ASSESSMENT

Factual Recall

1. Briefly describe how to set up a budget.
2. List five qualities of a good budget.
3. Should your budget be set up so that expenses each month are equal to income? Why or why not?

Critical Thinking

1. What might be some consequences of having a budget deficit?
2. If you have a budget surplus, what do you think is the best way to use it?
3. Why might a budget have to be revised from time to time?

CHAPTER 4 REVIEW AND ASSESSMENT

Chapter Summary

Section 1 Defining Your Goals

- A budget usually covers a given period of time and is based on how much income you can expect during that time.
- A budget should fit with your personal goals and values.
- The best way to start planning a budget is to look at your short-, medium-, and long-term financial goals. Making a goal chart can help you with this step.
- A good way to plan realistically is to look at your current money habits and consider how well they fit with your goals.
- Plan for your sharing, saving, and spending goals.

Section 2 Working Out Your Budget

- After you have defined your financial goals and values, you can begin making a budget.
- Estimate your income and expenses for the near future by computing your average earnings and spending over the past several months.
- Include only regular, predictable sources of income in your budget.
- Include both fixed and variable expenses in your budget.
- In addition to income and expenses, your budget should include money for sharing and saving.

Section 3 Using Your Budget

- Studying examples of other budgets can help you—but make sure the budget you create fits your own situation.
- A good budget is based on your values and geared toward your goals. It is practical, flexible, and easy to use.
- Monitor your budget by keeping track of your income and expenses.
- Review your budget regularly to see whether it needs to be revised.
- A budget is necessary for financial well-being and can serve you well throughout your life.

Reviewing Key Terms

For each of the following statements, choose the key term that best completes the sentence.

1. Saving to buy a house is an example of a ______.
   a. short-term goal
   b. long-term goal
   c. fixed expense
   d. variable expense
2. An auto insurance premium is an example of a ______.
   a. short-term goal
   b. long-term goal
   c. fixed expense
   d. variable expense
3. Planning to buy a birthday gift for a friend is an example of a ______.
   a. short-term goal
   b. long-term goal
   c. fixed expense
   d. variable expense
4. The cost of electricity for your home is an example of a ______.
   a. short-term goal
   b. long-term goal
   c. fixed expense
   d. variable expense
5. If you spend more than you earn, you will have a(n) ______.
   a. budget
   b. estimate
   c. budget surplus
   d. budget deficit
6. You can look at your past earnings to make a(n) ______ about future income.
   a. budget
   b. estimate
   c. budget surplus
   d. budget deficit
7. A(n) ______ can be used to pay for unexpected expenses.
   a. estimate
   b. emergency fund

c. variable expense
d. budget deficit

Understanding the Main Ideas

1. When planning for a goal that has a specific dollar amount, what two things do you need to consider?
2. If a financial goal is open-ended, how can you judge your progress toward that goal?
3. Name three examples of fixed expenses.
4. Name three examples of variable expenses.
5. Which expenses should be listed first in your budget? Why?
6. Why is it a good idea to put your emergency fund into a separate savings account?
7. What could you do if your expenses each month continue to be more than your income?

Practicing Math

1. Look at Mateo's worksheet on page 97. Suppose that his income increased to $650 per month. If he kept the same percentage goals, how much would he have each month for sharing, saving, and spending?
2. Look at Shauna's budget on page 109. Suppose Shauna wants to move into an apartment now instead of waiting. She will have a roommate, and Shauna's share of the rent, utilities, and groceries will come to $525. Create a new, balanced budget for Shauna that still includes savings. Explain your reasons for the changes you have made to the old budget.

Applying Critical Thinking Skills

1. Life is unpredictable. Things can happen that ruin your plans and make your goals impossible to achieve. Is it still worthwhile to make financial plans? Explain your answer.
2. Why is it important to develop healthy money habits now, rather than waiting until you are an adult?
3. What do you think are reasonable percentages for sharing, saving, and spending? Explain your answer.
4. "Stick to your budget" is good advice. So is "Be flexible and adjust your budget." How can they both be right?
5. Denise's expenses were more than her income. To solve the problem, she stopped putting money into her savings account. What are some possible consequences of this solution?

Working with Real-World Documents

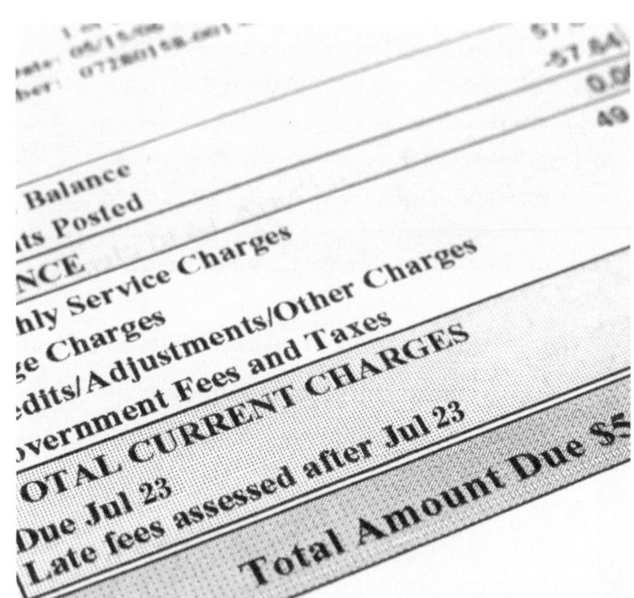

1. Your cell phone service is a fixed expense, but it can change somewhat from month to month. Examine your cell phone bills from the last two or three months. (If cell phone bills are not available, use utility bills or bills for landline phone service.) What items changed? Were any of these within your control?

Taking It Home

1. Do you wonder how other people think about goals for the future and budgeting for them? Ask! Start a conversation with a parent or grandparent about how he or she first started thinking about budgeting. What methods does he or she use today? Do you have an older sibling or cousin? Find out what he or she does (or does not do) to budget money. What seems to work for the people you talk to? What does not work?

CHAPTER 5

Checking Accounts

In today's world, everyone wants to turn their paychecks into usable money as quickly as possible. The fastest way is to cash a check at your bank for spending money. But cash is hard to use for some things, such as paying a bill or buying music online.

The most efficient way to pay some expenses is to use a check. Most banks also offer debit cards and electronic transfer services to their customers. You deposit your paycheck into your checking account. Then you transfer some of the money into your savings account, withdraw some cash, and leave the rest in your account to pay bills by either check, electronic transfer, or debit card. In this chapter, you will find out how to do all of these things.

SECTION 1	Basic Banking Concepts
SECTION 2	Checking Account Tools
SECTION 3	Using a Checking Account

Fact or Fiction

What do you think? Are the following statements true or false? If you think they are false, then say what is true.

1. A consumer always has to pay a fee to the bank to open and maintain a checking account.
2. Your money is insured whether you deposit it in a bank, an S&L, or a credit union.
3. You cannot open a checking account until you are 18 years old.
4. You should reconcile your checking account a least once a month.
5. You always have at least 24 hours to cover a check you have written by making a deposit of equal or greater value into your checking account.
6. Many banks charge a fee when their customers use ATMs that belong to other banks.

Answers on page 141.

Study Reminder

*Knowing how to study can increase your knowledge, improve your grades, and cut down on your study time. See the **Studying Personal Finance** pages at the front of the book for some tips to help you study this chapter.*

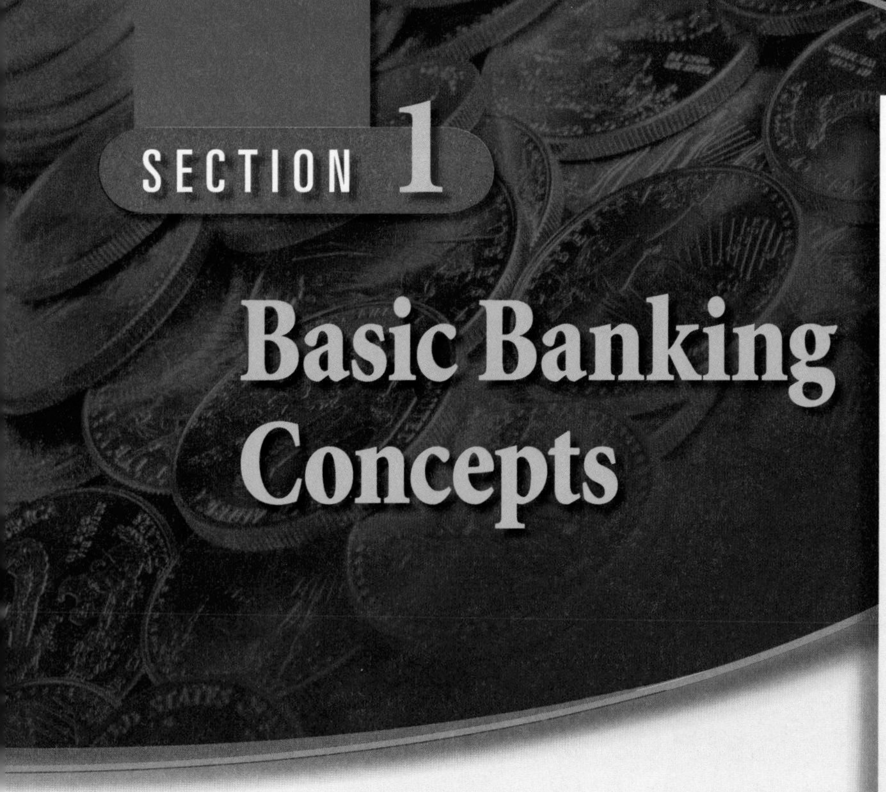

SECTION 1

Basic Banking Concepts

Focus Questions

1. How does a checking account work?
2. What is the difference between a bank and a credit union?
3. Why might a bank want its customers to use ACH transactions rather than checks?
4. What are some different types of checking accounts?
5. What factors should be considered when selecting a checking account?
6. What are some alternatives to writing traditional checks?

Key Terms

savings account
interest
checking account
check
debit card
commercial banks
savings and loan associations (S&Ls)
credit unions
payday lenders
financial transaction
deposit
withdrawal
debit
credit
transfer
loan
Automated Clearing House (ACH)

savings account a bank account in which money is deposited for safekeeping

interest the costs of using money—paid by banks to their depositors, and paid by borrowers to the institutions that provide their loans

checking account a bank account that allows the account holder to withdraw money, pay a bill, or make a purchase by writing checks

check a preprinted form ordering a bank to withdraw money from an account and pay it to someone else

debit card a plastic card used to withdraw cash from a checking account or make payments electronically without having to write a check

Banks and other financial institutions offer a variety of services. Your first experience with a bank was probably a small savings account that your parents helped you open when you were a child. A **savings account** allows you to deposit money at the bank for safekeeping. The bank uses your money to make loans to other people. It charges them a fee for the loan, and in turn pays you for the use of your money. These costs of using money are called **interest**.

You can withdraw money from a basic savings account, but it may not always be easy to get your money. There might be a limit on how many withdrawals you can make in a month, or you may have to pay a penalty when you withdraw it. If you are going to deposit and withdraw money from your account on a regular basis, a checking account might be a good idea.

You might have heard of checking accounts but are not sure how they work. With a **checking account**, you can withdraw money, pay a bill, or make a purchase easily, using checks.

A **check** is basically a written request to your bank to take money from your account and pay it to someone else—the *payee*, or person to whom you wrote the check. With most checking accounts you also get a **debit card**, which allows you to withdraw cash from your account or make payments electronically without having to write a check. In addition, you can have your paycheck electronically deposited into the account, and you can also make online payments from your account.

You Can Succeed Financially

One of 17-year-old Jason's early money memories is his first trip to a local bank in his hometown of Cleveland, Ohio, when he was just 8 years old. His parents took him to the bank just after the Christmas holiday so he could open his own savings account.

Jason was not sure about giving a stranger his entire life savings of $225—money he had earned doing odd jobs around the house, as well as birthday and holiday money he received from his grandparents. He wondered: "What are all these people in this big building going to do with *my* money?" Would the money still be there when he wanted to use it for something like buying a bicycle or going to camp?

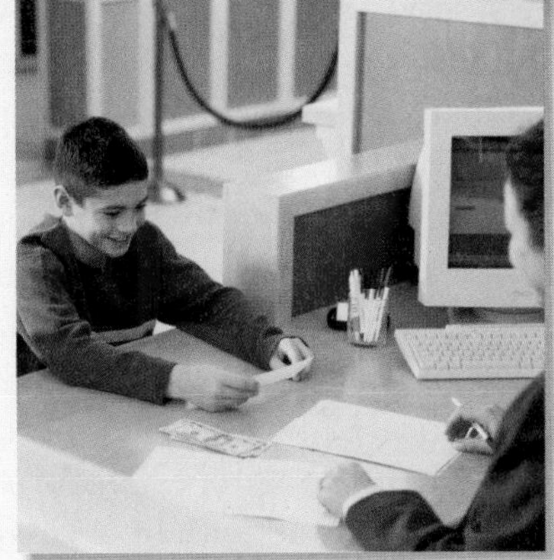

How It Works

Jason's parents, along with a very helpful banker, reassured him. Yes, not only was his money safe, but it would *grow.* The bank would lend his money to other people who needed it for things like buying a car or a house, or starting a new business. When the people paid back their loans, they would also pay interest—and so Jason's money would be *earning* money.

Jason still was not totally convinced that his money would be there when he needed it, but he trusted his parents. With their help he opened a savings account.

As the months passed, he deposited his gift money and the money he earned from odd jobs. In turn, the bank paid interest on his money. The interest earnings were added to his savings account balance. By age 10, his savings had grown to more than $500— a combination of money he deposited and interest he earned from the bank.

Advanced Banking

As time went on, Jason learned more about the bank's services. When he got his first part-time job at age 16, he opened a checking account. He even learned to successfully use and manage his debit card for some purchases. These practical lessons will serve Jason well as he graduates from college and gets a full-time job.

Learning to take advantage of the services at a local bank is an important foundation for developing healthy money habits. And to think—for Jason, it all started with a little savings account when he was just 8 years old.

What Would You Do?

1. How old were you when you opened your first bank account? What have you learned about banking since then?
2. How does having a checking account and a savings account help you achieve your financial goals?
3. What would you still like to know about the way banks operate? What would help you become a better banking consumer?

Types of Financial Institutions

Several types of financial institutions offer checking accounts. Financial institutions do not differ from one another very much, as far as consumers are concerned—but it is worth understanding the differences. That way, you will be better equipped to decide which type of institution you want to do your banking.

commercial banks the most common type of financial institution—privately owned, offering a wide range of services, and run to make a profit

savings and loan associations (S&Ls) financial institutions that originally provided home loans but now offer most of the same services as a bank

credit unions nonprofit financial institutions that are owned by their members and organized for the members' benefit

Banks, S&Ls, and Credit Unions

Commercial banks are the most common type of financial institution. They accept deposits, make loans, and offer a wide range of services to their customers. Many of them are nationally known, such as Citibank, Bank of America, U.S. Bank, and Wells Fargo. They have locations—or *branches*—all over the country. Others are smaller, often independently owned community banks that have only one or a few branches around town. Commercial banks are privately owned and run to make a profit.

The successful economic activity of the country relies heavily upon the large commercial banks. As a result, these institutions are closely regulated by a number of government agencies, including the Federal Reserve System, the Federal Deposit Insurance Corporation (FDIC), and state and federal banking agencies. Your money is extremely safe in a commercial bank—insured up to $100,000 per account.

Savings and loan associations (S&Ls) comprise another type of financial institution. Savings and loans were originally set up to accept savings and provide home loans to consumers. Today, S&Ls typically offer the same services that banks do. The government regulates them and insures the money deposited in them, just as it does for banks.

Credit unions are nonprofit financial institutions, owned and operated by the people who use them. If you have an account at a credit union, you are a "member" of the credit union—actually a part owner. Credit unions do not seek profits as banks do. Instead, they distribute any profits they earn to their members, either as higher dividends or in the form of lower interest rates on loans. Credit unions restrict membership—you must be eligible to join one. The members usually share something in common, such as where they work or where they went to college. Like banks and S&Ls, credit unions are regulated by the government, and their customers' money is insured up to $100,000.

If you do a lot of traveling or are planning to go away to college, it might be a good idea to open a checking account at a bank that has a lot of branch locations around the country. Then, if you need to make a withdrawal or deposit, or talk to a

▼ **You have many options when it comes to financial institutions. Do your research and find out what works best for you.**

Do Your RESEARCH

Most banks have company Web sites where they provide detailed information about the accounts they offer. You can research checking accounts and compare them without even leaving home. Look on the Web sites of the banks listed here. See what you can learn about their checking accounts. Then print out the information you find and compare the results.

- Wells Fargo (http://fin.emcp.net/wellsfargo)
- Bank of America (http://fin.emcp.net/bankofamerica)
- Citibank (http://fin.emcp.net/citibank)
- U.S. Bank (http://fin.emcp.net/usbank)
- Wachovia (http://fin.emcp.net/wachovia)

Remember also to look into a credit union for your banking needs. Many offer competitive rates and a variety of account services. Find out if you are eligible to become a member of a credit union. Visit the Web site of the Credit Union National Association (http://fin.emcp.net/creditunions) for more information and to find a credit union in your community.

Your Assignment

1. Do any of the banks offer attractive checking account features that others do not? Do any have negative aspects you would want to avoid?
2. Did you find that the banks and credit unions in your community had checking account services that were more or less similar, or that varied significantly? How would this influence your decision if you were going to open a new account?

banker, you have a better chance of finding a branch nearby, wherever you are. If you want to support a local community bank, you can choose a smaller institution close to home. If you have access to a credit union, you will likely want to take advantage of the lower costs and other benefits that credit unions offer.

Payday Lenders and Check Cashing Companies

According to the Center for Responsible Lending (http://fin.emcp.net/responsible), payday lenders and check cashing companies are some of the most expensive financial institutions in the country. Check cashing companies charge a fee to cash checks, primarily for people who do not have a bank account. Keep in mind, however, that if the person has proper identification the bank that issued the check would cash it for free.

Payday lenders make short-term, usually small loans to tide a person over "until payday." They target low-income working people including welfare-to-work women, members of the military, and others who have little or no savings, who live paycheck to paycheck. Most borrowers who get payday loans are not able to repay the entire loan within the standard two-week time frame. They end up having to renew the loan, paying multiple renewal fees. They become trapped in a never-ending cycle of debt—even paying much more in fees than the amount they originally borrowed.

payday lenders companies that make small short-term, high-interest loans to tide a person over "until payday"

What Is a Payday Loan? A payday loan is a small cash advance, usually $500 or less. The borrower gives the payday lender a *postdated* personal check (a check written with a date in the future, in this case usually two weeks in the future) or an authorization to withdraw funds from the borrower's bank account. In return, the borrower receives cash, minus the lender's fees. As an example, with a $300 payday loan, the borrower would give the payday lender a check for $300. About $45 might go to the lender in fees, and the borrower would get $255 in cash.

After about two weeks (usually the borrower's next payday), the borrower must either repay the loan or renew it if he or she cannot repay it. This renewal is called *rolling over* the loan. Another form of renewing the loan is a *back-to-back transaction*—writing a check for a new loan, and then using the new funds to repay the previous loan.

What Are the Costs of a Payday Loan? For a two-week payday advance, a borrower will pay at least $15 for every $100 borrowed. But do not be deceived—this is *not* an annual interest rate of 15 percent. These two-week loan fees translate to about *400 percent* a year! As Figure 5.1 shows, those who renew their loans often end up paying more in fees than they borrowed in the first place.

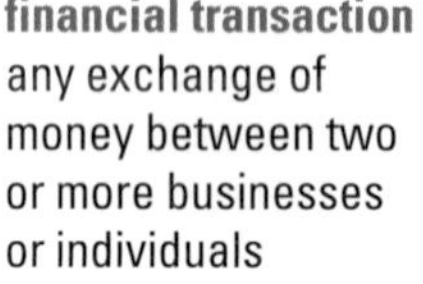

financial transaction any exchange of money between two or more businesses or individuals

Some borrowers will have five, ten, or sometimes even twenty repeat loans a year. For them, payday lending does not relieve their debt—and in fact creates more. The Center for Responsible Lending estimates that payday loans cost 5 million Americans as much as *$3.4 billion* annually.

A payday loan might be convenient at the moment, but you are better off steering clear of this financial option. Likewise, think about the costs before you use a check cashing store. You can avoid the high fees of payday lenders and check cashing companies by opening and using a basic checking or savings account at a bank, an S&L, or a credit union.

Types of Banking Transactions

A **financial transaction** is any exchange of money between two or more businesses or individuals. Deposits, withdrawals, debits, credits, purchases, transfers, loans, electronic transfers, payments, and written checks

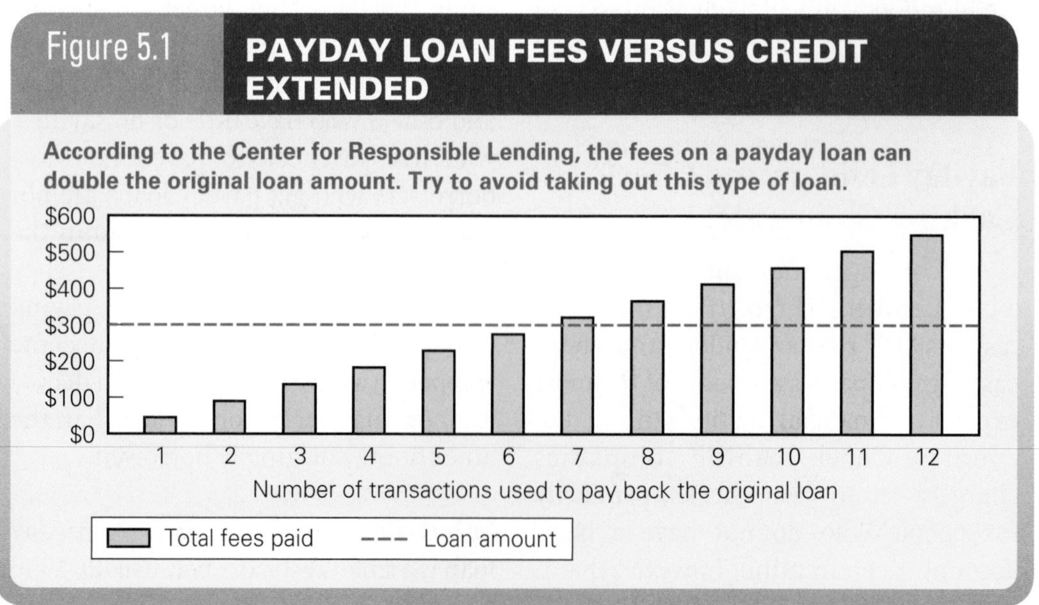

are all different types of transactions—but the meanings sometimes overlap. Here are brief descriptions of some common financial transactions:

- A **deposit** is any addition of funds to your account balance. Any time you put a paycheck, cash, or other money into your checking account you are making a deposit.
- A **withdrawal** is the opposite of a deposit. Any time you take cash out of your bank account—either in person at the bank itself or with a debit card at an ATM—you are making a withdrawal.
- A **debit** is any transaction that removes funds from your account. Besides withdrawals, debits also include checks written on the account and fees the bank charges to your account—such as monthly maintenance fees or check overdraft fees.
- A **credit** is any positive addition to your account. Credits include deposits, but other transactions too. If you return an item that you paid for with a debit card, for example, the store will credit your account for the amount of that purchase.
- A purchase is any payment made in exchange for a good or service.
- A **transfer** is a movement of funds from one account to another. You might deposit your paycheck into your checking account and then transfer a portion of it into your savings account.
- A **loan** is a temporary transfer of money from one person or institution to another. The loan must be repaid over time, with additional money paid as interest. *Interest* in this case is the money the bank charges the borrower in exchange for providing the loan.

Most of your financial transactions can be processed through the **Automated Clearing House (ACH)** network. The Automated Clearing House is an electronic system for transferring money between banks. In other words, an ACH transaction is an *electronic funds transfer* (EFT). ACH payments include the following:

- Payroll direct deposits
- Social Security and other government deposits
- Consumer payments such as mortgage payments, loan payments, and insurance premiums
- Business-to-business payments
- E-checks
- E-commerce payments
- Federal, state, and local tax payments

ACH transactions have increased in recent years as more and more people take advantage of direct deposit for their paychecks and other income. In addition, more than 50 percent of all consumer transactions are now done with "plastic"—credit and debit cards.

The paper check is becoming a less common form of payment—although a checking account is still called a "checking" account. The difference between the checking account of decades ago and today is simply that money is now commonly transferred electronically by computer. These electronic monetary transfers are much more efficient and

According to the National Postsecondary Student Aid Study, more than 65 percent of four-year undergrads borrow money for their college education. Costs for college tuition, books, and room and board add up, and many students turn to the bank for help. Student loans can get complicated, so do a little research before you take one out. As with any other loan, you will have to pay interest on the money you borrow. Shop around and find out which banks have the lowest interest rates.

deposit an addition of funds to an account balance

withdrawal the removal of cash from an account, either at the bank or at an ATM

debit any transaction that removes funds from an account, including cash withdrawals, checks written on the account, and fees charged by the bank

credit any positive addition to an account balance

transfer a movement of funds from one account to another

loan a temporary transfer of funds from one person or company to another, to be repaid over time with additional money paid as interest

Automated Clearing House (ACH) an electronic system for transferring money between banks

occur much faster than the old clearing process for a paper check. Instead of a week or ten days, for instance, ACH transactions can clear in 72 hours or less—and often almost immediately.

Types of Checking Accounts

If you go to a bank and request information about checking accounts, you will likely get some pamphlets or materials that describe several options. For basic or low-activity checking accounts, banks will likely charge you a small monthly fee and may limit the number of checks you can write each month without paying an additional fee. They may also require a minimum balance and may charge other fees for different types of transactions.

Many banks advertise free checking accounts, and who *wouldn't* want a free account? According to the law, a "free" checking account cannot require a minimum balance and cannot charge a maintenance fee or any activity fees.

On the other hand, free checking accounts usually do not pay interest. Some banks charge higher penalties on a free checking account. They might also have a maximum number of checks or ATM transactions per month. They may charge fees for certain services, such as use of a debit card or printing your checks. They can charge penalties if you have insufficient funds to cover a transaction and overdraw your account. Make sure you read the fine print before deciding that a bank's "free" checking account is the right one for you.

YOU DECIDE

Kent wants to open a checking account in one of the banks in the small town where he lives. His choices include the local branches of two big national banks and a smaller locally owned bank. He goes to each bank for information on their checking accounts. He finds that they have similar types of accounts, but some offer "teasers" or incentives to get him to sign up.

More specifically, for a limited time one large institution is offering a free iPod to anyone who opens an account and deposits $1,000 for at least six months. Kent has always wanted an iPod. But though it sounds tempting, Kent decides to do his homework on each bank's services before he jumps at the iPod offer.

What Kent discovers is that the local, independently owned bank offers a unique benefit to its checking account customers. The checking account has a free link to the account holder's savings account. Kent will be able to make free money transfers between his checking and savings accounts—so he can deposit his paycheck into the checking account and then easily move a portion of it into the linked savings account.

Kent also learns that the bank offering the iPod does not offer free money transfers and has fees for other services as well. Because he has several important savings goals, Kent wonders if the locally owned bank might be a better choice than the one offering the iPod.

Should he...

1. ...open an account at the locally owned bank, or at the bigger national bank? Explain your answer.
2. ...consider the cost of the iPod before making his decision? How might this make a difference?

◀ Joint checking accounts allow two or more people to share responsibility for managing their money. These accounts are often used by married couples. Opening a joint checking account with a parent or guardian is a great way to start learning about money management.

Interest-earning checking accounts require substantial minimum balances—usually $1,000 or more—but they pay interest on that money. Unfortunately, these accounts generally pay much lower interest rates than do other savings plans, so you are probably better off putting your extra money in a savings account (see Chapter 6).

Joint checking accounts are shared between two people. Both their names are listed on the account, and either person can write a check on the account. Correspondence from the bank is sent with both names on it.

Some banks prefer that young people open a joint checking account with a parent or guardian to make sure an adult is supervising the money coming in and going out. If you open a joint account with a parent or guardian, you will be able to make your own deposits and withdrawals and write your own checks—but your parent or guardian will assume responsibility in case of a mistake or problem. Opening a joint account now can help you learn money management skills and will make it easier to assume the responsibility of a regular checking account later on.

A person who is self-employed or who runs a small business may wish to open a business checking account in addition to a personal checking account. That way, he or she can keep business income and expenses separate from personal finances. Each week or two—whatever time frame the entrepreneur prefers—he or she can transfer funds from the business account to a personal account, to use for food, clothing, entertainment, and other personal expenses. The remaining money in the business account would pay for business expenses.

SECTION 1 ASSESSMENT

Factual Recall

1. What is the difference between a checking account and a savings account?
2. When dealing with a check, who is the payee?
3. What is the difference between a debit and a withdrawal?
4. What is the difference between a debit and a credit?
5. What is a transfer?

Critical Thinking

1. Check cashing companies charge high fees. Banks charge less, or nothing, to cash checks for their account holders. How can you be sure to avoid check cashing companies?

SECTION 2

Checking Account Tools

Focus Questions

1. How long does it take for a check to be processed and the amount to be deducted from your account balance?
2. What is the difference between a debit card and a credit card?
3. What are some of the fees that banks charge their checking account customers?

Key Terms

automated teller machine (ATM)
stop-payment order

Checks and Debit Cards

Your checking account provides you with different tools for making payments and obtaining cash. The two major tools are writing checks and using an ATM or a debit card.

Checks

Most banks offer checks that you order ahead of time and then use as needed. With some accounts, you must pay for the checks to be printed with your name, address, and phone number. The checks also include your account number and the individual check numbers. Banks generally charge a small fee for the checks, but at some banks the fee can be quite large. Ask the bank about this fee before you open a checking account.

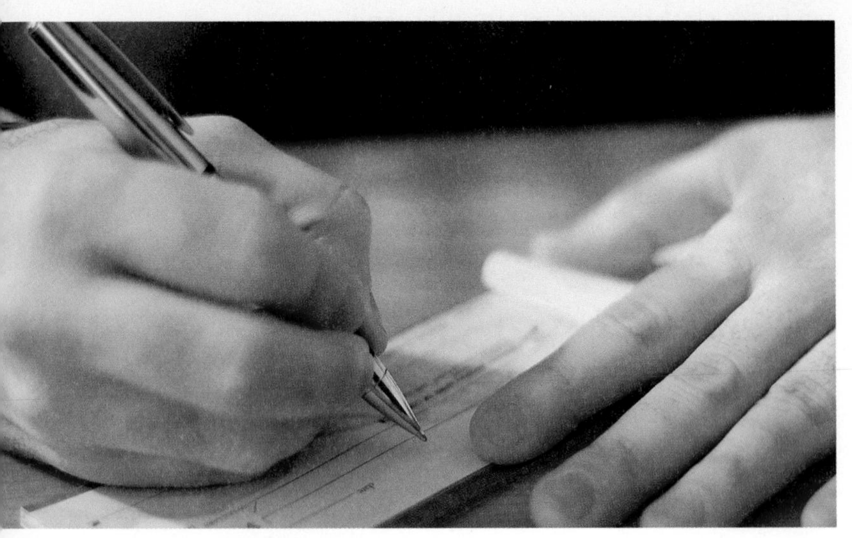

▼ You can order personalized checks through your bank. Your name, address, and phone number can be printed on the check, along with any other information you think is necessary.

A number of check-printing companies offer consumers a wide variety of check styles, often at prices similar to or lower than those the bank charges. These companies allow you to choose the design for your checks—personalizing them with your own photos, for instance, or decorating them with specialized lettering. Some, called *duplicate checks*, have convenient carbonless copy sheets under each one, giving you a ready-made copy of each check you write and making it easy for you to maintain a constant record of your spending.

Debit Cards

You can use a debit card just as you do a credit card—to make purchases or to withdraw cash from an **automated**

teller machine (ATM). Remember, however, that debit cards take the cash directly and *immediately* out of your checking account. When you use a credit card, the money does not come out of your account. Even when you write a check for cash, the money may or may not come out of your account immediately. But you can be sure that the money comes out immediately when you use your debit card.

Some banks limit the amount of money you can spend or withdraw with a debit card to $200 or $300 per day. Banks may also charge fees for using a debit card. There might be an annual fee, or perhaps a small fee of a dollar or two for each transaction. Those dollars can add up, though, so watch your money!

Using a debit card is fast and convenient, but remember to keep track of what you spend with it. Poor record keeping is the leading reason for overdrafts, but you can avoid them if you subtract the amount from your balance right away. It is easy to forget a purchase or withdrawal, so always get a printed receipt from the ATM or the merchant. (Recall the example of Darren in Chapter 3, the young man who had to pay overdraft penalties when he spent more money than he had in his account.)

ATMs have become a part of today's culture, appearing in many practical locations. But most banks will charge you a fee if you use an ATM that is not sponsored by your bank. The fee may range from $1 to as much as $5, depending on the bank. In addition, some ATMs themselves charge an additional fee just for using their "convenient" service. So think before you pop your debit card into an ATM—you may be spending up to $10 extra just to withdraw your money.

▲ You may be charged a fee if you use an ATM that is not sponsored by your bank. Be aware of such charges because they can add up.

How Checks and Debits Are Processed

Before 2004, every check that every consumer wrote had to go through the bank of the person or company it was written to, then on to a regional bank, and over to the consumer's bank to be processed—where the money would actually be taken out of the consumer's account. Since 2004, new regulations have made it easier for companies to process checks electronically. The company receiving the check can make an electronic image of the check and process it almost immediately.

People writing checks before this change typically felt safe "floating" a check. *Floating a check* means that Jane would write a check at the grocery store, even though she did not have enough money in her account. Her thinking

automated teller machine (ATM) a computerized electronic machine that performs basic banking functions

would be that she gets paid tomorrow, so she would be able to put money in her account then, to cover the check she wrote at the grocery store before it clears. But now the grocery store can process Jane's check immediately. She is no longer safe in assuming she has that 24-hour grace period. Jane should hold off on that grocery store visit until payday, after she has made her deposit.

Banks also process debits and cash withdrawals immediately. If you use a debit card at an ATM or at a retail store, the transaction may not be approved if you do not have enough money in your account to cover it at that moment.

What Are All Those Fees?

Banks can and often do charge fees on everything from using their online bill-paying service to having a negative balance—even for a matter of minutes. Some of these fees are small; others are quite high.

Types of Checking Account Fees

Some of the common fees that banks charge their checking account customers include monthly maintenance fees, ATM fees, fees for online bill-paying service, overdraft penalties, and stop-payment fees. The amounts vary from bank to bank and might also depend on the type of account you have.

Monthly Fees Some banks charge a monthly fee for maintaining the checking account, especially if the account balance is less than a certain amount. For instance, if the minimum balance is $50 at your bank, and your balance goes below that amount for even a few hours, the bank will charge you a fee.

ATM Fees According to Bankrate.com (http://fin.emcp.net/bankrate), banks charged nearly *$4.4 billion* in ATM fees in 2007. As pointed out earlier, many banks charge a fee for using ATMs that belong to other banks. If you are at the mall with your Wells Fargo debit card, but the ATM there sports a U.S. Bank logo, you will probably pay a fee to use that ATM. In fact, many times you will be charged *two* ATM fees—one by the company that owns the ATM, and another by your bank. Learn what those fees are likely to be, so that you can subtract them from your balance.

Online Bill-Pay Fees Many people like to pay their bills online instead of sending checks through the mail. After you log in to your bank account, you can set up the bill-pay service. It lets you make electronic payments from your checking account directly to your car loan company, insurance company, online music service, cell phone company, and others. Most banks charge a flat monthly fee for this service, regardless of the number of online bills you pay. Some banks offer the service at no charge. There will be more about online bill paying later in this chapter.

Overdraft and NSF Fees If you spend more money than you have in your account, your balance may fall below $0. If this happens, the offending check or transaction will result in overdraft or *non-sufficient funds* (NSF) fees. This oversight can be very costly. Many banks charge between $30 and $40 *per check* or transaction. Your bank will return the check—unpaid—to the person or company to whom you originally wrote it. Then you still have to pay the money you owe. And to make it worse—if you wrote the bad check to a place of business, you will probably also have to pay an additional fee for a "returned check."

Gia is a high school senior who wants to open a new checking account. She goes to three financial institutions and collects information on the features and fees of the checking account each one recommends for a new customer like her. Then Gia makes a chart to compare her options. You can review her chart here:

Features	Option 1	Option 2	Option 3
Description	Free account at large, national bank	Start-up account at local community bank	Free account at student credit union
Monthly fees	None	$2	None
Free checks	No	Yes	No
ATM/debit card	Yes	Yes	Yes
ATM/debit card fees	$2 per non-bank ATM transaction	25¢ per debit card transaction	None
Online banking	Yes	Yes	No
Interest paid	1% annual	No	No
Minimum balance	$100 to open	$50 to open	$0
	$100 to avoid fees	$200 to avoid monthly fee	$0
NSF fee	$34	$15	$30
Bill pay (online)	$10/month	$6/month	No
Requirements	Minors under 18 must have joint account with guardian	None	Student ID required

Should she...

1. ...open an account at the bank that provides free checks, even though it charges a monthly fee? What other information would she need to know before she did that?
2. ...open an account at the bank that will pay interest on her checking account, even though it will charge her for checks? What other information would she need to know before she did that?
3. ...consider how much she would use her debit card, as opposed to writing checks? Should she determine which institution has the most favorable policy regarding ATM and debit card usage?

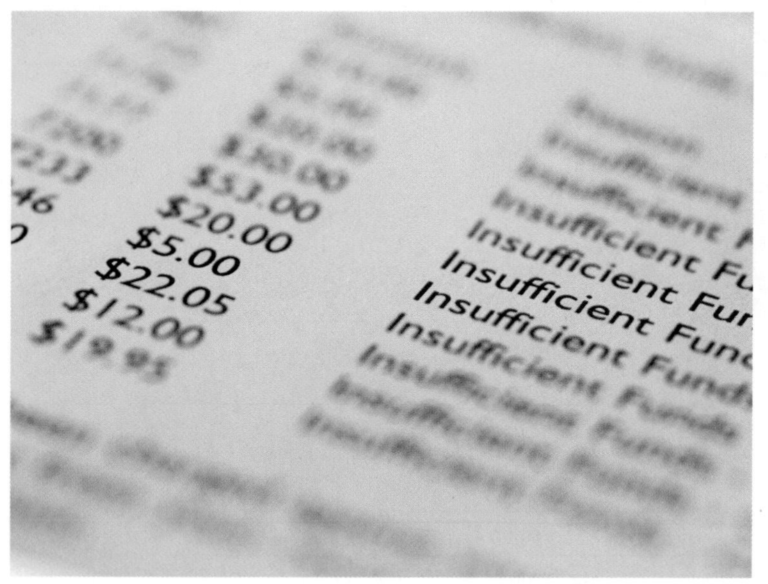

▲ Banks charge high fees if you go below $0 in your checking account. Those fees are deducted from your account, and they can lead to more overdrafts and more fees. Keep an eye on your balance!

Stop-Payment Fees If you write a check or schedule an automatic payment and then change your mind, you can ask your bank to put a stop-payment order on it. A **stop-payment order** is a request that a bank or another financial institution not cash a particular check. The bank will do its best not to clear the check or payment, but it will charge you to do so. The typical fee for stopping payment is $25, so you do not want to make this request often or without good cause.

stop-payment order a request that a bank or another financial institution not cash a particular check

You might request a stop-payment order for a variety of reasons—for example, if the goods or services you paid for are not acceptable, if the amount of the check was greater than what you owed, if you made the payment by mistake, or if your check was lost in the mail.

Avoiding Unnecessary Fees

Paying attention to all the fees that could be charged to your account can save you lots of money and headaches. If you do not have a bank account and are afraid to open one because of all the fees, don't worry—because you can ask for help. When you are comparing the accounts at different institutions, be sure to ask the banker to thoroughly explain all the fees. If you do not understand how everything works, ask the banker to start over and explain it again. The people who do best at managing their money ask lots of questions—especially when using a new financial tool.

Finally, keep in mind that at some point in your life you will probably have an unexpected or unwanted fee associated with your bank account—just like everyone else. Try not to get too stressed out if this happens. Managing your money is not about always being perfect. But it *is* about learning from your mistakes. If an overdraft or an unwanted ATM fee hits your account, do not ignore it. Find out what happened and make sure the fee is justified. If it is, adjust your spending so that you can avoid a similar unwanted fee in the future.

SECTION 2 ASSESSMENT

Factual Recall

1. How can you get checks for your checking account?
2. What is the advantage in having checks that include carbonless copy sheets?
3. What is the difference between a debit card and a credit card?
4. What does it mean to "float" a check? Why is this practice risky?
5. Name five examples of checking account fees.
6. What does *NSF* stand for?

Critical Thinking

1. Which do you think is better for making a purchase: a debit card or a credit card? Why?
2. You might be charged a fee for using an ATM. Do you think this is fair? Why or why not?

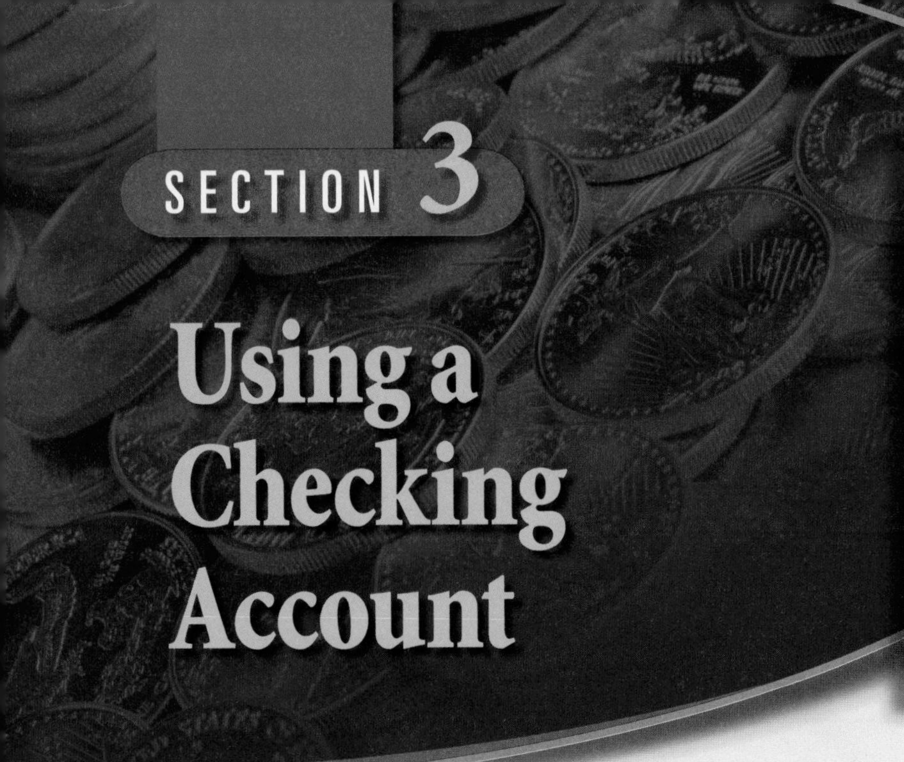

SECTION 3

Using a Checking Account

Focus Questions

1. What does it take to open a checking account?
2. How can a computer make using a checking account easier?
3. How can you know how much is in your account at any time?
4. Why is it important to reconcile your bank balance every month?

Key Terms

signature authorization form
deposit slip
reconciling
account statement

Opening an Account

When you open a checking account, you will be asked to fill out an application, like the one shown in Figure 5.2. You will also be asked to provide your Social Security number and sign an official **signature authorization form**. This document leaves your signature on file with the bank to prevent fraud. Checking account fraud occurs when a thief writes checks using your name to take money from your account. Finally, you will be asked to make an initial deposit.

Some banks require that teens open a special "student" checking account. There might be no monthly maintenance fee, but there will be certain restrictions, such as a limit on the amount of money you can withdraw in a single day—kind of like a checking account with training wheels. Other banks require teens to open a joint checking account with a parent or guardian to ensure that an adult is supervising the transactions.

Another important aspect to opening an account is getting to know your banker. Remember, bankers are there to support you. You are their customer, and they should be eager and willing to help you understand how their various accounts work.

Banks and credit unions will likely be a part of your financial life for years to come. Learn the ropes about checking accounts and other financial instruments, so you will be well prepared to utilize all the services they offer.

signature authorization form a document that leaves the account holder's signature on file with the bank to prevent fraud

◀ **Opening a checking account is easy. Some banks offer student checking accounts that are specially designed to fit a student's lifestyle. What are the benefits of a student checking account?**

Figure 5.2 CHECKING ACCOUNT APPLICATION

Checking Account Application

Type of account: _______ sole ownership _______ joint ownership

Opening deposit: $ ________________________________

Primary account holder

Full name: ________________________________

Address: ________________________________

City/State/ZIP: ________________________________

Length of time at above address: ________________________

Home phone: ________________________________

Workplace name: ________________________________

Work address: ________________________________

Work phone: ________________________________

Cell phone: ________________________________

E-mail: ________________________________

Requesting debit card: _______ yes _______ no

Link savings account to checking account: _______ yes _______ no

Applying for overdraft protection: _______ yes _______ no

Checking Account Activity

As you use your checking account, you write checks and make deposits. You also have to balance your checkbook—which means being sure the amount in your checkbook agrees with the amount the bank says you have.

Writing a Check

You may be thinking, "Who uses checks anymore? Doesn't everyone use a debit card or check card?" Although the use of these cards is certainly increasing each year, probably the best way to learn money management skills is to physically *write checks* for a period of time, recording each check in the check register provided by your financial institution. You will be able to "see" the money coming in and going out—and this in turn will help you understand how your account works.

Most people who get lazy about monitoring their account activity end up with overdrafts and unwanted fees. Whenever you open and use a checking account, it is best to establish a healthy pattern for keeping your checkbook up-to-date. Paying attention to the details can save you a lot of time, money, and aggravation.

When you pay for something with a check, you will fill out the blank spaces on the front of the check (see Figure 5.3). First you fill in the date and the *payee* (the person or business that will receive the money). Then you fill in the dollar amount, both in numeric form and spelled out. For example, if the amount is $145.83, you write that number in the box. Then you write out "One hundred

Figure 5.3 **THE PARTS OF A CHECK**

Learning the various parts of a check and how to fill out a check properly is one way to improve your financial savvy.

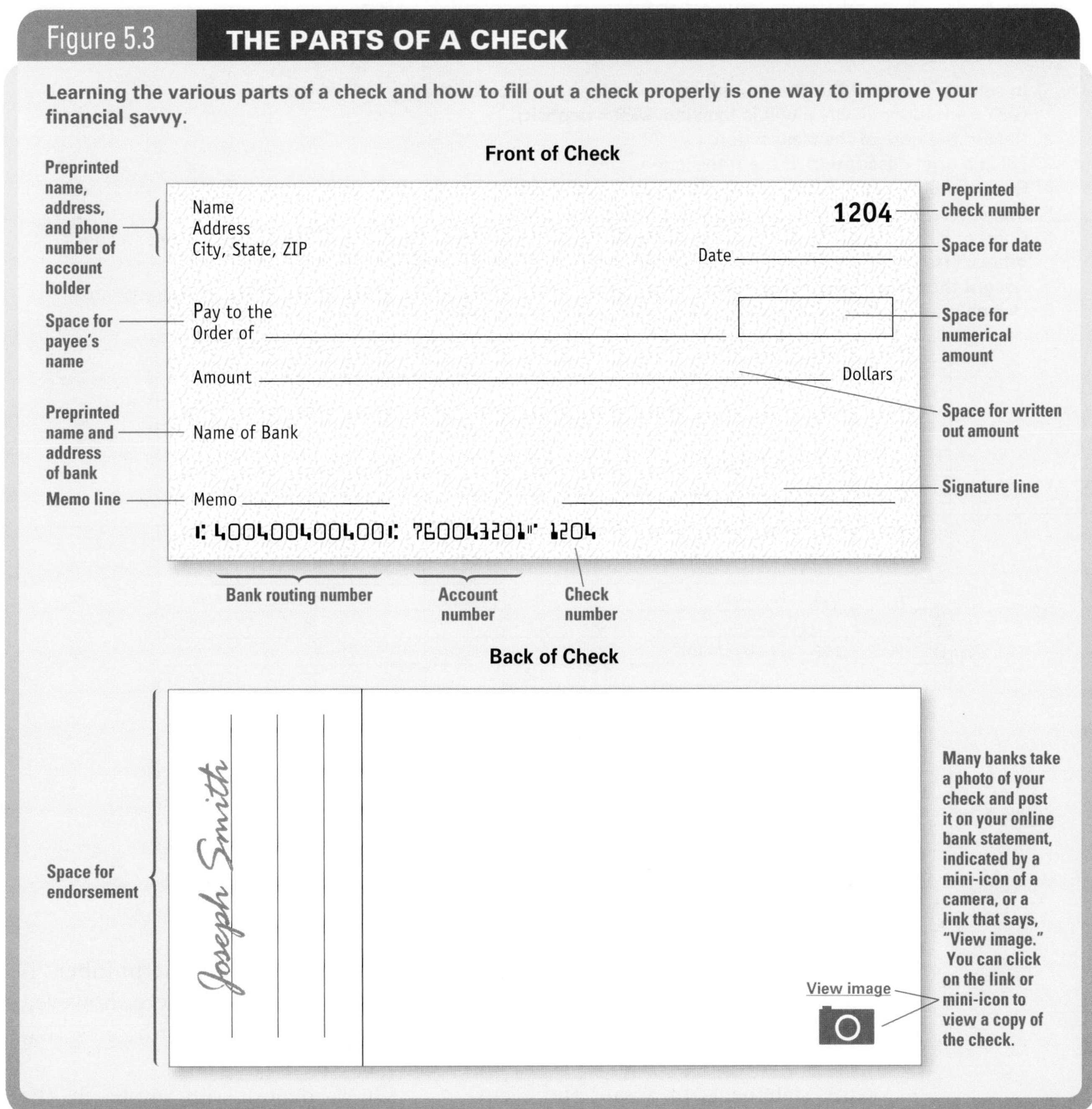

forty-five and 83/100" on the line underneath. Your signature goes at the bottom right. To the left of your signature is a memo line where you can add a note about the payment, such as "guitar lesson" or "lunch program."

After writing the check and using it for payment, make sure you have a record of it. Write it down in your checkbook register if you don't have check copies (see Figure 5.4 on the next page).

When you write a check, always use permanent ink (never pencil). Write legibly so no one will misunderstand the amount or the payee. If you make a small mistake, correct it and write your initials next to the correction. If you make a larger mistake, write "VOID" across the front of the check or tear it up. Make a note of the voided check in your register, as shown for check 1067 in Figure 5.4, and write a corrected check.

Figure 5.4 CHECKBOOK REGISTER

1. In column 1, record the check number or a code that indicates the type of transaction (WD = withdrawal, ON = online banking, DEP = deposit).
2. Record the date of the transaction.
3. Fill in a brief description of the transaction.
4. Record the amount of the payment or debit transaction.
5. Make note of any fee charged as a result of the transaction.
6. Column 6 is provided to help you reconcile your check register with your bank statement. You can check off each transaction as you go through your monthly bank statement.
7. Record the amount of any deposit or credit.
8. Use column 8 to keep a running total of your account balance.

1	2	3	4	5	6	7	8
Check # or trans. type	Date	Description	Payment/ debit (–)	Fee (–)	✔	Deposit/ credit (+)	Balance $292.70
1065	2/15	Target	54.68				–54.68
		sports bag, toiletries					238.02
WD	2/16	ATM withdrawal	20.00	1.00			–21.00
							217.02
ON	2/16	Int'l Insurance Co.	62.00				–62.00
		auto insurance					155.02
DEP	2/19	Paycheck				288.52	+288.52
							443.54
1066	2/23	Soccer Unlimited	125.00				–125.00
		league fee					318.54
1067		VOID	– –				– –
							318.54
FEE	3/1	Monthly fee		6.00			–6.00
							312.54
ON	3/3	iTunes	20.00				–20.00
		online music					292.54

Another important money management practice is to keep track of every check (used and unused) associated with your account. Keep all your checks and bank statements in a safe and secure place. Never throw away unused checks without first shredding them. Otherwise they could be used by another individual. Even if you close an account, you should still shred all the unused checks before you throw them away.

deposit slip a document that accompanies bank deposits, showing the account holder's name and account number and the amount to be deposited

Making a Deposit

To make a deposit, you will need a **deposit slip** (see Figure 5.5). Deposit slips are typically found at the back of each book of checks, printed with your name and account number. If you do not have any there, however, the bank will have blank ones that you can fill out.

On a deposit slip, write in the amount of each check you are depositing and the amount of any cash you are depositing. If you want some cash back, write in that amount as well and subtract it from the total. At the bottom of the slip, write in the total deposit amount.

Each check you are depositing will need to be *endorsed.* To endorse a check, turn it clockwise so that what was the left-hand edge is now on top, and then flip the check over to the back side and sign along the top (refer again to Figure 5.3). Most

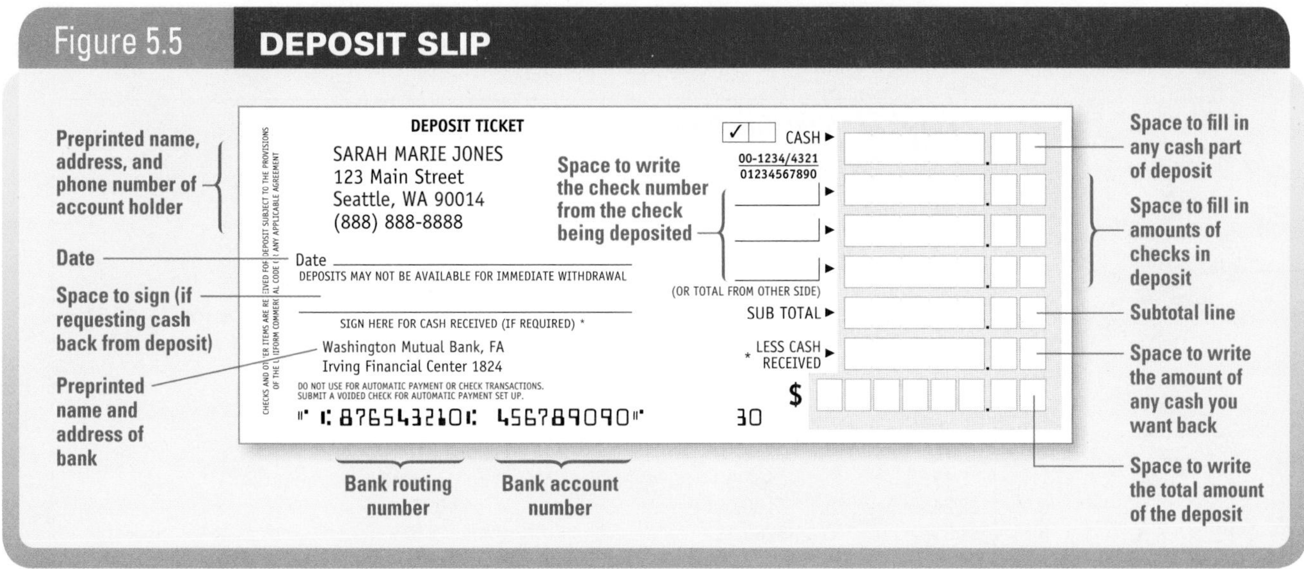

Figure 5.5 DEPOSIT SLIP

checks indicate where you are to sign with a line and text that says something like "Sign above this line." After you deposit your money, you will get a receipt for the transaction. Keep this receipt. Also write the amount in your checkbook register.

Your deposit should be added to your account on the next business day. If you have online access, check your account. If you notice a difference between what you deposited and what you see online, notify your financial institution immediately. The earlier you report a discrepancy, the easier it will be to fix it.

Reconciling Your Account

Reconciling your account means matching up your records with the bank's records. You compare the entries in your checkbook with the bank's records to be sure that neither of you has made mistakes. This is a good way to check your math and monitor your income and spending.

You can use online banking to reconcile your account. (There will be more about online banking later in this section.) If you do not have online banking, you can reconcile your account using your monthly **account statement**. This is a list of transactions that the bank has recorded for the month—all your deposits, checks, debit withdrawals, fees, and other transactions. Figure 5.6, on the next page, shows a sample bank statement.

When you reconcile your account, you go through the bank's list of transactions and compare it with the entries in your checkbook register. The checks will not necessarily appear in the same order. This is where you use column 6 in Figure 5.4—check off each transaction in your checkbook that is listed on the bank statement to be sure everything is accounted for.

You might have some stragglers—called *outstanding checks*—that do not appear on the bank's statement but that you have listed in your own records. Keep track of these checks to make sure they clear the following month. You might also have some recent deposits that do not show up on the bank's statement. These are called *outstanding deposits*.

On the back of the account statement you will find step-by-step instructions

reconciling matching one's personal account records with the bank's records

account statement the official monthly list of transactions that the bank has recorded

Figure 5.6 **BEN'S BANK STATEMENT**

MCB Mid City Bank
Southfield, NM 87075

Ben Voldt
6881 3rd Street SW
Southfield, NM 87075

Statement for July 1–July 31

Opening balance: $642.31
Ending balance: $444.21

Deposits/credits

Date	Amount	Description
7/15	$292.46	Branch #154
7/17	$32.50	Purchase return—Nordstrom
7/24	$100.00	ATM #620
7/31	$280.22	Branch #101

Checks

Check #	Date cleared	Amount
2099	7/2	$41.00
2102*	7/7	$159.33
2103	7/10	$200.00
2104	7/19	$92.71
	7/31	$138.54

*Check missing or check numbers out of sequence

Debits/withdrawals

Date	Amount	Description
7/3	$50.00	Withdrawal ATM #31
7/16	$201.50	Electronic payment
7/20	$15.20	Electronic payment
7/31	$5.00	Monthly service fee

for reconciling your account. Figure 5.7 illustrates the process, and here are the basic steps:

1. First, in your checkbook register, check off all the transactions listed on the bank's statement.
2. Now locate the *ending balance* shown on the statement.
3. Add any *outstanding deposits* to this ending balance.
4. Subtract any *outstanding checks* or other outstanding withdrawals or fees from this new balance.
5. The amount should match the current balance in your checkbook.

If your final amount and the bank's amount do not agree, first check your math. Be sure you did not transpose any numbers by mistake. Then be sure you counted all the outstanding checks and outstanding deposits. If the numbers are still off, make sure you deducted any fees or charges. You might have to go back and check off each item on your list and your bank's list again, one by one. If you still cannot reconcile your statement, you can make an appointment at your bank for help.

Checking Account Problems

If you keep your checkbook up-to-date and reconcile your account on a monthly basis, you should not have any problems. But what if something does go wrong?

Figure 5.7 RECONCILING A CHECKING ACCOUNT

Each month you will have two sources of information on the same checking account—your check register and the statement that the bank sends you. You can reconcile your checking account to see if you are missing any information and to see if the bank has any incorrect information. Here's how:

1. **Use your register to mark off each check, withdrawal (WD), deposit (DEP), online payment (ON), or credit (CR) that appears on your statement. All these items should match from one document to the next. If the bank statement indicates that new interest has been paid or fees have been assessed, enter those in your register and check them off.**

   In his check register, Ben Voldt checks off all the transactions that are listed on his bank statement (shown in Figure 5.6). He sees that the bank statement lists a new service fee for July, so he adds a line for that and checks it off too.

Check # or trans. type	Date	Description	Payment/ debit (–)	Fee (–)	✔	Deposit/ credit (+)	Balance $642.31
2099	7/1	A & M	41.00		✔		–41.00
		groceries					601.31
WD	7/3	ATM withdrawal	50.00		✔		–50.00
		county fair					551.31
2100		VOID	– –				– –
							551.31
2101	7/4	Mom	25.00				–25.00
		money for picnic					526.31
2102	7/5	Kars R Us	159.33		✔		–159.33
		auto loan					366.98
2103	7/8	Uncle Jake	200.00		✔		–200.00
		rent					166.98
DEP	7/15	Paycheck			✔	292.46	+292.46
							459.44
ON	7/16	Best Buy	201.50		✔		– 201.50
		card payment					257.94
CR	7/16	Nordstrom			✔	32.50	+32.50
		purchase return					290.44
2104	7/19	Al's Stereos	92.71		✔		–92.71
		stereo speakers					197.73
ON	7/20	Rockout	15.20		✔		–15.20
		online music service					182.53
DEP	7/24	ATM deposit			✔	100.00	+100.00
							282.53
DEP	7/31	Paycheck			✔	280.22	+280.22
							562.75
2105	7/31	Kmart	138.54		✔		–138.54
		stuff					424.21
FEE	7/31	Monthly service fee	5.00		✔		–5.00
							419.21

2. **If the ending balance in your checkbook register does not match the ending balance on your bank statement, you will need to find out whether any deposits and withdrawals are outstanding. Use a chart like this one to list any outstanding items.**

   The ending balance in Ben's register ($419.21) does not match the ending balance in his statement ($444.21). Ben looks through the check marks column in his register and finds that a $25 check to his mom has not cleared the bank. He records that check in his "Items outstanding" list. When he subtracts $25 from the $444.21 ending balance listed on the bank statement, he gets $419.21—which matches the amount he shows as an ending balance in his register. He has now balanced his account for the month.

Items outstanding	
#2101	$25.00

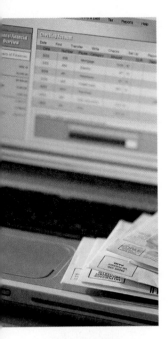

▲ Online banking is a convenient tool. Whether you bank online or not, remember to double-check the bank's records by balancing your accounts.

A computer glitch might create an error on your statement. Sometimes a deposit or credit does not go through. Other times there is simply what is known as a "bank error." If you catch a mistake, contact the bank right away. You will probably have little trouble sorting out the issue.

Online Banking

Most banks provide online banking. This service allows you to see your account balance, make transfers or payments, check your account history, and even pay your bills. Some banks charge a fee for online banking, but others provide it for free. Either way, it can be a handy (and sometimes indispensable) tool for keeping track of your account.

To use your bank's online features, you will need to register and select a password and a *PIN (personal identification number)*. You will use these to access your account information. Choose a password and PIN that are easy for you to remember but that others will not be able to guess easily. Record them in a safe place—not in your wallet or address book.

Every bank's online banking Web pages look slightly different. One bank's account information page is shown in Figure 5.8.

Online Money Transfers

One of the great benefits of online banking is the ability to move money instantly between accounts at the same bank. If your car loan came from your bank, for instance, instead of writing a check you can simply transfer funds from your checking account to make your monthly car payment. You can do the same thing to pay your credit card bill if your credit card was issued by your bank. And of course, you can transfer money

Figure 5.8 HOME PAGE OF A BANK'S WEB SITE

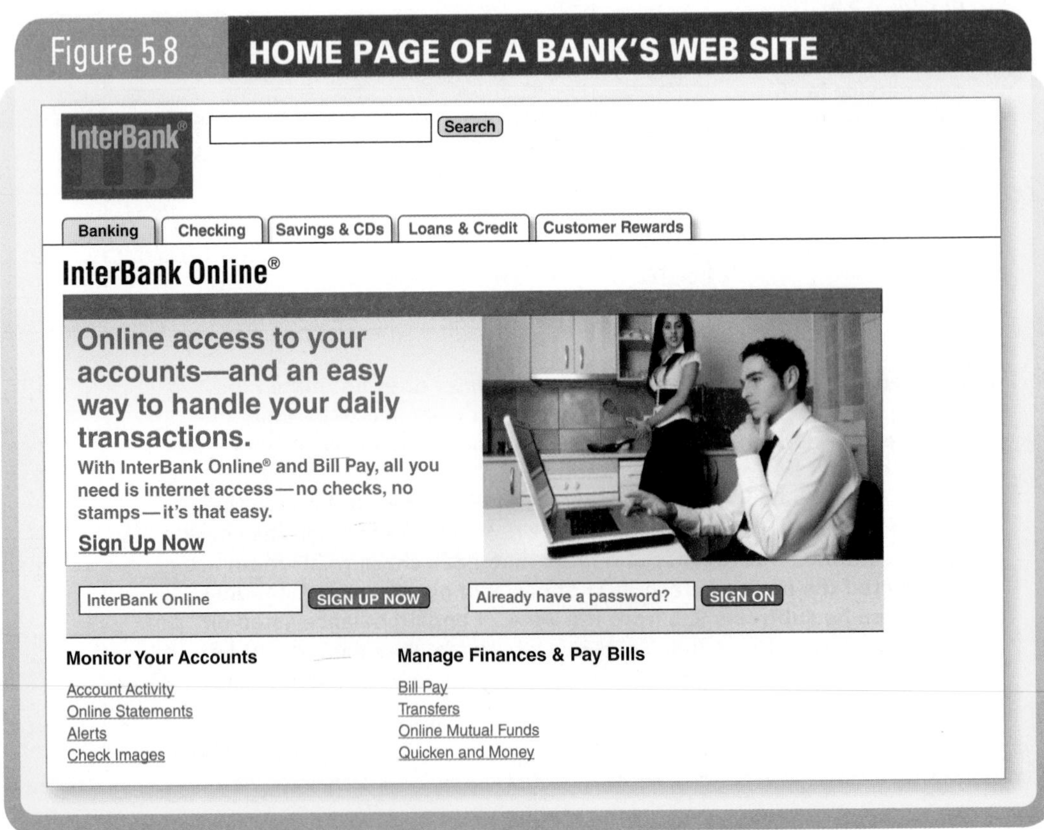

from your checking account into your savings account, and vice versa—instantly, without leaving home.

Paying Bills Online

Later in life you may decide to utilize your bank's online bill-pay feature (see Figure 5.9). Most accounts with online access allow you to pay certain bills—electric, phone, credit card, mortgage, and even doctor and dentist bills—online. After you enter the proper data about the payee, you simply type in the amount you want transferred to that account and click "Pay Bill"—and the bill is paid. (Remember to subtract this amount in your checkbook register!) Some banks charge a fee for online bill paying. Some will waive the fee if your balance stays above a certain amount. Others offer the service at no charge.

Many people who use online bill paying take advantage of the *auto bill-pay* feature. After you tell the bank which bills you want to include, the bank will automatically deduct money from your account to pay those bills when they come due.

Even if you have to pay a monthly fee for this service, it might be worth it because it ensures that your bills are paid on time. For some people, this is both a time-saver and a comfort factor. They do not have to worry whether their bills will get paid on the right date or for the right amount. It happens automatically each month.

Of course, if there is not enough money in your account to cover the automatic payment, you will get an overdraft. Even if you are not writing the checks yourself, be aware of when your bills are due and always be sure you have enough money in your account—and remember to subtract the amount from your balance when each bill is paid.

Answers to Fact or Fiction

1. False—Many banks will open a checking account with no minimum balance required; **2.** True; **3.** False—Most banks have special "student" checking accounts, or they will open a joint checking account for a young person and a parent or guardian; **4.** True; **5.** False—New banking regulations have made it easier for companies to process checks electronically and sometimes almost immediately, so consumers no longer have a 24-hour grace period; **6.** True.

Figure 5.9 A BANK'S ONLINE BILL-PAY FEATURE

Protecting Your Account Information

If your bank provides online access, be sure to guard your username and password information very carefully. Avoid checking your banking information on a public computer—like those at an Internet café or the library. There have been instances when a person's financial information was compromised because he or she did not properly log off the computer—and the information landed in the wrong hands. If you do not have access to a personal computer, most financial institutions allow you to check your account balance information by phone.

If for some reason you discover that your account information has been stolen, contact your financial institution immediately. They will tell you what steps to take to ensure the least possible damage. It is also helpful to have quick access to all your account information in the event something goes wrong. Store this information someplace that is secure but easily accessible.

LOOK Before You Leap

Have you ever received an e-mail like this one, with the name of your own bank in the first sentence?

> Here at XYZ Bank we like to keep all our records up-to-date to ensure that we can provide you with the best and most timely service in the industry. According to our records, we noticed a discrepancy in your Social Security number and date of birth. At your earliest convenience, please click on this link and update your records with the correct information. Thank you for attending to these important details and for helping us help you with all your banking needs.

Did you identify this scenario as a big-time scam? Unfortunately this practice—known as *phishing*—happens millions of times a day around the world. Its sole purpose is to steal a person's identity to open up fraudulent accounts. Of course it is illegal—but very difficult to stop because many of the "phishing" expeditions originate overseas. Authorities like the FBI or local police cannot do much about it. However, you should still file an Identity Theft Report, which will start legal action on your case.

Legitimate financial institutions do not request such information via e-mail. Be *very* suspicious when you are asked to share personal data like a Social Security number, date of birth, passwords, or account numbers. Never click on any links in the e-mail, and contact your bank to inform them about the suspicious e-mail. Unraveling the damage can be a hassle and take weeks if not months to sort out. For more information on identity theft and phishing, visit the Web site of the Federal Trade Commission at http://fin.emcp.net/ftc.

Before Responding

1. Why would it be a good idea to call the bank and ask if they sent you such an e-mail message? Even if you do not respond to the phishing request, report it to your bank so its fraud department can investigate.
2. Would you respond to a similar request if it came by telephone? Why or why not?

Get Good Advice

The use of checking accounts has changed dramatically over the past half-century. What used to be the norm—paying all of your bills with a paper check—has been replaced with paying most of your bills online. The very notion of *cashing a check* has come to mean getting cash from an ATM. To check their bank balance, people used to wait until the middle of the month to get a paper copy of the previous month's statement. Now you can get immediate access to your account information online, with a login ID and a secure password.

Are all these changes positive? Do you know anyone who started banking more than twenty or thirty years ago? Ask those people about their early banking experiences. Use the following questions as a guide:

1. What year did you open your first checking account?
2. Were you ever nervous about making a mistake in managing your first account?
3. How did you use your checking account to help manage your money?
4. How did you keep track of deposits and withdrawals?
5. Did someone (like a parent or a banker) teach you how to use the account, or did you learn on your own?
6. Some people like writing checks because it gives them a better sense for managing the money in their account. Do you agree? Why or why not?
7. What feature do you like best about your checking account today?
8. What feature about your past banking experiences do you miss the most?

Bring your answers back to the class and share what you learned. As a class, note the similarities and differences in the answers. Discuss these differences and how they will influence the decisions you make.

Sometimes the best lessons about what to do and what not to do come from people with a lot of life experience. Use their knowledge to your advantage. They may end up saving you hundreds or even thousands of dollars during your lifetime. You can learn from their mistakes—and in turn you will make better decisions about managing your money.

SECTION 3 ASSESSMENT

Factual Recall

1. What do you need to do in order to open a checking account?
2. Why is it still useful to write checks, even though debit and check cards are available?
3. What does it mean to endorse a check?
4. What is an outstanding check?
5. What is an outstanding deposit?
6. List the five steps for reconciling a checking account.

Critical Thinking

1. Why do you need to write the amount of a check in both numbers and words?
2. Why should you keep your checkbook updated and reconcile your account monthly?

CHAPTER 5 REVIEW AND ASSESSMENT

Chapter Summary

Section 1 Basic Banking Concepts

- Banks, savings and loan associations, and credit unions offer checking accounts.
- People who do not have bank accounts often turn to check cashing companies and payday lenders for financial services. These businesses charge high fees and high interest rates.
- A financial transaction is any exchange of money between two or more businesses or individuals.
- The Automated Clearing House (ACH) is an electronic system for transferring money between banks.
- Today, checking account transactions are often processed electronically, even if a paper check was written.
- Various kinds of checking accounts are available. Compare features and fees at several institutions before opening an account.

Section 2 Checking Account Tools

- When you use an ATM machine, you might be charged a fee if the ATM is not sponsored by your bank.
- Since 2004, new regulations have made it easier to process checks electronically, reducing the time it takes a check to clear.
- Banks charge a variety of checking account fees. The amounts vary from bank to bank and might also depend on the type of account.

Section 3 Using a Checking Account

- Banks have different checking account requirements for teens than for adults.
- Keep a record of every check you write and every deposit you make.
- Regularly reconcile you account—compare your records to the bank's records to make sure they agree. If there is a problem, contact your bank as soon as possible.
- Online banking allows you to use a computer to check your account balance and conduct transactions. If you use online banking, be sure to protect your account information.

Reviewing Key Terms

Match the following terms with their definitions.

a. account statement
b. loan
c. transfer
d. reconciling
e. credit
f. debit
g. withdrawal
h. deposit
i. payday lenders
j. credit unions
k. check
l. interest
m. commercial banks
n. debit card

1. The cost of using money.
2. A preprinted form ordering a bank to withdraw money from an account and pay it to someone else.
3. What you use to withdraw cash from a checking account or make payments electronically without having to write a check.
4. The most common type of financial institution, offering a wide range of services and operating for profit.
5. Nonprofit financial institutions, owned by their members.
6. Companies that make short-term, high-interest loans.
7. The addition of funds to an account.
8. Any positive addition to an account balance.
9. The removal of cash from an account.
10. Any transaction that removes funds from an account.
11. Matching one's personal account records with the bank's records.
12. Movement of funds from one account to another.
13. Temporary transfer of funds from one person or company to another, to be repaid over time and with interest.
14. Monthly list of transactions that a bank has recorded.

Understanding the Main Ideas

1. Which type of financial institution is a non-profit organization?
2. Which type of financial institution is likely to have the most branches?
3. Free checking accounts may still cost you money. How?
4. Name two drawbacks to interest-earning checking accounts.
5. What is a stop-payment fee?
6. You have just opened a new checking account. Why should you shred any unused checks from your old account?
7. What should you do if the ending balance on your monthly checking account statement does not agree with the amount you have calculated?
8. What is online banking?
9. What is an online money transfer?
10. If you want automatic online bill payments, what two things do you need to do?
11. What can you do to protect your account information when you use online banking?

Practicing Math

1. You and your brother have been saving coins in a jar for almost a year. You take the coins to the grocery store, where there is a coin-counting machine. It turns out you had $206 in that jar. The machine charges a 9 percent fee. How much money do you end up with? Are there other places that would have charged you less?
2. You want to open a checking account. Bank #1 requires no minimum balance, but there is a $3 monthly fee. The account does not pay interest. Bank #2 offers an account that pays 0.15 percent annual interest. There's no monthly fee if you maintain a $1,000 minimum balance. Which account is better?

Applying Critical Thinking Skills

1. How would you decide whether to open an account at a bank, an S&L, or a credit union?
2. Suppose you and your mom have a joint account, and you both write checks on that account. How can you keep the account in good order?
3. Why would an entrepreneur want to keep business income and expenses separate from personal finances?
4. How can you avoid paying bank fees?
5. Why do you think some banks place restrictions on teens' checking accounts?
6. You are paying a bill and accidentally write the wrong amount on the check. Why shouldn't you just cross out your mistake and write the correct amount next to it?

Working with Real-World Documents

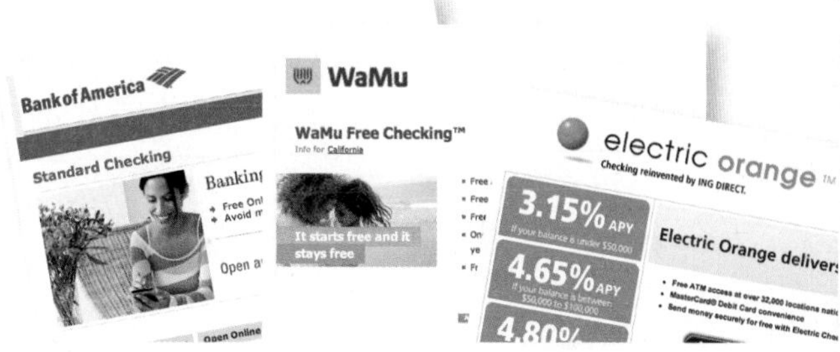

1. Obtain brochures about checking accounts from local banks, S&Ls, and credit unions. Make a chart similar to the one shown here comparing the features of the various checking accounts. Which accounts do you think are best? Give reasons for your answer.

	Name of institution	Name of institution
Minimum balance to avoid fee		
Monthly fee		
Annual interest rate		
NSF fee		
ATM fee		

Taking It Home

1. Ask adult family members where they go for financial services such as checking and savings accounts. What do they like and dislike about these institutions? How did they choose them? Summarize your findings.

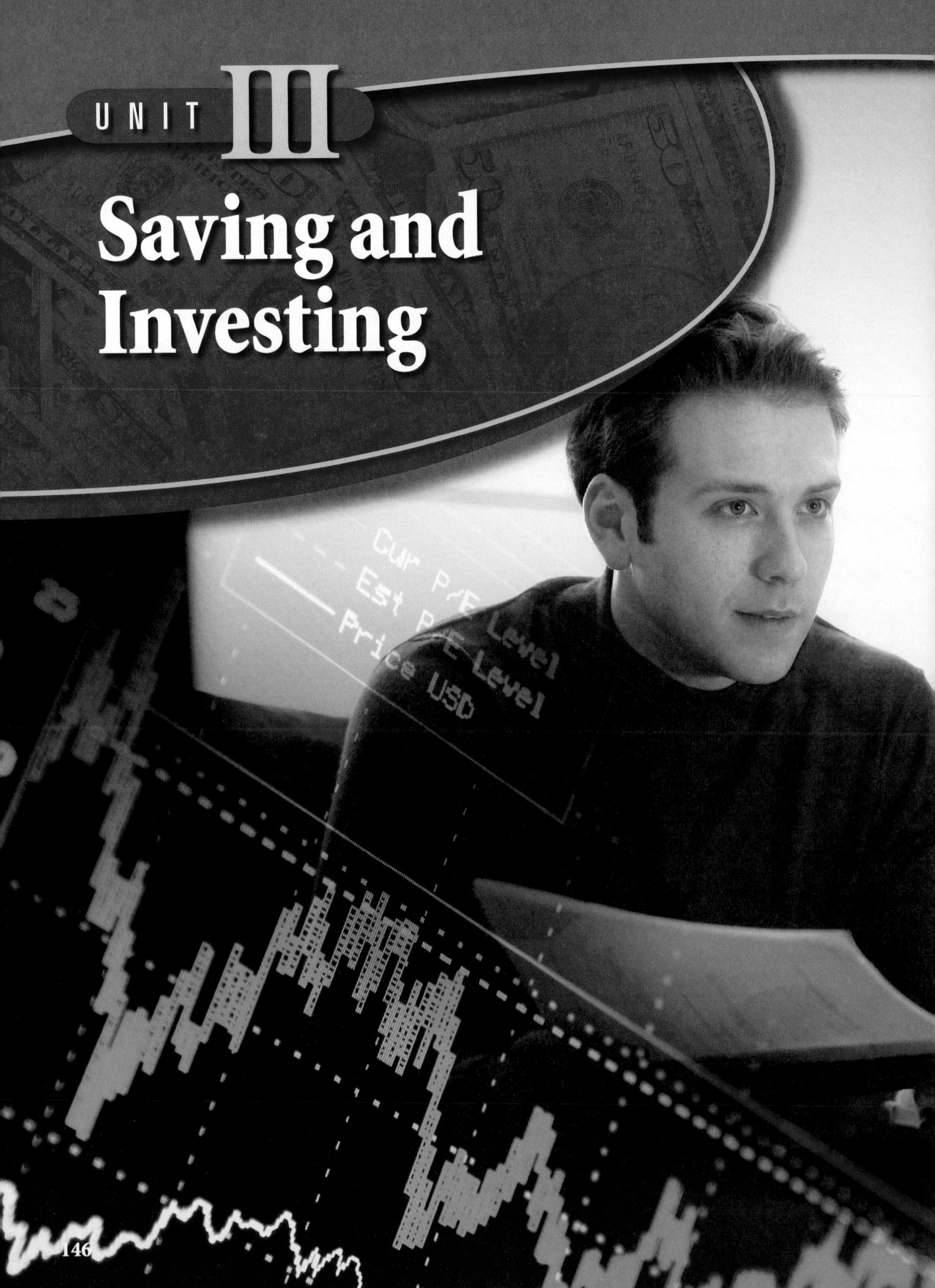

UNIT III
Saving and Investing

CHAPTER 6 Saving: Starting *Now!*

CHAPTER 7 Investment Options: Risks and Rewards

CHAPTER 6

Saving: Starting *Now!*

Saving money can be very exciting! Every time you tuck money away for later, you are investing in something positive for your future. Most people who reach their savings goals start from nothing and slowly build up their savings over time.

Saving can seem difficult at first, but it's not—especially if you make it a priority. Think of things you want. Make them goals that you will save for.

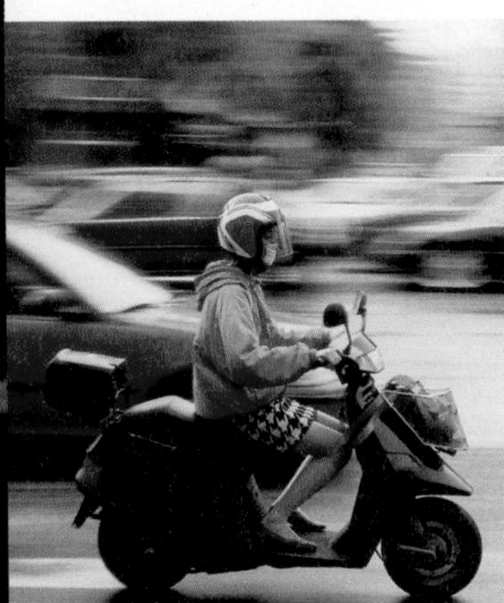

▲ **Saving money gives you the freedom to achieve your goals, such as owning a home, or driving a moped.**

Commit to saving a certain amount every week. Then put away that amount before spending money on anything else. In time, you will be well on your way to achieving your goals.

SECTION 1	Savings Goals
SECTION 2	Savings How-To

Fact or Fiction

What do you think? Are the following statements true or false? If you think they are false, then say what is true.

1. An emergency fund should have enough money to cover your expenses for a full year.
2. Buying things on credit is more expensive than saving for the same items.
3. The interest earnings on savings can vary, depending on the type of account.
4. The security that comes with having money in savings can improve your self-confidence.
5. You should wait until you have a high-paying job before you begin saving for retirement.

Answers on page 167.

Study Reminder

*Knowing how to study can increase your knowledge, improve your grades, and cut down on your study time. See the **Studying Personal Finance** pages at the front of the book for some tips to help you study this chapter.*

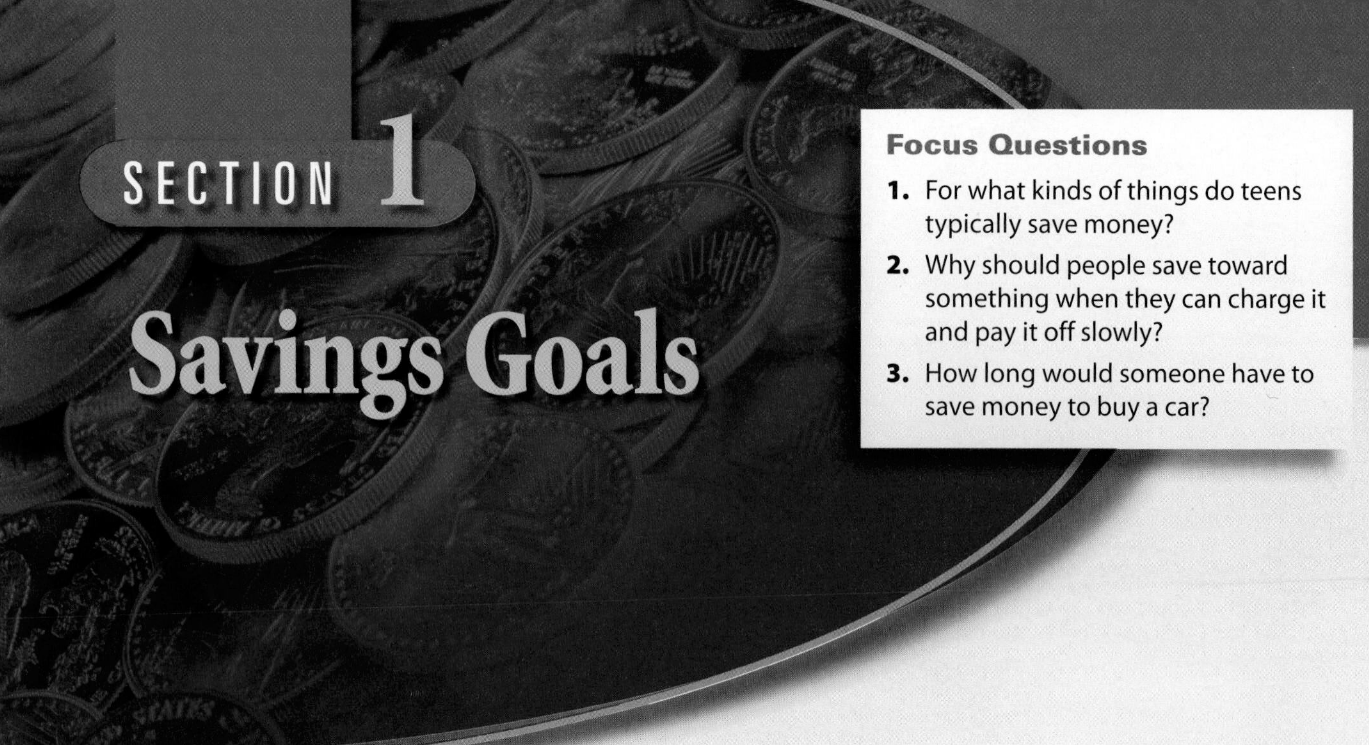

SECTION 1

Savings Goals

Focus Questions

1. For what kinds of things do teens typically save money?
2. Why should people save toward something when they can charge it and pay it off slowly?
3. How long would someone have to save money to buy a car?

Saving money is easy for some folks. But for others it seems nearly impossible: There is never any leftover money to save. And besides, *saving* money feels like taking it out of commission—almost like never having had it at all. The key is patience and discipline.

Reconsider what saving money means to you. Instead of considering it something you do with "leftover" money at the end of the month, think of it as the *first* bill you pay after getting your paycheck. Think of it as *paying yourself.*

As discussed in Chapter 4, consider what you want to do with your money. What are your values? What are your short-term, medium-term, and long-term goals? Work out a savings plan.

As you reach each of your short-term goals (new cell phone, sports gear, beginning college), you will feel a sense of accomplishment. You can then begin saving for *new* short-term goals, and medium-term goals (finishing college, buying a house). Meanwhile, you will continue to save year after year for your long-term goals (having a family, retirement).

Saving for the Short Term

Short-term savings goals are goals that you can obtain or achieve in the next five years. Meeting a short-term savings goal means you have saved enough money to buy something you want, take a vacation, or put your mind at ease about potential emergencies.

Setting Up an Emergency Fund

Planning for emergencies is an important short-term goal. Other savings goals might sound like more fun, but an emergency fund can help you avoid a lot of stress.

Consider this example. Benny's family lives about 10 miles outside of the town where he goes to school, works, and does just about everything else. So when he turned 16, Benny wanted his own car. He had a little cash set aside, so he settled on an older pickup that his neighbor was selling.

Benny knew that the purchase was not ideal. He had no idea when some-

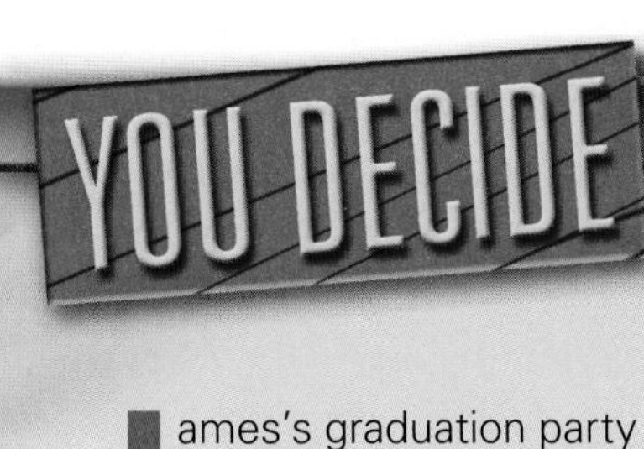

James's graduation party has been a huge success. All his friends from school came by, and so did many relatives and friends of his parents. After everyone leaves, James and his parents look through the cards that people left for him. In all, James has more than $1,500 in graduation gift money.

James is very excited—he has been thinking about traveling during the summer before starting college in the fall. His parents are also excited, but for a different reason. They think the money will give James a nice cushion as he begins his first year away from home. They think James should put the money in the bank. James is not so sure. "This is my last chance to have fun and be free!" he argues. "I want to enjoy this summer!"

What do you think James should do with the money?

Should he . . .

1. ...spend it all on a summer road trip—the trip of a lifetime? Why or why not?
2. ...put it all in the bank for an emergency fund during his first year at college? Why or why not?
3. ...put half in the bank and spend the other half on a scaled-down summer trip? Explain your answer.

thing might go wrong with his new set of wheels. Although he had used up his savings to pay for the truck, he continued to put aside the same amount of money each month in a "vehicle fund." That way, if something went wrong with the truck, Benny would be able to do something about it.

Sure enough, after six months the radiator went out. Benny used some of the savings to replace it. Then a year went by, and he had no more problems. In the meantime, he was able to increase his savings by doing odd jobs for people in the area: chopping wood, putting up hay, mowing, and other chores.

The summer he turned 17, Benny was able to sell the pickup for $500—which he added to his savings for an upgrade to a newer model. But Benny knew not to quit saving. He continues to have a vehicle fund ready and waiting.

What Is an "Emergency"? An emergency fund is used in emergency situations like these:

- Sudden illness or accident
- Vehicle breakdown
- Job loss
- Family emergency (perhaps requiring unexpected travel)

▼ **Every driver should have an emergency fund for unexpected car repairs. How much does it cost to have your car towed to a local repair shop?**

Many people like to have money set aside in case they suffer an accident or illness. Health problems can cause you to miss work and lose income. They can also cost a lot in medical bills. Having money set aside for medical emergencies will reduce the stress of the health crisis itself.

If you are like most young people, you are not driving a brand new car. You may not have a warranty that covers major repairs. If your transmission fails or if you have another unexpected major vehicle expense, an emergency fund will help you get back on the road sooner and with fewer headaches.

You never know when you might lose your job unexpectedly. Then you would need some money to get by until you find new employment. Even if you are not getting a regular paycheck, you still have bills to pay and other expenses—rent or possibly a mortgage, food, insurance, gas for your car, cell phone charges, and so forth.

How Much Should You Put In?

Many people wonder how much to put into an emergency fund. For adults, a general rule of thumb is to have enough money to cover living expenses for three to six months. If you lost your part-time job and did not find another one with comparable pay for six months, how much money would you need to sustain your lifestyle?

You may feel that six months' income is more than you need—and in fact, more than you can save in the short term. Be realistic and thoughtful when deciding how much is a reasonable amount. Maybe two months' income is enough for you. Having this money set aside will keep you from having to borrow from friends or get help from your parents—which can affect your self-confidence. It will also keep you from having to hurry into a new job that you may not like.

Saving for Something You Want to Buy

Not all short-term savings goals are for covering emergency expenses. Some are even fun! You can save money for things like vacations, major celebrations, or a car. Short-term purchases that cost more than an article of clothing but less than a house will require more time for saving. In other words, you would not buy them on a whim.

▼ By saving money, you could purchase these items in the next five years. How much does each cost? Could you afford them all?

Examples of these types of short-term purchases might include:

- Piece of furniture
- Computer or stereo equipment
- Summer camp
- Bicycle or car
- Pet and pet supplies
- College textbooks/materials

Saving for Summer Camp RaeAnne played on her school's junior varsity soccer team. She was working really hard and looking for ways to become a better player because she wanted to make the varsity squad next year. A couple of the girls on the team were talking about signing up for an elite soccer camp the next summer, which would help them improve their skills and prepare for tryouts. RaeAnne wanted to go to the camp but knew that her parents could help only a little with the high tuition. She would have to come up with $500 of her own money to go to the camp.

RaeAnne's income was not a whole lot. She refereed at little kids' soccer games and worked on weekends at a sporting goods store. Her income varied,

Like many teens, Siri has been waiting impatiently to get her driver's license. When she turns 16 and finally takes the driving test—and passes it—Siri asks her mother about getting a car.

Siri's mother thinks she should wait awhile and just borrow the family car when she needs it. Buying her own car would be expensive. Siri would have to get insurance, and there would be maintenance and repair bills too.

Her mother says that Siri could pay her the difference in insurance costs—the rate will go up with Siri added to the policy, but the amount would be much less than a new policy on a car that Siri would own. However, there would be restrictions on when she could borrow the car, where she could go with it, and who could go with her.

Siri tells her mother that she can scrape together enough money to buy an older car and pay for the insurance herself. She feels like a car of her own will give her a sense of independence. In addition, she will always have wheels, even if her mother has to go shopping or take Siri's younger brother to baseball practice or piano lessons.

Siri has a big decision to make. Since she still lives at home, using her mother's car right now does make sense. After all, she has gone sixteen years without needing her own car, and the family car would be available for her to use most of the times that she needs it. But she really wants the independence that comes from having her own car.

Should she . . .

1. ...listen to her mother's advice? That way, she can put away some money and get a nicer car in a couple of years. Explain why you do, or do not, agree.
2. ...get a car now? With her own transportation she can also get a job to pay for the upkeep. Is this a sensible plan? Explain your answer.

but in an average month she earned about $275. If she started saving in October, and she had only until May to pay for camp, she would have to set aside about $75 per month—nearly a third of her income.

As soon as RaeAnne got her weekly paycheck, she put one-third of it into a camp fund in her savings account. She did this each week until she reached her monthly goal of $75. By the end of January she had $300. By the end of March, $450. Before the end of April, RaeAnne was able to move $500 from her savings account into her checking account and write a check for soccer camp. She was on her way to camp—and hopefully to the varsity team in the fall!

Saving for a goal doesn't have to be painful if you are committed to it and are open to spending less. During the months when RaeAnne was saving toward her goal, she had to be frugal about spending money—after she put away one-third of each paycheck and paid for other necessities, there was not a whole lot of cash for things like movies and going out to eat. She and her friends spent more time just kicking around a soccer ball. Not only was it free entertainment, but also it helped them improve their soccer skills!

Why Not Charge It? Do you know anyone who wanted to buy something but did not have the money to do so?

Excited to see the new PlayStation console, Nate stopped at a Computer City store as soon as it came on the market. While he was trying it out, a sales associate approached him.

"How do you like the new PlayStation?" she asked.

"It's amazing," replied Nate. "I can't wait to get one. I've been saving for a couple weeks, but it will take me awhile to earn enough to buy it."

"Why don't you open a Computer City account?" the sales associate suggested. "Then you can buy it today. Plus, right now, the company is charging no interest for six months, so even if you take that long to pay it off, you won't have to pay any interest."

What the sales associate failed to mention to Nate was the so-called fine print. If Nate charged his purchase, he would have to make the minimum monthly payments starting the first month or be charged interest for the entire period. If he was ever late with a payment—even by just a day—he would be charged interest for the entire period. The interest rates on a Computer City credit card range from 26 to 30 percent!

Right now, Nate can afford one payment—but that is all. He will have to be very careful about saving money to be sure he does not miss a payment and get stuck paying high interest rates.

Without reading the fine print, Nate was tempted. Why should he wait to buy the PlayStation when he could open a charge account and have it now?

Before Buying

1. Should Nate open a charge account and get the PlayStation now? Or should he continue saving until he has enough money to buy it? Explain your answer.
2. What questions should Nate ask the sales associate about the credit card agreement?
3. What questions should Nate ask *himself* about his income and his saving habits?

Many people in this situation might choose to *charge it*—buy the item on credit instead of saving toward it. Some people even choose to live on credit indefinitely after a major crisis catches them unprepared with no emergency funds. Using credit instead of waiting and saving may seem like a painless solution—but is it?

Whenever you buy on credit and pay back over time, you pay back more than the actual cost of the item because you are also paying interest. Companies charge very high interest rates—sometimes up to 20 percent or more of the original cost. So if a jacket is priced at $200 and you charge it, over time it could end up costing you $240 or more. However, saving in a bank account *earns* interest for you.

Consider this example: Assume you lost your job when your employer decided to downsize. You were out of work for six months before you found another job. Take a look at the numbers. If your take-home pay had been $2,000 a month, you would still need most of that amount to cover your rent, utilities, food, auto insurance, gas for your car, cell phone, and so forth. Maybe you needed $1,500 a month just to cover basic expenses—$9,000 for six months, assuming you had no other unexpected bills. If you put all of those expenses on a credit card with a 15 percent interest rate, and if you paid only the minimum amount ($225) each month, how long do you think it would take you to pay off the debt?

The answer is fifty-six months. At the end of that time, you would have repaid a total of *$12,600*. However, if you had already set aside an emergency fund to cover those expenses, you would not have to live on credit. You would save thousands of dollars, and you could start your new job debt free. Saying "Charge it" might seem easy, but you will pay a price.

Credit card companies overwhelm college students with offers that seem terrific. However, students with little or no income, and little or no credit or budgeting experience, often end up deeply in debt after using the cards. Frequently, parents are the ones who end up paying off the debt. In 2007, Congress began working on a new law to help those families. Under the proposed bill, credit card companies could offer only one card to students with no income, and on students' and parents' joint accounts, spending limits could be raised only with parental approval. Go to http://fin.emcp.net/thomas and find out more about the bill, called The College Student Credit Card Protection Act.

Saving for College

College and other higher education are major expenses that you will likely begin paying for in the next few years. Some young people have the luxury of parents or grandparents who can foot the bill. A few earn scholarships that cover much of the cost. But the majority of students have to come up with at least some of the money themselves.

Many college students take out student loans to fund the educational expenses they cannot pay up front. If student loans can help you complete your college education and snag a well-paying job, then they are probably worth it. But you can save a lot in the long run if you put away money toward at least some of those expenses before heading to college.

Interest rates on college loans are not as low as they were in the past and could keep climbing. For example, if the interest rate for a Stafford Loan—one common source of student aid—is 7 percent, that means for every $100 you owe, you will pay an additional $7 per year in interest.

Considering that the average college student graduates with more than

$20,000 in loans, that interest adds up. In fact, a college loan of $20,000 would cost $1,400 in interest alone for the first year after graduation. Each year, the remaining balance on the loan would acquire additional interest.

Saving for college can help you avoid other money problems as well. College students are inundated with offers for credit cards. Many young people accept these offers and then use the credit cards to pay for books, transportation, tutoring, clothes, entertainment, phone bills, and other educational and noneducational expenses.

Those expenses add up fast—causing many students to pile up a lot of credit card debt before they even leave college. Putting some money away toward these expenses now can save you a lot of money in the long run.

Saving for the Medium and Long Term

Medium-term and long-term savings goals are your future goals. They are usually quite expensive—requiring you to put aside smaller amounts of

Get Good Advice

Shortly after Shaina turned 17, she decided to begin saving money for college. The idea was a good one, but Shaina had a hard time following through on her plan. Every time she accumulated a couple of hundred dollars, she found herself rushing to the mall to splurge on something she did not really need.

After six months of starting and stopping, she decided to talk with her mom about this inability to stay on track. Fortunately, Shaina's mom was an excellent saver, who had a process for turning her dreams into reality. Working together, they devised a plan for Shaina to achieve her goal of saving money for college.

When saving for a goal, it can be enormously helpful to seek out a savings "veteran"—someone you know who has the discipline and the know-how to achieve a savings goal. He or she can be a parent, grandparent, sibling, aunt or uncle, family friend, or even a financial adviser.

Many young people who do well at managing their money have a *money mentor* who can help them compare and evaluate a wide variety of financial decisions—like learning how and where to save.

To put this into practice, find someone you know who does well at saving money. Then interview that person by asking the following questions:

- Do you have savings goals?
- How do you save money?
- How does it feel to start at zero?
- What do you do with the money you save?
- Why do you work so hard to save?
- How do you stay on track?
- Who taught you about the importance of developing a saving routine?
- What was the most satisfying time you ever saved money?
- What made that instance so meaningful?

After you have completed the interview, consider how you can implement some of his or her advice into your own savings plan.

Talking with your parents and others about saving for college is a good idea. How much are your parents planning to contribute to your college education? What are other sources of funding for college? What other ideas might you come up with to save additional money for college?

LOOK Before You Leap

At the age of 17, Nolan was earning pretty good money at his part-time job in an auto parts store. His paychecks provided more than enough spending money, so Nolan was looking for a way to save or invest some of his pay.

Nolan's father brought home some information from the bank about a savings account that could be linked to a checking account like Nolan had. With that arrangement, Nolan could deposit his check into the checking account and then easily transfer some of it to savings each month.

Nolan's cousin Dave had a different idea about how Nolan could invest his money. An Internet wheeler-dealer, Dave told Nolan how people can make big money by buying newly released electronics and then selling them on eBay while demand is still higher than supply. "Video game consoles, new cell phones, handheld music players—whenever a new one comes out, we just buy as many as we can and then turn around and sell them for lots more than they cost us!" exclaimed Dave. "You can't lose!"

Before investing in anything—especially a get-rich-quick scheme, do your research. What can you find out about the real profits that people make? How risky is it? What if no one wants to buy what you are selling? Is there a chance you can lose money?

In a situation like this one, Nolan would probably want to check the Internet for information. He should look at unbiased sources to get both the pros and the cons of doing this type of business.

Before Investing

1. What kinds of information should Nolan try to locate on the Internet? Give examples.
2. How would the safety of his money in a savings account compare with the safety of investing in Dave's enterprise?
3. Should Nolan ask to see the financial records for Dave's Internet business? What information could he learn from them?

money regularly, over an extended period of time. People commonly set up savings plans for goals like these:

- Finishing college
- Second vehicle or "toy" (boat, motorcycle)
- Supporting a family
- Remodeling a home
- Retirement

Short-term goals are reached rather quickly, but achieving medium-term and long-term goals takes patience. Avoid the temptation to take out the money for some other purpose. Think about the long-term rewards you will reap. For instance, if you are saving toward buying a boat, imagine the day when you accomplish your goal. Or if you are saving to support a family, think about how the job you have today is more meaningful because it is connected to a life goal—not just another spending decision.

Achieving Medium-Term and Long-Term Goals

Saving money toward more distant purchases is just as valuable as saving for education. If you can use savings to make a down-payment on a house, for example, you can take out a much smaller loan than if you had no money for a down payment.

Other long-term savings goals—such as supporting a family and retirement—might seem too far in the future to matter much now. But saving some money toward them, even just small amounts, can help you in several ways. First of all, you are developing habits that will become part of your life and that will make it easier for you to continue in the future. Secondly, the money you save now will be earning interest for you for decades.

In addition, investing your money in savings options that earn you more interest will help protect you from inflation. *Inflation* is an increase in the price of goods, or average level of prices. If inflation occurs, you need more money to buy the things you want because your dollar does not stretch as far. This is known as the erosion of buying power. Take precautions by investing in high-interest savings options, such as those described below.

Savings Success Starts with a Plan

After you have been saving money for a few months, you still might not be convinced. Take a few minutes to examine your bank statement and admire what you are doing. Once you establish a routine for saving, accomplishing your goals will be much easier.

Avoid the temptation to withdraw the money and spend it on something else. Remember your long-term plan. Dream about your goals and then put your plan into action!

Krista's Savings Plan

Krista, a sophomore, decided to try a savings plan. She started out with short-term, medium-term, and long-term goals, as shown in Figure 6.1.

Krista then determined that she could save at least 25 percent of her income, or about $200 each month. She opened two savings accounts—one for short-term goals and one for medium-term and long-term goals. Then she ranked her goals in order of their approximate costs and when she hoped to reach them. Finally, she looked at how much she would have to save toward each one to meet those estimates, as shown in Figure 6.2.

Krista soon realized that reaching her goals would require her to save more than she thought. To meet all her goals when she wanted to, she would have to save nearly $1,280 per month! She does not even make this much money. So Krista decided to rethink her savings goals and time line. This time she would base her plan on a realistic amount of money she could save each month—$343.

Krista would be going to college in three years, so she knew she must save for textbooks. She decided not to buy a phone now because she can use her parents' phone. She also decided to go to Yosemite *after* graduation rather than before her senior year, giving her an extra 12 months to save. If she waits to buy a car until after graduation, she can borrow her mom's car and save money. Also, she will get

Figure 6.1 KRISTA'S LIST OF GOALS

Short-term goals	Medium-term goals	Long-term goals
• Buy an iPhone	• Volunteer 1 yr. in Belize	• Have a family
• Weekend trip to Yosemite	• Finish college	• Retire
• Buy a car	• Travel to Alaska	
• Establish emergency fund	• Buy a moped	
• College textbooks/materials		
• Donate to adoption agency		

a less expensive car and spend less than she originally thought.

By cutting her list of goals, Krista has a more realistic chance of achieving them. Other decisions Krista made include making smaller adoption donations for a longer period of time, rethinking whether she would go to Alaska, and making smaller payments into her long-term savings fund.

Krista knows she can adjust her goals in a few years. After college, she may sell her car and use public transportation. Then she could use the money from the sale for her trip. Maybe she will have a higher paying job after her college graduation, so she could put more money into long-term savings. She can adjust her goals and increase the amounts she saves, as she can afford to.

For now, Krista has decided to save 40 percent of her paycheck—rather than 25 percent. The emergency fund will get all of the money she saved in her piggy bank as a child, plus any windfall money from birthday gifts or bonuses. If she gets a summer job with additional hours or develops another source of income, she will put that into her "finish college" fund. See Krista's Revised Savings Plan in Figure 6.3.

Make a list of your short-, medium-, and long-term savings goals, using these charts as a guide. Show the total dollars required for each goal, the amount you will need to save per month, and the number of months you will need to reach your goal. When you break down your goals like this, you will have a more realistic picture of what it will take to pay for something.

Figure 6.2 **KRISTA'S FIRST SAVINGS PLAN**

	Cost $	Amount per month $	No. of months
Short-term goals			
iPhone	400	35	12
Yosemite trip	500	42	12
Car	3,000	167	18
Emergency fund	500	42	12
College texts & materials	2,000	56	36
Donations	300	25	12
		$367	
Medium-term goals			
Volunteer 1 year	2,500	35	72
Finish college	8,500	119	72
Alaska	1,500	25	60
Moped	2,500	35	72
		$214	
Long-term goals			
Family	50,000	278	180
Retirement	200,000	417	480
		$695	
Total	$271,700	$1,276	

Figure 6.3 **KRISTA'S REVISED SAVINGS PLAN**

	Cost $	Amount per month $	No. of months
Short-term goals			
Yosemite trip	500	21	24
College texts & materials	2,000	56	36
Emergency fund	500	42	12
Car	2,000	61	33
Donations	300	15	20
		$195	
Medium-term goals			
Finish college	8,500	118	72
(moped)	(2,500)		
		$118	
Long-term goals			
Family	50,000	15	(Increase
Retirement	200,000	15	when
		$30	possible)
New total savings per month		$343	

Krista's revised savings plan is realistic, and she can add to her goals as her income increases.

Post your chart in a prominent place so you can see how you are doing from month to month. When you reach one of your savings goals (especially a short-term goal), you might want to consider adding a new one to the list. That way you can get into a healthy rhythm for saving up money rather than getting into too much debt.

Jeff's and Jenna's Savings Plans

Jeff and Jenna were siblings and a year apart in high school. As a sophomore, Jeff got a job waiting tables at an ice cream parlor down the road from home. Soon after that, Jenna—a freshman—got a job there as well, busing tables and taking orders from the counter. They both opened bank accounts and began depositing their checks each payday.

Jeff's and Jenna's parents had always promised to take care of college tuition and room and board expenses if the kids would pay for their books and other minor expenses. When he opened his checking account, Jeff linked it to a savings account, so he could easily start putting away some money for college. Jenna also opened a savings account, but she did not develop a plan to save regularly for college.

After three years, Jeff had saved nearly $4,000. This meant he would be able to buy books and have enough spending money for at least his first couple of years in college. He would not have to take a part-time job during the school year, so he could focus on his studies. During the summers, he would work to replenish his savings account.

Jenna put some money in her savings account each month, but each summer she withdrew most of her savings for shopping, outings with friends, and other diversions. By the end of her high school days, she had only about $500 in her account.

Upset that she would have to work during the school year in college, Jenna asked her parents for help—but they stuck to their original decision. Jenna would have to sacrifice part of her valuable time during college to earn money for books and other expenses associated with college life.

The lesson here should be obvious. But another important point is whether Jenna will modify her habits today to be a responsible saver for her future.

Regularly depositing money into your savings account and leaving it there is an important part of responsible saving.

How Do Others Reach Their Savings Goals?

Most young people and adults who achieve their savings goals have four things in common:

1. They set achievable goals—goals they can realistically attain, like saving for an iPod, college, or a car.
2. They break down their goals into small amounts over a period of time—like $20 per week or $140 per month, instead of $7,280 a year.
3. They monitor their progress from start to finish—and if they get off track they make the necessary adjustments.

4. They have a money mentor—like a family member or financial adviser—who holds them accountable. There is nothing like a routine visit with a money mentor to help you stay on track.

You can also get good advice from your peers. On the Motley Fool Web site (http://fin.emcp.net/motleyfool), author Selena Maranjian's article "Ways to Save and Make Money" contains some saving tips from teens. Here are some of their suggestions:

- Daniel Carroll, 16, says, "I have a little bank that I put spare change and bills into. Whenever I have a significant amount in there, I'll invest it or put it in the bank. It's important to keep a routine. Every time I get money, I put some away."
- Adam Kaufman, 15, adds, "Start with small amounts. When I first started saving to invest, I was saving $1 to $2 each day, so by the end of the month, I had $30 to $60, depending on what kind of month it was."
- Jason Hart, 18, continues, "Take only what you *really* need for spending, and put the rest of it somewhere that's difficult to get to, such as into long-term CDs or money market accounts. Making it inconvenient to get to your money might help you avoid the urge to spend it. Also, decide exactly what percentage you will spend and what you will save, and follow your own rules."

If you put $100 in a savings account today, and the interest rate is 2 percent, by the end of one year you will have $102. If you then put another $100 in the account, by the end of the second year you'll have $206.04. Following this plan, by the third year you will have $312.16; year four: $420.40; and year six: $643.43. So after six years, you will have earned $43.43 in interest by saving only $100 per year. Imagine how much interest you could earn if you could save more than $100 each year!

The bottom line is this: Saving money, like being physically fit, is about patience and discipline. It is about resisting the temptation to spend money frivolously, which prevents you from reaching your goals. Once you get into the rhythm of setting—and achieving—your savings goals, you will be well on your way to a lifetime of financial success.

SECTION 1 ASSESSMENT

Factual Recall

1. Is planning for emergencies a short-term goal or a long-term goal?
2. What is an intermediate purchase? Name three examples.
3. Tell what is missing from this list of steps for reaching a savings goal: set an achievable goal; break it down into small amounts and short time periods; get help from a money mentor. Why is the missing item important?

Critical Thinking

1. Describe at least two scenarios in which an emergency fund would be useful.
2. What do you think are some advantages and disadvantages of saving for your goals?

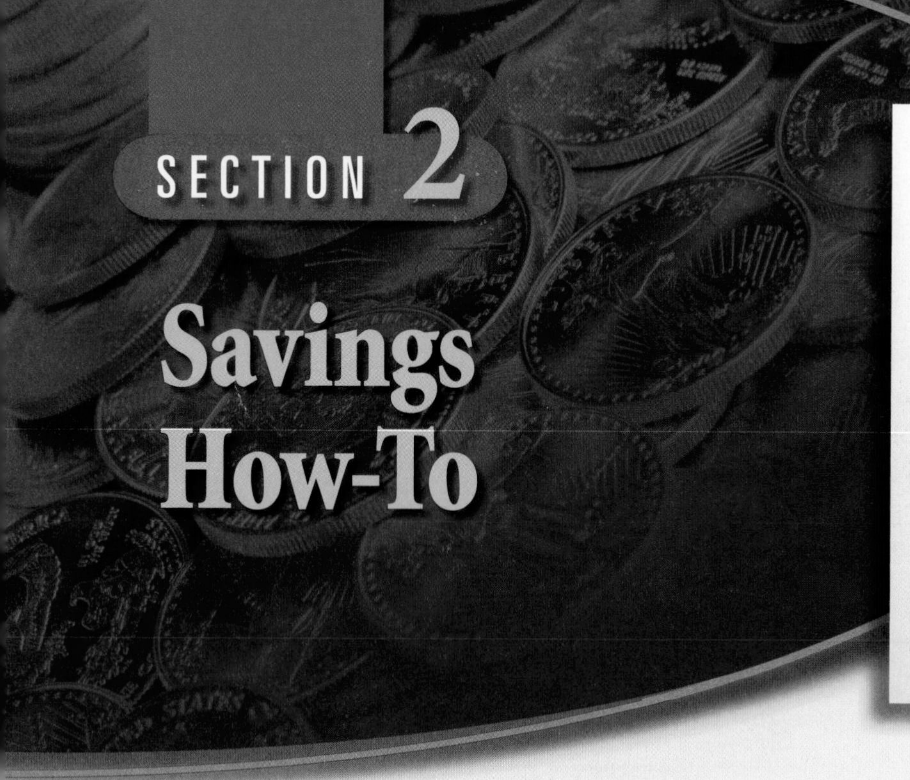

SECTION 2 Savings How-To

Focus Questions

1. How do I know what kind of savings account is right for me?
2. How does compounding interest increase my account balance?

Key Terms

discretionary income
liquidity
certificate of deposit (CD)
money market account
securities
savings bonds
compounding interest
annual percentage yield (APY)
return

discretionary income income left over after savings and essential expenses have been accounted for

To begin a savings plan, you have to be conscious about what you do with your money. As stated at the beginning of this chapter, saving should not be an afterthought. Saving money is possible if you make it a priority in your money routine. Here's how:

▶ Regularly putting part of your paycheck into savings helps you reach your financial goals. What percentage will you put into savings?

- First, decide how much you think you can save per month or per paycheck. You might want to think of this as a percentage of your income—say 25 or 40 percent, for example.
- Each month or pay period, pay *yourself* first. Put the money in a piggy bank, a jar, or—better yet—a savings account. If you are saving toward more than one goal, use a notebook or other tool (like a spreadsheet) to keep track of how much is reserved for each goal.
- Next, pay your fixed monthly expenses—such as transportation, food, and school needs.
- Finally, use the leftover money—called **discretionary income**—for entertainment, shopping, and other pleasurable spending.
- Whenever you receive unexpected money like a birthday or holiday gift, or an inheritance, put it away in savings. If saving all of that windfall is too difficult for you, consider splitting it in half. Save half, but earmark the rest toward something that fits with your values.

Saving for a Lifetime

So you have succeeded in meeting a savings goal. Should you stop there and use the extra money from each paycheck for fun from now on? No!

Once you are in the habit of setting aside an amount of money toward a savings goal each pay period, do not stop. Find a new goal, or start putting that money toward your long-term savings objectives.

Adding New Goals

Neva works at a natural foods co-op, earning $7.50 per hour. After taxes and Social Security are taken out of her check, she gets around $6 per hour. During the week, Neva works only one or two five-hour shifts. On weekends, she usually has an additional seven-hour shift. So every two weeks, she pockets about $180, for a monthly total of around $360. Neva wants to save for future college expenses and also for a laptop. She figures she can put one-fourth (or 25 percent) of her income in her savings account.

Every two weeks, when she deposits her paycheck in her checking account, Neva writes a check for $45 and deposits that into her savings account. She also puts any extra cash she gets from odd jobs or gifts into savings as well. Neva keeps track of how much of her savings should go toward the laptop and how much is for college. Her savings record is shown in Figure 6.4.

After six months, Neva has saved $790. Of that, she has earmarked $385 toward the laptop and $405 for college. Without causing herself too much pain, she has made huge strides toward her savings goals.

At this rate, Neva will be able to buy a really nice laptop by March of next year. Then she can begin working on a new short-term savings goal. If she does not have one, she can put the extra $20 per paycheck into her college fund.

Figure 6.4 NEVA'S SAVINGS ACCOUNT RECORD

In six months, Neva saved a total of $790.

Date	Deposits	Balance	Laptop	College
Sept. 15	$45	$45	$20	$25
Oct. 1	$45	$90	$40	$50
Oct. 10 (babysitting)	$20	$110	$60	$50
Oct. 15	$45	$155	$80	$75
Nov. 1	$45	$200	$100	$100
Nov. 15	$45	$245	$120	$125
Dec. 1	$45	$290	$140	$150
Dec. 15	$45	$335	$160	$175
Jan. 1	$45	$380	$180	$200
Jan. 5 (gifts)	$100	$480	$230	$250
Jan. 15	$45	$525	$250	$275
Feb. 1	$45	$570	$270	$300
Feb. 15	$45	$615	$290	$325
Feb. 20 (gift)	$25	$640	$315	$325
Mar. 1	$45	$685	$335	$350
Mar. 7 (misc. income)	$60	$745	$365	$380
Mar. 15	$45	$790	$385	$405
Total savings for six months		$790	$385	$405

Developing a Savings Plan

Once you decide that you want to save some of your money, consider how your ideas for saving fit with your values and goals. Reflect on your conversations with parents and others. Finally, think about your own personality.

Ask yourself how easy or difficult it is for you to control your impulses to spend money. Can you put away money and leave it there, or will you want to take it out of the bank and spend it? Will you be able to follow through on your plan in the long run? If you think your patience may be lacking and that you might have trouble saving money, you need to develop a saving plan that will help you be consistent.

Some people might start out simply —say, with a savings jar. At the end of every day, they will drop their spare change into the jar and watch it quickly accumulate. Others may find this too tempting. A jar half full of change—enough to buy a ticket to the movies, for instance—could be too easy to empty out when something comes along that they want to buy.

A better solution is to use a savings account. This way, once you put the money away, it is in the bank—far less accessible than a savings jar in your room. The other advantage of a savings account is that the bank *pays you* for keeping your money there. Recall that this money you earn on savings is called *interest.* Your savings can increase even faster than you think!

The most important thing about saving is being patient. In fact, for many young people, the temptation to spend is just too great. Do not give in. Remember your plan. Leave your money in savings until you reach your goal. If you do mess up and withdraw part of it for something else, try not to be too hard on yourself. Pick up where you left off. Keep working to develop healthy savings habits!

Savings Accounts

You might have had a basic savings account since you were young. You deposit money, and the money earns interest. You can make deposits or withdrawals at any time. Because this arrangement makes it easy to get your money out quickly, a regular savings account is said to have high **liquidity**. The downside is that this type of account earns less interest than other types of savings accounts.

liquidity the ability of an asset to be quickly and easily converted into cash

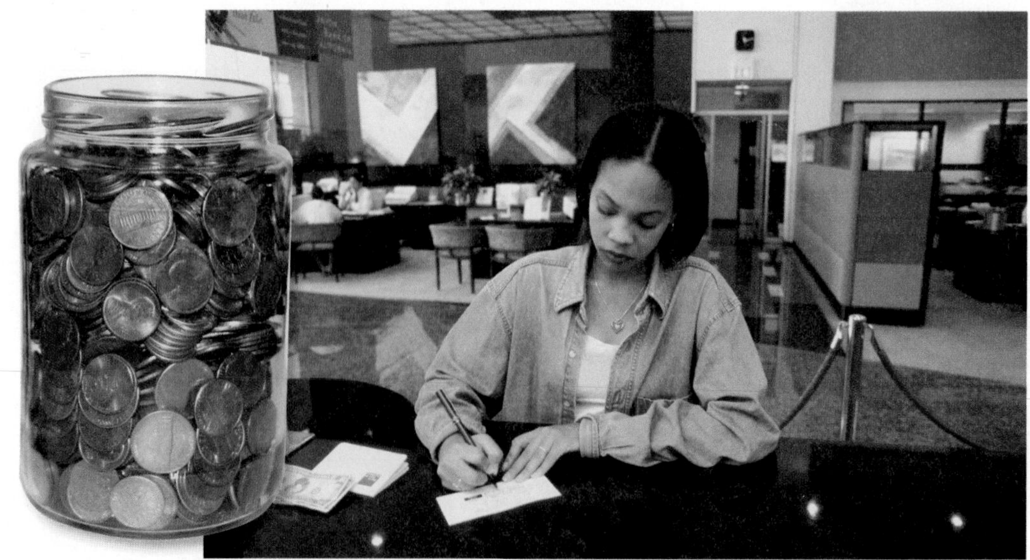

Inside a bank, depositing or withdrawing money from an account requires filling out a bank slip.

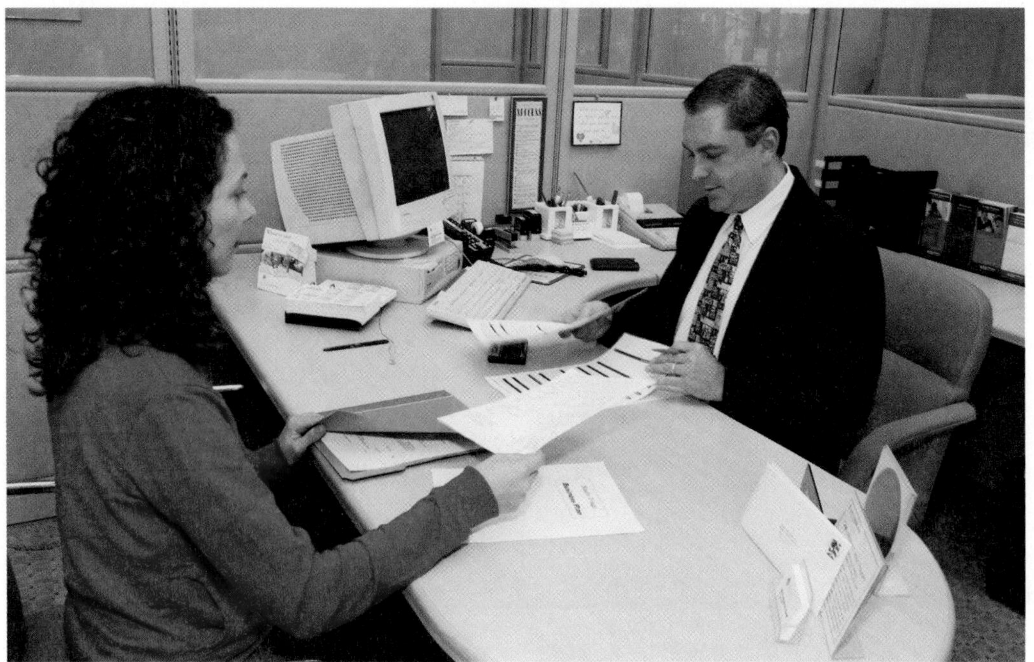

◀ Bankers at financial institutions are available to answer your investing questions. Meet with several before deciding where and how to invest.

Types of Savings Accounts

If you want to make more money with your savings, consider these other types of savings accounts.

A **certificate of deposit (CD)** is a savings deposit that earns a specific amount of interest over a fixed amount of time—say six months or a year. You have to put a minimum amount of money into a CD, and you have to leave it there for the entire time span. CDs have less liquidity than regular savings accounts, but they do pay higher interest rates.

A **money market account** is a type of savings account in which your money is invested in **securities**—documents indicating ownership, such as Treasury bills, savings bonds, and certificates of deposit, that can be bought and sold in the investment markets. A money market account requires a minimum deposit and a minimum balance. It might also limit the number of checks you can write per month. However, the interest earned is generally higher than earnings from a regular savings account or CD.

Savings bonds are another option for putting money away to earn interest. When you buy a U.S. savings bond, you pay half of the face value of the bond—in other words, you pay $25 for a $50 bond. When the bond reaches its maturity date, usually in twenty years, it will be worth the face value.

Some savings bonds continue to earn interest after they reach maturity—for thirty years from the date they are issued. After thirty years, they can be worth much more than their face value.

Unlike securities, savings bonds are *nontransferable*—they cannot be bought or sold in the investment markets. You can purchase Series EE savings bonds from a bank or directly from the U.S. Treasury at http://fin.emcp.net/savingsbonds.

Choosing a Savings Account Option

How do you know what type of savings account is right for you? To help you learn about different types of savings accounts, visit your local financial institutions and explore the options. In preparation for this excursion, consider the following questions:

certificate of deposit (CD) a savings alternative in which money is left on deposit for a stated period of time to earn a specific rate of interest

money market account a type of savings account that invests in securities

securities documents indicating ownership—such as stock certificates, bonds, or Treasury bills—that can be bought and sold in the investment markets

savings bonds nontransferable bonds issued by the U.S. government initially sold at half their face value

Do Your RESEARCH

Many financial Web sites have calculators that will tell you how much interest you will earn by saving a certain amount of money each year. Try the compound interest calculator at MoneyChimp.com (http://fin.emcp.net/moneychimp).

Your Assignment

1. Imagine your goal is to save just $20 per month, or $240 a year. Assume the interest rate is 5 percent. How much money would you have in your account in five years? In ten years?
2. Now try it with a $600 annual contribution, or $50 each month. What might you be able to do with that money in ten years?

1. For what purpose are you saving?
2. How long will you be able to "park" the money in the account before you need to get it out?
3. Do some accounts pay higher interest rates than others?
4. Are there penalties for early withdrawal?
5. Can you track your balance online?

After you have finished comparison shopping, think about your savings goals. Your decision will depend on what you are saving for, how long you intend to have the account, and how often you might need to withdraw funds from the account.

compounding interest figuring interest earnings on both the original amount *and* any previous interest that has been added to the balance

annual percentage yield (APY) the amount of interest that a deposit would earn after compounding for one year, expressed as a percentage

Earning Interest

You might be wondering how interest rates affect the amount of money in your account. As you learned in Chapter 5, the bank pays interest on your account—rates can range from less than 1 percent of the balance to as much as 5 or 6 percent, depending on the type of account and current economic conditions. Those interest earnings are added to your balance. Each time interest is recalculated, the amount you receive is based on the new, larger amount in your account. This is called **compounding interest**—figuring the interest earnings as a percentage of both the original deposit or balance (termed the *principal*) and any previous interest that has been added to that original amount. Physicist Albert Einstein said, "The most powerful force in the universe is compound interest."

Interest can be compounded monthly, quarterly, or annually. For example, if you start with $100, and the interest rate is 5 percent compounded annually, your earnings are $5 after one year. Now your balance is $105, assuming you do not add any deposits to your principal amount. The second year, the interest will be paid on the balance of $105. Your earnings for the second year are $5.25, and your new balance will be $110.25. If your account paid 5 percent interest compounded monthly or quarterly instead of annually, those numbers would change.

The amount of interest an account earns can be described in terms of its **annual percentage yield (APY)**. The APY, or *rate of return*, is the amount of interest your deposit would earn in one year, expressed as a percentage.

For instance, assume a bank offers a 5 percent annual interest rate on savings, compounded monthly. On a $100 deposit, the interest earned after one month would be 5 percent of $100 ($5.00), divided by 12, which equals 42 cents. Then the second month, you would calculate the interest rate based on a balance of $100.42, and so on. By the end of the year, your balance would be $105.12—12 cents more than if the interest were compounded annually. The APY in this case is 5.12 percent.

Some accounts compound interest quarterly—four times a year. On that same $100 deposit, you would earn $5.09 after twelve months. So by the end of the year, your balance would be $105.09—9 cents more than if the interest were compounded annually. The APY is 5.09 percent.

By comparing each bank's APY, you can get an accurate measurement of the actual **return** on your money—or amount of interest earned—from one bank account to another.

One or two percentage points can make a big difference in the long term. The *Rule of* 72 is a simple way to estimate the effect of interest rates. Dividing 72 by the interest rate will tell you approximately how many years it will take to double your investment. For example, if the interest rate is 4 percent, it will take 18 years to double your investment.

Current Yields
Member FDIC
PRODUCT
MINIMUM
APY
12 MONTH
$500
5.35%
15 MONTH
$500
5.40%
18 MONTH T.D.
$500
5.60%
2 YEARS
$500
5.65%
4 YEARS
$500
5.50%

This presents an opportunity to get to know your local banks and credit unions. Check out a few in your neighborhood to compare their rates. Some of them will offer higher interest rates on CDs in order to attract new business. For example, one institution might offer a $2,500 CD for five years at 4 percent compounded monthly, while another one down the street offers the same deal but at 5 percent compounded annually. Do the math to figure the difference.

◀ **Signs like this one appear in financial institutions to show investors the current APY rates. Which investment looks best to you?**

return earnings from a savings account or profit from an investment

Answers to Fact or Fiction

1. False—A general rule of thumb is to have enough money to cover living expenses for three to six months; **2.** True; **3.** True; **4.** True; **5.** False—You should begin now to save for retirement.

SECTION 2 ASSESSMENT

Factual Recall

1. This section recommends that you use discretionary income for entertainment and shopping. What is discretionary income?
2. Name four types of savings accounts or savings plans. Which one has the highest liquidity?
3. What is meant by "compounding interest"?

Critical Thinking

1. Suppose you are saving for a new phone, a car, and college, all at the same time. How can you keep track of how much is reserved for each goal?
2. You have saved $1,500, and you want it to earn more interest. What factors should you compare when deciding whether to put the money into a certificate of deposit or a money market account?

CHAPTER 6 REVIEW AND ASSESSMENT

Chapter Summary

Section 1 Savings Goals

- A savings plan should take into account your goals and values.
- Savings goals can be short-, medium-, or long-term.
- Money in an emergency fund can be used to pay for unexpected expenses or to support you if you are out of work.
- If you buy an item on credit and do not pay the entire bill at once, you will have to *pay* interest. If you save your money in a bank account, you will *receive* interest earnings.
- To save for a specific goal, determine how much money you will need and when you will need it. Divide the dollar amount by the amount of time to find the rate of savings.
- Successful savers set achievable goals, break down each goal into small amounts over a period of time, monitor their progress, and receive advice from a money mentor.

Section 2 Savings How-To

- To begin a savings plan, decide how much of your income you can save per month or per paycheck. Set aside this amount first, *before* you spend any money.
- Next, pay your bills.
- Use your discretionary income for entertainment, shopping, and other fun spending.
- Add unexpected money to your savings.
- Once you reach a savings goal, set a new goal or increase your savings for other goals.
- There are several types of savings accounts. What works best for you will depend on your circumstances.
- Interest can be compounded monthly, quarterly, or yearly. The frequency of compounding affects the amount of interest you earn (annual percentage yield).
- Saving money requires patience and discipline, but you will be rewarded with the achievement of your goals and a sense of accomplishment.

Reviewing Key Terms

For each of the following statements, choose the key term that best completes the sentence.

1. A regular savings account lets you make deposits or withdrawals at any time. Such an account has ______.
2. John put his money into a bank account that pays a specific amount of interest for a fixed amount of time. His money is in a(n) ______.
3. You can buy ______ directly from the U.S. Treasury.
4. Anita chose an account that pays higher interest than a regular savings account. However, she needs to maintain a minimum balance, and she can withdraw only a few checks per month. She has a(n) ______.
5. If Bank #1 has a higher APY than Bank #2, you would get a higher ______ on your money at Bank #1.
6. When you buy ______ at a bank or financial institution, you pay less than their face value.
7. Money that is left over after you have paid bills and set aside money for savings is called ______.
8. Documents such as Treasury bills, which can be bought and sold in the investment markets, are called ______.
9. Figuring interest earnings as a percentage of both the principal plus any previous interest is called ______.
10. The ______ is the yearly rate of return on your investment.

Understanding the Main Ideas

1. What does it mean to "pay yourself first"?
2. What is the difference between a short-term, a medium-term, and a long-term savings goal?
3. In general, how much money should an adult put into an emergency fund?
4. Name three examples of long-term savings goals.
5. Name two alternatives to getting a student loan for higher education.

6. What is windfall money?
7. What is a money mentor?
8. Once you have reached a savings goal, what should you do with income you no longer need for that goal?
9. When comparing interest rates, why should you look at the APY?

Practicing Math

1. Using the *Rule of* 72, how long will it take to double your money if the interest rate is 4.5 percent? What if the rate is 6 percent?
2. Suppose you want to double your money in 8 years. What rate of interest do you need to earn? Again you can use the Rule of 72. This time, divide 72 by the number of years. What interest rate will double your money in 8 years?

Applying Critical Thinking Skills

1. Does a teen, living at home, need to save money in an emergency fund? Why or why not?
2. The digital camera you have been wanting to buy is on sale. You do not have enough saved to pay for it. The sale ends in one week. Which would be better: to buy the item now on credit, or to pass up the sale and continue saving to buy it later? Give reasons for your answer.
3. Saving for college can help you avoid borrowing money or at least can reduce the amount you have to borrow. What other benefits might there be from saving for college?
4. Your friend has a hard time saving money and has asked for your advice. What would you say to help your friend become a better saver?
5. Your sister receives $100 for her birthday. She wants to spend it all on clothes. How would you convince her that spending it all is not the best thing to do?

Working with Real-World Documents

1. Many people need financial help to pay for college, trade school, or professional school. The federal government is the largest source of student aid, providing more than $80 billion per year. Go to http://fin.emcp.net/fafsa4caster to learn about federal student aid and answer the following questions.
   a. What are the three categories of student aid programs?
   b. Does federal student aid cover only tuition?
   c. What is the difference between a loan and a grant?
   d. After graduation, if you do not get a job in your field of study, can you have your loan canceled?
   e. How much does it cost to apply for federal student aid?

SECTION 1 – STUDENT INFORMATION

- **Use of this Worksheet is optional. It should not be submitted to Federal Student Aid or to your college.**
- Not all of the questions from *FAFSA on the Web* appear in this Worksheet, but questions are generally ordered as they appear online.
- Once you are online, you may be able to skip some questions based on your answers to earlier questions.

Your Social Security Number (Q8)	☐☐☐-☐☐-☐☐☐☐
Your last name (Q1)	
Your driver's license number (optional) (Q11)	
Are you a U.S. citizen? (Q14) If you are neither a citizen nor an eligible noncitizen, you are not eligible for federal student aid. However, you should still complete the application, because you may be eligible for state or college aid. If you are in the U.S. on an F1 or F2 student visa, or a J1 or J2 exchange visitor visa, or a G series visa (pertaining to international organizations), you must answer "Neither citizen nor eligible noncitizen.	❑ U.S. citizen (U.S. national) ❑ Eligible noncitizen Generally you are an eligible noncitizen if you are: • A permanent U.S. resident with a Permanent Resident Card (I-551); • A conditional permanent resident (I-551C); or • The holder of an Arrival-Departure Record (I-94) from the Department of Homeland Security showing any of the following designations: "Refugee," "Asylum Granted," "Parolee" (I-94 confirms paroled for a minimum of one year and status has not expired), "Victim of human trafficking," T-Visa holder (T-1, T-2, T-3, etc.) or "Cuban-Haitian Entrant." ❑ Neither citizen nor eligible noncitizen
Your Alien Registration Number (Q15) If you are an eligible noncitizen, enter your eight- or nine-digit Alien Registration Number.	A
Your marital status as of today (Q16) "As of today" refers to the day that you sign your FAFSA.	❑ Single, divorced, or widowed ❑ Married/remarried ❑ Separated
Month and year you were married, separated, divorced or widowed (Q17) (Example: Month and year: 05/1997)	M M Y Y Y Y
Your state of legal residence (Q18)	
Did you become a legal resident of your state before January 1, 2003? (Q19)	❑ Yes ❑ No

2. FAFSA stands for Free Application for Federal Student Aid. The application can be completed online, but it is a good idea to complete a worksheet first. That way, you can be sure that you have all your information ready when you go online. Download and print out the *FAFSA on the Web Worksheet*, which is available at http://fin.emcp.net/fafsa. (Look for it under step 1.) What documents and other information will you need in order to complete the worksheet?

Taking It Home

1. With the help of your parent(s) or guardian(s), visit the SallieMae Web site at http://fin.emcp.net/salliemae and find out about Stafford loans. What are the qualifications for obtaining these student loans? How much money can be borrowed? How much interest is charged? What are the repayment terms?

CHAPTER 7

Investment Options: Risks and Rewards

Once you have your financial goals, your budget, and your savings and checking accounts all in order, you are ready for the next important step. It's now time to think about investing money for long-term goals like supporting a family and retirement.

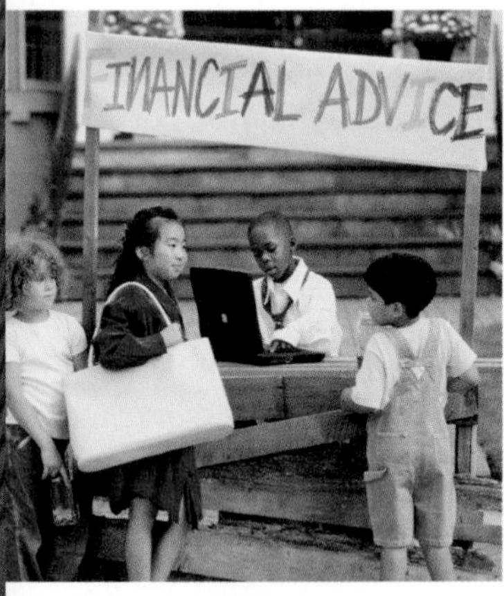

▲ These kids are smart! Establishing saving and investing habits at an early age leads to financial success later in life.

Investing is *saving* money in a way that *earns* money. Its purpose is to earn a *financial return*—more money back.

Investors have two main considerations: rate of return, and risk. How much money can be earned? How much could be lost?

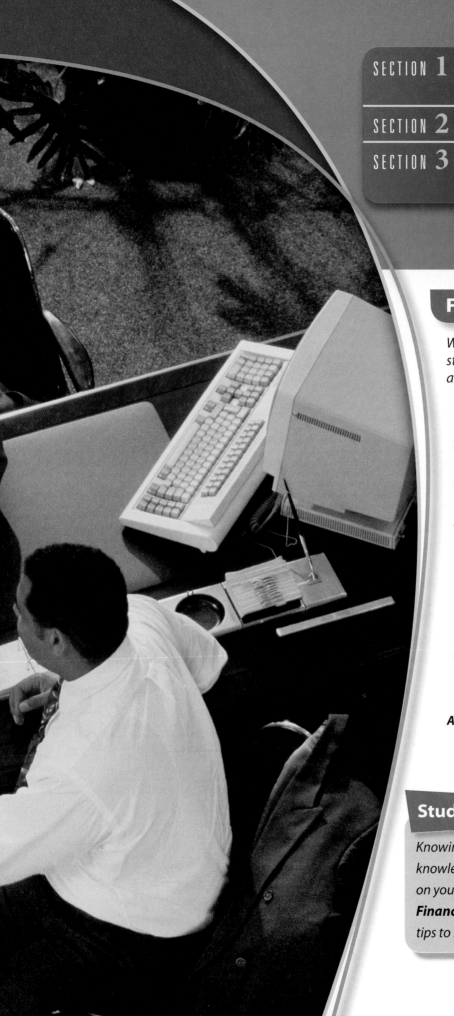

SECTION 1	Stocks, Bonds, and Mutual Funds
SECTION 2	Other Types of Investments
SECTION 3	Advice, Information, and Transactions

Fact or Fiction

What do you think? Are the following statements true or false? If you think they are false, then say what is true.

1. Only rich people invest money in the stock market.
2. Stocks and bonds are always risky places to put your money.
3. People generally begin saving for retirement around the age of 50.
4. Social Security was designed to be a primary source of retirement income.
5. Before investing in a company or mutual fund, you should follow the progress of the stocks to determine how successful your investment is likely to be.
6. Today, many companies automatically enroll their employees in retirement plans.

Answers on page 195.

Study Reminder

Knowing how to study can increase your knowledge, improve your grades, and cut down on your study time. See the ***Studying Personal Finance*** *pages at the front of the book for some tips to help you study this chapter.*

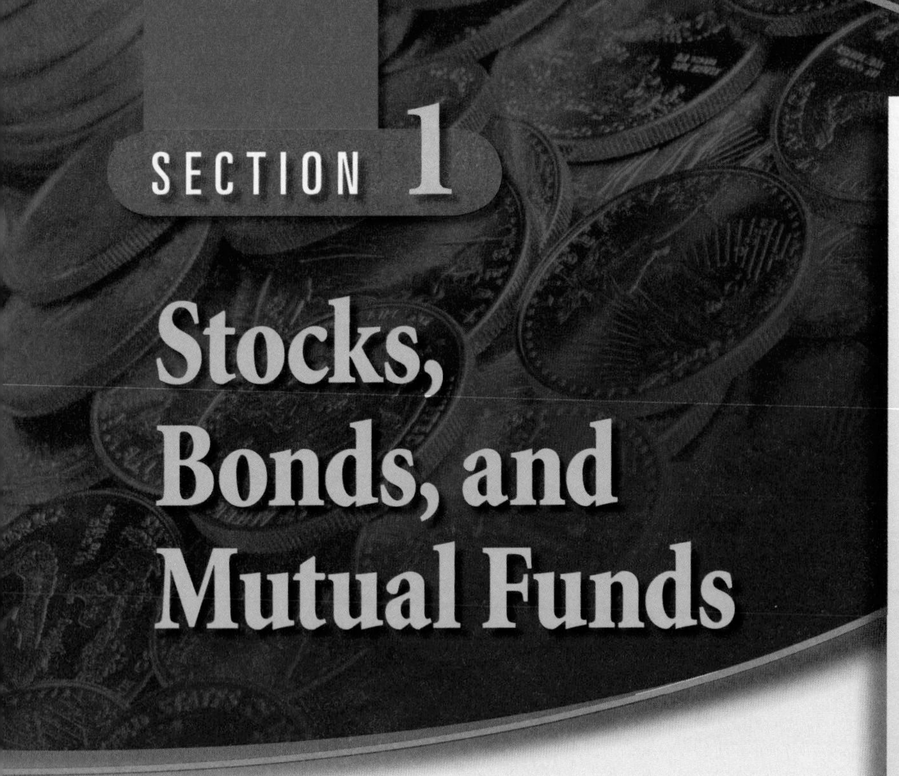

Stocks, Bonds, and Mutual Funds

Focus Questions

1. What is the difference between stocks and bonds?
2. What is a mutual fund? Is it risky?
3. Name several types of investments other than stocks, bonds, and mutual funds.

Key Terms

stock
dividends
capital gain
common stock
preferred stock
New York Stock Exchange (NYSE)
NASDAQ
blue-chip stocks
Dow Jones Industrial Average
bull market
bear market
S&P 500 index
Fortune 500
futures
commodities
options
penny stocks
bond
mutual fund
no-load funds
load funds

Stocks

stock an investment in the ownership of a corporation, usually represented by shares of the business

dividends company earnings distributed to shareholders, usually in the form of money or stock

capital gain the profit from the sale of assets such as stocks, bonds, or real estate

common stock a stock whose owner has voting rights and receives dividends based on company profits, paid out after preferred stockholders receive their dividends

preferred stock a stock whose owner has no voting rights, but receives a fixed dividend, paid before common stockholders receive their dividends

A **stock** is an investment in the ownership of a corporation, usually represented by shares of the business. Recall from Chapter 1 that a corporation is a company owned by stockholders (also called shareholders) instead of by a single person or small group of people. When you own stock in a particular company, you actually own part of the company.

A company's profits are paid to its stockholders in the form of **dividends**. If a company's value goes up, the value of its stock goes up as well. If you sell your stock at a higher price, the amount of your profit is called a **capital gain**. If a company's value decreases, on the other hand, so does the value of its stock. If you sell your stock at a lower price, the difference between what you paid for it and your selling price is called a *capital loss.*

Basic Types of Stock

Shares in a company can be issued as common stock or preferred stock. Owners of **common stock** receive dividends based on the company's earnings. They also have voting rights in electing the company's board of directors and deciding other important matters. The board of directors works with other company officials to run the company. Each share of stock has a vote. Major shareholders have more voice in company decisions and in electing the board of directors. For example, if you have 1,000 shares of stock and your neighbor has only ten, you have a much bigger say in what happens and in who gets elected than your neighbor does.

Owners of **preferred stock** receive a fixed dividend. In other words, the preferred stockholder earns the same dividend no matter what kind of profit the company is (or is not) making. If the company is doing poorly and there might not be enough profit to pay all stockholders, owners of preferred stock have first priority. They are paid before the common stockholders. However, if the company makes a huge profit, preferred stockholders still receive only the fixed dividend. Preferred stockholders have no voting rights.

◀ A typical day on the NYSE trading floor includes hundreds of brokers carefully monitoring stock prices and then trading stocks for their investors.

Stocks can be classified in other ways, too. For instance, *income stocks* are stocks that pay high dividends to shareholders. Companies that issue *growth stocks* do not necessarily pay high dividends. Instead, these companies put most of their profits back into the business. People invest in growth stocks in the hope that the value of their shares will increase over time.

The Stock Markets

Stocks are bought and sold on the stock markets (sometimes called the *stock exchanges*). Anyone who has the money to buy a share of stock can invest. The three major stock markets in the United States are the New York Stock Exchange, NASDAQ, and the American Stock Exchange (AMEX). The AMEX market handles about 10 percent of trades. The other two markets are more well known.

The New York Stock Exchange In terms of dollar volume, the **New York Stock Exchange (NYSE)** is the largest exchange in the world. It is also one of the oldest—it began trading securities in the 1790s. In the current age of automation and electronic communication, many financial transactions take place through computer programs and over satellite systems. But the NYSE still has floor traders who conduct many transactions face-to-face.

The NYSE is open Monday through Friday from 9:30 a.m. to 4:00 p.m., Eastern Time. It is closed on most U.S. national holidays. Activity on the trading floor is lively and sometimes chaotic throughout a typical day, as brokers bark out buy and sell orders. There are 1,366 members with trading privileges on the NYSE floor. The NYSE sells licenses to "seat holders" for these privileges. About 3,000 U.S. and foreign companies are listed on the NYSE.

NASDAQ Founded in 1971, **NASDAQ** represents the largest U.S. stock market

New York Stock Exchange (NYSE) the world's largest stock market in terms of dollar volume

NASDAQ the largest U.S. stock market in terms of number of companies listed and number of shares traded per day—all done electronically through a network of computers

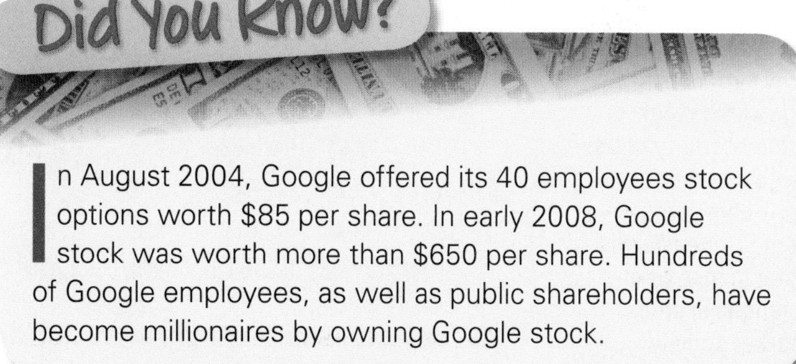

Did You Know?

In August 2004, Google offered its 40 employees stock options worth $85 per share. In early 2008, Google stock was worth more than $650 per share. Hundreds of Google employees, as well as public shareholders, have become millionaires by owning Google stock.

in terms of listings. It has approximately 3,200 companies listed and trades more shares per day than any other U.S. market. NASDAQ is an acronym for the National Association of Securities Dealers Automated Quotations system. Unlike the New York Stock Exchange, where you see floor traders buying and selling stock, NASDAQ is a "virtual" stock exchange, a network of computers.

Newspaper Stock Listings

Before you invest in a stock, you will want to learn more about it. What has it been doing for the past year or so? Has its price been going up, or going down? What kind of dividends does it pay? You can find this information online and in the financial pages of your newspaper (see Figure 7.1). Here is a list of the what you will see there and what the terms mean:

- **52-Week High** shows, in dollars and cents, the highest price paid for one share of the stock during the past fifty-two weeks.
- **52-Week Low** shows the lowest price paid for a share during the past fifty-two weeks.
- **Stock (Ticker)** gives the name of the company and its stock ticker symbol.
- **Div** indicates, in dollars, the amount of the dividend forecasted for the following year.
- **Yield %** indicates the rate of return, which is equal to the dividend per share of stock divided by the closing price.
- **P/E** shows the price-earnings ratio—the closing price per share of stock divided by the company's net earnings per share over the past year.
- **Vol (00s)** indicates the number of shares traded on that particular day, in hundreds.
- **High** is each day's intra-day high trading price.
- **Low** is each day's intra-day low trading price.
- **Close** shows the closing price—the price paid in the final transaction of the day.
- **Net Chg** states the difference between today's closing price and the closing price on the previous day. This number indicates whether the stock's value went up or down in that 24-hour period.

blue-chip stocks safe investments in the ownership of large, respected, and well-established companies

Dow Jones Industrial Average a daily average of the stock prices of thirty of the largest and richest blue-chip companies in the United States, used to measure changes in stock market activity

Figure 7.1 **READING THE STOCK MARKET PAGE OF A NEWSPAPER**

The text above explains how to read and understand listings like these, found in newspapers such as the *Wall Street Journal*.

52W high	52W low	Stock	Ticker	Div	Yield %	P/E	Vol (00s)	High	Low	Close	Net chg
45.39	19.75	ResMed	RMD			57.5	3831	42.00	39.51	41.50	−1.90
11.63	3.55	Revlon A	REV				162	6.09	5.90	6.09	+0.12
77.25	55.13	RioTinto	RTP	2.30	3.2		168	72.75	71.84	72.74	+0.03
31.31	16.63	RitchieBr	RBA			20.9	15	24.49	24.29	24.49	-0.01
8.44	1.75	RiteAid	RAD				31028	4.50	4.20	4.31	+0.21
38.63	18.81	RobtHall	RHI			26.5	6517	27.15	26.50	26.50	+0.14
51.25	27.69	Rockwell	ROK	1.02	2.1	14.5	6412	47.99	47.00	47.54	+0.24

Evaluating Stocks

Blue-chip stocks are safe investments in the ownership of large, respected corporations that have been established for many years—Disney, Coca-Cola, and AT&T, for example. Shareholders in these companies typically receive fairly regular dividends and few surprises. If you are looking for the names of blue-chip companies, there are several places to find them.

Hang on to your stocks! Many stock market analysts say that it is not necessarily a bad thing when the S&P 500 index shows a declining market. A market *correction*—a short-term change in the direction of stock prices—can relieve the excesses of both bull and bear markets.

Dow Jones & Company, which publishes the *Wall Street Journal* and other financial publications, also compiles a list of thirty of the largest and richest blue-chip companies in the United States. It computes a daily average of these companies' stock prices, known as the **Dow Jones Industrial Average**, or simply "the Dow." The Dow quotes the number of points a stock has risen or dropped, not actual stock prices. Each point is equal to one dollar per share. For example, if a stock increases 3 points, it has increased by $3 per share.

As it goes up or down, the Dow is indicating the overall performance of the stock market. A **bull market** exists if investors are generally optimistic about the economy and the market goes up. A **bear market** exists if investors are more pessimistic about the economy and the market goes down.

A benchmark, like the Dow, that measures how the stock market is doing, is called a *stock index*. Economic news, disasters, and other events can drastically shift the Dow. For example, after the 9/11 terrorist attacks, it dropped more than 14 percent.

Another stock index is the **S&P 500 index**, maintained by Standard & Poor's, a division of publisher McGraw-Hill. The S&P index is based on the performance of the top 500 U.S. companies. Standard & Poor's rates these companies in terms of price per share and number of shares owned by the public. Many consider the S&P 500 a better market indicator than the Dow because it includes far more companies than the Dow.

If you want another source of blue-chip company names, every year *Fortune* magazine publishes the **Fortune 500**. This is not a stock index. Instead, it is a list of the top 500 U.S. companies in terms of earnings. Most of these are publicly owned, although a few are privately owned, which means they do not sell stock to the public.

bull market condition that exists when investors are optimistic about the economy and the market goes up

bear market condition that exists when investors are pessimistic about the economy and the market goes down

S&P 500 index an indicator of overall stock market performance based on the average stock prices of 500 top U.S. companies, compiled by Standard & Poor's

Fortune 500 a list of the 500 U.S. companies with highest earnings, published yearly by *Fortune* magazine

◀ **Study a company's annual report to find out if you could receive a high return on your investment.**

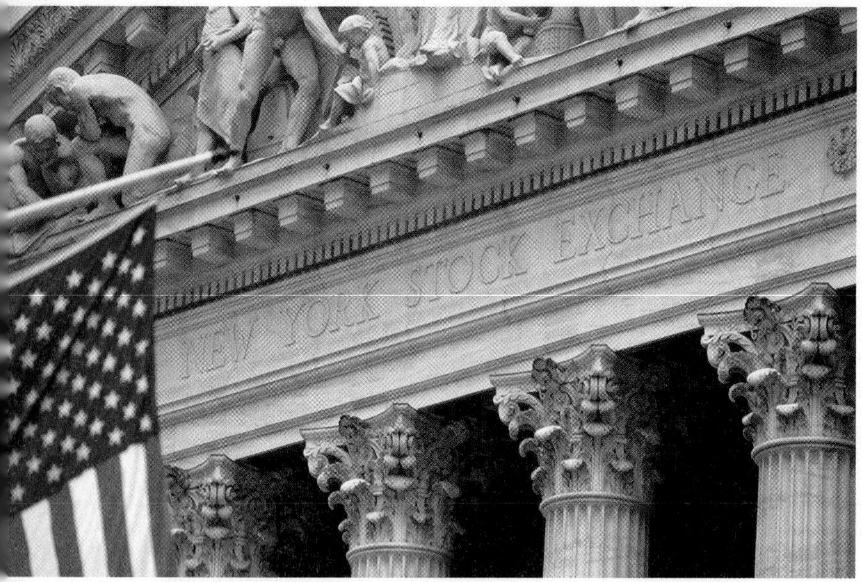

▲ The New York Stock Exchange is one of the oldest and largest stock exchanges in the world.

Risk and Return

Consulting with a financial planner is always a good idea when deciding how to invest your money. Some stocks represent a more risky investment than others. Usually, the greater the potential return on your investment, the greater the risk. How much risk are you willing to take? How much return are you hoping for? These factors will determine the type of stock you buy.

The other aspect of risk and return involves your investment philosophy. Are you buying stocks with the intention of selling them as soon as you make a decent profit? In that case, you might be willing to take a little more risk in order to get a quick return on your money. On the other hand, if you intend to hold the stocks for the long term, you would wait out the smaller ups and downs in stock prices that occur from day to day because you assume that your stocks will grow in value over a long period of time.

Warren Buffett, one of the most successful investors ever, is also one of the most generous. In 2006 he announced that he was giving $37 *billion* to the Bill and Melinda Gates Foundation over the next several years.

futures contracts to buy or sell a specific commodity or financial instrument at a set price on a set date in the future

commodities bulk items such as grains, metals, and food that are bought and sold on a commodities exchange

options contracts that give the owner the right, but not the obligation, to buy or sell a stock or commodity at a set price on or before a specified date

penny stocks high-risk stocks that typically sell for less than $1 per share when they are first offered

Higher-Risk Investments

Futures, options, and penny stocks are all higher-risk investment alternatives that offer the *possibility* of a high return. The high risk, though, can mean that you might not earn much from your investment—and you might even lose some or all of the money you invest.

Futures and Options

Futures are contracts to buy or sell a commodity, stock, or other financial instrument for a set price, at a specific date in the future. **Commodities** are bulk items including agricultural products—such as wheat, corn, or soybeans—as well as livestock, crude oil, heavy metals, and other goods. They are traded on large world commodities exchanges such as the New York Mercantile Exchange, the Chicago Board of Trade, and the London Metal Exchange.

A person investing in futures is basically betting that the price of a particular stock or commodity is going to rise or fall in the future. Because it is difficult to make short-term predictions about the stock market or the commodities market, this is a risky way to invest money.

Options are similar to futures. However, the owner of an option simply has the right—but not the obligation—to buy or sell a specific commodity or stock at a predetermined price, on or before a specific date. An option contract is just that: an option.

Penny Stocks

One type of stock that most investors consider risky is the penny stock. **Penny stocks** are low-priced stocks, usually less than $1 a share. They are issued by start-up companies or by companies that have not demonstrated reli-

Chelsea is a recent college grad with a degree in graphic design. She has no student loans or other debts, and she landed a fantastic job with a magazine publisher in Chicago.

Chelsea rents a nice place near downtown. She prefers public transportation to driving through the traffic-congested streets of the city, which also saves money. Now she wants to invest her savings in stocks.

Chelsea has always been a risk taker. She wants to find an up-and-coming company for her investment. She hopes the stock will take off and earn her a lot of money very fast.

Her father is less of a risk taker. He is trying to persuade her to stick with companies that have a proven track record. She might not earn as much so quickly—but she is less likely to lose money, because a stable company is not likely to fail.

Chelsea begins to investigate. One of her personal values is reducing automobile use in U.S. cities. She discovers that a company manufacturing electric- and battery-powered skateboards recently *went public*—that is, the company began selling stocks. Chelsea's father wants her to make a safer choice. He suggests that she invest her hard-earned money in companies like Apple, Sprint, Nike, or Harley-Davidson.

Chelsea is torn between investing as an adventure, and investing as a money management tool. The unknown company may be famous around the world by next year—or it might be bankrupt. Of course, the blue-chip company might tank as well, though it is less likely to do so.

Should she . . .

1. ...invest in the unknown company that makes a product that fits with her values—even if it means she might lose everything? Support your answer with several reasons.
2. ...play it safe for now, choosing a blue-chip stock for her first investment experience? Why or why not?
3. ...divide her investment dollars and buy some shares in the unknown company and some in a blue-chip company? How might this be a good choice for a first-time experience?

able growth patterns. There are many penny stocks out there—but they are not always easy to find because they are not traded on major markets or tracked in major financial publications.

Penny stocks represent high risk because the company issuing them does not have a proven track record. Many companies that issue penny stocks end up closing. If that happens, the investors lose their money. On the other hand, most companies start out small, and some of them obviously do succeed. If an investor finds a penny-stock company that does well in the long run, he or she could make a lot of money.

Bonds and Securities

Many different organizations sell bonds to raise money. You can buy bonds from corporations, as well as from towns, cities, counties, states, or the federal government.

Basic Types of Bonds

A **bond** is similar to an IOU. Organizations, corporations, and governments sell bonds to borrow money for things like building new facilities, starting new business ventures, or creating new transportation systems. As an

bond a promise to pay a certain amount on a certain date, issued by a corporation or government for the purpose of borrowing money

investor buying the bond, you are essentially lending money to the organization. The issuer of the bond must pay you back—plus interest—when the bond *matures*, or reaches its due date.

Corporate and Municipal Bonds

Corporations sell *corporate bonds*. These bonds must be repaid in full at maturity. In addition, the bond owner receives regular, periodic interest payments over the life of the bond.

Cities, towns, counties, and other local governments sell *municipal bonds*. Like corporate bonds, they must be repaid when they reach maturity. The interest earned on municipal bonds is often tax-exempt—meaning you do not have to pay taxes on the income you earn from the interest.

▼ Investing in Series EE savings bonds any time you receive extra money—such as for graduation or birthday gifts—can earn a lot of money toward your long-term goals.

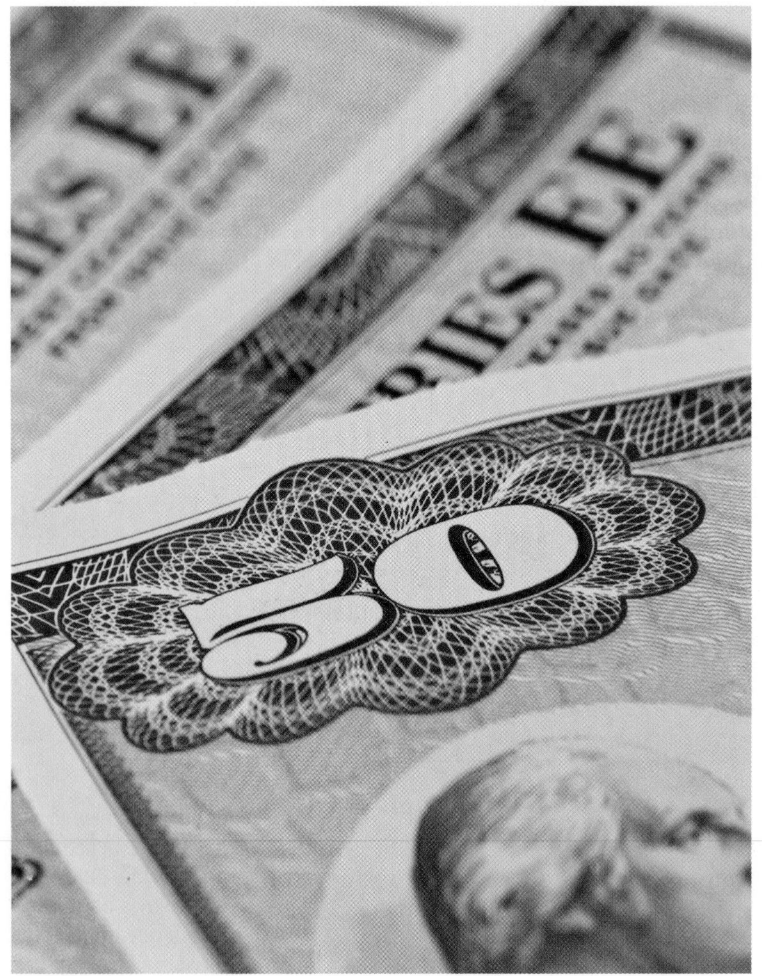

Savings Bonds and T-Bills The U.S. government sells a number of different bonds and securities. The one you may be most familiar with is the Series EE savings bond. Perhaps you received one as a birthday present from a relative or for some other occasion. This type of savings bond can be purchased at a bank or other financial institution for half its *face value*—which is the amount it will be worth when it matures. For example, a $50 Series EE savings bond costs $25.

Electronic EE bonds, purchased on the Internet directly from the Treasury Department, are bought at face value. Interest on the bond adds up over time and is paid when you *redeem* it—or cash it in. You need to keep the bond at least twelve months. After that, you can redeem it at any time, but if you redeem it in the first five years you will forfeit some of the interest. Most Series EE bonds mature in twenty years. If you do not cash in the bond at maturity, it can keep earning additional interest for up to thirty years.

The U.S. government also sells *Treasury bills*, commonly called T-bills. These cost much more than savings bonds. The lowest denomination for a T-bill is $1,000. T-bills mature in relatively short time periods—a year or less. *Treasury notes* and *Treasury bonds* are other investments available from the U.S. Treasury. They are sold in $1,000 denominations, and the maturity rates vary from a few years to thirty years.

Risk and Return

Bonds are popular among some people because they are not as risky as stocks. Investors who want to be certain that they do not lose their money, but who still want to earn some interest, are happy with bonds—particularly government bonds. However, people who are looking for a large return on their investment may not

Do Your RESEARCH

For as long as he could remember, C.J. had been getting savings bonds as birthday and holiday gifts. He even received a couple *before* he could remember—from grandparents and great-grandparents upon his birth in 1995. When C.J. was 12, he asked his parents if he could cash in the savings bonds to buy a new snowboard. They advised him not to redeem them yet. Instead, C.J. and his parents set up a plan to save for the snowboard. C.J.'s parents agreed to match his deposits, and soon he had enough to buy a new snowboard.

When C.J. turned 16, he asked about cashing in the bonds—this time to buy a car. Again, his parents advised him to hold onto the bonds so they would keep earning interest. Once again, C.J. formed a plan to save for his car and keep earning interest on his savings bonds.

After graduating, C.J. went on to college and stopped thinking about the bonds. After college, he got a good job and bought a small house. Eventually he met a young woman and became engaged. C.J.'s parents and his fiancée's parents helped with the wedding costs, but the couple really wanted to go on a romantic honeymoon. C.J. thought about the savings bonds. There would not be enough money from the bonds for a nice trip—or would there?

Look at the accompanying table. It shows the value of C.J.'s savings bonds from the time they were purchased until 2025. Even relatively small amounts in savings can really add up over time!

Your Assignment

1. What is the total value of the bonds in 2025? What was their total value in 2007?
2. Assume you purchased a $25 EE savings bond every month for 25 years. How much would you have at the end of that time? What if you bought a $100 EE savings bond each month—how much would you have after 25 years? Use the Growth Calculator on the Web site of the U.S. Treasury (http://fin.emcp.net/growthcalc) to see. Assume an initial investment of $100, an interest rate of 3 percent, and a federal tax rate of 28 percent.

C.J.'S SAVINGS BONDS

Year purchased	Type of savings bond	Value in 2007	Value in 2025	Number of bonds	Total value in 2025
1995	Series EE $100	$85	$328	3	$984
1995	Series EE $50	$42	$164	4	$656
1996	Series EE $100	$78	$315	2	$630
1996	Series EE $50	$39	$158	2	$316
1997	Series EE $100	$75	$303	3	$909
1998	Series EE $50	$37	$146	2	$292
2000	Series EE $50	$34	$135	5	$675
2002	Series EE $100	$70	$250	2	$500
2003	Series EE $50	$30	$120	2	$240
2005	Series EE $100	$60	$225	5	$1,125

be as concerned about losing some money from time to time if the long-term outlook is promising. They may choose other investment opportunities.

Mutual Funds

A **mutual fund** is an investment in which people pool their money to buy stocks, bonds, real estate, or other assets. This collection of assets is called a *portfolio.* Investors buy shares in the portfolio, which is maintained by a professional manager who receives a fee from the investors.

A mutual fund allows an individual to *diversify,* which means spreading money among several different investments. Diversifying is the opposite of putting all your money into a single investment. Smart investors diversify to help protect themselves against major losses.

Different funds have different specialties, each with varying degrees of risk and return. For example, some funds specialize in growth stocks. Others specialize mainly in different types of bonds.

Investing in a Mutual Fund

To invest in a mutual fund, you must choose a fund manager. Companies that offer fund management include Fidelity, Schwab, and Vanguard. Then you have to choose a specific fund for your investment. Most importantly, you need the money to invest. Most mutual funds require at least $500 to get started—and usually between $1,000 and $10,000.

mutual fund an investment in which people pool their money to buy stocks, bonds, real estate, or other assets selected by professional managers

Another important aspect—especially if you are a first-time investor—is deciding which mutual funds best fit your financial goals and objectives. In addition to consulting a financial adviser, you might also want to check an objective publication like the *Morningstar* newsletter, *Money* magazine, or *Forbes* to help you sort through all the choices.

Mutual funds are rated by analyzing risk and return. You can also find information on how various mutual funds have performed over the last one, three, five and ten years. Different types of funds have different performance records.

Socially Responsible Mutual Funds

In the past few years, socially responsible investing (SRI) has grown exponentially around the world, particularly in the U.S. This approach to investing takes many things into account, but especially the so-called ESG (environmental, social, and governance) factors. Many mutual fund companies include socially responsible mutual funds among their offerings. Some of the most common SRI fund groups are Calvert, Pax World Funds, Green Century Funds, and Ariel Mutual Funds.

Here are some guidelines to determine if a mutual fund company invests in a fund that is socially responsible:

1. The fund does not invest in such industries as tobacco, alcohol, pornography, gambling, or military production. It also rules out companies whose business activities include environmental pollution, human rights violations, community neglect, and poor employee relations.
2. The fund seeks to include companies with good ESG performance, and it bases its portfolio analysis and management on these companies' continued ESG policies.
3. The fund uses its shareholder power, if necessary, to influence corporate behavior. An example of how SRI has influenced not just business but also government policy occurred during the apartheid (segregation)

▲ Socially responsible mutual fund companies may invest in alternative energy sources like windmills or solar panels.

era in South Africa. Many socially responsible funds in the United States began to *divest*—to remove their investments from companies operating in South Africa. This economic pressure finally forced South African businesses to call for an end to apartheid.

4. The fund engages in socially responsible lending—screening potential borrowers for ESG factors and denying loans to companies that ignore ESG regulations.

Load vs. No-Load Funds Mutual funds also involve a variety of fees. Understanding how these fees work is important because it might influence your total return.

Some funds are called **no-load funds**. This means you do not pay any up-front fees to invest. You buy the shares directly from the fund company rather than through a broker. Others are called **load funds**, and you buy them through a brokerage firm or other sales representative. For these, you are re-quired to pay a percentage of your investment every time shares are bought or sold—it could be as much as 8.5 percent. The advantage is that with a load fund, the broker explains the fund and gives advice on when it might be a good time to buy or sell shares. The fee is in exchange for this extra service.

You might think that if you pay a fee, you will not earn as high a return on your money. Although that might be true, it is not always the case. At the end of the day, what matters is how different funds perform after all expenses are factored in. Again, this is where sources like *Morningstar* can be very helpful. Such sources have already done most of the homework on comparing mutual funds in various categories. The earlier you get in the habit of researching your

no-load funds mutual funds that do not require an up-front fee

load funds mutual funds that charge a commission every time shares are bought or sold

investments, the better you will be at making smart investment decisions.

Index Funds Earlier in the chapter, you learned about stock indexes—the Dow Jones Industrial Average and the S&P 500 index, for example. An *index fund* is a mutual fund whose portfolio matches one of the stock indexes. Standard & Poor's offers an index fund called the Standard & Poor's Depositary Receipts (SPDR Trust). The acronym SPDR led to the term *Spider.* An investor can buy into the fund by purchasing a Spider, which costs one-tenth of the index. For example, if the index is at 1,600, one share in the fund would cost $160.

Several other index funds also track the S&P 500. In addition, there are a variety of index funds designed to match the Dow Jones Industrial Average and other stock indexes such as the Wilshire 5000 and the Russell 2000.

Risk and Return

Like stocks and bonds, mutual funds vary in the level of risk and return they offer. Obviously, buying a mutual fund that specializes in growth stocks is a safer investment than putting all your money in a single stock. Because a mutual fund invests in a variety of companies, if one stock in the fund does poorly it will not completely wipe out your investment. On the other hand, if you put all your money in that one poorly performing stock, you might lose it all. The return on your mutual fund investment depends on the performance of the fund *as a whole* rather than on the performance of an individual stock.

Mutual funds can be characterized as either *growth funds* or *income funds.* A growth fund goes up in value over a longer period of time. This is because the fund contains growth stocks—issued by companies that reinvest their profits in the growth of the company, rather than by paying huge dividends to investors. If you invest in a growth fund, you will not count on dividends. Instead, your profit will come when you sell your shares in the future. Income funds, on the other hand, pay out interest in the form of dividends on a regular basis.

Do your homework before you invest. Warren Buffett became a successful investor for two key reasons: (1) he always did his homework before investing, and (2) he was patient—in other words, he did not expect to make loads of money overnight.

▼ **Licensed traders quickly wave their hands to buy and sell stocks from the NYSE floor. Would you prefer to invest on your own or to hire a brokerage firm to invest for you?**

Time Value of Money

All the investments discussed in this section and the next are connected to the *time value of money.* The time value of money assumes that an investor would rather receive a fixed amount of money today than an equivalent amount in the future. If you had the money now, you could invest it or deposit it in an interest-bearing bank account—where it would earn interest. Then, at that future date, it would be worth more than it is now. If you fail to invest and earn interest, it does not matter when you receive the money—now or in the future. By failing to invest, you would have wasted time by not increasing your initial amount. But if you invest and earn interest now, you take advantage of time by using the time to earn interest. This is called the time value of money.

Consider this example. Bob and Sheila work for the same company. Bob works in the marketing department and has been with the company for almost fifteen years. During that time, he had several opportunities to enroll in the company retirement program, but he never did. Instead, he spent money on a new boat for his family, a new car for his son, and several family vacations.

On his 45th birthday, Bob decided it was time to take the leap and invest $250 a month ($8 a day) in the retirement plan. Bob felt he had plenty of time to sock away enough money for his retirement—after all, he would not be retiring for another twenty years.

When Sheila started working for the company, she learned during employee orientation that she was eligible immediately to start investing in the retirement plan. She was only 25 at the time and was earning much less than Bob. But when Sheila was growing up, her parents told her that "time was her greatest ally" when investing money for the future. She decided to start investing $250 a month right away. After twenty years, she stopped contributing to the fund and let the interest accumulate. See Figure 7.2 for a good picture of how the time value of money worked for Sheila.

Figure 7.2 TIME VALUE OF MONEY: THE COST OF WAITING

Bob and Sheila saved the same amount of money for the same period of time, earning the same interest rate. The difference is that Sheila started saving at age 25, then stopped at age 45. Bob started saving at age 45. When they were ready to retire at 65, you can see how the time value of money enhanced Sheila's retirement fund!

	Sheila: age 25	Bob: age 45
Annual investment	$3,000 ($8/day)	$3,000 ($8/day)
Time	20 years	20 years
Rate of return	6% annually	6% annually
Value at age 65	$353,929	$110,357

The figure really tells the story. Even though Sheila stopped investing at age 45 and let her money accumulate for the next twenty years, she is still well ahead of Bob at age 65. The moral of the story: Nothing makes money like time.

You can learn more about this concept by visiting It All Adds Up, the Web site of the National Council on Economic Education, at http://fin.emcp.net/italladdsup.

SECTION 1 ASSESSMENT

Factual Recall

1. What are stock dividends?
2. What is a capital gain?
3. What are the three major stock markets in the United States?
4. True or False: Only governments can sell bonds.
5. What are ESG factors?

Critical Thinking

1. Suppose you bought some shares of stock. In what two ways could you get money from your investment?
2. Which type of stock is characteristic of a new company: growth or income? Why?
3. What is the main difference between a share of stock and a bond?

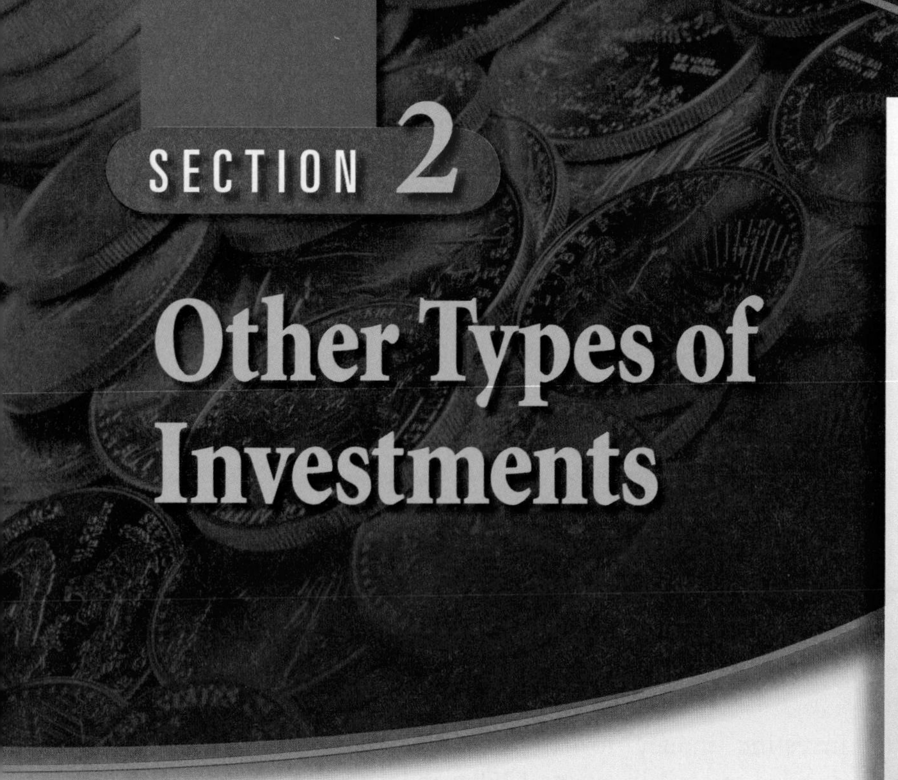

SECTION 2

Other Types of Investments

Focus Questions

1. What should you consider before investing in real estate?
2. What are some sources of retirement income in addition to Social Security?

Key Terms

real estate
collectibles
pension
vested
profit-sharing plan
stock-bonus plan
401(k) plan
403(b) plan
individual retirement account (IRA)
Roth IRA
Simplified Employee Pension (SEP-IRA)

People invest in a variety of things besides stocks and bonds, hoping to make some extra money. Smart investors develop specific plans—in addition to their savings accounts—to save for retirement.

Real Estate and Collectibles

Some investors put money into **real estate**—land and the houses or other buildings that are on it. Rental properties, such as apartment buildings, are common real estate investments. People also invest in single-family homes, vacation or retirement homes, business property, and vacant land with no buildings.

Investing in real estate often requires more than just an investment of money—it can also involve the owner's time. An owner of a rental property, for example, has to maintain the property's condition, including plumbing, electricity, heating and cooling, roof, and so forth.

real estate land and any houses or other buildings that are on it

collectibles items that appeal to collectors and investors, including stamps, works of art, antiques, and sports memorabilia

Some people like to put money in nontraditional investments, such as coins, antiques, art, sports memorabilia, and other **collectibles**. This can be an enjoyable way to invest money. As a collector, you can gain knowledge and happiness from buying and selling things you are passionate about. On the other hand, the market for selling collectibles is usually very small. Most people are not willing to pay what you believe a particular item is worth. Assigning value to collectibles, therefore, is difficult and unpredictable.

Before committing your money to a real estate venture, ask yourself and then do the research to answer questions like these:

- What changes are occurring in this neighborhood or area? Are there any pending changes in regulations, land-use policies, or zoning?
- Is this property equivalent in value to other properties in the area?
- What is the main reason I am considering this property? Do I want to live here, or is it solely for investment purposes?

- What kind of mortgage will I need (interest rate and length of term) to make this a profitable venture?
- Will I be able to afford the mortgage if the interest rate moves up?

The return on a real estate investment can vary greatly. People who invest in rental property are typically interested in the property as a long-term investment. It will often provide a steady income, but there is a risk that you might not get back the cost of your initial investment for many years—especially if you had to invest additional money up front to fix up the property. Also, you will have to factor in the cost of ongoing maintenance when determining the return on your investment. It is possible that if you invest in land and hold it for a period of years, and later sell it to a developer, you could see a huge return on your money.

▲ Investing in real estate is one way to enhance your savings.

Retirement and Estate Planning

One of the major reasons people save and invest money is to have funds available for their retirement. A majority of working adults hope someday to retire from their careers so they can travel, learn new skills, try new hobbies, and spend more time with family and friends.

Estate Planning

Many people continue to save and invest even *after* retirement so that they can leave money to their children or to a special cause. These people receive enjoyment from knowing that even after they have passed on, they will be making a positive contribution to people and causes that they care about.

The process of taking steps to maximize your wealth and to transfer it to others after your death is called *estate planning.* In legal terms your *estate* is everything that you own (and owe, if you have debts) at the time of death.

An effective estate plan clearly explains what you want to have happen with all the things you own at the end of your life. An important part of this plan is creating ways to transfer money and possessions in such a way that those receiving the money pay the minimum amount of taxes. For families with young children, deciding who should be the children's guardian should the parents die while the children are young is also very important.

Some estate plans include *trusts.* A trust is a legal arrangement in which one person manages money and property for the benefit of another. One common reason for creating trusts is to protect money for minors until they are old enough manage it themselves. Another reason is to minimize or avoid taxes. Trusts and other aspects of estate planning aimed at reducing taxes are often referred to as *tax shelters.*

The details of the estate plan and any trust that exists are spelled out in a *will.* A will, which people often refer to as a person's "last will and testament," is the legal document that tells your survivors

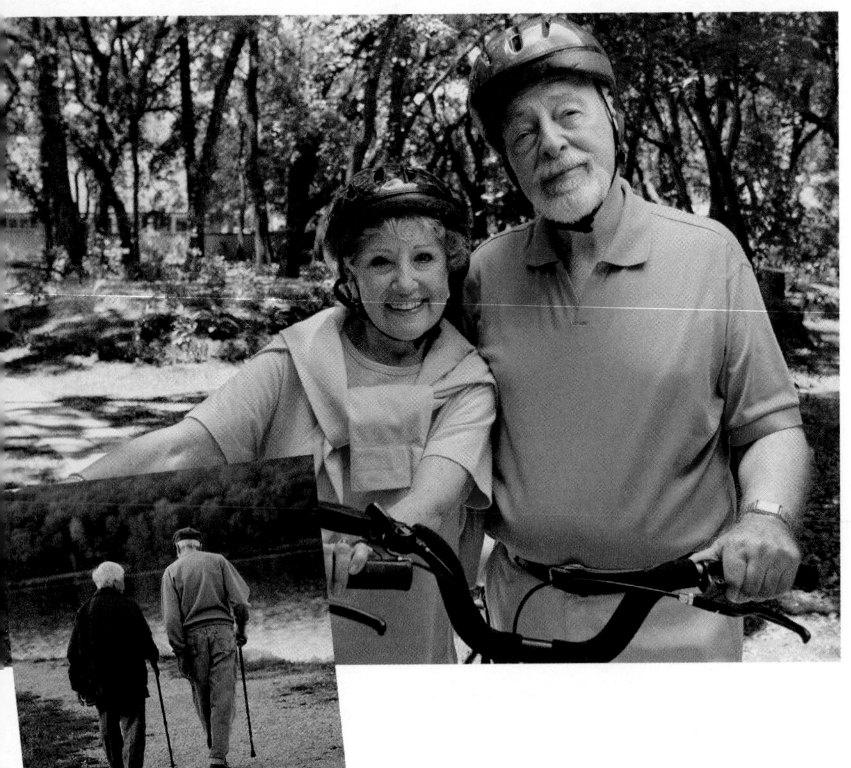

▲ People who save responsibly for retirement have a good chance of enjoying peace of mind, security, and happiness during their retirement years.

how you want your money and property distributed after your death. It spells out your estate plan and any other last wishes you might want carried out.

Most states require that your will be signed, witnessed, and notarized, although, contrary to popular belief, you need not have an attorney write your will. The larger your estate, however, the more important it is to have a knowledgeable attorney or financial advisor help you with all of your estate planning issues.

Did You Know?

Half of all working Americans aged 55 and older have accumulated less than $50,000 for retirement. It is a stunningly low number when you consider the high cost of health insurance and all the other financial unknowns that go with retirement. How can this be? One of the top reasons older Americans give for their retirement shortfall is that they didn't make it a priority in their early working years. Don't make the same mistake—plan for your retirement success by investing early and often.

When Should You Start Saving?

Your life is unpredictable. You cannot know how long you will live—but you can assume that you will live for many years after you retire. Likely, you would want to have as much money coming in after retirement as you did before. Recall the time value of money. The sooner you start putting money away for retirement, the more years you will be earning interest on it. And the longer you invest, the less you will have to put away each year.

Imagine that you are earning $100,000 per year at your job when you decide to retire at age 65. Chances are you would not want to go from a $100,000-per-year lifestyle to a lifestyle that goes with, say, only $20,000. You will probably get some income from Social Security. You might get some from a pension or profit-sharing plan offered by the company where you were employed. But everything else will have to come from your own savings and investments. Your retirement investments probably have to supply about half of your $100,000 income after you retire. In that case, you will have to have a retirement investment portfolio worth at least $1 million!

Surveys have shown that most people do not start saving for retirement until they are in their fifties. But if you wait until you are 50 to start putting away that $1 million, it will cost you a huge chunk of your paycheck—around $2,500 each month. But if you begin investing for retirement at an early age, say 25, you can meet the same $1 million goal by putting away just a little more than $125 each month.

To see how various retirement scenarios will play out, go to http://fin.emcp.net/choosetosave, the Web site of the Choose to Save education and outreach program and click on Ball-

Get Good Advice

Cheryl is a high school senior, planning to study business in college. Last summer, Cheryl, her brother Darnell, and their parents attended a family reunion in Washington, D.C. At the reunion, Cheryl particularly enjoyed talking with her Aunt Reatha. She wanted to know all about Aunt Reatha's experience working for a Fortune 500 company.

Cheryl listened intently as Aunt Reatha described how she rose in the ranks—from sales rep to manager, and eventually to president of her division. It took a lot of hard work and dedication, and whenever possible she went the extra mile to learn new skills. Aunt Reatha explained that when new opportunities came along—such as increased responsibilities or managing more people—she wanted to prove she was ready for any new challenge.

Cheryl was also curious how Aunt Reatha had managed to retire at the relatively young age of 59. Her aunt's response was straightforward and also very practical: "I started early, investing in the company retirement plan, and I also got the advice of an experienced financial professional to help me sort through my options." That is excellent advice.

Like Cheryl, seek out a money mentor or someone in your family who is good at managing money. Ask that person about his or her own investing history and see what you can learn. Here is what Cheryl asked Aunt Reatha at the reunion:

1. At what age did you make your first investment in the stock market?
2. Did your company offer a retirement plan? If so, did you participate in it?
3. What has been your biggest investment mistake?
4. What has been your biggest investment success?
5. What advice would you give a young person about investing for the future?
6. If you had it to do over again, what one thing would you do differently with respect to your overall investment plan?
7. Do you have an investment adviser?
8. Who helped you learn about investing? Was it a family member, a friend, or a professional?
9. What tools (the Internet, magazines, investment shows on radio or TV) do you read or watch, and how have they helped you?

Cheryl was very wise to take advantage of the family reunion—and more important, wise to seek out Aunt Reatha to get her perspective on working and investing. Note that Cheryl did not ask her aunt how much money she had. That would not be appropriate. Instead, Cheryl asked how Aunt Reatha learned about investing and asked about some of her mistakes and accomplishments. Sometimes the best learning opportunities about money come from the people in your own family.

park E$timate. The Ballpark E$timate is an easy-to-use, two-page worksheet. It will quickly estimate approximately how much you need to save if you want to have a comfortable retirement. The Ballpark E$timate takes complicated issues like future Social Security benefits and future interest earnings on savings—and turns them into language and numbers that are easy to understand.

Sources of Retirement Income

Retirement income typically comes from a variety of sources, including plans managed by the government, by employers, and by the retirees themselves.

Social Security Social Security provides retirement, disability, survivorship, and death benefits to people in the United States. The U.S. government has sponsored the Social Security system since 1935 when Congress passed the Social Security Act. The program is funded by payroll taxes, under authority of the Federal Insurance Contributions Act (FICA). These taxes are therefore called *FICA taxes*. As you learned in Chapter 2, your employer will match the amount of your FICA contributions.

The amount of Social Security income you will collect when you retire is based on the amount of money you pay into the system during your working years. However, Social Security contributions are not like a savings account. The money you put in is not "yours." Today's contributions are used to pay today's benefits. When you retire, your benefits will come from FICA taxes paid by people in the workforce at that time.

pension a retirement plan that is funded at least in part by an employer

vested being eligible to receive a pension or other employer-contributed benefits, usually after working at a company for a certain number of years

Most years, the government collects more money from FICA taxes than it pays out in benefits. The leftover money is put in the Social Security Trust Fund. This money is invested and saved for the years when not enough FICA money is collected. So far there have been only eleven years when Social Security did not collect enough in FICA taxes to pay the current year's benefits. In those years, Social Security Trust Fund money made up the difference.

▶ **Social Security partially funds the retirement of U.S. citizens. The amount of Social Security income you receive when you retire is based on the amount of money you pay into the system while you are working.**

The Social Security system has been controversial almost since it began. Early on, some objected to such a large-scale government program. Over the years, some have wanted to use the money in the Social Security Trust Fund for other purposes. But lately the issues surrounding Social Security have become even more serious. It remains uncertain whether the system is adequately funded for the future, that is, whether today's wage earners will even see Social Security benefits when they retire.

Keep in mind that Social Security benefits are not intended to be your entire retirement income—but merely to supplement it. This is an important factor in the retirement plans of most people. Keeping on top of new information regarding the Social Security system will help you understand how it may be part of your retirement planning.

Company-Sponsored Retirement Plans Many retirement plans are sponsored by employers. The employer might even make some payments into an employee's account as a fringe benefit. Here are some of the most common employer-sponsored retirement plans:

- A **pension** is a company-sponsored retirement plan that is funded at least in part by the employer. The amount the employer contributes is usually based on the employee's salary. The money put into the pension fund is invested and saved for the employee's retirement.

  In most pension plans (and other employer-based plans) an employee has to be **vested** in the company—officially eligible to receive employer-contributed benefits—before he or she can take possession of the money in the account. To become vested, an employee usually has to remain with

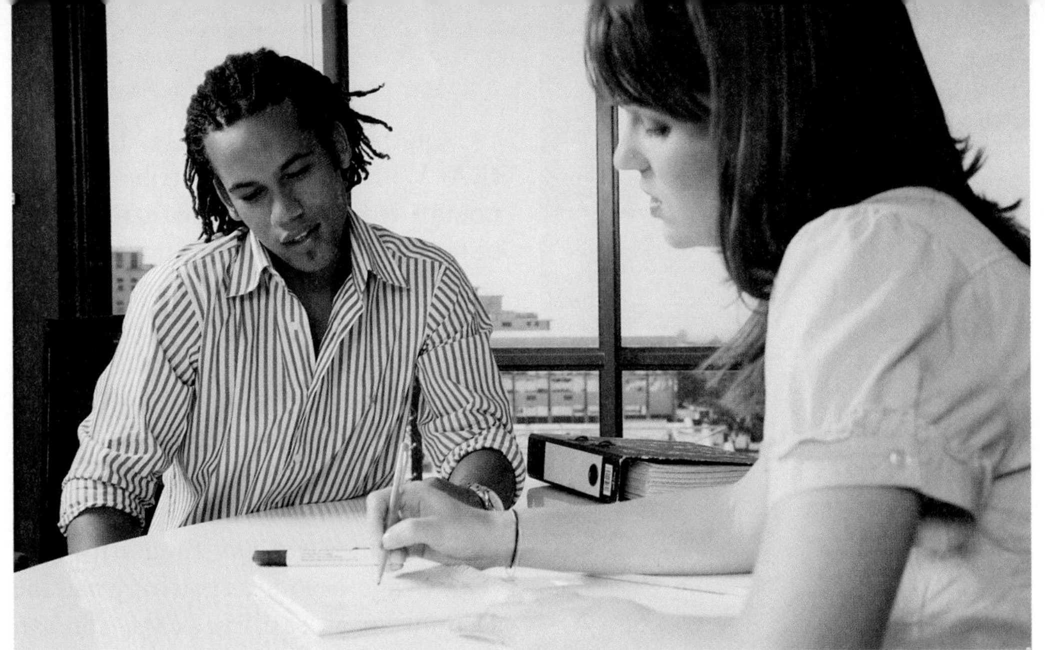

◀ Employees with little investment experience often decide on the best retirement plan after talking with a counselor from Human Resources or the brokerage firm that manages the company's retirement plan.

the company for a certain number of years.

▶ A **profit-sharing plan** is an employer-funded program that allows employees to share in company profits. The employer makes contributions to each employee's account based on the company's earnings.
▶ A **stock-bonus plan** is a type of profit-sharing plan in which the employer rewards the employee with company stock instead of cash. At retirement, the employee can either sell the stock or keep it as a source of income from dividends.
▶ A **401(k) plan** is funded by the employee. The employer offers various investment options but the employee decides how to invest the money. A 401(k) is a *tax-deferred* plan: Contributions are withheld from the employee's paycheck *before taxes*—thus reducing the employee's current taxable income—and the funds grow tax-free until they are withdrawn.

Many companies match their employees' contributions up to a certain amount. For example, if you choose to put $50 per paycheck into your 401(k) account, your employer might add an additional $50 per paycheck.

▶ A **403(b) plan** is similar to a 401(k) but covers employees of public schools and other tax-exempt organizations.

A recent development in company-sponsored 401(k) plans is something called the *opt-out provision*. Originally, all 401(k) plans were structured on an opt-in basis. This meant it was the employees' option to get in—they had to sign up if they wanted to participate in the plan. That sounds easy enough, but many employees would put it off far too long and miss out on valuable years when they should have been investing in the plan (again, recall the earlier discussion on the time value of money).

With an opt-out provision, employees are automatically enrolled from the first day of their employment, and they must opt out if they do not want to participate. More and more companies are now shifting their 401(k) plans to this opt-out mode and employee participation is indeed growing.

This is a welcome shift because too many workers would otherwise continue to put off saving for retirement. According to a 2007 survey by the Employee Benefit Research Institute, almost half of workers saving for retirement report that they have put away or invested less than $25,000.

profit-sharing plan a retirement plan that allows employees to share in the company's profits

stock-bonus plan a type of profit-sharing plan in which the employer rewards employees with company stock instead of cash

401(k) plan a tax-deferred retirement plan funded by regular contributions from the employee

403(b) plan a tax-deferred retirement plan for employees of public schools and tax-exempt organizations

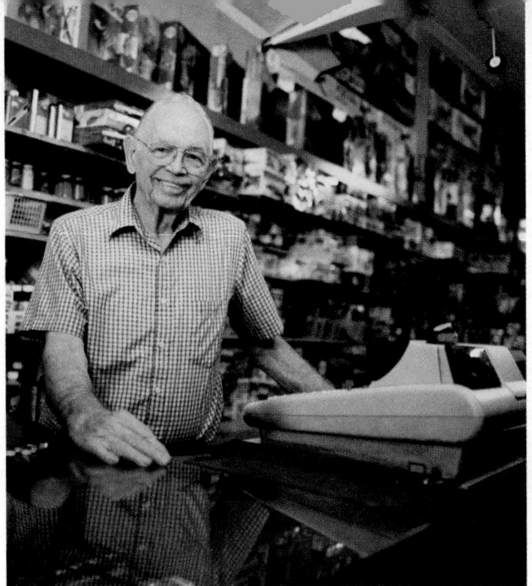

▶ **Simplified Employee Pension plans and IRAs reward smart, disciplined investors.**

individual retirement account (IRA) a personal retirement plan that permits individuals to set aside money; with the contributions and earnings not taxed until the funds are withdrawn

Roth IRA a personal retirement plan in which the original contributions are not tax-deductible, but the earnings are tax-free

Simplified Employee Pension (SEP-IRA) a tax-deferred retirement plan for small businesses and self-employed people, in which the employer makes contributions directly to employee IRA accounts

Other Ways to Save for Retirement

There are a number of other investment opportunities you can use to save for retirement. Lots of people—especially those who are self-employed or who work for companies that do not have a retirement program—invest in personal retirement plans.

The most common form of personal retirement plan is the **individual retirement account (IRA)**. With a traditional IRA, you can make annual contributions until you reach 70½ years of age. Unless your income is more than a certain amount, all or part of your contributions are tax deductible. The earnings are taxed only when you begin to withdraw the money at retirement. As of 2008, you can contribute up to $5,000 each year.

Another popular IRA is the **Roth IRA**. With this plan, contributions are not tax deductible, but the earnings will be tax-free when you withdraw the funds at retirement. The maximum amount you can contribute is the same as for a traditional IRA, with certain income restrictions.

You can continue making contributions to a Roth IRA even after you are 70½ years old, and you can start taking money out any time after 59½ years of age, as long as you have had the account for at least five years. You can also withdraw money from a Roth IRA to pay for qualified first-time homebuyer expenses—even before you are 59½ years old—if you have had the account for at least five years. A lot of young people are opening Roth IRAs to get a jump on investing.

A **Simplified Employee Pension (SEP-IRA)** provides a way for employees of small businesses and self-employed people to invest for retirement. Employees of a small business set up their own IRA accounts, and then the employer contributes directly to those accounts. For a small business, this is a practical alternative to an expensive pension plan. Contributions are fully tax deductible by the employer, and so are the earnings on those contributions. Self-employed individuals can set up their own SEP-IRAs and contribute in the same way.

SECTION 2 ASSESSMENT

Factual Recall

1. Investing in real estate often requires more than money. What else might be required?
2. Name four sources of retirement income besides Social Security.
3. Besides retirement income, what kinds of benefits does Social Security provide?
4. What are FICA taxes?
5. Who can participate in SEP-IRA plans?

Critical Thinking

1. Are collectibles a good investment? Why or why not?
2. Your cousin says that the amount of money you receive from Social Security will be equal to the amount you paid in, plus interest. Is he right? Explain your answer.

SECTION 3

Advice, Information, and Transactions

Focus Questions

1. How can people learn more about investing?
2. Where can investors find written information about a particular company and its stock?

Key Terms

broker
financial adviser
annual report

You can get advice and find information about investing from many different sources. Consulting more than one or two will give you several perspectives on investing your money.

Brokers, Advisers, and Planners

There are people in the business world who earn a living by telling people how to invest their money, when to invest it, and how much to invest. Many of these people provide valuable services to their clients. A few provide poor services. Finding the person who is right for you may take some work.

A **broker** works for a company called a brokerage firm. Brokers buy and sell stocks, bonds, and securities for their clients. A *full-service broker* will also provide clients with investment information and advice on how to invest. A *discount broker* works mainly with investors who need very little advice. Discount brokers charge less than full-service brokers, but they do not provide the knowledge base or the advice that a full-service broker offers. Popular brokerage firms include Merrill Lynch, Charles Schwab, Ameritrade, and Piper Jaffray.

A **financial adviser**, or *financial planner*, has the knowledge and capability to give extensive investment advice. Financial advisers tailor their advice to fit the individual client's financial goals, stage in life, income, budget, family situation, assets and liabilities, and other factors. Many charge an hourly rate. Some charge varying fees for different services. Still others charge a commission on the

broker a person who works for a brokerage firm and who buys and sells stocks, bonds, and securities for clients

financial adviser a person with the knowledge to give financial advice based on the client's goals, income, debts and assets, stage in life, and other personal factors

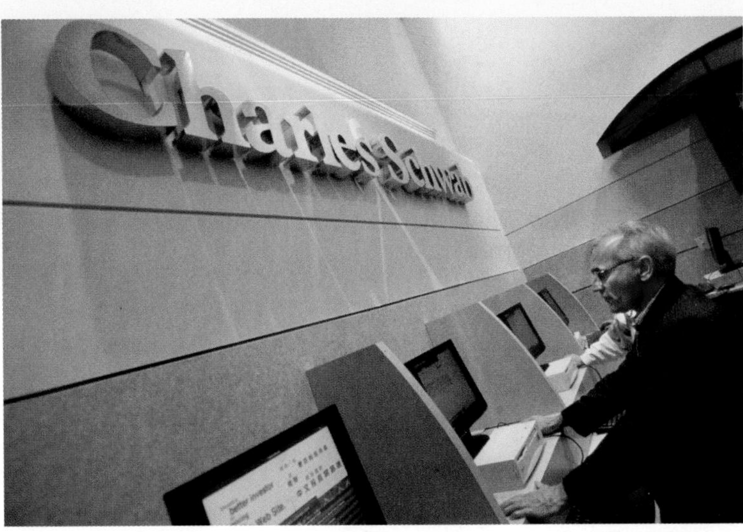

▼ **Brokerage firms help you invest your money wisely.**

sales they make on behalf of the client. Before choosing a financial planner, make sure you understand how he or she will be paid.

When choosing a person to help you with your financial planning, it is important that you select someone you can trust. Consider more than just the fee. Make sure you understand the person's educational background and experience. Is the person licensed? What type of investing does the person seem to prefer? Will this person take risks that you are uncomfortable with, or fail to listen to your input? What are his or her specialties, or areas of expertise? Will the person give you references?

Publications and Web Sites

Numerous publications—both print and online—can give you financial information. Newspapers and magazines like the *Wall Street Journal*, *Money*, and *Forbes* provide financial information and analysis of stocks and other investments. Your daily newspaper also has a business section with this kind of information. Standard & Poor's and Moody's Investors Service also offer financial planning publications with useful information on investing.

annual report a detailed report about the financial condition of a company, published each year

All publicly traded companies publish four quarterly reports and an **annual report** containing financial information about the company. Many of these reports can be found on the Web site of the Securities and Exchange Commission (SEC) at http://fin.emcp.net/sec.

Other online resources are—as you can imagine—abundant. Here are some of the most popular Web sites that provide information to investors:

- The Motley Fool (http://fin.emcp.net/motleyfool) offers stock market information and advice with a dose of humor.
- TeenVestor (http://fin.emcp.net/teenvestor) has a wealth of investment, business, and planning information and advice for young people.
- The National Association of Investors Corporation is a nonprofit organization that offers investment information through its BetterInvesting Web site (http://fin.emcp.net/betterinvesting).

Did You Know?

Because of inflation and increasing interest rates, the number of millionaires is on the rise. In 2006, Merrill Lynch reported that there were 8.7 million millionaires worldwide and 2.9 million in North America. Europe and Asia have the second and third largest population of millionaires. The rate is increasing rapidly in the Middle East, which is home to more than 300,000 millionaires. What does the increase in the number of millionaires mean to the financial community? to society? to you?

Getting Started

If you have some extra money in your saving or checking accounts—maybe you inherited some money, won the lottery, or received a birthday check—you are ready to begin investing. If you have at least $500 to $1,000, you can probably make a nice initial investment in some stock or in a mutual fund.

How do you get started? First, determine what kind of investor you are. Generally, younger people are more willing to take risks than older people are, because younger people have more time to invest. Older people tend to be more conservative. They want to make sure they do not lose the money they have accumulated over decades.

The two main ways of investing for the first time are to buy stocks or mutual funds. Many mutual funds require a

You Can Succeed Financially

As you use your money management skills to improve your financial future, you might discover a talent for financial matters. In that case, you can put your skills to work in another way—with a career in financial planning.

Financial advisers help people plan their financial futures and achieve their financial goals. They work with people of all ages and income levels—assisting them by setting up financial plans, beginning savings programs, or investing money for college and retirement. Many financial advisers work for large financial service companies like Ameriprise, UBS, and Wachovia. Some work for smaller banks and credit unions. Others own their own financial planning firm.

What are the qualifications? Most financial advisers have a college education, many with degrees in business, mathematics, or the liberal arts. All good financial advisers have a solid understanding of finance, banking, investing, and the stock market. They are up-to-date on current laws and trends in retirement accounts, college planning, and health care. And of course they understand cultural issues—like why it seems so hard to save and invest but so easy to spend, spend, spend. Additionally, the best advisers

have excellent interpersonal skills—in other words, they can relate and communicate well with others.

Some financial advisers become Certified Financial Planners® by passing the education, experience, and ethical requirements of the Certified Financial Planner Board of Standards. Like attorneys and accountants, financial advisers are required by law to complete a certain amount of continuing education credits each year. Their money management skills can help others—*and* themselves: financial advisers can earn an excellent living.

What Would You Do?

1. Does a career in financial planning interest you? Visit the Web site of the Certified Financial Planner Board of Standards (http://fin.emcp.net/cfp) and investigate the requirements for becoming certified by the CFP Board.
2. Assume you are finished with college and have been working for a year or two. You would like to increase your investments but are not sure where to start. Describe the steps you would take to find a financial adviser you could trust.

fairly large investment, but you can buy into some with a minimum investment of just $250 to $1,000. If you are younger than 18, your mutual fund account will probably be a *custodial* account—one that you open with a parent or guardian.

Choose a fund that you like and send the money to the fund manager. Then watch and wait. The fund manager makes all the decisions, so you will not need to be especially vigilant about how the fund is doing. It is a good idea, though, to check from time to time at the fund's Web site or by reading periodic account statements that you will receive.

If you want a more hands-on approach to investing, you may decide to put your money into the stock market. An easy way to invest in the stock market is to open an account with a discount

YOU DECIDE

The average wedding these days costs the bride and groom and their families an average of $27,000. Of course you have the wedding dress, rings, cake, flowers, reception, band, and other "standard" amenities. But people also fork over thousands of dollars on extra costs like wedding planners, limousine service, photographers and videographers, personalized water bottles, and even deluxe portable toilets.

Now, $27,000 is a lot of money, especially for an event that really doesn't *have* to cost much more than the marriage license (between $25 and $100, depending on the state and county). But U.S. culture dictates that you spend as much as it takes to guarantee that the day is special (in other words: *expensive*). Bridal expos, magazines, and books showcase a variety of services and items that brides and grooms can spend their money on—but you don't have to.

Imagine that you are getting married this year. You and your future spouse are discussing your plans. You can spend $27,000 on your wedding. Or, you can invest half that amount in an index fund for ten years, yielding a 10 percent return. This amount—$13,500—invested at 10 percent for ten years would grow to $35,015. The other half of the original amount will still provide an elegant wedding—$13,500 will cover all the basics and then some. And with $35,015 in ten years, you will have a decent down payment for a home.

Should you have the very *special* wedding you've always dreamed of—something to be vividly remembered forever? Or is it a better idea to save some of that money for your future?

Should you . . .

1. ...go ahead with plans for an extravagant wedding? Explain your answer.
2. ...have a less expensive wedding and invest some of the money toward your future goals? Give reasons for your answer.

online brokerage service, such as Ameritrade or E*TRADE. Once you have your account set up, you can log in to buy and sell stocks.

Although buying and selling stocks online is easy, do your research and be sure you are confident about each transaction—because even a discount brokerage firm charges a fee for the transactions you make.

What if you are not ready to invest in the stock market? You can still try your hand at stock trading—with an imaginary account. Begin a logbook, starting with an initial "investment" of $1,000. Decide which stocks you would buy for your portfolio, and then track their daily progress in the newspaper or online.

Notice how much the price of each stock rises or falls. If you do not like the way a stock is performing, or if you think it might begin to lose value soon, you can sell it and purchase a different one. Keep track of these transactions in your logbook. After three to six months, cash out and see if you made a profit on the initial $1,000. Following the stock market in this way is good practice for when you can invest for real.

◀ **Be vigilant! If a new product—like a game console—is coming out for sale, investing in that company before the product is released may earn you some extra dollars.**

You can also practice virtual investing on the Internet. Several Web sites offer free stock trading games that allow you to buy and sell stocks and watch your progress over time. Most give you a hypothetical $100,000 to invest, sometimes more. Here are some you can try:

- StocksQuest (http://fin.emcp.net/quest)
- Virtual Stock Exchange (http://fin.emcp.net/virtual)
- Wall Street Survivor (http://fin.emcp.net/survivor)

When you are deciding which stocks to purchase, think about which companies' stocks might rise in value. Evaluate your information and your reasoning. Make sure you have good evidence behind your decisions.

Keep track of local, national, and world news—especially news about business and the economy. For example, if fuel prices are rising, you might decide that companies involved in the manufacture of large, gas-guzzling vehicles will suffer. On the other hand, companies that sell electric cars, motorcycles, and other fuel-efficient vehicles might do very well. If a company will soon be releasing a hot new movie, game console, or cell phone model, you might expect that company's stock price to rise. Buying before the event could earn you some money.

In all your transactions, you should keep your values and goals in mind. Make investments that move you closer to your long-term goals. And invest in companies that fit with your values. Then you will be a "complete" investor—and well on your way to financial success!

Answers to Fact or Fiction

1. False—Anyone who has the money to buy a share of stock can invest; **2.** False—Some stocks are riskier than others, and bonds are usually less risky than stocks; **3.** True; **4.** False—Social Security benefits are not intended to fund a retired person's entire income, but to supplement it; **5.** True; **6.** True.

SECTION 3 ASSESSMENT

Factual Recall

1. What type of broker is likely to provide financial advice?
2. How are financial advisers paid?
3. Name at least three specific sources of financial information.
4. How much money should you have to begin investing?
5. What is a custodial account?

Critical Thinking

1. When you are choosing a financial planner, why is it important to select someone you can trust?
2. Stocks and mutual funds are two places to invest your money. What might be the advantages of investing in bonds?

CHAPTER 7 REVIEW AND ASSESSMENT

Chapter Summary

Section 1 Stocks, Bonds, and Mutual Funds

- When you buy stock in a corporation, you become a part owner of that corporation.
- Shares of publicly held stock are bought and sold on the stock markets.
- Before buying stock in a company, research online and print publications for reliable information.
- A stock index compares the average daily prices of a representative group of stocks with their prices on previous days. Major stock indexes provide a benchmark for the overall performance of the stock market over time.
- When you buy a bond, you are lending money to the company, organization, or government that issued the bond.
- Some investments carry more risk than others. Futures, options, and penny stocks are all higher-risk investments. Mutual funds and bonds are lower-risk investments.
- Before investing your money, always evaluate the potential risk and return.
- By starting to invest while you are young, you will have the time value of money working to your advantage.

Section 2 Other Types of Investments

- Real estate and collectibles are two alternative types of investments.
- One of the major reasons people save and invest money is to have funds for retirement.
- Retirement income can come from Social Security, employer-sponsored plans, and individual savings and investments.
- You are likely to live for many years after you retire, so you will need a large amount of money. Start saving as soon as possible.

Section 3 Advice, Information, and Transactions

- You do not need a large amount of money to begin investing.
- Advice and information about investing can come from many sources, such as brokers, financial advisers, print publications, and Web sites.
- To gain investing experience without risking your money, create an imaginary account in which you track stocks to see what could happen if you bought and sold those stocks.

Reviewing Key Terms

Indicate whether each of the following statements (featuring key terms) is true or false. If a statement is false, rewrite it to make it true.

1. A **financial adviser** might charge either an hourly rate or a fee for service.
2. A share of **stock** is a unit of ownership in a corporation.
3. **Real estate** includes property such as land and houses or other buildings.
4. A company's profits are paid to shareholders in the form of **commodities**.
5. Interest earned on bonds is called **capital gain**.
6. The **Fortune 500** is a stock index.
7. A **mutual fund** is an investment in which people pool their money to buy stocks, bonds, real estate, or other assets.
8. A T-bill is a government **bond**.

Understanding the Main Ideas

1. People investing their money have two main considerations. What are they?
2. What is the relationship between rate of return and risk?
3. Which type of investment carries more risk: stocks or bonds?
4. What is an index fund?
5. Why is investing in a mutual fund usually safer than investing all your money in the stock of a single company?
6. Why should you begin investing for retirement as soon as possible?

7. What does it mean when a 401(k) plan has an "opt-out" provision?
8. How does a traditional IRA differ from a Roth IRA regarding taxes *on earnings*?

Practicing Math

1. Whenever you make a choice, you are also making a decision *not* to do something else. For example, when you buy a restaurant meal, you are giving up the chance to use that money for something else. In finance, this idea is called *opportunity cost*, and it relates to the time value of money. Suppose you have $250. You could spend it on clothes or add it to your money market savings account, which has an APY of 4.75 percent. If you buy the clothes, what is your opportunity cost?
2. Prices of goods and services can vary from month to month, but over the long run they always increase. This increase is called *inflation*, and it means that the dollar you have today will buy less in the future. For example, a "basket of goods" that you could buy for $500 in 2010 may cost $521.27 in 2011. Important financial decisions, such as investment choices or retirement planning, need to take inflation into account. If you had invested that $500 in 2006, what rate of return would you need just to keep your investment at the same value?

Applying Critical Thinking Skills

1. Preferred stock pays a fixed dividend, regardless of the company's profit. Is this an advantage or disadvantage? Explain.
2. Your grandfather is close to retirement and wants to invest in stocks that will pay a high dividend. Would growth stocks be a good investment for him? Why or why not?
3. You are thinking about investing in XYZ Corporation. The company's Web site promises "fantastic returns." Should you buy stock based on this information? Why or why not?
4. In your own words, define "time value of money."
5. Is it better to enroll in a 401(k) plan or to invest in an IRA?

Working with Real-World Documents

1. Obtain an annual report. Many large companies post their annual reports online. Go to the company's Web site and look for buttons or tabs marked "Investors" or "Investor relations." In the annual report, look for the following:
   a. Overview of company sales. How does the company make most of its money?
   b. Stock price history. Has the overall trend been up or down, or have there been numerous changes in both directions?
   c. Income statement of company earnings. Is the company making a profit?
   d. Cash flow statement giving the movement of cash between the company and the outside world.
   e. Balance sheet showing what the company owns and what debts it has.
2. Before investing in a mutual fund, study the fund's prospectus. The *prospectus* provides information about the fund's objectives, investment strategies, risks, past performance, fees and expenses, management, and distribution policy (how the fund pays its investors). Obtain and report on the prospectuses from several mutual funds (many are available online).

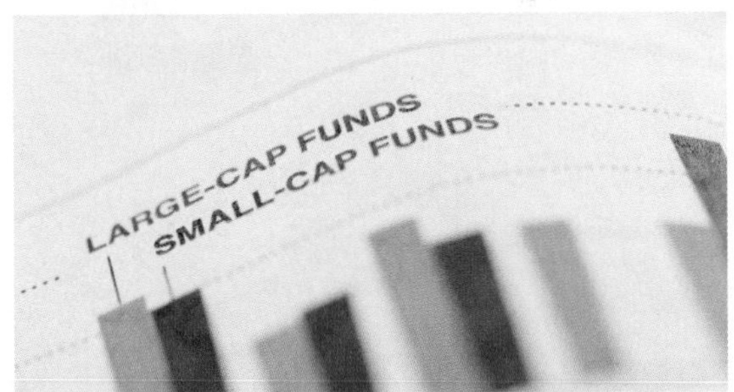

Taking It Home

1. Collaborate with a family member or friend and create an imaginary portfolio of stocks. Select companies that you think could provide a good return and "invest" an imaginary $20,000. Track your portfolio for two months. Did you make money? What factors affected the price of the stocks?

UNIT IV

Spending Wisely

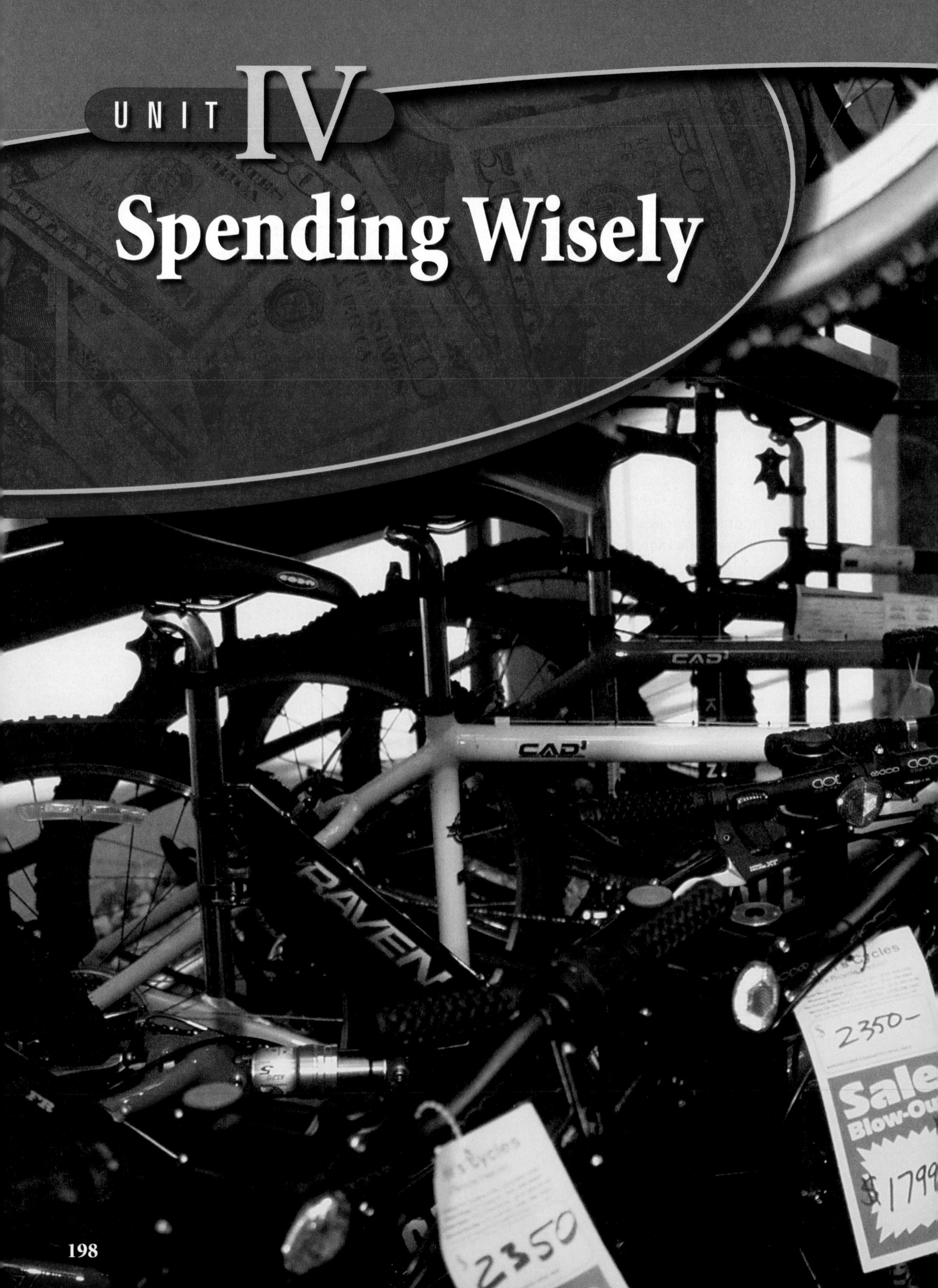

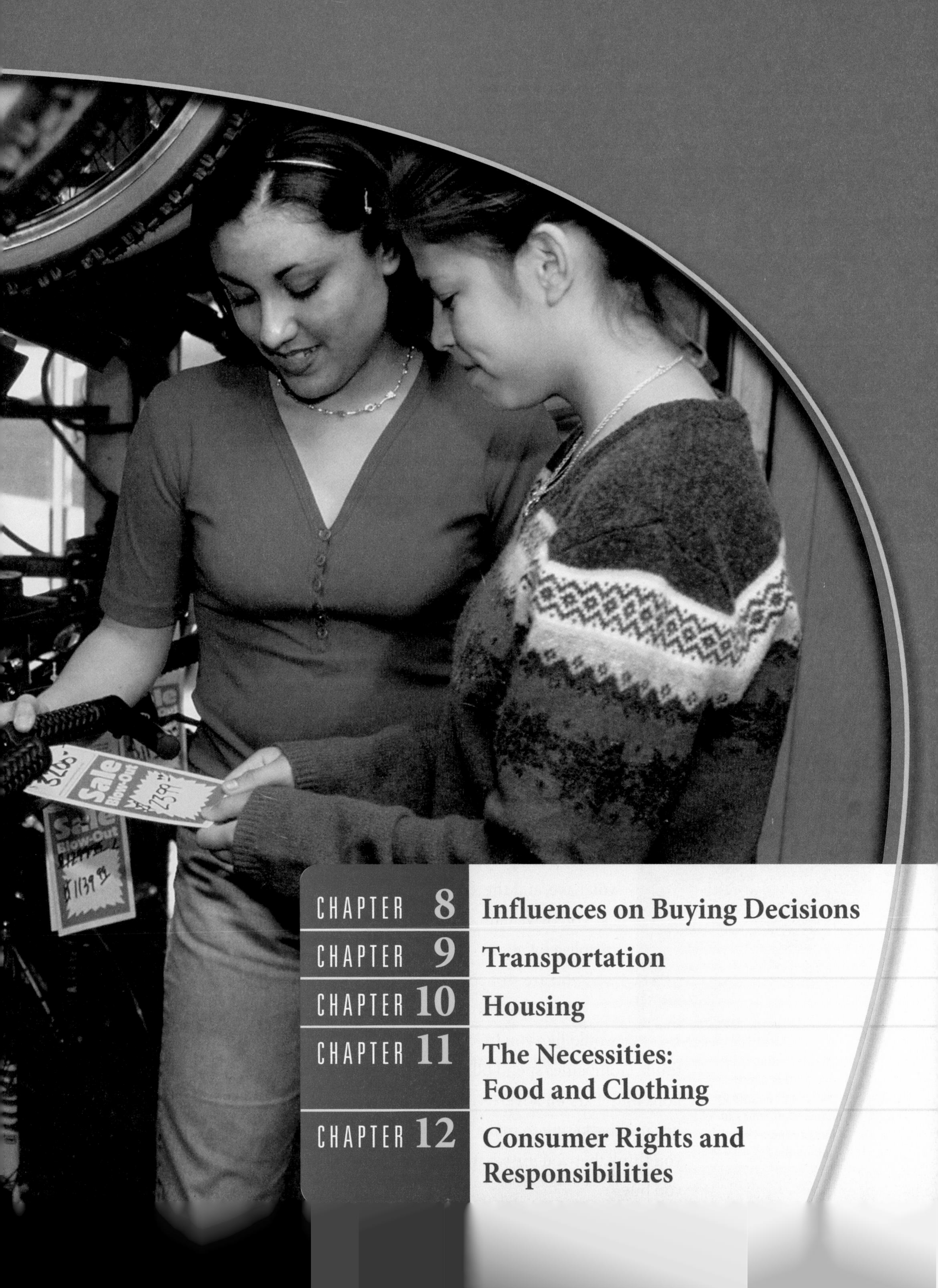
Sale
Blow-Out

CHAPTER 8

Influences on Buying Decisions

We live in a culture that emphasizes spending money and buying "stuff." We buy certain things to make an impression on the people around us. Our *stuff* gives other people clues about how much money we have and how old we are (or how old we would like to be). Our *stuff* can express our interests, our sense of style, and our personality.

▲ **Marketing companies make billions of dollars by convincing teens to buy products they do not need.**

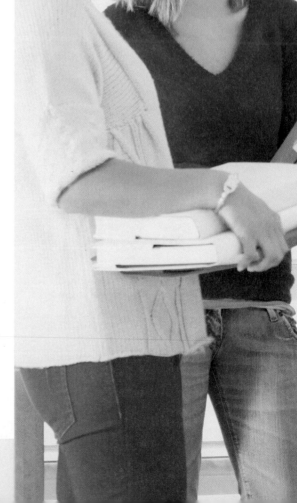

The brand of jeans you wear, the kind of MP3 player you have, and the car you drive tell people a lot about who you are—or so the big companies would like you to think. Companies spend billions of dollars on advertising and marketing to make you think that you *are* what you buy.

SECTION 1 Needs vs. Wants

SECTION 2 Advertising

SECTION 3 Making Buying Decisions

Fact or Fiction

What do you think? Are the following statements true or false? If you think they are false, then say what is true.

1. Television shows and commercials reflect the lives of typical people.
2. The U.S. government does not prohibit advertising companies from aiming manipulative TV ads at children.
3. Most people make their buying decisions after careful thought.
4. Higher-priced brand name products are better quality than lower-priced off-brand products.
5. Only a small part of a typical company's spending is budgeted for marketing.
6. Shopping around to compare features and prices can help save money.

Answers on page 218.

Study Reminder

*Knowing how to study can increase your knowledge, improve your grades, and cut down on your study time. See the **Studying Personal Finance** pages at the front of the book for some tips to help you study this chapter.*

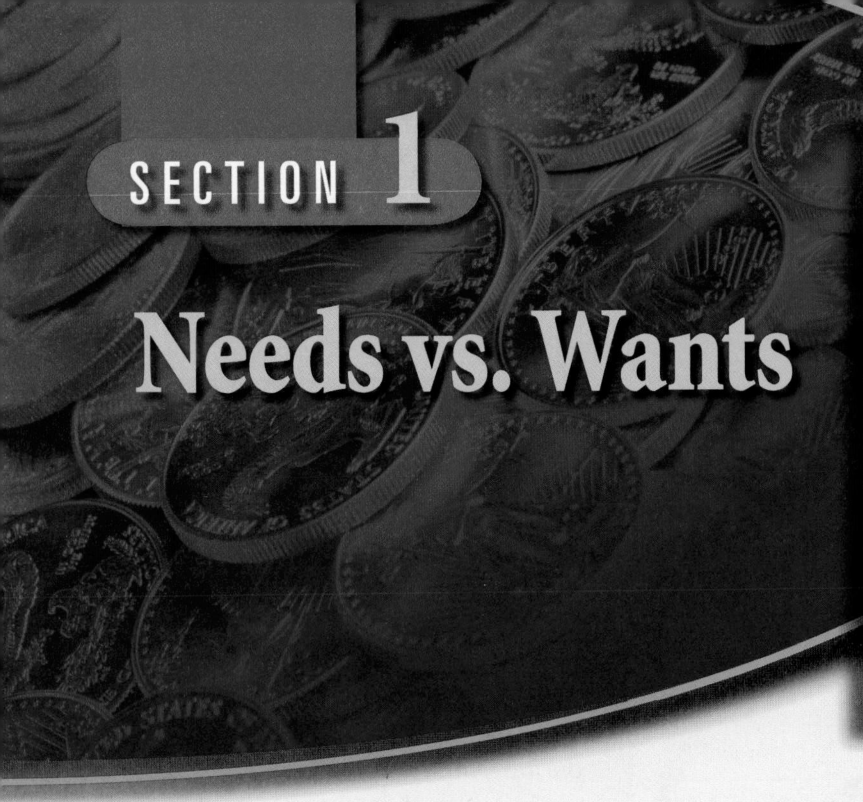

SECTION 1
Needs vs. Wants

Focus Questions

1. What is the difference between needs and wants?
2. What factors should you consider when you go comparison shopping?
3. What marketing tools and tactics do companies use to encourage you to buy more expensive brands or simply to overspend?
4. What elements make ads effective?

Key Terms

consumers
comparison shopping
opportunity cost

Turn on your television set at any given time, and you are likely to see advertising for something—and you do not even have to be watching a commercial. Television programs—as well as Web sites, cell phone screens, video games, and magazines—commonly show products and services that everyone "needs" to be popular, better looking, richer, or healthier. Today it seems that almost everything you view, hear, and read is encouraging you to spend, spend, spend.

▼ Certain TV shows try to convince teens to spend lots of money or feel bad if they cannot. Who benefits from these shows?

Rich-and-Famous Lifestyles

So-called "reality" TV programs like *Cribs*, *The Simple Life*, and *My Super Sweet 16* highlight rich-and-famous lifestyles. But logically, you know those lifestyles are not common for most people.

Cribs features the homes of sports stars, famous musicians, and other highly paid celebrities. Likewise, the parties on *My Super Sweet 16* take place in very wealthy areas such as Beverly Hills, California, and Scottsdale, Arizona. The parties carry estimated price tags of $80,000 to $250,000, in addition to the car—or two—that each "Sweet 16" receives. In fact, *My Super Sweet 16* is so over the top that other programs such as *MADtv*, *Saturday Night Live*, and *South Park* have created their own silly "Sweet 16" episodes.

But buying into the "spend today, save tomorrow" lifestyle will not make other people believe that you are a

▲ Doing things you want without spending a lot allows you to save money for things you need.

celebrity. More likely you will just seem foolish for draining your bank account to impress people you hardly know.

Acquiring Luxury Items

Buying into the rich-and-famous lifestyle is a risky undertaking. It means spending money on luxury items to create the rich-and-famous image—and this is often money you do not have. And yet, plenty of people of all ages do buy in, even though they jeopardize their financial futures.

Many **consumers**—people who acquire goods and services—spend large chunks of their income on designer clothes, electronics, music, restaurants, and salon visits. This might seem harmless, but remember: you can never get back the money you spend on luxuries like these. You cannot save it for the future or use it to support an important cause you believe in. Perhaps even worse, that money will not be available to you when you *need* it for something crucial, like car repairs or bus fare.

The truth is that most people do not consider the differences between what they *need* and what they *want*. They have money, so they spend it. In fact, most people find that their spending rises to match any increase in their income. It is more difficult to make their buying habits shrink to match a smaller income, as many people discover later in life.

Being able to tell the difference between needs and wants will not only ease your mind about finances, but it can also help you get what you really want in the long run. Differentiating between wants and needs is an important and valuable skill—and a mark of maturity. In the process, you discover the difference between what is truly important and what is, in the grand scheme of things, pretty trivial.

In Chapter 3, you learned that in financial and economic terms, a *need* is a necessity—a good or service that you must have to survive—like basic food, shelter, medical attention, and clothing. A *want* is something you desire; it is not necessary. Although you may need new shoes, you do not specifically need brand name shoes, no matter how much you might want them. And everyone

consumers people who acquire goods and services

Figure 8.1 NEEDS AND WANTS CHART

Needs	Wants

needs to eat, but you do not specifically need Quiznos subs, Old Chicago pizzas, or Panera sandwiches. The same goes for shelter. We all need somewhere to sleep—but a small, modest house or apartment fills that need just as well as a flashy, ostentatious mansion would.

Think about the purchases you have made in the past month. Copy a chart like the one shown in Figure 8.1 and list each item as either a "Need" or a "Want."

Now examine your chart. How many of your purchases were things you really did not need?

Addiction to Spending?

Recall from Chapter 6 that *discretionary income* is money left over after savings and essential expenses have been accounted for. In general, people spend these discretionary funds on products and services that make them feel good. For some people, acquiring unneeded items or going on fancy trips gives them the kind of "high" that other people get from gambling, extreme sports, or using drugs. When people plunge into debt by buying things they cannot afford, their behavior may be a kind of addiction.

Take, for example, people who buy things on eBay, the online auction site. Fox News quotes an eBay insider as saying that the popular site is "the world's biggest garage sale." According to some participants, part of the attraction to

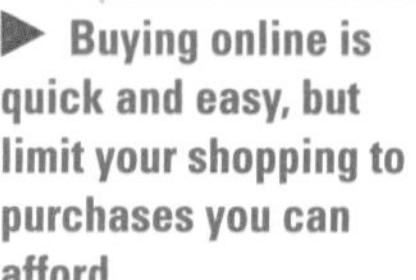

▶ **Buying online is quick and easy, but limit your shopping to purchases you can afford.**

Internet auctions is that the competition feels a little like playing blackjack or slot machines. For others, winning the bid gives them an emotional rush. Addiction to eBay auctions is so serious that the Center for Online Addiction has a specific program to help those who have spent their children's college funds or their own retirement funds on eBay.

To some young people, it might seem like no big deal to blow a week's allowance on CDs or a week's pay on new clothes. But the good feelings they get from satisfying their desires might mark the beginning of a lifelong struggle with poor financial habits. On the other hand, if you think about your spending decisions in terms of needs versus wants—and learn to cover your needs first—you will be far better prepared to manage your money as you move into adulthood.

Clearly, your generation is not alone. Past generations of teens have faced similar challenges. Many adults never learn the difference between needs and wants. The phrase "keeping up with the Joneses" has been around for a long time. It refers to people who continually try to outspend friends, neighbors, and family members. These very competitive types want to be the first on the block with the newfangled outdoor grill or latest sports car.

People of all ages have the urge to spend money on things they do not need because they believe that their possessions define them. *Things* make them feel important, trendy, or good looking. Often, however, the desire to have the newest and best things can start to control the person—rather than the person controlling his or her spending and possessions.

Breaking the Cycle

Okay, so you know you want to be more thoughtful about your spending. What do you do? How do you go about planning and making wise decisions? Here are a few ideas to get you started:

- Remove your emotions from your finances. This process will help you understand your own financial value system.
- Determine how you feel about spending, saving, and sharing money.
- Think through your *own* personal values, not those of advertisers or your peers.
- Think about what you need, based on your value system.
- Learn to separate your needs from your desires. If something cannot be classified as a need, accept that it is a want. Recognize that having this want will not change you as a person.
- Know your strengths and weaknesses. Do you have a hard time going to the mall without buying something? Can you go to the movies without splurging on a large popcorn and soda? Or maybe you cannot go online without downloading some music. Avoid these activities until you can limit your spending.

"Keeping up with the Joneses" is an old saying that means "trying to impress and surpass the neighbors." Increasingly, Americans spend more on items they cannot afford, like cars and expensive clothes, simply because "everyone else" has them. The truth is that Americans are going into debt as a result of trying to keep up appearances. Perhaps another old saying offers sounder financial advice: "living within your means." That means buying only what you can actually afford and saving for the things you want, rather than relying on credit cards. By living within your means now, you can build good financial habits to last a lifetime.

If you understand your personal spending habits, you can do a better job of changing them. Also, consider the conversations you have with others about spending. Do you talk with your parents or other trusted adults about how you spend money and what you spend it on? If so, how do those conversations affect your spending decisions? If not, think about starting up routine talks about spending with someone whose financial values or success you admire.

As already mentioned, peer pressure can influence your spending decisions. It is hard not to cave in and buy that iPod if all of your friends have one. But *knowing* that your peers are an important influence can help you make a wise decision.

When you think about buying something, ask yourself why you want it. Is it because "everyone" has it? If so, take a step back and reconsider your motives. You might even want to sleep on it. If you still really want it (and can afford it), you can always buy it tomorrow. Never let yourself believe that if you do not buy it now, the opportunity will be gone forever.

The Decision to Buy

After you have seriously thought through a spending decision and have decided to buy, you have other options to think about. You need to consider these things:

- What brand to buy
- Where to buy
- Whether to buy now, or later

YOU DECIDE

Kiara paged through the latest *Elle* magazine and saw some fabulous Miu Miu shoes. She and her friends were always talking shoes, so she showed these to her friends. They all agreed the shoes were fantastic. Then Anne pointed to the price tag: $500. Kiara had more money than most 15-year-old girls, but $500 was still a lot to spend on shoes.

Despite the price, Kiara saved her allowance and did extra chores for cash. She begged her grandparents for donations. She even improved her grades in hopes of earning extra bucks from her parents. It all paid off. After a couple of months, she had saved the money.

Should she . . .

1. ...run to the mall to buy the shoes? Everyone would just die to see her wearing them! After all, she worked so hard to save up for them.
2. ...research on the Internet to see if the price was lower somewhere else? Buying them at the lowest price possible would save her some money. Plus, then she would have extra cash to buy something else.
3. ...reconsider the purchase? After all, $500 is a lot of money to spend on a pair of shoes. Maybe she should put the money in the bank and let it earn interest instead. Explain your answers.

As an example, let's say you do need a new pair of jeans. But do you need to buy jeans that cost upward of $145 to $225? Learn to weigh the costs versus benefits of the upscale jeans instead of a more economical pair, such as Levi's for $20 to $40. You should become a *comparison shopper.*

Comparison shopping involves researching different brands to find out which one offers the highest quality for the least amount of money. It also involves looking around to see which store has the best price. Here you might even check out used-clothing stores. You would be amazed at how often you can find never-worn clothing with the price tags still attached—selling for a fraction of the original price. Why? Because the person who first purchased the item never wore it.

The Internet makes comparison shopping easy with sites like AOL Shopping (http://fin.emcp.net/AOLshop) and BestPrice.com (http://fin.emcp.net/bestprice). These Web sites allow you to order online or tell you where to go for the best value. This is the ultimate in comparison shopping—finding the item you want and getting a great deal as well.

comparison shopping researching various brands to buy the highest quality item at the lowest price

Do Your RESEARCH

One of the most important buying decisions a young person makes is a car. It can give you the freedom to go where you want, when you want. But it can also weigh you down with huge costs—car payments, gas, insurance, repairs, and more. This is definitely a decision you want to think about carefully before making the purchase.

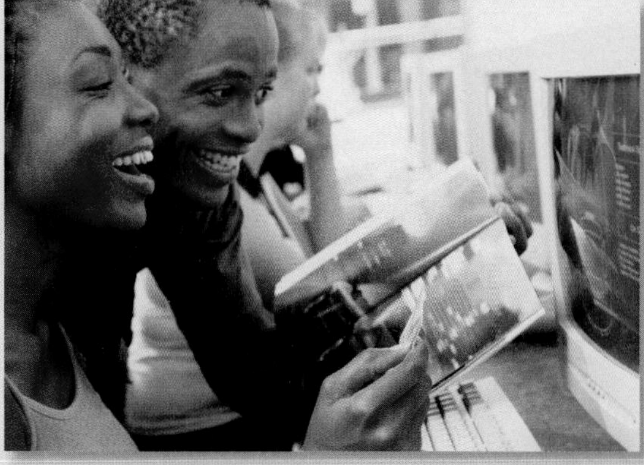

To start, check Kelley Blue Book (http://fin.emcp.net/bluebook), the trusted car resource, for the official Blue Book values of any cars you are thinking about buying. Another helpful Web site is Edmunds.com (http://fin.emcp.net/edmunds), which provides information about pricing, as well as unbiased car reviews, ratings, and expert advice to help you get a fair deal on a car.

When you have narrowed down your choices, consult with an insurance agent about insurance costs. Many times, the type of car you buy influences how much you will pay for insurance. Also consider the price of fuel. A bigger car or truck might seem like a good idea, but it may guzzle gas that you cannot afford. Some vehicles will have larger repair bills than others.

Doing your research and talking to knowledgeable people will help you find the most economical car to maintain—and help you negotiate a good price.

Before Buying

1. Do you know the Blue Book value of the car you want to buy? Visit the Kelley Blue Book Web site and find it.
2. Many Web sites have activities and games that you can play to practice making smart buying decisions. Log onto *It All Adds Up* at http://fin.emcp.net/italladdsup. Click on the car keys and try playing "Let's Wheel and Deal!" You will be asked to think about features that are important to you. Then the exercise will help you calculate the cost of buying a car.

When you go shopping for that pair of jeans, ask yourself the following questions: Is the most expensive brand worth four times as much as a standard pair? Is the quality better? Will the jeans last longer? Maybe the answers to your questions will lead you to buy the less expensive pair. Maybe you will not change your mind, because you value being at the cutting edge of fashion. The important thing is to ask yourself the questions, so that your decision is rational.

Of course you also need to consider matters other than price. Before you buy, ask yourself whether the item is something you need right now, or whether you can put off the purchase and wait for a sale. Maybe you can buy the item used. Should you try to save a little more money before making the purchase? Remember, it is a lot easier to live within your means—and you will be happier in the long run.

Your Spending Budget

Your income will play a large part in determining your financial decisions. Your ability to spend money, after all, is based on how much money there *is* to spend. So, how do you determine your spending budget?

Recall the Share Save Spend system introduced in Chapter 3. Think about how much you are going to set aside for sharing and saving even *before* you decide how to spend your money. If you spend it all now, you will not have anything in the bank for emergencies. You will not be able to take advantage of "once in a lifetime" opportunities, and you will not be able to support the causes you believe in. Remind yourself that you

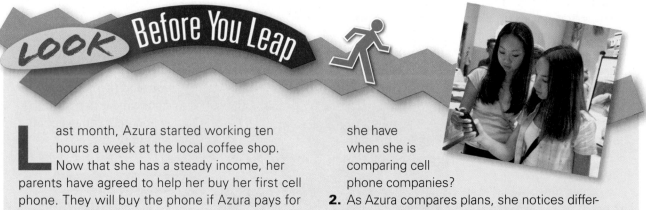

LOOK Before You Leap

Last month, Azura started working ten hours a week at the local coffee shop. Now that she has a steady income, her parents have agreed to help her buy her first cell phone. They will buy the phone if Azura pays for the monthly plan.

Azura reads every cell phone ad she can find, and her head starts to spin. She asks her two best friends which plan they recommend—and gets two different answers. She asks her parents, and they suggest yet another plan. Azura decides to get information about each of those three plans and figure out which one might be best for her.

Before Buying

1. Azura knows that a cell phone plan is a contract. She wants to be sure she makes a good choice because it is very expensive to switch plans before the contract is up. What resources does she have when she is comparing cell phone companies?
2. As Azura compares plans, she notices differences: length of contract, monthly charges for voice and text minutes, cost of exceeding allotted minutes, and charges for games and online use. What other features should she compare? How should she narrow down her plan options?
3. Azura also has to figure out how much time she will spend using her new phone each month. Her mother suggests that she estimate the number of minutes and then add 20 to 30 percent. Why?
4. Azura finds that she will have enough money for a basic plan that offers everything she needs. How can she keep track of her minutes to avoid any excess fees?

do not *immediately* need to spend all of the money you earn or get from your parents.

After you have determined how much to set aside for sharing and for savings, you are ready to set up a spending budget. Copy the chart from Figure 8.2 onto a sheet of paper, and estimate how much money you spend per month in each of the categories.

This is your preliminary spending budget. You can also use the "Needs vs. Wants" chart that you completed earlier to set up budget categories that reflect your values. For example, if you really love nice clothes, be honest with yourself and make a conscious decision to allocate your money accordingly. If you value entertainment, be sure to include some funds for going out.

No matter how you set up your budget, though, understand that if you spend money in one area you cannot spend the same money elsewhere. Economists refer to this as the **opportunity cost**, which means that the real "price" of an item is the value of what you gave up to get it —the cost of passing up the next item on your list. In other words, when you decide to buy something, the other options for spending that money become the item's opportunity cost. If you spend all your money today, the opportunity cost of those purchases might be not saving enough for college, or not being able to buy a car next year.

Figure 8.2 **SPENDING ESTIMATES CHART**

Spending category	Amount
Clothing	
Connectivity (cell phone, Internet)	
Entertainment (movies, music, video games)	
Food (eating out, snacks)	
Sports and hobbies	
Grooming (cosmetics, haircuts)	
Transportation (bus, car, gas)	

opportunity cost the cost of giving up one thing to get something else

SECTION 1 ASSESSMENT

Factual Recall

1. Name two ways you might comparison-shop.
2. How can peer pressure influence your spending decisions?
3. What is opportunity cost?

Critical Thinking

1. Imagine that you have a younger brother who loves to buy new video games and spends all his money on them. A new video game system is coming out next month, and he is desperately scrambling and begging for money to buy it. Based on what you have read, what kind of advice would you offer him about making this purchase?
2. You have always wanted a Vera Wang jacket, and you see one on sale for half price—today only. Even on sale, the price is still about twice what you would normally pay for a jacket. You have enough money in your checking account and would not have to withdraw from savings. You tell yourself you will not buy any other new clothes all winter, just to have this jacket. What are the pros and cons of such a decision?

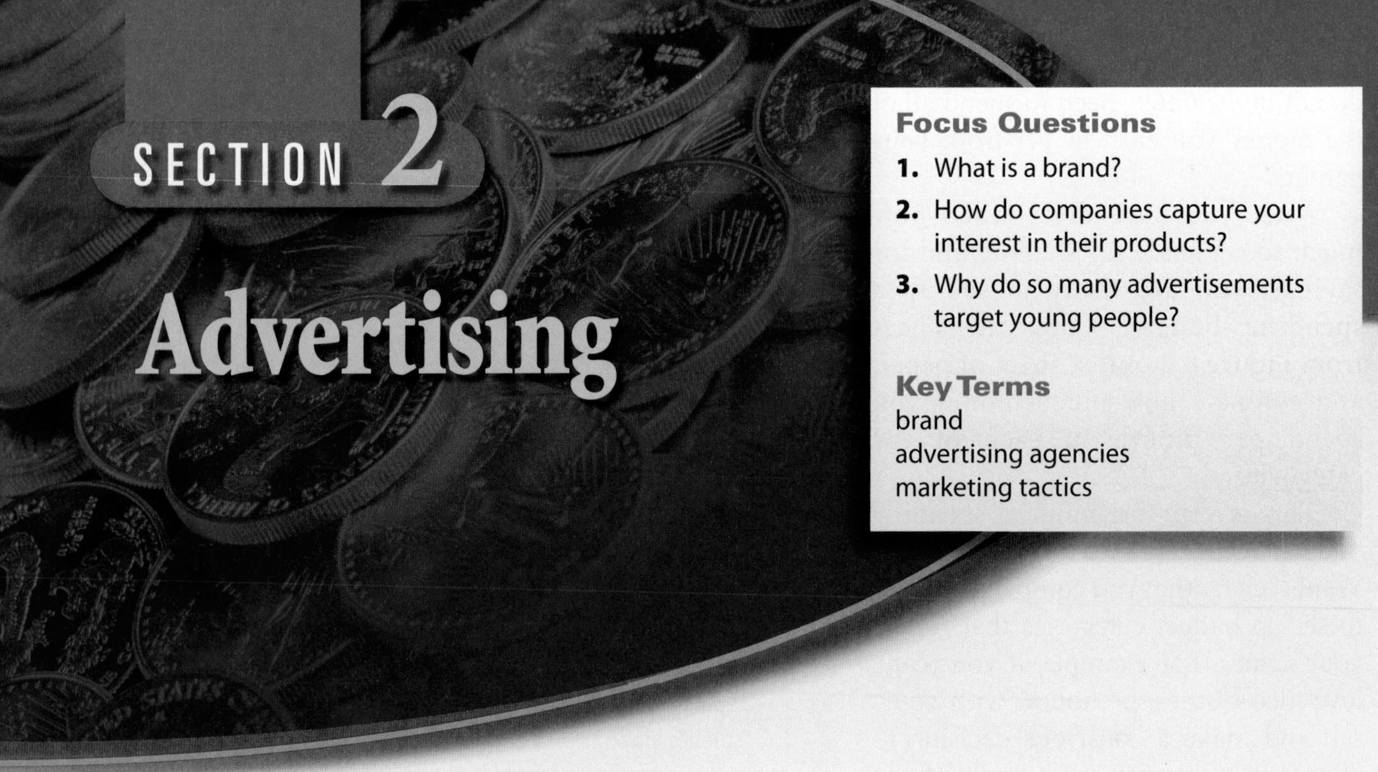

SECTION 2

Advertising

Focus Questions

1. What is a brand?
2. How do companies capture your interest in their products?
3. Why do so many advertisements target young people?

Key Terms

brand
advertising agencies
marketing tactics

Advertising affects the way you view things—perhaps more than you realize. As an exercise, what would you assume about people who . . .

- Always carry a Starbucks?
- Shop for clothes at Goodwill?
- Drive Volvo station wagons?
- Drive Dodge minivans?
- Wear expensive aftershave?
- Wear clothes from The Limited?
- Wear Chuck Taylor high-tops?
- Always wear black Tripp pants?
- Wear Ray-Bans, even indoors?
- Dress exclusively in clothes from Anthropologie?

You might have fixed ideas about people who show the behaviors listed above. If so, many of those ideas come from ads and commercials. Advertising promotes brand names, trying to convince you that one brand is better than another. Advertisers want you to think that you can be happier, healthier, or more admired if you buy their product.

brand the name that identifies a product or manufacturer

Brands Are Everywhere

Have you seen your favorite TV actor wearing Seven jeans? A famous athlete sipping Gatorade? Or a rock star showing off a Sony flat-screen TV? Images like these are everywhere, and not just in TV commercials, magazines, or billboards. Marketers are bright and creative people. They know that lots of consumers, especially teens, have learned to tune out traditional ads. So they use all sorts of strategies to get their brand names into the public eye.

A **brand** is the name that identifies a product or manufacturer. A *logo* is the graphic symbol or trademark that represents a brand. Look around your home. Brand names and logos stand out on everything: on the television set in your family room, the sports equipment in the garage, the food containers in your refrigerator, and the shampoo bottles in the bathroom. Companies want you to think that their brand name makes a product different from others—

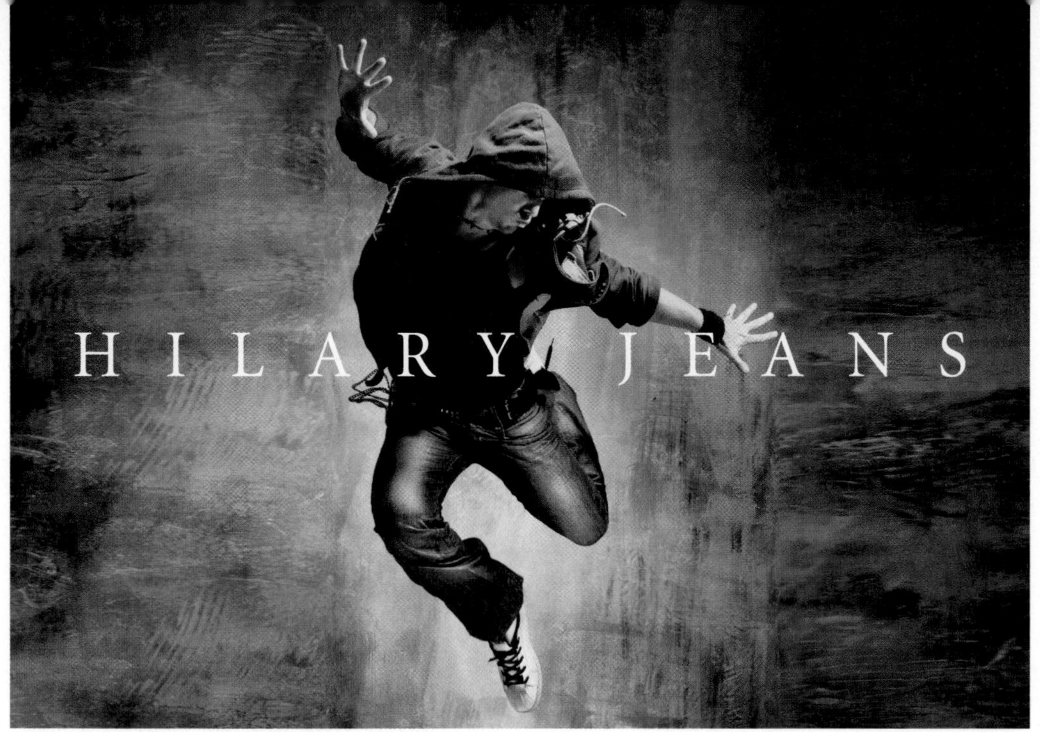

◀ In what way is the creator of this ad trying to appeal to you? Explain why the ad either is or is not effective.

superior to others. But this is not always the case. In fact, many off-brand products are actually manufactured in the same plants that make the high-end products, and often there is no difference in quality whatsoever.

Promoting Brands

To promote their brands and persuade consumers to buy their products, companies hire **advertising agencies**. Ad agencies are staffed by people with marketing, business, communications, and journalism backgrounds. Some have research departments led by psychologists or sociologists. They also have art departments that create the ads and logos you see all around you. These professionals are determined to convince you to spend your money on their products.

Analysts have calculated that the average U.S. teen is bombarded with more than 5,000 advertisements a day. You hear these ads on the radio and see them on television, at the movies, and on Web sites. The advertisements are in restaurant menus, on cell phone screens, on T-shirts—and just about anywhere else you can imagine.

A typical company earmarks the majority of its spending for marketing. In fact, companies spend more than $150 *billion* per year to get you and your friends to buy their products and services. Teens are an attractive audience for companies. Advertisers target young people because young people pay attention to trends and also because young people spend a lot of money. Young people usually do not stop to analyze

advertising agencies agencies whose job is to promote brand names and persuade consumers to buy goods and services

▼ Flashy Web sites are another catchy way to convince teens that shopping here is hip.

their spending—and retail companies want to keep it that way.

You might think that laws would protect consumers—especially young people—from deceptive advertising practices. Unfortunately that's not the case. In 1980, the U.S. Congress sided with businesses (and against children) when it passed Public Law 96-252. This law *prohibits* the Federal Trade Commission (FTC) from making any rules about advertising to children. So the only agency with the power to regulate marketing has virtually no ability to protect kids from manipulative marketing practices.

marketing tactics advertising methods that rely on human nature and emotional responses to sell products

Marketing Strategies

The purpose of advertising is not to provide unbiased information to consumers. Companies want you to buy their products. Ad agencies use psychological research to figure out how to win over customers, especially young people. They will try to tap your insecurities, weaknesses, and inexperience. They will tell you that buying a particular product will make you smarter, better looking, or more popular.

▼ Advertising executives spend hours figuring out what will make teens buy the items their clients want to sell.

Companies use a number of different strategies to get you to pay attention to what they are saying. For instance, Target Corporation launched a successful television ad campaign featuring a bouncy tune that repeated, over and over, the words "I want it, I need it" while displaying a visual array of fun products you can buy at Target stores. Gatorade ads often use famous sports stars to demonstrate how drinking the sports beverage can make an athlete faster and stronger.

Some strategies are obvious, others are more subtle. Most have been around for decades. These methods are referred to as **marketing tactics**. Instead of presenting facts, marketing tactics rely on human nature and people's emotional responses to particular images. Some examples are discussed next.

The "Beautiful People" Factor Companies spend millions of dollars trying to convince you that buying their products will make you a popular and beautiful person. Vans and other makers of sports shoes have truly outperformed in this area. You can find fancy sneakers for virtually every sport from skateboarding to basketball to cross country. Other shoes—like Coach sandals that sell for $100 and up—allow teens to present themselves as quite wealthy.

Jump on the Bandwagon Many advertisements try to get consumers to buy a product because everyone else is. Energy drink companies use this tactic a lot—"It Gives You Wings" for Red Bull energy drink and "Party Like a Rock Star" for Rock Star energy drink, for instance. Monster energy drink takes it a step further: The side of the can carries a health advisory cautioning consumers not to drink more than three 16-ounce servings per day. It says any more than that can cause increased heart rate, dizziness, nausea, or even death. It is an invitation to show how tough you are.

Celebrity Testimonial Advertising executives hope that you want to be like famous people and will buy the products the celebrities endorse. Advertisers use *celebrity testimonials*—famous people tell you that they use a product and you should too. For instance, in 2008, advertising agencies paid Tony Hawk to advertise skateboards, Beyoncé to promote milk, and Snoop Dogg to pitch clothing and sunglasses.

◀ **Nike hired golf superstar Tiger Woods to advertise its company, hoping people who like Tiger will buy Nike products.**

You Can Succeed Financially

Stephon Marbury can buy anything he wants—after all, the NBA star guard makes millions of dollars a year playing basketball. But Marbury grew up without a lot of money, and he knows that not every kid can afford Nike Shox, which cost well over $100 a pair. He also knows that lots of teens idolize professional athletes and want to buy top-quality sports shoes and clothing.

Marbury set out to create products with the brand name *Starbury,* a nickname of his since his high school days. All the Starbury products, marketed and sold by Steve & Barry's retail stores, are reasonably priced. The shoes, for example, cost less than $15. For that matter, so does everything else—including sweatshirts, jackets, and jerseys. Marbury says the products are high quality, and he proves it by wearing the shoes on the basketball court. Marbury insists that it costs less than $14 to make a shoe. He adds that for other brands, "all the prices are marked up. We don't do all the advertising that they do. We do word of mouth."

The product line is catching on fast, even without mass advertising. Marbury went on a tour around the country when he launched his line in 2006. Three million pairs of shoes sold in the first three months.

What Would You Do?

1. If you had a new product and no money for national TV and magazine ads, what role could a celebrity spokesperson play in your marketing strategy?
2. Do you think a new product could succeed without either a mass media campaign or a celebrity spokesperson? Explain your answer.

Emotional Appeal Many advertisements want you to think that a product will make you feel happier, more confident, or more loved. Some appeal to your desire to help others. Lance Armstrong started a mini-revolution when he introduced his yellow "Live-Strong" silicone bracelets to raise money for cancer research. Soon, other causes followed—pink bracelets to raise money to fight breast cancer and royal blue bracelets to pay tribute to Kentucky Derby winner Barbaro after his tragic leg fracture.

Catchiness Factor Lots of jingles and slogans work because they are catchy. You find yourself humming the tune—and repeating the name of the product as you do so. Think of the Campbell's soup jingle, "M'm! M'm! Good!" Or the ads for Meow Mix cat food. Cats sing "Meow, meow, meow, meow..." to a catchy melody, and then the announcer says, "Cats ask for it by name." Some companies use well-known music in their advertising, as Chevrolet has done in its "Like a Rock" campaign. The advertisement featured lyrics and music from a Bob Seger song.

Retail Sensory Overload Retail establishments bombard shoppers with an array of environmental stimulants to encourage you to buy. Walking through a mall or a store, you might hear jingles on the speaker system, catch the scent of perfume or chocolate-chip cookies in the air, or glimpse a video screen showing the latest fashions. All these appeals to your senses are intended to get you *subconsciously* thinking about buying something—and to disconnect you from cool, hard logic.

Gotta Have It Now Not only do marketers want you to buy their products, but they also try to convince you that you have to have the item *now*. They do not want you to think twice. If you stop to think, you might decide to wait for a sale, buy the item used, buy an off-brand look-alike, or not buy anything at all.

The gotta-have-it-now mentality has taken over American culture. What people want, they want now. Convenience foods and fast-food restaurants cater to people's desire to have a snack the instant they decide they are hungry. No one needs to look for a public telephone anymore because everyone has a cell phone. And to go shopping, you don't even have to wait for the stores to open. You can go online and shop for anything at any time of day or night.

Targeting You

In a number of ways, advertisers use their skills and resources to target teens. One form of marketing, called *social network marketing*, uses teens themselves to spread the word about new products. For instance, Procter & Gamble has identified young people who are popular, connected, and outspoken. The company then sends product samples, sometimes with entertainment tie-ins, to these teens. The teens then spread the word about a television episode in which the product will be advertised, or about the product sample itself.

Coca-Cola, Apple Computer, Procter & Gamble, Time Warner, and Sony have all tapped into youth networks through online social Web sites like MySpace, Facebook, Xanga, and hundreds of smaller, local systems. They promote their products on the Web sites' pages and on their advertisements for concerts, entertainment venues, and events that cater to teens.

Marketers use various other tactics to "spy" on young people. Some consumer research companies invite teens to participate in surveys or focus groups. Others invade spaces like malls, sporting

You Can Succeed Financially

The slogan was "You Target Us, We Target You"—when some enterprising teens in Minnesota turned the tables on the tobacco industry. They launched a successful antismoking campaign called Target Market. The youth-led movement was funded by the state of Minnesota, using part of the 1998 settlement from the state's multibillion-dollar lawsuit against the tobacco companies.

Target Market used the same marketing tactics that the tobacco companies use to target teens—but this time the teens targeted Big Tobacco. They wanted to show their peers how the tobacco companies use advertising to go after young people to get them hooked on cigarettes. Said Matt Novak, a co-chair of Target Market's executive committee: "I see my friends who smoke wanting to quit and they can't. I don't think it's cool that people are making money off disease and death."

The Target Market teenage volunteers created hard-hitting TV commercials like this one: *"I just want to say thank you. Thanks. Thank you Big Tobacco, for convincing me to smoke. And this filter just makes me feel so safe. Thanks. It's like a seat belt or an air bag. Thank you Big Tobacco for singling me out as a main target. For underestimating our intelligence. Thanks a lot."*

They also produced CDs and film shorts. They sponsored concerts and sports events, including a tour across the state aimed at educating young people and engaging them in the antismoking campaign. And they had a Web site, TMVoice.

Target Market operated from 1999 until 2003—and it worked. More than 40,000 young people joined the organization. More than 14 million TV ads hit the airwaves. The Web site registered more than 6 million hits. Experts believe the campaign reduced youth smoking rates in Minnesota by 11 percent—saving about 15,000 young people from becoming smokers. In the previous six years, teen tobacco use rates had increased more than 35 percent.

And the overall lesson? The Target Market campaign shows that social network marketing can be effective—and that it *is* possible to counteract the advertising huge companies use to target young people. Most importantly, it shows that you *can* make a difference in your community!

What Would You Do?

1. Budget cuts led the Minnesota legislature to eliminate funding for Target Market in 2003. Within six months, the number of teens who reported that they would consider smoking went up by 10 percent. Without state funding, what would you do in your own community to educate your peers about the tobacco companies' marketing tactics? What other agencies and organizations could you ask to become involved?
2. Is there another industry that you believe uses questionable advertising tactics? What can you do to counteract the effects?

events, and even schools to see what young trend-setters are doing, and then passing this information along to their clients, who use it to develop their marketing strategies. Look-Look, a leading market research company, recruits young people to report on their peers' tastes and attitudes about everything from fashion, entertainment, and beauty to food and technology.

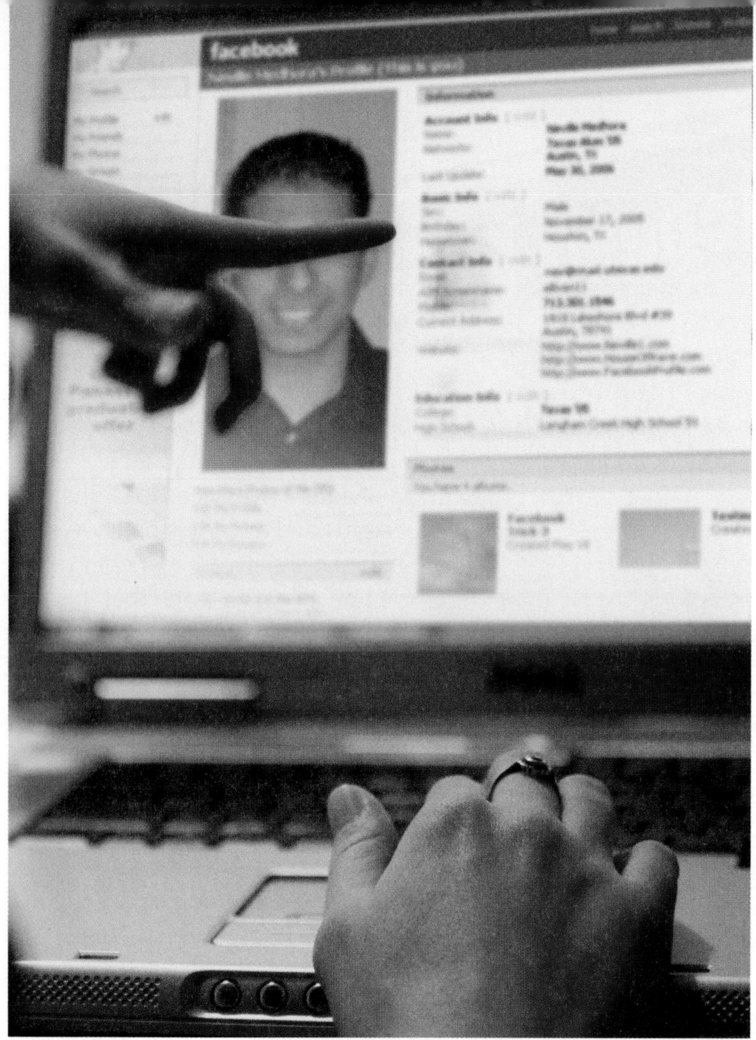

In Your School Lots of companies have moved their marketing efforts right into the schools. They know many school districts are strapped for money. For example, schools have allowed television companies such as Channel One to provide technological equipment in exchange for twelve minutes of the students' time each day. The students are asked to pay attention to the programming, which includes two minutes of commercials.

Companies that sell soft drinks and junk food have also taken advantage. Many school lunchrooms feature long rows of vending machines that sell these items. In return, the schools receive a portion of the profits. The medical community finally raised objections. Some of these companies are shifting their product lines to healthier alternatives such as juice, bottled water, and granola bars. But the fact remains that they are selling brand names in school settings.

▲ Advertisers use information from Web sites like Facebook to target ads to teens.

▶ Vending machines are subtle, daily advertisements for soda and snacks.

Start 'Em Young Chances are that you were a target for marketers even before you became a teenager. Kids as young as the 0-to-3 age range are targets, because research shows that even young children understand brands. Virtually every movie, TV show, and children's character can be found on licensed products—from Tickle Me Elmo to Pokémon cards. You may have the *Cheerios Counting Book*, Bob the Builder play sets, and Scooby-Doo Halloween costumes. Dora the Explorer appears on birthday hats, and movie characters of all kinds are found with kids' fast-food meals and on fruit stickers.

Did You Know?

About 17 percent of today's American households have DVRs—digital video recorders—according to Nielsen Media Research. So advertisers are coming up with creative strategies—including sneaking commercials into the shows—to be sure their messages get across even if people with TiVo fast-forward through the ads.

One tactic is to create commercials that feature little dramas or mysteries, enticing viewers to watch so they can find out what happens. Court TV aired an unsolved mystery with clues scattered throughout regular shows. Viewers could text-message or go online to answer questions about the story, and those who solved the mystery shared a $25,000 prize. As the story unfolded, the client's product played a central role.

Advergaming A lot of companies offer games to would-be buyers. Numerous contests, games, sweepstakes, polls, surveys, and online treasure hunts are aimed at young people. *Advergaming* can be used to promote a brand obviously, or the strategy might be more subtle.

The least subtle games appear on a company's own Web site and feature the company's products. Other games, usually designed for computers or video-game devices, prominently feature brand names like NASCAR, Major League Baseball, or the U.S. Army. In the most subtle form of advergaming, product logos appear in other companies' games. In a soccer video game, for example, you might see posters

◀ Advertisers use programming for children to hook them on toys and products that they will beg their parents to buy.

▶ Quiet the influences telling you to buy, and think for yourself about what you need.

Answers to Fact or Fiction

1. False—Most television shows and commercials depict the lives of super-rich celebrities or fictional people; **2.** True; **3.** False—Most people buy things without even thinking about what they are doing; **4.** False—Many off-brand products are actually manufactured in the same plants that make the high-end products, and often there is no difference in quality; **5.** False—A typical company earmarks the majority of its spending for marketing; **6.** True.

along the sidelines advertising Pepsi or Taco Bell.

In the Media Media companies represent the connection between products and consumers. These large companies include many smaller divisions and media outlets, which all try to reach you with their advertising messages. AOL Time Warner, for example, has about a dozen TV channels, a half-dozen magazines, and a number of record labels—plus several film studios, Internet service providers, and search engines. Viacom includes a number of TV channels, radio stations, video stores, book publishers, film studios, and a theme park. Walt Disney has TV stations, book publishers, radio stations, film studios, theme parks, newspapers, sports teams, and magazines.

Be a Smart Consumer

Knowing how advertisers are trying to influence your thinking will help you be a smarter consumer. Half the battle is just being aware of the messages encouraging you to spend. To be a smart consumer, ask yourself questions like these:

- What is this ad about?
- What product is it trying to sell?
- Does this product satisfy a need, or a want?
- Why do I need or want this product? Is that a good reason to buy it?
- Can I afford it?
- Will it take away from my ability to save for a goal or share with others?

Do you want to be financially successful? Most people do, but it means exercising self-control when you spend money. To avoid worrying about money, you need to be a thoughtful money manager and a smart consumer.

If you think carefully and plan your spending, you will be on your way to financial success as an adult. The most financially successful people are not necessarily those who have the most money. Rather, they are people who practice a healthy balance between sharing, saving, and spending—and who avoid going into debt to buy things just for the sake of buying.

SECTION 2 ASSESSMENT

Factual Recall

1. Why do companies target young consumers?
2. List at least three marketing tactics used to promote a company's products.
3. What is social network marketing?
4. What is a celebrity testimonial and why does it work?

Critical Thinking

1. If you were creating a marketing campaign to entice young people to buy a new energy drink for athletes, what are some of the ideas you would include? Why?
2. If you saw an ad telling you that a new model of cell phone would make you more popular, why should you be skeptical of this claim?

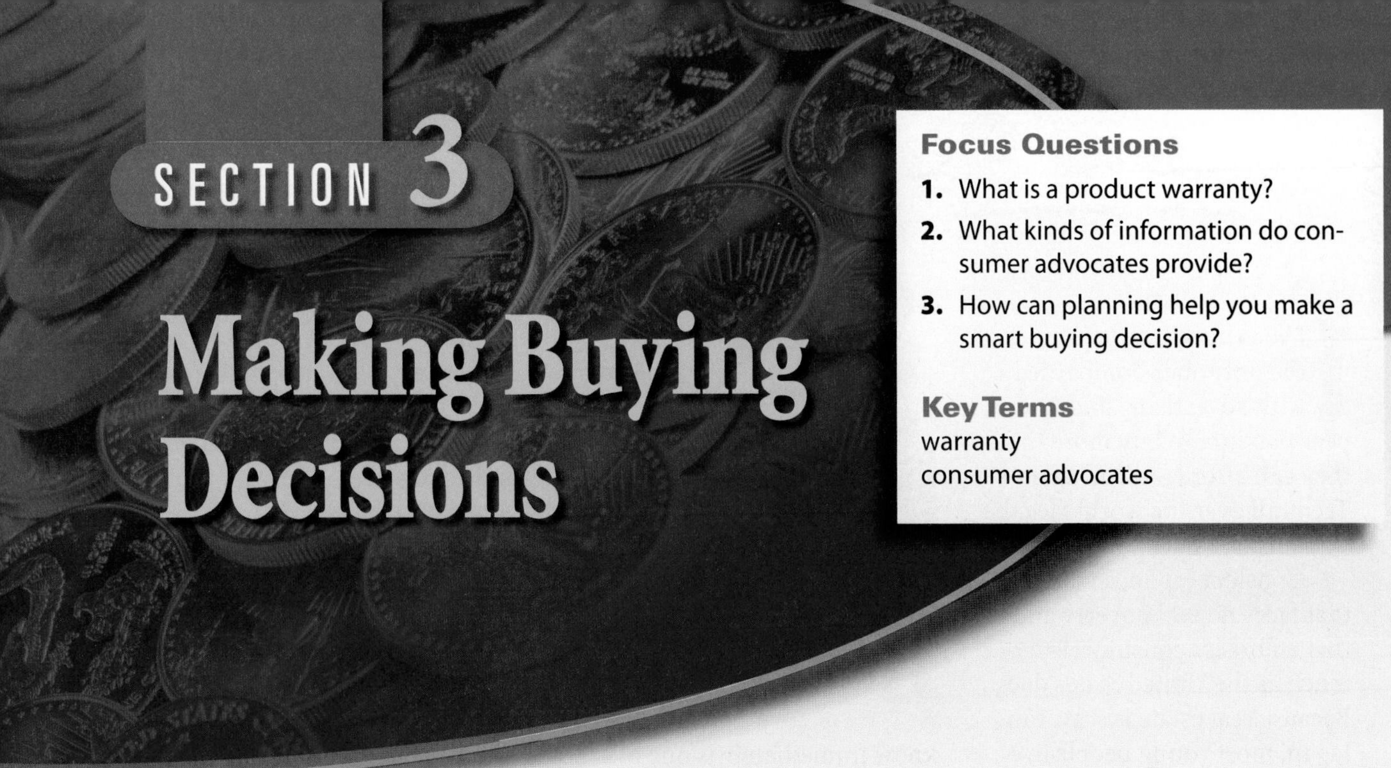

SECTION 3

Making Buying Decisions

Focus Questions

1. What is a product warranty?
2. What kinds of information do consumer advocates provide?
3. How can planning help you make a smart buying decision?

Key Terms
warranty
consumer advocates

If advertisers and retailers are spending so much time and money trying to brainwash consumers, what can you do to make good decisions about what to buy? It is not as difficult as you might think. Being aware of marketing tactics and being thoughtful about your decision making can take you a long way toward being a smart consumer. Then, you can go a step further by researching and learning about your potential purchases.

Gathering Information

Before you buy a new pair of jeans or shoes, a bicycle or stereo, a laptop or cell phone, gather information about the item. Use the Internet or scout out local stores—not to make an immediate purchase, but to see what your choices are. Check out the various brands of the product you want. How do the brands differ from one another? Which are more expensive? *Why* are they more expensive—because they are better quality, or just because the name is more well known? Does one store have a better price for the same item than other stores?

Where to Buy

Sometimes it makes a difference where you buy an item. Different stores offer different deals. One store might offer a **warranty**—a guarantee that if the product breaks down or does not work properly, it will be replaced or repaired. Some warranties are free but others are not, so you would need to evaluate whether a warranty is worth the extra money. Another store might not offer a warranty, but it might allow you to pay for the product a little at a time. And another store might offer a broader selection of colors or models of the item you are buying.

More and more shoppers are turning to the Internet for their purchases. Buying online may get you a better price, but make sure that what you save on the product is more than the shipping and handling costs. Also consider that buying online sometimes makes returns or exchanges more difficult. Most online

warranty an official guarantee to replace or repair a product that does not work properly

Going Global

If you think U.S. teens are the only ones bombarded with advertising and under peer pressure to buy more than they can afford—think again. Teens all over the world face the same situation.

Consider Japan, a country that faces no real poverty and that embraces consumerism as much as the United States does. Because real estate is scarce in Japan, most young people live with their parents well into adulthood. With no need to save for rent, cars, or food, they have a lot of discretionary income to spend on clothes, music, and entertainment.

Clothing manufacturers and retailers take advantage. They produce only a few of each hot item and then sell them for a small fortune. Young people, male and female, line up outside trendy stores, waiting for their turn to go inside and shop. They want to buy *the* unique piece of clothing that everyone else will

know immediately is one of a kind—and that it cost a mint. According to Japanese clothing designer Jun Takahashi, "Japanese people read magazines as their bibles, and when they see images in them they have to have them and will pay anything."

Just like blanket statements about people in the United States or anywhere else, this one should be accompanied by some healthy skepticism. Obviously all Japanese people are not so easily manipulated by marketers and are not so dependent on the opinions of others. But it does show that young people the world over are an attractive target for manufacturers, retailers, and advertisers.

Thinking Globally

1. If a Japanese clothing retailer wanted to create an ad campaign targeted at Japanese teens, do you think it would be more successful hiring a Japanese advertising agency (that understands Japanese culture) or an American ad agency (with more background in persuasive media strategies)? Give reasons for your answer.
2. If U.S. teens had as much discretionary income as Japanese teens, do you think they would be as eager to line up outside of stores and spend all their money on expensive one-of-a-kind items to impress their friends? Why or why not? Explain your answer.

sites, however, work hard to give you good products and services.

Consult with Others

consumer advocates those who support the interests of consumers through activities such as testing products and services, lobbying, and reporting on products and services

Besides doing your own research, you can find out what other people think. Talk to friends and relatives about their purchases, experiences, and opinions. Which brand did your uncle buy, and why? Is he happy with his decision?

You might also consult an independent source of information, such as the research carried out by **consumer advocates**. Publications like *Consumer Reports* offer unbiased information about product choices—everything from cars and exercise equipment to cameras and vacation packages, as shown in Figure 8.3. You can find articles about the various features of different brands, how to get the most for your money, and which models to avoid. You can also look at two or more brands of a particular product, side by side, to compare and contrast the features of each.

Figure 8.3 **Sample Product Information Page**

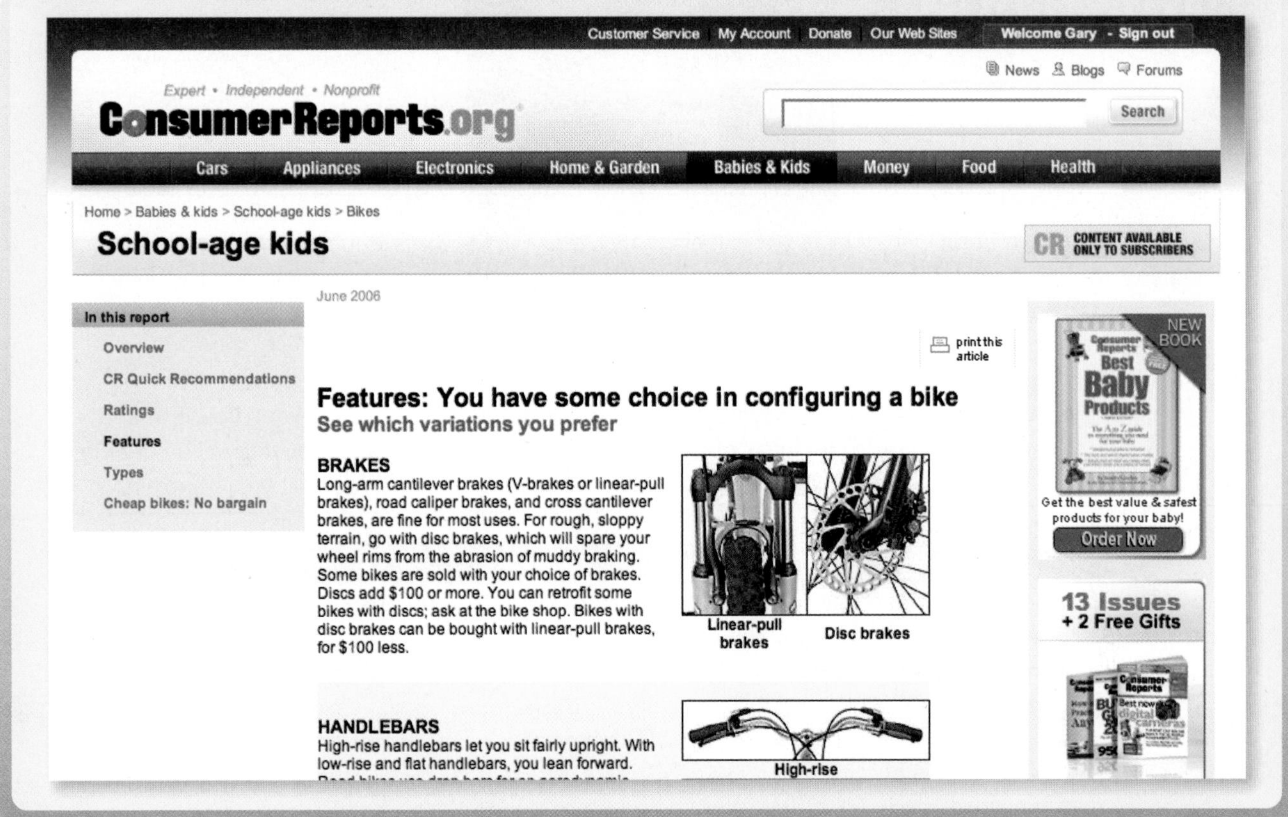

Customer Service | My Account | Donate | Our Web Sites | Welcome Gary - Sign out

News | Blogs | Forums

Expert • Independent • Nonprofit

ConsumerReports.org

Search

Cars | Appliances | Electronics | Home & Garden | Babies & Kids | Money | Food | Health

Home > Babies & kids > School-age kids > Bikes

School-age kids

CR CONTENT AVAILABLE ONLY TO SUBSCRIBERS

In this report
- Overview
- CR Quick Recommendations
- Ratings
- Features
- Types
- Cheap bikes: No bargain

June 2006

print this article

Features: You have some choice in configuring a bike

See which variations you prefer

BRAKES

Long-arm cantilever brakes (V-brakes or linear-pull brakes), road caliper brakes, and cross cantilever brakes, are fine for most uses. For rough, sloppy terrain, go with disc brakes, which will spare your wheel rims from the abrasion of muddy braking. Some bikes are sold with your choice of brakes. Discs add $100 or more. You can retrofit some bikes with discs; ask at the bike shop. Bikes with disc brakes can be bought with linear-pull brakes, for $100 less.

Linear-pull brakes | Disc brakes

HANDLEBARS

High-rise handlebars let you sit fairly upright. With low-rise and flat handlebars, you lean forward.

High-rise

NEW BOOK

Best Baby Products

Get the best value & safest products for your baby!

Order Now

13 Issues + 2 Free Gifts

There are also many online sources you can consult. Web sites like ConsumerSearch (http://fin.emcp.net/consumersearch), BizRate (http://fin.emcp.net/bizrate), and DealTime (http://fin.emcp.net/dealtime) offer product comparisons where you can see how each product rates in terms of price, quality, and feature availability.

Planning Your Purchases

Most people buy things without even thinking about what they are doing. However, *planning* can save you a lot of money. Before you go shopping for a particular item, make a list of the features you want, in order of importance. Then make another list of the features that are not important to you. Checking these two lists while you are shopping will keep your priorities straight. You will not end up paying more for a product that may catch your eye, but that has features you do not really need or will not use.

Say, for example, that you want to buy a new cell phone. Many cell phones

▼ The Internet offers a variety of resources for comparing goods, allowing you to be a careful shopper.

YOU DECIDE

You have been saving for months, and now you are ready to buy that MP3 player. You have been looking at three different MP3 players and made a chart to compare the features of each player. You have enough money to buy any of the three, but cost is not the only factor. Which one would you buy?

Paying close attention to the features of each, choose the player that suits your needs.

Should you . . .

1. ...buy the least expensive one and use the rest of the money for something else? What might be the drawbacks to this option?
2. ...think about how long you plan to keep your PC, and whether you will be getting a Mac next year? Explain.

Features	MP3 player #1	MP3 player #2	MP3 player #3
Internal memory	4 GB	8 GB	30 GB
Computer connection	USB cable included	USB cable included	USB cable included
Batteries	Built-in rechargeable lithium battery	Replaceable rechargeable battery	Internal rechargeable li-poly battery
Formats supported	MP3, WMA, WAV, ASF, TXT	MP3, WMA, WMV, AVI, QuickTime MOV, JPEG, TIFF, BMP, GIF	MP3, AAC, WAV, JPEG, GIF, BMP, MPEG-4
System compatibility	PC only	Windows XP only	Mac, PC
Warranty	None	None	One year
Additional features	FM tuner	Plays downloadable games	Earphones, AV output
Cost	$150	$200	$400

▲ Take time to think about the options that an expensive purchase offers, and get the version that matches your wants and needs.

have built-in cameras, video, music players, games, personal planners, Internet access, e-mail, text messaging, and other features. But many people would have no use for some or all of the extras. Which of these features would you want to be sure you had? Which do you really not care about? With your lists, you can eliminate the phones with unnecessary features—and you could save a bundle.

Planning is also important when you think about *when* to make your purchase. Look for sales. If you are buying a seasonal product, like a winter coat, consider waiting until halfway through the season. Stores will mark down coat prices to make room for spring apparel. If you are buying a swimsuit, think about waiting until the end of summer, when swimsuits go on sale. If you are planning to buy a higher-priced item, like a stereo system, you might want to wait until after your birthday—you might receive gift money to help pay for it.

Planning is important for any purchase—but the more expensive the item, the more thought you should put into it. Weighing the pros and cons of one soccer ball over another should not

LOOK Before You Leap

Pete was at the electronics store with some friends. As they wandered among the television sets, he thought to himself that it would be great to have a TV in his bedroom. He had not planned on buying a television set, but all of a sudden he saw an amazing flat-screen model —and it was on sale for a really good price. He just got his paycheck yesterday, so he could actually pull off the purchase if he wanted to.

Then his friend Nick stepped in with some words of caution: "How do you know the price really is a good one? Maybe there's a reason the set has been marked down. Maybe people have had bad luck with this particular model, and the manufacturer wants to get rid of it. Maybe the set is a display model that customers have been fiddling with, and it's messed up. Is the warranty still good? You'd probably be better off going home to think about it before buying."

Pete agreed and went home to think about it. He needed to decide three things: whether he should buy a TV at all, and, if so, whether this is the make and model he wants to buy, and whether the price at the electronics store is a good deal.

Before Buying

1. Pete went online and checked out customer reviews of that particular model. Then he checked out the manufacturer's reputation. How can this information help him decide whether this is the make and model he wants to buy?
2. Pete also checked out other stores' prices for the same TV set. He learned that the electronics store really did have a good deal. Should he spend his whole paycheck on the TV set? Give reasons for your answer.

take more than a couple of hours. But if you are making a decision about a bigger-ticket item, such as a computer or a car, you will need to take more time to compare various options. Talking to friends and relatives, consulting consumer advocate organizations, and comparison shopping should all be included as you plan. The work you do before your purchase will pay off. In the end, you will be happier with your purchase, confident that you made the right decision.

SECTION 3 ASSESSMENT

Factual Recall

1. What is a warranty?
2. How can consumer advocate organizations help you make a purchase?
3. How can you plan to make an important purchase? What factors should you consider in your planning process?
4. What are the pros and cons of shopping online?

Critical Thinking

1. If you wanted to buy a new laptop computer, what would be the best plan of action? List the steps you would take before your purchase.
2. Assume you bought a new digital camera that came with a six-month warranty. If the camera broke down after only three months and the retailer refused to honor the warranty, what action would you take? How could a consumer advocate organization help?

CHAPTER 8 REVIEW AND ASSESSMENT

Chapter Summary

Needs vs. Wants

- Needs are different from wants. Knowing what is a need and what is a want is important for every consumer.
- Comparison shopping is important in deciding what you want to buy. Think about a product's cost, quality, and features compared to those of other products.
- Create a budget that tells you how much you can afford to spend on wants. Stay within that budget to make sure you have money for your needs.

Advertising

- Advertising is everywhere. Being aware of the ways that advertisers try to influence your buying decisions helps make you an informed consumer.
- Do not believe everything companies tell you in their ads. Their objective is not to inform you. They want to persuade you to spend your money on their products.
- Know the persuasive techniques that companies use. Look at advertising with a critical eye.

Making Buying Decisions

- Plan before you make a purchase. Talk to friends and family members about buying decisions.
- Consult consumer advocate organizations. Compare different products to see which is best matched to your wants or needs.
- Consider waiting for sales and checking out different stores to find the best deal.
- Keep track of your spending, including small purchases, which will help you stick to your limits. A snack here and a magazine there can add up.
- Carry less cash with you when you go shopping because the less you have, the less you will be tempted to spend.
- Take care of the things you buy because replacing them can be expensive.
- Do not buy something just because it is on sale. Instead, make a list of what you need and take it with you to the store.
- Borrow from the library or friends if you need something that you do not have to own.
- Consider picking up used DVDs, music, video games, or other similar items.

Reviewing Key Terms

Choose the vocabulary term that best completes each sentence.

advertising agencies	**consumer advocates**
brand	**marketing tactics**
comparison shopping	**opportunity cost**
consumer	**warranty**

1. A(n) ______ is the name that identifies a product or manufacturer.
2. Some products come with a(n) ______, which is a guarantee to fix or replace a defect.
3. The strategies that companies use to persuade you to buy their products are called ______.
4. Making careful decisions about what to purchase involves ______.
5. ______ create(s) marketing campaigns for companies.
6. A(n) ______ is someone who acquires goods and services.
7. The cost of giving up one thing to get something else is called the ______.
8. ______ are organizations that offer unbiased information about product choices. One example would be *Consumer Reports*.

Understanding the Main Ideas

1. What is the difference between wants and needs?
2. What does a consumer do when he or she is comparison shopping?
3. What are some influences on the spending decisions of young people?
4. In what ways do companies try to get you to buy their products?

5. Name and explain a marketing technique used to persuade potential buyers.
6. What are the factors you should consider when comparing two products?
7. How can consumer advocate organizations help you make a purchase?
8. Name three things to consider when planning a purchase.

Practicing Math

Which of these sports drinks is the most economical purchase? Calculate which is the cheapest per ounce. Then consider the ingredients. Which gives you the most for your money?

Energee: contains carbohydrates, electrolytes
16-ounce bottle: $2.00

Sports-Ade: contains carbohydrates, electrolytes, protein
four 12-ounce cans: $4.00

Kwencher: contains carbohydrates
12-ounce bottle: $1.75

Applying Critical Thinking Skills

1. You earn an allowance and also work ten hours a week. You go shopping with your friends on the weekend and see a really nice shirt on sale. It is a brand-name shirt, on sale for $50. You really like it.
   a. Shirts are clothing. Is the shirt a need or a want? Explain your answer.
   b. You have seen ads for this brand of clothing, so you know it's a really hot brand. Because it is on sale, is it a good deal? Why, or why not?
   c. If you were already going to buy a shirt in the first place, what would you do to plan your purchase?
2. You are going to the mall with your friends. You only need to buy a few items and do not want to spend too much money on this shopping trip. What are some things that you can do to prevent yourself from spending too much money?
3. You have framed some of the photographs you have taken and want to sell them to make a profit. What are some ways that you can advertise your product? Who would be your target audience?

Working with Real-World Documents

Read through this page of a store advertisement circular. Imagine you already have a digital camera that works pretty well. Is buying a new one worth the cost? If you were in the market for a new digital camera, which of these would be the best purchase for you? Explain your answer.

Taking It Home

1. Talk to a parent or other adult about a recent big-ticket purchase. Ask questions about how he or she planned, budgeted, and determined what to buy. Ask the person to reflect on the purchase. Would the person make the same purchase again? Why or why not?
2. Ask a parent or other adult about the advertisements they remember from when they were a child. Do they still remember the products, people in the ads, or a specific jingle? Compare the ads they remember with the ads you are familiar with today?

CHAPTER 9

Transportation

Transportation refers to how you get to the places you need to go. You might live miles from school, or your part-time job might be miles from home. How do you get there?

Even if you can walk to school and the mall, there are times when you need to travel farther away. Most people use a mix of transportation methods. The important decisions you make about transportation will impact your finances, your schedule, your social life, and even the global environment. Thinking about your transportation options will help you make intelligent decisions.

▲ **Biking to work is economical, healthy, and good for the environment.**

SECTION 1	Transportation Choices
SECTION 2	Buying and Maintaining a Car

Fact or Fiction

What do you think? Are the following statements true or false? If you think they are false, then say what is true.

1. For mass transit, most cities use taxis.
2. In most areas, trains are used for commuter service.
3. Buses carry more passengers between U.S. cities than other forms of public transportation.
4. The main form of private transportation in the United States is the automobile.
5. Sales tax must be paid on new cars but not on used cars.
6. The fuel economy of motorcycles is one of their biggest advantages.
7. Hybrid cars have much lower fuel costs.

Answers on page 247.

Study Reminder

*Knowing how to study can increase your knowledge, improve your grades, and cut down on your study time. See the **Studying Personal Finance** pages at the front of the book for some tips to help you study this chapter.*

SECTION 1

Transportation Choices

Focus Questions

1. What is mass transit?
2. What is the most common form of private transportation?
3. What are some of the costs that come with owning a car?

Key Terms

mass transit
commuter service
intercity public transportation
Amtrak
Blue Book
preventive maintenance
miles per gallon (MPG)

mass transit public transportation in an urban area

▼ Taking the bus to work, to school, to the airport, or to visit friends or relatives is an energy-efficient means of public transportation in urban areas.

Walking was the first form of transportation and even today is often the best choice. It costs nothing and provides good exercise. However, not many people can walk everywhere they need to go. Other transportation choices depend on the situation.

Where you live has an impact on your transportation options. Public transportation is more available in areas with large populations. In other places, private transportation—typically the automobile—is the most common way to get around.

Public Transportation

The goal of public transportation is to move groups of people from one location to another as efficiently as possible. As the name implies, such transportation is available to everyone. The use of public transportation saves energy and other resources. The types of public transportation available to you will depend on your location and on where you are going. Areas with larger population usually offer the most options. Rural areas, towns, and small cities may have little or no public transportation. The three categories of public transportation are urban, intercity, and overseas.

Urban Transportation

Urban areas—large cities and their surrounding suburbs—are densely populated. Public transportation in an urban area, called **mass transit**, helps move people from place to place, usually through a system of interconnected buses. Some cities also have light rail systems, which are electrically powered railroad cars that run on tracks at street level.

The cost to use mass transit is often quite low. That makes it possible for people to get to work, to shopping, and to recreational areas for less than it would cost to drive a car. Cities favor mass transit over cars because more people can be moved, reducing traffic congestion as well as pollution.

Commuters are people who must travel some distance between their homes and where they work. The public transportation system that brings workers from the suburbs or nearby communities into cities—and takes them home again—is called **commuter service**. Commuter service runs mainly during business hours and usually relies on trains. In fact, commuters make up about three-fourths of all train passengers in the United States. Commuter trains include both regular surface tracks and underground subway lines. Light rail systems are another alternative. Waterside cities such as New York City, San Francisco, and Seattle also have commuter ferry service for passengers and cars.

Transportation Between Cities

Intercity public transportation connects cities by means of buses, trains, and airplanes. Bus travel is somewhat less expensive than going by train. Flying between locations is the most expensive option.

Amtrak, the National Railroad Passenger Corporation, operates passenger trains in the United States. Trains use less energy per passenger mile than planes, buses, or cars. Unfortunately, many parts of the country lack intercity train service. Because of this, Amtrak offers a system of bus routes that connect to some passenger trains.

▲ Taking the train is an economical and convenient way to travel between cities.

Airplanes carry more passengers between cities than either buses or trains, especially for longer trips. The main advantage of air travel is speed. However, airports are generally located on the outskirts of cities. Sometimes getting to and from the airport can take considerable time. And there are also delays once you get there—checking your luggage and undergoing long waits in security lines.

International Transportation

U.S. citizens do a great deal of international traveling. While ocean liners were once a favored method for overseas travel, planes are now the preferred choice. An important financial aspect of international travel is learning how to calculate exchange rates (see the currency exchange rates table in the Resource Center).

Private Transportation

Private transportation does not run on a schedule, and it is not available to the public. It is for the use of the owner (and

commuter service public transportation systems that bring people from the suburbs or nearby communities into cities

intercity public transportation public transportation connecting cities, usually involving buses, trains, and airplanes

Amtrak the federally subsidized National Railroad Passenger Corporation that operates trains in the United States

perhaps the owner's family and friends), whenever needed. The main form of private transportation is the car. However, there are other, more economical forms of private transportation to consider.

Bicycles

Bicycles are not just for kids. Especially for short distances, bicycles provide economical, nonpolluting transportation, combined with good exercise. Could you use a bicycle for at least part of your transportation needs?

Choose a bicycle according to its intended use, performance, and comfort. *Road bikes* are designed to be ridden on paved roads and bike trails. They are typically lightweight and responsive, with smooth tires and high gearing to allow for fast speeds and efficiency. Rugged *mountain bikes* have sturdy frames, lower gearing, knobby tires, and powerful brakes. They are more comfortable

Going Global

A huge increase in bicycle sales during the early 1970s resulted from gasoline shortages and a boom in cardiovascular exercise. Richard Burke wondered if his employer, Roth Distributing, should invest in bicycles. The idea faded, but a few years later Burke rekindled his interest. He convinced Roth to invest $25,000 into making bicycle frames. Trek started out as a bicycle frame maker, working out of a barn in Waterloo, Wisconsin, as a division of Roth Distributing. It began making complete bicycles in 1980, answering retailers' desire for an American competitor to Schwinn, which had a lock on the street bicycle market.

The company used a European welding technique that resulted in stronger, lighter frames. Later they built aluminum and then carbon fiber bicycles. Trek bikes became popular with racers—but bicycle racing is not a major sport in America.

Europe is a different story, however. There, bicycle racing is second only to soccer in popularity. In 1988, Richard Burke's son John went to Europe to test the waters. The company went global, gaining market share over more well-known European and Japanese brands. The real making of the brand in the global market came with Trek's sponsorship of the U.S. Postal team in the Tour de France, beginning in 1998. Trek made all the bikes Lance Armstrong rode in his seven victories in the Tour, the biggest bicycling event in the world. That made Trek bikes international favorites.

In the early 2000s, Trek expanded its marketing to China, which has the largest number of street bikes in the world. Though sales so far have not been profitable, the company is willing to wait. The thinking is that as the Chinese become wealthier and have more leisure time, the demand for high-tech bicycles will grow—and Trek will be there to meet it.

Thinking Globally

1. Do you think Trek actually will sell a large number of its high-tech bikes in China? Explain your answer.
2. Which would you choose: a high-performance bike built by Trek or a similar bike made in China. Why?

than road bikes and are ideal for riding in rough terrain.

Many people choose a cross between these two types, often called *hybrid, crossbreed*, or *fitness bikes*. They work well for both transportation and recreational biking. Meanwhile, lightweight, practical *commuter bikes* are becoming increasingly popular. They come in five-speed to eight-speed models, are comfortable and reliable, and are great for getting to work and back.

Talk to friends, check reviews, and take a test ride before you buy a bicycle. Look for easy pedaling, precise handling, good brakes, correct size, and overall quality. And of course, for safety, always wear a helmet when you ride a bike.

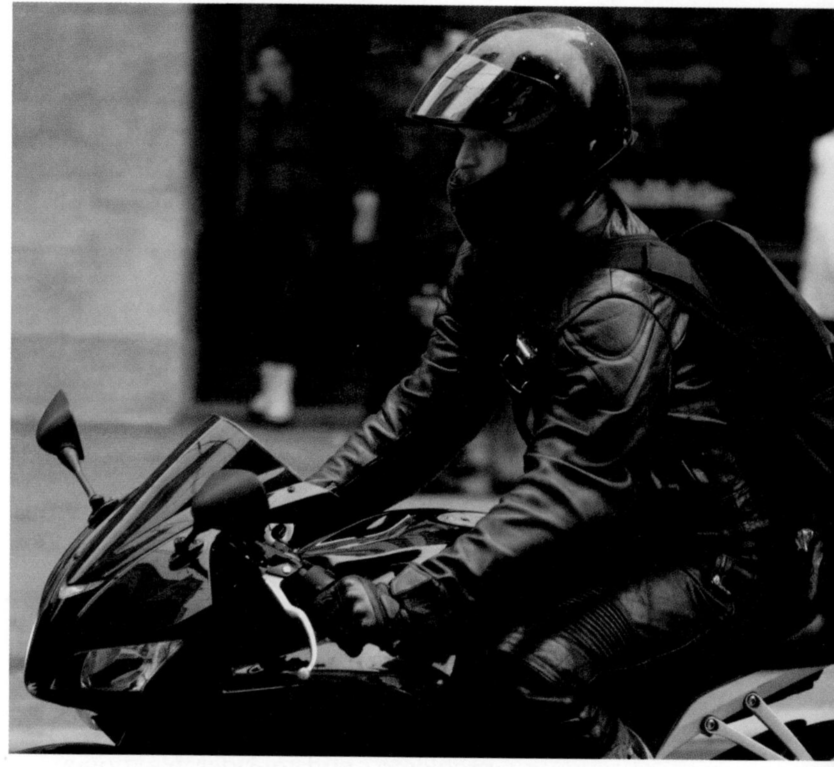

▲ Riding a motorcycle has the advantages of fuel economy, freedom, and quickness, but along with those advantages comes concern for safety.

Motorcycles and Scooters

Some people rely on motorcycles or scooters for transportation. Motorcycles are sometimes called "bikes" (not to be confused with regular bicycles, of course!). They come in many sizes and types, from large and heavy to small and light. You can spend less than $2,000 to more than $30,000 for a motorcycle, depending on the size, brand, and accessories. Scooters or mopeds are smaller, lighter, and less expensive. They can go from 30 mph to 75 mph and are a good option if you frequently travel short distances.

The fuel economy that motorcycles and scooters offer is one of their biggest advantages. Many motorcycles travel 50 or more miles on a single gallon of gas, and scooters can get 60 to 100 miles per gallon.

Motorcycles and scooters also have drawbacks—the primary one being safety. Riding one of these vehicles is far more dangerous than riding in a car. They have less stability than cars, and riders have little protection in a crash. Other drivers often have trouble seeing motorcycles and scooters. That increases the chance of having a serious accident. The high accident rate means that the cost of vehicle insurance is high.

If you purchase a motorcycle or scooter, safety should be your primary concern. Choose one with a rear-view mirror so you can monitor traffic. It should also have a roll bar to provide some protection in a spill. A windshield helps keep dirt and insects away from your face or safety visor.

Always wear protective gear when you ride. A safety visor or goggles help protect your vision. A helmet may save your life in an accident—and in fact, many states require helmets. Heavy clothing, gloves, and boots will help protect you in case of a minor accident. Also remember that motorcycle and scooter riding is safest in good weather. Find other transportation when there is ice, snow, or heavy winds.

Cars and Other Vehicles

Cars—and similar vehicles—are the top choice for private transportation. They are immediately available and can get you there in comfort, in all kinds of weather. This category includes small economy cars, midsize cars, luxury cars, vans and minivans, sports utility vehicles (SUVs), and both small and large trucks. For simplicity, they will all be referred to in this chapter as *cars.*

Cars are convenient, but they are expensive—and the costs do not stop with the purchase price. Ongoing expenses include interest on the auto loan, insurance, taxes and licenses, routine maintenance, repairs, and fuel costs. These expenses almost always total more than the buyer expects. There are many things to consider when purchasing a car, so make sure you know what you are getting into. If you can meet your transportation needs without a car, you will save yourself a lot of problems—and considerable money.

▼ Having access to a car conveniently allows you to go where you want and need to go. But do you need your own, or can you borrow your parents' car or ride with a friend?

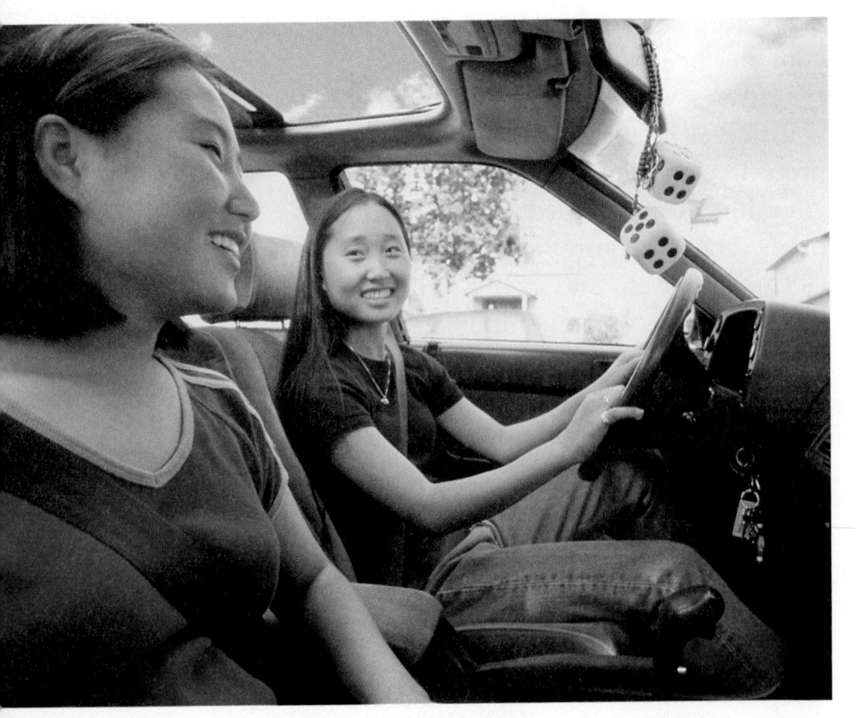

Car Ownership

Regardless of the pros and cons, if you are like most people you will rely on a car for private transportation—either now or someday in your future. Even if you already have a car, you might not realize the true costs involved. Your parents or other relatives probably pay at least some of those costs now. This discussion explains the basic decisions and general costs involved in car ownership. Then, Section 2 of this chapter will outline the specific steps necessary for buying a car and for protecting that investment.

The two major factors to consider are *needs* and *costs.* As you read about choosing a car and estimating the costs involved, think carefully about your own situation. Do you really need a car? Could you afford one? If so, what type of car can you afford? If your income is limited, buying and maintaining a car might be out of your reach until you have saved enough to afford one.

Narrowing Your Choices

You probably have an idea about what your *ideal* car would be. You may picture yourself driving around in a black pickup or a sporty red convertible. However, most people do not start out being able to afford their dream car.

A better place to begin is to think about the type of driving you will do and how you will use your car. A two-door compact model might be a smart choice if most of your driving will be around town. A four-door model might be more convenient if you frequently have several passengers or if you transport lots of items.

Smaller cars tend to cost less—both to buy and to operate. Check out models in the subcompact and compact categories. Because gas prices are high, many people are choosing smaller cars.

The demand for *hybrids* has also increased. Hybrid cars run on two fuel sources—a small gasoline engine and a battery-powered electric motor. The electric motor and batteries help the gasoline engine operate more efficiently. Hybrids are generally more expensive to buy, but

Do Your RESEARCH

The Internet is a great resource for finding new cars and used cars alike. You can browse the listings on sites such as eBay, Autobytel, or Cars.com. You can find information about reliability and repair costs at ConsumerReports.org.

Even if you are not ready to buy a car just yet, you can build your virtual dream car online. Go to the Web site of a car or truck manufacturer you admire, and look for an option such as "Build Your Car," usually located on the home page of the site.

As you follow the on-screen instructions, interactive Web software lets you choose the model, body type, interior and exterior colors, option packages, and accessories. Thinking of adding 20-inch wheels to your truck? Watch them appear on the screen before your eyes. At the same time, you can see the total price change as you add or subtract options.

After you have built the virtual car of your dreams, you may even be able to use it in a video game. The popular Xbox game Project Gotham Racing allows you to "drive" one of more than twenty-five high-performance cars—including a Ferrari, a Porsche, and a BMW—to test your driving skills in the world's most exciting cities.

Your Assignment

Go to the Web site of one your favorite auto makers, and build the car of your dreams. Then find out how much your monthly payments would be on the vehicle using the manufacturer's financing.

their money-saving fuel efficiency is worth considering for the long run.

Of course you should also consider your general price range. How much have you saved for a down payment, and how much can you afford to borrow? Remember that most people purchase a used car as their first car. Do not limit your search to new models only.

Estimating Ownership Costs

When you have a fair idea of the type and size car you would like, pick one or two models and research the costs of ownership. You should investigate the initial purchase price as well as loan interest rates, auto insurance, taxes, and upkeep costs. As just mentioned in the preceding paragraph, for most people their first car is a used car—so the following information is based on doing research for a used car.

Purchase Price You can research the prices of used cars in general, or specific car models, using a variety of sources. Check your local newspaper, or one from a nearby city. Visit used-car lots to see how the overall condition of cars relates to their prices. As mentioned in Chapter 8, one of the best sources of average prices for specific models of used cars is the *Kelley Blue Book*, often called simply the **Blue Book**. Ask for it at your local library or car dealerships. You can also access the Internet version (http://fin.emcp.net/bluebook).

Keep in mind that used-car prices are negotiable. Owners are often willing to sell for 5 to 10 percent less than their asking price.

Blue Book a widely used guide to used-car values, published by the Kelley Blue Book Company

▲ Shop around when buying a car. Compare what the dealers offer with ads from the newspaper and Internet to ensure you get the best deal.

Finance Costs Unless you have saved enough money to pay cash, you will be taking out a loan to pay for a car. To determine the approximate amount of the loan you would need, subtract the amount you have saved for the down payment from your estimated purchase price. Car loans are available from banks, S&Ls, credit unions, finance companies, and sometimes from a dealership itself.

preventive maintenance automotive service intended to keep a car running well and to prevent major problems

To estimate the monthly payments for the amount you are likely to borrow, find an online calculator that determines monthly payments. Section 2 in this chapter gives more information about car loans.

Insurance The cost of car insurance, particularly for young drivers, is a significant expense. Call several insurance companies for estimates. Sometimes getting insurance from the same company as your parents or other family members is less expensive. Tell the agent your age and the make and model of the car you are considering. Find out whether you are eligible for a "good student" discount. For your estimate, ask for the agent's recommendations on coverage. You will learn more about auto insurance in Chapter 15.

Taxes Taxes on cars vary from state to state. Most, but not all, states charge a sales tax. If a sales tax is charged, it applies to both new and used cars. All states require cars to be registered with the Department of Motor Vehicles and to display license plates (sometimes called *tags*). The registration and license fees are another form of taxation. Some states also tax cars separately as personal property, as mentioned in Chapter 3. Find out about the vehicle-related taxes in your state, and take them into consideration when you are estimating the costs of car ownership.

Maintenance Costs Car ownership includes paying for preventive maintenance and repairs. **Preventive maintenance** is automotive service that keeps a car running well and prevents major problems. This service includes engine tune-ups, oil changes, and replacing the battery and tires as needed. Of course, even with preventive maintenance, some repairs are likely—following an accident, for example, or as parts wear out from normal use over time. The more miles you drive and the older the car, the more likely you are to need repairs.

Many potential buyers fail to plan for these expenses. When you figure

Did You Know?

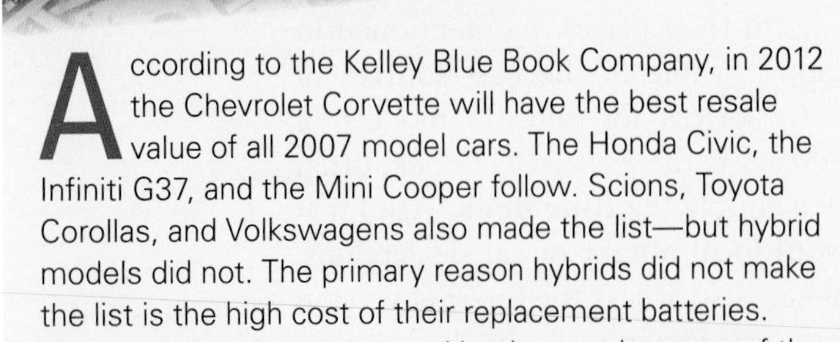

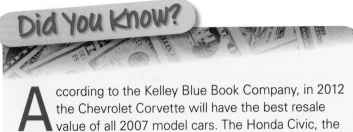

According to the Kelley Blue Book Company, in 2012 the Chevrolet Corvette will have the best resale value of all 2007 model cars. The Honda Civic, the Infiniti G37, and the Mini Cooper follow. Scions, Toyota Corollas, and Volkswagens also made the list—but hybrid models did not. The primary reason hybrids did not make the list is the high cost of their replacement batteries. Most owners are not deterred by the cost because of the hybrid's many benefits, including impressive fuel savings. Additionally, environmentally friendly hybrids support the ecological values of many young drivers.

your estimate, you can assume that *average* yearly maintenance costs will range from about $650 for a small car to more than $2,000 for a large car or SUV.

Fuel Costs Practical buyers always consider fuel costs when choosing a car. Total fuel costs are influenced by the number of miles you drive, the **miles per gallon (MPG)** your car delivers, the type of gas your car uses, and the price of gasoline. Some big SUVs and pickups get just 12 to 15 MPG and also require more expensive premium fuel. The smallest cars and hybrids deliver 35 to 50 MPG and run on the lowest grade of fuel.

To estimate fuel costs, divide the number of miles you expect to drive (15,000 per year is average) by the expected MPG for the car you are thinking about. That will tell you approximately how many gallons of gas you will buy per year. Then multiply that result by the average price per gallon. You now have a rough estimate of the yearly fuel costs for that car.

Totaling the Cost of Ownership Use what you learned from your research to develop cost estimates for the car you are considering. Identify the expenses that occur at the time of sale—down payment, sales tax, license fee, and so on. That tells you how much money you need up front. Next, divide your yearly estimates for the other expenses—car payments, insurance premiums, maintenance, fuel—by 12 to get the monthly cost for each. Then, add up all the monthly costs to arrive at an overall estimated monthly cost of owning that particular car. (Remember that there will also be unexpected expenses. Be sure you have an emergency fund to cover those situations, as you learned in Chapter 4.)

Based on your cost estimates and your income, decide whether you can afford to buy a car. If your anticipated income is not enough to buy the car you selected, try running the numbers for a less expensive car. If your income is likely to increase in the near future, you might decide to wait and buy a car later.

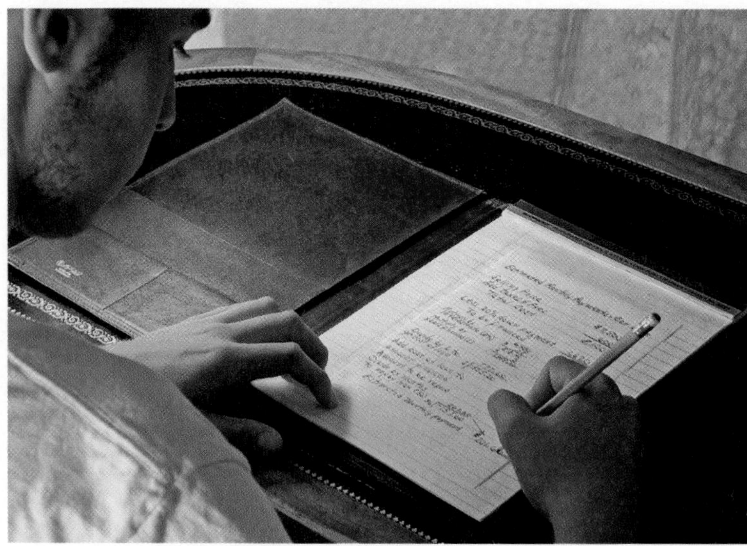

▲ Actually making a list of the expenses involved in car ownership will help you determine the kind of car you can afford.

miles per gallon (MPG) the average number of miles a car travels on one gallon of gasoline

SECTION 1 ASSESSMENT

Factual Recall

1. What is the least expensive form of transportation?
2. What is mass transit?
3. What is the most common form of intercity transportation for long distances?
4. What two major factors should you weigh when you consider the decision to buy a car?
5. What is MPG and how does it influence the cost of owning a car?

Critical Thinking

1. What are the advantages and disadvantages of public transportation versus private transportation?
2. Would riding a bicycle meet most of your transportation needs? Why or why not?
3. If you determine that the car you want costs more than you can afford, what can you do to make owning that car a reality?

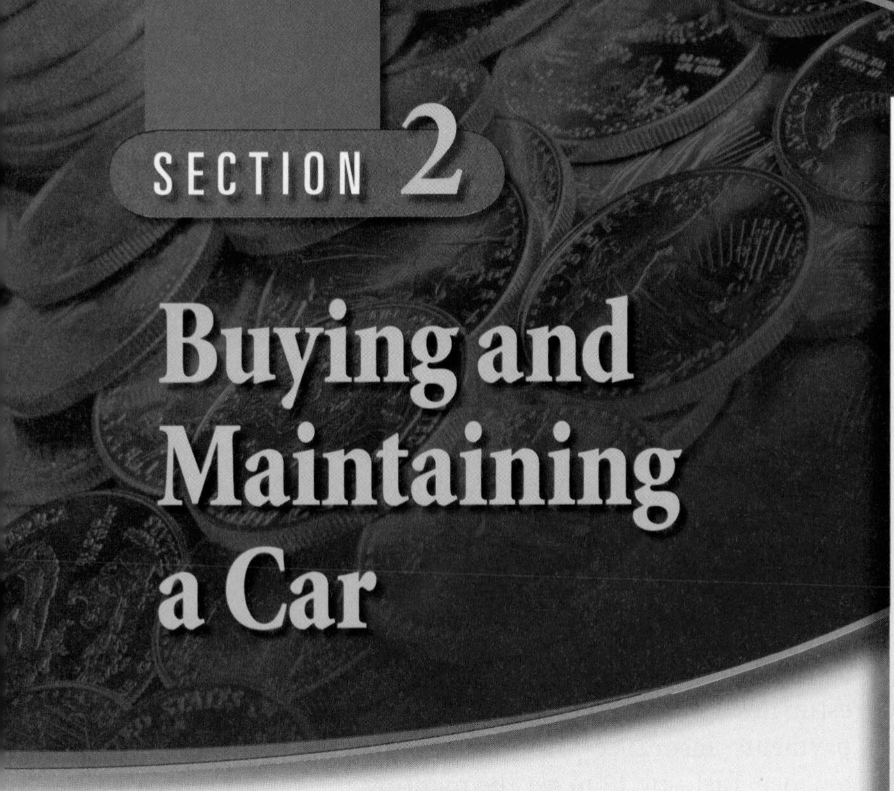

SECTION 2

Buying and Maintaining a Car

Focus Questions

1. What are some publications that provide information on different makes and models of automobiles?
2. Where can you look to buy a used car?
3. What are the things to check when examining a used car?
4. When should you *not* buy a car?
5. What is the purpose of "lemon" laws?
6. What can you do to reduce the need for major car repairs?
7. If you buy a new car, where are you likely to get good service?

Key Terms

depreciation
trade-ins
repossessed
vehicle identification number (VIN)
title
Used-Car Rule
invoice price
sticker price
"lemon" laws
cosign

In Section 1 of this chapter you explored the basic decisions and the general costs involved in car ownership. You did some research on a car that you would consider buying. Once you know what type of vehicle you need and what you can afford—it's time to shop.

For such a large purchase, you need sharp negotiation skills. You should also know how to take care of your car and to protect your investment after you make the purchase. This section explains how to buy and maintain a car.

▼ All cars look their most appealing on the showroom floor. Know what you want, and how much you can spend, *before* beginning to shop.

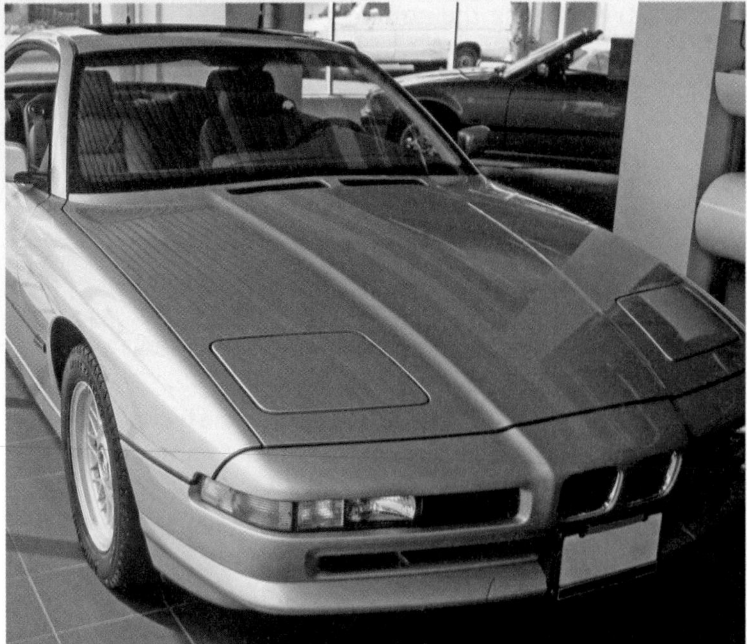

Making Informed Decisions

As you learned in Section 1, evaluating your needs and the costs of car ownership is the first consideration when you are getting ready to buy a car. After determining what will best fit your needs, you can research specific makes and models.

Take advantage of the resources available to you. Various print materials and Internet sites have buying guidelines, tips for evaluating vehicles, and other information about costs and reliability. For example, the Bureau of Transportation Statistics—part of the U.S. Department of Transportation—publishes the *Transportation Statistics Annual Report,* which you can access online (http://fin.emcp.net/transportationreport). Among other facts, this report contains a chart on the "Average Cost of Owning and Operating an Automobile." The American Automobile Association (http://fin.emcp.net/aaa) and Edmunds (http://fin.emcp.net/edmunds) publish several helpful guides on buying a new or used car. January through April issues of *Consumer Reports* magazine (http://fin.emcp.net/consumerreports) include maintenance records of most models of used cars. In addition, you may know people who can help you evaluate potential vehicles. If others know you are looking for a car, they might give you leads about vehicles that are not advertised.

Shopping for a Used Car

Due to **depreciation**—the declining value due to age—the price of a car usually drops thousands of dollars by the time it is just two years old. Buying a used car can have advantages. The price is more affordable, and major problems often have already been discovered and corrected. A used car with low mileage is often a very good buy.

As stressed throughout this book, however, be sure you have done your homework before you shop. For instance, you might want to check the *Consumer Reports Annual Buying Guide*, which has a list of best buys in used cars. With careful shopping, you may find an excellent car at a bargain price—but there are also cars that are no bargain at *any* price. The average used-car buyer seldom inspects a car closely enough to find all the flaws.

Where to Look

When you have in mind the type of car you want to buy (and perhaps the make and model), check several sources to see what is out there.

Private Sales by Owners The best buys in used cars are often from private individuals. These are often advertised in local newspapers or on the Internet. You also may hear about them from people you know.

Vehicles up to three years old are usually still under the manufacturer's *warranty*—written guarantee against specific defects. Ask the owner about the warranty and whether it can be transferred to you.

Also, ask if you can see the maintenance records. These will show how often the car has had oil changes and what kinds of repairs have been made. Write down the name of the garage where the car has been serviced, then stop by and see the mechanic. Ask about the general condition of the car and about problems that the mechanic has observed. You should also ask whether the car was ever in an accident.

New-Car Dealers Almost half of all used cars are sold by new-car dealers. These dealers usually keep only the best of their customers' trade-ins to sell. **Trade-ins** are the used cars that new-car buyers turn in as partial payment on their new-car purchases. Many new-car dealers have their own service departments check out the trade-ins before offering them for sale. They also might make some repairs. New-car dealers may offer a limited warranty with the used cars they sell. If so, read the warranty carefully before you buy, to see what is included and what is excluded.

Used-Car Dealers The lowest-priced cars are often advertised by used-car dealers. These are usually older models or cars with high mileage. Many are trade-ins that new-car dealers did not keep to sell. Used-car dealers are less

depreciation the decline in value of a car or other property due to age

trade-ins the cars that new-car buyers turn in as partial payment on their new-car purchases

likely to have their cars checked and repaired before sale. You must evaluate these cars very carefully. Look for dealers who have been in business for many years and have a good reputation.

Banks and Finance Companies Cars that have been **repossessed**—taken back because of missed loan payments—are sometimes sold by banks and finance companies. Repossessed cars are usually advertised in local newspapers. Sometimes you can buy one simply by paying off the amount due on the loan. Sometimes a *sealed bid* is required. In this case, you write down the amount you are willing to pay, put it in a sealed envelope, and mail it or take it to the seller's office. When the bids are opened, the car goes to the highest bidder. Vehicles from these sources are usually sold "as is"—in other words, without a warranty.

repossessed taken back because of missed loan payments

▶ **Carefully inspect the outside of a used car, looking for dings, body repair work, and other signs of mishandling or bad conditions.**

Rental-Car Agencies Some rental-car agencies buy new cars every year. They advertise their one-year-old models for sale through newspaper ads. These cars typically have been driven a lot of miles in a short time. On the other hand, they are generally well maintained. Some even come with a limited warranty.

Online Listings Many Web sites advertise and sell cars. Some sites list cars for sale by established new-car or used-car dealers. Others include listings by private individuals. Use extra caution when considering a purchase on the Internet. Always carefully check out *in person* any car that interests you, and do not reveal your personal financial information over the Internet.

What to Look For

The purchase of a car is one of the largest investments you will make. Thoroughly examine any car you are thinking about buying. Besides checking it out yourself, it usually pays to have someone who knows cars well take a look at it.

Check the Exterior and Interior Check the outside for any evidence of an accident (dents, faint ripples along the sides, and paint that does not quite match). Do all the windows and lights work? Is the car level? If not, a spring may need replacing. Push down hard on each corner of the car several times and then let go. If the car continues to bounce, it probably needs new shock absorbers.

Tires are expensive to replace. Check for any bulges, and make sure the tire tread shows even wear.

If the interior is clean and undamaged, the owner probably took good care of the car overall. Signs of excess wear on the seats or surfaces may indicate that it has not received such care.

Go for a Test Drive If you like the car, take it for a test drive. Actually drive the car for ten or twenty minutes in town and on the highway—not just a quick spin around the block. This will give you a good idea of its condition and can help you decide how well it handles.

As you drive, see whether the motor runs and shifts smoothly. Does it have good acceleration when you step on the gas? On a straight, level surface like an empty parking lot, test the brakes. Accelerate to about 45 miles per hour, then brake. The car should stop quickly without pulling to either side. Repeat this two more times and note any changes. Try out both the air conditioner and the heater.

Go through the following questions to make sure the car is right for you.

- Does the car shift smoothly?
- How does the car handle? Is it firm and stable?
- How are the brakes? Can you stop quickly?
- Is there enough headroom and legroom?
- Is your driving position comfortable?

LOOK Before You Leap

Briley, a high school senior, has saved $3,500 over three years. He decides the time is right to buy a truck. He's been thinking about a Toyota Tacoma. He checks *Consumer Reports* and sees that the frequency-of-repair records look good for that model.

Searching through the newspaper classifieds, Briley spots a 5-year-old short-bed Tacoma with 50,000 miles on the odometer for $6,500. *Kelley Blue Book* online tells him that this truck, in good condition, should sell for around $7,000 in his town. Great—maybe he can get a good deal. He can afford to finance the other $3,000.

So Briley checks out the truck. The body looks pretty good, but when he drives it, the ride seems bouncy. The owner tells Briley that he's a newspaper distributor, and he used the truck to deliver papers around the southern part of the state. Briley asks if he can take the truck to a mechanic friend. The owner seems a little reluctant, but agrees.

The mechanic tells Briley that the truck will need new shocks—the constant weight of the newspapers has worn them. And the mechanic also suggests that Briley get a vehicle history report on the truck from Carfax.com. He is suspicious of the low mileage reading, since the owner says he made deliveries over a large area. He tells Briley that the report can also reveal major repairs and can track ownership of the truck since it was new.

Sure enough, when Briley gets the report, it turns out the truck had 50,000 miles on it *two years ago*, when it had some repairs to the transmission. The truck is starting to look like it might not be such a bargain after all. Briley is glad he spent the money to check out the truck's condition—better to spend a little money now than discover major problems too late.

Before Deciding

1. What are some other sources of information that Briley could use in his search for a good truck at a fair price?
2. Briley told the truck's owner what he learned, and the owner offered to cut $2,000 off the asking price. Should Briley buy the truck at the lower price of $4,500, using the money he saves to make the needed repairs? Give reasons for your answer.

▶ **Have a trusted mechanic look over any used car you want to buy. The inspection can prevent you from buying a bad car and save you lots of money.**

- Are the controls and gauges easy to use?
- Check your visibility. Can you see clearly on all sides of the car?

Check the Vehicle History Report You can use the Internet to check the history of any car built since 1981. Log on to Carfax (http://fin.emcp.net/carfax), and you can find out how many owners the car has had, whether the car has been in a major accident, or if the manufacturer has recalled the car for any reason. You will need the car's **vehicle identification number (VIN)** to look up information on Carfax. The VIN is a number assigned at the factory, identifying the individual car. It can be found on a small metal plate attached to the dashboard, on the driver's-side doorjamb sticker, and on the title document. Each car has a different VIN.

Get a Mechanic's Evaluation If the car passes your inspection, ask a trusted mechanic to check it over more thoroughly. The mechanic should look underneath the car for excessive rusting or cracks in the frame. He or she should check all the major mechanical systems, look for signs of fluid leaks, and examine the belts and hoses. The steering, braking, electrical, and exhaust systems need to be checked. Ask specifically about anything you noted during your test drive. Paying for a thorough, independent evaluation can save you from buying a car that has serious problems.

All cars manufactured in recent years have an onboard computer called an *electronic control module* (ECM) that controls the engine operation and emissions system. For trained auto mechanics, the ECM helps diagnose problems, but it is difficult for the average person to check how well all the electronic components are functioning.

Get a Clear Title Make sure the owner can give you a clear title before you buy. The **title** is a document that proves you legally own the car. Some buyers get stuck with a car that is about to be repossessed or one that is stolen. If the seller says he or she will get the title for you later, wait until it arrives before agreeing to buy the car. You can check Carfax to learn if there is a problem with a car's title.

vehicle identification number (VIN) a unique number assigned to a car at the factory for identification purposes

title a document that indicates the legal owner of a vehicle

When Not to Buy

There are many reasons *not* to buy a car—even if it is the model you want at a good price. Is the salesperson pressuring you too much? Are you told that you must decide immediately? Were you refused a test drive or the chance to have your mechanic check out the car? Is it an online purchase that you have not evaluated in person? Be sure you look the car over carefully in daylight on a dry day. Even cars with bad paint jobs look good when they are wet. You are always better off passing up an "opportunity" that does not seem right than getting stuck with a problem vehicle.

Getting the Best Deal

When you have found a car that satisfies you, ask the dealer or owner for the lowest price. Whatever the answer, he or she will almost always accept even less—so you can save money by bargaining. Make the lowest offer you think might be accepted. If it is not accepted, you can always offer more.

The Federal Trade Commission (FTC) wrote the **Used-Car Rule** to protect used-car buyers. This rule requires dealers to place a sticker called the Buyers Guide on every used car offered for sale. It tells the buyer whether the car is being sold "as is" or with a warranty. If the car comes with a warranty, the Buyers Guide tells how much (if any) of the repair costs the dealer will pay. Cars sold by a private individual are not covered by the Used-Car Rule.

Used-Car Warranties

Warranties on used cars, when offered, differ from dealer to dealer. Some warranties provide for all parts and labor for thirty to ninety days. Others pay half the cost of repairs for a certain period of time. If you receive a dealer's warranty and you suspect something is wrong with your car, take the car back right away. If the dealer does not fix it to your satisfaction, keep taking the car back until it is done right. Do not accept an excuse such as "You don't have an appointment—bring your car back next week." The warranty period could expire before the car is fixed correctly.

Some states require motor vehicle inspections. If the dealer guarantees that a car will "pass inspection," get it in writing.

Shopping for a New Car

A new car costs more than a used one, but shopping for a new one is more straightforward. You can get a new car with exactly the options you want—although you may have to wait a month or two. By doing so, you will not have to pay for a lot of extra features that you don't care about.

Even with a new car, it is important to do research and evaluate the options. Car magazines, consumer publications, and Web sites carry evaluations of new models. Take a test drive to see whether you feel comfortable in the car. Are the controls easy to operate and easy to reach? Try sitting in the backseat, as well as the front, to check for comfort.

New-Car Warranties

One of the advantages of buying a new car is that you will receive a warranty covering most major repairs for several years or until you have driven the car a specified number of miles. Terms of new-car warranties vary considerably among car manufacturers and sometimes even from model to model. You can also purchase an *extended warranty* from new-car dealerships that extends the original warranty for a longer period of time and for more miles.

Negotiating the Best Price

For new cars, comparing prices is easier than for used cars. The **invoice price**, sometimes called the *factory invoice*

Used-Car Rule a federal trade rule requiring dealers to place an informative sticker on every used car, telling the buyer both whether the car is being sold "as is" or with a warranty, and how much of the repair costs the dealer will pay

invoice price the price the dealer pays the manufacturer for the car

▲ You can usually buy new cars for less than the sticker price.

price or the *dealer invoice price*, is what the dealer paid the manufacturer for the car. The **sticker price** or manufacturer's suggested retail price (MSRP) is the retail price that the manufacturer sets for the car. It may be 10 to 15 percent above the dealer's cost, but does not include transportation (so-called "destination charges") and dealer-installed options. The sticker price is only a suggested price—dealers can charge more or less.

To negotiate a fair price, you really need to know only the dealer's invoice price and the sticker price. Decide on the exact make, model, color, and options you want, then go online and check Edmunds (http://fin.emcp.net/edmunds) to learn the dealer's invoice price, which is not shown on the car. Armed with this information, ask the dealer for the lowest price the dealer will accept.

sticker price the retail price that the manufacturer sets for the car

"lemon" laws laws providing relief for people who buy new cars that do not meet basic standards of quality and performance

Just as with a used car, you can almost always buy a new car for less than the stated "lowest" price. You might be able to negotiate a price that is just $300 to $500 above the dealer's invoice price. Dealers often receive incentive payments that boost their profit on sales, so the dealer usually makes money even by selling at near cost. If possible, compare prices from several dealers. If you are looking for a popular new car in short supply, then you might have to pay the sticker price.

If You Have a Trade-In

Learn the approximate value of the car you intend to trade in by checking *Kelley Blue Book* or another source, such as the National Automobile Dealers Association's *NADA Price Guide* (available online at http://fin.emcp.net/nadaguides). Keep in mind that mileage and condition will affect the actual value of your trade-in. Wait until you have negotiated the lowest price for your new car before offering to trade in your current car. By keeping the purchase and trade-in deals separate, you will know exactly how much you are paying for your new car—and how much they are allowing for your trade-in.

If you are patient, you usually can get a higher price for your old car by selling it yourself. Advertise it in your local newspaper or on the Internet. However, if you need the money from selling your current car to purchase the new one, you may not be able to wait until you can sell it on your own.

New-Car "Lemon" Laws

New cars ought to run well for a long time, but sometimes a new car will have one problem after another, or maybe the same problem over and over. These cars, which leave a bitter taste in the mouths of their owners, are known as *lemons*. Most states have laws that provide some relief for the owners of such cars.

These **"lemon" laws** vary from state to state, but most define a "lemon" as a new vehicle that has been in the shop at least four times for the same repair, or is out of service for thirty days or more during the first year. You can find out your state's "lemon" law from your local consumer protection office or state attorney general's office, or by looking online.

Financing a Car

If you pay for your car with cash, you will not have to pay any interest or loan fees. However, if you are like most car buyers and cannot afford to pay cash, you will have to borrow some money. Many lenders require that you pay at least 20 percent of the selling price as a down payment. If you have an older car to trade in or sell, that may be enough to serve as your down payment. You can apply for a loan for the rest.

Arranging a Loan

Unless you have an established credit rating, the lender may require a responsible adult with good credit to **cosign** your loan. That means the person guarantees that you will make the payments. A cosigner takes on considerable risk.

As mentioned in Section 1 of this chapter, auto loans are available from banks, S&Ls, credit unions, finance companies, and sometimes the dealers themselves. Dealers might offer very low interest rates on certain cars—but be aware that there are trade-offs. The dealer might not be willing to negotiate on the price or might require you to buy *credit insurance* that will pay off your loan if you die or become disabled. Arranging financing through a new-car dealer may save time, but you might be able to save money by arranging it on your own.

Exploring Your Options

Take time to gather information about various loan options before you actually buy a car. Check rates and conditions at local banks and credit unions. Will you be required to have a cosigner? Compare their terms with the terms offered by the dealer. If you do not qualify for a loan through these sources, then check with a consumer finance company. These loans typically have higher finance charges and interest.

To pay off your loan, arrange for the highest monthly payment you can afford. This will eliminate the loan in the shortest time possible and hold down the total cost of your loan by reducing interest charges. Find out if you can pay off the loan early—by making larger payments or extra payments. The contract should specifically allow for a reduction of the finance charges if you pay it off early.

Buying Insurance

When you test-drive a car, the dealer or former owner has insurance on it. When you buy a car, you should have your own insurance before you drive it home. If you finance a car, the bank or loan company will probably require proof of insurance to protect its money in case the car is badly damaged. In many states, car insurance is a legal requirement. Even if it is not required in your state, you will need insurance for your own protection. For example, a lawsuit resulting from an accident could cost you hundreds of thousands of dollars. As mentioned in Section 1 of this chapter, you should contact several insurance companies before you purchase a policy. Car insurance is discussed in greater detail in Chapter 15.

cosign to act as joint signer on a loan or contract, guaranteeing payment if the primary signer does not meet the requirements

Did You Know?

You probably know that if you hit another car, your insurance company will increase the premium for your car insurance. But most people don't know that their credit scores can also have a major impact on the cost of their car insurance. It is a good idea to know your credit score before you shop for car insurance—and of course, to keep your credit record clean in the first place.

What About Leasing a Car?

Leasing a car is something like renting it for a specific period of time. It seems like all ads for new cars mention low monthly payments if you lease the vehicle. Have you wondered whether it is better to lease than to buy?

Advantages of Leasing

Leasing a car has several advantages. Among them are the following:

- You can drive a new or nearly new car with a lower down payment than if you purchased the same car.
- Your payments are lower than if you purchase a car. You are not paying for the whole life of the car, just for the time of the lease period.
- Often the dealer will provide an excellent service package to be sure the car stays in good condition for resale at the end of your lease.
- At the end of the lease you just give back the car to the dealer or agency.

Disadvantages of Leasing

Of course there are some disadvantages. Among the drawbacks are these:

- You do not own the car. At the end of the lease, you have nothing to show for the money you have paid.
- You might have to pay a security deposit and other fees at the beginning of the lease.
- If you drive more miles than specified in the lease, you will have to pay an extra fee.
- Your insurance costs might be greater because the dealer could require you to carry a higher level of coverage.
- You will always have a car payment. People who buy a car and pay off the loan can drive for years without making any car payments.
- If you want to end the lease early, you will probably have to pay a significant penalty.
- You can buy the car at the end of the lease period, but you will pay much more than if you had purchased the car in the first place.

Deciding Whether to Lease

If you decide that you want to lease rather than buy, remember to get every detail in writing. Also, work out a fair price for the car *before* you ask about a lease. That way the dealer cannot hide the price of the car under lease terms.

There are no clear-cut answers about whether leasing or buying is better. If you want to drive a newer car but do not have the necessary down payment to buy it, then you may decide to lease. If you plan to drive the same car for more than a few years, you will save money in the end by purchasing your car.

Protecting Your Investment

It's a great feeling to drive home in the car you have just purchased. Whether you will continue to be happy and satisfied with your choice depends on how well your car continues to run and how economical it is to drive.

Maintaining Your Car

All vehicles need to be repaired now and then. Regular preventive maintenance makes major repairs less likely. See Figure 9.1 for a list of things to check regularly and see Figure 9.2 for a list of tips for economical driving. Every new car comes with an owner's manual that provides information about the car and how to care for it properly. Follow the

Figure 9.1 REGULAR CAR MAINTENANCE CHECKUP

Do these checks at home when you have not driven your car for several hours. A cold engine will give more accurate readings. Check your owner's manual if you have any trouble with the instructions.

Tire Tread Tires need to have at least 1/16 inch of tread. You can use a pencil to measure the tread. Another option is to insert a penny into the tread groove with Lincoln's face showing upside-down. If you can see all of Lincoln's head, the tire needs replacement.

Tire Pressure Use a pressure gauge to check the pressure in each tire. The recommended pressure is posted on the driver's doorjamb, glove box, or fuel cap.

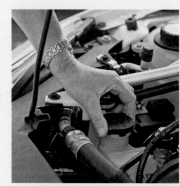

Belts Check belts for cracks, glazing, or missing ribs on the underside. Replace belts if any of these problems are found.

Washer Fluid If the washer fluid level is low, fill the tank to the top.

Brake Fluid Many cars have see-through reservoirs and easy-to-read markings. Make sure not to let any water or dirt in the compartment. Fill to the FULL line if necessary.

Coolant Check the coolant overflow tank and add a 50-50 mix of coolant and water until it reaches the MAX mark. If the coolant appears rusty or oily, there is a problem and you should contact a mechanic.

Power-Steering Fluid If the engine is cold, the fluid should reach the COLD mark. Check the dipstick and add fluid if the level is low.

Transmission Fluid Warm up your car a few minutes and then check the dipstick. Fill to the FULL mark if necessary. If your car does not have a dipstick, check with a mechanic.

Hoses Check hoses for bulges, cracks, and mushy spots. Replace the hoses if any of these problems are found.

Oil If the oil level is low, add oil up to the FULL mark on the dipstick. If the oil is gray or black, you probably need an oil change.

Figure 9.2 CHECKLIST FOR DRIVING ECONOMY

The following tips for gas-saving maintenance and driving really work. Try them all, and see how many added miles you can get from a tank of gas.

Maintenance

- ☑ Keep your car properly tuned.
- ☑ Inflate tires to the correct pressure. Check them when they are cold.
- ☑ Keep the air filter clean.
- ☑ Keep the fan belt tightened.
- ☑ Use radial tires to improve mileage.

Driving

- ☑ On the highway, drive at a steady speed no higher than 65 miles per hour (or lower if the posted limit is lower).
- ☑ Keep the windows closed when driving over 40 miles per hour. Open windows cause resistance, and that uses more gas.
- ☑ Whenever you stop for more than a minute, turn off the ignition and restart the engine when you are ready to go. Of course, you will have to decide whether it would be difficult to restart in very hot or very cold weather.
- ☑ When starting your car in cold weather, do not let it sit still to warm up for more than a minute.
- ☑ Fast, erratic ("jack-rabbit") starts waste gas, so do very slow takeoffs. A medium-fast start is the most economical. Accelerate slowly on gravel and sand, and on snowy, icy, or rain-slick roads.
- ☑ Look ahead to traffic lights. If a light is red, take your foot off the accelerator and coast to a stop. Avoid using the brakes when you can. When the light turns green, accelerate smoothly.
- ☑ Accelerate slightly before starting up a hill. Do not try to gain speed going up. Once over the top, let up on the gas pedal and let gravity help carry you down the other side.
- ☑ Do not cut in and out of traffic.

regular maintenance schedule outlined in the manual. You will save money in the long run by keeping repair bills down and by saving gas.

Arranging for Repairs

If you buy a new car, you will probably get the best service by having it maintained and repaired at the dealership. The same goes for a used car bought from a new-car dealer. If you buy from a private individual, ask where the car has been serviced, and ask whether the owner was satisfied with the garage's maintenance and repair service. Members of your own family or family friends are other good sources of information on auto mechanics with good reputations.

When your car needs service or repairs, make an appointment. Arrange to leave the car long enough for the repairs to be done properly. Unless you are certain about what's wrong with your car, just describe the symptoms. Leave the diagnosis to the mechanic. When the problem is identified, ask to be contacted with an estimate of the cost of the repairs, before the work is actually done.

Take common sense precautions before leaving your car. Even though a repair service is honest, many people come and go daily. Remove any valuable items from your car. Also leave *only* your car key, not your whole set of keys. Write down the odometer mileage as well, so you will know that your car was not used improperly while it was out of your possession.

When you return for your car, look it over carefully. As you drive away from the

◀ Taking your car in for regular maintenance and repairs helps to prevent bigger breakdowns and saves you money in the long run.

garage, notice whether the original problems have been solved. If they have not, drive right back and talk to the mechanic or service manager. You may have to make another appointment and bring the car back later, but at least you will not be charged for something that was not fixed.

Driving for Economy

The average driver uses about 800 gallons of gasoline each year. With high gas costs and concerns about the global oil supply, it makes sense to drive in ways that conserve fuel.

Some newer cars display the current MPG while you are driving. You can see the numbers change as you accelerate, coast, or drive up or down a hill. If your car does not have this feature, you can add an accessory called a *vacuum gauge*, available at most auto accessory stores, that will do the same thing. By monitoring the MPG your car delivers, you will learn to drive more economically.

Even without such equipment, you probably already know some driving habits that waste gas. Jack-rabbit starts, jamming on the brakes instead of coasting to a stop, and driving too fast would all be on that list. You can find many more ideas online. For instance, "Driving Tips for Tree-Huggers" at CarTalk (http://fin.emcp.net/cartalk) has tips for saving fuel and other ideas for helping the environment.

Answers to Fact or Fiction

1. False—Cities favor buses for mass transit; **2.** True; **3.** False—Airplanes carry more passengers between distant cities than either buses or trains; **4.** True; **5.** False—Sales tax must be paid on new and used cars; **6.** True; **7.** True.

SECTION 2 ASSESSMENT

Factual Recall

1. What publication provides a list of the best buys in used cars?
2. What are three sources for an auto loan?
3. What are three precautions you should take when leaving your car for service or repair?
4. What are two advantages and two disadvantages of leasing a car instead of buying it?

Critical Thinking

1. How can knowing both the sticker price and the dealer's invoice price help you figure out what is a fair purchase price for a new car? Where can you find these two pieces of information?
2. How would you decide where to take your car for maintenance and repairs?
3. What are some ways that you can save money while driving your car?

CHAPTER 9 REVIEW AND ASSESSMENT

Chapter Summary

Section 1 Transportation Choices

- Urban public transportation is usually provided by buses. Commuter service usually relies on trains.
- Transportation between U.S. cities is usually by bus, train, or airplane. Transportation to locations overseas is usually by airplane.
- When shopping for a bicycle, take a test ride—and look for easy pedaling, precise handling, good brakes, correct size, and overall quality.
- When thinking about what type and size car you might want to buy, consider the kind of driving you do and the number of passengers you usually have.
- One of the best sources of prices for specific models of used cars is the *Kelley Blue Book*.
- All states require cars to be registered with the Department of Motor Vehicles and to display license plates.

Section 2 Buying and Maintaining a Car

- Buying a used car is much cheaper than buying a new one, but you may not get your choice of accessories.
- The *Consumer Reports Annual Buying Guide* publishes a list of best buys in used cars.
- One advantage of buying a new car is that you get a warranty that covers major repairs for several years.
- You can almost always buy a new car for less than the sticker price.
- When taking out a car loan, choose the highest monthly payment you can afford, to reduce the overall cost of the loan.
- You need auto insurance to protect yourself and your car. Many states require it.
- Leasing a car has fewer up-front costs and lower monthly payments, but also has extra fees and penalties if the lease terms are not strictly followed.
- To keep your car in good condition, take it to a reputable mechanic for maintenance and repairs.

Reviewing Key Terms

Indicate whether each of the following statements (featuring key terms) is true or false. If a statement is false, rewrite it to make it true.

1. Local public transportation in large urban areas is called **mass transit**.
2. **Commuter service** transports people from one city to another distant city.
3. **Intercity public transportation** refers to the system of buses, trains, and airplanes that transport people from one city to another city.
4. **Amtrak** is a high-speed commuter train linking major cities in the eastern corridor of the United States.
5. The **Blue Book** is an excellent source for finding dependability ratings of used cars.
6. **Preventive maintenance** is expensive and unnecessary work that a mechanic will try to sell you.
7. **MPG** is a measure of how many miles a car can travel on one gallon of fuel.
8. The declining value of a car due to its age is called **depreciation**.
9. **Trade-ins** are cars that dealerships have used as demonstration cars.
10. The **vehicle identification number (VIN)** is different for each car.
11. The **title** is a legal document showing who owns the car.
12. The FTC's **Used-Car Rule** protects the dealer from having to take a car in poor condition as a trade-in.
13. The **sticker price** is the price the dealer pays for the car.
14. **"Lemon" laws** allow buyers to return new or used cars they don't want for a refund.

Understanding the Main Ideas

1. Name the three categories of public transportation.
2. Mass transit most commonly uses which mode of transportation?

3. Name the three most commonly used means of transportation for intercity service.
4. What is the most common form of public transportation to locations overseas?
5. List three advantages of riding a bicycle for private transportation.
6. What are three important qualities to consider when purchasing a bicycle?
7. Why do the insurance premiums for motorcycles tend to be high?
8. What are the two major factors to consider when you are thinking about buying a car?
9. Name four sources where you might shop for a used car.
10. What are four ways you can check on the condition of a used car?
11. What are the two things you need to know in order to negotiate a fair price on a new car?
12. Why is it important to follow a regular maintenance schedule for your car?

Practicing Math

1. The *odometer reading* (number of miles driven) on Evelyn's car was 41,205. She filled up her gas tank and drove to another town to visit her mother. When she returned from her trip, she purchased gas again. It took 8.9 gallons to fill her tank. This time the odometer reading was 41,415. How many miles per gallon did she get on her trip? Round your answer to the nearest tenth of a mile.
2. Using the information from question 1, calculate the fuel cost per mile if Evelyn paid $3.09 per gallon of fuel. Round your answer to the nearest cent.
3. If Evelyn is planning a 2,500-mile trip, what should she estimate for her fuel cost for the trip?

Applying Critical Thinking Skills

1. Select a location in the United States that you would like to visit. The location should be distant from where you live. Then explain what factors you would need to consider in deciding which form of transportation would be the best way for you to travel to that location.
2. Examine the forms of public and private transportation that are available to you locally. Decide which of these best fit your current needs and wants. State your decision and explain how you arrived at it.
3. Imagine that you saved $3,000 to buy a car, which is all the money you can afford to put toward a car purchase at this time. Create three scenarios for how this money may be used, based on the following options: (a) Buy a used car, (b) Lease a car, or (c) Make a down payment on a new car. In creating your scenarios, list how much you would spend on fees, insurance, and maintenance to determine how much money you will spend in total. Will you spend more than $3,000? If so, how much more will you spend?

Working with Real-World Documents

1. Compare loan applications and loan terms from an auto dealership with those from a conventional lending institution. Write a summary of the similarities and differences.
2. Examine what a new-car warranty covers for at least three cars. Also, examine what actions an owner must take to make certain that the warranty is not voided upon purchase of the car. Summarize your findings.

Taking It Home

1. Make comparisons on three vehicles owned by family and friends. Compare the MPG and the total cost of fuel and maintenance for one month. Which car has the best miles per gallon rate?
2. Ask an adult family member or friend to help prepare a summary of their *actual* costs of owning and operating a car for the last six months. Gather receipts for fuel, repairs and maintenance, insurance, car payments, license tags, smog test fees, parking fees, road tolls, car washes, and any other expenses they can remember. Total these expenses and divide by 6 to obtain their average monthly expense. This will give you an indication of what you can expect to pay, too.

CHAPTER 10

Housing

Having a place to live meets some of your most basic human needs—shelter, safety, and security. It also helps fulfill higher-level needs such as interaction with others and self-esteem.

However, if needs were the only things that mattered, a cave or hut would be satisfactory. But housing choices are also shaped by wants—personal desires and preferences. Wants are influenced by culture and the media, personal experiences, and likes and dislikes.

▲ Housing needs vary depending on personal desires.

At various stages of life, people consider different things to be most important. A single person or a young couple may find apartment living very comfortable, while a family with children may prefer a house with a yard.

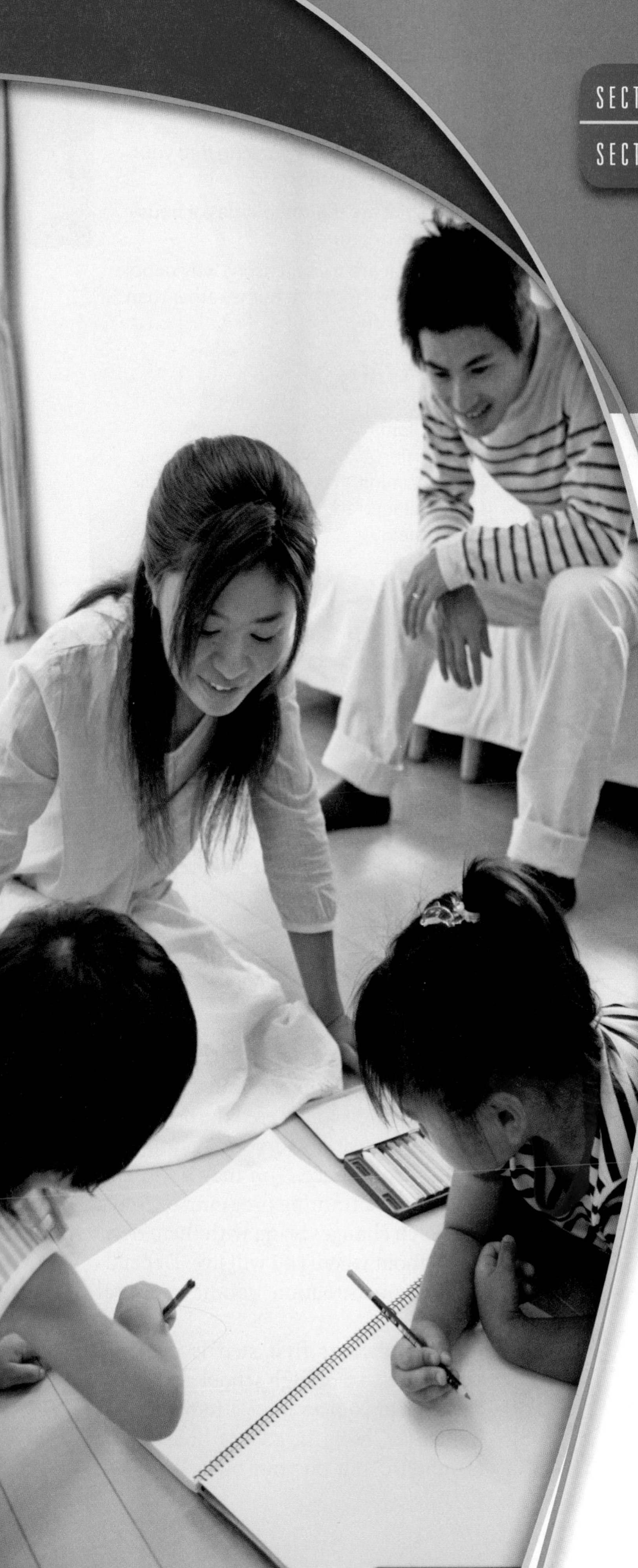

SECTION 1 Alternatives in Housing

SECTION 2 Buying a Home

Fact or Fiction

What do you think? Are the following statements true or false? If you think they are false, then say what is true.

1. The increased cost of housing in the United States has led to more young people remaining in their family homes longer than in the past.
2. The single-family home is the most popular type of housing in the United States.
3. More than one-third of all Americans choose to rent rather than buy a home.
4. Your credit score will not affect your cost of repaying a home loan.
5. When you make an offer on a house, you should offer more than the asking price.
6. Homeowners are entitled to certain tax advantages.
7. The interest rate on a conventional mortgage always remains the same.

Answers on page 271.

Study Reminder

*Knowing how to study can increase your knowledge, improve your grades, and cut down on your study time. See the **Studying Personal Finance** pages at the front of the book for some tips to help you study this chapter.*

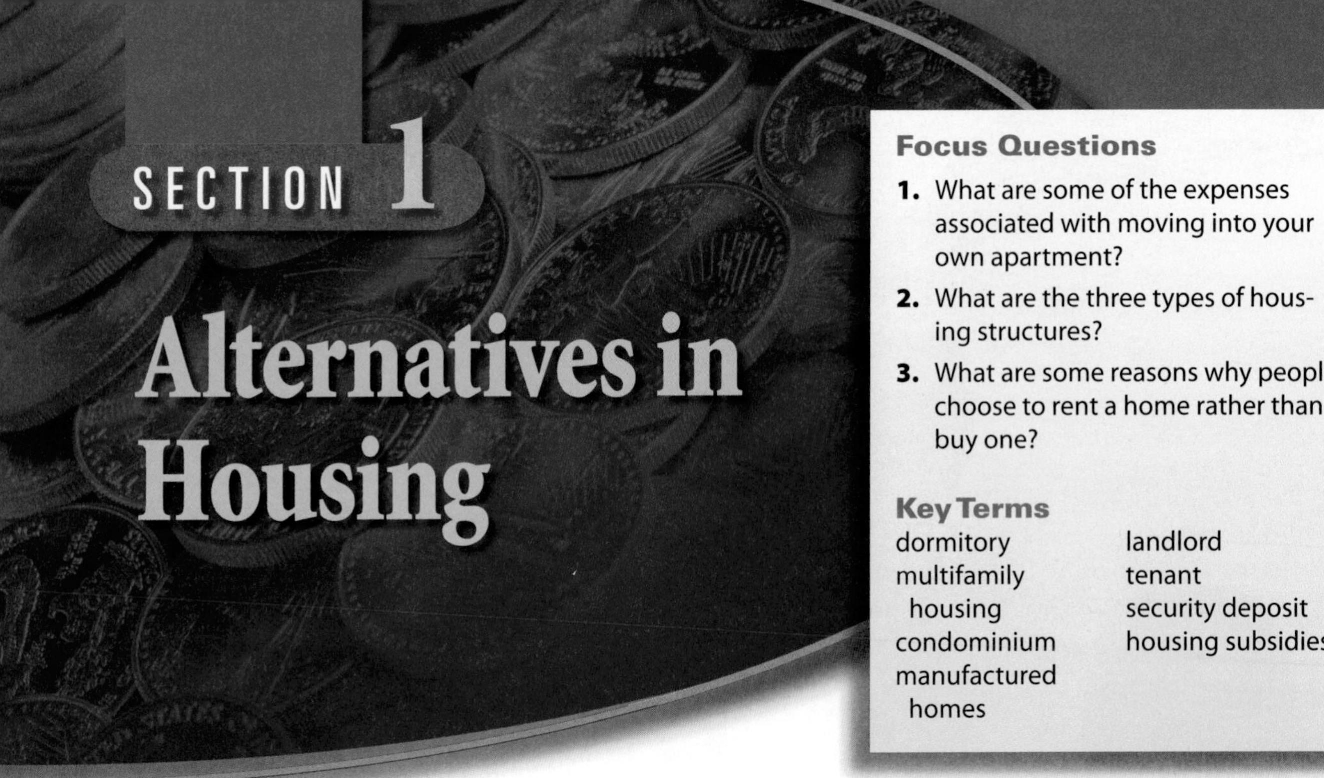

SECTION 1

Alternatives in Housing

Focus Questions

1. What are some of the expenses associated with moving into your own apartment?
2. What are the three types of housing structures?
3. What are some reasons why people choose to rent a home rather than buy one?

Key Terms

dormitory
multifamily housing
condominium
manufactured homes
landlord
tenant
security deposit
housing subsidies

Right now, housing may not be one of your top concerns. However, it is one of the major decisions you will soon be facing. Housing-related expenses average up to one-third of a person's income. The choices you make will have a real impact on your finances and other areas of your life.

▼ In areas where land is scarce, homes are built close together to provide housing for many people.

The types, availability, and costs of housing vary considerably across the country. In areas with a fast-growing population or limited space for new homes, competition limits choices and drives up prices. In places where demand is lower, you can get more for your money.

Identifying Housing Alternatives

In America, graduation from high school is often considered the beginning of your transition to young adulthood and independence. You may go to college, begin a training program, or find a job. Such changes bring with them decisions about where you will live. Depending on your situation, you have several options.

The obvious first step is deciding where to live. For high school graduates, the typical choices are (1) remaining at home, (2) living in college housing, or (3) moving out on your own. What are

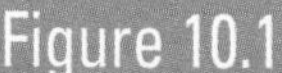

DECISION-MAKING MODEL FOR HOUSING ALTERNATIVES

There are many alternatives to choose from when deciding on housing. The first consideration, however, is finances. Be sure the housing option you choose fits within your budget.

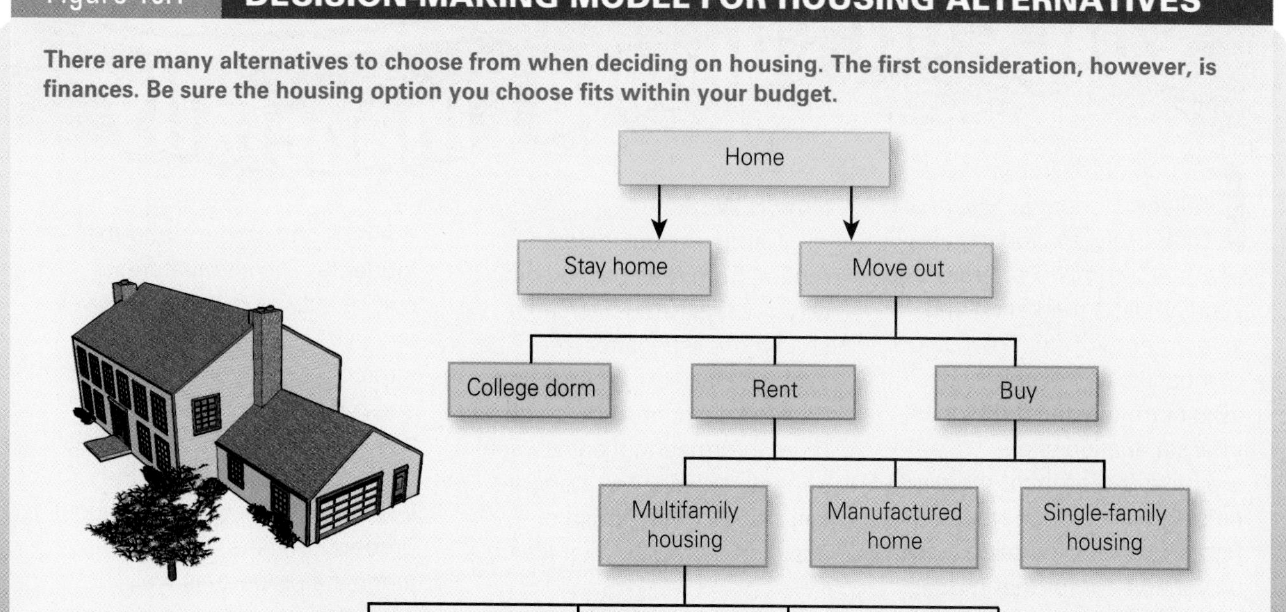

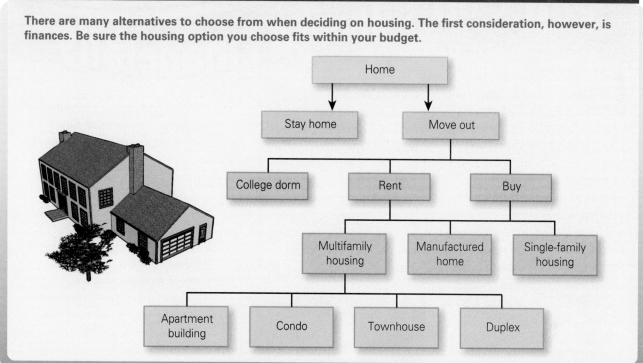

your housing alternatives? Figure 10.1 is a decision-making model that shows the possible alternatives at each point in the process. One decision leads to another until satisfactory housing is obtained.

Living with Your Family

Many teens continue to live with their families for at least some time after graduation. If you and your parents agree that this is the best choice, it is important to discuss the practical aspects of day-to-day life early, before they become troublesome issues. Even though you will still be at home, your status is changing. That brings new independence, but new responsibilities too. You and your family will have to adapt to these new circumstances.

Your Changing Status Think through possible issues and make a list. Give your parents your list and set a time to talk about it. What rules will you be expected to follow? Will you pay rent? Will you be on your own for meals and do your own laundry? What household chores will you take on? How will you handle disagreements?

This type of change in status presents real challenges for everyone involved. It is important to be able to see your parents' point of view, as well as your own. A cool head and a sense of humor will make the transition go more smoothly.

Boomerang Children Returning Home More and more recent college graduates are moving back home with their families until they can make it financially. Other times, economic circumstances bring young adults home after they have been on their own for a period of time. Of course, these twenty-somethings are no longer children—but some have tabbed them *boomerang children* because they have been away and now come back.

You Can Succeed Financially

In 2004, Jake Burns was a college student at Miami of Ohio. He was working as a summer intern at Petters Group Worldwide, a marketing and investment firm that owns such companies as Polaroid and uBid.com, the second-biggest Internet auction site.

Jake realized that there was no single source for students to find off-campus housing at his university—or for that matter, anywhere in the country. He had an idea: create an auction Web site for housing. It would serve students, landlords, and university administrators—and he thought it could be a profitable business, too.

How They Did It

Burns partnered with a friend and classmate, Joe Condit. Together, the two traveled throughout the Midwest, doing market research at forty-five university campuses. They learned that their original idea would have to be expanded. A Web site listing *all* available housing at each university—not just an auction site—would fill a giant hole. Condit calls it "a one-stop shop for every off-campus housing need."

The business plan presented to the Petters Group was accepted, and with funding from Petters, Burns and Condit set up Campus1Housing.com in 2005—before they had graduated from college themselves.

How It Works

Campus1Housing earns money from fees paid by property owners. Students can search the listings for free. The Web site includes photos and detailed descriptions—much more information than newspaper ads provide—so students can decide if the house or apartment will suit their lifestyle.

The site lists prices for each school according to what is customary in the area. The more popular properties are offered at auction to the highest bidders. Students can get together with friends to bid on a great house to share. Once students have narrowed down their choices, they can click on a button to contact the property manager for more information or to see the place in person.

Where It's Going

After their first year, Burns and Condit realized that for real success they would have to maintain good relationships with three groups—the universities, the property owners, and the students. The site features a community blog for each university in its catalog. It also has interactive maps so students can see exactly how close to campus the properties are. There is even a parents' page on the Web site with information about property owners. Parents can judge if a property is well managed and safe—concerns a student might overlook.

In its first year, Campus1-Housing served five midwestern universities and had more than 2 million hits on the Web site. By 2006, it had expanded to nine midwestern campuses. In February 2007, Campus1Housing announced a merger with LiveByCampus, an off-campus housing resource in the Southwest that was founded in 2006. The partners hope their enterprise will expand to serve universities nationwide.

What Would You Do?

1. How could including a community blog on their Web site benefit Campus1Housing's business?
2. Why is it a good idea for Campus1Housing to have properties available to individuals as well as groups of students?
3. As a student, what kind of information about possible housing units would you want to see on the Web site?

YOU DECIDE

Nadia, a high school senior, has been working part-time in a bookstore for two years. She is planning to be a librarian, and her first step is getting an associate's degree in library science from her local community college. It's going to be hard work, and she will have to study hard.

Nadia shares a bedroom with her 12-year-old sister and wants to move out of her parents' house when she graduates, so she can have some privacy. Her sister is always on the phone with her friends while Nadia is trying to study.

Nadia has been searching the classifieds for a private room in a house with shared kitchen privileges. She finds one near the college, in a house with a swimming pool—which sounds great to Nadia. If she works more hours at the bookstore next year, she might be able to afford that one.

Nadia tells her school guidance counselor about her plans. The counselor is concerned that if Nadia works more hours, she will not be able to keep up with the course work in college. That might jeopardize her long-term goal.

Nadia's parents offer to turn the family room into a private bedroom for her, so she will not have to share. If she stays at home another year, Nadia can save more money for her education. The swimming pool is calling to her, but maybe it can wait.

Should she . . .

1. ...move to the house with the swimming pool? Give reasons for your answer.
2. ...stay at home one more year? Besides saving money, what are other benefits to staying in the family home rather than renting a room in someone else's house? Explain your answer.

For example, college graduates often have many thousands of dollars in loans to repay. They simply cannot afford their own place. Difficulty finding a job, credit card debt, and divorce are other common reasons for moving back home. For boomerang children, the adjustments are even more challenging. Parents might set time limits for such a stay.

Living in a College Dorm

If you will be attending a college or university, you may live in a **dormitory**, or *dorm*, for at least a year or two. Besides solving your housing problem, dorm living is a good way to get acquainted with other students and make new friends.

Typically, the rooms are fairly small and you will probably have at least one roommate. The furnishings are limited but include the basics. Laundry equipment, social areas, and other facilities are shared. Meals are usually provided or available.

If you will be living in a dorm, deciding what additional furniture and personal items you will take requires careful planning. You might need to pare down your list several times, because you will probably be living in half of a small room. Coordinate with your roommate to avoid too much duplication. Most students find that life is much easier with just the basics than with an overcrowded space.

Moving On

At some point, you will move out of your parents' house or the dorm and

dormitory a college or university building containing living quarters for students

into a place of your own. School, a job, or simply the desire for more independence may be the reason. You might live in a dorm during your first year or two in college, then decide to rent an apartment with friends. This is a good way to learn how to be responsible for living on your own—and how to handle friends who do not take this responsibility seriously.

Whatever the reason, this move will probably be only the first of many moves that you make. The average American family moves once every five years—and single adults move even more often. With each move, you will need to reassess your needs, your wants, and your finances.

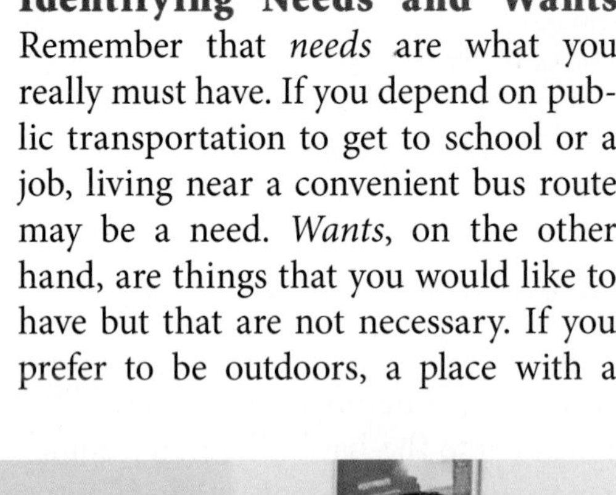

Identifying Needs and Wants Remember that *needs* are what you really must have. If you depend on public transportation to get to school or a job, living near a convenient bus route may be a need. *Wants*, on the other hand, are things that you would like to have but that are not necessary. If you prefer to be outdoors, a place with a swimming pool may be on this list. However, other things are likely to rank higher—such as good security features, plenty of storage, or a garage for your car. The best plan is to list your needs and wants, then rank them in order of importance. Convert this to a chart that you can use to compare various housing options you look at. Remember that choosing housing usually requires trade-offs.

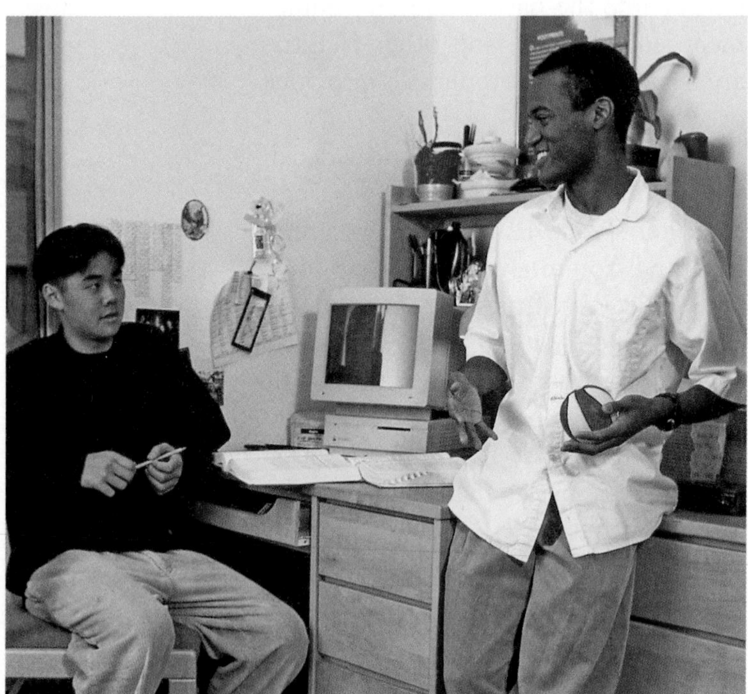

▼ College students often live in a dormitory for their first year or two to save money and meet other students. **What expenses can you avoid by talking with your roommate before moving in?**

Estimating Housing Costs You might actually find a place that meets all of your needs and wants. But would it also be affordable? Whether you will be renting or buying, make an estimate of the obvious expenses—and also those that are less obvious, such as insurance or trash pickup. Remember that these are estimates. Higher costs or changing prices could mean that you will pay more. Experts recommend that your housing expenses equal no more than one-quarter to one-third of your income. If you start out at your upper limit, dealing with increases or emergencies may be difficult.

The location of the place you choose to live will also influence your overall expenses. The farther away you live from where you shop, work, or go to school, the more your transportation costs will be. Over time, the difference between driving 3 miles to work versus 30 miles would amount to thousands of dollars.

Also include the cost of furniture and kitchen equipment in your estimate. Furnished apartments are available but cost more. You can often buy used furniture, dishes, or pots and pans inexpensively from secondhand stores or garage sales. Your family and friends might be willing to give you a few items, but you should figure on spending some money to get set up.

Just the act of moving itself is expensive, even if you do most of the work

YOU DECIDE

Eddie lived in a dorm his freshman year at college, but for his sophomore year he wants to move into an apartment with his friends Amit and Ray. They found a two-bedroom place for $1,180 per month. His two friends would share one bedroom, and Eddie would have the other to himself.

Amit and Ray each agree to pay $365 and Eddie would pay $450 of the rent. They estimate their monthly utilities—gas, electricity, phone, and Internet service—to be around $240, or $80 apiece. So Eddie figures his monthly total for housing will be about $530.

Eddie knows he will spend more on food than he did in the dorm, where meals were part of his $980 monthly fees. His mom thinks he should plan on $150 a week—$600 a month—especially if he wants to eat out sometimes instead of cooking. At that rate, Eddie figures it will cost about $150 a month *more* to live off-campus than in the dorm. But he thinks the freedom of having his own place would be worth it.

Eddie's parents are willing to pay the cost of dorm housing, but no more than that. Eddie thinks he can afford the extra amount for apartment living if he works an additional ten hours a month at his part-time job.

He has almost made up his mind to sign a ten-month lease for the coming school year. However, while reading the lease agreement, he learns that if one of the roommates moves out, the other two will be responsible for all the rent until they find another roommate. Eddie doesn't think that will happen—all three enjoyed school last year, got good grades, and intend to stay at this college until they graduate. Still, Amit suggests that they try to find a fourth roommate. He says that would reduce their individual costs, and also lessen the amount of risk if one of them leaves.

If there were four roommates all paying equally, Eddie's share of the rent and utilities would drop from $530 to $355, a difference of 33 percent. Still, Eddie is not sold on the idea. He was hoping to get that bedroom to himself.

Should he . . .

1. ...look for a fourth roommate? Why or why not?
2. ...reconsider living in the dorm? List some possible advantages for Eddie to stay in the dorm another year.

yourself. If you do not hire a moving company, you will probably have to rent a truck. Utilities like electricity, gas, phone, and cable TV usually charge a fee to set up service, and some require a deposit, especially if you are a new customer. Renters typically pay two months worth of rent up front—one for the first month and one held for the last month. If you have a pet, you might have to pay a deposit to cover any possible damage to the property. Further costs associated with buying a home are discussed in Section 2 of this chapter.

Types of Housing

When you are ready to move out on your own, what type of housing will you choose? There are three major categories of housing structures: single-family houses, multifamily housing, and manufactured homes.

Single-Family Housing

The single-family home is the most popular type of housing in the United States. These homes are built on their

▲ Single-family homes offer privacy, storage space, and freedom.

▶ Townhouses benefit families living in areas where land is scarce, offering the joys of a home with shared luxuries like swimming pools.

own lots and usually have a lawn or other kind of outdoor living area. People who choose single-family homes often say they want greater living and storage space—and more privacy and freedom.

Most single-family houses are occupied by their owners. However, they can also be rented. Living in a single-family home, even if you rent, usually means you are responsible for the yard as well as the house itself. A chance to garden may bring joy to your living experience.

multifamily housing housing that features two or more family dwellings within the same building

condominium multifamily housing in which the units are owned by individuals and the common grounds and building structure are owned jointly by the unit owners

Multifamily Housing

Multifamily housing features two or more family dwellings within the same building. Structures such as apartment buildings, townhouses, and duplexes provide homes for more people on less land. Rising prices for land and construction, along with population and environmental pressures, would seem to tip the balance toward more multifamily housing in the future.

Most multifamily housing units are rented, but some are owned. One common form of ownership is the **condominium**, or *condo.* Each unit in the building or group of buildings is individually owned. The common grounds and building structure are owned jointly by the unit owners. Each owner pays a monthly maintenance fee to cover costs such as lawn care and maintenance of the exterior and shared interior spaces, such as elevators and parking garage. A homeowner's association sets rules. Some associations allow owners to rent out their unit, while others do not.

Apartment Buildings An apartment is likely to be your first home away from home. Apartments are available in all sizes, and their rental costs vary from a few hundred dollars to thousands per month. Most apartments are located in buildings built specifically for apartments. You may also find single-family houses that have been converted into a few apartments. *Apartment complexes*—groups of apartment buildings that share some facilities, such as a pool or tennis courts—are popular, but they often cost more. Desirable characteristics, such as a convenient location, more space, or lots of parking, also affect the rental price.

Townhouses Townhouses are individual housing units with two or more floors, often attached at the side walls to other units. Outdoor space is usually limited. Some townhouses are rented. Some are owned, often in a condominium arrangement.

Duplexes A *duplex* is a building with two living units, resembling two houses joined together. (A building with three units is called a *triplex*.) The living units in a duplex may or may not be of equal size. Both might be rented, or the owner might live in one unit and rent the other. Duplexes often offer advantages similar to single-family homes, such as outdoor living space, a garage, and location in a residential neighborhood.

▲ Manufactured homes provide affordable housing with the possibility for landscaping and decorative exteriors.

Manufactured Homes

Manufactured homes include modular homes and mobile homes. These houses are built in factories, using assembly-line techniques. They generally come equipped with furniture and appliances. Once completed, a manufactured home is towed to a housing site in one or more pieces. Then it is installed and the utilities are connected.

Some communities require manufactured homes to be located only in certain areas—for example, they may limit mobile homes to mobile home parks. Others do not place restrictions on the location of manufactured homes. Manufactured homes are considerably less expensive than most single-family houses. Most are owned by the people who live in them, but some are available for rent.

About half the people who buy manufactured homes rent the land their house will sit on. Sometimes the leases are short-term—and if the landowner decides to sell, it may be more expensive to move the house than the house is worth. In that case, the buyers could lose their entire investment. Consumer groups therefore advise potential buyers to find a site for their home *before* buying, and to be sure that installation of the home is part of the sale package. Finding an installer yourself can be very difficult and expensive.

Most manufactured housing is sold with a warranty against defects. As with any warranty, it is important to read and understand all the terms.

Renting a Home

For the same quality and space, is it better to rent or buy? Each has its advantages and disadvantages. Finances are a major consideration, of course, because buying a home requires considerable money at the time of purchase. Section 2 of this chapter will cover the steps involved in home ownership. The following discussion explores decisions related to renting a home.

Reasons for Renting

More than one-third of all Americans choose to rent rather than buy a home. Most renters are single people, young married couples, or retirees. Renting provides some advantages over owning a home. For example, renters are able to

manufactured homes homes that are built in a factory and towed to the home site, where they are installed

change housing more quickly than owners. They also are better able to estimate their monthly housing expenses, because they are not responsible for repairs or maintenance. Other reasons frequently given for renting rather than buying include these:

- "I need to be able to move quickly if my employer transfers me."
- "I'm not ready for the responsibility of ownership."
- "I prefer to invest my money in other ways."
- "I don't have enough money to buy and maintain a house."

Drawbacks of renting include having less privacy, limitations on changes, and nothing to show for rent payments.

Finding a Roommate and an Apartment

Renters—especially first-time renters—often share housing to make the costs more affordable. If you consider this type of arrangement, take the time to make a good choice. Then, discuss and agree upon how expenses will be split, how responsibilities will be divided, and how problems will be solved. Ask yourself whether you can share space with this person on a day-to-day basis. Choose someone who follows through on promises and responsibilities. You do not want to end up paying the entire rent or electric bill.

You can find out about places available for rent in many ways—newspaper ads, online listings, signs, and real estate agents. Tell your friends you are looking for a place to rent. Arrange for personal tours of the places that seem most promising.

When you have located a house or apartment that you want to rent, contact the owner or rental agency to fill out a rental application. It's common to be asked for *personal references*—people who will verify that you are a responsible person. You will also need to provide some credit information. Figure 10.2 on the next page shows an example of a rental or lease application.

The Cost of Renting

Monthly rent is often related to the size and location of the rental unit and any extras provided, such as parking or an exercise room. Rent may or may not include utilities—so find out if electricity, water, trash pickup, cable television, Internet connection, and other services are included or if you would be paying for them yourself.

Don't forget about the importance of insuring your possessions. A renter's insurance policy covers your furniture, computer, TV, jewelry, or other possessions if any is lost or damaged by theft, fire, flood, or wind.

Legal Issues for Renters

When you rent a house or apartment, you are assuming major financial responsibilities. Study the lease or rental agreement before signing it, and know your legal rights.

The Lease or Rental Agreement Study the lease or rental agreement carefully. Be sure you understand and agree to the information in it before you sign it.

Did You Know?

Young, single people are not the only ones looking for roommates these days. With housing costs rising in most regions, some older adults have begun looking for roommates, too. Their reasons are the same as anybody else's: companionship, security, and sharing household chores are often named—but the major reason is that it's almost always cheaper to live with others than to live alone.

Figure 10.2 SAMPLE RENTAL (OR LEASE) APPLICATION

When filling out a rental (or lease) application, you will be asked to share a lot of personal information. Use your personal data sheet to help you fill it out.

Application for Residency

(Every additional live-in resident over the age of 18 as of the lease commencement date must submit a separate application and sign the lease)

APPLICANT

Full Name (Last) ______ (First) ______ (MI) ______ Date of Birth ______

Home Phone Number (___) Area Code ______ Cell Phone Number (___) Area Code ______ Work Phone Number (___) Area Code ______

E-mail Address ______ Gender ______ Male/Female Marital Status ______ Smoker (Y / N) Circle One

Education ______ Social Security Number ______

Proof of Identification: Type ______ (Examples: Driver's License, Passport, etc.) Identification Number ______

How did you hear about us? ______

LIST OTHERS WHO WILL RESIDE IN APARTMENT ON A PERMANENT BASIS
(To be used only for additional live-in residents of apartment under the age of 18 as of the lease commencement date)

Full Legal Name	Social Security Number	Relationship to Applicant	Date of Birth

RESIDENCY INFORMATION (please include at least 2 years of prior residences)

Present Address: ______ Apt # ______ Phone (___) Area Code ______

City ______ State ______ Zip ______ Monthly Payment $ ______

Rent or Own? ______ Dates: From ___/___ Month/Year To ___/___ Month/Year

Landlord/Lender Name ______ City ______ State ______ Phone (___) Area Code ______

Previous Address: ______ Apt # ______ Phone (___) Area Code ______

City ______ State ______ Zip ______ Monthly Payment $ ______

Rent or Own? ______ Dates: From ___/___ Month/Year To ___/___ Month/Year

Landlord/Lender Name ______ City ______ State ______ Phone (___) Area Code ______

Most rentals are based on a *lease*—the legal document stating the responsibilities of the **landlord** (the property owner) and the **tenant** (the person renting). The lease will identify the property being rented, the length of the rental period, and the amount of the rent and when it is due. It also should include other key information, including which utilities the tenant must pay for separately, the penalty for moving out before the lease ends, and special restrictions, such as "no pets."

A *rental agreement* is often simpler than a lease. Rental agreements usually run "month-to-month." That means you can continue renting as long as you pay the rent each month—but you can move out any time after giving a month's notice.

The language in a rental lease can be confusing. It can end up costing you money if you do not take the time to read it—and make sure you understand everything in it—before signing. Here is an example:

> **Security Deposit.** The $500 security deposit is to be applied against damage to any part of the premises leased hereby, *including the common areas*, or to the furnishings therein, unpaid utility bills, unpaid rent, late-payment

landlord the owner of property that is leased or rented to a tenant

tenant someone who rents or leases property from a landlord

> charges, cleaning expenses, attorney fees, court costs, or any other costs or losses related to the aforesaid apartment and premises *regardless of which of the tenants allegedly causes the loss,* unless the damage is paid for prior to the end of this lease. Owner expressly agrees to itemize all deductions from the security deposit. When there is no such damage or loss, the security deposit shall be refunded to tenant within thirty (30) days after expiration of this lease term.

The *italicized* phrases in this lease are important, and you should object to this particular wording. Common areas include hallways, basements, laundry rooms, and other shared public spaces. In many states, your liability for these areas is limited and you cannot be held liable for damage to common areas unless you committed the damage yourself—or if you signed a lease with a clause like this. An example of a residential lease agreement is shown in Figure 10.3 on the facing page.

Care of the Premises Inspect the house or apartment before you take possession. Document any existing conditions or damage in writing and with photographs. Also make a list of all items in the apartment, describing their condition. Sign and date these documents *before* moving in—and ask the landlord or manager to sign them, too.

You should make this inspection because when you rent, the landlord will usually require a **security deposit**. This is a sum of money (usually one month's rent) that will cover, or help cover, any damage to the property while you are the tenant. You will lose your security deposit if the property owner thinks you caused damage. On the other hand, if you take good care of the property while you live there, you will get your security deposit back when you move out.

security deposit a sum of money a tenant gives to the landlord before moving in, to cover any damage to the property while the tenant lives there

During the course of your lease, tell the property owner about any problems as soon as possible. The landlord is responsible for making repairs, but you are responsible for notification.

Your Legal Rights Be familiar with laws that protect renters. A local tenants' organization or the housing code department can assist you. Check the telephone directory for listings.

The Fair Housing Act Discrimination in housing is against the law. That does not mean owners must rent to anyone, including someone with a record of not paying rent. However, the federal Fair Housing Act protects people who want to rent or buy a home from discrimination based on race, color, national origin, religion, gender, family status, or disability. Specifically, no one may discriminate in the following ways:

- Refuse to rent or sell housing
- Refuse to negotiate for housing
- Make housing unavailable
- Deny housing
- Set different terms, conditions, or privileges for the sale or rental of housing
- Provide different housing services or facilities to certain groups
- Falsely deny that housing is available for inspection, sale, or rental
- Use fear tactics to persuade owners to sell or rent (a practice called *blockbusting*)
- Deny access to or membership in a facility or service (such as a Multiple Listing Service) related to the sale or rental of housing

In addition, if you are a renter with a disability, your landlord must allow you to make reasonable changes to the property so that you can use the housing.

Figure 10.3 SAMPLE RENTAL (OR LEASE) AGREEMENT

A rental (or lease) agreement is a long document that lists the rights and responsibilities of both the landlord and the tenant. Be sure to read all of the fine print carefully before you sign it.

16. **VACANCY:**
a. Tenant agrees to notify the Lessor (or their agents) if the house will be vacant for a period of 5 days or more with the exception of school break periods

11. **ACCESS AND LOCKS:**

"Inspection Sheet." Normal and/or reasonable wear and tear are expected.

5. **UTILITIES:** Electricity, fuel, cable, telephone services, rubbish removal, and charges for snow/ice

LEASE AGREEMENT

THE UNDERSIGNED LESSOR/OWNER has let and demised unto the undersigned LESSEE(S) herein called "Tenant", this ___ day of ____________________, 20__:

Rental Address: ______________________________

____

Lessee/Tenant Name(s): ______________________ ______________________

______________________ ______________________

______________________ ______________________

Lessor/Owner Name(s): ______________________

____

Rental Amount: ______________ Security Deposit: ______________

TO HAVE AND TO HOLD THE SAME, with the rights and privileges thereof, for the term of ______________________________ on condition of payment to said Lessor of a rent therefor of ______________________________ on the ______________ next hereafter; that the demised premises shall not be altered, mutilated, damaged, sublet, or underlet without the knowledge and written consent of the Lessor; and that for any condition broken, the Lessor, so choosing, may enter upon and resume possession of said premises, without prejudice to his/her/their other rights or remedies against the Tenant, hereunder, pursuant to Rhode Island General Laws.

1. **DEPOSITS:** Security Deposit is due at signing of lease or no later than ______________. First Month/First Payment, Last Month Rent and Rubbish Removal Fee is due by ______________. Checks should be made payable to ______________________ and delivered to ______________________________. If any of the present students are re-renting the same property, ______________, (hereinafter "Realty Agency") is entitled to the full commission.

2. **SECURITY/DAMAGE DEPOSIT:** The security deposit is to be held to reserve rental for ______________________________. Upon Tenant's arrival, it becomes a damage deposit. If the Tenant changes his/her/their mind, the security deposit is **non-refundable and will be forfeited**. The damage deposit will be returned within 20 days of the expiration of the Lease pursuant to Rhode Island General Laws, turning in the keys (**$10.00** for each missing key), and providing forwarding addresses, provided there is no physical damage to the premises and its furnishings, other than ordinary wear and tear, and no outstanding bills as provided. Tenants agree to allow Lessor to deduct from the security deposit the following charges if they apply: (a) The costs of any repairs, replacements, redecorating, and or refurnishing of the premises, or any fixtures, systems or appliances, caused by other than "ordinary" wear; (b) any damages caused by smoking inside the house as smoking is not permitted; (c) a reasonable cleaning expense; and (d) any outstanding bills (e.g. cable, internet, phone, electric, fuel). **THE SECURITY DEPOSIT MAY NOT BE USED FOR RENTAL PAYMENTS.**

3. **DELINQUENT AND/OR RETURNED CHECKS**: Lessor's ability to provide services rests upon the prompt receipt of monthly/semester rental payment. Lessor's failure to receive Lessee's monthly/semester rent within **5 days** of the due date will result in a late fee of **$25.00** for each late payment, and an additional **$2.00** fee per day will be assessed until payment is made. If a check has been returned by the financial institution, all future payments will be required in cash or by certified check. In addition, Lessee shall pay a **$35.00** returned check fee. Eviction process for all tenants will begin on the **16th day** any payment from **any one** individual is in arrears. All fees, late fees, and service charges incurred by the Tenant as well as any expenses including reasonable attorney's fees incurred by Lessor in instituting and prosecuting any actions by reason of any default of Tenant hereunder shall be deemed to be additional rent and shall be due from Tenant to Lessor immediately following the incurring of the respective expenses, the nonpayment of which shall be a breach of this agreement for nonpayment of rent.

4. **INSPECTION:** Lessee shall have 3 days from the beginning of the Lease to inspect the premises and return the "Inspection Sheet." Lessee shall be responsible for any damages not identified on the

▶ The U.S. government gives grants of money to citizens with low incomes to help improve their living situations.

The Fair Housing Act provides similar protection from discrimination for anyone applying for a mortgage. Report any violations to the nearest office of the Department of Housing and Urban Development (HUD). You can learn more about the protections offered in this law, and what to do if you have a problem, by reading "Fair Housing—It's Your Right" at the HUD Web site (http://fin.emcp.net/fairhousing).

Help for Those in Need

Low-income families often find it difficult to afford decent housing. This is especially true in places where housing is scarce or prices are high. Housing accounts for the largest part of a family's monthly expenses. Many people on very limited incomes must choose between paying housing costs and buying food or medicine.

housing subsidies grants of money from the U.S. government that help low-income families pay their housing costs

Consider this example. Alice is a divorced mother who works as a clerk in a supermarket. She has two preschool children. After she pays for child care, transportation to work, and food, Alice has less than $200 per month available to pay for housing. Even a small apartment costs much more. She needs help.

Since the early 1960s, the federal government has provided **housing subsidies** (grants of money) to low-income households. In general, these government programs help pay part of the family's rent, so the family can have adequate housing. The amount of the subsidy will depend on the family's income and how many children there are. There are also special rent supplement programs to assist the elderly with their housing costs.

SECTION 1 ASSESSMENT

Factual Recall

1. For high school graduates, what are three typical choices when deciding where to live?
2. What percentage of income can safely be allocated to housing?
3. If you are renting a home and not buying it, why should you still get insurance?
4. You want to rent an apartment, but your employer might soon be transferring you to another city. Should you get an apartment with a lease or with a rental agreement? Why?

Critical Thinking

1. Suppose you have decided to continue living with your family after graduation. Why is it important to discuss this arrangement with family members?
2. What are some advantages and disadvantages of living in a dorm?

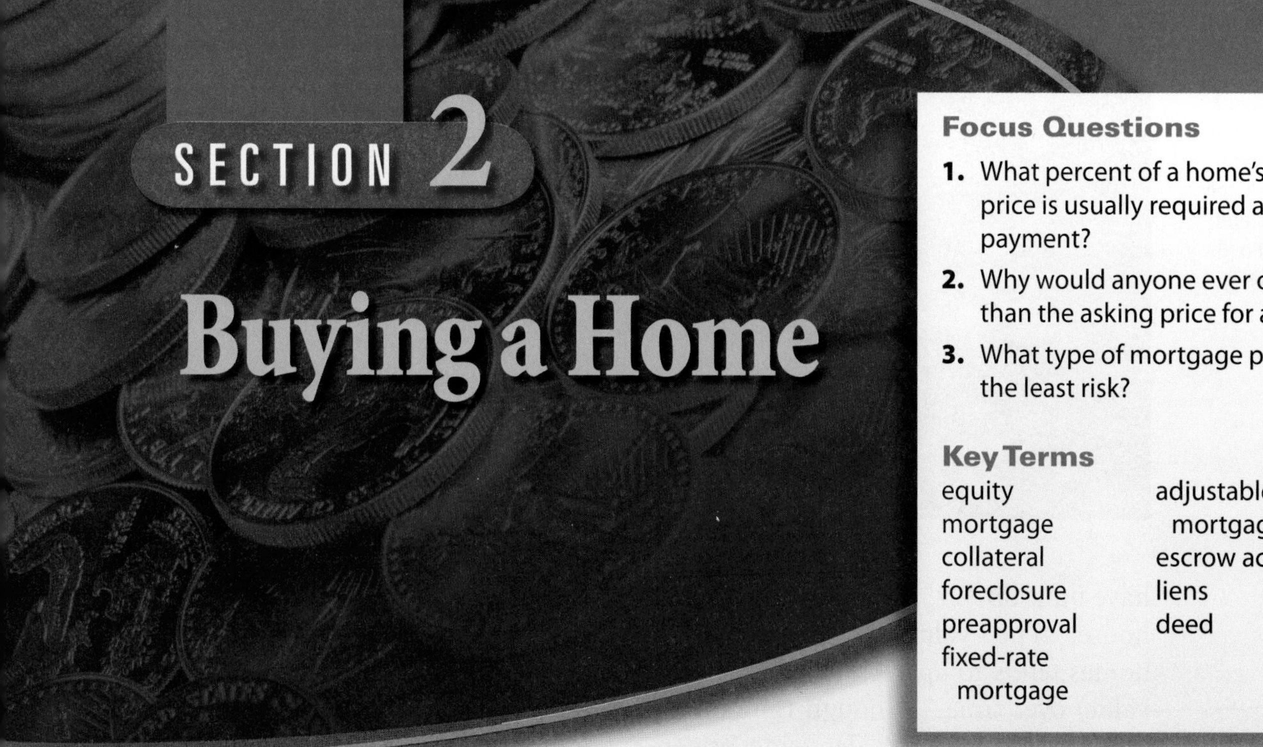

SECTION 2

Buying a Home

Focus Questions

1. What percent of a home's purchase price is usually required as a down payment?
2. Why would anyone ever offer more than the asking price for a home?
3. What type of mortgage presents the least risk?

Key Terms

equity
mortgage
collateral
foreclosure
preapproval
fixed-rate mortgage
adjustable-rate mortgage (ARM)
escrow account
liens
deed

For most people, a home is the most expensive purchase they will make during their entire lifetime. It might also be the best financial investment they will make. Under the right economic conditions, a home can increase significantly in value.

When you take the time necessary to learn about home ownership, you are much more likely to make a good choice. You can buy an existing home or build a new one. Building a new home is more complicated, but the decision-making process is similar for each. The discussion that follows, however, is based on buying an existing home.

Advantages of Home Ownership

Owning your own home has been a major part of what is known as the "American dream" for generations. The advantages can be personal as well as financial. The obvious advantage, of course, is that a growing family needs more room. But for both families and single people, there are other benefits as well. Home ownership provides more privacy and freedom. Unlike rent payments, some of the money you use to pay off a home loan counts toward your ownership of the property. Buying a home also has certain tax advantages.

Privacy and Freedom

In your own home, you will have more privacy than in most rental units. No one will knock on your door to check the heating system. You will not have to share a laundry room with other tenants in your building. In your own home, you can redecorate whenever you want to, in any style you want.

Building Equity

As you pay off your loan, you will be building equity. **Equity** in a home represents your amount of ownership. It is the value of the home minus the amount you still owe on it. For instance, if the house is worth $300,000 and you have paid off all but $75,000, then you

equity the value of a home minus the amount still owed on it

▶ Home ownership offers the freedom to enjoy your property. For example, you can have barbecues and entertain family and friends whenever you like.

have built up $225,000 in equity in the house. The value of single-family homes tends to *appreciate* (increase in value) over time—although the rate of appreciation can vary. Housing prices have also been known to decrease. This means that if you buy a home at an inflated price, you might later have to sell it at a loss.

Tax Advantages

Homeowners are entitled to several tax advantages. When you are filing your income tax return, you can deduct the interest you pay on your home loan from your total income. This will reduce your income tax bill. Property taxes on a home are also tax-deductible. If your home increases in value over the years, much or all of the profit when you sell is usually free of federal tax.

Costs and Responsibilities

The advantages of home ownership are appealing, but there are also some disadvantages. You will have considerable costs and ongoing responsibilities that renters do not have. (Some of the costs directly related to the purchase of a home are explained later in this chapter.)

The Down Payment

Many people want to own a home—but a substantial amount of money is needed to buy one. The *median price* for a home in the United States in 2005 was $297,000. (That means half the homes in the country sold for more than $297,000 and half sold for less.) Most lenders require a minimum of 10 to 30 percent as a down payment on a traditional loan. A *down payment* is cash paid against the purchase price, lowering the amount you have to borrow. If you hope to purchase a home for $200,000, you will probably need to save at least $20,000 to $60,000 for a down payment.

Even though that amount might seem out of reach, it *can* be done without winning the lottery. If one of your long-term goals is home ownership, follow the budget and savings plans already outlined in this book—and you will be on the right path.

One way to increase your savings is to live economically. If your household has two incomes, live on one and save the other. Skip or scale back on vacations and big purchases. Eat out less often. Limit clothing purchases. Enjoy free or inexpensive entertainment. For now, choose to live in housing a little less expensive than what you can afford. Every dollar you save will bring you closer to your goal.

Other Costs

Your monthly mortgage payment is a predictable cost of home ownership. There are other ongoing costs, both predictable and unpredictable. These include yearly real estate taxes on the home, monthly utility bills, and repair costs that can come at any time. Lenders require borrowers to carry homeowner's insurance to protect their investment. There are many online and print materials available to help you identify and estimate these expenses.

Another potential drawback is that owning your own home limits your mobility. Some people simply do not like to stay in one place very long. Others might have a job that requires them to move frequently. Selling your home every time you move, can be costly in both time and money.

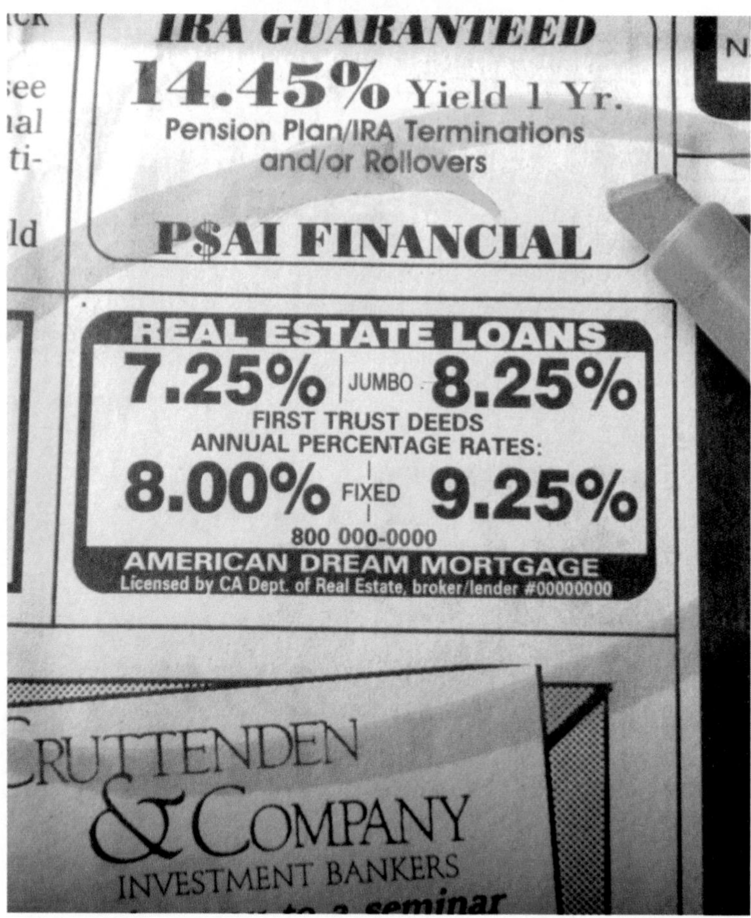

▲ Finance companies compete with each other by offering a variety of mortgage loans at various rates.

Obtaining Financing

When buying a home, most people borrow money in the form of a **mortgage**, which is a long-term home loan. The home you buy is the **collateral**—a valuable asset that serves as a kind of security deposit. If you fail to repay the loan, the lender can *foreclose* on the property. **Foreclosure** is the legal process that the lender can use to take possession of the house and sell it.

When you are ready to buy, a good first step is to contact two or three mortgage lenders (banks, credit unions, mortgage companies) to find the best terms and to see if you can obtain preapproval. **Preapproval** means that the lender has done all the work necessary to commit in writing to lending you money. With preapproval you will know how much you are able to borrow and how much you can spend on a house.

Lenders base their maximum loan amount on how much money you have for a down payment, your other savings, and your employment record, monthly income, and credit score. The lender may "lock in" or promise you a certain interest rate for a specific time period. Note that a good credit score can lower your interest rate by as much as 3 or 3.5 percent, saving you tens of thousands over the life of your loan.

If you have preapproval for a loan, it speeds up the process when you are ready to make your purchase. Without a preapproval, you will have to complete lots of paperwork and may still fail to get the loan.

Mortgage Rates

In general, interest rates are influenced by national economic factors. Different lenders' rates may vary, so it pays to check a number of places when you are ready to apply for a mortgage. Even small differences in the rate can

mortgage a long-term loan made on a home or other real estate property

collateral a valuable asset that a borrower must give up if the loan is not repaid

foreclosure the legal process that a lender uses to take possession of a house and sell it when a borrower fails to make mortgage payments

preapproval the process of obtaining an official commitment for a mortgage loan prior to making an offer to buy a home

LOOK Before You Leap

Patricia and Felipe, both 24, have been married for three years. Patricia manages a carryout pizza restaurant, and Felipe is assistant manager of a shoe store at the mall. They are both valued employees who regularly receive pay raises. Together, they bring home $47,000 a year after taxes.

A new development on the edge of town has two-bedroom units selling for $225,000. The floor plan suits them, the landscaping is attractive, and Patricia and Felipe believe the value of the units will go up over time. They do not want to miss out on the benefits of home ownership. They have $15,000 saved, and their parents have offered to help with the down payment.

A mortgage broker tells Patricia and Felipe that he can get them pre-approved for a 90 percent fixed-rate mortgage at 6.8 percent interest. The monthly payment would be $1,320. That's about 35 percent of their after-tax income. They can handle that, so they leave the loan office excited.

Their parents ask them how much the property taxes and insurance will be on the unit, and what the monthly condominium fees are. The couple realizes they don't have all the facts yet. They'll have to check with the condo developer and the county tax collector for more information.

They decide to check the Web site of the National Association of Realtors (http://fin.emcp.net/realtor) to track price changes in the condo market in their area. Maybe prices have topped out already. In that case, Patricia and Felipe cannot count on their investment increasing much in value any time soon. Next, they check out LendingTree.com (http://fin.emcp.net/lendingtree) for current mortgage rates from other lenders and banks. Maybe they can find a lower interest rate somewhere else.

Patricia and Felipe decide to slow down. They want to be certain that this is the right time and the right home for them to buy.

Before Deciding

1. Where can Patricia and Felipe find out how much property taxes and condo fees will be?
2. If the taxes and fees will make their monthly payments too high, should Patricia and Felipe go for a longer mortgage (with smaller payments), find a less expensive condo, or put off home ownership for another year while they save more money? Give reasons for your answer.

make a huge difference in what you pay over the life of a mortgage.

Four factors will affect the amount of your monthly mortgage payment:

1. The price of the home
2. The amount of the down payment
3. The interest rate of the loan
4. The length of the loan

Negotiating the lowest price possible, making the biggest down payment that you can, and obtaining a loan with a low interest rate all help to lower your monthly payment. Increasing the length of a loan will also lower your monthly payment—but this will substantially increase the total amount you will pay for the home, because you will be paying interest for a longer term.

Most home loans are *amortized* over the term of the loan. That is, the total debt is gradually eliminated over the life of the mortgage. Each monthly payment includes some interest, and the rest goes toward reducing the amount of the original loan—called the *principal*—so that the loan is completely paid off by the end of the term.

Most loans today are written for a term of thirty years, but some loans may be offered for a shorter or longer term. If you sell your home before you have paid off the loan (most people do), the balance that you owe will be taken from the proceeds of the sale.

Paying Points As mentioned earlier, interest rates charged by different lenders will vary, sometimes significantly. Some lenders might offer a lower rate on some loans, but to qualify for such a loan you will have to pay *points* (an extra fee) when your transaction closes. A point is equal to 1 percent of the loan amount. For example, you might be offered a $200,000 loan at 7½ percent with no points, or 7 percent plus one point. The *point* in this case would be $2,000, to be paid when the loan is granted. Over the years, the amount you would save on the lower 7 percent loan would make up for the point charged at the beginning. Ask what other fees you will be charged for the loan, then compare the *total* cost of the loan, including interest and loan fees, to help you choose the best lender.

Government Financing The Federal Housing Administration (FHA) arranges financing for first-time homebuyers, members of minority groups, and some borrowers who do not have enough money for a down payment. Interest rates are comparable to conventional rates. However, loan amounts are limited (in 2006, it was $359,650). Borrowers must prove they have sufficient income to make the mortgage payments.

The Department of Veterans Affairs (VA) helps eligible veterans obtain financing for up to 100 percent of the sale price. Interest rates are comparable to conventional and FHA loans.

The U.S. government does not provide the money for these loans. However, it does assist with obtaining the loans from regular sources—and it guarantees that the loans will be repaid.

Types of Mortgages

There are two basic types of mortgages available to homebuyers—a fixed-rate mortgage and an adjustable-rate mortgage.

Fixed-Rate Mortgages Sometimes called a conventional mortgage, a **fixed-rate mortgage** is a loan whose rate of interest does not change. If you obtain a loan for 8½ percent interest, you will pay 8½ percent for the entire life of the loan—or until you sell your home or refinance the mortgage. If you expect to own your home for more than five years,

fixed-rate mortgage a home loan with an interest rate that does not change during the life of the loan

The U.S. Census Bureau reports that, in 2006, more than 1.5 million American households spent over 30 percent of their income on housing costs. This figure is considered the limit of affordability. At the same time, nearly 14 percent of mortgage holders and 25 percent of renters spent over 50 percent of their incomes on housing costs. These people are definitely living beyond the limit of affordability.

adjustable-rate mortgage (ARM) a home loan with an interest rate that might increase or decrease during the life of the loan

a fixed-rate mortgage presents the least risk and is usually the best choice.

Adjustable-Rate Mortgages The interest rate for an **adjustable-rate mortgage (ARM)** might increase or decrease during the life of the loan. The lender can change the rate on your loan according to current economic conditions. If you are interested in an ARM, ask the lender to provide an explanation in writing of how often and how much the rates and the payments are allowed to change—and what index will be used to determine changes in the rate.

The beginning rate for an ARM is usually lower than the rate for a fixed-rate mortgage. For instance, an ARM might be offered at 4 percent, but the lender can increase the rate to 8 percent or higher if interest rates increase in the overall economy. Some lenders offer a beginning rate of just 1 or 2 percent. Consider this just a "teaser" rate and count on it to go up as soon as the lender can legally raise it.

Most ARMs have a *rate cap* that limits rate increases to 1 or 2 percentage points per year and 5 points during the life of the loan. These caps provide some protection. Still, changes in interest rates can push some buyers out of their homes.

▼ **Looking in the newspapers and online, you can find details about homes that are for sale in your area and around the world.**

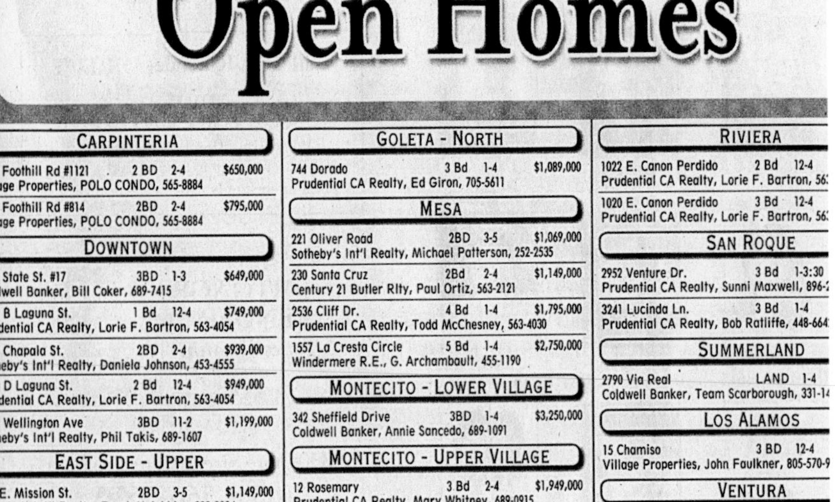

Open Homes

CARPINTERIA

5 Foothill Rd #1121 2 BD 2-4 $650,000
lage Properties, POLO CONDO, 565-8884

5 Foothill Rd #814 2BD 2-4 $795,000
lage Properties, POLO CONDO, 565-8884

DOWNTOWN

5 State St. #17 3BD 1-3 $649,000
dwell Banker, Bill Coker, 689-7415

0 B Laguna St. 1 Bd 12-4 $749,000
udential CA Realty, Lorie F. Bartron, 563-4054

5 Chapala St. 2BD 2-4 $939,000
heby's Int'l Realty, Daniela Johnson, 453-4555

0 D Laguna St. 2 Bd 12-4 $949,000
udential CA Realty, Lorie F. Bartron, 563-4054

2 Wellington Ave 3BD 11-2 $1,199,000
heby's Int'l Realty, Phil Takis, 689-1607

EAST SIDE - UPPER

E. Mission St. 2BD 3-5 $1,149,000
heby's Int'l Realty, Frank Hotchkiss, 898-2084

GOLETA - NORTH

744 Dorado 3 Bd 1-4 $1,089,000
Prudential CA Realty, Ed Giron, 705-5611

MESA

221 Oliver Road 2BD 3-5 $1,069,000
Sotheby's Int'l Realty, Michael Patterson, 252-2535

230 Santa Cruz 2Bd 2-4 $1,149,000
Century 21 Butler Rlty, Paul Ortiz, 563-2121

2536 Cliff Dr. 4 Bd 1-4 $1,795,000
Prudential CA Realty, Todd McChesney, 563-4030

1557 La Cresta Circle 5 Bd 1-4 $2,750,000
Windermere R.E., G. Archambault, 455-1190

MONTECITO - LOWER VILLAGE

342 Sheffield Drive 3BD 1-4 $3,250,000
Coldwell Banker, Annie Sancedo, 689-1091

MONTECITO - UPPER VILLAGE

12 Rosemary 3 Bd 2-4 $1,949,000
Prudential CA Realty, Mary Whitney, 689-0915

RIVIERA

1022 E. Canon Perdido 2 Bd 12-4
Prudential CA Realty, Lorie F. Bartron, 56

1020 E. Canon Perdido 3 Bd 12-4
Prudential CA Realty, Lorie F. Bartron, 56

SAN ROQUE

2952 Venture Dr. 3 Bd 1-3:30
Prudential CA Realty, Sunni Maxwell, 896-

3241 Lucinda Ln. 3 Bd 1-4
Prudential CA Realty, Bob Ratliffe, 448-664

SUMMERLAND

2790 Via Real LAND 1-4
Coldwell Banker, Team Scarborough, 331-14

LOS ALAMOS

15 Chamiso 3 BD 12-4
Village Properties, John Faulkner, 805-570-9

VENTURA

Unless other arrangements can be made, failure to keep up payments might result in the lender foreclosing on the loan and a complete loss of investment. Some lenders offer *convertible* ARMs that can be changed to a fixed-rate mortgage after a specified period of time at a slightly higher rate than the current conventional loan.

If you know that you will be moving in less than four or five years and expect to sell your house at that time, then a low-rate ARM may be a wise choice. However, it's best to consult with a real estate lawyer before signing to make sure you understand all the conditions.

Not all mortgages are fully amortized over the life of the loan. *Balloon mortgages* are low-interest loans with short terms, usually five to ten years. During that time, the buyer makes monthly payments toward principal and interest. At the end of the loan term, whatever principal is left becomes due—in full. Most buyers don't have the cash, so they refinance.

Many of the ARMs made in the early years of the twenty-first century were subprime loans. A *subprime loan* is a high-interest loan made to high-risk borrowers. These are people who have poor credit records, few assets, or a lot of debt. By 2006, about 20 percent of mortgage loans were subprime. When the housing market declined in 2007, many people found themselves with houses they could not sell but could not afford to keep.

Working with a Real Estate Agent

When considering buying a home, many people start by checking out the current real estate market. They identify areas where they would like to live, the types of houses for sale in that general area, and the average prices for homes with the features they want. They might go to some *open houses*, where homes for sale are open to the public.

However, most people soon get the help of a real estate agent. Agents are trained to help buyers (and sellers) through all the steps of buying (or selling) a home. There are quite a number of steps involved—and some have legal consequences. A qualified real estate agent can be a helpful guide.

Agents earn a commission for their work, which is paid by the seller when the transaction is completed. In most areas, real estate commissions total about 6 percent of the selling price—and are split between the seller's agent and the buyer's agent.

Ask people you trust to recommend a real estate agent. Talk to two or three before deciding on one.

Location, Location, Location

There's an old saying in real estate that the three most important things to look for are *location, location, location.* That's just a simple way of saying that where the property is located is often more important than anything else. Everyone prefers a home located in a safe neighborhood, near shopping and good schools. The buyer is more likely to be happy living there, and the home will be easier to sell later.

Check the real estate ads in your local newspaper or on the Internet to find out the types of homes for sale in the area you prefer and how much they cost. Your real estate agent will be able to help narrow your search. He or she might also have leads about other houses in the area that fit your wish list.

Size and Feature Preferences

In addition to your location preference, the real estate agent will need to know approximately how large a home you want and also what features you think are important. With an accurate picture of your needs and preferences, the agent can identify the properties that most closely match your description.

▲ Real estate agents can explain issues relating to home ownership to help you find the best and most affordable house for your circumstances.

Making an Offer

When you find a home you want to buy, the agent can advise you about making an offer. In most situations, you would offer less than the seller's asking price. Here's how it works:

Your agent presents the offer to the seller's agent, and the seller decides whether to accept the offer. The seller might simply say "No" and reject an offer considered too low. You would then have to decide whether to make a new offer at a higher price. Often, the seller's agent will contact your agent with a *counter offer*—a figure higher than your offer but still less than the original asking price. In that case, your agent can help you decide whether to accept the seller's counter offer. Sometimes both the seller and buyer make counter offers before an agreement is reached. Sometimes no agreement is possible.

If the demand for homes is greater than the supply and homes are selling fast, buyers can end up in a *bidding war*, with several people making offers on the same home. In such a situation, it might be necessary to offer the full

Answers to Fact or Fiction

1. True; **2.** True; **3.** True; **4.** False—A good credit score can lower your interest rate by as much as 3 or 3.5 percent, saving you hundreds of dollars a month and tens of thousands over the life of your loan; **5.** False—In most situations, you would offer less than the seller's asking price; **6.** True; **7.** True.

Do Your RESEARCH

The Web has revolutionized real estate marketing. You should work with an agent when approaching a seller, but now you have much more freedom to browse and compare before reaching that point. In fact, it's possible to get a brief look online at virtually every property listed for sale in most areas.

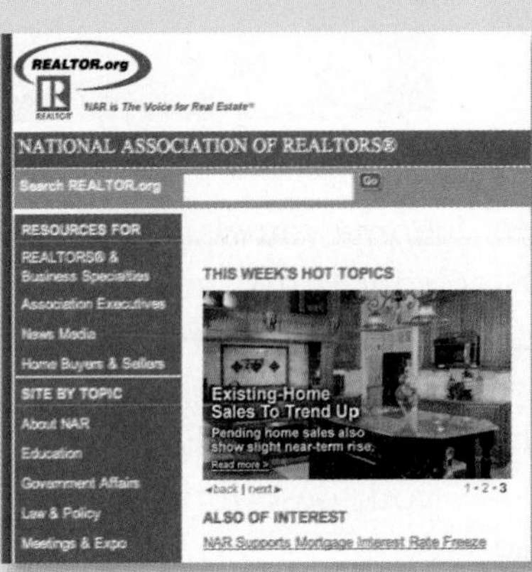

Try it for yourself. Make a list of all the features that you want in a home. Then check the Multiple Listing Service in your area at the MLS Web site (http://fin.emcp.net/mls). Browse the listings for houses and condominiums. Find the home that most closely matches your list. Now, go to a mortgage lender's site, such as CapitalOne (http://fin.emcp.net/capitalone) or LendingTree (http://fin.emcp.net/lendingtree), and find out how much your monthly payment would be on the home. Assume a 10 percent down payment for starters. Then try a down payment of 30 percent.

You can even browse real estate in a different part of the country, or a different country altogether. What city or town would you most like to live in—Honolulu? Paris? Tokyo? You can find real estate listings for houses, condos, and apartments all over the world. In the United States, most areas are covered by the MLS site. General international sites include EscapeArtist (http://fin.emcp.net/escape) and the International Real Estate Digest (http://fin.emcp.net/ired). You can also use search engines like Google.

Compare prices in different parts of the country—or in different countries—for houses with all or most of the features on your list. You can find a table comparing median prices of houses and condos in U.S. metropolitan areas at the Web site of the National Association of Realtors (http://fin.emcp.net/realtor).

Your Assignment

1. How much income would you need to afford the home you chose from the MLS site, assuming you will spend 25 percent of your income on housing?
2. How do prices in your area compare with those in other cities or towns you researched? Which areas are more expensive than your area? Less expensive?

asking price, or even more, to get the property. Agents will discuss this with buyers before any offers are submitted.

The Purchase Agreement When the buyer and seller agree on a price, both must sign a *purchase agreement*. This contract states their intention to complete the sale. A purchase contract may also include certain conditions that must be met in order to close a deal. For example, the sale obviously depends on the buyer's ability to obtain a loan. The contract also usually says that a qualified home inspector must inspect the property, and the seller must agree to make any needed repairs. Sometimes the seller includes a clause requiring the sale to be completed within a certain number of days.

The Escrow Account In most cases, as the buyer you must make a deposit, usually several thousand dollars, to show that your offer is serious. The deposit, along with the purchase agree-

Get Good Advice

Buying a new home brings up so many questions that it's easy to feel overwhelmed. You want to be smart with your money, but who can know everything about interest rates, locations, inspections, down payments, and monthly payments? What you need is the advice of a professional real estate agent—someone who understands real estate and works with home buyers and sellers.

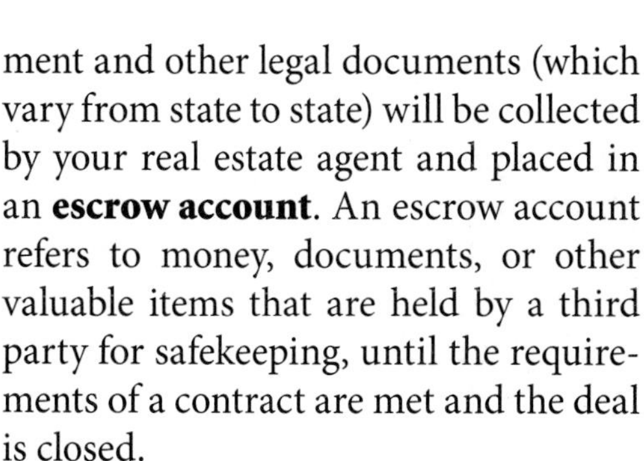

The question is: Who can you trust? Should you just put your finger on a name in the phone book? If you have no experience working with a real estate agent, finding the right one seems like reaching into a grab bag—what you get is a random pick. But finding a good agent does not have to be left to chance. Even if you don't know a good real estate agent yourself, someone you know probably does.

If your parents own a home, ask who helped them. Or try asking a trusted family member, maybe an aunt or uncle. At least one of your relatives is likely paying a mortgage. Your family is a good place to start when looking for a dependable real estate agent because your family will have your best interests at heart. Also, family members can steer you away from bad or disreputable agents, so you do not get burned.

Maybe you have a relative who sells real estate. He or she might make a good agent for you. If that person lives out of the area, he or she might be able to recommend someone. Referrals are a great way to find an agent, because the one you hire knows you will report back to the person who made the recommendation—and the agent wants your report to be positive!

Do not be afraid to ask your friends, too. One of them might know a good agent. Also ask trusted neighbors, teachers, or others you know. By asking around, you will be more likely to find a good agent—and that means you will be more likely to get the house you really want.

ment and other legal documents (which vary from state to state) will be collected by your real estate agent and placed in an **escrow account**. An escrow account refers to money, documents, or other valuable items that are held by a third party for safekeeping, until the requirements of a contract are met and the deal is closed.

The Walk-Through Inspection

You should schedule a walk-through of the house and property about a week before you expect the transaction to close. This is the time to inspect it for any needed repairs or *contingencies* (conditions in the purchase agreement) that have not yet been met. If you find any, tell your agent. He or she will contact the seller's agent, who will contact the seller and get things in order in a matter of days.

Closing the Transaction

The process of *closing*—finalizing the sale of property by transferring the title from seller to buyer—can vary from state to state. Before the closing, a third party receives your down payment, along with the purchase contract, and

escrow account money, documents, or other valuable items that are held by a third party for safekeeping, until the requirements of a contract are met and the deal is closed

Going Global

It might be a long time before you build your own home, but there's a huge building boom right now in Chinese residential housing—and Putnam Lumber of Jacksonville, Florida, is getting in on the ground floor.

The company has been selling southern pine timber since 1945, both in the U.S. and to foreign markets. When China opened its markets to imports, many U.S. suppliers jumped in. Putnam was among them.

The company's president, Ellis Crosby, has a vision for expanding Putnam's influence in China. He is introducing finished wood products, but these finished products will *not* be imported from America. After all, the low labor costs in China and the huge number of available workers mean there will not be much of an import market—it is much cheaper to make the goods there. And that is what Crosby proposes to do.

Under his leadership, Putnam Lumber joined forces with local investors to build a mill in China where raw timber can be cut to custom lengths and pressure-treated to protect it from insect or fungal damage. The mill also produces finished door and window frames, moldings, and some furniture.

It was a bold decision. Crosby says Putnam never could have afforded to expand into manufacturing in the U.S., but low labor costs made it possible to do so in China. Other timber exporters will most likely follow suit. China has a population of 1.3 billion. Even if only 20 percent of the population buy new homes, that is a market as big as the entire United States.

Thinking Globally

1. The cost of lumber for house building in the United States has increased dramatically in recent years. What connection might there be to the Chinese building boom?
2. Do you think a profitable global business could be based on other U.S. raw materials that are manufactured into building supplies in China? Give examples of raw materials and final products.

all the necessary documents from the escrow account. Then there is a *title search.* This process examines all the relevant records to verify that the seller is indeed the legal owner and that there are no **liens**, or financial claims against the property. If the search turns up no claims against the property, the title is considered clear.

liens financial claims against a property

deed a written document transferring ownership of property from one person to another

At the closing, you receive the title to the property. This is a legal document in the form of a **deed** that transfers ownership from the seller to you. (The bank or loan company's name will also be listed on the deed if a mortgage exists on the property.) You might also receive a *title insurance* policy protecting against any claim that might have been missed. You will be charged for the title search as well as the title insurance policy, plus a number of other services. Some of the typical closing costs and services are shown in Figure 10.4, on the facing page.

The mortgage lender usually requires you to set up an escrow account. This is not the same account that the real estate agent established when you were buying the house. This time, the mortgage company uses the escrow account to hold funds to pay property tax and homeowner's insurance during the term of your mortgage.

Just before closing, the lender will prepare the loan documents and tell the person handling the closing when the loan funds will be available. If all the conditions listed in the original purchase agreement have been met, the transaction normally closes on the day after the lender provides the funds for the mortgage. The sale is complete and you (along with the lender) now own the property.

◀ The rewards of home ownership are worth the time and energy of securing a mortgage.

Figure 10.4 REAL ESTATE CLOSING COSTS

Notice the items in the far left column. Each item is a necessary part of closing a real estate deal, and each has a hefty price—all of which add up! The chart below shows actual closing costs from 2007 in three U.S. cities. What are these costs where you will live? Find out, and be sure to factor the closing costs into your budget.

Closing costs	Westlake Village, CA	Oklahoma City, OK	Washington, DC
Title insurance premium	(Varies)	(Varies)	(Varies)
Title search	$195	$195	$195
Tax research	$50	$50	$30
Document preparation	$100	$100	$100
Settlement coordination	$399	$399	$399
Disbursement fee	$125	$125	$125
Recording of mortgage (estimate)	$110	$110	$110
Recording processing	$30	$30	$30
Total	**$1,009 + Title insurance premium**	**$1,009 + Title insurance premium**	**$989 + Title insurance premium**

SECTION 2 ASSESSMENT

Factual Recall

1. List three advantages of home ownership.
2. What four factors affect the amount of a monthly mortgage payment?
3. If you pay two points on a mortgage of $120,000, what is the dollar cost of those points?
4. What is the purpose of a walk-through inspection?
5. What does it mean to "close" a real estate transaction?

Critical Thinking

1. Why do you think most mortgage lenders require a down payment?
2. If you move frequently, is home ownership a good option? Why or why not?

CHAPTER 10 REVIEW AND ASSESSMENT

Chapter Summary

Section 1 Alternatives in Housing

- The average American family moves once every five years, and single adults move even more often.
- There are three major types of housing structures: single-family homes, multifamily housing, and manufactured homes.
- There are some advantages to renting rather than buying. More than one-third of Americans rent their housing.
- Be sure to inspect an apartment thoroughly before you rent it. Take time to read and understand the lease agreement before you sign it.
- The Fair Housing Act protects people who rent or buy a home from discrimination based on race, color, national origin, religion, gender, family status, or disability.

Section 2 Buying a Home

- For most people, a home is the most expensive purchase they will make during their lifetime.
- Homeowners are entitled to several tax advantages.
- A qualified real estate agent can help guide you through the process of buying a home.
- Where a home is located is often more important to the buyer than anything else.
- When making an offer, buyers usually offer less than the seller's asking price.

Reviewing Key Terms

For each of the following statements, choose the answer that best completes the sentence.

1. A security deposit is paid ______.
   - **a.** by a tenant to cover damage to rental property
   - **b.** by a buyer as part of a purchase agreement
   - **c.** by a seller to cover repairs to a home
   - **d.** by a borrower to cover the cost of paperwork for a loan
2. A financial claim against a property is called a(n) ______.
   - **a.** escrow account
   - **b.** deed
   - **c.** lien
   - **d.** mortgage
3. Money, documents, or other valuables may be held in a(n) ______ until the requirements of a contract have been met.
   - **a.** security deposit
   - **b.** lien
   - **c.** equity
   - **d.** escrow account
4. A type of housing that has two or more family dwellings within the same building is called ______.
   - **a.** a dormitory
   - **b.** a condominium
   - **c.** a manufactured home
   - **d.** multifamily housing
5. Housing subsidies are ______.
   - **a.** grants of money from the government to landlords
   - **b.** grants of money to low-income households
   - **c.** programs to build multifamily housing
   - **d.** no longer provided by the government
6. A written document that transfers ownership of property from one person to another is a ______.
   - **a.** deed
   - **b.** lien
   - **c.** foreclosure
   - **d.** mortgage
7. Equity refers to ______.
   - **a.** a sum of money a tenant gives to the landlord before moving in
   - **b.** a valuable asset that a borrower must give up if he or she does not repay a loan
   - **c.** the value of a home minus the amount still owed on it
   - **d.** valuable items that are held by a third party for safekeeping until the requirements of a contract are met

Understanding the Main Ideas

1. When you are looking for a place to live, why should you consider the distance from work, school, or shopping?
2. What is the most popular category of housing in the United States? Why?
3. Why might more people be living in multifamily housing in the future?

4. Describe the advantages and disadvantages of renting a home.
5. Why should you document the contents and condition of an apartment before moving in?
6. What are three tax advantages of home ownership?

Practicing Math

1. Use an online amortization table to find answers to the following questions. One site that provides such tables is the mortgage calculator at Bankrate.com (http://fin.emcp.net/bankrate). Suppose you have a mortgage loan of $240,000. The interest rate is fixed at 6.25 percent, and the loan term is 30 years.
   a. What will be the amount of your monthly payment?
   b. With your first payment, how much will go toward the principal and how much will go toward interest?
   c. How many years will you be paying the mortgage before the amount for the principal is greater than the amount for interest?
   d. How much interest will you have paid at the end of 30 years?
   e. What will your $240,000 loan have cost you in principal plus interest?
2. Suppose you are looking for a two-bedroom home with a garage. Make a table comparing the costs of renting an apartment, renting a house, and buying a house in your community. Be sure to include costs for utilities and taxes.

Applying Critical Thinking Skills

1. When boomerang children return to the family home, the adjustment might be more difficult than for those who never left. Why?
2. Choosing housing usually requires trade-offs. Describe some possible trade-offs.
3. Compare the three kinds of housing structures, listing advantages and disadvantages of each.
4. You are about to rent an apartment, and the landlord seems very nice. He hands you a lease, tells you it's "just a formality," and expects you to sign right away. What should you do?
5. Renting a home and buying one both have advantages and disadvantages. Which do you think is better? Why?
6. If you are going to be moving in less than five years, why might an ARM be a good type of mortgage for you?
7. What do you think are some advantages of working with a real estate agent rather than searching for a home on your own?

Working with Real-World Documents

1. Standard apartment leases include: (1) the names of the tenants; (2) the address of the apartment; (3) the amount and frequency of rent; (4) the amount of security deposit; (5) the lease's duration (length of time the lease will remain in effect); and (6) the signatures of the tenants and the landlord (or agent). Examine a lease for renting an apartment or house. What is the duration of the lease? What does it say about a security deposit? How often must rent be paid? Are there any clauses about special matters, such as keeping pets or redecorating?
2. Research newspapers, local lenders, and online sources to find information about at least three different types of mortgage loans—for example, a fixed-rate mortgage, a balloon mortgage, and an option ARM. Compare and contrast the various types of loans. Consider down payment options, interest rates, and length of loan. Which type of loan seems most expensive? Which carries the most risk for the borrower?

Taking It Home

1. Suppose you will soon be moving to your own apartment. Talk with relatives and friends about what to look for—and what to avoid. Use their input to create a checklist of the features you would look for in an apartment.
2. Do you know someone who has moved frequently? If so, interview that person about his or her experiences. What advice does the frequent mover have about making moving easier?

CHAPTER 11

The Necessities: Food and Clothing

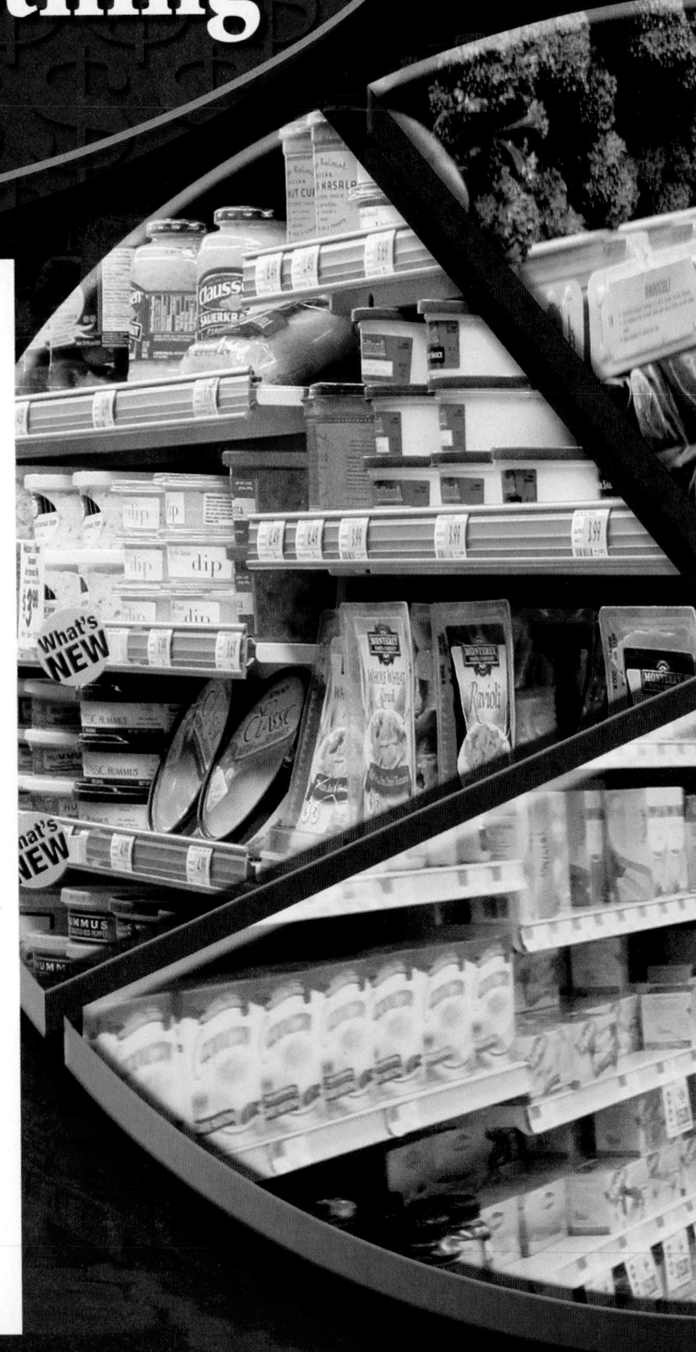

Big-ticket items, such as housing and cars, are major purchases that require research and a lot of thought. However, the items that you purchase over and over—*everyday purchases*—also have a big impact on your finances.

This chapter will help you sharpen your decision-making skills and feel more satisfied with your food and clothing choices. You can use the same skills when you make other everyday buying decisions. As a smart shopper of the things you need all the time, you will have more money to save for your short-, medium-, and long-term goals.

▲ House brands of some foods contain the same ingredients as more expensive ones. Why are name brands more expensive than house brands?

SECTION 1 Buying Food

SECTION 2 Buying Clothing

Fact or Fiction

What do you think? Are the following statements true or false? If you think they are false, then say what is true.

1. Online food shopping is becoming more popular every year.
2. All food products must have a label identifying the nutrients contained in the product.
3. House brands and generic products can often be smart food choices.
4. The clothes you buy are required to include instructions for how to clean them.
5. Clearance sales offer some of the biggest price reductions for clothing.
6. You can always return a clothing purchase, as long as you have not worn it.

Answers on page 297.

Study Reminder

Knowing how to study can increase your knowledge, improve your grades, and cut down on your study time. See the ***Studying Personal Finance*** *pages at the front of the book for some tips to help you study this chapter.*

SECTION 1

Buying Food

Focus Questions

1. What are some current food-buying trends?
2. What nutrition information is listed on the product label?
3. How can you judge the freshness of foods you buy?

Key Terms

organic foods
universal product code (UPC)
nutrient density
national brands
house brands
generic products
pack date
pull date
expiration date
unit pricing

You grab a bite to eat with your friends after practice. You skip breakfast because you are running late. You stop at the store on the way home to pick up ingredients for tonight's dinner. Even if you are not living on your own, you already make many of your own food choices and purchases all the time. How many of those decisions are automatic? How many do you really think about before making them?

Influences on Food Choices

You have probably heard the term *comfort foods.* They are the foods that you associate with good memories. Oatmeal cookies might be what you reach for when you are stressed, because your grandmother used to make them, and she always made you feel better.

Why people choose the foods they do is a complex subject. Certainly, your preferences are shaped by your personal likes and dislikes. Culture and geography also play a role, as can the food choices of your family and friends. If you are health conscious, you will try to choose nutritious foods. If you are budget conscious, you will try to find inexpensive foods. Advertising and food packaging are aimed at getting you to buy particular products without realizing why you do so. Food costs, on the other hand, might be on your mind every time you shop or eat out.

Money and Food Decisions

You have an interesting vantage point for observing how people—classmates, friends, and other families—make food choices. You might know some teens who always seem to have plenty of money to spend on snacks and eating out, even though they don't have a job. Others might bring their own lunch and walk past vending machines without a second glance. How much money you have available, and how hard you personally worked for it, will influence your attitude toward all types of spending, including food. Your priorities play a role, too: You are likely to spend more money on the things that are important to you.

You Can Succeed Financially

Kenny Lao had a goal of owning his own restaurant chain. He thought it would be smart to go to business school, so he enrolled at New York University's Stern School of Business. In his first semester, he met Andrew Stenzler, an earlier Stern graduate and founder of Cosi, a popular chain of informal restaurants. Stenzler would become Lao's future major investor.

The Plan

Meanwhile, Lao entered Stern's Maximum Exposure Business Plan competition. His business idea was an Asian dumpling bar—a restaurant concept that Lao termed "fast-casual." Patrons would be able to eat quickly and inexpensively, but the food quality would be much higher than the usual fast-food outlet. He designed the business to be expanded easily if successful.

His plan won second prize in the contest—$150,000. He used the prize money, and an additional $450,000 from Stenzler and other investors, to open Rickshaw Dumpling Bar in the Chelsea neighborhood of New York City in 2004.

Lao also knew the importance of having a good chef. With the help of Stenzler's contacts in the food world, he met Anita Lo, a well-known New York gourmet restaurant chef. She agreed to develop a menu and recipes for Rickshaw. Having a famous chef on board gave the restaurant immediate credibility.

The Food

The restaurant's dumplings are made fresh daily. The stuffings are inspired by many Asian cuisines—from Peking duck to Thai basil. There are also pork, chicken, shrimp, and vegetarian dumplings.

▲ **Kenny Lao is the founder and owner of Rickshaw Dumpling Bar, a fast-casual restaurant in New York City.**

Dumplings can be fried or steamed. They are served either with dipping sauce or in soup and can be accompanied by salad if desired. The restaurant also serves dessert dumplings and Asian-inspired beverages—including a green tea milkshake. Six dumplings with a salad costs less than $8.

Rickshaw Dumpling Bar was an immediate success in the fickle New York food world. MTV did a documentary about Lao. He and chef Anita Lo appeared on Martha Stewart's television program. That publicity and word-of-mouth recommendations soon had customers lined up out the door and onto the sidewalk. Celebrities took to the food, adding to its popularity. "Dumplings aren't something you need to learn how to love. We just brought a food people really like to a mainstream audience," Lao says.

The Business Angle

Once the concept proved itself in the Chelsea location, Lao began to develop plans for other outlets. He says the restaurant is designed for urban areas with large populations. Because of the high quality of the ingredients, the profit margin on each item is small. This means that outlets need a large turnover each day to be profitable.

The first location employed thirty-five workers and had $1.5 million in sales in 2006. That year Lao and Stenzler began looking for more investors to finance five more Rickshaw Dumpling Bars in the New York area.

What Would You Do?

1. What menu options do you think would be healthiest when eating at Rickshaw? What options should you avoid to keep your meal lower in fat?
2. Based on American food-spending habits, does opening a restaurant seem like a good career move? Give reasons for your answer.

The same is true for families, but more factors must be considered. A family's available income must meet the needs—and some of the wants—of all its members. Food is both a need and a want. Everyone needs enough nutritious food to stay alive and healthy. However, most families buy not just the basics, but also many extra foods that they like.

Unfortunately, some people do not have enough money to buy even the most essential foods. They might be out of work. They might be retired and living on a small, fixed income. Some people have to choose between buying food or medicine and paying their utility bills.

For people in situations like these, the federal government's food stamp program can help them buy the food they need. Those who qualify for food stamps receive monthly benefits on an electronic card that they can use like an ATM card at most grocery stores.

Where to Eat?

You and your family make decisions every day about where to eat. You can prepare meals at home, eat out, or grab some take-out food. Each has advantages and disadvantages. Each uses different amounts of available resources, money, time, and skills.

▼ Eating at restaurants is fun and introduces you to foods you might not make at home.

Eating In Preparing food at home from fresh ingredients can provide tasty meals, good nutrition, and often, cost savings, too. Cooking requires both time and skill. Even if your kitchen skills are limited, however, you can still fix meals at home. Many fresh, frozen, and canned foods are easy to prepare. For instance, an easy, nutritious meal could be frozen lasagna warmed in the microwave, frozen or canned peas, whole-grain rolls, and oranges for dessert. You could pack a lunch of yogurt, carrot sticks, and granola, then buy milk or juice at school.

By trying out new recipes, you expand your cooking skills. If you cook more than you need for one meal, reheating the leftovers gives you a second meal.

Eating Out Going out for a restaurant meal is an opportunity for good food, plus time with friends or family. No one has to spend time in the kitchen. Everyone can order something different.

On the downside, when you eat out it's hard to know what ingredients were used. You cannot be sure how the food was prepared. It's easy to take in many more calories than you imagine—especially with the extra-large portions so common today. Instead, you can ask for a half-portion, share a main dish, or take home part of your meal to eat later. That way, you will be cutting calories and cutting restaurant prices at the same time.

Fast-food restaurants present additional challenges. Many choices are high in fat, sugar, salt, and calories. Be a smart consumer: Look for, and order, the more nutritious options. Salads with fat-free dressing, baked foods instead of fried, and low-fat dairy drinks are good choices. Resist the pitch to *super-size.* Several online sites, such as Calorie-

Counters (http://fin.emcp.net/caloriecounters), provide nutrition information on major fast-food chains.

Take-Out Food When everyone in the household is rushing to evening activities, there might not be time to cook. Take-out food, plus a few items from home, can be one solution. Get a baked take-out chicken, toss a quick green salad at home, and heat up some frozen rolls for a no-fuss meal. The cost is much less than if the family ate out. The deli departments in many grocery stores now include salad bars and take-out sections with a variety of salads, entrees, side dishes, and desserts.

A food label you are probably seeing more and more these days is "Certified Organic." Organic fruits and vegetables are grown without the use of pesticides, hormones, or chemical fertilizers. They are processed without preservatives or other artificial ways of keeping them fresh and attractive. Organic meats, milk, and eggs come from animals that are fed only organically grown food and not given hormones or antibiotics.

But the question is: Are organically grown foods healthier for you? There have been many studies, but no definite proof. Still, some people prefer organic food, even though it is usually more expensive than conventionally grown products. Judging by the growth in demand for organic foods in the early 2000s, many people believe they are worth the extra expense.

Food-Buying Trends

Two trends are influencing the food choices and food-buying habits of some consumers. The demand for organic food is on the rise. Online shopping is also growing in popularity and availability.

Organic Foods Foods grown without the use of pesticides, chemical fertilizers, antibiotics, and hormones are termed **organic foods**. Organic foods have been around for years. Until recently, however, there were no standards identifying what *organic* meant. Availability varied and prices were high.

Today, foods labeled as organic must meet strict government regulations. With rising concern about pesticides and other contaminants in the food supply, demand for organic foods is up. Grocery shoppers now find more organic choices. In addition, some specialty groceries sell only organic foods. Prices can be slightly higher—or much higher—than for similar nonorganic choices. Some consumers choose organic only when buying foods that might otherwise be high in harmful chemicals, such as apples, peaches, milk, spinach, and beef. Others buy only organic.

Online Food Shopping In 2006, 5 million shoppers bought groceries online—and the number was expected to double by 2010. Shopping for groceries online appeals mainly to people who want to save time. However, online food shopping is also used by people with limited mobility and people who do not have transportation to the supermarket. Online grocers plan to expand throughout the country, but this option is likely

organic foods healthy foods produced without the use of pesticides, chemical fertilizers, antibiotics, or hormones

▼ Organically grown foods are a good source of nutrition.

to be limited to large cities for quite some time.

Online grocery prices and in-store prices tend to be about the same. However, online shoppers can expect to pay more for home delivery, usually between \$10 and \$20. Many customers also tip the delivery person.

Getting the Best Food for the Money

When you walk into a supermarket, you are faced with more than 10,000 choices. Even if you have planned ahead and made a shopping list, you will still be bombarded with decisions. Green beans are on your list. Will you buy fresh? If not, do you want frozen, or canned? What brand and size should you buy?

More information than you might realize is available to help you make informed choices. Much of it is right in the store, on the product labels.

universal product code (UPC) the pattern of black and white lines on a package, forming a bar code that identifies the product

Reading Food Labels

You have probably noticed the pattern of black and white lines on food packages. This is a **universal product code (UPC)**, and it identifies the food processor and what the package contains. A scanner at the supermarket "reads" the code and records the price.

The labels you find on foods do a lot more than tell you what's inside the package. Government laws and regulations specify certain information that must be included. Food manufacturers and processors add their own information, as well.

Basic Information The Fair Packaging and Labeling Act sets the basic requirements for information on food labels. Most must include the following:

- The name of the product
- The name and place of business of the manufacturer, packer, or distributor

▶ Grocery stores offer a variety of foods, so you can choose the ones that fit your budget and nutritional needs.

- The net contents by weight, measure, or count
- The ingredients, listed in order from the greatest in weight to the least (some common products, such as ketchup and mayonnaise, are exempt because their ingredients must match government specifications)
- Any additives used to flavor, color, or preserve the product
- Any specific ingredients known to cause allergic reactions in some people or known to be related to certain other health problems
- The nutritional content of any food for which nutritional claims are made or that have nutrients added to the food

Food companies have long used terms such as "fat free," "low fat," "lean," "light," and "cholesterol free" to help sell their products. Now these terms can appear on food labels only if a product meets strict government standards. Figure 11.1 defines some of the terms you might see on a food label.

Figure 11.1 FOOD LABEL TERMS

The government has recently established standards for use of some words commonly found on food labels. Now when consumers see these words on food labels, they know what each means.

Definitions of Food Label Terms

fat free:	contains half a gram or less of fat per serving
low fat:	contains 3 grams or less of fat per serving
lean:	contains not more than 10 grams of fat, not more than 4 grams of saturated fat, and less than 95 milligrams of cholesterol per serving
light:	(1) a serving provides one-third fewer calories or half the fat of the regular product; (2) a serving of a low-calorie, low-fat food provides half the sodium normally present; and/or (3) the product is light in color and texture (A product needs to meet only **one** of these meanings to be considered light.)
cholesterol free:	contains no cholesterol or a trivial amount

Nutrition Information By law, additional nutrition information must be shown on the labels of many foods. Usually this is organized on an easy-to-find "Nutrition Facts" box on the label (see Figure 11.2 on the next page). The information, based on one serving of the product, must include the following:

- The serving size and number of servings in the package
- The number of calories in one serving
- The fat, cholesterol, carbohydrate, and protein content (given in grams)
- The percentage of the recommended daily intake (Daily Values) of protein, vitamin A, vitamin C, thiamine, riboflavin, niacin, calcium, and iron in a serving, if the food contains them (Other nutrients might also be shown.)

The nutrition information on food labels can be useful in helping you decide what to buy. Because it lists the nutritional value right on the label, you can easily compare different products. This information can help you choose foods with the best **nutrient density**—the most nutrition with the fewest calories. For instance, you can compare the calories, fat, and salt in two frozen dinners. You can evaluate differences in "low-fat" and regular versions of products. In doing so, you may find that *low-fat* does not always mean *low-calorie.*

Having this nutrition information printed on the label is especially helpful for people on restricted diets. Some people need to limit sodium. Others must

nutrient density the amount of nutrients in a food, compared with the number of calories

Figure 11.2 SAMPLE NUTRITION LABELS

The percentages of nutrients listed on a Nutrition Facts panel are based on a 2,000 calorie diet.

What percentage of a 2,000 calorie diet does one serving of this tuna fulfill for sodium? For total fat? What is the size of one serving of this tuna? How many servings in a can?

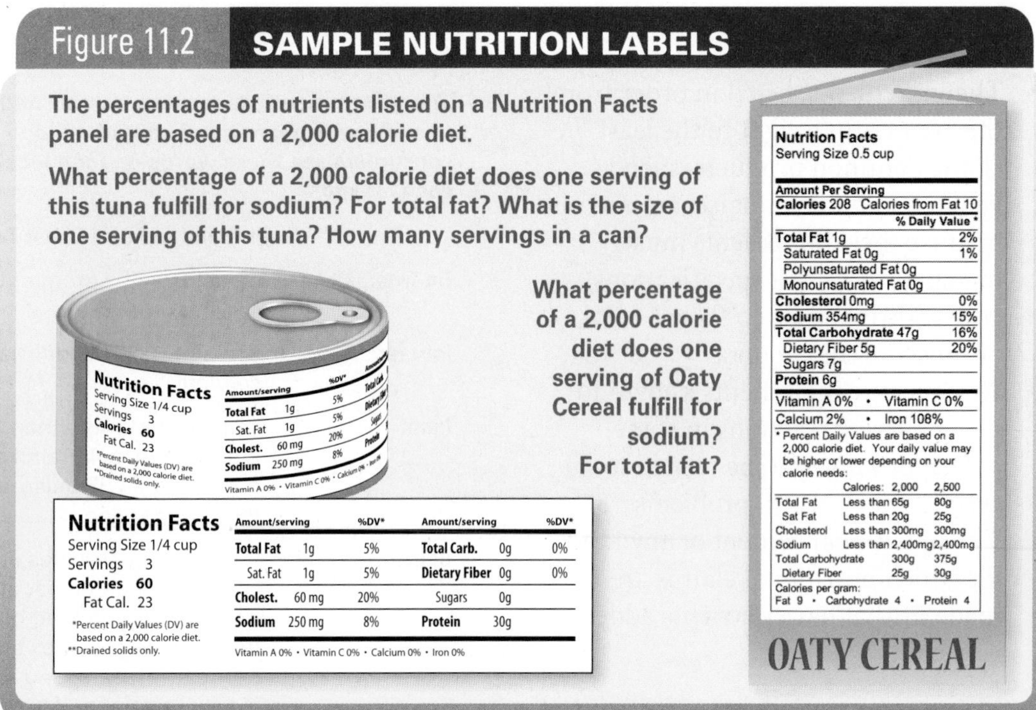

national brands heavily advertised product names that are found in stores around the country

house brands "private label" product names found only in one chain of supermarkets

cut down on their sugar or fat intake. People who are trying to lose or gain weight can keep track of calories. In addition, identifying the ingredients that can cause dangerous allergic reactions is vital for those people at risk.

Did You Know?

Many people in the mid-twentieth century stopped eating solid animal fats like butter or lard and started eating hydrogenated vegetable oils—*trans fats.* Nutrition science told them that the saturated fats in animal fats were harmful to their health. But research over time has shown that trans fats lead to unhealthy changes in cholesterol levels—and to heart and vascular disease. All fats and oils should be eaten sparingly, but trans fats are worse for your body than any others.

Until recently, trans fats were found in almost all snack foods and fast foods. Most margarines and all solid shortenings still contain them. Federal laws require all food labels to list trans fat content. Makers of snacks and fast foods are gradually removing these fats from their products—but as a consumer it is important to check labels yourself.

Evaluating Product Brands

A product's brand name is usually prominently displayed on the label. Food companies hope consumers will become loyal to their brand and automatically buy other products they make. Brand names can help you buy a particular product—perhaps a frozen pizza—that you liked before. In the store you will find national brands, house brands, and generic products.

- **National brands** are sold across the country in many different stores. They are heavily advertised. These products are usually the most expensive, unless they are on sale, but you can count on consistent quality.
- **House brands** are sometimes called *private labels.* A supermarket chain generally stocks many products with its own brand. (The name may or may not be the same as the name of the store.) The quality of house brands is usually as good as for national brands. In fact, they are often produced by the same manufacturer—but packaged under the store's label. House brands

LOOK Before You Leap

Teresa knows that being overweight puts her at risk for many serious diseases, including diabetes. And she already gets out of breath climbing a flight of stairs. She is determined to get more exercise and lose weight. She wants to lose 30 pounds.

There's a new diet in a popular magazine—you eat nothing but steak and grapefruit. A celebrity lost 60 pounds on the diet in six months. If she lost weight at the same rate, Teresa would reach her goal in just three months.

She's ready to go shopping when her friend Larry stops her. Larry took a nutrition class last semester and knows the steak-and-grapefruit diet is not well balanced—and could even be dangerous. Larry thinks Teresa should use the plan he did—Weight Watchers—or at least some plan that encourages a wide range of healthy foods.

The two go online and look at the Weight Watchers Web site. Teresa is disappointed because it doesn't promise she can lose 10 pounds a month. Larry points out to Teresa that she needs to eat a variety of foods. "Let me show you what your body needs," he tells her.

While online, Larry shows Teresa the Department of Agriculture's Food Guide Pyramid (http://fin.emcp.net/pyramid). They click the link to the MyPyramid Plan—a diet program that follows the Pyramid guidelines. Teresa enters her age, sex, weight, height, and activity level onscreen and gets a list of foods she needs for health and energy. She sees that if she learns more about good nutrition she can choose a better way to lose weight than eating only steak and grapefruit.

Before Starting

1. Why is it a good idea to know what foods your body needs before trying to lose weight?
2. Use the MyPyramid Plan to find out what foods you need. How does your actual diet shape up?

generally cost a little less than national brands.

- **Generic products** list no brand name. You are likely to see a plain box or can labeled "Macaroni and Cheese" or "Baked Beans." These products typically offer the same nutrition as national brands or house brands, but they cost less. You might notice a difference in quality. For example, a can of generic peaches might contain chunks of varying sizes, compared to a national brand's uniform slices. When such differences are not important, choosing generics could save you money.

Assessing Quality

High-quality foods are more appealing. In some cases, they are also more nutritious. Food safety is also a quality issue. If food manufacturers or suppliers allow contaminated or spoiled food to go on the market, many people can become ill, or even die. Of course, foods can also lose quality or spoil after they leave their source.

The federal government—through laws, regulations, and other methods—oversees the food system. The two main governmental units responsible for these efforts are the United States Department

generic products products that carry no brand name, with packaging that simply describes the contents

Get Good Advice

How do you get the most for your food dollar? You can look through the sale ads in your newspaper or check for red tags along the market aisles to find products with reduced prices. Sometimes, though, your best bet is simply talking with people in the stores.

Employees at specialty shops and in the specialty departments of supermarkets can recommend good, inexpensive food. They have extensive knowledge about their products and can tell you what is freshest, what is a good deal, and what is on sale.

For example, butchers are meat specialists who work in butcher shops or the meat department of your local supermarket. Trained butchers know the various cuts of beef, their costs, and how to cook them. They will tell you which is freshest and which daily cuts are the best deal. Fresh meat often has higher quality than frozen meat from the frozen foods section (even though the nutritional value is about the same).

Butchers can also help you find the best cuts of pork and chicken. They can tell you how to prepare duck, quail, buffalo, or even llama. For a real bargain, they can tell you how inexpensive organ meats and some leftover animal parts can improve your nutrition. For example, liver is used in pâtés, and animal bones are used for soup stock and gravy—and both of these can be purchased for pennies a pound.

Other knowledgeable food specialists include the employees in the seafood department, bakery, and produce sections. The folks in the seafood department can tell you the catch of the day—and in some stores they will even prepare your seafood purchase at no charge. The bakers make fresh breads daily. The produce specialists can tell you what is in season—and therefore what is less expensive than usual.

If you have a friend or relative who likes to cook, or who cooks professionally, ask him or her for grocery recommendations. Then don't hesitate to get more good advice from the various specialists in the store.

of Agriculture (USDA) and the Food and Drug Administration (FDA).

As a consumer, you have a role to play as well. As you shop, be alert for bulging cans and opened packages, because the food inside might be spoiled or contaminated. Never purchase or eat such items. Foods that must be stored in your refrigerator should be cold when purchased and kept cold until stored. Frozen foods should be frozen solid.

Product Grades About half of all the money spent on food goes for meat, eggs, and dairy products. The USDA has established a system of food grades, or quality ratings, for these foods and others. The higher the grade, the better the quality—and the more expensive the product. It is important to remember that a higher grade does not indicate anything about the nutritional value of the food. Food grading is voluntary, so not all products have grades.

Because not all foods are graded in the same way, take time to learn about some of them, as follows:

- *Meat:* Beef is graded from highest to lowest: *Prime*, *Choice*, and *Select.* A *Prime* cut is the most tender, juciest, and most flavorful of the grades. A *Choice* cut is more tender and flavorful than one graded *Select.* A *Select* cut is less flavorful but leaner. Pork is not graded because it is generally tender.

- *Eggs:* Eggs are graded AA, A, and B. The grade is determined by the interior quality of the egg and also by its outer appearance. Grade AA and A eggs are good for all purposes, but especially those where appearance matters. Grade B eggs are fine for general cooking and baking.
- *Dairy products:* Almost all dairy products can be graded, but the system is used mostly for butter, Cheddar cheese, and nonfat dry milk. Inspectors also grade other cheeses, dry whey, dry buttermilk, and dried and condensed milk. Grades AA and A are found in stores.

Keys to Freshness If you are buying *produce*—fresh fruits and vegetables—you will not see any product grades. The quality of these foods begins to deteriorate as soon they are picked, and that process continues until they are eaten. Through technology, deterioration can be slowed, but it cannot be stopped entirely. You must evaluate the quality of produce on your own. The freshest produce has good color and firmness. It does not look dried out or have spots of decay.

Fresh meat, poultry, and seafood are also subject to spoilage. Because these items are usually packaged at the store, most stores put a date on the labels indicating how long the items may be sold as fresh. This date allows a few days' time for you to cook and use the food at home.

Many food processors also put dates on their food packages to help consumers judge freshness. This process, called *open dating*, helps store owners and shoppers know when a product has passed its peak of quality or should no longer be eaten. Three different types of dates are used. The **pack date** is the day the food was manufactured, processed, or packaged. The **pull date** (sometimes shown as a *Sell by* date) identifies the last day a store should sell the food (but not the last day it can be eaten). The **expiration date** is the last day the food is acceptable to eat. For example, milk might begin to sour after the expiration date.

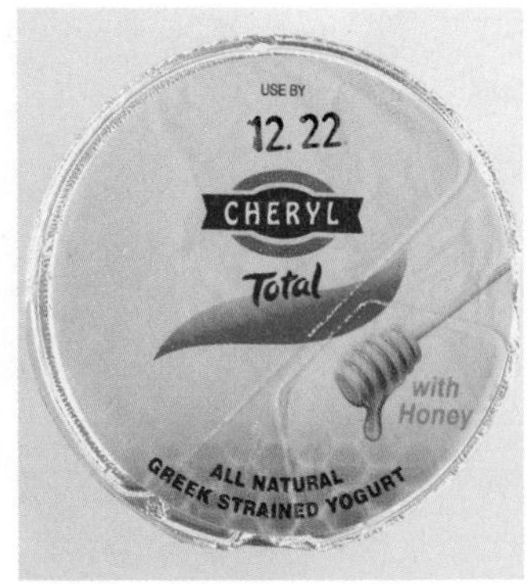

▲ Finding an expiration date can be tricky, but it should be there. If it is not, use your food knowledge to decide if the food is safe to eat.

The length of time before a product begins to lose quality varies considerably. Some packaged, canned, and frozen foods can retain quality for months or years. Even after they begin to lose quality, most are still safe to eat. Stores sometimes offer food that is slightly past the pull date for sale at a lower price. If the food still looks fresh and you will be using it within a day or two, it can be a good buy.

Food Safety Inspection helps ensure that foods have been labeled and packaged properly, are wholesome, and are safe. In the United States, the grading of raw meat and poultry is voluntary, but inspection of those items is mandatory. Both packing plants and raw meats and poultry are inspected for sanitation and contamination.

In-store handling can also affect the safety of food, especially of meat and produce. Fresh foods in particular must be processed, packaged, and displayed properly and at the correct temperatures.

pack date a date printed on food packaging that indicates when the item was manufactured, processed, or packaged

pull date a date printed on food packaging that indicates the last day a store should sell the item (but not the last day it can be eaten)

expiration date a date printed on food packaging that indicates the last day a food is acceptable for its intended use

Deciding on Quantity

Deciding how much of a food to buy depends on a number of factors. If you

▲ **Bulk purchases often save money, but only if you eat what you buy.**

are planning to make a certain recipe, it may specify "one 28 oz. can of whole tomatoes." If you are fixing pork chops for five people, you need to buy at least five pieces.

You might think buying larger quantities always saves money. A 25-pound bag of flour might save money compared to a 5-pound bag—but not always. Think about how much of the product you will use in a reasonable time. The flour in that 25-pound bag will not be nearly as fresh if you are still using it a year from now. You might have to throw some (or most) of it away. Remember, too, that large quantities require more storage space.

unit pricing a method of expressing the price of an item per unit of measure, such as cost per ounce or cost per piece

Comparing Prices

The cost of any food product can vary significantly from store to store and from one week to the next. Most stores provide price comparison information using a system called **unit pricing**. This system expresses the cost of food per unit of measure—for example, the cost per ounce. It helps you compare costs for different sizes of packages. Unit price tags are usually located on the shelf beneath the product. If the unit price is not given, you can calculate it by dividing the total cost by the number of units. Suppose a 48-ounce bottle of apple juice is priced at $2.16. Divide $2.16 by 48 to get the unit price of 4.5 cents per ounce.

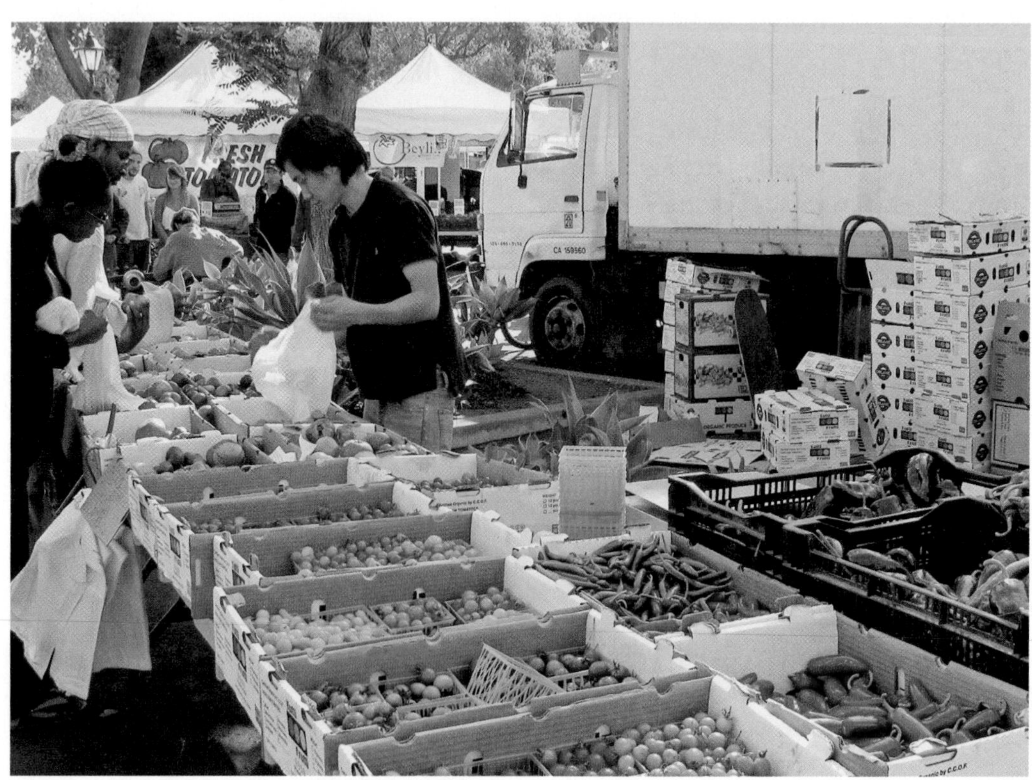

▶ **Farmers' markets offer locally grown, healthy foods and a chance to chat with neighbors.**

Choosing Where to Shop

For your primary grocery shopping, choose a store that has the products and services you want. Compare quality, prices, and the sales promotions offered. Travel distance may also be a consideration.

In addition to their primary grocery stores, many people shop at other places on a less regular basis. They might drive a little further once a month to stock up on items at a store with lower prices. If a farmers' market is in the area, you might buy seasonal produce there. Specialty stores, such as bakeries and meat or fish markets, focus on particular types of foods. Some national retail chains like Wal-Mart and Target also sell grocery products.

As people move away from farms and into cities, they are eating more processed foods, a significant cause of obesity. Many environmentalists and other experts, including writers Bill McKibben and Wendell Berry, stress the importance of eating locally grown foods to improve both nutrition and community life.

Berry suggests that as farms go through foreclosure and rural communities disappear, many people come to feel isolated and depressed. Both Berry and McKibben promote one small, important step to recovering happiness: Shop at local farmers' markets—the food is fresh and the neighbors are friendly.

Understanding Food Promotion

Food manufacturers spend billions of dollars each year on advertising. Advertising costs make products more expensive. About 3.5 cents of every dollar spent on food goes to help pay for advertising and promotion. One out of every five commercials on TV is for food or beverages.

Displays and packaging with bright colors and logos are also part of advertising. Attractive food displays make it hard to resist buying foods. Studies show that during each visit to a grocery store, the average consumer buys three more items than planned.

Weekly food ads and coupons help bring customers to particular stores. Some coupons are issued by food manufacturers. Others come from the stores themselves. Many stores offer discount cards to their regular customers. This allows them to take advantage of reduced-price items. You might also find coupons online.

SECTION 1 ASSESSMENT

Factual Recall

1. Is food a need or a want?
2. List at least three advantages of cooking at home.
3. What are three ways to reduce calories from a restaurant meal?
4. What are three reasons for people to buy groceries online?
5. Must all food labels list nutritional content? Explain.
6. Why might reading a food label be helpful if you have an allergy?

Critical Thinking

1. Eating at home is usually cheaper than eating out or buying take-out food. Why, then, is it not always the best option?
2. Suppose you wanted to buy organic foods but had limited funds. What kinds of foods should you choose to get the most benefit for your money?

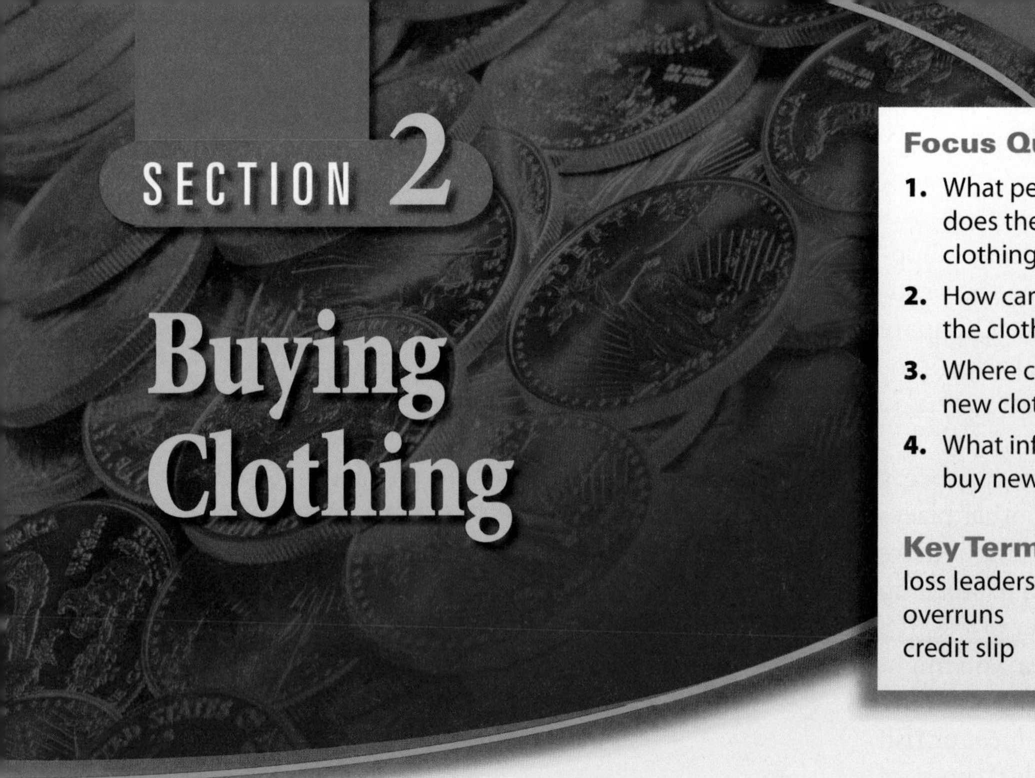

SECTION 2

Buying Clothing

Focus Questions

1. What percentage of total expenses does the average family spend on clothing?
2. How can you check for quality in the clothes you buy?
3. Where can you find bargains on new clothes?
4. What influences your decision to buy new clothes?

Key Terms

loss leaders
overruns
credit slip
sales receipt
layaway plan

Clothes help form people's first impression of someone else. What would your clothes suggest about you? For most teens, clothes are a sign of self-expression—but also a way of fitting in with peers. It's not surprising, then, that clothing purchases are one of the largest categories of teens' spending. Do you feel like you never have the right clothes? Perhaps you spend more than you should on clothes. With a little know-how, you can become a better shopper.

Influences on Clothing Choices

Clothing manufacturers try to predict what you will want to buy. They even try to influence trends through their advertising—projecting certain images as being the "popular" way to dress. When entertainers and stars wear manufacturers' clothes, it does have an influence. Certain brands, often expensive ones, become status symbols.

There are many other influences on clothing choices. You only have to look around your school to see the variety. Some people have their own style, unconcerned about whether they dress like anyone else. Others use clothes to portray an image, make a statement, or show what group they belong to.

Teens generally have more freedom than adults to dress the way they want. But family and society do have expectations about what clothes are appropriate for certain situations. Schools do, as well. Dress codes are meant to prohibit clothes that are inappropriate or distracting.

Most businesses and industries have rules—implied, or sometimes written into the company handbook—about what clothes are acceptable. Some require uniforms, either for safety reasons or job position recognition, or as a way of promoting the company's image. For other jobs, clothes that project a professional image are expected.

Analyzing Your Wardrobe

You could have a closet overflowing with clothes, but not the ones you need. Most people wear only about 20 percent of their clothes on a regular basis. They tend to buy clothes they like when they see them. If you rely on spur-of-the-moment decisions, you might be spending more than you should. Clothes chosen this way might not go with anything else you have. Do you have some things you have never worn? Taking a more systematic approach can help you spend less by making better choices.

The most important step is to take a close look at the clothes you already have—your *wardrobe*. Begin by emptying your closet, drawers, and other storage areas. As you take out each piece, put it in one of four groups, as shown in the list that follows. Then go through each group using the guidelines given.

- *Group 1: Clothes you wear often.* Organize these clothes by type (all pants together, all shirts, and so on) or by color.
- *Group 2: Clothes you wear occasionally.* What keeps you from wearing each item more often? See if you can combine any of these items with clothes you already have in a new way. Perhaps adding an accessory would make it more wearable. Move clothes you want to keep to Group 1. Move those that do not fit or that you do not want to Group 4.
- *Group 3: Clothes that need attention before you can wear them again.* What's the problem? Some might no longer fit. Others might need simple repairs or cleaning. Decide which you can make wearable again. Move the others to Group 4.
- *Group 4: Clothes that you have not worn for more than a year or no longer want.* First check to see if you want to return anything to your active wardrobe. Decide what to do with the clothes you no longer wear. Can anything be passed down to a younger sibling? Are others suitable for donation or sale?

◀ Going through your clothes so that you know what you have and what you need may prevent impulse buys.

Before you put away the clothes you are keeping, make a list of the parts of your life that have distinctive clothing needs. For example, your list might include school, a part-time job in an office, working out, time with friends, and special occasions. Identify the clothes or outfits you have that fit each category. If you find any gaps, write them down. Try combining what you have in new ways to expand your options, based on your analysis. Make a list of clothes you need and clothes you want. You will use this list to plan what you will buy.

Getting the Most for Your Money

Clothing costs are rising. Except for meeting basic clothing needs, these purchases are considered *discretionary*, not essential, spending. Think about what else you and your family could use the money for if you spent less on clothes.

Setting a Clothing Budget

On average, families spend just under $2,000 per person per year on buying and caring for clothes. That is about 6 percent of the family's total expenses.

As you learned in Chapter 4, families and individuals who are good money managers set up a budget. They decide how much they will spend on a monthly basis for various categories of expenses. This helps them avoid overspending.

Many people who do not budget will end up spending more than they can afford. If they consistently spend too much on clothes—or anything else—they either increase their debt or have to go without other things.

The best way to set up a clothing budget is to start by tracking what you actually spend on clothes over several months. Then evaluate your spending. Decide how much you can and should spend on clothes each month. Budgets can be readjusted later, if needed. And remember—you don't have to spend your entire clothes budget each month. If you keep some in reserve, you will have extra money for bigger purchases like a winter coat or a prom dress.

► **Color, fabric content, and price are some aspects to consider when buying clothes.**

Planning What to Buy

Your list of needs and wants is a starting point for setting up a plan to improve your wardrobe. You have analyzed how well the clothes you have meet your needs. Now, expand that picture. Are there any upcoming changes in your life that might change your clothing needs? Will you be graduating soon and going on to school or a job? Are you still growing? If so, it does not make sense to buy expensive clothes that will not fit a few months from now.

There is no "correct" number of pants or sweaters to have. What is important is to have individual pieces that can be matched in a variety of ways to create many different outfits. Clothing specialists suggest choosing two or three main colors as the basis for your wardrobe. That way, it's easier to mix and match pieces. Navy and tan are good colors in every season, but you should also consider what colors look best on *you.*

Another good tip is to choose classic styles, rather than fads, for more expensive purchases. Classic styles change little over the years. Fads come and go and quickly look out-of-date.

One good way to consider what to spend on particular clothing items is to calculate the *cost per wearing.* This is a rough estimate of how much value you get from a clothing purchase. Take the price you would pay and divide that by how many times you think you will wear the item. If you buy a prom dress and wear it once, the cost per wearing equals the purchase price. If you buy a pair of pants for $36 and estimate that you will wear them once a week for the next year, the cost is less than 70 cents per wearing. You can see that it can pay to buy better quality for clothes that will get a lot of use.

Understanding Clothing Labels and Tags

When you are shopping, read and compare the labels and tags that are attached to clothes. They provide important information that can help you make good choices. Over the years, Congress has passed laws designed to protect and inform consumers. As a result, clothing labels and tags must identify the manufacturer, the country where the garment was produced (if outside the United States), the fiber content of the fabric, and what care is required.

Fiber Content If you gently pull apart a natural cotton ball, the individual strands are fibers. Fibers are the building blocks of fabrics. The fibers used to make clothes determine their appearance, comfort, and ease of care.

There is no perfect fiber. *Natural fibers*—including cotton, wool, silk, and linen—come from plants and animals. *Manufactured fibers*—such as polyester, nylon, and acrylic—are made from chemicals. In general, clothing made from natural fibers is more comfortable but harder to take care of. Clothing made from manufactured fibers is generally stronger but may pick up stains easily. A shirt made of a combination of cotton and polyester has the comfort of cotton and the wrinkle-resistance of polyester.

Take a look at the fiber content of clothes you own and like. You will soon learn which types to look for. Laws such as the Wool Products Labeling Act and the Textile Fiber Products Act require clear labeling of fiber content.

Care Labels Since 1972, the Federal Trade Commission (FTC) has required manufacturers to attach permanent care labels to the clothes they produce. These labels must provide consumers with clear instructions for care. They must specify whether a garment should be dry-cleaned or washed. Water temperatures and how to dry the item must also be included.

Consider this information before you buy an article of clothing. Dry cleaning adds a lot to the overall cost. Washing by hand takes extra time and effort. If you do not like to iron, avoid clothes that require it.

60% WOOL
40% POLYESTER
MACHINE WASH COLD
WITH LIKE COLORS.
NON-CHLORINE BLEACH
AS NEEDED.
HANG TO DRY
IRON ON LOWEST SETTING
AS NEEDED OR DRY CLEAN
CA 00480 RN 83427
MADE IN MEXICO

▲ Clothing labels provide information that helps you make wise buying decisions. **What would prevent you from buying a piece of clothing?**

Special Finishes Many fabrics undergo special processing before being made into clothes. The resulting finishes include wrinkle-resistance, stain-resistance, and waterproofing. You will usually find this information on the garment label. One special finish—flame-retardance—is required by the Flammable Fabrics Act for all fabrics used to make pajamas, robes, and children's sleepwear.

Checking Signs of Quality

Well-made clothes last longer than clothes that are poorly constructed. Look for signs of quality—or lack of it. Does the fabric seem sturdy? Are the inside seams straight and secure? Check details such as buttons and trim. They should be correctly placed and tightly attached. When you try on the garment, does it look good and hang straight? High prices and high quality do not always go together. It pays to check.

Using Sales to Your Advantage

You can always find sales on clothes. Just open a newpaper, read flyers in the mail, or check online. Throughout the year, stores hold many types of sales. Some stores have different items on sale every week. You can often buy what you want and need at a significantly reduced price.

Did You Know?

ShopSmart Mobile is the *Consumer Reports* text messaging service that can help you make safer and wiser buying decisions. It provides brief reviews and the latest ratings for thousands of brand-name items, including televisions, phones, DVD players, bikes, and video games. If you are not sure which is the best model or what is the best price, ShopSmart Mobile will send unbiased test results and up-to-date online and in-store prices directly to your cell phone in seconds—right there, while you are in the store. *Consumer Reports* calls it "buying power in your pocket!"

Not all sales are equal. Clearance sales, which sell clothes near the end of a season, usually offer some of the best reductions. You might save 50 percent or more. Late in a season, however, the selection is more limited. If you buy a winter coat in January or a swimsuit in September, be sure you can and will wear it the following year.

Sometimes store ads offer a few specific items at surprisingly low prices. These are called **loss leaders** because they are often sold for less than the store paid for them. The number of these items in stock might be limited. The store is willing to take a loss on these items because their main purpose is to bring you into the store. Once you are there, the store hopes you will buy other items, too.

Stores might offer storewide percent-off coupons, especially when they need to reduce inventory. Sometimes you can combine this type of coupon with the sale price on a specific item—and get a real bargain. Read coupons carefully to see what restrictions they have. Also, remember that no bargain is a true bargain if you don't need it or will not use it.

loss leaders sale items deliberately sold at a loss but designed to attract customers into the store

Comparing Prices

Even though a store advertises a sale, it does not mean the store has the lowest price on something you want. Check the prices of items on your list at several stores. Write down the prices you find. Then, when one of the things you are looking for goes on sale, you can judge whether it is a good buy.

Shopping for Clothes

You have a plan and are ready to shop for the clothes you need. Your choices give feedback to manufacturers about what their customers like and dislike. Your purchases pump money into the U.S. economy.

The clothing industry has undergone tremendous changes. Technology has greatly improved the comfort, performance, and care of fabrics used in clothes. At the same time, the costs of raw materials and labor have brought a shift in manufacturing. Today, most clothes are produced outside the United States because labor costs are lower in other parts of the world. This has helped control costs to the consumer, but it has resulted in plant closings and layoffs here.

Some people choose to buy only clothes made in the United States. Others see the changes as inevitable. Whatever your position, realize that many people are involved in turning fibers into the clothes you wear.

Considering Where to Shop

You have many options for where to buy clothes. Large cities have the most variety. However, even if you live in a small town or rural area, the Internet links you to an almost unlimited number of clothing retailers.

Department Stores More clothes are sold in department stores than

Going Global

Janet Freeman's sister was tired of wearing the baggy outerwear that male snowboarders favored. So Freeman started BettyRides, a women's snowboard clothing company. There were no snowboard apparel lines specifically for women at the time.

Freeman surveyed local high school girls in search of styles they would like to see. The result is a youthful, urban look—with fit, colors, and patterns that are obviously feminine.

BettyRides began in 1989 on a shoestring. Freeman had employees sewing clothes in their homes all around Portland, Oregon. Always financially cautious, she preferred to borrow from banks rather than venture capitalists.

▲ Janet Freeman created a niche in a male-dominant industry by creating snowboarding clothing for women.

When the number of orders grew, Freeman explored other manufacturing options. Going offshore seemed best. Many of her Oregon employees were Vietnamese immigrants, so she naturally looked to Vietnam for outsourcing.

Globally outsourced production allowed BettyRides to move into foreign markets. It was a smart move. Of more than 55 million snow-sport participants in the United States in 2004, only 5 percent were female snowboarders—a total of about 2.75 million.

Compare this to Japan, with almost 20 million snow-sport participants. Nearly 35 percent of these are women—a total of about 7 million, obviously a much bigger market. The market share for women's snow-sport apparel is similar in Europe as well.

Thinking Globally

1. What alternatives to snowboard clothing would be less expensive than clothes made specifically for the sport?
2. When production costs for BettyRides decreased, its clothing prices remained stable. What effect would this have on company profits?

anywhere else. They typically offer clothes for all ages at a variety of prices. Department stores offer many services, including knowledgeable salespeople. They rely upon their reputation and service to keep customers coming back.

Specialty Stores Specialty stores cater to very specific buyers. They tend to carry a limited selection of items. They might specialize in a particular type of clothes, such as shoes. They might offer special sizes. For example, stores for "tall men" or for "petites" provide more variety in those sizes than you would find in regular stores. Some stores specialize in costumes or leotards for ballerinas and gymnasts.

Boutiques Boutiques are specialty stores that concentrate on fashionable clothes, accessories, and gifts. Depending upon the store, merchandise might be inexpensive or very costly. Boutiques attract consumers who are very interested in fashion. Their customers tend to be younger and willing to spend more on clothing.

Discount Stores Discount stores generally sell clothing at lower prices than the department or specialty stores. The trade-offs are less service and fewer

Answers to Fact or Fiction

1. True; **2.** False—Nutritional content is required on the label only if nutritional claims are made; **3.** True; **4.** True; **5.** True; **6.** False—Stores almost always require a sales receipt as proof of purchase, along with the returned item.

overruns garments or products resulting from excess production

credit slip a document, also called a *store credit*, stating that a customer is entitled to merchandise from the store equal to a certain dollar amount

sales receipt a document that verifies the purchase of an item from a particular store, including the date of sale and the price paid

frills. Labels are sometimes removed from name-brand clothing, or the store might have its own private label. Some clothes are of lower quality. You might not be able to make returns. These stores count on a high volume of sales.

Factory Outlets Factory outlet stores sell a manufacturer's **overruns** (excess production) and less-than-perfect products at discount prices. They also sell clothes from the previous season. The damaged or flawed clothing is marked as *seconds* or *irregular*. Before buying, examine these items carefully for flaws.

Sometimes clothes that are usually expensive can be bought for a reasonable price at a factory outlet. Many outlet stores locate together in *outlet malls*.

Online and Mail Order Shopping online continues to grow in popularity. It has gradually replaced mail order, although many companies offer both printed and online catalogs. The Internet brings a huge potential customer base. Specialty items, as well as more general offerings, are available no matter where you live.

With online shopping and mail order, you cannot actually see and feel the clothing before you buy it. You have to rely on descriptions, photos, size charts, and the company's reputation. Be sure items can be returned before you order. Also check shipping and handling fees. What looks like a good selling price might not be so good after you add in these other costs.

▼ Flashy window displays lure consumers into stores to spend money on expensive clothes.

Other Shopping Options A creative shopper can find many other sources of clothes. For instance, some of the items sold in secondhand stores were originally quite expensive and have had very little wear. Garage sales, flea markets, thrift shops, and swap meets may also yield good bargains. There are no returns, so you must shop with care.

Return Policies

Not all stores allow returns. Those that do have varying policies. Before you buy an item that you might need to return, make sure you understand the store's policy. Even if a store accepts returns, it might not give cash back. Instead, it might give you a **credit slip**, sometimes called a *store credit*. This slip of paper entitles you to buy an equal amount of other store merchandise. If you made the purchase by credit card, the store might simply credit the amount back to your account.

You usually need the **sales receipt**—verifying the item bought, the purchase price, and the date of sale—when you return something. Some stores will allow you to return a gift without a receipt. However, if the item has gone on sale in the meantime, you will get credit for only the current sale amount. Your sales receipt is also important if you find that what you bought is defective. Always return defective items as soon as possible.

Cash, Debit, or Credit

Buying clothes with cash or a debit card—which is the same as cash—is the best option. You cannot spend what you do not have. Saving for larger purchases will help give you the financial discipline you will need to manage your money throughout life.

YOU DECIDE

Jeannie is putting together an outfit to wear to a holiday party. She has her eye on a black velvet skirt at a boutique downtown. It's a little over her budget—but it's beautiful, and it looks great on her. She's almost ready to go downtown with her credit card to buy it when her sister Diane calls her to the computer.

Diane found the Web site of a women's specialty clothing chain. On the screen, Jeannie sees a skirt that looks very similar to the one she tried on downtown. It's on sale for about half what she would pay at the boutique.

Jeannie begins to think she can stay within her budget after all. She puts the skirt in her online shopping cart and proceeds to the checkout page. She enters all her information, and the final confirmation page comes up. Jeannie sees that the shipping charges are going to be $11.95.

Jeannie also knows that if the skirt does not fit well or look as good as she hopes, she'll have to pay for postage and insurance to return it. She goes back to the Web page that had details about the skirt, and sees that it must be dry-cleaned. The skirt she liked at the boutique is washable, which would save her some money over time.

Should she . . .

1. ...buy either of the two skirts? Explain your decision.
2. ...shop for a lower-priced skirt than the ones at the boutique or online? Where else could she shop?
3. ...learn to sew and then make the skirt she wants?

More and more consumers are using credit cards to buy clothing. There are benefits. You can buy specific items when you need them and take advantage of sales. Your credit card bill also provides back-up proof of your purchase. Unfortunately, many people, including many teens, get themselves into credit card debt. As discussed in Chapter 13, this problem has far-reaching consequences.

Some stores have a **layaway plan**. This purchase option allows you to make a small down payment, and then the store holds the item until you can pay the full price. Many stores will also allow you to put an item *on hold* for a few days. They will set aside the item and give you time to think about the purchase or do some comparison shopping.

layaway plan a purchase option in which the customer makes a small down payment and the retailer holds the item until the customer pays in full

SECTION 2 ASSESSMENT

Factual Recall

1. When analyzing your wardrobe, you should sort your clothes into what four groups?
2. Describe advantages and disadvantages of natural and manufactured (synthetic) fibers.
3. A package of socks is labeled "seconds." What does this mean?

Critical Thinking

1. Your friend asks if it's okay for her to wear a rock concert T-shirt and jeans to her job interview at an insurance office. She says she doesn't "feel like herself" in more formal clothes. What advice would you give her?
2. What are some ways to get more value for your clothing dollars?

CHAPTER 11 REVIEW AND ASSESSMENT

Chapter Summary

Section 1 Buying Food

- Food choices are influenced by many factors, such as personal likes and dislikes, culture, geography, family and friends, advertising, and cost.
- You can choose to cook and eat at home, go to a restaurant, or bring home take-out food. Each requires different amounts of resources, money, time, and skill.
- Two current food-buying trends are organic foods and online grocery shopping.
- Reading food labels can help you determine which food best meets your needs and wants.
- National brands, house brands, and generics differ in cost and sometimes in quality.
- To assess quality in foods, look for product grades; pack, pull, or expiration dates; and (with fresh foods) their appearance.
- Buying larger quantities might save money, but storage and spoilage might be problems.
- To compare prices of food, look at the cost per unit.
- Advertising informs consumers but also adds to the cost of products.

Section 2 Buying Clothing

- The key to a good wardrobe is not the amount of clothing but how well it meets your needs. Before buying new clothes, analyze your wardrobe and then decide what else you need.
- To set up a clothing budget, start by tracking what you currently spend. Evaluate your spending and decide how much you can and should spend each month.
- Read and compare clothing labels and tags. Look for information about fiber content, care instructions, and special finishes.
- Check clothes for quality construction. Well-made clothes look better and last longer.
- Use sales to your advantage. Look for news about sales and compare prices at different stores.
- You have many choices about where to shop, including various types of stores, mail order, and online sites. To save money, consider additional options, such as thrift shops and flea markets.
- Not all stores allow returns under all conditions. Make sure you understand the return policy for any item you buy.

Reviewing Key Terms

Match the following key terms with their definitions.

a. credit slip
b. national brands
c. unit pricing
d. pull date
e. sales receipt
f. generic products
g. loss leaders
h. house brands
i. expiration date
j. pack date

1. Items that are priced for less than they cost the store.
2. A date on food packaging that indicates when the item was made, processed, or packaged.
3. A document stating that a customer is entitled to merchandise equal to a certain dollar amount.
4. Private label product names unique to a particular chain of supermarkets.
5. Expressing the price of an item per unit of measure.
6. Heavily advertised product names that are found in stores around the country.
7. A date on food packaging that indicates the last day a store should sell the item.
8. A document that verifies the purchase of an item from a particular store.
9. Products that carry no brand name.
10. A date on food packaging that indicates the last day a food is acceptable for its intended use.

Understanding the Main Ideas

1. What kinds of foods do *not* have to include a list of ingredients on the label?
2. Which is likely to cost most: a house brand, a national brand, or a generic product?
3. What is a "private label"?

4. Which two government units are primarily responsible for regulating food quality?
5. Are foods with a higher grade more nutritious? Explain.
6. What should you look for when buying fresh produce?
7. Is it safe to eat food that is past its *Sell by* date? Explain.
8. What are some signs that a garment is well made?
9. Why is it better to buy clothing with cash or a debit card rather than with a credit card?

Practicing Math

1. Which is cheaper by unit price: a 12-ounce package of cookies for $2.75 or a 16-ounce box for $3.25?
2. Make a list of ten food products your family buys most often. Visit at least three stores and note the prices of these items in each store. Record your findings in a table. What conclusions can you make?

Applying Critical Thinking Skills

1. When comparing in-store and online grocery shopping costs, what factors should you consider in addition to the prices of the products?
2. Your cousin, a busy young father with two jobs, complains that there are too many choices to make in a grocery store. He says that time is wasted making decisions about products that are not very different from each other. Do you agree? Why or why not?
3. Why is it good to select foods with high nutrient density?
4. How would you decide whether to purchase a Choice or Select grade of meat?
5. You accidentally left an opened package of sandwich meat on the counter overnight. The expiration date stamped on the package is still a week away. Does this mean the meat is safe to eat?
6. The grocery store has 5-pound boxes of blueberries on sale at a very good price. Your family loves blueberries but cannot eat that much before the berries spoil. How could you still take advantage of the sale?
7. Advertising helps food producers and sellers improve sales. How might advertising help a consumer?
8. Is it always cheaper to buy items for which you have a coupon?
9. Describe advantages and disadvantages of shopping for clothes online.

Working with Real-World Documents

1. Shown here are portions of two Nutrition Facts labels from cereal boxes. Refer to them to answer the following questions.
   a. Look at the serving size. If the amount listed is less than you usually eat (or more), how will that affect the rest of the information?
   b. The serving *size* is the same for both cereals. Why do you think the serving *weight* differs?
   c. Which cereal has more total carbohydrates? What is the main reason for the difference?

Nutrition Facts
Serving Size 3/4 cup (49g)
Servings Per Container about 10

Amount per serving		with 1/2 cup skim milk
Calories	180	220
Calories from Fat	30	30
	% Daily Value**	
Total Fat 3g*	5%	5%
Cholesterol 0mg	0%	1%
Sodium 230mg	9%	12%
Potassium 180mg	5%	11%
Total Carbohydrate 38g	13%	15%
Dietary Fiber 5g	19%	19%
Sugars 14g		
Other Carbohydrates 19g		
Protein 4g		

Nutrition Facts
Serving Size 3/4 cup (30g)
Servings Per Container about 10

Amount per serving		with 1/2 cup skim milk
Calories	100	140
Calories from Fat	5	10
	% Daily Value**	
Total Fat 0.5g*	1%	1%
Cholesterol 0mg	0%	1%
Sodium 190mg	8%	11%
Potassium 90mg	3%	8%
Total Carbohydrate 23g	8%	10%
Dietary Fiber 3g	10%	10%
Sugars 15g		
Other Carbohydrates 15g		
Protein 2g		

2. Some clothing care labels use drawings rather than words. Find out what the following symbols mean:

   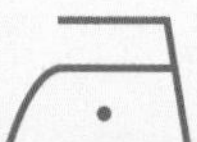

Taking It Home

1. Survey several friends and/or relatives about their grocery shopping preferences. Where do they shop? What are the two most important factors in deciding where to shop? Do they buy organic foods? Do they buy groceries online?

CHAPTER 12

Consumer Rights and Responsibilities

Consumers are the basis of the American economy. Not only do they buy products and services, but they produce them as well. Consumers are also citizens with rights and responsibilities. How are your needs met as a consumer? What role can you play in maintaining and improving consumer rights?

▲ **Always read warranties to know your rights in relation to the products you buy.**

This chapter will focus on the various ways you, as a consumer, can ensure that businesses continue producing products and services that work. You will learn how to make an effective complaint. You will also learn about your role as a responsible consumer.

SECTION 1 Increasing Consumer Awareness

SECTION 2 Basic Consumer Rights

Fact or Fiction

What do you think? Are the following statements true or false? If you think they are false, then say what is true.

1. *Consumer Reports* provides consumers with independent test results on consumer products.
2. Product warranties are usually written in "legalese" language that is hard to understand.
3. Certification seals promise that a product will perform "as advertised."
4. A contract is legal only if it includes mutual assent, consideration, and competent parties.
5. Some 90 percent of people who get involved in a pyramid scheme will lose their money.
6. The Better Business Bureau will take a consumer complaint to the business in question, and if the business refuses to act, the BBB can force it to do so.

Answers on page 324.

Study Reminder

Knowing how to study can increase your knowledge, improve your grades, and cut down on your study time. See the ***Studying Personal Finance*** *pages at the front of the book for some tips to help you study this chapter.*

SECTION 1

Increasing Consumer Awareness

Focus Questions

1. How did President Kennedy help the consumer movement in 1962?
2. What are some ways that manufacturers communicate with consumers?
3. How can consumers provide feedback to companies about their products?
4. What are some government agencies that address consumer issues?

Key Terms

caveat emptor
certification seals
boycott
product standards
deregulation

Your rights as an American consumer are far greater now than at any time in history. This did not happen overnight. Those who provide the products and services you use did not suddenly decide to be better to their customers. It happened gradually, after many years of consumer complaints—protesting poor quality, unsafe products, and unfair business practices. Government policy makers had to be convinced to change the laws. As a consumer today, it is your responsibility to appreciate the rights you have by providing your input on consumer issues.

▶ Find out which products have the highest rate of quality and safety before making a big purchase decision.

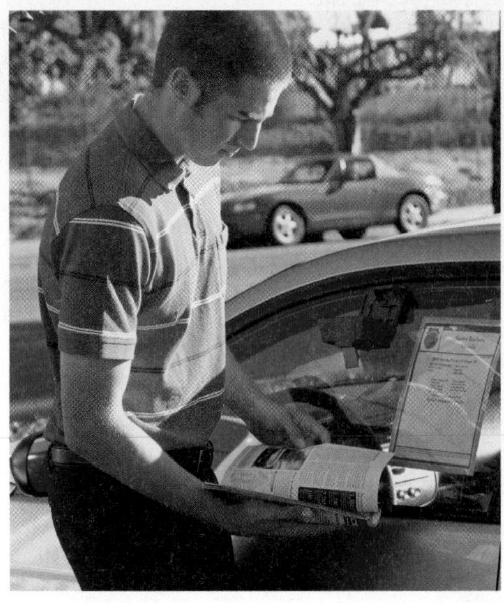

The Consumer Movement

The U.S. consumer movement began in the late 1800s. Society was growing more industrialized. As people streamed into the cities, poor housing and unsafe working conditions were reported. Finally, concerns about food safety led to the formation of the first consumer groups. Inspections of meatpacking plants found poor sanitation and impure food. This led Congress to pass the Pure Food and Drugs Act and the Meat Inspection Act in 1906.

The next major push for consumer rights came in the 1960s. Critics spoke out against American industry—against its lack of concern for the environment and the effect of its economic policies on the poor. They also questioned the safety of many consumer products. In 1962, President John F. Kennedy presented a Consumers' Bill of Rights to Congress (see Section 2 of this chapter). In 1964,

President Lyndon B. Johnson appointed the first federal consumer affairs officer, Esther Peterson. In the late 1960s, Ralph Nader became known nationally as a consumer advocate. He worked tirelessly for consumers, attempting to improve automobile safety. The push for reform had an impact. Consumer laws were passed. Many industries set up policies to handle consumer concerns.

Today's business community understands that consumers expect it to be accountable to society. Government has played a needed role by passing laws that protect the people and the environment. Still, the need for involvement in consumer issues continues.

In the mid-1800s, traveling salesmen sold "snake oil" from the back of a wagon. They claimed that it cured everything from indigestion to heart disease. Often the concoction was little more than water, some flavorings, and a bit of alcohol. Sometimes it contained harmful substances. In those days, there were no laws governing truth in advertising. Consumers were on their own.

The truth-in-advertising movement actually began within the business community to deal with outlandish claims. But until the federal government passed laws covering truth in advertising, unscrupulous companies were still free to use their imaginations to lure consumers, whether their products were safe and useful or not. For decades, cigarette ads promoted smoking as a healthy activity that could calm your nerves and even sweeten your breath!

The Federal Trade Commission issued its Deception Policy Statement in 1983, defining what *deception* means in terms of advertising. It said an ad is considered deceptive if it contains a statement (or leaves out information) that is likely to mislead consumers—as long as that statement (or omission) is important to the consumer's decision to buy the product.

The Consumer Story

There are three roles in the economic system—producers, consumers, and citizens. Each role impacts the individual, society, and the economy. You will play all these roles at one time or another.

The Producer

Do you work, either for pay or as a volunteer? If so, you are a producer—helping to provide the goods and services that others consume. Consumers will choose those that best meet their needs or wants. Producers want to create a desire for their own products and services. They also need to provide consumers with information to help them make decisions. Finally, producers must think about what consumers will buy—and then develop new products based on those predictions. The key to successful sales is communication, which can take a variety of forms.

Advertising Advertising is one-way communication from the producer to consumers. As you learned in Chapter 8, its main purpose is to persuade consumers to buy products or services. Ads can also be informational. They might introduce new products or describe product features. They might give information about stores, prices, or sales.

You have to separate fictions from facts as you view ads. Recall the discussion of marketing strategies in Chapter 8. Sellers might exaggerate the good side of their products, or they might leave out important information.

The slogan **caveat emptor** (a Latin phrase, pronounced *CA-vee-aht EMP-ter*) is what people say as a warning about a seller's claims. It means, "Let the buyer beware."

caveat emptor a Latin phrase meaning "Let the buyer beware," warning consumers about a seller's doubtful claims

Toll-Free Numbers Many companies provide toll-free telephone numbers. Consumers can call the company directly and get immediate responses to their

You Can Succeed Financially

In 2001, Jeff Grady was 30 years old and unemployed. He lost his job when the 1990s dot-com bubble burst. He spent his afternoons looking for work, but each morning he was at the gym working out—and listening to his new gadget, a first-generation iPod.

Filling a Need

One thing that bothered him about his new music player was that it did not come with a case. He had to either hold it or put it in a pocket—neither of which was a great option while exercising. As a consumer, Grady saw a need for a product that did not exist.

Even though his background was in sales, not industrial design, he designed a case for his iPod. Then he contacted an Apple accessories buyer to talk about his creation. Within ten minutes, Grady got a callback with an order for 2,000 cases.

Suddenly it looked like Grady had a new job—and a new company! He named the company Digital Lifestyle Outfitters (DLO). He launched a Web site and had orders for 3,000 more cases in the first month. Production could barely keep up with demand. Soon MacWarehouse and other Apple accessory suppliers were selling his products. Grady's company developed other iPod accessories and even began reselling items from other retailers on its Web site.

DLO was the first company to make not just cases for the iPod but other accessories too—including the iBoom boom box designed specifically for iPods and systems for playing an iPod through a car stereo or TV set. The iBoom was named

"Product of the Year" by *MacWorld* magazine in 2003. That same year, Apple itself entered a partnership with Grady and began selling DLO's products from the Apple Store Web site. Best Buy signed on the same year.

Grady's company had a line of 100 products by mid-2006 and expects to bring out twenty to thirty new products each year. In 2005, it had $84 million in sales.

Making It Work

Grady attributes much of his company's success to its being first on the market with so many of its products—even though other producers have copied some of DLO's ideas. In many cases, DLO is an entire year ahead of the competition. Being first on the market allows the company to make improvements to its products before others even make an appearance.

Grady says his management style is fairly hands-off. One thing he is passionate about, however, is the DLO brand. "Our brand is everything, so we have to keep establishing it," he says. "We need to keep stressing our name and our logo until everyone knows it."

He wants his employees to have fun at work. He wants the challenge of inventing and designing new "toys," as he calls them, always to be creative and enjoyable. That creative fun at work has so far given DLO a big edge over the competition.

What Would You Do?

1. If DLO makes accessories to be used with other products besides iPods, what happens when the market for those other products slows down?
2. How does it benefit the DLO brand to have its products featured on the Apple Store Web site?
3. As a consumer, name two products you wish existed. Would either of them be practical to make? Who would buy them?

questions or complaints. The companies sometimes use these opportunities to conduct brief consumer surveys. Consumer complaints and comments are logged into computers and analyzed to improve customer satisfaction.

Manufacturers' Warranties Producers also provide information to consumers through their warranties and guarantees. A manufacturer's warranty promises that a product will be replaced or repaired if it does not work properly, and it spells out your rights as a consumer. Check warranty provisions before you buy. A warranty that runs longer and covers more could save you a lot of money, especially with expensive items.

Manufacturers might offer a full warranty or a limited warranty. With a *full warranty*, a defective product will be fixed or replaced without charge. A *limited warranty* covers less. For instance, if a repair is needed, it might cover the cost of parts, but not labor. In addition, when you buy a product you automatically have an implied, *unwritten warranty* that the product will serve the purpose for which it was made. A toaster will toast, and a furnace will heat.

The Magnuson-Moss Warranty Act of 1975 was passed by Congress to help clarify the language used in warranties. It requires warranties to be written in ordinary language—not "legalese"—so that consumers will know exactly what they are getting.

Energy Star Choices Energy Star is a joint program of the Environmental Protection Agency and the Department of Energy. It identifies products that meet certain energy-efficiency standards. When you see the Energy Star label on a package of lightbulbs, a water heater, or a dishwasher, the manufacturer is telling you that this product can help you save money and protect the environment.

ABC Electronics Inc.

CD/DVD Player

LIMITED WARRANTY

ABC Electronics Inc. ("ABC") warrants this Product (including any accessories) against defects in material or workmanship as follows:

1. LABOR: For a period of one (1) year from the date of purchase, if this Product is determined to be defective, ABC will repair or replace the Product, at its option, at no charge, or pay the labor charges to any ABC authorized service facility. After the Warranty Period, you must pay for all labor charges.

2. PARTS: In addition, ABC will supply, at no charge, new or rebuilt replacements in exchange for defective parts for a period of one (1) year. After the warranty period, you must pay for all parts costs.

3. ACCESSORIES: Parts and labor for all accessories are for one (1) year.

To obtain warranty service, you must take the Product, or deliver the Product freight prepaid, in either its original packaging or packaging affording an equal degree of protection, to any authorized ABC service facility.

This warranty does not cover customer instruction, installation, set up adjustments or signal reception problems.

This warranty does not cover cosmetic damage or damage due to acts of God, accident, misuse, abuse, negligence, commercial use, or modification of, or to any part of the Product, including the antenna. This warranty does not cover damage due to improper operation or maintenance, connection to improper voltage supply, or attempted repair by anyone other than a facility authorized by ABC to service the Product. This warranty does not cover Products sold AS IS or WITH ALL FAULTS, or consumables (such as fuses or batteries). This warranty is valid only in the United States.

Proof of purchase in the form of a bill of sale or receipted invoice which is evidence that the unit is within the Warranty period must be presented to obtain warranty service.

This warranty is invalid if the factory applied serial number has been altered or removed from the Product.

REPAIR OR REPLACEMENT AS PROVIDED UNDER THIS WARRANTY IS THE EXCLUSIVE REMEDY OF THE CONSUMER. ABC SHALL NOT BE LIABLE FOR ANY INCIDENTAL OR CONSEQUENTIAL DAMAGES FOR BREACH OF ANY EXPRESS OR IMPLIED WARRANTY ON THIS PRODUCT. EXCEPT TO THE EXTENT PROHIBITED BY APPLICABLE LAW, ANY IMPLIED WARRANTY OF MERCHANTABILITY OR FITNESS FOR A PARTICULAR PURPOSE ON THIS PRODUCT IS LIMITED IN DURATION TO THE DURATION OF THIS WARRANTY.

▲ Companies describe their responsibilities to consumers in their product warranties.

Seals of Approval As you shop, you may see seals of approval on various products. What do they mean?

Certification seals placed on items indicate that they meet standards set by industries or other private organizations. For example, you might see the American Gas Association (AGA) seal on a gas appliance. If so, it has met or exceeded the standards of durability and safety set by the AGA. Underwriters Laboratories (UL) is an independent, nonprofit organization that tests thousands of products and materials. The UL label means the product has met UL safety standards.

Some seals are awarded by magazines. However, these are little more than promises that products will perform "as advertised." *Good Housekeeping* magazine's seal does guarantee replacement of or reimbursement for any product if it is found to be defective within two years.

Other magazines, most notably *Consumer Reports*, provide independent

▼ Using products with an Energy Star graphic is good for the environment.

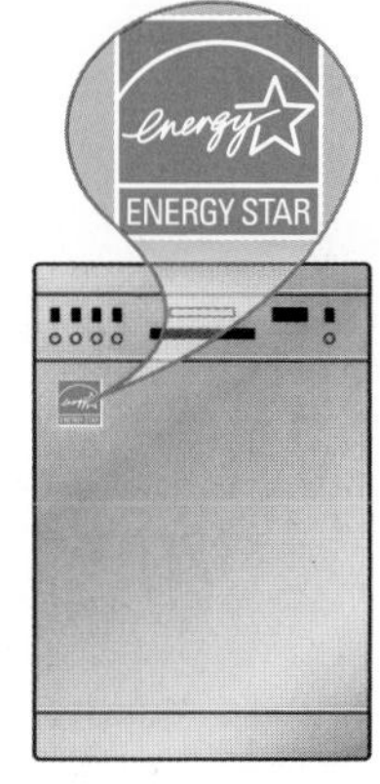

certification seals labels placed on products certifying that they meet safety or performance standards set by an industry or private organization test results to help consumers make decisions. The products will not receive a seal of approval, but consumers can check product ratings in the magazine.

The Consumer

As a consumer, you are responsible for gathering information and examining the alternatives before making a purchase or choosing a service. The consumer's role in the economic system also includes giving feedback about products and services, in order to improve the responsiveness of producers.

Making Informed Choices Research your options before making a purchase—but use common sense. Spend the most time and effort on the most important, most expensive purchases. Choosing a T-shirt that does not wear well is quite different from buying a flat-screen TV that has a poor-quality picture.

There are a variety of fairly simple ways to put the odds in your favor. For important purchases, learn as much as you can about the following:

- *Product information.* Manufacturers' Web sites usually give specific information about their products and various models. In addition, many products come with use-and-care booklets. Ask to read these before you buy. The information included might help you either eliminate or choose the product.
- *Product comparisons.* Some magazines and Internet sites rate products. This can be helpful, but check how the rating process is handled. For example, if a magazine rates products, does it accept advertising? If it rates the products of its advertisers, those ratings might be biased. *Consumer Reports* magazine accepts no advertising. Its product ratings are highly respected.
- *Recommendations.* Ask people you know who are "experts" or recent purchasers. Some online sites include consumer feedback on various products.

Articles in consumer-oriented magazines like *Consumer Reports* can be helpful even if they do not rate the specific models of a product you are considering. You can use them to identify the points to consider and problems to avoid. Then make your own chart and compare the features of the models you are thinking of buying. Most of these magazines have Internet sites, as well.

Communicating Consumer Opinions Consumers also have a responsibility to provide feedback to producers and sellers. Maybe your hair dryer broke after only one week. Maybe your eyeliner smeared after swimming, even though the ad said it would not. When you inform the retailer, manufacturer, or service provider, it becomes aware of the problem and can address it.

Also take time to report when products and people perform exceptionally well. Positive feedback is also valuable because it lets producers know what they are doing right.

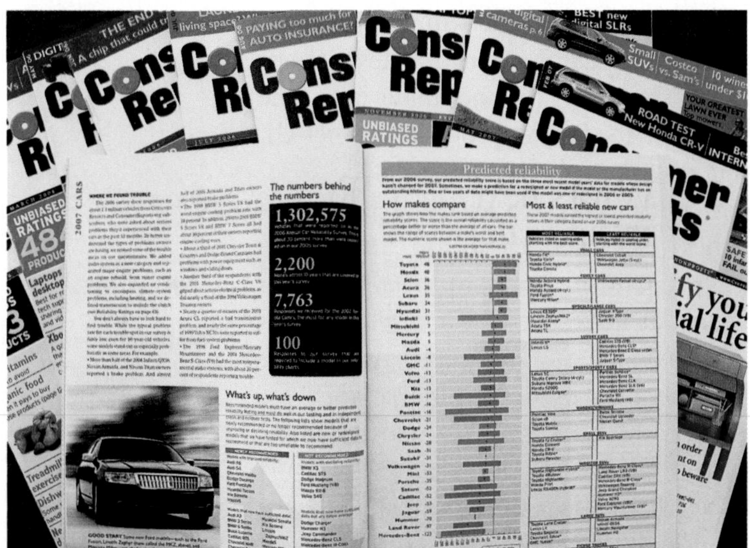

▼ *Consumer Reports* **articles are respectable sources of helpful product information. What other resources can you use to help make purchasing decisions?**

Do Your RESEARCH

As a high school graduation gift, Heather's parents want to buy her a laptop computer that she can use when she goes to college. Heather begins shopping online, comparing the features of different computers at manufacturer and retailer Web sites. There are so many brands and models to choose from!

Does she want a laptop that comes with photo and music software already installed, or should she get a basic model and buy the software separately? One manufacturer offers a one-year warranty, and another only ninety days. She can get a two-year extended warranty from a retail electronics chain—for an extra $200. Is it worth it? Heather asks her older brother Ron for help.

He tells her to make a list of the features she thinks are important, the software applications she'll need for college, and the programs that suit her lifestyle and interests. After she completes the list, they identify five computers that satisfy her needs.

Next, Ron and Heather go to Epinions.com, a Web site that has unbiased customer reviews and price comparisons. Heather reads what people have to say about the laptops she is considering. They also visit the *Consumer Reports* Web site, where Heather again checks the ratings and assessments of the five laptops.

After Heather decides which laptop she wants, she has to decide where to buy it. She and Ron plan to search for the best price at stores around town and also from reputable Web dealers.

Your Assignment

1. Visit Epinions.com (http://fin.emcp.net/epinions) and the *Consumer Reports* Web site (http://fin.emcp.net/consumerreports). Compare three laptop computers that you would like to buy. Summarize your findings. Were the reviews helpful? Why should you check out customer reviews and independent ratings before buying a computer?
2. How can it help to have a list of the features you need in any product you are shopping for?

Consumers Working Together

When consumers join together to express common concerns, the business community and the government listen. Improved product labeling and pollution controls are two examples of consumer successes.

As a group, consumers might **boycott** a product by refusing to buy it because of their feelings about the product or about the company, industry, or government that produces or sells it. They might think the product is unsafe, or they might disagree with the methods used to produce it. Communicating with producers by means of a boycott can be dramatic when many consumers join together.

Even without boycotts, consumers are more likely to achieve common goals when they work together. Government and industry are more likely to respond to requests from large groups of people. For years, producers have been hiring *lobbyists*—people to represent their interests in Congress and in state legislatures. *Consumer interest groups*, on the other hand, have been much slower to organize and speak with one voice—mainly because consumers are such a diverse group. Today, however, a number of national

boycott to protest a product by refusing to buy it

Nutrition Facts

Serving Size 1 cup (228g)
Servings Per Container 2

Amount Per Serving	
Calories 260	Calories from Fat 120
	% Daily Value*
Total fat 13g	**20%**
Saturated Fat 5g	**25%**
Trans Fat 2g	
Cholesterol 30mg	**10%**
Sodium 660mg	**28%**
Total Carbohydrate 31g	**10%**
Dietary Fiber 0g	**0%**
Sugars 5g	
Protein 5g	
Vitamin A 4% •	Vitamin C 2%
Calcium 15% •	Iron 4%

*Percent Daily Values are based on a 2,000 calorie diet. Your Daily Values may be higher or lower depending on your calorie needs:

	Calories:	2,000	2,500
Total FatLess than		65g	80g
Sat Fat	Less than	20g	25g
Cholesterol	Less than	300mg	300mg
Sodium	Less than	2,400mg	2,400mg
Total Carbohydrate		300g	375g
Dietary Fiber		25g	30g

Calories per gram:
Fat 9 • Carbohydrate 4 • Protien 4

▲ **Nutrition labels help you make informed food choices.**

organizations represent consumers, including these:

- Consumers Union, publisher of *Consumer Reports*
- Citizens for Health, promoting policies that allow individuals to make informed health choices
- Consumer Federation of America, advancing pro-consumer policies at the levels of federal and state governments

The Citizen

Besides being a producer and a consumer, you are a citizen. That role has certain responsibilities. For example, citizens pay taxes. They also need to let their government know what is important to them. Voting is one way of doing this. Attending public meetings is another.

Become an active citizen consumer. Communicate with your government representatives at the local, state, and national levels. Give them feedback on the issues that concern you. Consider joining or helping to organize a consumer interest group.

Federal and state governments respond to citizens' concerns in various ways. They pass laws to make products safer, and they work to ensure that producers are truthful. In general, handling consumer problems is divided among many different government agencies. Some are described here. Addresses for these and others are listed in the Appendix in the back of the book. You can also go to Consumer.gov (http://fin.emcp.net/consumer) for more links to consumer information from the federal government.

Government Agencies You will find consumer protection agencies at every level of government. These agencies generally do not resolve individual consumer problems—but they do investigate companies that have a record of many complaints from consumers. When serious problems arise, it is important to contact the related agencies to make them aware. Some of the key federal agencies that deal with consumer issues include the following:

- The *Federal Trade Commission (FTC)* has the responsibility of checking advertising, making sure that false or misleading claims by manufacturers are corrected.
- The *United States Postal Service* is responsible for controlling and stopping mail fraud. Advertisements for "get-rich-quick" schemes and "work-at-home" moneymakers are popular types of mail fraud.
- The *Surface Transportation Board* is responsible for regulating the shipment of goods across state lines.
- The *Federal Communications Commission (FCC)* grants licenses to radio and TV stations.

Did You Know?

Another kind of consumer advocacy group is called a PIRG—public interest research group. PIRGs are funded by contributions from citizens. They work at the state level on environmental, economic, and public health issues. They often appear before government agencies and legislative bodies to speak on behalf of consumers.

There are independent PIRGs in twenty-nine states and a national PIRG that represents the states that don't have their own. PIRGs use grassroots organizing, media publicity, research, and legal action as tools in their work. They depend on volunteers—and many of their employees are idealistic young people, recent college graduates in law, public health, and economics.

- The *Food and Drug Administration (FDA)* is responsible for the safety and labeling of food products.
- The *Consumer Product Safety Commission (CPSC)* sets product safety standards and can ban any products found to be unsafe.

State, county, and local consumer protection agencies can also help with consumer problems. In addition, state regulatory agencies license and oversee professionals such as physicians, lawyers, and real estate brokers.

Government Regulation Congress has given some government agencies the power to *regulate* certain products and processes. This means that rules written by the agencies must be followed. Government regulations can influence production, distribution, advertising, and selling.

One form of regulation is setting **product standards**. Government agencies will sometimes specify the requirements for a particular type of product. For example, the Food and Drug Administration has set a standard for mayonnaise. Any product labeled "mayonnaise" must contain specific ingredients. Lightbulbs must conform to standards of safety and size. There are also standards for car tires and energy standards for appliances.

Government regulation is controversial. Many people in industry think it is too restrictive, costly, and time-consuming. They believe it decreases competition and innovation. Still, they would rather have federal regulation than state regulation. State regulation would mean having to comply with fifty different sets of rules. With federal regulation, a company can sell the same product in every state.

Most consumers believe some regulation is needed. Many of the rules focus on health and safety. For example, the FDA can order unsafe products to be removed from stores.

For both the producer and the consumer, there is a trade-off in terms of costs. A product might have a higher purchase price because of regulation. For example, pollution-control devices can make cars more expensive. At the same time, however, the regulations calling for pollution controls will conserve natural resources for the next generation.

Deregulation is the removal of government restrictions on business. This is usually done to encourage free operation in the marketplace. Those who favor deregulation believe it leads to more competition, higher productivity, and lower prices for consumers. The effects, however, are mixed. During the 1980s, deregulation of the savings and loan associations—combined with inflation—caused many S&Ls to fail. The U.S. government stepped in to prevent major losses to consumers. Congress then passed new legislation to regulate the industry once again.

product standards standards, set by government agencies, that specify requirements for particular products

deregulation the removal of government regulations on businesses in order to encourage free operation in the marketplace

SECTION 1 ASSESSMENT

Factual Recall

1. A manufacturer's warranty guarantees the product will work. What else does the warranty describe?
2. Name three national organizations that represent consumers.
3. Which level of government—federal, state, or local—includes consumer protection agencies?

Critical Thinking

1. Honoring a warranty could cost a company money, yet most producers guarantee their products. Why do you think they do this?
2. What do you think are some consequences of *not* giving feedback to producers?

SECTION 2

Basic Consumer Rights

Focus Questions

1. What are the four basic consumer rights?
2. How does competition among producers help consumers?
3. What are some ways to resolve disputes with a producer or seller?
4. How can you recognize pyramid schemes, phishing, and other types of consumer fraud?

Key Terms

Consumers' Bill of Rights
contract
mutual assent
consideration
competent parties
pyramid scheme
monopoly
oligopoly
quotas
tariffs
arbitration
North American Free Trade Agreement (NAFTA)
Better Business Bureau (BBB)
consumer action panels (CAPs)
small-claims courts
mediator
class-action suit

Rights and responsibilities cannot be completely separated. They are like two sides of the same coin. Many consumers are not aware of their rights under the law, so they fail to be responsible consumers. Well-informed consumers protect their rights by living up to their responsibilities.

Basic and Expected Rights

In 1962, President John F. Kennedy presented the first **Consumers' Bill of Rights**. This list included these four basic rights:

- The right to safety
- The right to be informed
- The right to choose
- The right to be heard

In addition, consumers expect additional rights in a free enterprise system. These rights include the following:

- The right of all consumers to have equal access to available goods and services
- The right to learn about and compare available alternatives
- The right to be treated with courteous service
- The right to expect producers to consider the environmental effects of their products
- The right to expect product quality
- The right to consumer education

Consumers' Bill of Rights a list of consumer rights, including the right to safety, the right to be informed, the right to choose, and the right to be heard

The Right to Safety

As a consumer, you ask questions about the products you buy. You ask about prices, materials, or colors—but how often do you ask, "How safe is this product?"

Consumer Rights and Responsibilities

Not long ago, the Consumer Product Safety Commission conducted a survey to see what factors consumers actually considered when buying a product. Thousands of consumers were surveyed, but not one listed safety as something they looked for. When asked why, they said they just assumed that if a product was for sale, it was safe.

As a consumer, you have a right to expect that the products you purchase are safe. Still, even though government regulations promote safe products, there are no guarantees. A product design might be flawed. Sometimes the only way to identify a safety hazard is when consumers report injuries or incidents.

Some imported products do not meet U.S. safety standards—but they still get into U.S. stores. In late 2007, a number of imported products from China, mainly children's toys, were found to have hazardous lead levels. Even very small amounts of lead in a child's system can permanently reduce brain function. Follow the news so you know about these unsafe products.

As a consumer, you have other safety responsibilities, too. Be sure to read and follow the directions before using a product. Use products for only their intended purpose. Store and dispose of products properly.

CPSC and NHTSA News

U.S. Consumer Product Safety Commission
www.cpsc.gov

National Highway Traffic Safety Administration
www.nhtsa.gov

Fall Hazard Prompts NHTSA, CPSC and Evenflo to Announce Recall of Embrace™ Infant Car Seat/Carriers

WASHINGTON, D.C. - The U.S. Consumer Product Safety Commission and the National Highway Traffic Safety Administration (NHTSA), in cooperation with Evenflo Company Inc., today announced a recall of the following consumer product.

Name of product: Evenflo Embrace™ Infant Car Seat/Carriers

Units: About 450,000

Manufacturer: Evenflo Company Inc., of Vandalia, Ohio

Hazard: When used as an infant carrier, the handle can unexpectedly release, causing the seat to rotate forward. When this happens, an infant inside the carrier can fall to the ground and suffer serious injuries.

Incidents/Injuries: Evenflo has received 679 reports of the handle on the car seat/carriers unexpectedly releasing, resulting in 160 injuries to children. These reports include a skull fracture, two concussions, cuts, scrapes and bruises.

Description: The recall involves Evenflo Embrace™ Infant Car Seat/Carriers made before April 8, 2006. The recalled car seat/carriers have model numbers beginning with 317, 320, 397, 398, 540, 548, 549, 550, 556, 597, 598 or 599. The model number and production date information can be found on a white label on the bottom of the carrier and on the top of the convenience base. Models beginning with "5" are units sold with the travel system (compatible stroller). "Evenflo" is on the carrying handle and car seat base. Embrace™ infant car seat/carriers made on or after April 8, 2006 are not included in this recall.

Sold at: Department and juvenile products stores nationwide sold the car seat/carriers from December 2004 through September 2006 for between $70 and $100 when sold alone and between $140 and $200 when sold with a compatible stroller.

Manufactured In: United States and China

Remedy: Consumers should not use the handle until the repair kit has been installed. The product can continue to be used as a car seat when secured in a vehicle. Contact Evenflo to receive a free repair kit that strengthens the handle latch. Recall notice will be sent to all registered owners of the recalled product. The recalled units

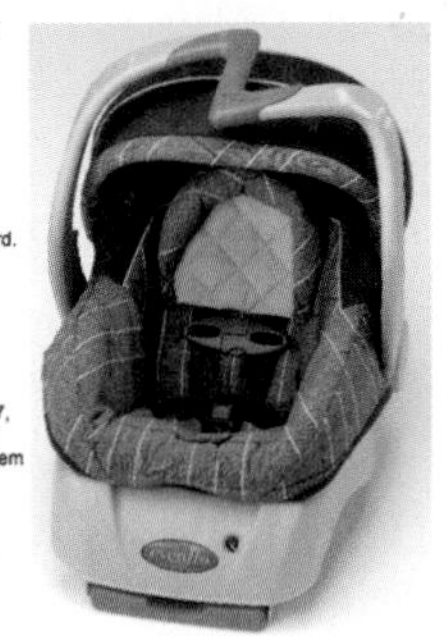

▲ **If a product is defective, the Consumer Product Safety Commission will issue a recall.**

Producer Responsibilities

Safety is a joint effort between the consumer and the producer. Manufacturers do have a responsibility to produce safe products. Some products (such as knives) can never be completely safe—but sometimes the producer can make a product safer for very little additional cost. The Consumer Product Safety Commission can remove unsafe products from the market.

The Right to Be Informed

Generally, today's consumers have access to plenty of information about products—and most of this information is free of charge. You can find it in newspapers and magazines, on TV, on the Internet, and on the radio. Informative brochures are published by the government, by local consumer agencies, and by the extension services affiliated with colleges and universities. Additional information is available at your public library.

Once you gather information about a product or manufacturer, how do you decide which sources to believe? How can you tell if advertisements contain accurate—or exaggerated—claims? You need to know about and read reliable sources. Then you can make good, well-informed decisions.

Did You Know?

The Federal Trade Commission publishes a handy guide to help people make wise buying decisions and understand their rights as consumers. The booklet is called *How to Be an Informed Consumer.* To get a copy, go to http://fin.emcp.net/consumerguide. For other free information about consumer issues, visit http://fin.emcp.net/ftc or call 877-382-4357.

Taking Time for Research

You can expect better results from your consumer decisions if you research a product or service before buying or investing. Of course, research takes time and can be costly. You might have to spend money on telephone calls or gasoline for the car. Many people start on the Internet. Most of the time you will be able to get the information you need there. Some people enjoy shopping and don't feel like they are giving up anything to conduct a search for information. You are generally willing to spend more time shopping if you are buying an expensive item, such as a car.

▼ **Be sure a company is reputable before you order products online or by phone. How can you verify that a company is reputable?**

Home Shopping

Despite the lure of shopping malls, home shopping is a growing business. Two key reasons for this are convenience and a wider selection.

Catalogs, TV, and the Web Catalog shopping has been around since the late 1800s. Ordering from the Sears catalog, for instance, families could buy everything from long underwear to a complete kit for building a house. Today, catalogs tend to be more specialized, catering to every interest.

Television offers additional buying opportunities. Entire stations are dedicated to home shopping. "Infomercials" have become a popular way to get information about products and services to the public. These paid advertisements run as long as twenty or thirty minutes and include product demonstrations and discussions.

Most companies have Web sites that let you place an order on your home computer. In fact, many companies (perhaps tens of thousands) sell *only* on the Web.

Shopping at home is more than a convenience for some people. It is

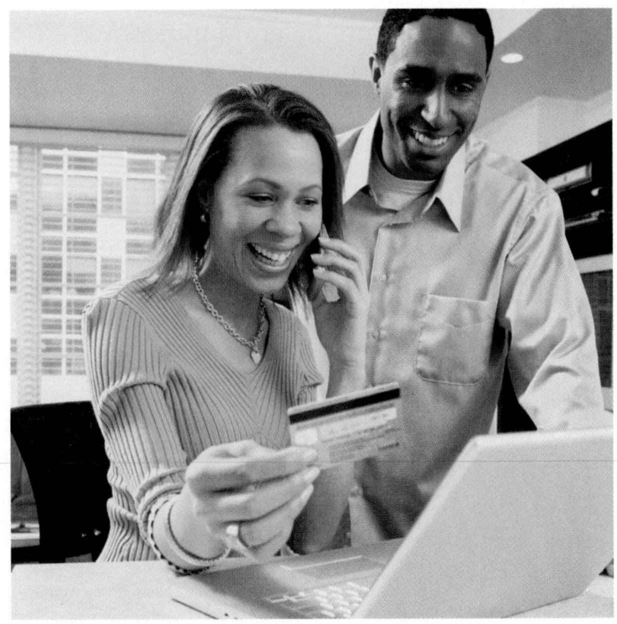

entertainment—or even an addiction, as discussed in Chapter 8. Ordering is as easy as a few clicks on a Web site or a phone call to a toll-free number.

Either way, you will likely pay with a credit card. You may also pay with a personal check or a money order. (A *money order* is a form that you purchase for a specific amount of money and make payable to a particular person.) It is important to remember that it's easy to buy products you don't need—and quickly overspend.

Buyer Beware Any time you shop, remember that some companies are reputable and some are not. Just because a product is advertised on TV and a celebrity says it's fantastic does not necessarily mean the product is reliable or something you need. Check out a product or service before you buy it whenever possible. If the item is available locally, call a store to compare the price. If you are dealing with an unfamiliar

Fifty years ago, you might have seen a well-dressed man walking down a residential street, carrying a heavy leather case, and knocking at each front door. Selling encyclopedias door-to-door was common practice then. *Britannica* was the most highly regarded encyclopedia printed in English. It had twenty-four thick volumes of information on thousands of subjects—describing in brief information on a vast number of subjects. Customers often bought the sets on credit, paying a few dollars a month over many years.

With the dawn of technology, the printed encyclopedia—though it still exists—is rarely found in homes any more. *Britannica* is still the most highly regarded collection, but it now focuses sales on CD-ROM, DVD, and online editions. An online encyclopedia can be updated constantly as new information becomes known.

A competitor to *Britannica* and other formerly print-based encyclopedias is *Wikipedia*, the online free encyclopedia, written and edited by its readers. Since it is maintained by the readers, the credibility of the information is not always assured. In 2007, there were about 2.2 million articles on the English version of Wikipedia.

YOU DECIDE

The newest MP3 player was released eight months ago. Justin thinks the player is really cool. It costs $350 but he just has to have it. He already has an earlier version, which he bought for $200 a year ago. He thinks he can sell the old one for $50 or so. He's also saved a couple hundred dollars from his job. By adding some birthday money, he thinks he can afford the new purchase.

Justin and his friend Bart go shopping at the discount electronics store where Bart's brother works. Bart's brother tells the guys that the store has sold a huge number of the new MP3 players, and people really like them. He also tells them confidentially that a new model is coming out in five months. It will have twice as much memory and twice as many cool features. That one might be worth waiting for—but it will cost $400.

Justin figures he can buy the current one now, and then sell it on eBay when the new one comes out. Bart's brother warns him that once the new one is on the market, the current model won't be worth much.

Should he . . .

1. ...wait five months to buy the next model? If he does, will Justin benefit?
2. ...buy the current player for $350, then try to sell it in four months for $150 and buy the new one for $400? Give reasons for your answer.

company, look for this motto: "Satisfaction guaranteed, or your money back." This means the company is willing to stand behind its product.

Telemarketing

How often do you or your family get phone calls from companies wanting to sell you something that you don't want? Using the phone to sell or promote something is called *telemarketing.* Many people find these calls disrupting, especially when the caller tries to pressure them into buying.

As with any purchase, do your research. Think before you buy. If the product or service is not something you were going to buy anyway, you are probably better off saying "No thanks."

The federal government set up the National Do Not Call Registry in 2003. If you do not want to receive telemarketing calls, you can register your phone number and most calls should stop. (A few types of calls are exempt.) To register online, go to http://fin.emcp.net/donotcall. You can also call toll-free 1-888-382-1222 from the number you want to register.

contract a legal agreement between two or more parties

mutual assent the requirement in a contract that all parties agree on the terms

consideration the requirement in a contract that money or something of value is exchanged

competent parties the requirement in a contract that all parties understand what they are doing

pyramid scheme a fraudulent system in which money from new investors is used to pay profits to earlier investors

Contracts

Consumers today buy many items with installment credit plans (to be discussed in Chapter 13) or other long-term contracts. A **contract** is an agreement between two or more parties that is enforceable by law. The requirements of a contract include these three points:

- **Mutual assent**—The parties must agree on all terms.
- **Consideration**—There must be money or something of value exchanged.
- **Competent parties**—The parties must understand what they are doing.

A credit contract is established when a consumer fills out an application and the creditor approves the application. The Equal Credit Opportunity Act helps consumers stay informed when they apply for credit. This law prohibits lenders from denying credit because of race, sex, color, religion, national origin, age, or marital status. Lenders also cannot ask about an applicant's spouse or child support or welfare payments. Anyone who is denied credit must be told the reason for denial.

Other credit laws, including the Fair Credit Reporting Act and the Truth in Lending Act, are discussed in Chapter 14.

Consumer Fraud

Consumer fraud—manipulation of consumers for personal gain—takes many forms. Examples range from forging a person's signature on a check to fake "sweepstakes" and foreign money offers. Victims might be contacted by phone, mail, or e-mail.

Remember: Claims that seem too good to be true usually are. If a pill could magically melt pounds away, or increase your IQ, wouldn't it be a top news story? Does it make sense to buy land you have never seen? Some fraudulent schemes offer correspondence courses that provide useless training at very high prices. Have you seen ads for work-at-home jobs? Are you being urged to contribute to a charity you've never heard of? Investigate before you commit.

Among the many acts of criminal consumer fraud are false advertising, identity theft, and pyramid schemes. A **pyramid scheme** is an illegal investment scam set up like a pyramid. It starts with somebody at the top and then spreads downward.

A pyramid scheme can take several forms. Basically it works like this: Some-

LOOK Before You Leap

Fabiana's friend Betsy gave her a lipstick she really likes. It's not a brand she knows, but Betsy brought along the product catalog. Fabiana sees a lot of tempting items, but the prices are high.

Betsy tells Fabiana that her aunt is a distributor for the brand. If Fabiana signs up to be a distributor, then she will get a discount on all of her purchases. What's more, if Fabiana signs up other people to sell the products, then she'll get a commission on *their* sales, too. "I'm going to do it. Everybody makes money, and you get great deals on the cosmetics," Betsy says.

This sounds great to Fabiana—a little too great. She wonders, "If you and your aunt sell this stuff, and I'm selling it—and then we both get our friends to sell it, and they get more people to sell it—who else can we contact to buy it?" Betsy had not thought of that.

Fabiana remembers hearing something on the radio about *multilevel marketing*, or MLM. She does some research on the Federal Trade Commission Web site and at the site of a watchdog group, MLM Watch. She learns that multilevel marketing is actually a type of pyramid scheme.

Distributors of products get their customers to be distributors, and then those people get *their* customers to be distributors. The distributors at each level earn a commission from everyone below them. Sometimes people have to pay fees to the parent company before they can begin to sell products. They might be required to keep large stocks of inventory on hand, even if they are not selling much.

Betsy is sure her aunt's company isn't like that. Anyway, her aunt makes money at it, and Betsy is sure she will, too.

Before Signing Up

1. Visit the Web site of MLM Watch (http://fin.emcp.net/mlmwatch) and read about multilevel marketing. Should Betsy sign up as a distributor with her aunt's company? Why or why not?
2. If there are five layers of distributors, each receiving a commission on the sale of one lipstick, what does that tell you about the price?
3. What do you think makes MLM schemes attractive to potential distributors?

one contacts you about an investment. You send this person money, say $1,000. Your contact says to contact ten other people and get them to invest. You call ten people, who send you $1,000 apiece. Those ten people each contact ten people, and so on. All new investors are required to send money to the person who recruited them.

The "investment" is a fraud because no product has been sold and no wealth created. The scheme will eventually collapse and people will lose their money. In fact, it is estimated that 90 percent of people who get involved in a pyramid scheme will lose their money.

The Right to Choose

The American market system is a free-enterprise, capitalist system. As a consumer, you have the opportunity to choose the goods and services you pay for. You are offered a wide variety of goods from all over the world, at all price levels.

Did You Know?

A *Ponzi scheme* is an illegal pyramid-type scam named for Carlo Ponzi, who swindled thousands of New England residents in 1919 and 1920. Ponzi developed a very complicated "investment opportunity" involving foreign currency exchanges and international mail coupons. He promised investors that they could earn a return of almost 50 percent in just ninety days, compared with 5 percent yearly on their money in bank savings.

Ponzi was flooded with money from investors who were attracted by the promise of such high returns over a short period of time. He took in $1 million during a single *three-hour* period! Early investors were paid off to make the investment look legitimate.

But there was no actual investment. It was just money transferred from new investors to earlier ones. Eventually the influx of new money dried up, and the scam collapsed.

Ponzi was convicted of embezzlement and deported to Italy after he served his sentence. Eventually, he died in poverty in Brazil.

Of course, not all individuals have the same opportunities to choose. Those with more money have more options. Sometimes those with very limited incomes have to pay higher prices because they cannot afford transportation to the stores with better deals. Location is another variable. Small towns and rural areas offer fewer shopping choices than cities do. But regardless of circumstances, prepared shoppers make better choices.

Competition

monopoly a market with only one seller or producer

oligopoly a market with a limited number of sellers or producers

Competition provides consumers with the opportunity for choice. There are more than forty brands of athletic shoes on the market. Most communities have more than one doctor or lawyer, so you can choose the person you think will provide the best service.

Competition encourages producers to operate efficiently in order to keep their prices low and quality high. They have to make existing products better and develop new products too. Sometimes, though, competition is restricted.

Restrictions on Competition In the 1800s, some industries were dominated by a single company that had stamped out the rest of the competition. A market like this, with only one seller or producer, is called a **monopoly**. In a monopoly, one company controls the supply and price of a product. In 1890, Congress passed the Sherman Antitrust Act to stop the creation of large monopolies and to help guarantee competition.

In the 1930s, investor-owned gas and electric utilities were granted monopoly status—but they are regulated, and rate increases must be approved. The government concluded that regulated monopolies could provide better service at a fair price than could competitors—each stringing its own electrical wires or putting in its own gas pipes. Since the late 1990s, some states have opened their utilities markets to other suppliers. These states are concerned about rising energy costs and limited supplies. The pros and cons of monopolies continue to be debated.

When a limited number of producers control the market for a product, it is called an **oligopoly**. For example, there are many different types of cereal and detergent on the store shelves, but just a few companies make most of them. You may not have as much choice as you thought.

Government Import Policies Many of the products on store shelves come from around the globe. Some government policies are meant to limit imports, primarily to save manufacturing jobs in the United States. Other import policies

Going Global

In the early 1990s, global positioning system (GPS) technology began to make being lost a thing of the past. Twenty-four satellites in orbit send data to earth. Small devices receiving data from at least three satellites at once can pinpoint the user's exact location. The system was developed for the military by the U.S. Department of Defense. It works in any weather, anywhere in the world, twenty-four hours a day.

In 1989, Gary Burrell and Min Kao founded Garmin Ltd. as a small Kansas company. They shared a vision that GPS technology could serve not only the military but also ordinary consumers. Garmin produced handheld GPS systems for soldiers in the 1991 Persian Gulf War. These devices have a video screen that shows a map with the locations of roads and landmarks. They can even show gas stations and fast-food outlets.

By 1993, Garmin was making receivers for commercial and private aviation. The company soon began producing other GPS products for hikers, climbers, boaters, and travelers.

Even though the GPS satellite system is an American creation, anyone on earth could use it—and Burrell and Kao saw the potential for a worldwide market. The company expanded to London and now sells its devices across Europe. An office was opened in Taiwan, Min Kao's original home country, for Asian sales.

European and Asian airline companies were among Garmin's biggest business customers around 2003. Today, the StreetPilot in-car device, the Edge GPS device for cyclists, and the Fishfinder are among its products sold internationally. In 2008, Garmin announced entry into the mobile phone market. Global positioning has certainly paid off for Garmin: It is now the world's leading GPS manufacturer.

Thinking Globally

1. What other products or technologies were developed for the military and then spread to civilian consumer use?
2. Why did GPS technology allow Garmin to expand so easily into a worldwide market?
3. As a consumer, what area landmarks would you like to see displayed on a GPS device screen?

are designed to encourage trade with foreign countries. These policies affect your choice of products and the prices you pay.

The two main policies for limiting imports are quotas and tariffs. Import **quotas** are limits on the amount of certain goods that can be imported into the country each year. **Tariffs** are taxes on imported products. A tariff raises the price of a product. The government's purpose in charging tariffs is to make sure the prices of imported goods are competitive with the prices of U.S. products.

The **North American Free Trade Agreement (NAFTA)** is a treaty that called for gradual elimination of tariffs and other trade restrictions on goods produced and sold in North America. The United States, Mexico, and Canada signed the agreement, which became effective on January 1, 1994. The goal was to encourage trade among the countries. Most tariffs were eliminated immediately and others took fifteen years to phase out.

quotas legal limits on the amount of a good that can be imported

tariffs taxes on goods imported into a country

North American Free Trade Agreement (NAFTA) a treaty signed by the United States, Mexico, and Canada that called for gradual elimination of tariffs and other trade restrictions on goods produced and sold in North America

The Right to Be Heard

The right to be heard relates to what you learned in Section 1 of this chapter about communicating your opinions to producers and sellers. Were you ever so dissatisfied with a product or service that you contacted the company that produced it? You might buy something that turns out to be defective or of inferior quality. Sometimes the service you receive is unacceptable. In these cases, as a consumer, you have an obligation to yourself and others to complain. At the same time, you have a right to expect the producer or seller to listen to your complaint and act on it.

Complaints to responsible manufacturers and businesses help all consumers. Reliable companies want to know why their products have failed or how they can improve their service. Most businesses want to please their customers.

▼ Good salespeople will listen to your complaint and solve the problem.

Complaining Effectively

Today, the people who sell products are generally not the same people who produced them. That can make it hard to reach the right person when you have a problem with something you have purchased. You usually cannot go directly to the manufacturer with your complaint. Instead, you must talk with a salesperson or retailer. With online and catalog shopping, you might be talking to someone thousands of miles away. You must rely on that person to understand your problem and decide who is at fault. This can be very frustrating—but if you believe something is wrong, it is important that you complain.

Lodging a Complaint The first step in lodging a complaint about an unacceptable product is to return it to the place of purchase, if possible. Before you go, decide what a fair resolution of the problem would be. For example, are you asking for a refund or replacement item? If the store clerk or customer service department fails to solve your problem, ask to see the manager.

Be sure to take the receipt with you. In addition, any time you have problems with a product, start keeping notes. Write down when you first noticed the problem and a summary of everything you did to resolve it. Include names of the people you talked to, as well as when, where, and what was said.

Following Up If the store will not agree to your reasonable request—or if the purchase is not from a nearby store—call, e-mail, or write a letter to the manufacturer. Keep your explanation clear, polite, and to the point. You will get a reply much more quickly than someone whose letter is angry and who is not sure of all the facts. Figure 12.1 is

Figure 12.1 **FORM FOR WRITING A LETTER OF COMPLAINT**

Be sure to give your complete contact information.

Your Address
Your City, State, ZIP
Date

Address the letter to a specific person or department.

Name of Contact Person (if available)
Title (if available)
Company Name
Consumer Complaint Division (if you have no specific contact)
Street Address
City, State, ZIP

Dear (Contact Person):

Re: (account number, if applicable)

Give specific information, such as date of purchase, identification of product, and place of purchase.

On (date), I (bought, leased, rented, or had repaired) a (name of the product, with serial or model number or service performed) at (location, date and other important details of the transaction).

State the problem clearly and concisely.

Unfortunately, your product (or service) has not performed well (or the service was inadequate) because (state the problem). I am disappointed because (explain the problem: for example, the product does not work properly, the service was not performed correctly, I was billed the wrong amount, something was not disclosed clearly or was misrepresented, etc.).

State how you would like the problem resolved. Be sure to enclose copies of receipts or other documents.

To resolve the problem, I would appreciate (state the specific action you want—money back, charge card credit, repair, exchange, etc.). Enclosed are copies (do not send originals) of my records (include receipts, guarantees, warranties, canceled checks, contracts, model and serial numbers, and any other documents).

Give them a time limit to respond to your complaint. Give your phone number as another way to be contacted.

I look forward to your reply and a resolution to my problem and will wait until (set a time limit) before seeking help from a consumer protection agency or the Better Business Bureau. Please contact me at the above address or by phone at (home and/or office numbers with area code).

Sincerely,

(Signature)

Your name (typed out)

a form for writing a good letter of complaint.

If you are dealing with a local company, you could try contacting the nearest **Better Business Bureau (BBB)**. This nonprofit organization, funded by local businesspeople, follows up on consumer complaints. If a business refuses the recommendation, the Better Business Bureau cannot force a solution—but problems are often solved. The BBB also provides information to people who want to check the reputation of a company before hiring it. For this reason, companies try to avoid a bad reputation.

Some communities have *consumer action lines* operated by local radio or TV stations. A call from the station often causes a manufacturer or retailer to respond to your concern quickly. The public discussion also helps other consumers with their own problems.

Better Business Bureau (BBB) a nonprofit organization that tries to resolve disputes between consumers and businesses

Resolving Difficult Problems

Most complaints can be settled easily, but you might not be satisfied with the action of a particular company. Or you might be upset by the lack of action. If so, you can take other steps.

Consumer Action Panels Many industries have established **consumer action panels (CAPs)** to listen to customer complaints and help find solutions. These panels are composed of people who are not employees in that industry, so the decisions will be unbiased. For example, automobile dealer associations have set up automotive consumer action panels (AUTOCAPs).

Arbitration More and more consumer complaints are being handled through **arbitration**. By this process, the complaint or dispute is referred to an *arbitrator*, an impartial third party. Both the consumer and the seller must agree to accept the decision of the arbitrator. The decision is final and cannot be reversed.

Small-Claims Court In the United States, **small-claims courts** are often used to solve disputes between a seller and a buyer. Claims must involve relatively small amounts of money—in most states less than $1,500. Court costs are relatively low, and usually no lawyers are involved.

The seller and the consumer present their information to the judge, who makes the final decision. The judge might tell the seller to pay the consumer—but if the seller does not pay, the consumer has to file a formal lawsuit to collect.

Many small-claims courts have *mediation* programs to help people settle their own disputes and work out their own agreements. A **mediator** is an outside person who works with two opposing parties to reach an agreement. Mediation is different from arbitration. A mediator helps the parties work together to settle the dispute, while an arbitrator decides on a solution that is final.

Legal Action Consumers can take legal action beyond small-claims court. To file a lawsuit, however, means hiring a lawyer and often going to court. It requires the most time and money—but might be worthwhile if you have strong evidence and the dollar amount of your claim is large.

Class-Action Suits When many consumers have similar complaints against the same company or person, one of them might file a **class-action suit** on behalf of all. In other words, the lawsuit will cover an entire group (or "class") of individuals. The lawsuit is considered in a single court case. If the consumers win, the company usually pays damages to all consumers who bought the product. Figure 12.2 shows articles about a class-action suit brought against Target.com.

Consumers' Voices in the Government

Government decisions affect the products and services available to you. As an active consumer, you need to be aware of these decisions. Be sure your voice is heard when the decisions are being made. Consumer action groups speak for your interests at the state and federal levels—but you can get involved locally. Learn what is happening in your city and county. Take an interest in water rates, housing codes, street-widening projects, and other issues.

Government decisions need consumer input. You have a responsibility to let the decision makers know what you think.

consumer action panels (CAPs) groups of people not employed in an industry who try to resolve consumer complaints about the industry

arbitration a process for settling disputes by allowing an unbiased third party to decide the outcome

small-claims courts courts without lawyers, settling disputes over small amounts of money

mediator a person who helps two parties settle a dispute

class-action suit a lawsuit filed by one party on behalf of a large group of individuals who all have the same complaint

Figure 12.2 SAMPLE CLASS-ACTION SUIT DESCRIPTION

In 2007, a California judge certified a class-action suit against Target.com. The *class* being served is the visually impaired who want to shop at the Target.com Web site using advanced computer screen technology. Find out more about this case. Do you think the case is fair? What do you predict will be the outcome? Explain your answers.

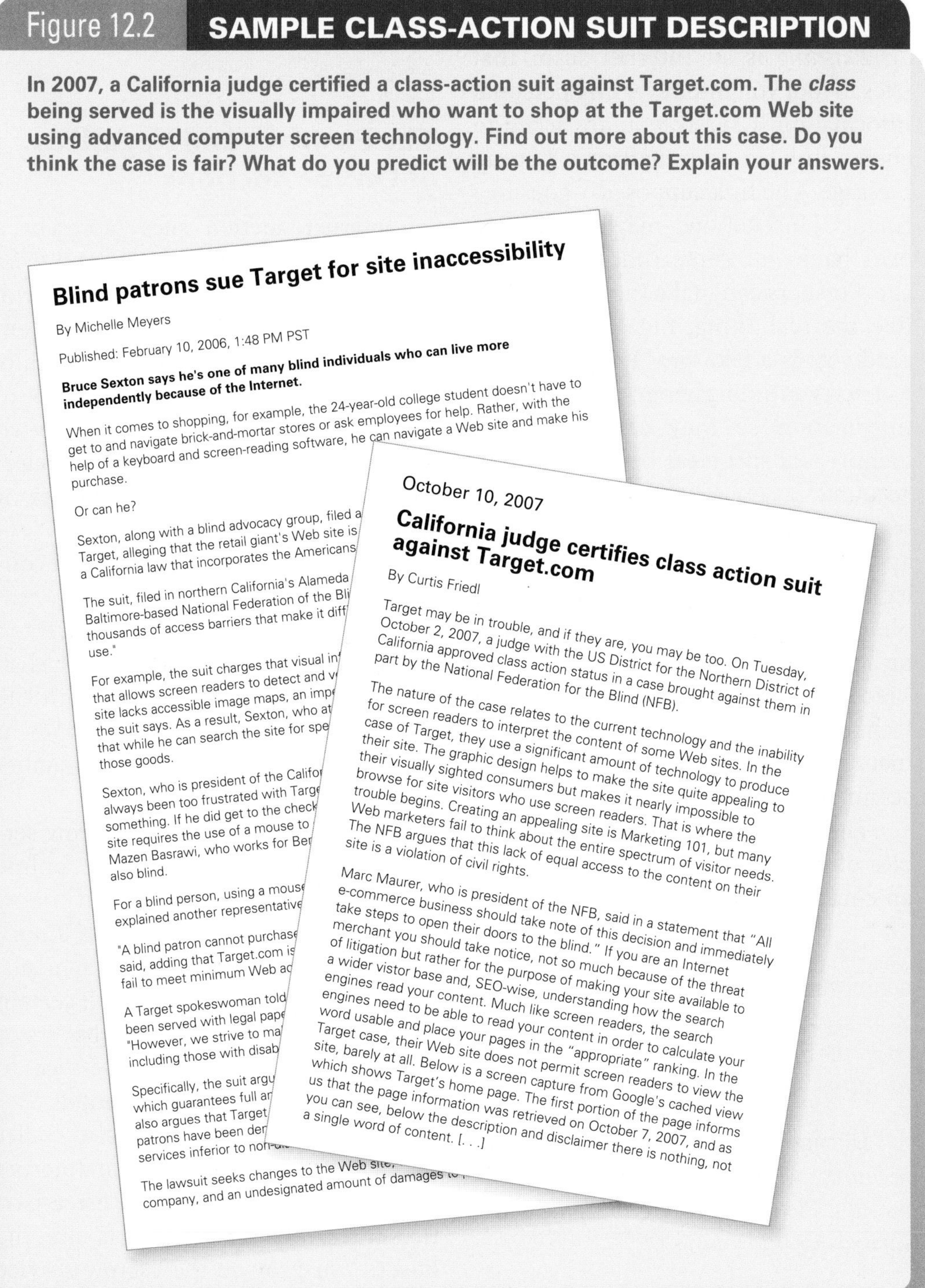

Blind patrons sue Target for site inaccessibility

By Michelle Meyers

Published: February 10, 2006, 1:48 PM PST

Bruce Sexton says he's one of many blind individuals who can live more independently because of the Internet.

When it comes to shopping, for example, the 24-year-old college student doesn't have to get to and navigate brick-and-mortar stores or ask employees for help. Rather, with the help of a keyboard and screen-reading software, he can navigate a Web site and make his purchase.

Or can he?

Sexton, along with a blind advocacy group, filed a
Target, alleging that the retail giant's Web site is
a California law that incorporates the Americans

The suit, filed in northern California's Alameda
Baltimore-based National Federation of the Bli
thousands of access barriers that make it diff
use."

For example, the suit charges that visual in
that allows screen readers to detect and v
site lacks accessible image maps, an imp
the suit says. As a result, Sexton, who at
that while he can search the site for spe
those goods.

Sexton, who is president of the Califor
always been too frustrated with Targ
something. If he did get to the check
site requires the use of a mouse to
Mazen Basrawi, who works for Ber
also blind.

For a blind person, using a mous
explained another representative

"A blind patron cannot purchase
said, adding that Target.com is
fail to meet minimum Web ac

A Target spokeswoman told
been served with legal pape
"However, we strive to ma
including those with disab

Specifically, the suit argu
which guarantees full ar
also argues that Target
patrons have been der
services inferior to non-

The lawsuit seeks changes to the Web site,
company, and an undesignated amount of damages

October 10, 2007

California judge certifies class action suit against Target.com

By Curtis Friedl

Target may be in trouble, and if they are, you may be too. On Tuesday, October 2, 2007, a judge with the US District for the Northern District of California approved class action status in a case brought against them in part by the National Federation for the Blind (NFB).

The nature of the case relates to the current technology and the inability for screen readers to interpret the content of some Web sites. In the case of Target, they use a significant amount of technology to produce their site. The graphic design helps to make the site quite appealing to their visually sighted consumers but makes it nearly impossible to browse for site visitors who use screen readers. That is where the trouble begins. Creating an appealing site is Marketing 101, but many Web marketers fail to think about the entire spectrum of visitor needs. The NFB argues that this lack of equal access to the content on their site is a violation of civil rights.

Marc Maurer, who is president of the NFB, said in a statement that "All e-commerce business should take note of this decision and immediately take steps to open their doors to the blind." If you are an Internet merchant you should take notice, not so much because of the threat of litigation but rather for the purpose of making your site available to a wider vistor base and, SEO-wise, understanding how the search engines read your content. Much like screen readers, the search engines need to be able to read your content in order to calculate your word usable and place your pages in the "appropriate" ranking. In the Target case, their Web site does not permit screen readers to view the site, barely at all. Below is a screen capture from Google's cached view which shows Target's home page. The first portion of the page informs us that the page information was retrieved on October 7, 2007, and as you can see, below the description and disclaimer there is nothing, not a single word of content. [. . .]

Consumer Fraud and the Internet

The Internet has brought enormous economic benefits to both world economies and individuals everywhere. It has also become an efficient tool of online scammers, identity thieves, and others involved in fraud. Among the illegal activities affecting the greatest number of Internet users are phishing and online auction fraud.

Answers to Fact or Fiction

1. True; **2.** False—The Magnuson-Moss Warranty Act requires warranties to be written in ordinary language, not "legalese," so that consumers will know exactly what they are getting; **3.** False—Certification seals indicate that products meet the standards set by industries or private organizations; **4.** True; **5.** True; **6.** False—If a business refuses to act, the Better Business Bureau cannot force a solution.

Phishing

Phishing is an Internet scam that tries to fool you into revealing personal information. Usually, you are asked to click a link on an e-mail or a pop-up message. The link supposedly goes to a financial institution—maybe even your own bank—or some other legitimate site. Phishers can make these links look like the real thing, but they actually send you to a fake site. The purpose is to trick you into giving them personal information so they can steal your identity—or just steal from your bank account!

For example, phishers might send an e-mail that appears to be from a legitimate business, asking you to call a phone number to update your account or access a "refund." Because they use Voice over Internet Protocol (VoIP) technology, the area code in this fraudulent message does not reflect where the scammers are located.

The following messages are examples of phishing scams. Never reply to an e-mail similar to these:

We suspect an unauthorized transaction on your account. To ensure that your account is not compromised, please click the link below and confirm your identity.

During our regular verification of accounts, we couldn't verify your information. Please click here to update and verify your information.

Remember that legitimate financial institutions do not request personal information by e-mail. To reach an organization you do business with, always call the number on your financial statements, look up the number in the phone book, or type in the Web address yourself.

If you receive spam that is phishing for information, forward it to spam@uce.gov and also to the company, bank, or organization being impersonated.

The Positives and Negatives of Online Auctions

Internet auction sites represent a virtual flea market with new and used merchandise from around the world. Sellers have a global storefront from which to market their goods. Practically any type of product you can think of can be found for sale online—and often at a lower price than you could find elsewhere. But whether you are buying or selling, online auctions have risks.

The FTC receives thousands of consumer fraud complaints every year. Those dealing with online auction fraud consistently rank near the top of the list. The complaints generally deal with late shipments, no shipments, or shipment of products that are not the high quality advertised.

Even though legitimate escrow services are available to handle online transactions, there have been many complaints about online *escrow scams.* Escrow is a situation in which payments, for example, are ineffective until certain conditions are met. In scams, buyers or sellers pose as an escrow service to improperly obtain money or goods.

For example, the so-called seller puts goods up for sale on an Internet auction and insists that you use a particular escrow service if you are the buyer. You provide the escrow service with your payment information, but the escrow service does not hold the payment. Instead, it sends the money to the fraudulent seller. You never receive the promised goods, and you cannot locate the seller. Because the escrow service was part of the scam, you cannot get any money back.

Figure 12.3 has helpful tips for buyers and sellers using an online auction site.

Being a Responsible Consumer

As a consumer, you have certain rights under the law. You have the right to expect safe products and services. You have the right to obtain truthful and useful information. You have the right to choose among a variety of products and services. You have the right to be heard—through the complaints you make and through your votes on important issues.

Along with these rights come responsibilities. You are responsible for researching the safety of products. You should always be alert to the possibility of consumer fraud. You have a responsibility to complain effectively when necessary—and to make sure your complaints are settled to your satisfaction. Failing to meet these responsibilities can mean higher costs for producers or retailers. Higher costs for them mean higher prices for consumers. Avoiding your responsibilities means that everyone suffers the consequences.

Consumer decisions are not made in a vacuum. Every product you buy or service you use can affect others. Think back to your values, the things that are important to you, and to your goals. You have the responsibility as a consumer to choose products and services with these values and goals in mind. Your choices should be safe for the environment and should not infringe upon the rights of others.

Figure 12.3 TIPS FOR USING AN ONLINE AUCTION SITE

If you are a buyer . . .

- Become familiar with the auction site by reading all the rules.
- Find out what protections the site offers to buyers.
- Read and understand the seller's product description. If you have questions about the product, send an e-mail to the seller.
- Determine the approximate value of an item before you bid.
- Learn about the seller. Pay attention to the seller's ratings.
- Check the seller's return policy.
- Establish a top price and stick to it.
- Print copies of all transaction information.
- Protect your identity. Never give out your Social Security number or driver's license number.
- Protect your payment funds. If you use an escrow, make sure it is legal, first.

If you are a seller . . .

- When describing your item and its condition, state whether it is new, used, or reconditioned.
- Try to anticipate questions that buyers might have. Address them in the description of your item.
- Include photographs showing different views of the item.
- Specify the minimum bid you are willing to accept.
- Specify who will pay for shipping and if you ship internationally.
- State your return policy, including who is responsible for paying shipping costs.
- Respond as quickly as possible to bidders' questions.
- When the auction closes, print all information about the transaction.
- Contact the buyer as soon as the auction closes. Confirm the final cost and shipping charges, and tell the buyer where to send payment.

SECTION 2 ASSESSMENT

Factual Recall

1. Which president presented the first Consumers' Bill of Rights? What four basic rights were covered in this bill?
2. Does the Consumer Product Safety Commission guarantee that all products sold in the United States are safe? Explain.
3. How can you stop or reduce telemarketing calls?

Critical Thinking

1. Your friend saw an infomercial about a new line of hair care products. She wonders if the products are as good as the program claimed. How could your friend obtain more information?
2. Describe pros and cons of online auctions.

CHAPTER 12 REVIEW AND ASSESSMENT

Chaper Summary

Section 1 Increasing Consumer Awareness

- The consumer movement has made businesses more accountable to society and has prompted the U.S. government to pass laws that regulate businesses.
- There are three characters in the consumer story—the producer, the consumer, and the citizen—and we each play all of these roles at one time or another.
- Producers communicate information about their products and support services through advertising, toll-free phone numbers, warranties, Energy Star labels, and certification seals.
- As a consumer, you are responsible for gathering information and examining alternatives before you make a purchase. You also are responsible for giving feedback to producers about the products or services you buy.
- Government agencies that handle consumer issues include the Federal Trade Commission (FTC), the United States Postal Service, the Interstate Commerce Commission (ICC), the Federal Communications Commission (FCC), the Food and Drug Administration (FDA), and the Consumer Product Safety Commission (CPSC).
- Product standards are requirements for particular products and are generally set by government agencies.

Section 2 Basic Consumer Rights

- The Consumers' Bill of Rights includes the right to safety, the right to be informed, the right to choose, and the right to be heard.
- Even though safety standards exist for many products, consumers must still be alert to possible safety problems.
- Consumer fraud takes many forms, and you must guard against becoming a victim.
- Competition among producers of goods and services is healthy. It encourages the producers to keep prices low and quality high. It provides consumers with more choices.
- In some cases, the government restricts competition by allowing monopolies in certain industries and by using quotas and tariffs to limit imports.
- To complain effectively, you need to know where to and how to make your complaint. Various business, consumer, and government organizations exist to deal with consumer problems.
- Consumers have an obligation to themselves and to others to complain when the goods or services they receive are not satisfactory.
- Difficult consumer problems can be resolved through arbitration, small-claims court, legal action, or class-action suits.

Reviewing Key Terms

For each of the following statements, choose the key term that best completes the sentence.

1. If you want to know whether a product meets safety or performance standards, look for ______.
2. When one company controls both supply and price, that company has a(n) ______.
3. Government can limit the amount of goods coming into a country by setting ______.
4. When consumers ______ a product, they refuse to buy it because of their feelings about the product or the company.
5. In ______, a judge listens to both sides in a dispute and decides the outcome.
6. When all parties agree to the terms of a contract, there is ______.
7. In a(n) ______, new recruits into a business or investment project are required to give money to the person who recruited them.
8. The ______ set by government agencies might require products to contain certain ingredients, to include safety features, or to meet other specifications.

9. The prices of some imported goods might be raised when the government imposes taxes called ______.
10. Some disputes between consumers and businesses can be settled with the help of a nonprofit organization called the ______.

Understanding the Main Ideas

1. What is the difference between a full warranty and a limited warranty?
2. What is the Energy Star program?
3. Why is government regulation controversial?
4. Name three ways consumers benefit from competition among producers.
5. What are the two main tools the government uses to limit imports?
6. If you are not satisfied with a company's response to your complaint, what other steps can you take?

Practicing Math

1. You are thinking about buying a laptop computer. It costs $1,168 with an extended warranty, or $1,026 without one. Because laptops are more likely to need repairs than desktop computers, you are thinking about buying the extended warranty. You will charge your purchase to a credit card and pay it off in twenty-four months, at 21 percent interest. How much will you really be paying for the extended warranty?
2. Compact fluorescent lamps (CFLs) save energy and money. If you replaced a standard 100-watt lightbulb with a 25-watt CFL and used it for 1,000 hours, how much money would you save in energy costs? Assume the cost of electricity is 10 cents per kilowatt hour. (*Hint:* 1,000 hours of use for a 100-watt bulb is equivalent to 100 kilowatt hours.)

Applying Critical Thinking Skills

1. How could reading a use-and-care booklet for a product help you decide whether to buy it?
2. How can you protect yourself against consumer fraud?
3. Which product or service providers have a monopoly in your community?

Working with Real-World Documents

1. Two months ago, you bought a watch for your mother's birthday. The watch stopped working after only one week. You took it back to the jewelry store, where you were told it was probably just a defective battery. The battery was replaced free of charge, but the watch stopped again after about ten days. In fact, you have now had the battery replaced three times, and the watch is again not working. You asked the store manager for a replacement watch but were told the store's policy is "no returns after thirty days." You still have your receipt. Write a letter of complaint to the manufacturer, Tymely, Inc.
2. Examine a credit card contract (agreement) and answer the following questions.
   a. Most contracts go into effect when all parties have signed, but credit card agreements typically do not require a signature. What action on the part of the consumer indicates acceptance of the terms?
   b. Can the credit card issuer change the consumer's credit limit or cash advance limit without notice?
   c. Are finance charges the same for all types of credit card transactions?
   d. What happens to the interest rate if the consumer fails to make at least the minimum payment by the due date?
   e. What kinds of fees can be charged?

Taking It Home

1. Has anyone you know been a victim of consumer fraud? If so, write a report about what happened. Be sure to get the person's permission first.
2. Make a list of organizations in your community that provide help with consumer problems. Describe the kind of help offered. Include addresses and phone numbers of the organizations.

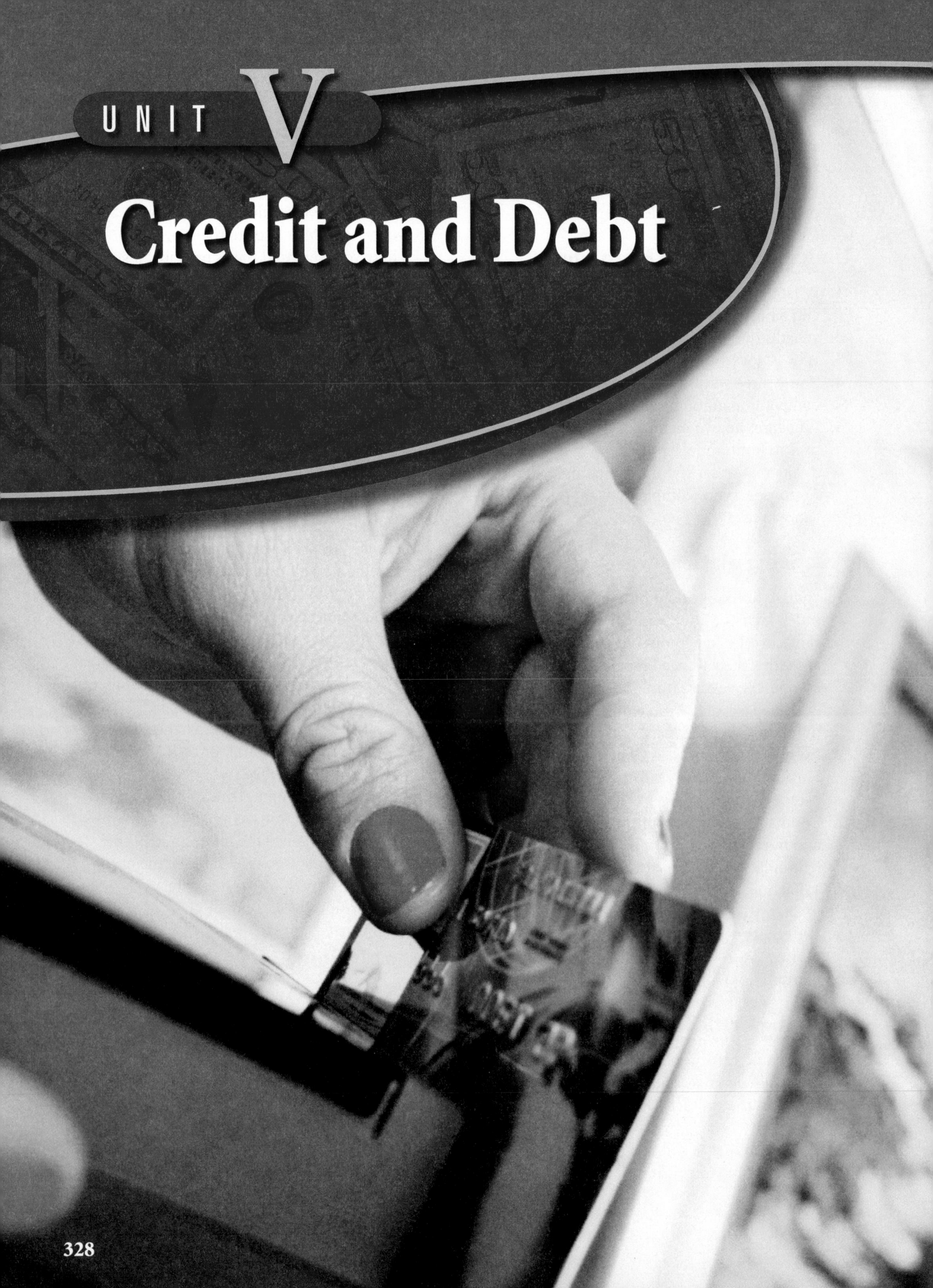

UNIT V
Credit and Debt

CHAPTER 13 Credit: Helpful or Hurtful?

CHAPTER 14 Using Credit Wisely

CHAPTER 13

Credit: Helpful or Hurtful?

You make a purchase in a local store, and the sales clerk asks, "Cash or charge?" When you say "Charge it," you are accepting *credit*—promising to pay later for something that you buy now. If you take out a loan, such as a student loan to pay for college, you are also using credit. You are receiving money and promising to pay it back later.

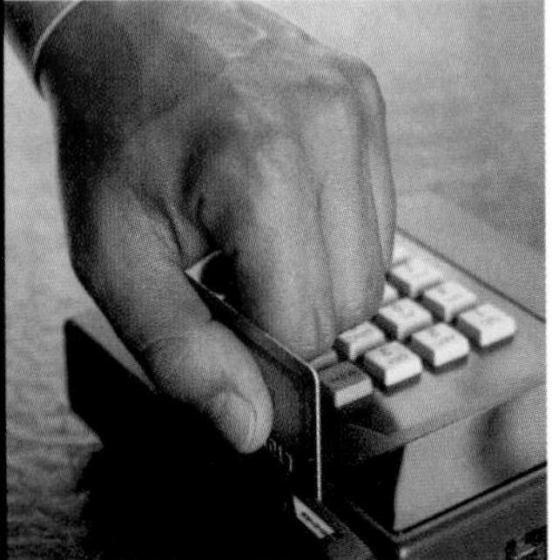

▲ Using a credit card is easy, but paying off the balance can be difficult.

Consumer credit has become an important part of the American economy, as almost everyone owes someone for something. In fact, nearly 75 percent of American families have some kind of consumer debt. Credit is used so often that some economists have predicted there may come a day when America will be a cashless society.

SECTION 1	Advantages and Disadvantages of Credit
SECTION 2	Types of Credit

Fact or Fiction

What do you think? Are the following statements true or false? If you think they are false, then say what is true.

1. Using credit can lead to serious problems.
2. When you charge a purchase with a credit card, you can withhold payment if the product is defective.
3. A credit card company cannot raise your interest rate as long as you pay all your bills on time for that account.
4. Credit reports usually cost $10 to $20.
5. If a thief charges items to your credit card, you will be responsible for all payments.
6. Debit cards work the same as credit cards.
7. Payday loans can cost more than 400 percent interest (APR).
8. If a loan is unsecured, you do not have to repay it.

Answers on page 353.

Study Reminder

*Knowing how to study can increase your knowledge, improve your grades, and cut down on your study time. See the **Studying Personal Finance** pages at the front of the book for some tips to help you study this chapter.*

SECTION 1

Advantages and Disadvantages of Credit

Focus Questions

1. What are the advantages of using credit?
2. What are the disadvantages of using credit?
3. What can you do to avoid credit fraud or identity theft?

Key Terms

grace period
universal default
bankruptcy
credit fraud
identity theft

Credit is tempting to use—"buy now, pay later." If you use it properly, credit can help you manage your finances. But other times, using credit can lead to serious problems. You might get what you want right away—but you might end up with financial troubles later on. Knowing the advantages and disadvantages of credit will help you decide when to use it and when not to.

Advantages of Credit

Have you ever borrowed against next week's allowance or borrowed lunch money from a friend? Think about a purchase that you or someone you know made on credit. Why use credit instead of cash? There are many good reasons for buying on credit.

Improved Standard of Living

Credit lets you purchase items now, instead of having to wait until you have enough cash to pay for them. It could take years to save enough money for expensive things like a car, a college education, or a house. A college degree improves your earning potential, but a college education can cost $50,000 or more. How many years would it take you to save that much money? With a student loan, you can get your degree now and then repay the money after graduation. Or suppose you decide to buy a new car. How long would it take to save up, say, $20,000? With credit, you can have the car immediately and enjoy using it while you are paying for it.

Convenience and Safety

Buying on credit is convenient. If you are short of cash when a special sale comes up, you can buy on credit and take advantage of the sale price.

Suppose you plan to purchase a DVD player. You know which model you want and you've been checking prices around town. Then, while buying some notebook paper one day, you see it on sale for a great price. But you have not brought your checkbook, and you don't have enough cash to pay for something as expensive as a DVD player. If you charge it, you can get the

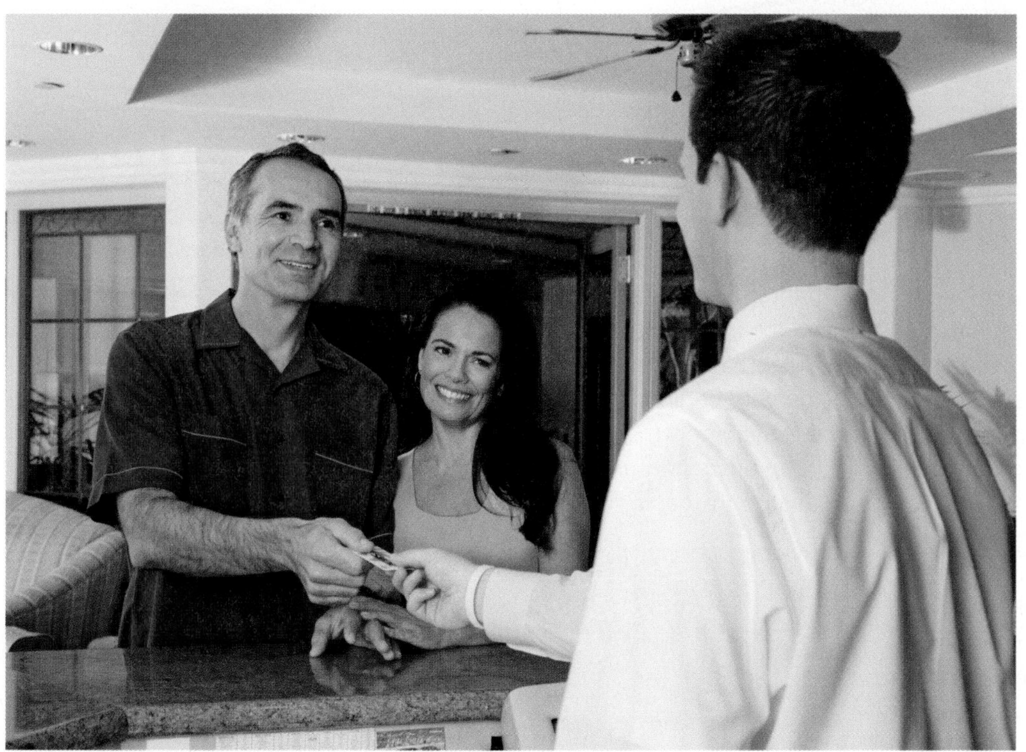

Credit is helpful and convenient when used responsibly.

sale price and take your new DVD player home that day.

Another convenience is using your credit card to "secure" a purchase. For example, many car rental companies require a credit card, even if you are not going to charge the rental to that card. If you don't show up, they can bill your account. That is one reason most hotels require a major credit card to make a reservation. In fact, credit cards are useful for almost all travel and entertainment expenses. (The first credit cards were designed specifically for travel and entertainment.) You don't have to carry large sums of cash when you travel or go out. You can even leave your checkbook at home if you wish.

Buying items by mail order or online is easier with a credit card—and can be safer than paying by check. A personal check includes information that a thief could use to access your account. If your credit card number is stolen, you will not be liable for unauthorized charges if you report the theft promptly to the institution that issued your card.

Buying on credit can also provide consumer protection. When you make a purchase with a credit card, you can withhold payment if the product is defective.

Help in Emergencies

Although it is important to save for emergencies, many people do not have enough savings to take care of all unexpected expenses. If your car needs an emergency brake job, would you have enough to pay for it? If you were seriously ill or injured and unable to work for several months, could you pay for food, housing, and other necessities? If your emergency fund is low, credit can be helpful in managing unexpected expenses.

Help in Record Keeping

Using credit can help you manage your finances. For example, when you use a credit card, you get a monthly statement. Each statement lists all the purchases you made that

You Can Succeed Financially

Marc Katz and Dave Christensen, a pair of 1998 Harvard University graduates, founded CustomInk in 2000. The company is a Web-based store where customers can design their own T-shirts, sweatshirts, caps, and mugs. Its first customers were college fraternities and athletic teams that wanted their logos on clothing.

That market has expanded to include anyone who wants to create a design and have it printed on merchandise—for family reunions, rock bands, political campaigns, or just about any conceivable theme or event. Its patented online "Lab" allows customers to create their own designs—almost like playing a video game.

At first the minimum order was six T-shirts or twelve caps, but in 2006 CustomInk began selling single items, widening its market significantly. The company printed 100,000 T-shirts in its first year. In 2007, it sold 35 times that many. Alexa, the Web rating service of Amazon.com, says CustomInk is the most popular seller of customer-designed merchandise on the Web.

Many companies offer printed T-shirts and other logo merchandise. What has made CustomInk so successful? From the very beginning, Katz and Christensen's main focus has been on customer satisfaction. CustomInk has a no-questions-

asked return policy and live support for customers seven days a week. But perhaps the company's biggest innovation is to ask for *and publish* feedback from every customer it serves. All feedback, whether positive or negative, is posted uncensored on the company Web site.

Some business advisers have suggested that Marc Katz is a little crazy to provide space for people to complain publicly. But Katz says it's a way to share the kind of word-of-mouth praise that businesses need to grow. A typical order is around $400, and he says people are more willing to spend that much for an unseen product if they know that others have been satisfied.

When people see that 99 percent of the CustomInk feedback is positive, they feel more confident. As a result, sales continue to increase each year.

When asked about the future of the business, Katz points out that "jeans and T-shirts are never going to go out of style." He says, "If you want something unique, design it yourself." And he's right. The business concept that Katz and Christensen designed is indeed one of a kind.

What Would You Do?

1. How do you think most customers pay for merchandise from CustomInk? Explain your reasoning.
2. For each credit card sale, retailers pay a commission to the bank that issued the card. How is this likely to affect prices for the customer?

month—so it is fairly easy to keep track of where you spent your money (see Figure 13.1 on the next page). Because the purchases are all on one statement, you need to write only one check (or make one online transaction) to pay the bill.

Some credit card companies categorize your purchases and send out quarterly or year-end summaries showing how much you spent in each category. This service can help you determine whether you are staying within your budget for various items.

Figure 13.1 SAMPLE CREDIT CARD STATEMENT

ACCOUNT NUMBER	NAME	STATEMENT DATE	PAYMENT DUE DATE
1234-000-321	John Doe	2/13/09	3/09/09
CREDIT LINE	**CREDIT AVAILABLE**	**NEW BALANCE**	**MINIMUM PAYMENT DUE**
$1200.00	$1074.76	$125.24	$20.00

REFERENCE	SOLD	POSTED	ACTIVITY SINCE LAST STATEMENT		AMOUNT
483GE7382		1/25	PAYMENT THANK YOU		-168.80
32F349ER3	1/12	1/15	RECORD RECYCLER	ANYTOWN USA	12.83
89102DIS2	1/13	1/15	BEEFORAMA REST	ANYTOWN USA	30.55
NX34FJD32	1/18	1/18	GREAT EXPECTORATIONS	BIG CITY USA	27.50
84RT3293A	1/20	1/21	DINO-GEL PETROLEUM	ANYTOWN USA	12.26
873DWS321	2/09	2/09	SHIRTS 'N SUCH	TINYVILLE USA	40.10

Forced Savings

Some people never seem able to save enough money for expensive items. For them, buying on credit is actually a kind of forced savings program. If they did not have to make payments on their major purchases, they might otherwise fritter away their money on lots of small, unimportant things.

However, it is important to note that credit used in this way is very costly. You are paying interest or finance charges in addition to the cost of the

Going Global

When Jacquelyn Tran graduated from college in 1999, she had the idea of starting a perfume business on the Web. Her parents already had a perfume business in California, but Tran recognized the global potential of the Internet. Even though Web marketing was still a new idea then, her parents loaned her $50,000 to start, and Perfume Bay was born.

The company offers more than 800 fragrances, including rare and difficult-to-find European perfumes. This benefits global sales—but shipping perfume overseas is complicated. Postal authorities consider perfume to be a hazardous product, so it requires special handling, which is expensive.

The business has not suffered because Perfume Bay charges a flat rate for any size package. This encourages customers to buy more items at one time.

Because the business has grown, Perfume Bay now ships to thirty different countries. Sales doubled between 2002 and 2005—to $9 million.

Thinking Globally

1. Would a global mail order business be practical without the use of credit cards? Explain your answer.
2. How would having a credit card influence your decision about how much perfume to buy, if the shipping charge is the same for any size order?

goods purchased. You are also losing the interest earnings that you would be getting in a true savings program.

Disadvantages of Credit

Because credit is useful, you might think that you should use it often. However, there are some disadvantages as well. Be aware of these drawbacks and avoid financial problems.

grace period a period of time, usually twenty to thirty days, when interest is not charged on current credit card purchases

universal default a provision in some credit card contracts that allows the company to review its customers' credit reports and charge a higher default interest rate if a customer's credit score goes down for any reason

Interest Charges and Fees

The primary disadvantage of using credit is the cost. If you pay your credit card bills in full each month, you will get a break of twenty to thirty days when the company does not charge interest on your purchases. This is called the **grace period**, or *free period*. However, if you do not pay the bill in full, you will be charged interest on the remaining amount. The interest is added to next month's bill. If you do not pay in full the following month, you will be charged interest not only on what's left of your original bill, but also on the interest charges from last month.

Some credit card companies have added (in fine print, of course) a provision called **universal default**, which gives them permission to change the terms of your agreement and charge a higher *default rate* under certain circumstances. Universal default allows the company to review your credit reports regularly—and if your credit score goes down for any reason, your interest rate goes up. Any of the following could increase the rate on your credit card:

- Late payments (even one) on a credit card, utility, or car payment
- Going over the limit on any credit card
- Carrying too much debt overall (their interpretation)
- Having too much available credit
- Too many credit inquiries
- Getting a new car loan

There are also other charges associated with using credit. These are discussed in Chapter 14.

Increased Impulse Buying

Sometimes credit purchases are too easy. Suppose you see something that you would like to have, but you do not have the cash to pay for it. If you can charge it and pay just a few dollars a month, you might not think about the total cost. You might end up buying things you really cannot afford.

You might also buy an item that you do not really need. Only later will you realize it was just a passing impulse. You might regret making the purchase, but it will be too late to return the item.

Bank deregulation in the 1980s made it easier for young people to obtain credit—but also made it more expensive. Nearly 70 percent of young adults aged 25–34 now have credit cards. Compared to people in other age groups, young adults pay less of their balance each month, paying more interest as a result. Consider these facts:

- Between 1992 and 2001, average credit card debt among the 25–34 age group rose by 55 percent—to almost $4,100. Households in this age range spent almost 24 percent of their income on debt payments.
- For younger Americans aged 18–24, the average level of debt was lower, at $2,985—but that average had more than doubled since 1992. This group spent an average of 30 percent of income paying off debt.
- Some 83 percent of college students had credit cards, with college seniors owing an average of $3,262.

It's much easier to get credit than to use it wisely. If misused, it can have long-lasting negative effects.

YOU DECIDE

One Saturday in September, Alicia sees a gorgeous red silk dress at the mall—it will be perfect for holiday parties! She's short of cash, but the dress is at a department store where Alicia has a revolving credit account. She spent $150 on clothes there before school started, but does not have to pay the full amount before she buys more.

If Alicia buys the red dress now, her balance will be up to $300. Her minimum payment will go up to $30. That won't be easy for her to come up with—but she knows the dress will look great on her, once she loses 10 pounds. If she gives up fast food and exercises a little more, she can lose some weight and save money, too.

Alicia will need new shoes and an evening bag to go with the dress. But she thinks she can probably convince her parents to help pay for those. Holiday dresses always go on sale in November—but she is sure it will be gone by then.

Should she . . .

1. ...wait to buy the dress until after she pays off her credit balance at the store? How would that benefit her?
2. ...buy the dress and count on losing the 10 pounds? What if she cannot lose the weight?
3. ...buy the dress now? Give reasons for your answer.

Financial Problems

A lot of people do not know how to set up a spending plan. Others are not willing to follow a plan. When they run out of cash, they start charging everything they buy and become overextended with credit debt.

People are constantly urged to buy now and pay later. This allows for immediate gratification. Many folks, particularly young adults, seem compelled to borrow in order to satisfy their wants. Some spend everything they earn and use all the credit they are allowed. This lack of discipline in the use of credit can cause financial problems. The interest on your credit payments eats up your hard-earned dollars. Overextended credit could lead to repossession of your car, foreclosure on your home, or even bankruptcy.

Bankruptcy is a legal process in which a *debtor* (a person who owes money) declares the inability to repay debts over a reasonable period of time. It is a drastic move and should be used only when there is no other way out of financial ruin.

Bankruptcy can help some people make a fresh start by canceling or refinancing debts, but there are consequences. When businesses lose money through their debtors' bankruptcies, they pass the cost along to other customers. That means everyone pays the cost of bankruptcies—in the form of higher prices for goods and services, and lower returns on savings. This topic is discussed more fully in Chapter 14.

Credit Fraud and Identity Theft

Credit fraud is the theft and illegal use of someone else's credit information. It usually involves purchasing goods and charging them to someone else. Credit thieves can get your credit information by using lost or stolen credit cards, stealing from your mailbox, going

bankruptcy a legal process in which a person or business declares the inability to repay debts

credit fraud the theft and illegal use of someone else's credit information

through your trash, making a fake phone solicitation—even by looking over your shoulder.

One type of credit fraud is **identity theft**. Identity theft occurs when someone gathers enough personal and financial information about you to assume your identity—and then uses your identity to commit fraud or other crimes. The thief might steal money from your bank account, charge large amounts to your credit card, or even buy property or get a loan in your name. In a 2006 case in Texas, someone stole another man's identity—and had major surgery. The innocent victim received a hospital bill for $44,000. It took a year before he could straighten out his finances and reestablish credit.

Safeguarding Your Information

What can you do to protect yourself? First and foremost, be careful about giving out personal information. Here are some actions that will help keep your identity your own:

identity theft the act of gathering enough information about a person to assume his or her identity, and then using that identity to commit fraud or other crimes

- Don't give your Social Security number to anyone unless it is absolutely necessary. You have to give your number to your employer, your bank, and other places that report your income for tax purposes. Most places have no right to your number.
- Do not deal with a company or person you don't know who calls you on the phone or sends you an e-mail message. Do not provide your personal information over the phone or by e-mail to anyone, even if they claim to be from your bank, credit card company, or some other institution you do business with. Instead, contact the company directly by phone or e-mail—but *not* by using a phone number provided by the caller or a link embedded in the e-mail. These could be fake.
- Remove mail from your mailbox as quickly as possible. If your mailbox is far from your home, get one that requires a key.
- Carefully examine all bills that come in the mail. Thieves mimic your real bill by including most of your information and a fake logo on a false bill and then ask you to send them a payment. They even include a return envelope.
- Use a shredder to cut up all of your personal documents, including old billing statements that you no longer wish to keep. Shred any new credit card applications you will not use.
- Never let anyone look over your shoulder when you are using a credit, debit, or ATM card.
- Always keep your wallet in a buttoned or inside pocket, or in your purse.
- Keep all receipts and check them against your credit card statements. Look for purchases you did not make.

▶ **Protect your identity by shredding all of your personal documents that you do not keep.**

You may take all these precautions and still have your personal information stolen. Some people buy identity theft insurance. Some home insurance policies include identity theft protection; if yours does not, adding such protection to the policy may be less expensive than buying separate identity theft insurance.

Monitoring Your Credit History

Another way to protect yourself against identity theft is to obtain your credit report and monitor your credit history. The *only* authorized online source for free credit reports under federal law is AnnualCreditReport.com (http://fin.emcp.net/annualcreditreport). You can also get one by calling the Annual Credit Report Request Service, toll-free at 877-322-8228. Figure 13.2 shows a sample page from a credit report.

Figure 13.2 SAMPLE PAGE FROM A CREDIT REPORT

Personal Information Since 11/1/86 FAD 5/22/01		
		Reported
Name	CONNORS, MICHAEL A	
SSN	201-10-1222	
Address	41 N, OAK DR, COLUMBIA, SC, 55679	8/1/98
Address	424 MAIN ST, LANCASTER, SC, 55724	11/1/95
Address	315 PINE ST, STATESVILLE, NC, 55857	
Phone	(679) 555-1247 Personal	

Add-On Products Summary

Product: HAWK
Status: Requested product delivered
Search: Available and Clear

Credit Summary From 11/1/86 To 5/22/01

Public Records	3	Collections	4	Negative Trades	1
Hist Neg Trades	0	# Trades	1	Revolving	0
Hist Neg Occurr	0	Installment	0	Mortgage	0
Open Trades	1	Inquiries	3		

Type	High	Limit	Balance	Past Due	Payment	%Avail
Closed	$0	$0	$202	$202	$0	—
Totals	$0	$0	$202	$202	$0	—

Public Records

Reported/ Amount	ECOA/ Subscriber	Assets	Type/Plaintiff/ Attorney	Docket/ Paid	Court/ City, State
05/95 984	C Z 0573214		Civil judgement Pltff: BUDGET OIL CO	95CVM11X	Superior Court
			Attn: VQM P1		
03/98	I Z 0621593		Chapter 7 bankruptcy discharged	9802PN6 05/99	Federal District
08/98 1903	I Z 0146321		Civil judgement Pltff: PETER PARKER	21BD7	Common Pleas

Collection Accounts

Firm/ID Code	Paid/ ECOA	Placed/ CLSD	VRFD/CS (MOP)	$PLCD/ BAL	Acc#	Creditor Name	Remarks
ATTN L.L.C. Y 01246591	I	05/99	05/00A O9B	83 83	8821	COMMON CARE MEDICAL CENT	Placed for collection
CREDBURSYS Y 08857661	I	09/98	03/00A O9B	216 216	2244871223	REGIONAL HOSPITAL	Placed for collection
CREDBURSYS Y 08857661	I	02/98	03/00A O9B	201 201	8256234780	REGIONAL HOSPITAL	Placed for collection
CAP RCV SVC Y 0667724	I	07/94	07/96A O9B	57 57	2239	FOOT CLINIC	Placed for collection

Figure 13.3 **WARNING SIGNS THAT SOMEONE IS USING YOUR CREDIT INFORMATION**

- You are receiving credit cards that you have not applied for.
- You have been denied credit or have been offered less favorable credit terms, such as a high rate of interest, for no apparent reason.
- You have not received bills or other mail for a while. A missing bill could mean that an identity thief has taken over your account and changed your billing address to cover his or her tracks.
- You are getting calls or letters from debt collectors or businesses about goods or services that you did not buy.

Once you get your report, review it carefully. Look for inquiries from companies you did not contact, accounts you did not open, and debts on your accounts that you cannot explain. Check to be sure all your personal information is correct—including your name, Social Security number, address, and employers' names. Figure 13.3 presents warning signs that someone is using your credit information.

If you find fraudulent or inaccurate information, get it removed as soon as possible. Under the Fair Credit Reporting Act (FCRA), both you and the business that sent incorrect information to the credit bureau (such as a bank or credit card company) are responsible for correcting the information on your report.

You must contact both the credit bureau and the information provider *in writing*. The information provider is required by law to investigate your complaint and report its findings to the credit bureau. If your credit information was indeed inaccurate, the provider must notify all nationwide credit bureaus to correct your file. If the investigation does not resolve your dispute, your statement about the inaccuracy must be included in your file.

▶ If you are a victim of identity theft, notify the authorities right away.

Reporting Fraud and Identity Theft

If it seems clear that you have become a victim of credit fraud or identity theft, report the crime immediately and take action to prevent further damage to your finances and your reputation. Keep a record of all conversations, dates, names, and phone numbers. Record the time and cost of all the work you do to clear your name. Following are some actions that you should take to protect yourself.

Notify the Authorities Contact at least one of the three national credit bureaus (Equifax, Experian, or TransUnion). Tell them that you believe you are an identity theft victim. (When you notify one bureau, it will notify the other two.) Ask that a *fraud alert* be placed on your credit file. Also ask for a *security freeze.* A security freeze locks access to your credit report and credit score until you instruct the credit bureau to unfreeze your report. To see if your state allows a security freeze, check the Consumers Union Guide to Security Freeze Protection at http://fin.emcp.net/freeze.

Of course you should also report the crime to your local police or sheriff. Report the crime to the Federal Trade Commission (FTC) as well. The FTC serves as a federal clearinghouse for identity theft information.

Notify Your Creditors If your credit report lists new accounts in your name—accounts that you did not open—notify those creditors immediately by phone and in writing.

If your current credit, debit, or ATM cards were stolen or used fraudulently, immediately report this crime by phone and in writing to the card company. Request new cards with new account numbers. If your checks were stolen or if bank accounts were set up fraudulently in your name, instruct your bank to report it to Chex Systems. Chex Systems is a network of financial institutions that report on mishandled checking and savings accounts.

Other Precautions If you suspect that someone changed your address with the U.S. Postal Service, notify the local postal inspector. If you suspect that an imposter has opened a cell phone account in your name, contact the company immediately. If someone has obtained a student loan in your name, report it in writing to the school where the loan was opened. If someone is using your driver's license number for identification on bad checks, call the Department of Motor Vehicles (DMV) in your state to see if another driver's license was issued in your name. You might have to get a new license number.

Do not pay any bill that is a result of fraud. It might later be considered an admission of guilt. Do not cover checks that were written fraudulently. Do not file for bankruptcy.

If debt collectors try to collect on the fraudulent accounts, tell them that you are a victim of fraud and are not responsible for the debts. Ask for the name of the person contacting you, the name of the collection company, the phone number, and the address. Also get the name, phone number, and address of the creditor, as well as the amount of the debt and dates of the purchases. Share this information with law enforcement authorities.

SECTION 1 ASSESSMENT

Factual Recall

1. How can using a credit card help you manage your finances?
2. If you go over your credit limit on one card, can your interest rate on another card go up? Explain your answer.
3. How can you get a free copy of your credit report?
4. If there is an unauthorized purchase on your credit card, should you pay it to avoid interest and fees? Explain your answer.

Critical Thinking

1. How might using a credit card save you money?
2. If you have a credit card, do you still need to save money for emergencies? Explain your answer.
3. Why should you shred unwanted credit card applications that are addressed to you, even though you have not filled them out?

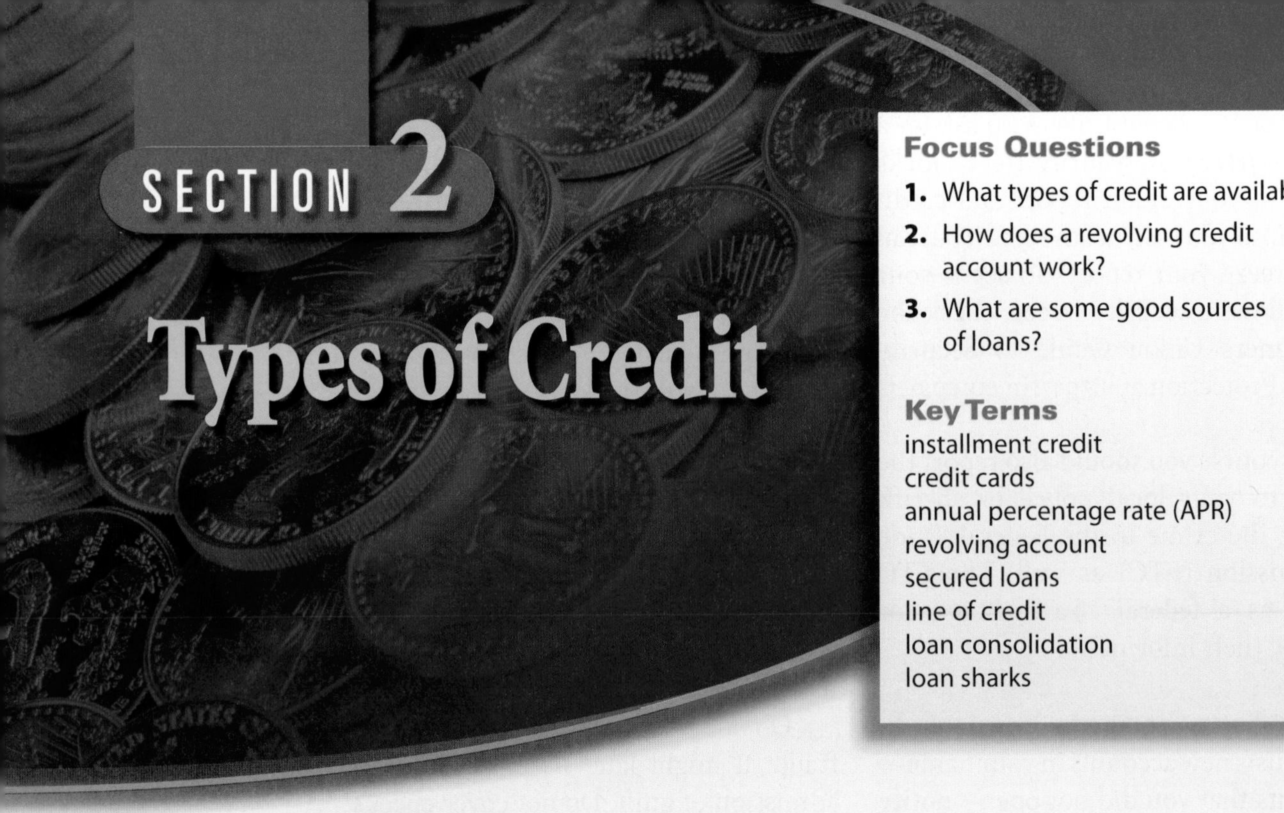

SECTION 2

Types of Credit

Focus Questions

1. What types of credit are available?
2. How does a revolving credit account work?
3. What are some good sources of loans?

Key Terms

installment credit
credit cards
annual percentage rate (APR)
revolving account
secured loans
line of credit
loan consolidation
loan sharks

Nearly everyone who lives in the United States will make use of consumer credit at some point. You, too, will use it for many of your future purchases. *Consumer credit* refers to credit extended for personal or household use, as opposed to business or commercial lending. You are probably already familiar with credit cards. You might not be as familiar with service credit and installment credit. And did you know that loans are also a form of credit?

▼ When you visit the dentist, you may not have to pay until the first of the next month.

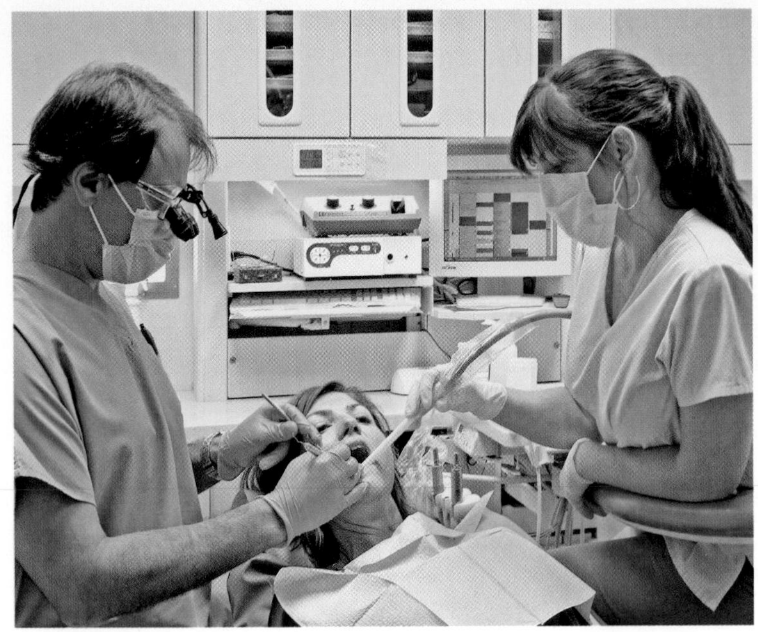

Short-Term Consumer Credit

Short-term credit usually refers to debts that are paid within one year, although the term might be longer. Short-term credit for consumers can take the form of service credit, installment credit, or credit cards.

Service Credit

Many people are using *service credit* without even knowing it. The most widely used service credit is for utilities such as electricity, gas, telephone, cable TV, water, and garbage collection. The service is provided before you pay for it. Each month, you receive a bill.

If you have a telephone, you can call a friend in another state or even another country and talk for hours, but you don't pay for the call until the next month. When you visit your dentist or doctor, you might be given credit until the first of the following month. In some areas, plumbers and appliance repairers perform their services and wait until the next month for payment. If the bills are paid on time, there is usually no interest charge for service credit.

Installment Credit

Installment credit is repaid in equal amounts over a set period of time. Many companies offer installment credit to customers who buy expensive items, such as a TV. Usually a down payment is required. A finance charge (interest) is added to the amount owed, and the total is divided by the number of weeks or months that payments will be made. The buyer signs a contract agreeing to make the payments on the due dates. With interest and added charges for credit checks and other costs, the buyer might end up paying more than double the original price of the item.

Installment credit allows you to use the goods while you are paying for them. Actual ownership remains with the seller, however, until you have paid the total amount. If you *default* (miss a payment), the seller can repossess the goods. Even if the seller repossesses the goods, you can still be required to keep up the payments.

How much can you safely buy on installment credit? That depends on many factors, including your personal values. Many financial advisers recommend that no more than twenty percent of your take-home pay should go for installment payments other than your mortgage (home loan). Some financial advisers include credit card debt in this twenty percent guideline.

This is a general guide. Some people spend as much as thirty percent—but such a large debt usually means they have to cut back on other expenses. You are the best judge of your own finances, but remember that large debts can leave you with no way to meet future needs or emergencies.

▲ **Using installment credit allows you to enjoy programs while paying for the TV. How might this lead to bad habits?**

Credit Cards

It seems like everyone has a credit card. Reggie is a high school senior with a part-time job at a music store. He just got his first credit card, with a $500 spending limit. The first item he buys is a video game console for $215. When he gets his first billing statement, the minimum payment is $15. The interest rate is 18 percent. If he pays the $15, Reggie will owe $200 on the console plus $3 in interest after the first month. He likes the idea of having plenty of cash to spend during the month. The $3 interest on the remaining balance doesn't seem like much of a trade-off.

But wait. If he keeps paying the $15 minimum and makes *no other purchases* with his credit card, it will take more than a year to pay for the console—and he will have paid more than $45 in interest on top of the price. Also, because there is no grace period if he has a balance on his account, when he makes other pur-

installment credit a loan repaid with interest in equal amounts over a set period of time

LOOK Before You Leap

In Jeb's first semester at City College he received offers for six different credit cards in the mail. The credit limits ranged from $500 to $1,500. Jeb plans to go for the one with the highest limit.

Jeb's girlfriend, Larissa, asks him what the annual fees and interest rates are for each card. Jeb isn't sure—he is focused on the credit limit. They go through the card offers together, reading the fine print. They discover most of the cards have an annual fee of $50, and interest rates vary between 17 and 24 percent. Larissa suggests they go online to compare offers that other card companies are making to students. Card companies are eager to do business with college students, hoping they will remain loyal customers after they begin earning higher incomes.

Each major bank that offers credit cards has details on its Web site. There is also a site—CreditCards.com—where Jeb and Larissa can compare different credit cards, including those for college students. They learn that there are many cards with no annual fee for students who have good credit—but Jeb has no credit history at all, so he cannot qualify for those. Some offer rebate awards on certain kinds of purchases. Maybe he can get one of those.

Finally Jeb identifies a card with very good terms, and he can qualify for it. The credit line is $1,000 to start, the annual fee $35, and the interest rate 16 percent.

Before Applying

1. Jeb goes to the home page of the company issuing the card. He reads through the application form. What other features should he check out before applying for the card?
2. If you have received credit card offers in the mail, compare those rates and incentives with cards offered by the banks in your area. Are the direct-mail offers as good as they seemed at first, or does the bank offer a better rate?

chases with his card he will owe interest on the cost of those items from the day he buys them. However, if Reggie pays as much as $60 a month, he will still have enough left from his paycheck for car expenses and a few evenings out—and he will pay off the console in just four months. More importantly, he will pay only $6.50 in interest.

Reggie decides to be a smart money manager and pay off the game console quickly. Credit cards allow you to increase your buying power, but the interest rates are often more than you might think. You have to use these tools wisely.

credit cards plastic cards issued by banks, retail stores, and other businesses that allow the user to buy products or services on credit, with an interest charge if the balance is not paid in full by the due date

Using Credit Cards Sometimes called "plastic money," **credit cards** are probably the most convenient way to make purchases. They are issued by banks, retail stores, or other businesses and allow you to buy gasoline, clothing, food, airline tickets—in fact, almost anything—and pay for it later. If you do not pay the balance in full by the due date, however, you will be charged interest.

Cards issued by retail chains or oil companies may be usable only at those businesses. All-purpose cards—such as Visa, MasterCard, and Discover—can be used at thousands of places. Sellers of goods and services accept credit cards because they know it will increase their sales. Consumers with credit cards tend to buy on impulse more than those who pay with cash.

Credit Card Rates Before you apply for a credit card, be sure you understand the terms and conditions. Find out the **annual percentage rate (APR)**, which is the amount of interest expressed as a yearly rate. For instance, if a credit card company advertises an interest rate of "only" 1½ percent a month, you would multiply the monthly rate by 12 months —and find the APR is actually 18 percent a year.

There are other things you need to know. Will that rate change after a few months? What is the grace period? If there is no grace period, finance charges begin on the day you make a purchase, even if you pay the bill in full when you receive your statement. What fees might be charged? Are there rewards programs?

Credit cards are a form of *revolving debt*. With a **revolving account**, you do not have to pay in full each month. As long as you make the minimum payment, you can keep charging items. There is a dollar limit, however, on how much you can charge. That limit is set by the store or company that issues the card, based on your income and credit record. And of course you are charged interest on the unpaid balance, as illustrated in the earlier example of Reggie and the video game console.

If you continue adding to your revolving account—making purchases each month but never quite paying the balance in full—the interest charges will go up as your balance goes up. You are paying interest on interest.

Electronic credit systems can use radio waves to provide a quick way to gas up your car. ExxonMobil calls it the Speedpass. Similar to the electronic toll technology used for subways, buses, and highway systems, it is a key tag with a built-in computer chip and a radio frequency antenna that communicates with the gas pump. You simply wave the tag in front of a reader on the pump, and it transmits a code into the computerized payment system. The computer locates your credit account, and the gasoline you buy is immediately charged to the credit or debit card linked to your Speedpass account.

Charge Cards Charge cards are similar to credit cards because they allow users to charge purchases—but the full balance must be paid each month. Because no balance is carried over to the next month, there are no interest charges. However, many charge cards require an annual fee. In fact, some cards cost hundreds of dollars per year in fees—but they offer benefits such as free upgrades for airline travel or hotel rooms. In the past, many department stores and other

annual percentage rate (APR) the amount of interest expressed as a yearly rate

revolving account a charge account that has a credit limit but does not have to be paid in full before the borrower can make further purchases

▼ Choose the credit card with the lowest interest rate.

merchants issued charge cards, but most of these retailers now favor revolving credit accounts.

Diners Club and American Express are two well-known issuers of charge cards. A good credit rating and higher than average income are required to obtain these cards.

Safeguarding Your Cards

If you have any credit card or charge card accounts, there is always the possibility that an unauthorized person may obtain your card or your card numbers. To protect your cards, follow these tips:

- Sign your cards as soon as you get them.
- Carry only one or two cards.
- Photocopy both sides of all of your cards, and keep the copies in a safe place.
- Keep your eye on your card during transactions and get it back as soon as possible.
- Do not let anyone borrow your card.
- Cut up expired or canceled cards.
- Do not give your card numbers and expiration dates over the phone to unfamiliar people or businesses.
- Keep sales and card receipts and check them against your statements.

If one of your cards is lost or stolen, immediately call the bank or company that issued it. Give the number of the card and when it was lost or stolen. Then write a letter confirming your phone call—again providing the card number and the date it was lost or stolen. Make a copy of the letter for yourself, and send the original by certified mail. Keep the receipt that you get at the post office—it has an "article number" that will allow you to go online and verify delivery.

If you do this immediately, you will not be charged more than $50 for goods charged to your card by someone else. The bank or company that issued your card will notify stores not to accept that card and will send you a new one.

▼ Debit cards, gift cards, and prepaid cards are other types of credit.

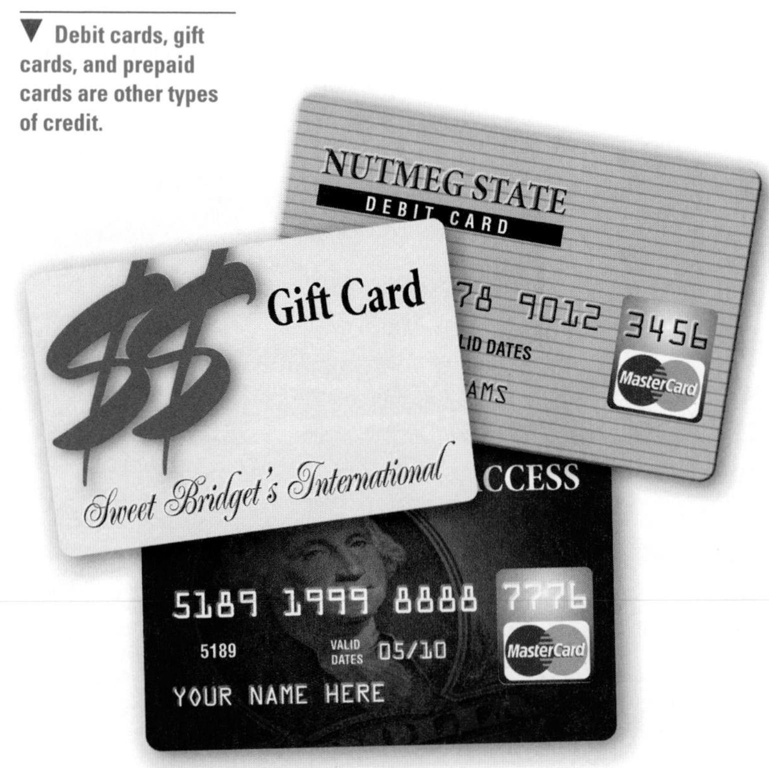

When Is a Credit Card Not a Credit Card?

Credit cards are not the only kind of plastic money. Three others are debit cards, prepaid cards, and gift cards.

Debit Cards *Debit cards* look like credit cards, but they do not allow you to buy on credit. They are a substitute for writing checks. (In fact, they are sometimes called *check cards* or *cash cards.*) When you use a debit card, the amount of the purchase is immediately deducted from your checking account.

Merchants like debit cards because they do not have to risk a possible bad check. They also know that customers typically buy more than they would if paying with cash. Surveys have indicated that customers spend as much as fifty percent more when using a debit card than when they pay with cash.

Do Your RESEARCH

Online banking and credit are becoming commonplace. You can open an account, apply for either credit or a loan, and manage your credit account—all from your computer, without leaving the comfort of home.

You can have an account at a traditional bank that has online services in addition to its bricks-and-mortar locations around town—or at a Web-only bank. You can apply online at either type of bank for a credit card or a loan. Two full-service Web banks are First Internet Bank (http://fin.emcp.net/firstib) and ING Direct (http://fin.emcp.net/ingdirect).

You can also apply online for credit from credit card companies, consumer finance companies, and mortgage brokers. Among the largest U.S. credit card issuers are Citibank (http://fin.emcp.net/citicard), Capital One (http://fin.emcp.net/capitalone), and Discover (http://fin.emcp.net/discovercard).

Most MasterCard, Discover, Visa, and other major credit card accounts can be managed online. Check your current balance, track your purchases, and make payments by direct debit from your bank account. If you want, you can even set up an automatic monthly payment schedule—so you do not have to write checks and mail payments to the card company.

Your Assignment

1. Go to the site of a Web-only bank and check out its loan rates. Compare them with the rates at your local bank. If there is a difference, what do you think accounts for it?
2. The rates that borrowers pay on Web-only bank credit cards are comparable to other banks and card companies. Why do you think online credit card services do not offer lower interest rates than land-based banks?

Prepaid Cards A *prepaid card* is sometimes called a *prepaid credit card*, but it works much like a debit card. You begin by depositing money into an account. You can then use your card to make purchases. However, your limit will be the amount in your account.

You can increase your limit by adding money to the account. You receive no interest charges or bills. However, there usually are fees to set up the account, make a deposit, or conduct other transactions. There might even be an "inactivity fee" for *not* using the card within a certain time limit.

Gift Cards A *gift card* is also prepaid. Many retail stores offer gift cards. So do restaurants, shopping malls, and even gas stations. They also are offered by credit card companies like Visa and MasterCard. You purchase the card for a specific amount, say \$25 or \$50. The person who receives the card can use it to pay for merchandise.

Many people never use up the entire amount of their gift cards. Some states now require merchants to refund small amounts of unused gift card money to the customer.

Loans

A loan is anything that is provided for temporary use. Borrowing a library book is a type of loan. If someone borrows a DVD from you, that is a loan. In financial terms, a loan is money. As with the library book and the DVD, loans of money have to be returned. Unlike the community library or your own generous self, those who provide money loans charge interest.

Types of Loans

Loans may be secured or unsecured. **Secured loans** are backed by collateral. Recall from Chapter 10 that *collateral* is a valuable asset that a borrower must give up if he or she does not repay a loan. The collateral for a secured loan is usually whatever the loan money was used to purchase—for example, a car or a house. If the loan is not repaid, the lender keeps the collateral.

Unsecured loans are not backed up by collateral. This does not mean that you don't risk losing anything with an unsecured loan. If you cannot repay the loan, the lender can have money taken from your wages. You can also lose your good credit rating—or even go bankrupt.

secured loans loans that are backed up by collateral

Loans can be short-term or long-term. The *term* of a loan refers to the amount of time you have to repay it. Most are repaid in equal amounts at regular intervals over a specified length of time. Loans that have to be repaid in less than one year are considered short-term loans. (Short-term loans are a form of installment credit.) Loans with longer repayment times are long-term loans.

Some people take out a loan to purchase a specific item, such as a car or a house. Other loans can be used for anything the borrower wants.

Personal Loans Personal loans are usually unsecured and are used for personal use—something like a vacation, a new computer, or debt consolidation. They can be either short-term or long-term. For big-ticket items like a TV or furniture, it might be cheaper to get a loan and pay cash than it would be to buy on credit and make installment payments to the retailer. You can often get a cash loan at a lower interest rate than installment credit.

Auto Loans Auto loans are available from banks, S&Ls, credit unions, finance companies, and sometimes from a dealership itself. Gather information about

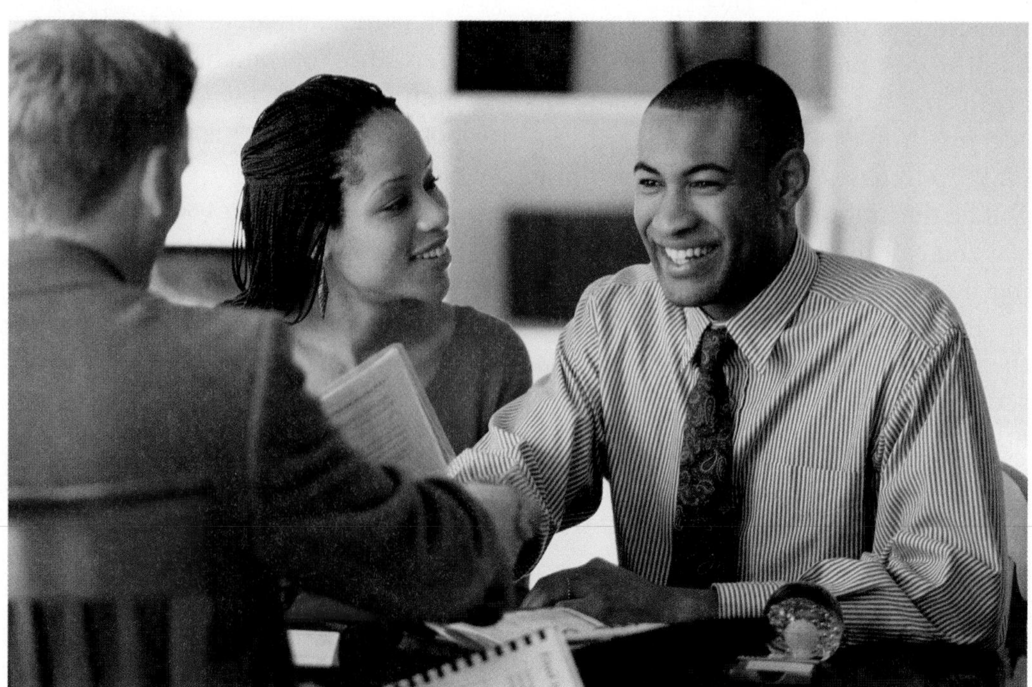

▶ **Getting a personal loan is often cheaper than making installment payments to a retailer.**

LOOK Before You Leap

"No credit? No job? No problem!" Mio and Paul were surprised when the man at the door offered to install new siding on their house and even arrange a home equity loan to finance it. Their credit wasn't so good since Paul was laid off, but they had built up quite a bit of equity in the house—only a few more years and it would be paid for. They needed new siding and were tempted to sign the contract. The interest rate sounded good, and they knew a home equity loan can be a smart use of credit.

First they talked it over with their neighbor, Liz. Schemes like these were familiar to Liz, who warned her friends, "You sign a contract for the siding, and later he returns with loan documents you have to sign in order for work to continue. He probably wasn't fully truthful about the interest rates, either. Maybe the loan was secured by the equity in your home. Soon, the work slows to a halt. But if you stop paying, the lender can take possession of your house!"

Liz suggested that they get advice from a nonprofit consumer credit counseling agency. Paul and Mio learned that they were misled. They decided not to take out the loan or do any work on the house right now, but to wait until Paul was working full-time again.

Before Borrowing

1. Always be suspicious of loan offers that quote very low interest rates and do not seem to care about your credit. How can Mio and Paul select a reputable lender when they are ready to take out a home equity loan?

various loan options and make careful comparisons before buying a car. Some dealers advertise "0%" auto loans. Being able to pay for a car in installments without paying interest might sound pretty good. But do your research: These loans usually require large down payments —as much as twenty to thirty percent— and must be paid off more quickly than conventional car loans. That means your monthly payments will be high. You might be better off with a conventional auto loan.

Auto loans are secured loans. Remember from Chapter 9 that if you do not repay, the car will be repossessed.

Student Loans Student loans are made to help pay for education beyond high school. They are available through the federal government and from private sources. Student loans are unsecured; you do not need to provide collateral. However, you do have a legal obligation to repay the loan after graduation. More information about student loans can be found in Chapter 6.

Home Loans Many years or even a lifetime would be required for most people to save enough money to pay cash for a home. Instead, people who buy homes usually obtain a *mortgage* (a secured loan with the home as collateral). They usually make a down payment of ten to twenty-five percent of the selling price and arrange for a long-term loan to cover the balance.

Buying a home might be the most expensive purchase in your life. Make

line of credit an approved loan amount that can be used at the borrower's discretion

loan consolidation combining two or more existing loans into a single new loan, usually to reduce monthly payments or obtain a lower interest rate

sure you do a careful analysis of your long-term goals and your ability to pay.

Generally, you are well advised to borrow no more than two to three times your total yearly income for the purchase of a home. In recent years, many people have borrowed up to five times their yearly income—but they have had to cut back severely on other costs of living. Another rule of thumb for purchasing a home is that your monthly mortgage payment should not be more than twenty-five percent of your monthly income. Details about obtaining a home loan are covered in Chapter 10.

Home Equity Loans After you have owned a home for several years, its market value will probably be more than the amount you still owe on the mortgage. Recall from Chapter 10 that this difference is called *equity.* Homeowners can obtain cash by getting a *home equity loan* or a *home equity line of credit.*

A **line of credit** is a preapproved loan amount that you can use anytime you want, for any purpose. It is a form of revolving credit, with a variable interest rate and no set term. Like a credit card account, it can go on indefinitely.

As an example, if you had built up at least $50,000 worth of equity in your house, you could get a $50,000 home equity line of credit. You would have up to $50,000 available to use whenever you need it. You could draw funds for home improvements, medical bills, a vacation, college tuition—anything. The bank would charge interest only on the amount you use, not the entire $50,000. Your monthly payments would be whatever you wanted to pay, as long as you paid the minimum each month.

A home equity loan, on the other hand, has a fixed rate of interest, fixed payments, and a fixed term, usually five to fifteen years. For both of these types of loans, your house would serve as collateral.

▼ When applying for a home equity loan, speak with a banking professional who will explain your options.

Consolidation Loans Some people are burdened with numerous credit card bills, auto loans, student loans, and other consumer debts. The interest on these loans can be staggering. If your credit becomes overextended, one solution is **loan consolidation**—combining all the existing loans into a single new loan. You use the money from the consolidation loan to pay off the other debts.

A consolidation loan can reduce monthly payments, offer a lower interest rate, and provide the simplicity of a single loan. On the other hand, loan consolidation will lengthen your repayment period, so it greatly increases the amount of interest you pay in the long run. There is another drawback as well. Once the pressure of unpaid bills is lifted, there is a temptation to go shopping! Debt begins to pile up again, and you might find yourself in a deeper hole than before. A better idea is to use credit wisely and avoid becoming overextended in the first place.

Sources of Loans

Where can you go for a loan? The best sources include banks, credit unions, S&Ls, and consumer finance companies.

Banks Obtaining a bank loan is not as simple as just asking for money. First you must complete an application form, and then the bank checks your credit history. If you can qualify, banks are good sources for loans. They often charge a lower interest rate than many other sources because they loan only to applicants with good credit records.

Most bank loans require collateral, but not always. If you obtain a loan to buy a car, you will almost surely have to pledge the car as collateral. As discussed in Chapter 9, you might also need someone to cosign the loan—particularly if you are under the legal age limit or have not yet established a credit history. Banks also tend to give preference to their own customers.

Credit Unions To borrow from a credit union, you must be a member. If you do belong to a credit union, that is probably the best source of a loan. As you learned in Chapter 5, a credit union is a nonprofit financial institution owned and operated by its members, who share a common bond. They might be employees of the same company or members of the same organization.

Because the members are associated with one another, the cost of checking loan applicants' credit records is lower. Other costs can be lower, too, because the officers and committee members often serve without pay. For these reasons, it is often easy to get a loan at a credit union—and the interest rate is usually lower than you would pay elsewhere.

Credit unions usually require collateral for larger loans, but *signature loans* (unsecured loans) are often available for amounts under $3,000. By signing your name, you are promising to pay back the loan on time.

S&Ls The original purpose of savings and loan associations was to provide money for home loans. Now they make loans for other purposes as well. Regulations vary from state to state, but many S&Ls provide loans for education and for other personal reasons if your credit is good. If you have a savings account with an S&L, you can probably borrow an amount equal to your deposits. When you need cash for only a few weeks or months, this is sometimes less expensive than withdrawing the money from your savings account.

▲ Credit unions, banks, and other financial institutions offer low loan rates, especially if you have good credit.

Consumer Finance Companies Consumer finance companies were once called *small loan companies* because their loans were limited to $300. Now they can loan much larger amounts. These companies operate under state law, and the maximum amount they can loan varies from state to state. In California, for example, the amount is unlimited.

Consumer finance companies often make loans to people who cannot get a bank loan, and sometimes their loans are not repaid. Because of this, they charge a higher rate of interest than other lending agencies. The typical rate can range from eighteen percent to more than forty percent on amounts up to $5,000.

Did You Know?

Some lenders lie to their customers or fail to give them complete information. They charge unnecessary or excessively high fees, or pressure customers into taking high-risk, high-interest loans. These unfair or abusive practices are called *predatory lending.*

Federal and state laws protect you against some—but not all—forms of predatory lending. For example, lenders are allowed to charge people with low incomes higher interest rates because those people are more likely to default on their loans—that is, not to pay.

Laws cannot entirely protect you from predatory lenders. You must protect yourself. When looking for a loan, know your rights, shop around, and don't let anyone pressure you into making a quick decision. You can find more information about predatory lending at the Web site for the U.S. Department of Housing and Urban Development (http://fin.emcp.net/hud).

Loans to Avoid

Some people need to borrow money but do not believe a bank—or any of the other sources discussed—would loan the cash needed. Maybe their credit cards are maxed out. Maybe they have declared bankruptcy in the past. Whatever the reason, these people might seek out other loan sources that any finance counselor would definitely *not* recommend. Some of these sources are described below, so that you know what they are—and can avoid them.

Credit Card Cash Advances It is tempting to use your credit card to get a cash advance. You don't have to fill out any forms or wait for your money. However, these cash advances come at a high price. A fee is added to process the transaction. The interest rate will be higher than the rate you pay on regular credit purchases. With no grace period, interest charges begin as soon as you take the advance. Payments you make to your credit card account are applied first to purchases. No money will go toward repaying the cash advance until after you have paid off *all* the purchases. In the meantime, interest will continue to build up on that cash advance.

Payday Loans Recall from Chapter 5 that payday loans are small, short-term, high-interest loans. They sometimes go by other names, such as *cash*

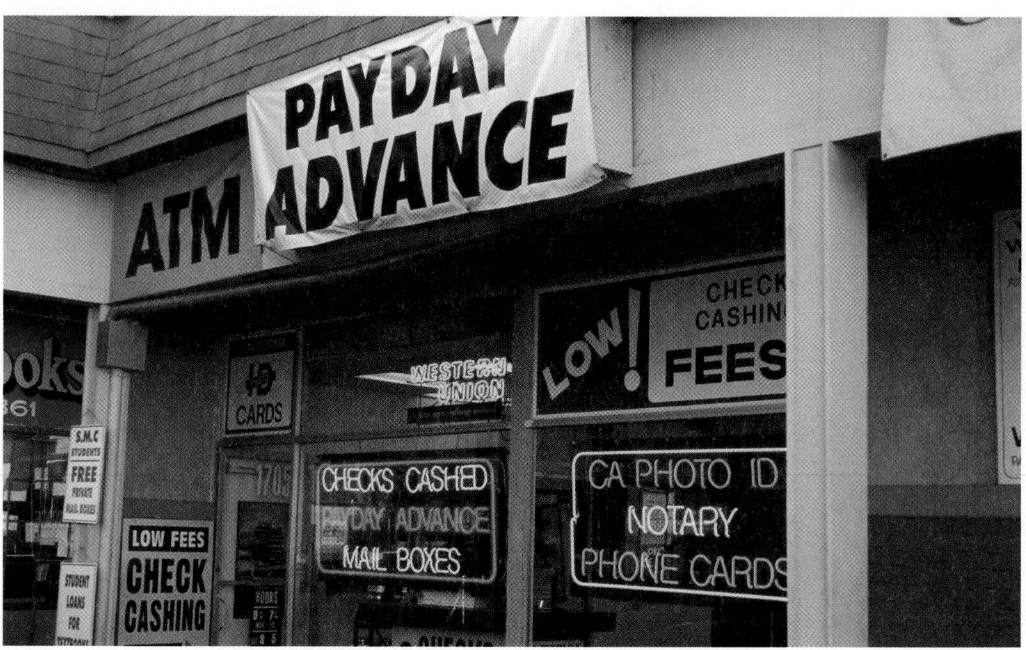

▶ Avoid taking out payday loans and do not borrow from pawnshops or loan sharks.

advance loans, check advance loans, post-dated check loans, or *deferred deposit check loans.* For an average payday loan of $300 for eight days, the fifteen percent interest rate actually comes out to an APR of 459 percent! Even a cash advance on a credit card would be much less expensive than a payday loan.

Refund Anticipation Loans You've probably seen commercials for "instant tax refunds." Tax preparation companies emphasize the convenience. You come to their office, they prepare your income tax return, and you walk out with your refund check in hand.

These "instant refunds" are actually *refund anticipation loans.* You are borrowing an amount equal to your tax refund, and you will end up using a large part of that refund to pay the high fees and interest rate on the loan. The APR on some of these loans is over 700 percent. Add the cost of the tax preparation and various fees, and you might get only $1,100 from a $2,000 refund.

Refund anticipation loans do not even save much time. If you file electronically and have the refund deposited directly into a bank account, you will usually receive your money in ten to fourteen days.

Remember, your tax refund is your own money. You should not have to pay someone else just so that you can have your money a few days earlier.

Pawnshops The cost of borrowing money from a pawnshop can be greater than almost any other source. You leave something of value, such as jewelry or a camera, as collateral. The amount of your loan will be much less than the item is worth—usually about one-third of its value, or even less. There is no application to fill out, few questions are asked, and you get the money immediately. If you repay the loan by the due date, the item you left as collateral will be returned. If not, the item will be sold, and the pawnbroker will keep the money. Interest rates on the loan are very high—often more than 100 percent APR. In addition, the pawnbroker will charge numerous fees for handling, appraisal, storage, insurance, and so on. You can see that this is not a smart way to borrow money.

Loan Sharks People who feel really desperate borrow money from loan sharks. This is a dangerous thing to do because **loan sharks** are people who loan money illegally. A state or federal license is required to operate a loan business legally.

Some states limit the amount of interest that can be charged—but loan sharks do not have licenses. They set their own interest rates, and the rates are very high. Paying back such a loan is difficult. Loan sharks usually stop at nothing to collect. They may threaten violence or actually use violence. Never borrow money from a loan shark!

Answers to Fact or Fiction

1. True; **2.** True; **3.** False—Under universal default provisions, a company can charge a higher rate if your credit score goes down for any reason; **4.** False—Credit reports can be obtained free of charge; **5.** False—If you report the theft promptly, you will not be charged more than $50; **6.** False—They look like credit cards, but they do not allow you to buy on credit; **7.** True; **8.** False—You are still responsible for repaying the loan.

loan sharks people who loan money illegally and set very high interest rates

SECTION 2 ASSESSMENT

Factual Recall

1. What is consumer credit?
2. What is service credit?
3. How do charge cards differ from credit cards?
4. How does using a debit card differ from using a credit card?
5. If you obtain a student loan from the government, are you required to repay it?

Critical Thinking

1. Your family is going to buy a new refrigerator. They could sign up for the store's installment plan or use their credit card. What factors should they consider when deciding how to pay for the refrigerator?
2. Is an auto loan a revolving debt? Explain your answer.

CHAPTER 13 REVIEW AND ASSESSMENT

Chapter Summary

Section 1 Advantages and Disadvantages of Credit

- Consumer credit has become an important part of the American economy, with almost everyone owing someone something.
- Advantages of using credit include improved standard of living, convenience, help in emergencies, help in record keeping, and forced savings.
- Some disadvantages of using credit are the interest charges and fees, increased impulse buying, and financial problems that can result from misuse.
- Identity thieves have many ways of stealing and using your personal information.

Section 2 Types of Credit

- Short-term consumer credit includes service credit, installment credit, and credit card accounts.
- Credit card accounts are one example of revolving credit.
- Debit cards look like credit cards, but they do not allow you to buy on credit. They automatically deduct the amount of the purchase from your bank account.
- A loan can be anything that is provided for temporary use. People get loans of money for many reasons, such as to pay for education, a car, or a home.
- Some sources of loans are banks, credit unions, S&Ls, and consumer finance companies.
- Some loan sources should be avoided because of high interest rates and fees. Examples of these are cash advances on your credit card, payday lenders, pawnshops, and loan sharks.

Reviewing Key Terms

Indicate whether each of the following statements (featuring key terms) is true or false. If a statement is false, rewrite it to make it true.

1. During a **grace period**, interest is not charged on credit card purchases.
2. Stealing from your mailbox is one way thieves obtain information to commit **credit fraud**.
3. The legal process in which a person or business declares the inability to repay debts is **universal default**.
4. With **installment credit**, you repay a loan in equal amounts over a set period of time.
5. If you have a **revolving account**, you can charge new purchases before you have finished paying for earlier purchases.
6. **Credit cards** are an example of **installment credit**.
7. Combining two or more existing loans into one loan is called making a **secured loan**.
8. The amount of interest expressed as a yearly rate is the annual **line of credit**.

Understanding the Main Ideas

1. How can using credit improve your standard of living?
2. What does it mean to "secure" a purchase with a credit card?
3. How can a grace period help you save money on credit card payments?
4. What are some ways that credit thieves can get your credit information?
5. Who has a right to know your Social Security number?
6. What is a security freeze?
7. If your credit card is lost or stolen, what do you need to do in order to limit your financial loss?
8. What is the difference between a secured loan and an unsecured loan? Name one example of each.
9. What is the difference between a home equity line of credit and a home equity loan?
10. Why are credit card cash advances not a good way to borrow money?

Practicing Math

1. Suppose you had a credit card balance of $1,000. The APR is 14 percent, and the minimum payment is 4 percent of the balance. Use an online credit payment calculator to answer

the following questions. One site with credit payment calculators is Bankrate.com (http://fin.emcp.net/bankrate).

   a. If you made only the minimum payment each month, how many months would it take to pay off the entire balance? How much would you pay in interest during that time?
   b. If you paid $60 per month, how many months would it take to become debt-free? How much interest would you pay?

2. Suppose you take a payday loan of $250. The finance charge is $15 for every $100 borrowed, and the term of the loan is two weeks. Use online calculators to find answers to the following questions. An online calculator for payday loans can be found at PayDay Loan Consumer Information (http://fin.emcp.net/payday). Other loan and credit card calculators can be found at Bankrate.com (http://fin.emcp.net/bankrate).
   a. What is the APR for the payday loan?
   b. How much interest will you pay for the two weeks?
   c. Many people get payday loan renewals. If you keep renewing the loan so that the actual term is 26 weeks (six months), how much interest will you pay?
   d. Instead of a payday loan, suppose you obtain a $250 cash advance on your credit card at an APR of 21 percent. If you take six months to repay, how much interest will you pay?
   e. Try a third alternative: a signature loan from your credit union. Suppose you borrow $3,000 for six months at 10 percent APR. How much interest will you pay on this loan?
3. Make a table comparing the cost of borrowing $1,000 for one year from a bank, credit union, S&L, and consumer finance company. If possible, use information from institutions in your community.

Applying Critical Thinking Skills

1. Many people with credit cards have trouble controlling their impulse to buy. What advice would you give them?
2. How might a stranger's bankruptcy affect you financially?
3. Someone calls you and says she is with your credit card company. She then reads a number—which is *not* your card number—and asks if that is correct. What should your response be?
4. Which sources are likely to charge the lowest interest rate for a loan?
5. How can people avoid having to borrow money from payday lenders, pawnshops, or loan sharks?

Working with Real-World Documents

1. Examine a credit card statement and answer the following questions. Some items might have different names from the ones listed here—for example, "Total Credit Line" rather than "Credit Limit."
   a. The statement shows the Minimum Payment Due. What percentage of the balance is this minimum payment?
   b. Look at the Credit Limit. Is it more or less than the Cash Advance Limit?
   c. Look at the Finance Charges. Is the APR the same for all categories—Purchases, Cash Advances, and Balance Transfers?
   d. Is there anything on the statement that tells you how long it will take to pay the balance if you make only minimum payments?
2. Look at the fine print on a gift card. Does the card have an expiration date? Are there limits on the ways you can use the card? For example, can it be used for in-store purchases but not for online purchases? What can you do if the card is lost or stolen?

Taking It Home

1. Check news sources for information about consumer fraud, such as online or telephone scams. Prepare a fact sheet to alert people to these scams and help them avoid being conned.
2. When using a debit card, you often have a choice of a PIN-based transaction or a signature-based transaction. Which do you and/or your family prefer, and why? Research this topic and write a report. What difference does the type of transaction make to the user? To the merchant? To the card issuer?

CHAPTER 14

Using Credit Wisely

Almost everyone uses some form of credit. You will probably need a loan to pay for a car, a house, or your college education. For everyday purchases, credit cards are convenient. Sometimes they are a necessity—as when you rent a car or make hotel reservations.

But credit can be a double-edged sword. It is easy to get into more debt than you can handle. A bad credit report can limit your opportunities.

Companies use credit reports to decide whether you will get a car loan, a mortgage, a rental apartment—and even a job offer. The best protection against crushing debt is to educate yourself in the wise use of credit.

▲ Too many credit cards? Keep one that has low interest, and then pay off and cancel the rest.

SECTION 1	Obtaining Credit
SECTION 2	Using Credit

Fact or Fiction

What do you think? Are the following statements true or false? If you think they are false, then say what is true.

1. When shopping for a loan, the most important thing to look for is low monthly payments.
2. For large loans, small changes in the interest rate make a big difference in the total amount paid.
3. When you sign a credit contract, you are agreeing with everything it says—whether you read it or not.
4. Credit bureaus obtain their consumer credit information from creditors such as banks, credit card companies, and other lenders.
5. All the major credit bureaus have the same information about your credit.
6. High-interest credit cards cause the biggest credit problem for young people just out of school or getting started in a career.

Answers on page 377.

Study Reminder

*Knowing how to study can increase your knowledge, improve your grades, and cut down on your study time. See the **Studying Personal Finance** pages at the front of the book for some tips to help you study this chapter.*

SECTION 1

Obtaining Credit

Focus Questions

1. When figuring the cost of credit, what four factors need to be considered?
2. How do credit card contracts differ from loan contracts?
3. What are four laws that protect the consumer in credit transactions?

Key Terms

principal	assets
finance charges	liabilities
appraisal	net worth
origination fee	credit bureau

When you take out a loan or apply for credit, you are assuming a big responsibility. To use credit wisely, you should understand the factors that determine its cost. You also need to know what credit contracts require. Finally, if you know how lenders decide to grant credit, you can start building your own good credit history.

Understanding Costs

Every type of credit costs something. These costs vary, depending on several factors: the source of the credit, how much you use, and how long you take to repay. The state of the economy plays a role too, of course. The economy affects interest rates.

Before you can compute the cost of credit, you have to know four things: (1) the amount you are borrowing (the principal), (2) how much time you will take to repay it, (3) the rate of interest, and (4) any fees and other charges. Then you can determine whether or not you want to make the purchase using credit.

principal the amount of money originally borrowed or still owed, on which interest is charged; also the amount of money deposited or invested, on which interest is credited

Principal

Obviously, you cannot compute the cost of credit without knowing how much you are borrowing. Recall that if you have a savings account, the amount of money you deposit in your account is known as the principal—and you earn interest on the principal. When you get a loan, the amount that you originally borrow or still owe is also called the **principal**—but this time you *pay* interest on the principal.

As you pay off a loan, the principal decreases. For example, suppose you borrow $12,000 to buy a car. As you make payments, part of each payment goes to pay interest on the loan, and the rest goes to paying off the principal.

Time

You might be tempted to spread credit payments over as much time as possible. When the repayment time is longer, your monthly payments are lower. However, taking longer to repay means that the total cost of your loan will be higher—usually *much* higher.

YOU DECIDE

Amber is buying her first car, a seven-year-old compact. Her mechanic checks it out and says it's in good shape. She wants to keep it for five years, until she finishes college and begins her career. She works part-time at a grocery store and will continue working while she attends college.

The price of the car is $6,000. Amber is making a down payment of $1,000. A local bank agrees to loan her the rest at 6 percent. The loan officer at the bank tells her that she can repay the loan over three, four, or five years. The difference in monthly payments is significant—she would pay $97 a month over five years, $117 over four years, or $152 over three years.

If Amber decides to pay off the car in three years, the total interest over the life of the loan will be about $475. If she pays the car off in five years, the total interest will be about $800—$325 more. But the $325 difference doesn't bother her—it will be spread out over several years, and she thinks it's worth it for the lower monthly payment.

She is debating between the four-year and five-year terms. Monthly payments are $117 versus $97. She can afford the $117 on a four-year loan, but she would rather have another $20 in her pocket every month. Still, the fact that she won't completely own the car for five years—until she's ready to sell it—bothers her.

The loan officer tells Amber that there is no prepayment penalty on the loan. If she signs up for the five-year plan, she can pay it off sooner if she wants.

Should she . . .

1. ...sign up for the four-year or the five-year loan? Why do you think the loan officer encourages Amber to sign up for the longest term loan? Give reasons for your answers.
2. ...take the five-year term and pay off the remaining balance of $1,123 after four years? She will save $37 in interest. Do you think that's a good idea? Why or why not?

Suppose you have a credit card balance of $500, at a yearly interest rate of 18 percent. If you make monthly payments of about $90 (including interest), you can pay off the entire amount in six months (assuming no new purchases). The total amount you pay for interest will be about $27. Or, you can have lower monthly payments by taking twenty-four months to pay off the balance. Your payments will be about $25 a month, but you will end up paying almost $100 in interest.

When you borrow large amounts of money, as for a car or a home, taking more time for repayment is even more expensive. For example, if you repay a 6 percent $200,000 loan in fifteen years, you will pay about $103,800 in interest. If you borrow $200,000 at the same rate and repay it over thirty years, your total interest will be about $231,650. You will save $127,850 by paying off the loan in fifteen years instead of thirty. You can save a great deal of money by taking a shorter term whenever possible.

Interest Rates

Another factor in the cost of credit is the interest rate. During the ten-year period ending in 2006, interest rates that banks charge for car loans went from a high of about 10 percent down to about 6 percent. On a five-year $10,000 loan, a change in the interest rate from

10 percent to 6 percent will lower the total cost of the loan by about $1,148.

On larger loans that are repaid over a longer time, small changes in the interest rate make a big difference. For example, on a thirty-year home loan of $200,000, if the interest rate goes from 6 percent to 8 percent, the total cost *for interest* will increase by $96,634—from $231,676 at 6 percent to $328,310 at 8 percent. If the rate on the same loan goes up from 6 percent to 10 percent, the cost for interest would be $431,851, or $200,175 *more* than at 6 percent.

Fees and Other Charges

Finance charges are the costs you pay for credit. Interest is one finance charge, but there are others. You might be asked to pay for credit insurance. You might be charged various other fees as well. When you apply for a loan, there are fees to cover the costs of credit reports and appraisals. (An **appraisal** is a professional estimate of the market value of property.) There might be an **origination fee** (a fee for starting the paperwork). When you use a credit card, you might be charged a fee for getting a cash advance or for making a late payment.

These charges can make a big difference in the total cost of credit. When shopping around for credit, don't compare only interest rates. Find out what other finance charges will apply.

finance charges the costs of using credit, including interest, late charges, and other fees

appraisal a professional estimate of the market value of a property

origination fee a fee for starting the paperwork on a loan

Computing the Cost of Credit

Some people spend a great deal of time shopping for the lowest price on a car, microwave oven, or flat-screen TV—but they never think about how much they will be paying for credit. Their only concern is whether they can afford the monthly payments. Certainly that is important. However, the total cost is even more important. Saving $200 on the price of a car—but then paying $400 more for credit than you would elsewhere—doesn't make sense.

To compute the cost of credit, follow these steps:

1. Multiply the amount of your monthly payment times the number of months you will be paying off the loan.
2. Add the down payment, if any.
3. Subtract the price of the item if you had paid cash, or subtract the amount of cash you receive if you are getting a loan. The difference is the cost of using credit.

For example, suppose the cash price of the car you are buying is $5,500. You make a down payment of $500 and borrow the rest. The loan requires you pay $225 a month for twenty-four months. Compute the cost of credit:

$225 × 24 months	=	$ 5,400
Plus down payment		+ 500
Total amount paid		$ 5,900
Less cash price of car		− 5,500
Cost of credit	=	$ 400

Online calculators can help you compute the cost of credit, whether it's for a loan or a credit card purchase. You will be able to compare the credit costs for different interest rates and different lengths of time. One site that has a number of useful calculators is Bankrate.com (http://fin.emcp.net/bankrate).

Understanding Contracts

If you use credit, you will have to sign a credit contract. When you sign a credit contract, you are agreeing to everything it says—whether or not you read it—so always read any contract very carefully before you sign it. If anything is not clear to you, ask for an explanation before you sign. Finally, always get a copy of any contract that you sign.

Some loan contracts have a *grace period*—an amount of time after the due date when a payment can be made without penalty. For instance, even if your payment is due on the tenth of the month, you might be able to pay as long as two weeks later without getting a late charge. You might also recall from Chapter 13 that a *grace period* is the period of time, usually twenty to thirty days, when interest is not charged on current credit card purchases. These terms will appear in the credit card agreement. Always know the grace period and make sure you pay within the time allowed.

Credit card agreements are different from other credit contracts. Figure 14.1 compares the terms of loan contracts with the terms of credit card agreements. You can see how credit card agreements make it easy for consumers to charge more than they can afford—and go deeper into debt. Remember also that a credit card company can raise the interest rate whenever it wants.

Microlending is not only for undeveloped countries. It can be a useful tool for young American entrepreneurs just starting out or who cannot get business financing from ordinary sources. For instance, the U.S. Accion Network is a nonprofit organization that uses microloans to help small business owners from New York to New Mexico, from Chicago to Texas.

The network focuses on loans ranging from $500 to $25,000. Sometimes that's all the financial help a business needs to get on its feet. Applicants can also get help with writing a business plan. Character and business experience count as much as credit scores—because the organization recognizes that there are lots of people who are fully employed and paying their bills on time, but who cannot get conventional business loans from a bank.

Qualifying for Credit

To obtain a loan or a credit card, you usually have to fill out an application form. The form asks you to supply information about yourself and your finances. Lenders want to know how much risk they will be taking if they grant credit to you. They estimate this risk by analyzing

Figure 14.1 **COMPARISON OF LOAN CONTRACTS AND CREDIT CARD AGREEMENTS**

Most auto and cash loan contracts include:	Most credit card agreements include:
• Total amount loaned	• Amount of credit available
• Amount of down payment (or trade-in)	• (No down payment required)
• Interest rate you will pay	• Interest rate—but even "fixed" rates can change at discretion of company
• Special charges you will pay	• Fees that the company can change
• Total amount you will pay	• No total amount listed because it will vary
• Total amount and due date of each payment	• Minimum payment, but no set time frame for total repayment

You Can Succeed Financially

In 1974, Muhammad Yunus was a 34-year-old economics professor in Bangladesh. He took his students on a class field trip to a small village. There, he interviewed a woman who made bamboo chairs. To buy the raw materials for the chairs, the woman had to borrow the equivalent of 25 cents—at an interest rate of 10 percent per week (520 percent per year). Her profit was 1 cent per chair.

The Idea: Microloans

Yunus realized that with cheaper credit, this woman and millions like her could make more profit from the work they did. They could bring themselves out of poverty, which has a big impact on an entire community's economic well-being. He reached into his own pocket and loaned the village cooperative about $30. This was a tiny loan, a *microloan*. It was the beginning of Yunus's experiment making very small loans to people who do not qualify for conventional credit.

Banks and government agencies did not think much of the idea. But Yunus had a vision of stamping out poverty "from the bottom up." He and a few others continued making personal loans to villagers. In 1983, Yunus created Grameen (meaning "village") Bank.

How It Works

Grameen's loans are quite different from those of a conventional bank. Borrowers typically have no collateral—they own nothing that could serve as security for the debt. Borrowers come to the bank in cooperative groups of at least five people. Rather than looking at the borrowers' credit history, the bank looks at their potential for future earnings. If one member of the borrowing group defaults on a loan, the others will become ineligible to borrow. This creates peer pressure to repay—and also develops a sense of community in the group. According to Yunus, group members aid each other as a result.

Most of the bank's loans are made to women. The loans are repaid in small weekly installments. Interest rates on the loans are much higher than you would expect to pay conventional lending sources because of the bank's high costs and its mission to lend money to as many people as possible. Yet, the bank has a policy that no borrower will ever pay more in interest than the amount of the original loan. If a borrower is behind in her payments, the bank does not impose late fees. Instead, it restructures the loan to fit the borrower's budget. More than 98 percent of Grameen's loans are repaid fully—a much higher rate than at any conventional bank.

The Result

By 2006, Grameen Bank had more than 6.75 million borrowers in 72,000 villages throughout Bangladesh. Each day the bank was collecting $4.5 million in weekly installments. That same year, Muhammad Yunus and his bank won the Nobel Peace Prize for their efforts.

In his autobiography, Yunus wrote, "If I could be useful to another human being, even for a day, that would be a great thing." Clearly, Yunus has achieved that great thing—and millions of lives are better for it.

What Would You Do?

1. Why do you think 98 percent of Grameen's loans are fully repaid, even though the borrowers are very poor and have no collateral?
2. Most microlenders charge between 30 percent and 70 percent interest on loans. Does that seem fair to you? Why or why not?

three factors: character, capacity, and capital. These are often called the "three C's" of credit:

- *Character* is your willingness to pay your bills on time.
- *Capacity* is your ability to pay your bills.
- *Capital* is represented by things of value that you own, such as your car.

You might be asked to pledge some of your capital as collateral. For larger loans, it is usually necessary to provide a statement of your net worth. To do this, you will need to list your **assets**—all the things of value that you own. You must also list your **liabilities**—amounts that you owe. The value of your assets minus your liabilities is your **net worth**, as shown in Figure 14.2.

assets money or anything else of value that a person or an organization owns

liabilities money or other debts that a person or an organization owes

net worth the difference in value between total assets and total liabilities

Figure 14.2 **SAMPLE NET WORTH STATEMENT**

Net Worth Statement

Name *Lambert Farm* Date *January 1*

Farm Assets	$ Cost Value	$ Market Value	Farm Liabilities	$ Market Value
Checking and savings accounts	*6,146*	*6,146*	Accounts payable (Sched. N)	*23,523*
			Farm taxes due (Sched. O)	
Crops held for sale or feed (Sched. A)	*228,166*	*228,166*	Current notes and credit lines (Sched. P)	*203,200*
Investment in growing crops (Sched. B)	*22,923*	*22,923*	Accrued interest—short (Sched. P)	*6,520*
Commercial feed on hand (Sched. C)	*31,230*	*31,230*	Accrued interest—fixed (Sched. Q)	*11,200*
Prepaid expenses (Sched. D)	*31,500*	*31,500*		
Market livestock (Sched. E)	*31,920*	*31,920*	Due in 12 months—fixed (Sched. Q)	*15,487*
Supplies on hand (Sched. F)	*15,548*	*15,548*		
Accounts receivable (Sched. G)	*5,966*	*5,966*	Other current liabilities	
Other current assets	*2,000*	*2,000*		
Total Current Assets	*$ 375,399*	*$ 375,399*	***Total Current Liabilities***	*$ 259,930*
Unpaid coop. distributions (Sched. H)			Notes and contracts, remainder (Sched. Q)	
Breeding livestock (Sched. I)	*25,250*	*25,250*	Machinery	*61,139*
Machinery and equipment (Sched. J)	*79,916*	*110,500*	Land	*73,587*
Buildings/improvements (Sched. K)	*60,000*	*100,000*		
Farmland (Sched. L)	*140,000*	*288,000*		
Farm securities, certificates (Sched. M)				
Other fixed assets			Other fixed liabilities	
Total Fixed Assets	*$ 305,166*	*$ 523,750*	***Total Fixed Liabilities***	*$ 134,726*
a. Total Farm Assets	*$ 680,565*	*$ 899,149*	***b. Total Farm Liabilities***	*$ 394,656*
c. Farm Net Worth (a – b)	*$ 285,909*	*$ 504,493*	Current Assets (market) / Current Liabilities = 1.44 Current ratio	
d. Farm Net Worth Last Year	*$ 256,820*	*$ 477,049*	Total Liabilities / Total Assets (market) = 44% Debt-to-asset ratio	
e. Change (c – d)	*$ 29,089*	*$ 27,444*		

Personal Assets		Personal Liabilities	
Bank accounts, stocks, bonds	*$ 38,065*	Credit cards, charge accounts, other loans	*$ 1,568*
Automobiles, boats, etc.	*14,000*	Automobile loans	
Household goods, clothing	*10,000*	Other loans, taxes due	
Real estate	*75,000*	Real estate, other long-term loans	
f. Total Personal Assets	*$ 137,065*	***g. Total Personal Liabilities***	*$ 1,568*
h. Total Personal Net Worth (f – g)	*$ 135,497*	Total Personal Liabilities / Total Personal Assets = 1% Debt-to-asset ratio	
i. Total Net Worth, Market Value (c + h)	*$ 639,990*		

Credit Bureaus

Your application will provide creditors with information about your character, capacity, and capital. However, creditors obtain most of their information from a **credit bureau**—an agency that keeps records of the credit activity of individuals. There are three major credit bureaus in the United States: Equifax, Experian, and TransUnion. All three are run for profit and are owned by their shareholders. They receive no government funding. Local, independent credit bureaus throughout the United States are most often affiliated with one of these three national bureaus.

credit bureau an agency that collects and sells personal credit information about individuals

Your Credit Information The credit bureaus obtain their consumer credit information from creditors such as banks, credit card companies, and other lenders. In return, creditors are allowed

Do Your RESEARCH

Many Internet resources are available to help you learn about wise *and unwise* use of credit. Type "using credit" into your Web browser, and you can turn up more than 4.5 million listings. How do you know which sources are trustworthy? You can usually rely on government sources and the Web sites of reputable financial institutions. Here are some examples:

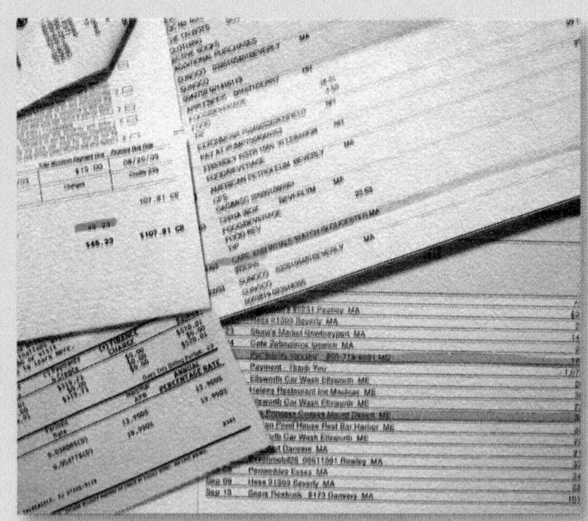

- The Bureau of Consumer Protection (BCP) is a branch of the FTC. Its Web site (http://fin.emcp.net/bcp) has consumer information about credit and loans. Click on the "Consumer Information" tab and then click on "Credit & Loans."
- The three major credit bureaus—Equifax (http://fin.emcp.net/equifax), Experian (http://fin.emcp.net/experian), and TransUnion (http://fin.emcp.net/transunion)—all offer helpful credit advice on their Web sites.
- *Forbes* magazine is a respected source of financial news. The articles on the Personal Finance page at the Forbes.com Web site (http://fin.emcp.net/forbesfinance) contain information about using and abusing credit.
- Tomorrow's Money (http://fin.emcp.net/tomorrowsmoney) offers financial advice aimed at young people. The site is operated by the Bond Market Foundation, a nonprofit educational entity funded by investment banks and other bond marketers.
- The National Student Loan Program (http://fin.emcp.net/nslp) is a private nonprofit agency that offers advice about student loans and can even help you apply for one.
- Major credit card providers also offer good credit advice at their Web sites.

When you search for credit advice online, be suspicious of sources that try to sell you something or try to convince you that they can help you "fix" bad credit ratings. Stick with reputable sources.

Your Assignment

1. If you or your parents have a credit card, go to that company's Web site and read what it says about using credit wisely. Summarize your findings. Why would credit card companies want to give you such advice?
2. Why is it smart to pay off the entire balance on your credit card each month?

to use the system to check the credit information of consumers. Whenever you apply for credit, the lender will check your credit report and your credit score.

As you learned in Chapter 1, your *credit score* is a three-digit number based on the information in your credit report. Fair Isaac Corporation developed computer software that calculates a credit score called the *FICO score*. It takes into consideration things like whether you pay your bills on time, how much debt you have, and how long you've had established credit. The major credit bureaus might use their own version of the FICO score or another method entirely, since there are types of credit scores other than FICO. The scoring methods are different, so a consumer may have varying credit scores.

The score is meant to be a quick way for creditors to determine whether you are a good risk. The higher your credit score, the better. Many employers now check the credit score of job applicants before offering employment. For a number of reasons, it is important that you maintain a good credit record and a good score.

Checking Your Credit Report Many people check their own credit reports and scores from time to time. Because the three national bureaus are competitors, they do not share their credit information except in special circumstances. Therefore, when you check your own credit report, you will need to get separate reports from each of the three bureaus.

The Fair Credit Reporting Act (FCRA) requires each bureau to provide consumers with one free credit report every twelve months, upon request. (Credit *scores* may not be free.) The bureaus have set up a central Web site (http://fin.emcp.net/annualcreditreport) where you can order your free reports. You can order them from all three bureaus at the same time, or you can order a report from one company at a time.

Note that AnnualCreditReport.com is the *only* authorized site for obtaining free credit reports. There are many sites with similar names. Some will ask you to sign up for a credit monitoring service in order to get your "free" report. Others are outright scams designed to get your personal information. Be sure to request your report only from the authorized Web site.

You might wonder what types of information cause your score to go up or down. Figure 14.3 shows the components of the credit score and how much weight is given to each.

Consumer Protection Laws

Several laws protect consumers in credit transactions. These laws are meant to help you understand your financial rights and obligations.

Equal Credit Opportunity Act The Equal Credit Opportunity Act (ECOA) prohibits discrimination against a

Figure 14.3 COMPONENTS OF A CREDIT SCORE

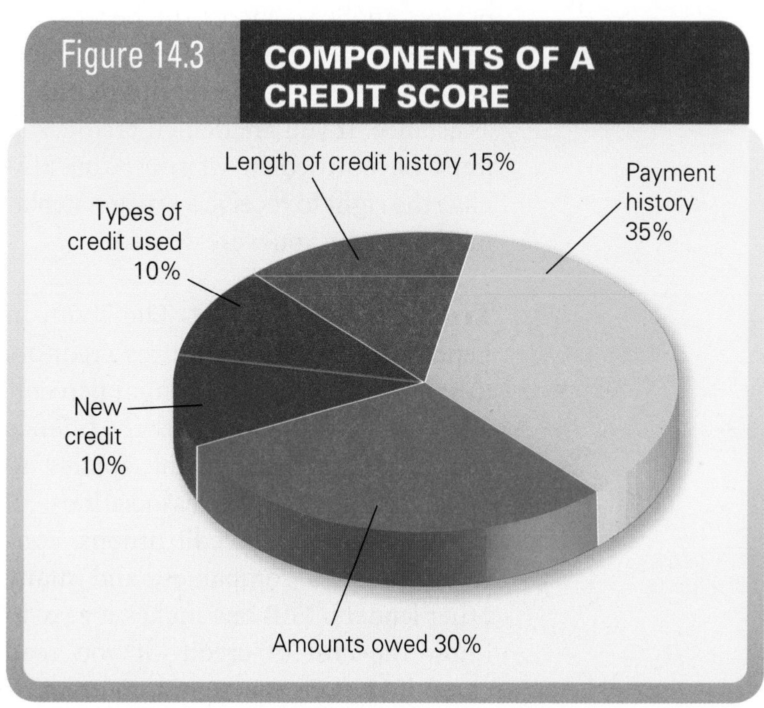

LOOK Before You Leap

Julio is moving to an apartment with two friends. The three have been shopping for furniture at garage sales, secondhand stores, and thrift shops. They have almost everything they need, except a TV. All three are sports fans, and they're looking forward to watching basketball and football games together in their new place.

They have seen plenty of used TVs as they shopped, including several on Craigslist. It seems as though folks are selling their old TVs and buying the newest and thinnest flat-screen models. Julio thinks they should be able to get a good 42-inch used TV for around $250, because so many people are switching.

The friends are downtown when they see a 51-inch flat-screen on sale. It's showing a football game, and the picture is crystal clear. The price is $1,799 plus 8 percent sales tax.

None of the boys has a credit card with a high enough credit limit to charge the TV—but the store offers one-year financing, with payments of $179 a month. That would mean each person will pay about $60 every month for a year—a lot of cash, Julio thinks.

Before Buying on Credit

1. Julio asks about the annual percentage rate (APR), which is 19 percent. This means the total cost of the TV, including finance charges, will be $2,148. Do you think a bigger screen is worth the difference between $250 and $2,148? Explain your answer.
2. Think about why the salesman did not reveal the APR until asked. How does the availability of credit persuade people to spend more money than they would otherwise?

person applying for credit because of age, sex, marital status, religion, race, national origin, or the receipt of public assistance. If you are denied credit, you must be notified in writing. You also have the right to receive a written explanation of why you were denied.

Truth in Lending Act The Truth in Lending Act (TILA) requires creditors to state, in writing, the annual percentage rate (APR) and other finance charges. This requirement applies to banks, savings and loan associations, all credit card issuers, credit unions, consumer finance companies, and many other lenders. This law makes it easy to know the cost of credit—if you read carefully before you sign a contract. It also allows you to compare the credit plans of different lenders.

Fair Credit Reporting Act As mentioned earlier, the Fair Credit Reporting Act (FCRA) gives you the right to see your credit record and to correct errors. If you are denied credit because of a bad credit report, you must be told the name and address of the credit bureau that gave the report.

If you find untrue statements in your credit record, give a corrected statement (in writing) to the credit bureau and ask them to check it out. If their investigation shows that you are right, the credit bureau must correct its records. If you are not satisfied, you can write a statement about the inac-

Going Global

Fashion designer Tracy Reese was not always a successful entrepreneur. In fact, at first she had trouble even qualifying for a business loan. But with creativity and determination, she has become a global success.

The Detroit native graduated from the prestigious Parsons School of Design in New York. She launched her own clothing line at age 23—but it lasted less than two years because she ran out of money. No one denied her talent, but lenders were not willing to make loans to someone so young. She spent the next several years learning the fashion business, and then she tried again.

In 1995, an older and wiser Tracy Reese partnered with an Indian investor, Om Batheja. They arranged to manufacture the clothes in India to keep expenses down. This time the business, Tracy Reese Designs, was profitable.

In 2004, the Tracy Reese line began to be sold in Europe. Her global reach was further extended in 2006, when she contracted with shoe designer Steve Madden to create an accessory and handbag line. It will be marketed wherever Madden's brand is sold—in the United States, Canada, Central and South America, and Europe. Today you can find Tracy Reese's classic signature line as well as Plenty, a casual and youthful line influenced by Indian styles, in hundreds of stores around the globe.

Thinking Globally

1. As a young entrepreneur, how would you convince a lender that you were a good credit risk?
2. How did it help Tracy Reese to have a partner from India?

curacy. Your statement must be attached to your file on record with the credit bureau, and it will be included in future reports about your credit record.

Fair Debt Collection Practices Act When a consumer breaks a credit contract, the lender usually tries to collect the money owed. For example, in 2005, about 150,000 debt collection agencies recovered more than $39 billion in consumer debt. The Fair Debt Collection Practices Act (FDCPA) controls those agencies. Before the law was passed, some collectors used harassment and even threats to collect the money owed. These practices are now illegal.

Building a Good Credit Record

You might not be interested in obtaining a loan now, but the chances are good that you will consider borrowing money within the next few years. Young people without a work history or a credit record sometimes have difficulty establishing credit. You might have been turned down for credit already. Perhaps you are afraid that you will be turned down if you apply. If so, you need to lay some groundwork. Here are some things you can do to build a good credit record:

1. *Open a bank account.* A good first step is to establish a checking or savings account (or both) and use it

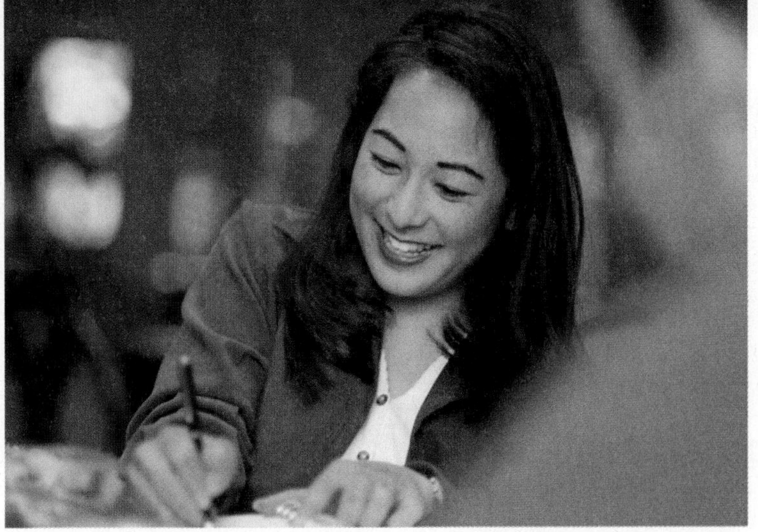

▲ Apply for credit from a store that is looking for young customers—but watch out for high fees.

responsibly. Even though bank accounts usually are not part of your credit score, the fact that you have bank accounts will show that you have money. Having a good relationship with a bank will make it easier to obtain a loan or a credit card from that bank.

2. *Open a store charge account.* Getting approval for credit is easier if you have been granted credit by another firm. Apply for credit from a store that is looking for young customers. Such a store is more likely to approve your application. Your limit might be low—perhaps only $250 or so—but use the account. Charge small amounts, and only for things you would buy even if you did not have the account. Always pay promptly. In a few months, your charge account will show up on your credit record.
3. *Avoid credit cards with high fees.* Some companies offer credit cards to people who have no credit history or have a poor credit record. These cards have a credit limit of only a few hundred dollars and have high annual fees, high maintenance fees, late charges, and other costs. Such cards are called *subprime cards.* After paying the fees, you are left with very little available credit. These expensive cards are not useful for building a credit record.
4. *Take out a small loan.* Some young people take out a small loan and put the money into a savings account. When the payments on the loan are due, they take the money out of savings to pay the lender. (Usually, additional money must be added for interest.) Because they have responsibly paid off the loan, they can more easily get a larger loan later.

To help make their decisions, some lenders give "points" for things they believe indicate character, capacity, and capital. They use this type of scoring in addition to a loan application form and a credit report. Your final "score" helps the lender decide whether or not to grant you credit.

SECTION 1 ASSESSMENT

Factual Recall

1. In order to compute the cost of credit, what four things do you need to know?
2. Is it a good idea to spread out credit payments for as long as possible? Why or why not?
3. Compare the total cost of a $9,000 car loan at 8 percent interest over three-year, four-year, and five-year periods.
4. What are the "three C's of credit"? How do lenders use them?
5. How many free credit reports can you obtain in twelve months?

Critical Thinking

1. On large loans that are repaid over a long time, even small differences in the interest rate make a big difference in the cost. Why?
2. When you are getting a loan, why is it important to know the cost of credit?

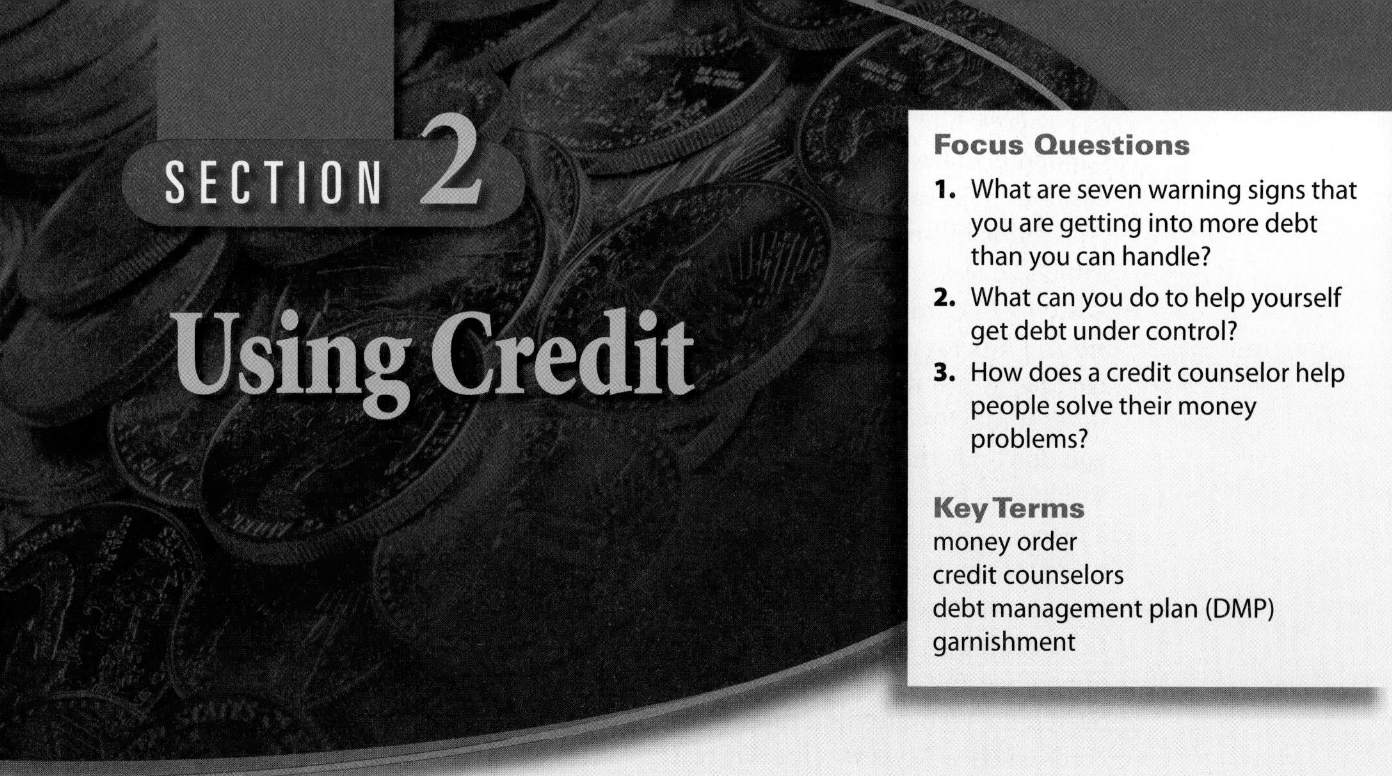

SECTION 2

Using Credit

Focus Questions

1. What are seven warning signs that you are getting into more debt than you can handle?
2. What can you do to help yourself get debt under control?
3. How does a credit counselor help people solve their money problems?

Key Terms

money order
credit counselors
debt management plan (DMP)
garnishment

Used wisely, credit can work to your advantage. A student loan can help you get an education and improve your earning power. A home obtained with a mortgage loan can help improve your quality of life. Credit can even save you money. People with good credit records often get better interest rates and other perks.

Using Credit to Your Advantage

Using credit wisely requires taking control of your finances. Make a realistic assessment of how much money you take in and how much you spend. List your income from all sources. Then list your fixed expenses—those that are the same each month, like rent, car payments, and insurance premiums. Next, list your variable expenses—like clothing, repair bills, and entertainment. Write down all of your expenses, even those that seem insignificant. Doing this can help you track your spending patterns, identify necessary expenses, and prioritize the rest. The goal is to make sure you can meet the basics of housing, food, health care, insurance, and education. Refer back to Chapter 4 for a detailed discussion of budgeting.

Once you have a budget, you can determine how much debt you can afford. Many bankers and others in the lending business believe it is all right to use up to 25 percent of take-home pay for paying off debt. After all, that's how they earn their money. When borrowers go over that 25 percent level, they increase their chances of going bankrupt—and then the lenders might lose money, too.

But don't play by bankers' rules. Why should you lead a stressed-out life, just so lenders can have more of your money? Realistically, you need to keep your debt—including your car payment—to no more than 20 percent of your take-home pay. (Rent or a house payment is not included in this 20 percent.)

Here are some tips for using credit wisely:

- *Pay your bills on time.* Monitor your spending and your debt, and be sure to pay your bills by the due dates. Computer software can make it easier to monitor your finances. Automatic bill-pay can help you avoid late fees.

- *Use only free, low-interest credit cards.* Look for a credit card that charges no annual fee and has a low interest rate (in case some month you don't pay the whole balance). It would be a bonus if the card also has a reward—such as a cash bonus, discounts on purchases, or "miles" that you can redeem for airline tickets. Mainly, though, look for no annual fee and a low interest rate. Search for Web sites that rate credit cards, such as Myvesta (http://fin.emcp.net/myvesta).
- *Pay more than the minimum.* Making only minimum payments can keep you in debt virtually forever. Coral owed a balance of $4,500 on her credit card. If she made only the minimum payment each month and never used the card again, it would take her *forty-four years* to pay off her debt. The bank would collect $17,000 in interest over those forty-four years. If possible, pay your credit card balance in full every month. That way, you will not have to pay any interest.

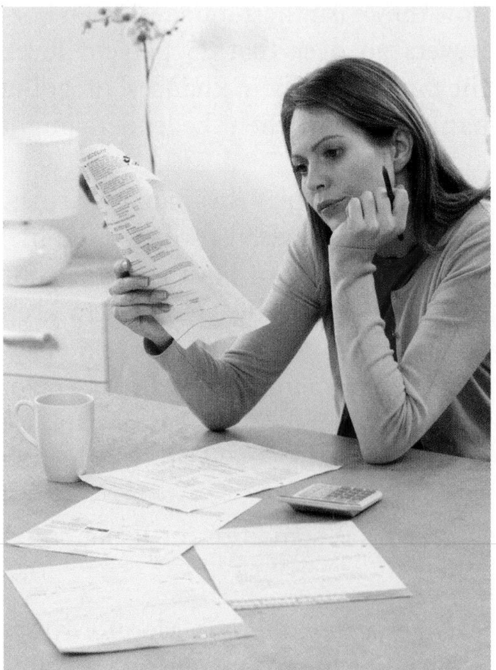

Read your credit statements closely to avoid getting overwhelmed by debt.

Solving Credit Problems

Jordan, an 18-year-old college freshman, was excited when he received his first credit card application in the mail. He was glad to see that the application did not require his parents' signature. It was strictly his decision and it would be his own credit card. A few weeks later, he received the card in the mail, along with an information sheet that said his credit limit was $1,200. With a limit on how much he could charge, he could not get into too much trouble, could he?

Within a few months, Jordan had maxed out the card and added two more. By his sophomore year he owed almost $6,000—and most of it was costing him 10 percent APR. He had a part-time job after class each day, but he barely earned enough to make the minimum payment on all three cards.

One night, he figured out that if he kept paying just the minimum each month—and never charged anything more—it would take more than nine years to pay off his debt. He knew he had to make bigger payments. He might have to drop a class so he could work more hours. He decided to talk things over with his parents.

Warning Signs

Soon you will be on your own, with the responsibility for paying your bills. As you can see from Jordan's story, falling into debt can happen very easily. Getting buried under a mountain of debt is a problem that you can avoid if you use credit wisely.

How will you know if you're taking on more debt than you can handle? Here are seven warning signs:

1. *Are you making only the minimum payments?* If you have been paying only the minimum on your credit card, you will need to review and revise your budget—and make some lifestyle changes. Note the highlighted numbers in Figure 14.4. You should do whatever is legally necessary to pay $278.50, not the $20 minimum.
2. *Have you applied for more than two credit cards?* If you feel like you need more than one or two credit cards, you might be trying to increase your credit limit—but you will probably end up in financial trouble. You might run up balances on several cards, or you might get desperate and get a cash advance on one card to make payments on others. One or two credit cards are plenty.
3. *Are your credit cards close to or even over your credit limit?* If you ever begin maxing out your cards, it's a sure sign that you are spending too much. If this is happening to you, face facts and set up a plan to pay off your balances as quickly as possible.
4. *Have you been denied a credit limit increase?* Creditors set limits on how much you can charge based on your credit history, income, and outstanding debt. If an increase in your limit is denied, it means the credit card company believes your finances are close to being out of control. When your creditors are concerned, it's time for you to be concerned, too.
5. *Do you rely on cash advances to pay other bills?* Always being "just a little behind" is proof that your income cannot support your lifestyle. Robbing Peter to pay Paul puts you on the fast track to financial ruin. It is absolutely necessary to take some drastic action—and soon.
6. *Do you live from payday to payday?* Do you sometimes write a check and hope that it does not get to your bank until after you deposit your next paycheck? Have you ever bounced a check? Have you ever used a payday loan? Do you sometimes wonder if your entire life will continue this way? It doesn't have to—but you need to begin paying off your debts and start saving at least a few dollars from every paycheck.
7. *Are creditors calling you?* This does not happen if you are using credit wisely. It does not happen after just a couple of spending sprees. When your phone starts ringing and you dread answering it because you think it might be another creditor, you are in trouble and you need help.

Did You Know?

Leveraged debt is a risky proposition. You probably learned in science class that you use a lever to lift a weight you cannot move by yourself. In finance, *leverage* refers to using borrowed money to make an investment—in other words, using debt to help you make much more money than if you used just your own funds.

For instance, suppose you want to buy a house so you can rent it out for income. You might not have enough cash to buy the house, so you borrow most of the money. You figure on using some of the rent money from your tenants to repay the loan. If all goes well, you will make a profit. But what if your tenants move out and you have trouble finding new ones? You will not have rental income, but you will still need to make payments.

At this point you could sell the house—but if prices have fallen, you might not get enough to pay off the loan. Unless you have plenty of income from other sources, you could lose the house to foreclosure—or go bankrupt.

Figure 14.4 **SAMPLE CREDIT CARD STATEMENT**

Statement of Personal Credit Card Account

AA BANK

☐ Check here if address or telephone number has changed. Please note changes on reverse side.

Account Number	Statement Closing Date	Current Amount Due
1234-567-890	01-31-08	$278.50

SUE EMPLOYEE
456 SKYVIEW DRIVE
HOMETOWN, USA 99900-1234

MAIL PAYMENT TO:
AA BANK
132 VINE STREET
ANYTOWN, USA 67500-0010

872919345 0017825500000000003

Detach here and return upper portion with check or money order. Do not staple or fold.

Statement of Personal Credit Card Account

AA BANK

Retain this portion for your files.

Cardmember Name	Account Number	Statement Closing Date
SUE EMPLOYEE	1234-567-890	01-31-08

Statement Date:	02-01-08	Payment Due Date:	03-01-08
Closing Date:	01-31-08		
Credit Limit:	$500.00	Credit Available:	$221.50
New Balance:	$278.50	Minimum Payment Due:	$20.00

Account Summary

Previous Balance:	+74.24	Transaction Fees:	+3.00
Purchases:	+250.50	Annual Fees:	+25.00
Cash Advances:	+0	Current Amount Due:	+250.50
Payments:	-74.25	Amount Past Due:	+0
Finance Charge:	+0	Amount Over Credit Line:	+0
Late Charge:	+0	NEW BALANCE:	$278.50

Reference Number	Sold	Posted	Activity Since Last Statement		Amount
43210987	01-03	01-13	Payment, Thank You		–$73.25
01234567	01-12	01-13	McBurgers	Anytown, USA	$25.25
78901234	01-14	01-17	Cell phone bill	Anytown, USA	$40.00
45678901	01-14	01-17	Sport Master	Anytown, USA	$75.25
3210987	01-22	01-23	Auto World	Anytown, USA	$20.75
76543210	01-29	01-30	Electric Planet	Anytown, USA	$89.25
23455678		01-30	Transaction Fees		$3.00
34567890		01-01	Annual Fee		$25.00
			PAGE 1 OF 1		

Rate Summary

Finance Charge Summary	Purchases	Advances
Periodic Rate	20.45%	20.45%
Annual Percentage Rate (APR)	19.80%	19.80%

For account information and customer service, please call 1-800-555-5555.

Payments or credits received after closing date above will appear on next month's statement.

Self-Help

At any point in your life, if you realize that you have to answer "yes" to any of the seven warning signs, the first thing to do is take stock of your debt. How much do you owe? What portion of your take-home pay is going toward paying off debt? How much can you realistically afford to pay each month?

The high-interest debt brought on by credit cards causes the biggest problem for young people just out of school or getting started in a career. If you find yourself in that situation, you can take steps to correct it. There are three basic steps to getting out of debt: You have to (1) take control of your finances, (2) reduce your spending, and (3) look for ways to earn money.

For some people, shopping is not simply about finding what they need. It can be an obsession. Kate Bingaman-Burt is a graphic artist who recognized this problem. She actually started documenting everything she bought—right down to a toothbrush or single postage stamps. She described the items and their prices. She told where she bought each item, and often drew pictures of her purchases. Then she put it all on her Web site, Obsessive Consumption.

The site became a business when she began selling the records of her purchases as art. Later, she added products like pillows in the shape of dollar signs and handkerchiefs with dollar signs on them. There's a blog on her Web site, too—a kind of consumer diary. She says it's all intended to get people to "think about consumption and obsession and their aftereffects"—the credit card bills that result.

Take Control To take control of your finances, first contact your creditors. Explain why it's difficult for you to make your payments. Try to work out a plan that reduces your payments to a more manageable level. Do not wait until your accounts have been turned over to a debt collector!

Next, stop all spending for anything that is not essential. Too often, buying nonessential items is what gets people into trouble. Cutting out things you do not need is a great place to begin a getting-out-of-debt plan.

Then, reduce the temptation to use plastic by cutting up any credit card you have maxed out. A card that has been spent to its limit is of no use—so get rid of it. Contact the company that issued the card and formally cancel it. If you have any cards with high interest rates, in the neighborhood of 18 to 24 percent, give them the scissors treatment too, and cancel the accounts. You will still have to pay off existing debt, of course, but at least you will not be adding to it.

Transfer as much debt as you can to the credit card with the lowest interest rate. Then pay off the credit card balances with the highest interest rates first. Continue making minimum payments on the other cards. When one card gets paid off, increase your payments on the next. Sometimes, if you call your credit card company and request a lower rate, it will actually do it. It's worth a try.

Consider a debt consolidation loan. Instead of several payments at different times of the month, you will have a single payment to one lender. Check carefully, though. Be sure your monthly payments—including principal, interest, and fees—will really be less than what you are paying now. Compare interest rates. Compare total costs over the life of the loan. And, if you do get a

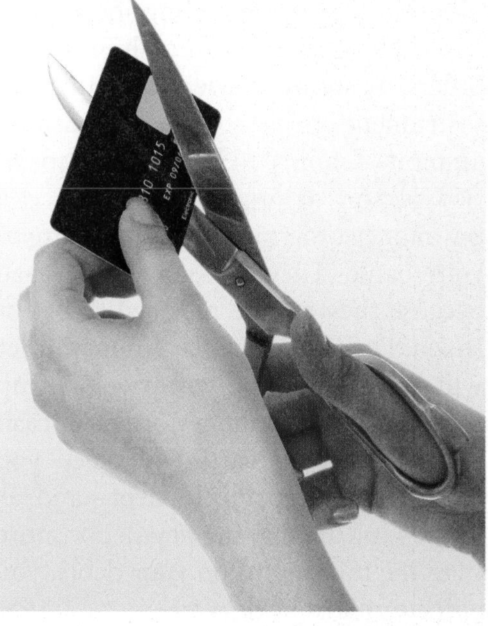

◀ **Pay off, cancel, and then cut up credit cards that you have maxed out.**

Do Your RESEARCH

During high school, Samantha worked part-time at a florist shop. She earned enough money to buy clothes and other things she liked. She never thought about living expenses. She was living at home with her parents, so all her income was hers to spend.

In college, things were different. Her parents paid for her housing, and she had grant money, plus a part-time job. But Samantha also had taken out student loans and had three credit cards. She used the cards to handle the shortfall when her checking account ran low. She figured all college students get into debt.

After six months, she was barely keeping her head above water. Two of her cards were almost maxed out—and she wasn't even sure where the money had gone. She was thinking of transferring all her credit card balances to the card with the highest credit limit.

Samantha's older brother Mike could see his sister was stressed. They went online, and Mike pointed her to the advice about budgeting at Nellie Mae and at American Consumer Credit Counseling. He showed her how to use Quicken personal financial management software. The two worked together to create a budget for Samantha.

Getting rid of two credit cards was a smart idea, Mike said. But he advised Samantha to keep one card—the card with the lowest interest rate, not the highest credit limit.

Your Assignment

1. Read about budgeting at the Web sites of Nellie Mae (http://fin.emcp.net/nelliemae) and American Consumer Credit Counseling (http://fin.emcp.net/consumercredit). How can having a budget help you use credit wisely?
2. If you have three credit cards with the *same* interest rate, what is the advantage of getting rid of two of them?

debt consolidation loan, do not celebrate your newfound freedom from high monthly payments by going shopping!

Try to pay only with cash or money orders. A **money order** is a financial instrument that orders a specified amount of money to be paid to a specified person or organization. You can buy money orders at the post office or at your bank. They are safer than cash because they can be replaced if lost or stolen. There is no chance a money order will bounce because you pay for it up front. Paying with money orders or cash instead of credit cards will keep you from going deeper into debt—and as long as you are making payments (more than the minimum) on your debts, you will eventually be debt free.

money order a financial instrument, purchased at a bank or post office, that orders a specified amount of money to be paid to a specified person or organization

Reduce Spending One way to cut back on your spending is to shop at thrift shops and secondhand stores. The savings can be huge. Another way to save on necessities is to look for special low prices on the Internet. One such shopper found new $60 shirts for just $7. (A company was closing out the popular western Barn Fly shirts.)

You can save money if you cook from scratch and eat at home. If you eat out a lot—whether in fine restaurants or fast-food spots—you have been paying far more for meals than if you cooked at home. Even convenient, microwave-ready meals are more expensive than actually cooking from scratch. If you have not had much practice in the art of cooking, this is a good time to learn.

You can save more money than you might imagine. Use the cash to help pay off your debt.

Another way to reduce spending is to reduce your housing expenses. Move to a less expensive apartment or get a roommate.

Look for Ways to Raise Money

Finally, see if you can come up with some extra money. For instance, cash in your savings bonds, if you have them, or use money from a savings account to pay off debt. Chances are, the interest on your debt is more than the interest you are earning from savings. (Just be sure to keep something in savings for emergencies.) After you become debt free, you can build up your savings again. See Chapters 6 and 7 for information about saving and investing.

Another way to raise money is to sell some assets. Look around your house or apartment, and you will probably see some things you can live without—but someone else would buy. Maybe you have sporting goods that you no longer use. Small items that are easy to ship can be auctioned on a Web site. If you are having trouble making car payments, consider selling the car. Even if your car is paid for, if you can do without a car until your other debts are paid, selling it could bring in some real cash.

Get a second job. Working two jobs might not make for a carefree life, but then neither does living under a mountain of debt. You might be able to work part-time or on weekends until you can get out of the credit crunch.

Should you borrow from family or friends? This is really a tough one, and normally it's not recommended. If you do not pay back a friend or family member on time, it usually causes unpleasant feelings. Still, if your debt load is heavy enough, you might consider doing this. It is especially important to pay back such a loan on time and (to be fair) with interest.

Credit Counseling

What if you are not disciplined enough to create a workable budget and stick to it? What if you cannot work out a repayment plan with your creditors, or cannot keep track of mounting bills? In these cases you should consider getting help from a credit counselor. **Credit counselors** discuss your entire financial situation with you and help you develop a personal plan to solve your money problems. Many work at nonprofit credit counseling organizations (also called *adjustment service companies*).

Be aware, though, that just because an organization says it's "nonprofit" does not guarantee that its services are free, affordable, or even legitimate. Figure 14.5 lists things to watch out for when you choose a credit counseling service.

credit counselors individuals who are trained to give advice on handling money and getting out of debt

Reputable credit counseling organizations can advise you on managing your money and debts. They can help

Figure 14.5 CREDIT COUNSELING PRACTICES TO WATCH OUT FOR

Be suspicious of any credit counseling organization that engages in the following practices:

- Charges high up-front or monthly fees for enrolling you in credit counseling or a debt management plan (DMP)
- Pressures you to make "voluntary contributions" (another name for fees)
- Will not send you free information about its services unless you provide personal financial information, such as credit card numbers and balances
- Tries to enroll you in a DMP without spending time reviewing your financial situation
- Offers to enroll you in a DMP without teaching you budgeting and money management skills
- Demands that you make payments into a DMP before your creditors have accepted you into the program

▶ Certified counselors can help you with debt management and budgeting.

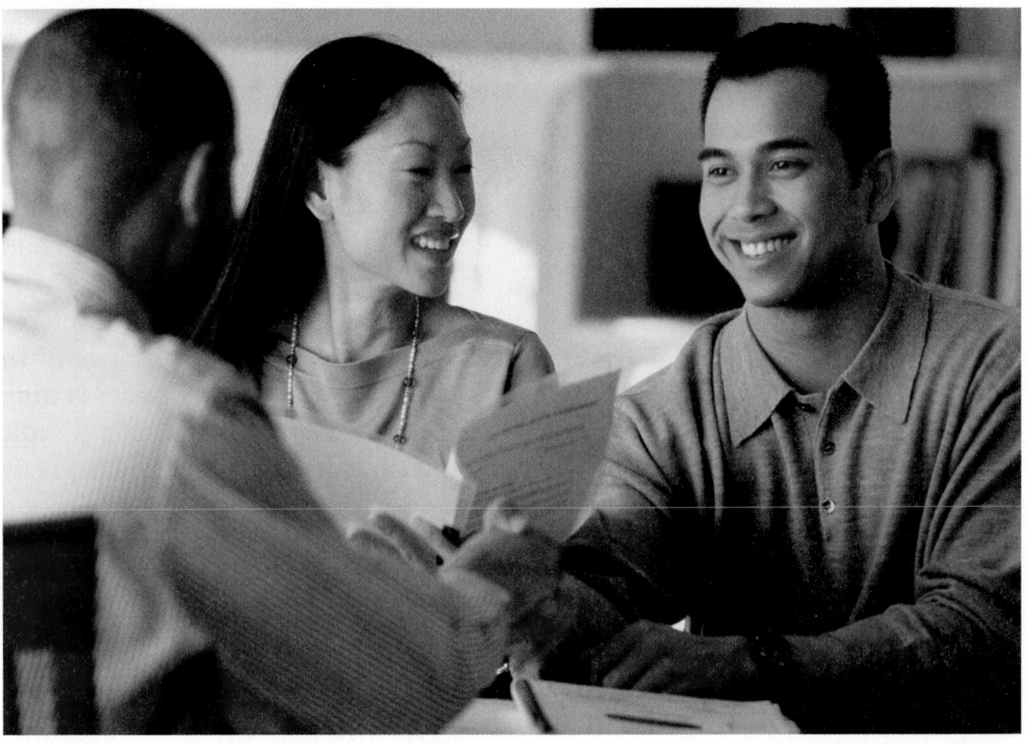

you develop a budget, and they offer free educational materials and workshops. Their counselors are certified and trained in the areas of consumer credit, money and debt management, and budgeting. An initial counseling session typically lasts for an hour, with an offer of follow-up sessions.

Most credit counselors offer services through local offices, the Internet, or on the telephone. Try to find an organization that offers in-person counseling. Many universities, credit unions, housing authorities, military bases, and branches of the U.S. Cooperative Extension Service operate nonprofit credit counseling programs. Your bank, local consumer protection agency, and friends and family might also be good sources of information and referrals.

debt management plan (DMP) a plan for paying off debt, in which the consumer deposits money each month with the credit counseling service, and the service uses the money to pay the debts

Debt Management Plans

If your financial problems come from too much debt or an inability to repay your debts, a credit counseling agency might recommend that you enroll in a **debt management plan (DMP)**. In a DMP, you deposit money each month with the credit counseling organization. That organization uses your deposits to pay debts such as your credit card bills, student loans, and medical bills.

The DMP operates according to a payment schedule that the credit counselor develops with you and your creditors. Your creditors might even agree to lower your interest rates or waive certain fees. However, check with all your creditors to be sure they offer the concessions that the credit counseling organization describes to you.

A successful DMP requires you to make regular, timely payments and could take forty-eight months or more to complete. Ask the credit counselor to estimate how long it will take for you to complete the plan. You might have to agree not to apply for—or use—any additional credit while you are participating in the plan.

Finally, remember: A DMP alone is not credit counseling, and DMPs are not for everyone. Sign up for one of these plans only after a certified credit counselor has spent time thoroughly reviewing your financial situation and has offered customized advice on managing your money. Even with a DMP, a reputable credit counseling organization will also help you create a budget and teach you money management skills.

Bankruptcy

There are two main types of personal bankruptcy: Chapter 13 and Chapter 7. Each must be filed in federal bankruptcy court. It costs money to file, plus attorney fees. The Bankruptcy Abuse Prevention and Consumer Protection Act (BAPCPA) of 2005 revised the rules and qualifications for filing bankruptcy. These changes give consumers more incentive to seek Chapter 13 bankruptcy relief, rather than Chapter 7.

Chapter 13 vs. Chapter 7 Chapter 13 bankruptcy allows people with a steady income to keep property, such as a mortgaged house or car that they might otherwise lose through the bankruptcy process. Instead of surrendering property, they are allowed to use future income to repay all or part of their debts. This repayment plan is approved by the court and usually takes three to five years. After all the payments have been made, most remaining debts are discharged. A discharge means the creditor no longer has the right to collect on the debt.

Chapter 7 is known as "straight bankruptcy." It requires giving up all assets that are not exempt. Exempt property might include cars, work-related tools, and basic household furnishings. Some property might be sold by a court-appointed official—a *trustee*—or turned over to creditors. Most debts are discharged within a few months.

Anyone whose debts have been discharged through Chapter 7 must wait eight years before filing again under Chapter 7. The Chapter 13 waiting period is much shorter and can be as little as two years between filings.

Both types of bankruptcy can get rid of unsecured debts. They can also stop foreclosure (the legal process used by a bank to repossess property), **garnishment** (a court order that allows all

Answers to Fact or Fiction

1. False—Low monthly payments often mean you will pay more in total amount of interest; **2.** True; **3.** True; **4.** True; **5.** False—The bureaus do not usually share information with each other, so they might each have different information about you; **6.** True.

garnishment a court order allowing all or part of a person's wages to be paid directly to the person's creditors

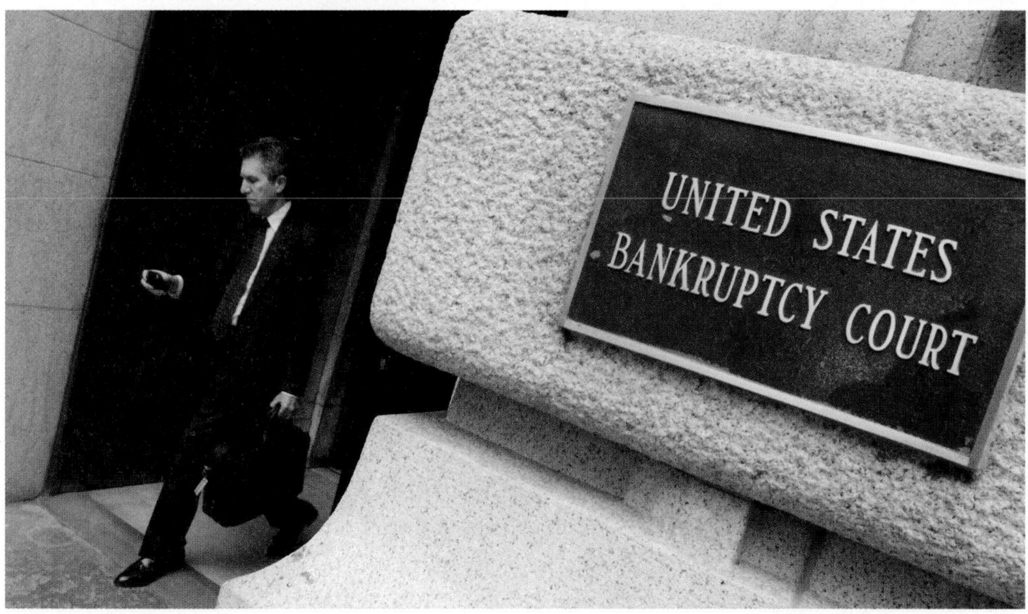

◀ **Bankruptcy will hurt your credit score and may prevent you from getting a loan or a job.**

Get Good Advice

Do you have some plastic with your name on it? You might use a credit card to buy concert tickets online, to pay your school tuition, or to contribute to a favorite charity. Some people use credit cards instead of carrying large amounts of cash. Credit cards will affect your ability to rent an apartment, buy a car, apply for a loan, start a business, and even get a job.

Credit cards will almost certainly be part of your overall financial picture. Learning to use them wisely will help you keep that picture looking good. The key is understanding how credit cards work *before* you sign on the dotted line.

Most adults have some experience—both positive and negative—with credit. Choose three people from three different age groups—twenties, forties, and sixties. Ask them how they learned about credit. Then, more importantly, ask how they use credit today. Here are some questions to get your interview started:

- When did you first apply for a credit card?
- What kind of paperwork did you have to fill out? What kind of questions did you have to answer?
- Were you instantly approved? Why or why not?
- What types of purchases have you made with a credit card?
- Do you pay the balance in full at the end of each month? If not, how do you handle the accumulating debt?
- What is the greatest benefit of having a credit card?
- What is your worst experience resulting from using a credit card?
- How often do you check your credit score or report?
- Have you ever uncovered a problem or an error in your credit score or credit report? If so, what did you do?
- What advice would you give to young people applying for their first credit card?

After your interviews, meet with a partner or a small group and share what you learned. What are the common themes from the interviews? What are some differences in the answers of people from the different age groups? What are some benefits and drawbacks of having a credit card?

What is the most important thing you learned from each age group? How will you apply what you learned in the interviews to your own good use of credit?

As a group, prepare a three-fold brochure or other print piece advising teens on how to use credit wisely.

or part of your paycheck to go directly to your creditors), utility shut-offs, and debt-collection activities. Both types allow people to keep some assets, although this varies state by state. Personal bankruptcy usually does not erase child support, alimony, fines, taxes, and some student loans. Unless you have an acceptable plan to catch up on your debt under Chapter 13, bankruptcy usually does not allow you to keep property if a creditor has an unpaid mortgage on it.

Before Filing There are certain hurdles that debtors must clear before they can file for bankruptcy. They must get credit counseling from a government-approved organization within six months before filing. You can get a state-by-state list of government-approved organizations from the U.S. Trustee Program (http://fin.emcp.net/trustee), the organization within the Department of Justice that supervises bankruptcy cases and trustees.

Before filing for Chapter 7 bankruptcy, debtors must satisfy a "means test." This test requires them to prove that their income is not more than a certain amount. The amount varies by state and is publicized by the U.S. Trustee Program.

The Aftermath Personal bankruptcy generally is considered the debt management option of last resort. That is because the results are so long-lasting and far-reaching. Bankruptcy information (both the date of filing and the later date of discharge) stays on a credit report for ten years. That can make it difficult to obtain credit, buy a home, get life insurance, or sometimes get a job. Still, bankruptcy is a legal procedure that offers a fresh start for people who have gotten into deep financial difficulty and cannot pay their debts.

▲ Use credit carefully—filing for bankruptcy can cost you your most prized possessions, or even your home.

Your Credit Decisions

You will be faced with many opportunities to say "Charge it." There are times when credit should be used, but you have to be careful. It can be very easy to get into the habit of spending next month's—or next year's—income today. A study by the MIT Sloan School of Management concluded that consumers using credit cards are willing to spend up to 100 percent more than when they use only cash. The study referred to this willingness to spend as the "credit card premium."

You must decide for yourself, based on your own spending plan, when to use credit. Before making a credit purchase, always ask yourself this question: "What else can I spend this money on if I don't spend it on this credit purchase? Should I save it?" Think about your answer, and then use credit wisely.

SECTION 2 ASSESSMENT

Factual Recall

1. Debt—including your car payment but not including your rent or house payment—should be no more than what percentage of your take-home pay?
2. If you are to use credit wisely, what are two important things to look for when comparing credit cards?
3. Name seven signs that a person has taken on too much debt.
4. You have decided that you don't need three credit cards, so you shred one and throw it away. What else do you need to do?
5. What are the two main types of personal bankruptcy?

Critical Thinking

1. Your credit card statement says that payment is due on the 17th of the month. When should you mail the check?
2. What is the danger in owning more than two credit cards?
3. Write an essay or create a fictional scenario to convince oth[illegible] ers that they should always p[illegible] the full amount of credit ca[illegible] bills. Be persuasive.

CHAPTER 14 REVIEW AND ASSESSMENT

Chapter Summary

Section 1 Obtaining Credit

- Every type of credit costs something. The costs depend on the source of the credit, how much you use, how long you take to repay, and the overall state of the economy.
- To compute the cost of credit, you need to know the principal, the repayment time, the rate of interest, and the amount of fees and other charges.
- Read credit contracts carefully, ask for an explanation of anything that is unclear to you, and always get a copy for your records.
- Before granting credit, lenders obtain information about you to determine how much risk they will be taking. Much of this information comes from credit bureaus.
- You have the right to examine your own credit report and score.
- Several federal laws protect consumers in credit transactions. These laws are meant to help you understand your financial rights and obligations.

Section 2 Using Credit

- To use credit wisely, first make a budget and determine how much debt you can afford.
- Select credit cards with no annual fee and a low interest rate, pay your bills on time, and pay more than the minimum amount.
- Be alert for warning signs that you are taking on more debt than you can handle.
- Self-help measures for dealing with debt include taking control of your finances, reducing spending, and looking for ways to raise ney.
- counselors can provide professional you should check their qualifications on before signing on.
- a debt management plan can ebts.
- term consequences, bank- nly as a last resort for

ay
d
edit 379

Reviewing Key Terms

For each of the following statements, choose the answer that best completes the sentence.

1. The costs of using credit, including interest and late charges, are called ______.
   a. finance charges
   b. appraisals
   c. origination fees
   d. liabilities
2. Net worth is ______.
   a. the total amount you owe to creditors
   b. something businesses calculate, not individuals
   c. the difference between total liabilities and your collateral
   d. the difference between total assets and total liabilities
3. If you are having trouble paying your debts, you can get advice from ______.
   a. a credit counselor
   b. a credit bureau
   c. both a and b
   d. neither a nor b
4. A(n) ______ is a professional estimate of the market value of property.
   a. appraisal
   b. principal
   c. garnishment
   d. asset
5. A court order allowing all or part of a person's wages to be paid directly to a creditor is a ______.
   a. garnishment
   b. debt management plan
   c. money order
   d. finance charge
6. An origination fee is charged for ______.
   a. acquiring a credit report
   b. starting paperwork on a loan
   c. transferring a credit card balance
   d. filing for bankruptcy

Understanding the Main Ideas

1. Name three examples of fees that you might have to pay for obtaining or using credit.
2. You did not know your credit card company would charge a higher interest rate for a cash advance. Do you still have to pay that rate? Why or why not?
3. True or false: The three national credit bureaus are government agencies.
4. Which law prohibits unfair discrimination against people applying for credit?
5. What can you do if you find untrue statements in your credit report?
6. Name at least three ways to reduce spending.
7. Is a debt management plan (DMP) the same as credit counseling? Explain.

Practicing Math

1. Your family needs new living room furniture. An ad from the Rent It/Buy It store shows a sofa and matching chair that can be rented for only $27.99 per week. If you rent it for 104 weeks, the furniture is yours. An ad from Parker Brothers Furniture offers a similar sofa and chair, payable in installments of $125 per month for fifteen months. Which store charges more per month? Which store has the lower total price? (*Hint:* Assume one month equals four weeks.)
2. A five-year loan of $15,000 at 6 percent interest will cost your family $289.99 per month. If the interest rate were only 5.5 percent, you would pay $286.52 per month. What is the difference in total payments for the five-year term? You can round to the nearest dollar.

Applying Critical Thinking Skills

1. Why should you obtain your credit report from each of the national bureaus instead of just one or two?
2. Bank accounts are usually not part of your credit score—so how can opening a bank account help you build a good credit record?
3. You see a credit card advertised as ideal for people with no credit history. It sounds good to you, but what should you look out for?
4. What are the pros and cons of a debt consolidation loan?
5. Describe advantages and disadvantages of borrowing money from friends or family.
6. Your friend has found a credit counseling organization. It is "nonprofit," so he believes it will work in his best interests. What advice would you give him?

Working with Real-World Documents

1. Bring to class at least one ad for a credit card. Working with other students who have brought ads, create a table comparing features of the cards, such as APR, annual fees, rewards, and so forth. Which cards seem the best? Why?
2. You bought shoes from Hansen's Shoe Depot and charged them to your Hansen's card. You returned the shoes, but your credit card continues to be billed. Write a letter of complaint to Hansen's Retail Services Department.

Taking It Home

1. Ask family and friends for tips on how to reduce spending. Make a "top ten" list of the tips you consider most useful.
2. Look at the bankruptcy notices in the newspaper. These notices list assets and liabilities. What is the *average* difference between the amount of assets and the amount of liabilities?

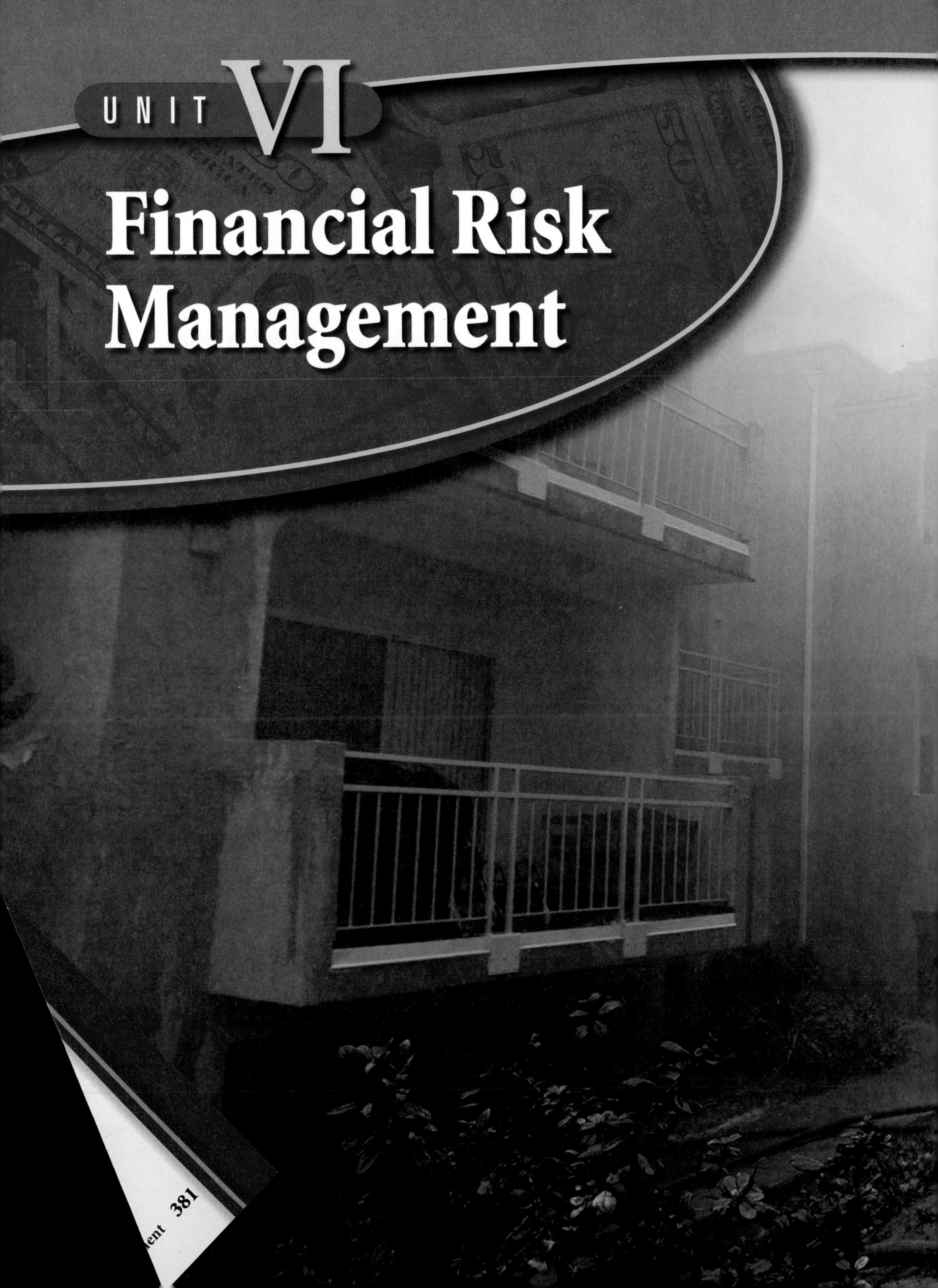

UNIT VI

Financial Risk Management

CHAPTER 15 Auto and Home Insurance

CHAPTER 16 Health and Life Insurance

CHAPTER 15

Auto and Home Insurance

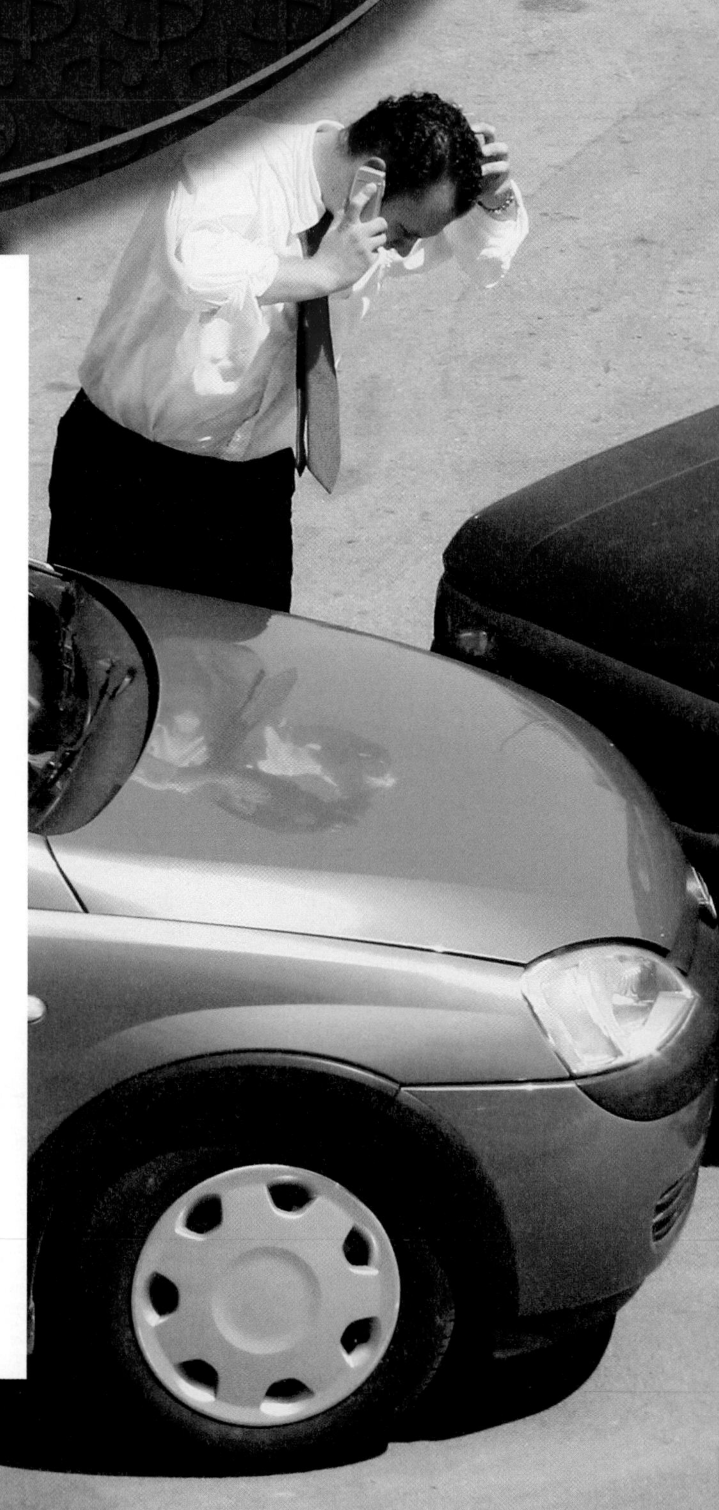

No one knows what tomorrow will bring. Insurance is a way to protect yourself against the risks that you face each day. You might pay for insurance for years and never have a claim. If you have an accident or loss, however, the amount you receive might be much more than the sum of what you paid over the years.

▲ Having insurance will protect you financially if you are involved in an accident.

Few people can absorb the whole cost of a car accident with injuries, or a house fire that destroys the family's home and belongings. Even a flooded apartment could wipe out many people financially. By taking out insurance, you choose to pay an insurance company a regular sum of money in return for the assurance that if a disaster strikes, the insurance will help with the costs.

SECTION 1 Insuring Your Auto

SECTION 2 Insuring Your Home and Property

Fact or Fiction

What do you think? Are the following statements true or false? If you think they are false, then say what is true.

1. Liability coverage protects you whether you are driving your own car or someone else's car.
2. Bodily injury liability coverage pays both medical and legal expenses.
3. Collision coverage is usually the least expensive portion of an auto insurance policy.
4. Comprehensive insurance covers losses if your vehicle is stolen.
5. A homeowner's policy includes liability protection whether you are at home or elsewhere.
6. Renters do not need property insurance because they don't own the building where they live.
7. If you live in a high-risk area, you cannot get home insurance.

Answers on page 401.

Study Reminder

*Knowing how to study can increase your knowledge, improve your grades, and cut down on your study time. See the **Studying Personal Finance** pages at the front of the book for some tips to help you study this chapter.*

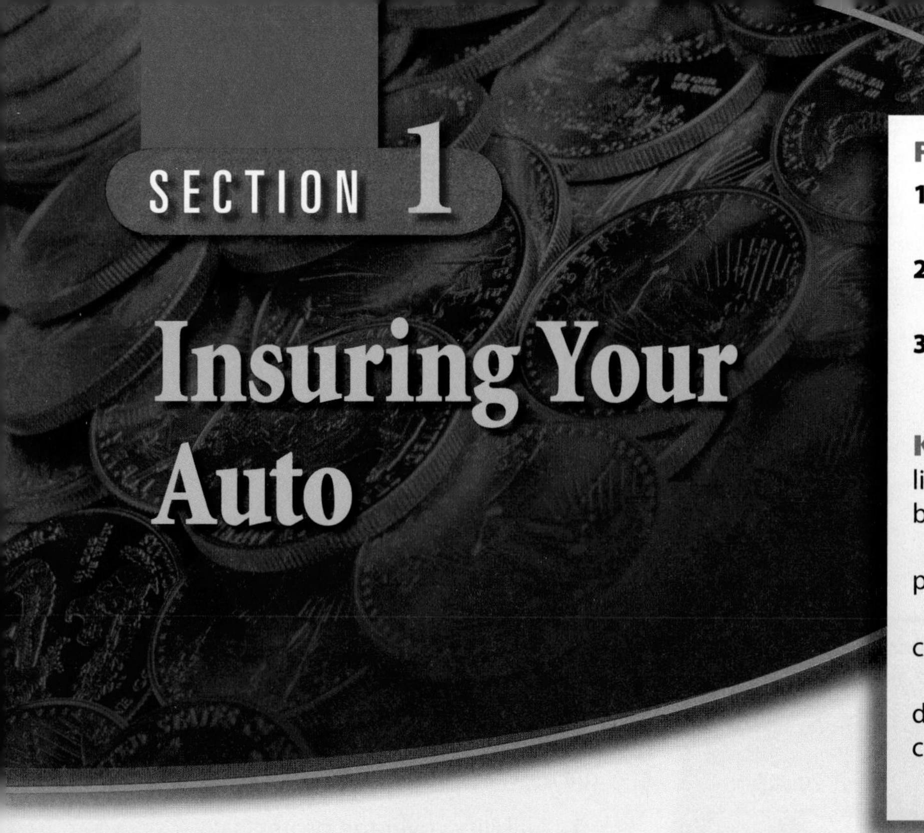

SECTION 1

Insuring Your Auto

Focus Questions

1. What are the basic types of car insurance coverage?
2. What are some ways to control your car insurance premiums?
3. What steps should you take if you have an accident?

Key Terms

liability
bodily injury liability coverage
property damage liability coverage
collision coverage
deductible
comprehensive coverage
medical payments coverage
personal injury protection (PIP)
endorsement
exclusions
premium

About one out of every ten vehicles in the United States is involved in an accident each year, and 1.5 million autos are stolen each year. Even a slight fender-bender can easily cost $1,000 in damages. Without auto insurance, you would have to bear the full cost of damages if you have an accident or if your car is damaged or stolen.

Almost all states require vehicle owners to have specific types and amounts of insurance. If you buy a car with an auto loan, the lender will require additional coverage on the car itself. That means that every vehicle on the road *should be* insured. Unfortunately, this goal is not always met.

Individual states regulate insurance within their borders. Most have a *traditional* system of insurance. That means the person at fault in an accident pays for all the damage and medical expenses. A few states use a modified *no-fault* system for auto insurance. If there is an accident, each driver's insurance pays for that driver's medical bills, car repairs, and any damage. Even if one driver was clearly at fault, both insurance companies pay. Lawsuits are limited.

liability in insurance, responsibility for damages caused

bodily injury liability coverage auto insurance coverage that pays for expenses related to injuries or deaths caused by the policyholder's car

property damage liability coverage auto insurance coverage for damage caused by the policyholder's car to another person's property

Basic Coverage Options

Insurance on motor vehicles from Bugs to Hummers is commonly called *auto insurance* or *car insurance.* It consists of six basic types of coverage. Some are mandatory. Others are optional. Figure 15.1 shows the types of coverage and what each pays for.

Liability Coverage

In insurance, **liability** means responsibility for damages caused. Auto insurance includes two types of liability coverage: (1) bodily injury liability and (2) property damage liability. Both are required. Liability coverage protects you (the insured) against any claims for injury or damage to another person's property. It protects you whether you are driving your own car or someone else's car (with the owner's permission). It even protects you if someone else is driving your car. Liability coverage does *not* pay anything

Figure 15.1 UNDERSTANDING AUTO INSURANCE

Type of coverage	Pays for
Bodily injury liability	Injuries to others when you are at fault (Required)
Property damage liability	Damage to the other car or to property when you are at fault (Required)
Collision	Damage to your car from an accident that is your fault (Optional)
Comprehensive	Damage to your car due to theft, vandalism, glass breakage, weather (Optional)
Medical payments or personal injury protection (PIP)	Injuries to you or your passengers (Optional; PIP required in states with no-fault insurance laws)
Uninsured/underinsured motorist	Injuries to you or your passengers, or damage to your vehicle, in an accident when the driver at fault does not have adequate insurance (Usually required)

toward your own injuries or damage to your own property.

If you are injured or your car is damaged in an accident that is someone else's fault, you can make a claim against that person's auto insurance company for bodily injury or property damage. However, you would need to prove that the other person was at fault.

Bodily Injury Liability Coverage If your car injures or kills someone else—passengers in your own vehicle, people in other vehicles, or pedestrians—**bodily injury liability coverage** will pay for the expenses related to the accident. These might include medical bills, loss of income, or pain and suffering. It does *not* cover injuries to you or anyone else covered on your policy (such as a spouse). Those expenses would fall under medical payments coverage or personal injury protection, to be discussed a little later in this section.

Property Damage Liability Coverage When personal property is damaged in an accident, and you are at fault, **property damage liability coverage** pays for repair or replacement. This includes another person's car—but also things like a damaged light pole, a fence, landscaping, or a building. It does not include damage to your own car or your own property.

▼ If you are in an accident—or if you hit someone else with your car—having bodily injury liability insurance could save you a lot of money.

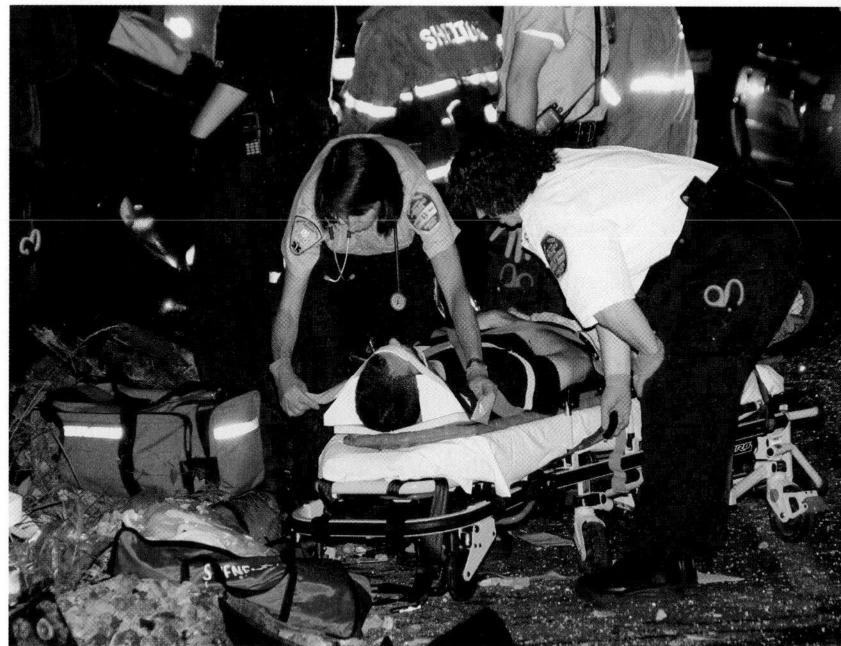

Going Global

The American Automobile Association (AAA) is a nonprofit organization that started as a service club for auto owners in 1902, when cars were a novelty. Today, AAA has 50 million members in affiliated auto clubs throughout the United States and Canada. It began by providing free emergency roadside assistance and towing. As early as 1903, AAA supported legislation in Congress to build better roads and highways.

As car travel became the most common type of transportation, AAA introduced other services. It publishes maps and guidebooks and acts as a travel agency for its members. Now AAA offers international travel planning as well. It also sells traveler's checks and European rail passes. It developed reciprocal agreements with automobile associations in many foreign countries—so that AAA members are eligible for those clubs' services when traveling abroad.

In many areas, AAA affiliates offer automobile insurance. Because U.S. insurers do not cover losses that occur in Mexico, drivers who want to take U.S.-registered vehicles into Mexico have to buy separate auto insurance issued by a Mexican company.

To make it easier for travelers to purchase Mexican insurance, many AAA affiliates offer Mexican policies. Some offer policies for AAA members driving in other parts of the world.

Thinking Globally

1. Why do you think U.S. auto insurance policies do not cover travel in Mexico?
2. Some AAA affiliates offer boat, business, and life insurance. Why would an auto club offer those possibilities?

collision coverage insurance coverage for accident damage to the policyholder's car

deductible the amount paid out-of-pocket by the policyholder before the insurance company pays benefits on a claim

comprehensive coverage insurance coverage for damage to the policyholder's car resulting from things other than an accident, such as a natural disaster, theft, or vandalism

Collision Coverage

Collision coverage pays for repairing any accident damage to your vehicle. Collision coverage is optional, but if you have an auto loan, the lender will probably require collision coverage. Collision coverage is usually the most expensive portion of auto insurance. It is especially important to have it for newer cars that are worth more. To reduce the cost of this coverage, most policies include a **deductible**. In case of damage, you would pay the first $250 or $500 (or whatever your deductible is). Then the insurance company pays the rest. The higher your deductible, the less you pay for coverage.

Collision coverage will pay only up to the *fair market value* of your car, minus the deductible. The fair market value is considered to be the average cost of a car of the same model, age, and condition. If the cost to repair your car is estimated to be greater than its fair market value, the insurance company will usually declare the car a total loss—or "totaled"—and issue you a check for the market value of your car.

Comprehensive Coverage

If your car is damaged by something other than an accident—such as fire, flood, earthquake, hurricane, hail, vandalism, or collision with an animal—**comprehensive coverage** pays for repairs. It also covers the loss if your vehicle is stolen.

As with collision insurance, comprehensive coverage will pay only up to the fair market value of your vehicle, minus your deductible. Comprehensive insurance is not required by any state, but if your car is financed, the lender will most likely require it before granting the loan.

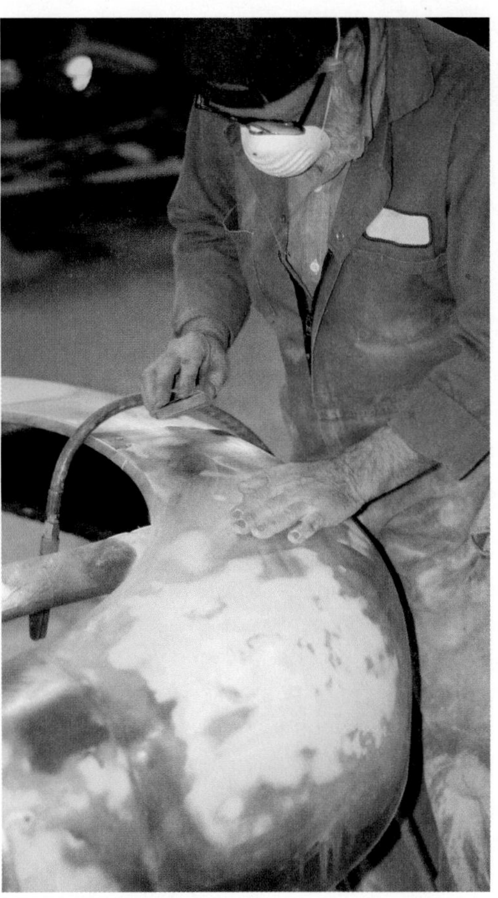

◀ **If your car needs repairs as the result of an accident, collision coverage will help pay for the costs.**

Medical Payments and Personal Injury Protection

Medical payments coverage is for medical bills that you or your family members have because of an accident, no matter who caused it. You are also covered if you are riding in or driving someone else's car (with permission), or if you are struck by another car while walking.

Personal injury protection (PIP) is a form of no-fault insurance that provides a broader form of medical payments coverage. It pays for medical care, lost wages, and certain other services. PIP is required in states with no-fault auto insurance laws. It is sometimes an option in states that do not have no-fault laws.

Uninsured/Underinsured Motorist Coverage

Some states require vehicle owners to carry insurance against uninsured and underinsured motorists. This pays medical bills—and sometimes car repairs—from your policy if a hit-and-run, uninsured, or underinsured motorist causes an accident. Even if not required, this coverage could help you avoid a major financial loss.

Additional Options

In addition to the basic coverage included in most auto policies, there are a number of other options available. Some may be written into policies as endorsements. An **endorsement**, also called a *rider*, is a modification to the master policy. For example, your basic policy might not cover the electronic equipment in your car, but you could add that coverage as an endorsement. Other optional types of coverage must be written as separate policies.

Towing Coverage and Rental Reimbursement

Towing coverage is a low-cost add-on. If your car has to be towed after an accident, or because you have a dead battery or a damaged tire, the towing charge could be equal to or more than the yearly cost of the towing coverage. Auto clubs usually offer free towing services with membership.

If your car is seriously damaged, it may take weeks to get it repaired. In the meantime, your transportation is gone.

medical payments coverage insurance coverage for medical bills of the policyholder and his or her family members involved in an accident

personal injury protection (PIP) optional insurance that pays expanded benefits for the policyholder's medical care, lost wages, and certain other services

endorsement a modification or addition to an insurance policy; also called a *rider*

Did You Know?

In the early 1600s, Lloyd's of London was a coffeehouse where sailors, ship owners, and merchants gathered to hear the latest shipping news and conduct business. It became the major meeting place for wealthy individuals who joined together into "syndicates" to insure ships and their cargo. The ship owner would pay a fee (a premium) to the syndicate. If the ship reached its destination safely, the syndicate would keep the premium. But if the ship was lost, the members of the syndicate, who were called "Names," had to pay the ship owner for his loss. This could be very costly to the Names, because there was no limit to their liability.

Lloyd's of London has continued into the present day. It is still not a true insurance company, but an association of syndicates. There are still some Names involved, but now corporations with limited liability are also involved. Lloyd's is famous for insuring things that normal companies think are too risky—like Tina Turner's legs or Jimmy Durante's nose.

Renting a car is one alternative, but it is an expensive one. Many consumers do not realize that most insurance companies offer rental reimbursement coverage at a very low fee.

Assigned-Risk Policies

You are required to carry insurance, but what if you've had speeding tickets or caused some accidents in the past—and none of the insurance companies you call will accept you? Then, in order to register and drive your car, you will probably have to get insurance from your state's *insurer of last resort*—also known as the *assigned-risk pool.*

Every company that sells auto insurance in your state must participate in the program. In that way, the state makes sure that almost everyone can get liability coverage. Assigned-risk insurance policies are very expensive because only high-risk drivers are included. The number of driving mistakes determines the rate that the driver will pay. If this is the only insurance you can get, try to maintain a perfect driving record for at least three years, so that you can get out of the assigned-risk pool and qualify for regular car insurance.

Some private insurance companies advertise that they will insure people with poor driving records. Be sure to compare costs and check out such companies before you buy.

▶ Shop around before settling on an insurance company—many good ones are out there, so find the one that matches your needs.

Buying Auto Insurance

When you first learn to drive, your family might add you as a driver on their car insurance policy. However, before long you will buy insurance on your own. It might seem hard to know just what coverage you need. You might choose to buy through a local insurance agent who can give advice on coverage and can help if you have a claim. Or you might get rate quotes and buy your insurance over the phone or online.

Once you decide on a company, you will be asked to fill out a detailed application form. If the insurance company accepts your application, you will be issued a policy. The policy is a contract spelling out what is and is not covered. Items that are specifically listed as not being covered are called **exclusions**. For example, companies often exclude personal belongings and any equipment not permanently installed in the vehicle.

The first page of the policy is usually a summary of what is covered under the policy, what is excluded, and how much you will pay—the **premium**. Auto insurance is generally paid twice a year. However, for a small additional fee, most companies allow smaller payments, either monthly or quarterly.

How Much Do You Need?

How much insurance you need depends on your situation. The absolute minimum is the amount of coverage your state requires for bodily injury liability and property damage liability. These minimums are designated by a three-part number that indicates the amount of damage covered by the policy, as shown by the example in Figure 15.2. The required amounts vary from state to state. Keep in mind, however, that the cost of an accident is often much greater than the minimum legal limits of most states.

How Much Bodily Injury? If you were sued for damages after an accident, legal fees alone could cause you to go bankrupt. You might be sued even if an accident was not your fault. Bodily injury liability coverage pays both medical expenses and legal fees. It also pays for lost wages of a person who could not work because of an accident. You want enough insurance to cover a judgment against you in case you are involved in a serious accident.

How Much Medical and PIP? The high cost of medical care also makes medical payments coverage and personal injury protection (PIP) very

exclusions items that an insurance policy does not cover

premium the rate charged for an insurance policy

Figure 15.2 DECODING LIABILITY INSURANCE (50/100/25)

The amount of liability coverage per accident is indicated by a three-part number, such as 50/100/25. The actual required amounts will vary from state to state. Because of the high costs of medical care, it is wise to carry higher limits than your state requires. Liability coverage does not pay for your own medical costs or property damage.

"50"	"100"	"25"
Maximum paid *per person* for injuries from one accident: $50,000	Maximum paid for *all injuries* from one accident: $100,000	Maximum paid for *property damage* from one accident: $25,000

LOOK Before You Leap

Carly has been helping her grandmother, Nana, who has severe arthritis, with shopping and housework for several years. Lately, she has been driving Nana to doctor appointments and to visit friends. Nana tells Carly that she has decided not to drive any more at all, and she'd like to give Carly her car in gratitude for all her help.

The car is a luxurious German sedan, only two years old. It has a powerful engine, leather upholstery, a high-end stereo, even a GPS system. Carly cannot believe it. She looks at her sturdy little 10-year-old Corolla and mentally begins to wave good-bye.

Carly tells her mom about Nana's offer. Her mom agrees it is very generous, but she asks Carly if she can handle the increased insurance and upkeep costs. Carly knows Nana pays a lot for service, but she had not thought about insurance. She calls her agent to ask how much more the premiums would be if she accepts Nana's offer.

Carly's current auto insurance premium is $219 every six months. She does not have collision coverage. She has a good driving record and good grades—but even so, for Nana's car the premium will be about $600 every six months for the same amount of coverage as the Corolla has.

However, Carly will need collision coverage for Nana's car. When she adds that, the premium will be $800 every six months—assuming she keeps her grades up and does not get any tickets. "There must be cheaper rates out there," Carly insists. But after checking around, she sees there is not much difference. Still, she's thinking, "I'd be crazy to turn down such a fabulous car!"

Before Deciding

1. Why does it cost more to insure an expensive car? What would you do in Carly's place? Explain your reasoning.
2. Might there be other options for Nana to show her appreciation? For instance, Nana could sell the car and deposit the money into a savings account for Carly's college education. Can you think of other alternatives?

important. It also provides coverage in some other accident situations. This coverage is relatively inexpensive, so it is best to carry the highest amount you can afford.

Collision and Comprehensive Coverage: How Much? Whether you need collision coverage depends upon the age of your vehicle and whether you have a loan. Most lenders require coverage. But if your vehicle is old and its value low, you might decide not to carry collision coverage. This can save you a lot of money. On the other hand, could you afford to repair or replace your car without reimbursement from insurance?

Comprehensive coverage is optional. As for collision coverage, it makes the most sense for newer vehicles.

The Premium: Risk Factors Count

Car insurance rates vary widely. Insurance companies continually analyze their customers' claims to identify common characteristics of drivers and

Do Your RESEARCH

Automobile and homeowner's insurance rates vary widely from company to company. It pays to shop for the best deal. You can get out the phone book and call different insurance companies around town. You can get quotes by mail. But probably the easiest way to compare offers is online.

You can fill out forms at the Web sites of various insurance companies and then compare the premiums. Some sites show side-by-side quotes from several companies. One online insurance agency that represents many different companies and provides side-by-side quotes is Insurance.com (http://fin.emcp.net/insurance). Another Web site that allows you to compare rates is DMV.org (http://fin.emcp.net/dmv).

You might be required to enter your name and address before receiving a quote. That raises privacy issues—and you are also likely to receive marketing e-mails from those companies in the future, whether you want them or not. To deal with this issue, you can set up an alternate e-mail account with a free provider such as Yahoo! or Hotmail. Any e-mails from those insurance companies will go to this other e-mail account instead of filling up your primary inbox.

Finally, remember: Never share your Social Security number or financial information online in order to get an insurance quote. If you decide to buy a particular auto insurance policy, however, you will have to provide your driver's license number so the company can check your driving history. Before offering to insure you, a company will also need to do a credit check.

Your Assignment

1. Go to Insurance.com or DMV.org and get three quotes to insure your car (or your ideal car, if you do not own one). Is there a big difference in these quotes? Why or why not?
2. An online auto insurer is offering you coverage at half the price you are currently paying. How can you know if the company is legitimate?
3. An insurance company has agreed to offer you car insurance, and asks if you have any debt on the car. Should you tell them? Why or why not?

vehicles involved in accidents. Each company calculates its rates based on the risk factors it identifies. The more risk factors you have, the higher your premium will be.

The Driver Your driver classification is based on your age, sex, marital status, and driving history. Drivers under age 25 have the most accidents. Men (primarily young men) have more accidents than women. Married people are less likely to have accidents than those who are single. In addition, if you have any tickets for driving violations or have had any accidents that were your fault, the cost of your insurance will go up.

Every driver listed on the policy is evaluated. Some companies also check credit ratings. Their research shows that people with good credit ratings are more careful and less likely to have accidents.

Where You Live Insurance companies also take location into consideration. Rates are higher in big cities because of heavier traffic and more accidents, theft, and vandalism. Rates are lower in small towns and rural areas, with less traffic and fewer accidents.

Automobile crashes are the primary cause of death for young people 15 to 20 years old. Only about 6.3 percent of licensed drivers in the United States are in this age group—but they are the group most likely to be drivers in both fatal and nonfatal accidents.

In 2006, drivers 15 to 20 years old accounted for the following:

- 12.9 percent of drivers involved in fatal crashes
- 16 percent of drivers involved in all police-reported crashes
- 16.5 percent of drivers in single-vehicle fatal accidents
- 11.1 percent of drivers in multiple-vehicle fatal accidents

Although these percentages are alarmingly high for this age group, the percentages are not as high as they used to be. In 2006, both girls and boys aged 15 to 20 years old were actually 8 percent *less likely* to be the driver in a fatal car crash than they were ten years earlier, in 1996.

How Much You Drive If you will be driving a lot less or a lot more than average, your premium might be affected. If you drive a long distance to work, that increases your risk of an accident. Using your vehicle on your job will raise your premium.

▼ Many young people have their own cars, which creates both mobility and expense.

The Vehicle The type of vehicle you drive can make a big difference in the cost of insurance. You will pay more for the following:

- Models that are more often involved in accidents
- Sporty, high-performance cars that often attract buyers interested in speed
- Models that have an above-average rate of injury or damage in a crash
- Models that are more expensive to repair
- Vehicles that are favorite targets of thieves

Controlling Insurance Costs

Car insurance is a major expense. You cannot change some risk factors, such as your age, but there are other ways you might be able to cut costs. Here are some examples:

- *Keep your driving record clean.* This has the biggest impact on the price of insurance. Any accident or ticket for a driving violation counts against your insurance for three years. Driving too fast and not paying attention are two common causes of problems.
- *Qualify for a good student discount.* Students who earn at least a B average in school are also safer drivers. If you have these good grades, many companies will give you a discount on car insurance. Passing a driver's education class might also qualify you for a discount.
- *Check for safety feature discounts.* You might qualify for discounts if your car has safety features such as antilock brakes or antitheft devices. Ask if your car has any that qualify.

- *Take advantage of multiple-car or multiple-policy discounts.* You might qualify for discounts if you buy your insurance from the same company as your family or if you have your car and home insurance together.
- *Consider increasing deductibles.* Increasing your deductible on collision and comprehensive coverage will save money. If you opt for a higher deductible, try to keep the amount of your deductible in savings so it will be there if you need it.
- *Compare options.* The cost of insurance varies by company, even for the same coverage on the same car and the same owner. Check online, call for rates, or ask a local agent who represents several companies. Beyond price, it is important to pick an insurance company with a strong rating. Check rating services online—such as A. M. Best, Standard & Poor's, and your state's online insurance site.

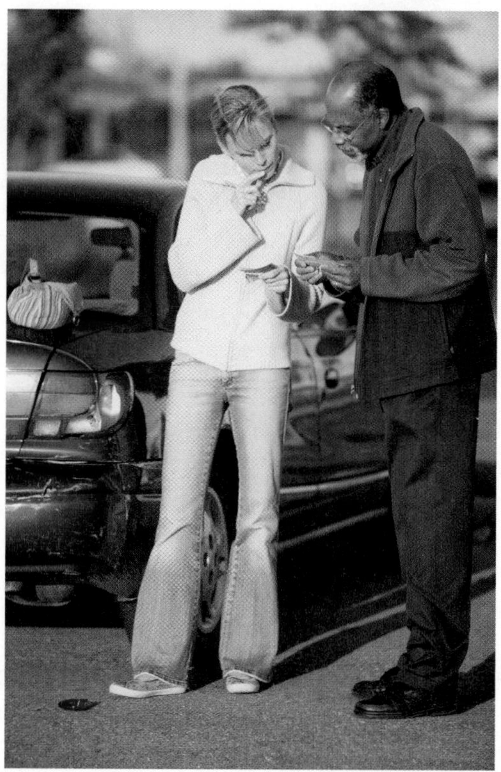

◀ Accidents can happen to anyone at any time, so be prepared with an accident kit that includes your information, and be ready to exchange information with the other driver.

If an Accident Occurs

At some point, you might be involved in an accident. Would you know what to do? If you take the appropriate action, you can help prevent further injuries, reduce costs, and speed the clean-up and repair process.

Sometimes it is hard to think clearly after an accident. Be prepared by carrying a cell phone and keeping an accident kit in your glove compartment. Figure 15.3 shows what to include in the accident kit.

Figure 15.3 WHAT TO KEEP IN YOUR ACCIDENT KIT

- Your vehicle registration card (issued by the state)
- Your insurance card verifying that you have insurance, along with notes about what coverage you have
- A pen and paper for taking notes
- A disposable or digital camera (if your cell phone doesn't have a camera) to take pictures of the accident scene
- A card naming a person to be notified in case of accident, plus any medical information that would be important if you needed emergency medical treatment
- Phone numbers of local and state law enforcement agencies in case 911 is not available

YOU DECIDE

Andy and his friend Todd are stopped at a red light when Andy's car is hit from behind by a pickup truck. The boys are shaken up but uninjured. They get out to check the damage. It doesn't look too bad—the bumper will have to be replaced and the trunk lid won't close, but that's all. The pickup's bumper is pushed in a little.

The driver gets out of the pickup and immediately apologizes, telling the boys he just learned that his father is in the hospital. His mind is not on his driving.

The boys say they are sorry about his dad. Andy asks for the man's personal and insurance information. Todd is dialing the police to report the accident when the man stops him.

"Can't we take care of this now?" he asks. He offers to write a check for $700. He says he will go to the bank with Andy while he cashes it. "I don't want to be messing around with insurance and waiting for the police to show up with my dad so sick," the man says.

Andy guesses $700 ought to take care of the damage to his car. Why wait for the police and fill out a bunch of insurance forms? This will be so much simpler.

Should he...

1. ...accept the man's offer? Can Andy be sure the man's check will not bounce? Do you think $700 would pay for a new bumper and repairs to the trunk? Check prices for bumpers online.
2. ...politely decline the man's offer, and then get the man's insurance and personal information and report the accident? Explain.

If you are involved in an accident, the following steps will help you take the necessary actions:

▼ **Call the police at 911 for immediate help if a serious accident occurs—especially if someone is injured.**

1. *First, be safe.* If you can, take several photographs of the accident scene. Then, if the accident is minor and no one is injured, move the vehicles off the road. If the cars cannot be moved or if someone inside is injured, turn off the ignition and turn on the hazard lights. If you must stay in the vehicle, keep your seat belt on.
2. *Call the police and ambulance, if appropriate.* Call the police if there is an injury, severe damage to the vehicles or property, or if a traffic violation occurred or alcohol might be involved. Any serious injuries need immediate attention from emergency medical personnel. Give the police factual information about the accident, but do not try to say who was to blame. If the police are not called, it is still important to file a state vehicle accident report. Forms for this are available at police stations and also, in many states, online at the Department of Motor

Vehicles Web site. A police report usually speeds up the processing of any claims.

3. *Exchange information.* Exchange information with the other driver. You will need each other's name, address, phone number, insurance company, driver's license number, and license plate number. If the other driver is not the owner of the vehicle, write down both names and their relationship. Also take the names of any passengers. Write a description for yourself of exactly how the accident happened, including each vehicle's make, model, year, and color. Be polite, but do not place or assume blame.
4. *Call your insurance company.* As soon as possible after an accident, notify your insurance company and file a claim. You can call your local insurance agent, but most companies have toll-free numbers to call. The claims representative will give you further instructions.
5. *Know your insurance coverage.* You might have to make some immediate decisions after an accident. If you know what coverage you have, you will make better decisions. For example, if your car is not drivable, do you have towing coverage? Does your policy cover a rental car while yours is being repaired?

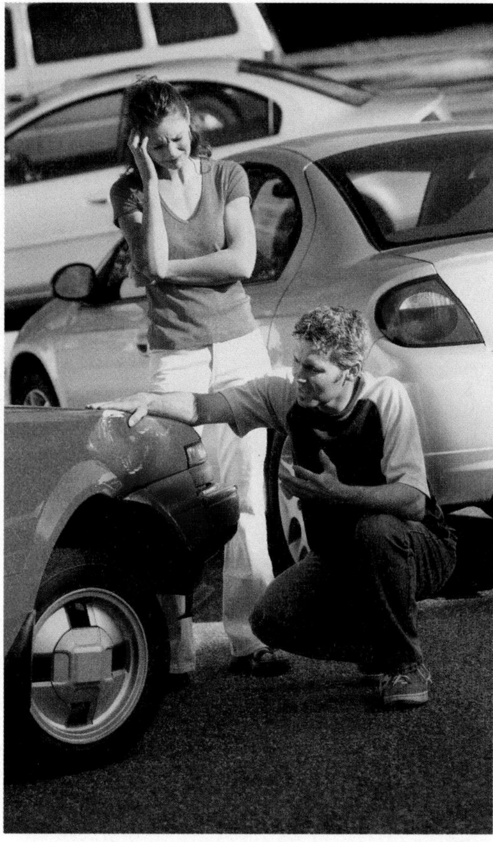

◀ Inspect accident damage to your car so that you can give details to your insurance company.

Finally, remember that insurance claims are not always settled quickly and to the satisfaction of the policyholder. If you have problems in dealing with your insurance company, call the company's policyholder office to get your questions answered. You can also contact your state's department of insurance by phone or online if you are still not satisfied.

SECTION 1 ASSESSMENT

Factual Recall

1. Who regulates auto insurance?
2. What is the difference between traditional and no-fault auto insurance?
3. What is liability coverage?
4. What is generally the most expensive portion of auto insurance?
5. When you buy insurance, you will receive a contract that spells out what is and is not covered. What is this contract called?

Critical Thinking

1. What is the purpose of insurance?
2. Why do you think the lender of an auto loan requires insurance coverage on the car?

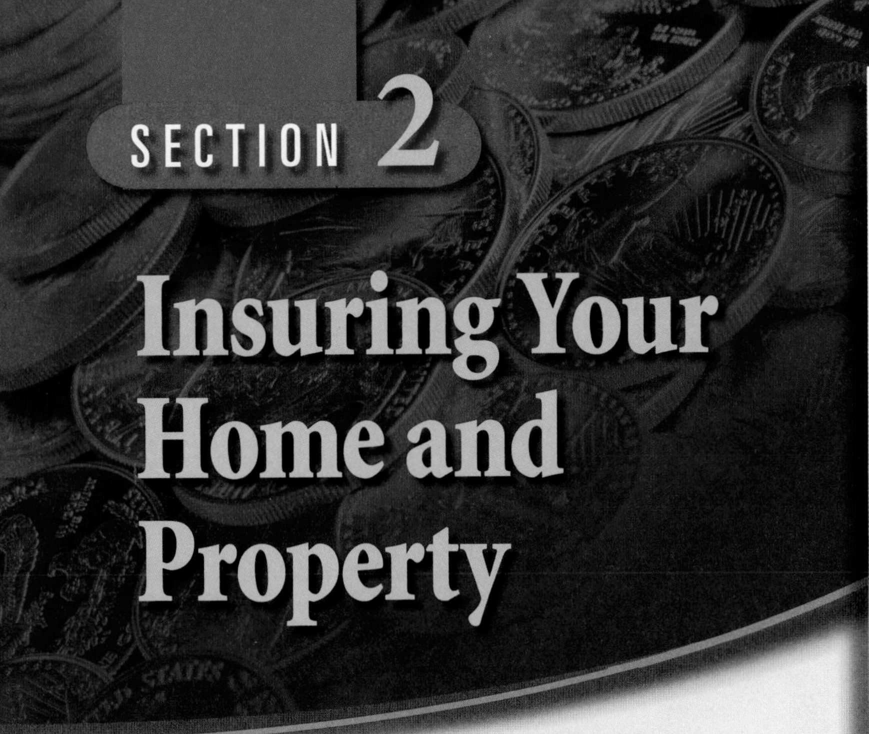

SECTION 2

Insuring Your Home and Property

Focus Questions

1. What four types of coverage are found in a standard homeowner's policy?
2. What kinds of things are covered under the liability portion of a homeowner's policy?
3. Why do renters need property insurance?
4. What kinds of discounts are available to reduce the cost of a homeowner's policy?
5. What are three situations that are considered "high risk" by insurance companies?

Key Terms

structural damage coverage
personal property coverage
replacement cost coverage
Fair Access to Insurance Requirements (FAIR) Plan

Your first decisions about home insurance might come more quickly than you think. You will soon be living away from home—in a dorm or apartment, depending on where life takes you. Although you will not own the building you are living in, you will probably have a lot of your personal property with you. If your things are stolen or destroyed in a fire, would you have insurance coverage?

In some cases, your belongings might be covered under your parents' homeowner's insurance while you are in school. It's important to check. Once you are living on your own—even if you are renting—you will need your own insurance.

Home Insurance Options

Home and property insurance—often called *homeowner's insurance*—actually comes in a variety of forms. In all, there are four types of coverage, but not all are included in every policy. The four types are as follows:

1. Coverage on the physical structure of your home
2. Personal property coverage, ranging from clothes to furniture
3. Liability coverage in case someone is injured on your property or hurt by a family member or a pet
4. Coverage for living expenses if you have to live elsewhere while damage is repaired

Various combinations of these types of coverage are available for renters, people who own their own houses, condominium owners, and those who own manufactured homes. Figure 15.4 shows the *forms* (types of policies) available, for whom they are designed, and what coverage is included for each.

Looking at a table of insurance forms that are available to you and then comparing them will help you decide which form includes the coverage you need for your situation.

Figure 15.4 **SORTING OUT HOME INSURANCE POLICIES**

Policy form:	Designed for:	Coverage includes:	Notes:
Basic form (HO-1)	Homeowners	Personal property, liability, physical structure, living expenses	Covers most common hazards
Broad form (HO-2)	Homeowners	All categories of coverage	Includes additional hazards such as electrical surges
Special form (HO-3)	Homeowners	All categories of coverage	Covers all hazards except flood, earthquake, nuclear accident, war
Tenant's form (HO-4)	Renters	Personal property, liability	Covers same hazards as HO-2
Condominium form (HO-6)	Condo owners	Personal property, liability, portion of structure owned but not common areas, living expenses	The condo association policy covers common areas
Manufactured homes	Owners	Coverages vary	Prices are higher than for conventional homes

A Closer Look at Coverage

If you rent or own a home, you could suffer a financial loss in a variety of ways. A fire breaks out in the apartment below you and your belongings have smoke and water damage. A neighbor's child falls down your steps and needs stitches. High winds snap a large limb off a tree and it falls on your roof. Damage due to hazards—called *perils* in insurance policies—is eligible for reimbursement, if you have the right coverage.

Structural Damage Coverage

Those who own their homes need **structural damage coverage** in case the house is damaged or destroyed by fire, severe weather, or any other disaster listed in the policy. Flood and earthquake damage are not included. Separate policies are available for those, but the cost is high for locations that are at increased risk.

Most policies also cover damage to other buildings on the property, such as a separate garage. Claims for these outbuildings are covered for up to 10 percent of the insurance coverage on the home. For example, if the insurance coverage on a house is $200,000, a detached garage would be covered for up to $20,000.

Personal Property Coverage

All types of home insurance include **personal property coverage**. This coverage pays if your personal possessions are stolen, damaged, or destroyed by fire or some other disaster listed in the policy. For homeowner's policies that insure a house or condominium (the structure), most companies cover personal property for up to 50 percent of the amount of coverage on the structure. Some people pay extra for added coverage. People who have renter's policies

structural damage coverage insurance coverage for damage to the physical structure of a home resulting from fire, severe weather, or other disasters listed in the policy

personal property coverage insurance coverage that pays if personal property is stolen, damaged, or destroyed by fire or some other disaster

need to estimate the value of their belongings to determine appropriate coverage.

Personal property coverage extends beyond your own home. If your trumpet is stolen from your car, it is covered. Companies often limit how much they will pay on portable personal items, such as laptops, cameras, audio equipment, and more expensive items, such as jewelry. For additional coverage, you can buy a special personal property endorsement.

Typically, the amount paid on a personal property claim is based on *actual cash value*. That is determined by the cost of replacement minus *depreciation*—the decline in value due to age. Often the amount of depreciation is much more than you would expect. For a higher premium, you can get **replacement cost coverage**. This reimburses you for the total cost of replacing an item.

replacement cost coverage insurance coverage that pays to replace the insured item at today's prices

Liability Coverage

All forms of homeowner's insurance include liability coverage. This provides protection against lawsuits for injuries or property damage caused by the policyholder, family members, and even pets. This coverage applies whether you are at home or elsewhere. It will pay for the cost of defending you in court and for any damages the court says you must pay—up to the maximum amount allowed in the policy. The basic limit for liability coverage is usually $100,000, but experts recommend that you have at least $300,000 of liability coverage. There is no deductible.

The liability portion of homeowner's insurance also provides some no-fault medical coverage. If someone is injured on your property, he or she can submit medical bills directly to your insurance company. By handling medical payments in this way, it is not necessary for the injured party to file a liability claim

▶ Some of the toys in your yard that are the most fun may also be the most risky—a trampoline injury can hurt people, as well as your pocketbook.

◀ Insuring your new home allows you to enjoy this investment with peace of mind since you are covered in case of accidents, disasters, or emergencies.

against you. Medical payments coverage is usually limited to an amount between $1,000 and $5,000.

Additional Living Expenses Coverage

With additional living expenses coverage, the insurance company will pay for a temporary place to stay if your home cannot be lived in during repair or rebuilding. The typical homeowner's policy will cover additional living expenses in an amount up to 20 percent of the coverage for structural damage to the home.

Different Policies for Different Needs

Whether your home is an apartment, a house, a condominium, or a manufactured home, there is a homeowner's insurance policy to protect you from many types of loss. Banks and others who lend money for home loans require borrowers to have a homeowner's policy for at least the amount of the mortgage.

Renter's Insurance

If you live in a rented apartment or house, having renter's insurance can give you significant protection at a reasonable cost. Tenant's form (HO-4) is designed to provide the coverage renters need most.

The personal property portion covers you against loss or damage to your personal possessions due to theft, fire, smoke, lightning, wind, and water (other than flood). The liability portion protects you and the family members living with you against liability for injury to others—in your home or elsewhere. If you are sued over an injury, it will pay for your defense. Finally, if your home is damaged, the insurance will pay for you to live elsewhere while it is repaired.

Choices for Home Owners

Homeowner's policies cover personal property, liability, and additional living expenses, just like renter's insurance. In addition, they provide financial relief if the home or surrounding property is damaged by any of the causes listed on the policy.

Answers to Fact or Fiction

1. True; **2.** True; **3.** False—Collision coverage is usually the most expensive portion of auto insurance; **4.** True; **5.** True; **6.** False—Even renters need property insurance to protect their personal belongings; **7.** False—More than thirty states participate in the FAIR Plan that provides insurance for people who live in high-risk areas.

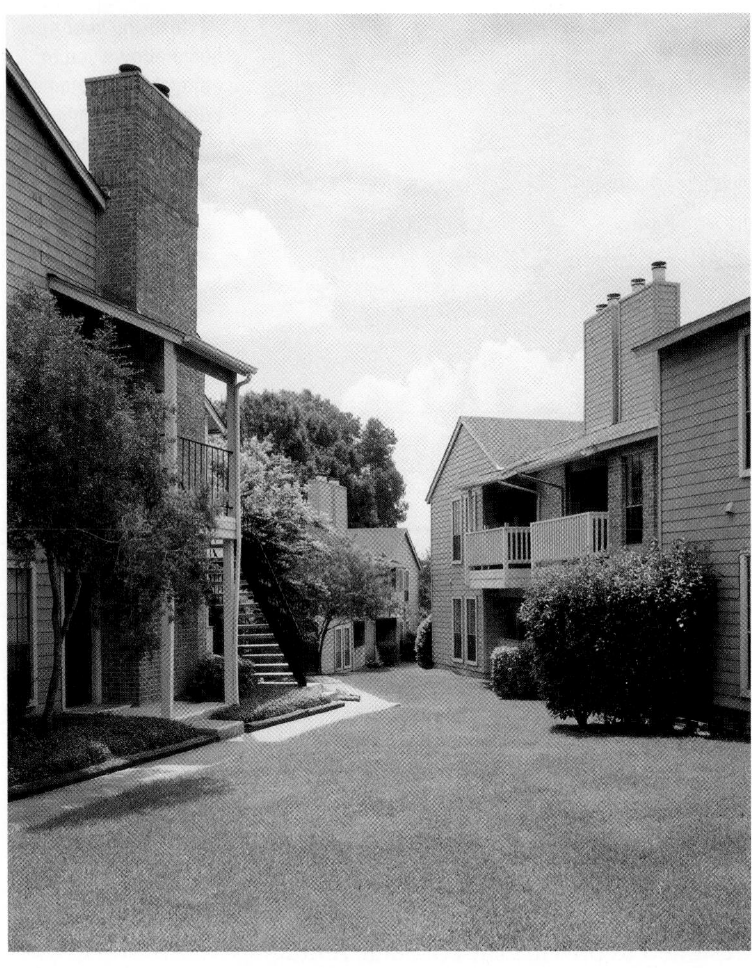

▲ Common areas in condominium developments are jointly owned, which means all owners pay for both maintenance and damages that occur.

As indicated by Figure 15.4 on page 399, homeowner's policies offer a choice of three levels of protection: Basic form (HO-1), broad form (HO-2), and special form (HO-3). The HO-3 includes coverage for almost every hazard.

Condominium Insurance

As you learned in Chapter 10, homeowners in a condominium own their individual living spaces. They share ownership of the overall building and common spaces, such as elevators, lawn areas, and parking garages. The condo owners' association usually has an insurance policy for the building and shared spaces. Individual owners need their own separate policies for things not covered by the association's insurance.

If you purchase a condominium using a mortgage, the lender will require that you have insurance to protect its investment in your home. You will need the coverage provided by a condominium form (HO-6) policy. This coverage is similar to a homeowner's policy. It covers the interior of your individual unit but not the common areas of the building.

Before finalizing your insurance coverage, it is important to read the group policy that covers the building and the liability coverage. A good insurance agent can help you identify any gaps in coverage.

Manufactured Home Insurance

If you buy a manufactured (mobile) home, you will need a special homeowner's insurance policy written specifically for these homes. It will include coverage for damages to the structure, theft, and liability protection (which includes medical payments).

Not as many companies offer this type of insurance. More restrictions apply, and premiums tend to be higher. It might be difficult to insure an older manufactured home. Some of these policies require deductibles for wind and hail damage and limit damage amounts. Unlike stationary houses built on and bolted down to concrete foundations, manufactured homes are quite vulnerable to damage from high winds. Policies for these homes are written based on the actual cash value, so the depreciation will be considered at the time of a loss.

How Much Coverage?

Choosing the appropriate amount of insurance coverage is a balancing act. Some people try to avoid the financial

LOOK Before You Leap

Nicole is learning about homeowner's insurance in her personal finance class. She asks her parents to look at the coverage on their house. They bought the place for $200,000 ten years ago, and it has increased quite a lot in value.

The policy is up for renewal. It currently has coverage limits of $120,000 on the structure, and $60,000 on personal property. Nicole tells her parents they should talk to their insurance agent or an appraiser. They need to find out what it would cost today to rebuild. If the house is not fully insured for replacement, they might not get enough from their insurance if there's a fire or storm, or some other catastrophic loss. She also tells her parents to find out from the insurance company if their policy has an endorsement to cover required building code upgrades.

Nicole says her parents should also update the replacement cost of their furniture and appliances. Those are much more expensive today than ten years ago. She offers to go online with them to check prices. She also offers to help them put together an inventory of their household personal property. There are many things to know before renewing the policy.

Before Renewing

1. Why is homeowner's insurance written for replacement cost rather than original cost?
2. Nicole's parents called the city building department. They learned that if their house ever had to be rebuilt, it would require expensive electrical and plumbing upgrades. Why would they need to know this before renewing their insurance policy?

consequences of risk altogether and buy too much insurance, often duplicating coverage. Other people—especially renters—have too little insurance. When your local news shows the rubble left from an apartment building after a tornado, chances are more than a few of the tenants have no insurance. They will be starting from nothing, trying to rebuild their lives. The main goal of insurance is to protect against the biggest losses.

Whether you live in a house, a condominium, or a manufactured home, you will need enough insurance to cover the following:

- The cost of rebuilding your home
- The loss of your personal possessions
- The cost of additional living expenses if you have to move temporarily to a motel or apartment
- Your liability to others

Review your home insurance coverage periodically (at least once a year) to make sure that your coverage keeps pace with rising building costs and any major improvements or purchases.

Other Insurance Considerations

Whether you own or rent your home, there are some other things to consider when you are buying or renewing an insurance policy. Three of these are

▲ Installing security systems in your home helps reduce insurance costs.

(1) learning about discounts to reduce the cost of your policy, (2) taking an inventory of your personal possessions, and (3) knowing where to obtain coverage if you cannot find a company that will sell you a policy on your home.

Reducing Insurance Costs

Every insurance company has its own set of special discounts to attract customers. Ask each company's agent what discounts are offered for the type of policy you want. You will want good insurance coverage but at the lowest price possible. Here are some of the most common types of discounts:

- Multiple-policy discounts for carrying more than one type of insurance with the same company, such as auto and home insurance
- Home security discounts for having smoke and burglar alarms, sprinkler systems, or monitored security systems
- Discounts for the use of fire-resistant building materials

Taking a Home Inventory

If your home were destroyed by fire, would you be able to remember all of your personal possessions? For insurance reimbursement, you may need to document what you lost and its worth. Making an inventory is not difficult if you begin now—then you will be prepared in case a disaster strikes. An up-to-date inventory of all of your personal possessions will relieve you of trying to remember all of the things you have accumulated over the years. Having this list will also help get your claim settled faster and can verify losses for your income tax return. It can also help you know how much insurance to purchase in the first place.

Begin by making a list of all of your possessions. To get started, type "home inventory form" into an Internet search engine, and you will find a number of different forms. Then use one of these or use your computer's word processing program to create your own list. Describe each item and note where it was purchased. Attach to your list all of the receipts and purchase contracts that you have saved. For electronic equipment and major appliances, record the serial numbers. Take photos or videos of what you have. Keep one copy of your inventory in a secure place away from your home, such as in a safe deposit box or with a friend.

What If You Can't Get Insurance?

If your home is located in an area considered "high risk," you might have difficulty getting insurance coverage. Insurance companies consider the following situations to be high risk:

- Your home is in an area subject to severe weather, such as hurricanes.
- You live in an area known for vandalism, theft, or other crime.
- You live in an older home with outdated electrical wiring, an old heating system, or old plumbing. These conditions mean there is a higher chance of fire or water damage.

Several companies might turn you down for insurance coverage. You still have options. If you are in the process of purchasing the home, ask the real estate agent for suggestions or find out from the seller who currently insures the home. Neighbors might be helpful.

If you still cannot get insurance, contact your state department of insurance. More than thirty states participate in the **Fair Access to Insurance Requirements (FAIR) Plan**. This is a property insurer of last resort. The plan provides insurance for people whose property is located in areas with high exposure to hazards that the owners cannot control. Similar to the assigned-risk auto insurance policies described in Section 1 of this chapter, FAIR Plan policies are created from insurance pools—more expensive than private insurance, but which provide protection in areas where none would otherwise exist.

◀ Homes in areas that are frequently hit by hurricanes are considered high risk for insurance policies—FAIR policies offer insurance to these homeowners.

Fair Access to Insurance Requirements (FAIR) Plan a program to provide property insurance for those whose property is located in areas with high exposure to hazards they cannot control

SECTION 2 ASSESSMENT

Factual Recall

1. Tell which of the following are *not* included in structural damage coverage: fire, hail, flood, lightning, earthquake.
2. Why do some people buy extra insurance for jewelry and other valuable items?
3. What is the difference between the replacement cost of an item and its actual cash value?

Critical Thinking

1. Suppose you rent an apartment. The building's owner has home and property insurance. Would you still need insurance? Why or why not?
2. If you rent a house, which type of insurance do you need: homeowner's or tenant's? Why?

CHAPTER 15 REVIEW AND ASSESSMENT

Chapter Summary

Section 1 Insuring Your Auto

- Auto insurance protects you against having to pay the full cost if you have an accident or your vehicle is damaged or stolen.
- The six basic types of auto insurance coverage are bodily injury liability, property damage liability, collision, comprehensive, medical or personal injury protection, and uninsured/underinsured motorist.
- Other types of insurance coverage—such as towing or rental reimbursement—can be added to a policy as options called *endorsements* or *riders*.
- State laws require a minimum amount of liability coverage. The amount varies from state to state and is represented by a three-part number that reflects the dollar limits (per accident) on (1) medical costs per person, (2) medical costs for all injuries, and (3) property damage.
- Insurance companies set rates by analyzing risk factors. The more risk factors you have, the higher your rate will be.
- If you are involved in an accident, you first need to ensure safety—then get help, exchange information, and call your insurance company. You should also know your own insurance coverage.

Section 2 Insuring Your Home and Property

- The four basic types of home and property insurance include coverage on the physical structure of the home, personal property, liability, and living expenses.
- People who rent their home need insurance to protect against liability and to cover loss or damage to their personal property.
- For people who own their home, the type of insurance varies with the type of structure: a house, condominium, or manufactured home.
- You can reduce your insurance costs by taking advantage of various discounts offered by insurance companies.
- Take an inventory of your personal possessions so that you have an accurate record in case they are damaged or stolen.

Reviewing Key Terms

Match the following terms with their definitions.

a. liability
b. deductible
c. endorsement
d. exclusions
e. premium
f. structural damage coverage
g. personal property coverage
h. replacement cost coverage

1. Not covered by an insurance policy.
2. Pays current prices to owners who have to buy new things because their property has been stolen, damaged, or destroyed.
3. Responsibility for damages.
4. Paid by the policyholder before the insurance company pays benefits.
5. Pays if your possessions are lost, damaged, or destroyed, even if they were not in your house at the time.
6. A modification or addition to an insurance policy.
7. The amount you pay for insurance.
8. Pays for damages to a building resulting from fire, severe weather, or other disasters listed in the policy.

Understanding the Main Ideas

1. Which type of auto insurance coverage would be involved if you ran over someone else's bicycle?
2. Which type of insurance coverage pays for repairing accident damage to your car?
3. Which type of insurance coverage pays if your car is damaged by something other than an accident?
4. True or False: If you have good medical payments coverage, there is no need to buy uninsured/underinsured motorist coverage. Explain your answer.
5. What are the four risk factors that auto insurance companies consider when determining your rates?

6. List four ways you can control your auto insurance costs.
7. If your dog bites the mail carrier, which part of your homeowner's policy would be involved in paying the medical bills?
8. If you own a condominium, whose policy covers the building itself?
9. How can making a home inventory be useful?
10. What can you do if you live in a high risk area and are turned down for home insurance?

Practicing Math

1. Daniel is working to improve his grades so that he will qualify for a good student discount of 10 percent. His annual premium now is $1,950. What would it be with the discount?
2. Depreciation refers to the decline in value over time. One way to calculate depreciation is the *straight-line method*. With this method, the purchase price of the item (in dollars) is divided by its life (in years). For example, a computer's useful life is considered to be 3 years. A $900 computer will therefore depreciate by $300 each year. Use the straight-line method to calculate the following:
   a. Your sister buys a microwave oven for $100. Useful life of the oven is 10 years. What is its depreciation, in dollars, after 5 years?
   b. A refrigerator's purchase price was $795. Useful life is 15 years. The refrigerator has depreciated by $371. How old is it?
   c. If the useful life of clothing is 5 years, by what percentage does it depreciate each year?
3. A storm damaged Mr. Johnson's roof, allowing rainwater to leak into the house. Mold began to grow in the attic. It cost $4,700 to repair the roof and $3,000 to clean up the mold. Mr. Johnson's policy has a $400 deductible, and it excludes mold damage. How much did the insurance company pay Mr. Johnson?

Applying Critical Thinking Skills

1. Why is it more important to have collision coverage on a new car than on an old one?
2. States have minimum coverage requirements for auto insurance. Is it a good idea to buy only the minimum coverage? Why or why not?
3. Matt is on a very tight budget, and he drives a 10-year-old car. To save money, he wants to drop some of his auto insurance coverage. What should he consider dropping?
4. Why should you review your home insurance coverage at least once a year?
5. Why do you think an insurance company would provide a discount to policyholders who install smoke alarms?

Working with Real-World Documents

1. Find out what your state's requirements are for auto insurance. What types of coverage are required? What are the minimum liability limits? This information is available from the Insurance Information Institute (http://fin.emcp.net/iii). Your state's Department of Insurance might also have a Web site with this information.
2. Examine a bill for homeowner's insurance. What does it tell you about types of coverage and limits? Were any discounts applied? Does the customer have a choice of payment plans?

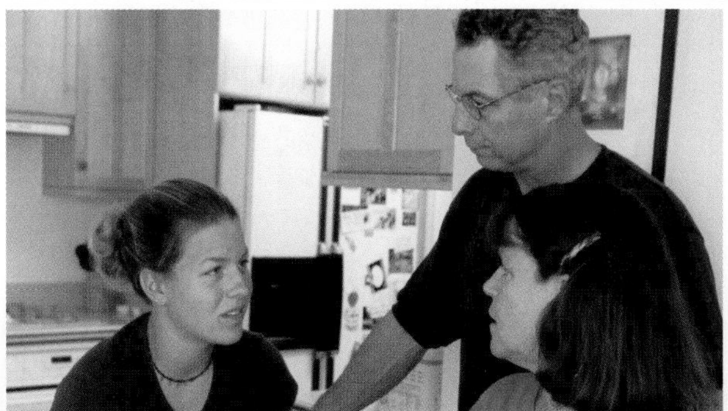

Taking It Home

1. Talk with your parents or other adults about their experience with auto or home insurance companies. Have they ever changed insurance companies? If so, why?
2. With the help and permission of your parent or guardian, find out what kinds of auto insurance discounts you might be eligible to obtain. For example, what would be required for you to get a good student discount? How much would the discount be?

CHAPTER 16

Health and Life Insurance

If you are young and healthy, life insurance and health insurance might not seem like anything to worry about now. But in fact, these are key parts of financial planning. You will have to make decisions about them soon after you graduate.

The costs of health care have skyrocketed. Without medical insurance, even a relatively simple surgical procedure could leave you in debt for years. In addition, life insurance can be a lifeline for family members who once depended on your income for survival. Even if you do not have dependents, life insurance can be a smart long-term investment.

▲ **Dental insurance is just one type of coverage that falls under the umbrella term "health insurance."**

SECTION 1 **Choosing Health Care Insurance**

SECTION 2 **Buying Life Insurance**

Fact or Fiction

What do you think? Are the following statements true or false? If you think they are false, then say what is true.

1. When you get a job, you automatically have a health insurance plan.
2. If you lose your job, you can continue your group health insurance coverage temporarily while you seek a new plan.
3. Disability insurance replaces 100 percent of your pretax income.
4. Even people in their twenties should think about purchasing life insurance.
5. If you do not have a spouse or children, you do not need life insurance.
6. The two main types of life insurance include term and permanent.

Answers on page 423.

Study Reminder

*Knowing how to study can increase your knowledge, improve your grades, and cut down on your study time. See the **Studying Personal Finance** pages at the front of the book for some tips to help you study this chapter.*

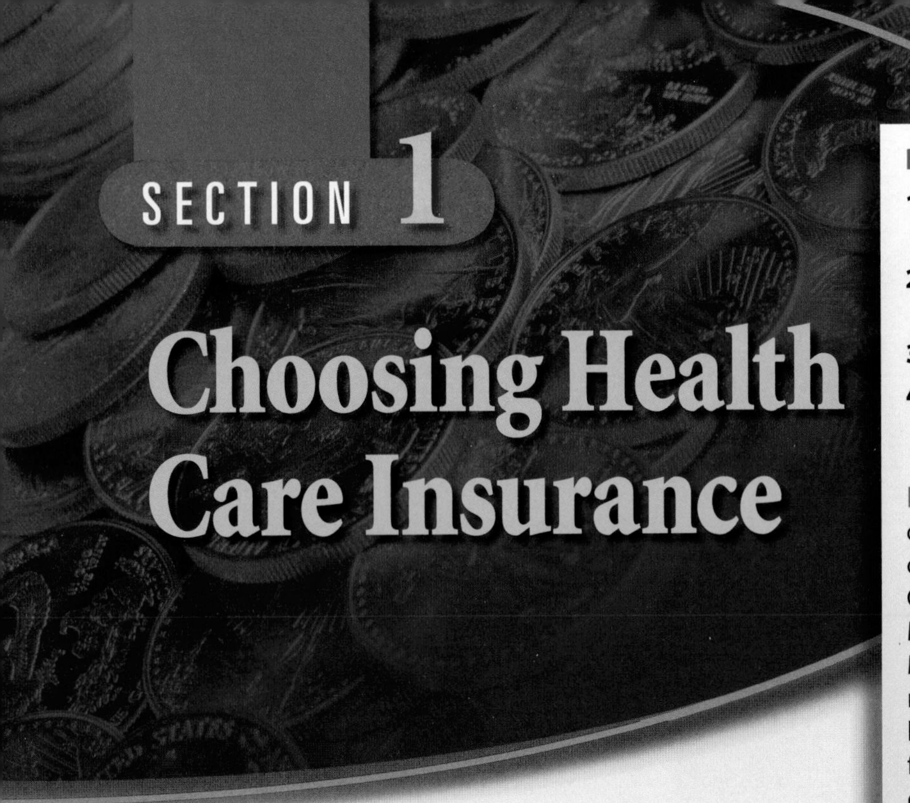

SECTION 1

Choosing Health Care Insurance

Focus Questions

1. What are the types of health care coverage?
2. How do you get health insurance if your employer does not offer it?
3. What is managed care?
4. What does disability insurance cover?

Key Terms

coinsurance
co-pay
COBRA
Medicare
Medicaid
managed care
health savings account (HSA)
flexible spending account (FSA)
disability insurance

Gayle had worked part-time during college, but now she was looking for her first full-time "career" job. Her dad made her realize that she had to consider more than salary. Benefits like health insurance would be important too. He said, "A good benefits package can be worth thousands of dollars a year. Actually, if you had a major illness or injury, it could be worth many times that amount. If you are serious about a job offer, find out all you can about the benefits that come with it."

In today's workforce, fewer jobs are considered "full-time, permanent"—the type of jobs that traditionally come with benefits like health insurance. More and more people are being hired as "independent contractors" or "freelancers," even though they might work full-time. Some of Gayle's friends are already working, and they have jobs like these. But her friends have no job security, and they are not eligible for the benefits their companies offer other employees.

Hiring people on this basis is meant to make companies flexible, allowing them to add staff on a temporary basis when they need it. There is another consequence, however: The practice saves money for the companies, but it leaves many people without health insurance.

Types of Health Care Coverage

Health care goes beyond doctor visits and hospitalizations. The term *health care* is an umbrella term for a number of types of health-related insurance plans, including medical, dental, and vision coverage. Disability coverage and long-term care are also included.

As the cost of health care—and the insurance that pays for it—rises, fewer people have total coverage and many have none at all. If you understand the types of insurance that are available, you can determine what should be your highest priorities now—and in the future.

Medical Coverage

For almost everyone, it's not a matter of whether or not you will need medical care—but how often. Illnesses can come on quickly, and accidents are never planned. Even if you are basically healthy, seeing a doctor for preventive care is important if you want to stay that way. Basic medical coverage helps pay for doctors' fees, medical tests, hospitalization, and surgery. Medications might also be covered. Basic medical is usually combined with *major medical* coverage, which helps pay for very expensive treatments such as long-term rehabilitation, organ transplants, or sophisticated cancer therapies.

Health insurance for pets is gaining in popularity. As advances in veterinary medicine have made more therapies available, the cost of health care for animals has gone up just as it has for humans. Many people consider their animal companions to be part of the family. They will spare no expense to keep their pets healthy and active.

Spot, a dog in Louisiana, became ill after eating some leaves from a poisonous plant. His care cost more than $3,500. But because Spot's owner had pet insurance, she had to pay only half the bills. Some policies pay an even higher percentage.

Insurers determine premiums for pet insurance based on risk factors. Large dogs tend to have more diseases and get injured more often, so they cost more to insure than small dogs. Cats, which often spend more time indoors, are less expensive to insure than dogs. Policies are available for other household pets as well.

Dental and Vision Coverage

You have other health-related expenses besides going to the doctor. Dental and vision expenses are not usually included in a regular health care plan. Sometimes they can be added for a higher premium. Sometimes you would have to purchase a separate policy.

Dental coverage would apply to the cost of fillings, crowns, and similar procedures. Preventive dental care—such as periodic checkups, teeth cleaning, and X-rays—is often included for a higher premium. Some plans also cover orthodontic care such as braces.

Vision coverage helps pay for eye examinations, glasses, and contact lenses. Vision correction surgery is often included. Treatment of eye injuries is covered under medical insurance on many policies.

Disability Coverage and Long-Term Care

The last pieces of the insurance puzzle are disability coverage and long-term care. These would usually not be covered in a regular health care plan. Like dental and vision coverage, protection in these cases might require separate policies.

Disability coverage is a good thing to have. The chance that you might become disabled is probably greater than you think. Studies show that a 20-year-old worker today has a 3-in-10 chance of becoming disabled before reaching retirement age.

▼ An office visit with the eye doctor can be expensive—but having vision insurance lowers your out-of-pocket costs.

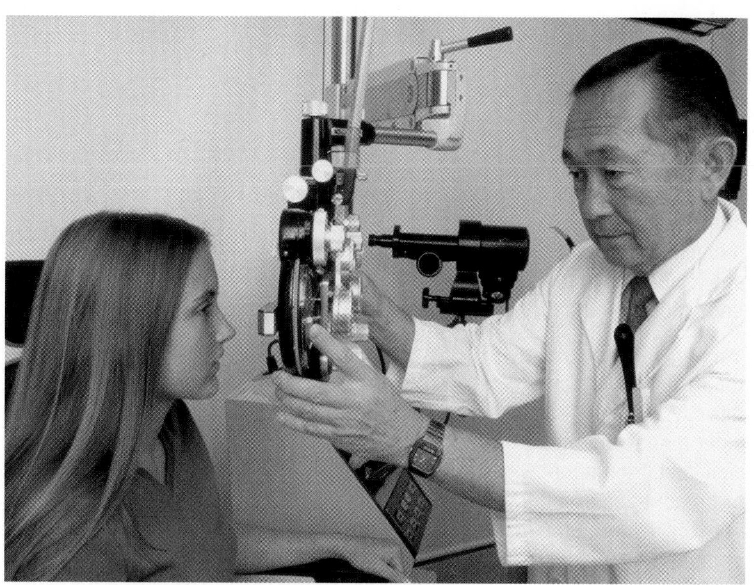

▲ **Employers may offer insurance to their employees, who then choose a plan from a variety of offerings.**

Coverage for long-term care is meant to help pay for extended nursing care that is not covered by medical plans, including Medicare. When a person is unable to care for himself or herself and needs someone to provide care in the home or in a nursing home, long-term care can be very important.

Understanding Costs

coinsurance the percentage of expenses the policyholder must pay in addition to the deductible amount

co-pay a flat fee that the policyholder pays directly to the provider for each doctor visit, test, treatment, or prescription drug, with the insurance company paying the balance

Health care insurance costs, and the way they are determined, vary significantly among insurance plans. However, the insurance industry uses some standard terms that will help you understand and compare the costs of different plans:

- *Premium.* The premium is the amount you pay to the insurance company for your policy. For health coverage, premiums increase as you get older. Premiums are also higher if you have other risk factors that increase the likelihood of claims.
- *Deductible.* Many policies have a deductible. This is a set amount that you pay toward your yearly expenses before your insurance coverage kicks in. Deductible amounts range from $100 to thousands of dollars, depending on the policy.
- *Coinsurance.* With some policies, after you meet your deductible you still pay part of each medical bill. **Coinsurance**, usually expressed as a percentage, indicates how you and the insurance company will share the charges. If your coinsurance is 20 percent, you would pay 20 percent of the hospital bill and the insurance company would pay 80 percent.
- *Co-pay.* When policies have a **co-pay**, you pay a flat dollar amount each time you go to a doctor, have a medical test or treatment, or buy a prescription drug. The insurance company pays the rest. In policies with a deductible, the co-pay begins after the deductible is met.
- *Out-of-pocket expenses.* The amounts that you pay for coverage are called your out-of-pocket expenses. They include your premiums plus any deductibles, coinsurance, and co-pays.

Sources of Health Insurance Coverage

The source of your health care insurance coverage—whether it is a group, individual, or government plan—largely determines the premium that you will pay. Many people are offered health insurance through their employers. By being part of a group plan, they save money. Those who do not have that opportunity can apply for an individual health insurance policy, although it will

Going Global

Health care costs in most developed nations make up between 10 and 15 percent of a country's entire economy. Many nations fund health care—at least partially—for all their citizens.

In most developed countries, people believe that health care is a fundamental right, like education, and that it should be available to everyone. This type of system is often referred to as universal health care. Germany, France, Sweden, and the United Kingdom have such systems. In fact, among developed nations, the United States is the only country in which most private citizens pay for their own health care.

The health care system in the United Kingdom is run by the National Health Service. In England, health care service centers—called *trusts*—are classified as either primary or secondary. Consumers can go to local primary care trusts as they wish, to receive the services of general practitioners, dentists, opticians, clinics, and pharmacists. Secondary care includes ambulance, hospital, mental health care, and other specialized services. Patients are referred to secondary care personnel by their primary care trusts.

Because some secondary service providers have long waiting lists in England, people who can afford private health insurance often buy it. A private health care system does exist in England, though on a small scale. Some National Health Service providers have separate private practices that are part of the private health care system.

Thinking Globally

1. Do you think countries should provide universal health care to their populations? Give reasons for your answer.
2. Should the United States move toward a more universal type of health care system? Use the Internet to research your position. Then discuss these ideas with your classmates.

probably cost a lot more. Still other people are covered through government programs.

Group Insurance Plans

The primary advantage of taking part in group health insurance is the cost. When many people are covered under the same policy, premiums are considerably less than they would be for an individual policy. Many health plans are employer-sponsored, which means the employer pays some of the cost of the insurance. If you do not qualify for employer-sponsored group insurance, you might still be able to take advantage of the lower costs of group coverage. Check with other groups you belong to or could join—such as a labor union or professional organization—to see if they offer group plans.

With employer-based group plans, several types of health care coverage might be offered, such as medical, dental, vision, and perhaps even disability. Usually once a year, employees can choose which plan or plans they want to enroll in. See Figure 16.1 for an overview of what a group plan could look like.

COBRA

What happens when you leave a job that had health care benefits? If you are moving directly to another job with

▶ **A group plan allows you to change your insurance coverage as the needs of your family change.**

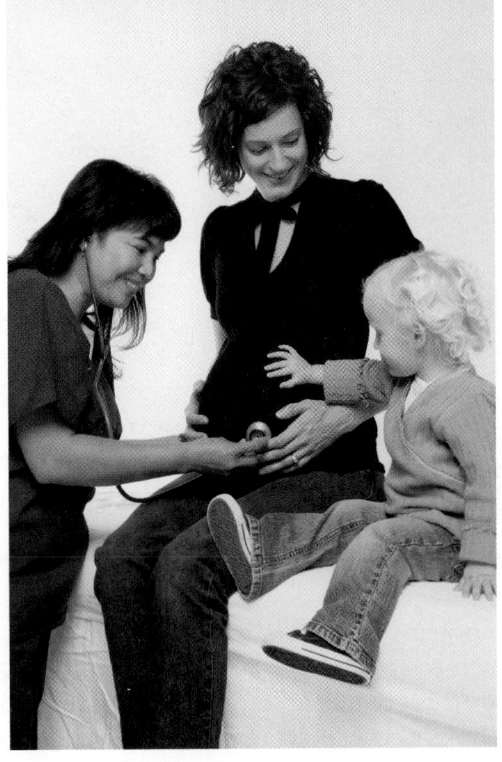

COBRA a federal law (the Consolidated Omnibus Budget Reconciliation Act) that allows employees, spouses, and dependent children to continue their group insurance coverage for a period of time after they leave the job or lose insurance coverage for some other specified reason

comparable insurance, there is no problem. But many workers are not that fortunate.

COBRA is an acronym for the Consolidated Omnibus Budget Reconciliation Act. It is a federal law that requires employers to let workers temporarily continue with their health insurance plan after leaving the company, usually for up to eighteen months. This gives them time to find a new health insurance arrangement, either individually or as part of a new group. While on COBRA coverage, the former employee pays the entire premium for the policy, which is usually significantly higher than before, when the employer was paying part of the cost. COBRA coverage also applies for a period of time after

Figure 16.1 SAMPLE EMPLOYER INSURANCE BENEFITS OVERVIEW

Some employers offer insurance benefits to their employees. They may provide a set plan or a variety of options from which employees are allowed to choose. Below is an overview of the various insurance benefits that one large corporation offers.

Insurance category	Brief annual benefit explanation
Medical	Medical insurance is available to employees who work over 30 hours per week. • Deductible is $500 for individuals, $1,000 for families. • Out-of-pocket maximum is $1,500 for individuals, $3,000 for families. • Office visit co-pay is $30. • Prescription co-pays are $15 for generic drugs, $30 for brand-name drugs approved by the plan, and $45 for brand-name drugs not approved by the plan.
Vision	Vision insurance is included as part of medical insurance, at no additional cost to employees. • One regular eye exam per year is covered at 100%. • Plan includes $100 toward hardware (glasses or contact lenses).
Dental	Dental insurance is available to all employees at an additional cost determined by the employee's salary. • 100% of charges provided for preventive care are covered. • 90% of charges provided for basic care are covered. • 60% of charges provided for restorative care are covered.
Disability	Two kinds of disability insurance are provided, both at no cost to employees. • Short-term disability insurance covers 100% of the employee's pay beginning on the eighth day of a qualified illness and continues for up to 26 weeks. • Long-term disability insurance covers 66.7% of the employee's pay beginning after 26 weeks of a qualified illness.
Flexible spending	Employees may participate in a flexible spending program to pay for medical and dental expenses that are not covered by insurance.

you graduate from college or reach a certain age, if you have been covered under your parents' insurance policies until then.

Individual Health Insurance Policies

Not everyone works for a company that offers health insurance to all its employees. Buying an individual health insurance policy is another option.

Pros and Cons One advantage of an individual policy is that you can keep it even if you change jobs. However, individual policies come with drawbacks. Most of these plans have very high monthly premiums and large deductibles. Insurance companies might deny coverage for people with a *preexisting condition*—a medical condition that was present before they bought the policy. These include conditions such as chronic asthma, diabetes, or a previous diagnosis of a serious disease.

Short-Term Policies Some insurance companies offer short-term plans for people who want coverage for only one to six months. These plans are intended to fill the gap if a person becomes temporarily uninsured due to job loss or some other incident. Most of these short-term plans do not let you reapply after the six-month period. In fact, some states regulate the number of days per year that a person can be covered by short-term insurance.

Typically, short-term plans are similar in scope and price to regular individual plans, but the process for applying is shorter and not as detailed. While you are covered under a short-term policy, you will need to investigate coverage in a long-term plan and get your new policy instated before the short-term policy runs out.

You have rights with regard to health insurance. In 1996, Congress passed the Health Insurance Portability and Accountability Act (HIPAA). The act protects you in the following ways:

- HIPAA makes it illegal for group insurance plans to deny coverage based on your health status. It also limits the length of time a group insurance plan can exclude coverage for preexisting conditions.
- HIPAA sets strict rules about disclosing your health-related information. These privacy and security rules protect both paper and electronic versions of your medical records.

Government Programs

Federal and state governments run health care programs for specific segments of the population. They are primarily meant to help people who have no private coverage. These government programs include Medicare, Medicaid, state-run programs, and workers' compensation.

Medicare The best-known federal health care program is **Medicare**, which provides health insurance to senior citizens and people with certain disabilities. Senior citizens must be at least 65 years old to qualify for coverage. Medicare Part A pays for hospital care, nursing home care, hospice care, and home health care. Medicare Part B pays for doctor visits and other medical services.

Medicare does not pay for everything. Individuals are responsible for their deductibles and co-pays. To help pay those costs, they can buy *Medigap* insurance, also called *supplemental insurance*. Medigap policies are sold by private insurance companies and will pick up some of the costs that Medicare does not cover.

Medicare a federally funded health insurance program for people at least 65 years old and others with certain disabilities

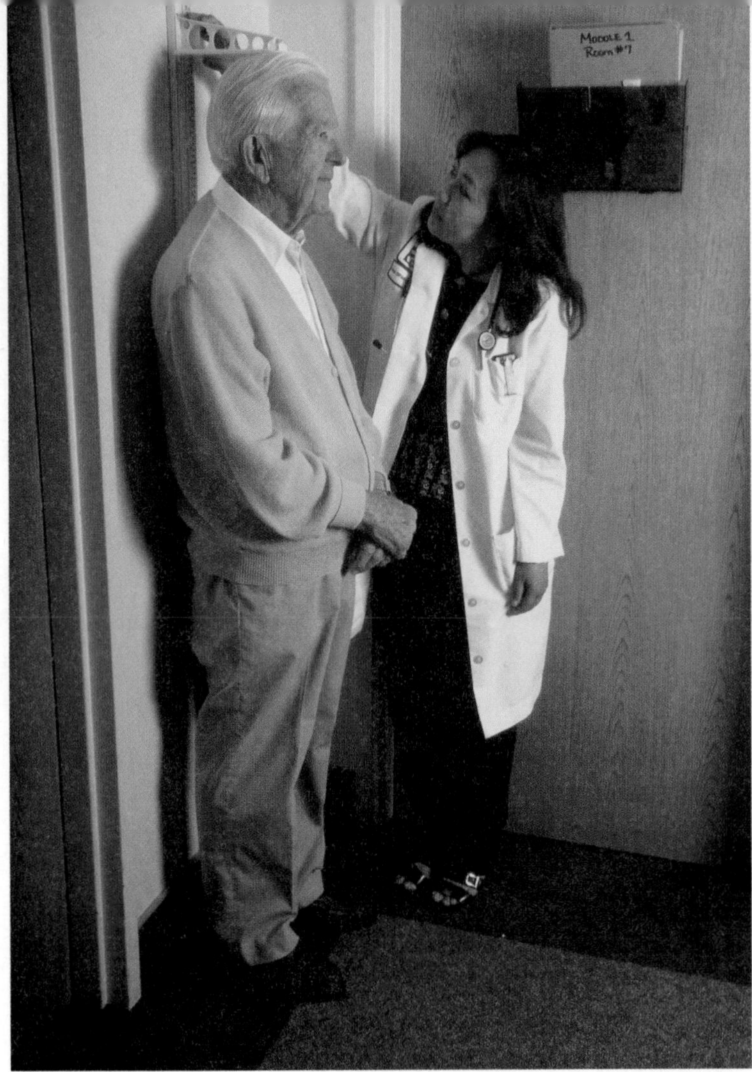

▲ People spend most of their working lives paying a Medicare tax so that when they retire, they are able to use the medical services that the program provides.

Medicaid The other major health care program run by the government is Medicaid. **Medicaid** is subsidized health insurance for low-income people and families who cannot afford private health insurance or their own medical care. Medicaid assistance is paid with funds from both federal and state governments.

State-Run Health Care Programs Many states offer health care programs for people who cannot afford their own private health insurance but do not qualify for Medicaid and are not offered health care benefits where they work. Some of these state-run programs focus on insuring children. Others offer coverage for families and individuals. More than half the states offer health care plans to people who have medical conditions that prevent them from getting insurance elsewhere.

Medicaid a government-funded medical assistance program for certain low-income individuals and families

Not all of these state-run programs are inexpensive or easy to obtain. Many require extensive paperwork and significant monthly premiums. However, they help millions of people who otherwise would have no health care coverage.

Workers' Compensation Employers pay into a state-run *workers' compensation* plan that covers people injured or killed on the job. Workers' comp indemnifies (protects against loss) the injured worker's salary. In addition, the medical portion of workers' comp helps cover medical bills. Those who accept workers' comp payments must give up their right to sue the employer.

Types of Health Care Policies

The type of policy you have is important because it determines what is covered, how free you are to choose your health care providers, and how much you will pay when you use your benefits. The plans explained here apply to medical, dental, and vision coverage. Disability and long-term care insurance are different types of policies, to be discussed later in the chapter. The two kinds of health care policies include traditional plans and managed care plans.

Traditional Plans

If your health care coverage is through a traditional plan (sometimes called an *indemnity* or a *fee-for-service* plan), you have the greatest choice of health care providers. You can choose to stay with your family doctor, select the best surgeon in the town, or go to a hospital near your home.

You are also likely to pay considerably more for this privilege. Each plan is somewhat different, but most require you to pay a yearly deductible before the insurance payments start. After you have met your deductible, your policy might have coinsurance, or you might have a co-pay amount for each service provided—or perhaps both.

If you are offered a traditional plan, ask questions up front so you know exactly what is covered and what you may have to pay. Traditional plans are becoming less common.

Managed Care Plans

Managed care insurance plans focus on managing the overall cost, use, and quality of the health care system. The specific details can vary, but these plans usually have agreements with health care providers to accept lower fees. As a result, you are likely to be limited in your access to and choice of doctors, hospitals, and other medical providers. You might have to get preapproval from the insurance company before you can have surgery or other expensive medical treatments. Managed care plans are typically less costly than traditional plans.

HMOs The oldest type of managed care plan is the *health maintenance organization* (HMO). HMOs emphasize wellness by encouraging checkups, immunizations, and screenings for diseases. You have a *primary care physician* (PCP) who provides most services or refers you to a specialist in the plan, if necessary. In most HMOs, you cannot see another plan doctor without a referral from the PCP, and there is no coverage for care by anyone outside of the plan. There is usually no deductible, and out-of-pocket expenses are often lower than for other plans.

PPOs A second type of managed care plan is the *preferred provider organization* (PPO). This is similar to an HMO, with a few differences. A PPO consists of a network of doctors and other health care providers, called "preferred" providers. You can go to a provider outside the network, but you will pay considerably more. There is usually a deductible, and you typically have to fill out more paperwork than HMO participants do.

POS Plans There are some hybrid plans that combine the features of both HMOs and PPOs. One of these is a *point-of-service* (POS) plan. As with an HMO, you have a primary care physician who makes referrals to other providers in the plan. However, as with a PPO, you can also choose providers outside the plan—at a higher cost. The amount the insurance company will pay depends on where the service is obtained—the "point of service." There is usually no deductible if you use network providers, but a deductible would apply if you choose providers outside the network.

Evaluating Medical Insurance

Some people are able to choose medical coverage from two or more options. Even if that is not the case for you, knowing how to evaluate medical coverage can help you better understand your coverage. You can plan ahead for expenses that you might have to pay yourself. No insurance pays medical costs completely, but some cover more expenses than others.

With the variety of insurance plans on the market, comparing them can seem difficult. It is not just a matter of finding the one with the lowest premium. You need to know what kinds of care the plan pays for, the choices you have about that care, and what your overall out-of-pocket costs will be. If you made a chart to compare plans, you

managed care
health insurance that focuses on managing the overall cost, use, and quality of the health care system

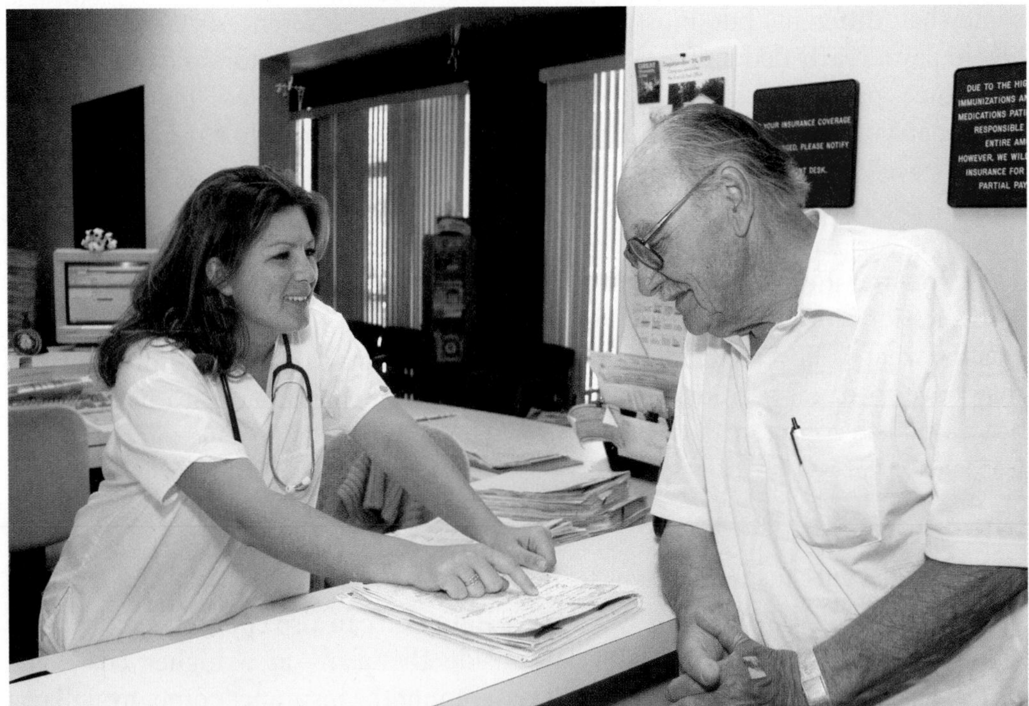

▶ Hospital employees and other health care professionals are used to working with insurance companies and can explain many details about your policy. Why is it a good idea to know what is in your policy before you go to the doctor's office?

would want to include answers to these questions:

- *How much are the premiums?* You will make payments on a regular basis to the insurance company. What are those costs per year? If you get medical insurance through your employer, the premiums might be deducted from your paycheck. Many medical insurance plans offer family coverage for a higher premium.
- *What is covered under the policy?* Most medical plans combine basic medical with major medical coverage for extraordinary events. However, some plans are very specific, perhaps providing only cancer coverage. Even among the broader plans, exactly what is included can vary. Are mental health, dental, vision, and prescription drug coverage also part of the plan?
- *How much freedom do you have in choosing your health care providers?* With some plans, particularly most HMOs, you can see only the physicians in the plan and only with your primary physician's referral. In other plans, you can choose your own physicians or pay more for using providers outside the network.
- *Are preexisting conditions excluded?* Some policies require a waiting period, often six months to a year or longer, before they will pay to treat conditions that already existed when you bought the policy. Find out what rules apply.
- *How much will you pay toward claims?* Some policies have a yearly deductible. You also need to know whether your policy has a coinsurance provision or if there is a co-pay required every time you visit your doctor or fill a prescription. These out-of-pocket expenses add up.
- *Is there a maximum out-of-pocket for the year?* Some plans pay at 100 percent after you meet a yearly maximum for out-of-pocket expenses.
- *Are there lifetime maximum benefits?* Some plans stop paying completely when you reach a maximum benefit. If your health insurance has such a

YOU DECIDE

Elena has a good job as a graphic designer. It's a small firm with only five employees. She loves the job—but it does not have a health insurance plan.

Elena is no longer eligible to stay on her parents' insurance plan. She might have to look for a new job that offers health insurance benefits. She would rather stay where she is and buy an individual health insurance policy—or maybe even go without health coverage.

Zach, one of Elena's coworkers, has an individual health care plan. His premium is only $100 a month. But his yearly deductible is $5,000. Zach says that now he pays for his own health care—annual exams, prescription drugs, visits to the doctor's office or emergency room. But he knows that if his medical expenses during the year ever reach $5,000, the insurance policy will kick in and pay everything over that amount. Including his monthly premium, Zach's out-of-pocket health care expenses could reach $6,200 per year, but never more than that. Elena wonders if she should get a plan like Zach's—but the deductible is so high!

She also thinks about opening a health savings account. She could deposit $100 a month —the same as Zach's monthly premium—and use the money in the account to pay for doctor visits and medicines. Any money she does not use for medical expenses will earn interest, so the account can grow over time. But what if she has an accident or needs an operation sometime soon? That would be many thousands of dollars. If her health care expenses are ever more than she has in the account, where would she find the money?

Casey, who also works with Elena, has another idea. He says people who have policies with high deductibles can have a health savings account in addition to their insurance. "You can get an inexpensive policy like Zach's," he says, "to protect yourself against huge hospital bills—but in the meantime you can also start a health savings account to cover normal health care expenses."

Elena is not sure if she wants to set aside money each month in *two* different plans.

Should she . . .

1. ...buy an inexpensive individual health care policy, with a high deductible, like Zach's? Give reasons for your answer.
2. ...skip health insurance and open a health savings account? Describe the pros and cons of this decision.
3. ...follow Casey's suggestion and open a health savings account in addition to a high-deductible insurance policy? Explain your reasoning.

maximum, how would you protect yourself against the high costs of a catastrophic medical condition?

Considering Other Options

A variety of alternatives—some more useful than others—are available to help reduce the high cost of health care. Three of these are health savings accounts (HSAs), flexible spending accounts (FSAs), and discount health plans.

Health Savings Accounts

The purpose of a **health savings account (HSA)** is to set aside money that can be used to pay for health care expenses not covered by insurance. Such an account would allow you to lower your health insurance premiums by switching to a

health savings account (HSA) a tax-free savings account that the owner can use to pay for medical expenses not covered by insurance; available only to people with high deductibles

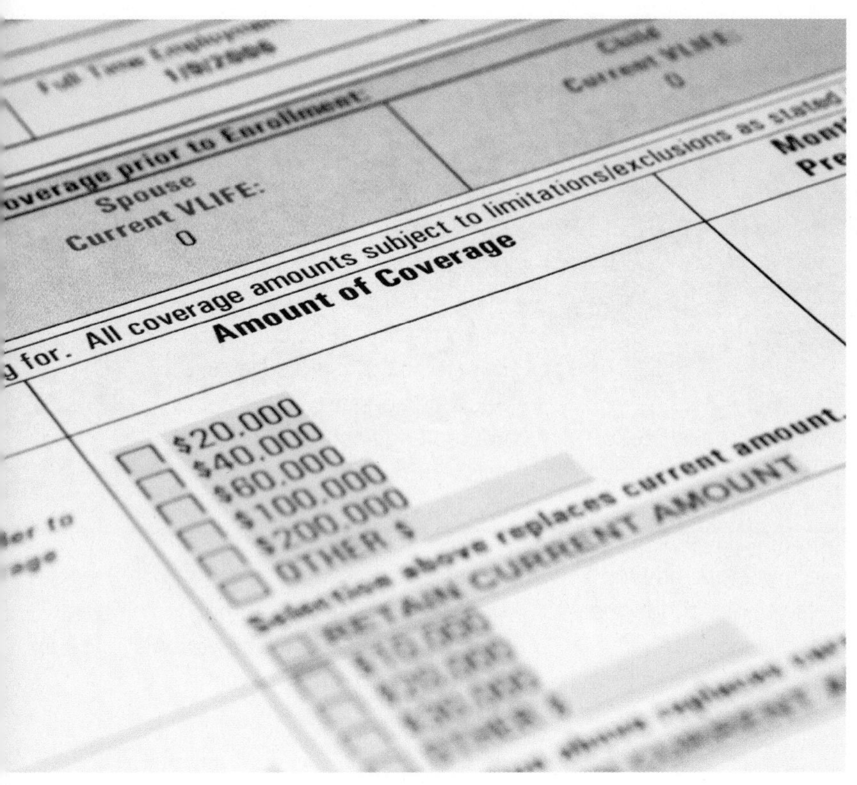

▲ Take time to go over your insurance plan carefully to be sure that you get the coverage you need and can afford.

health care policy with a very high deductible. In addition, HSAs provide three-way tax advantages: (1) tax-deductible contributions to the account, (2) tax-free earnings, and (3) tax-free withdrawals for medical expenses.

Only people who have medical insurance with a deductible in the thousands of dollars qualify. If you have such a high-deductible plan, you can deposit money from each paycheck into your health savings account, where it earns interest. You make withdrawals as needed to pay for services not covered by insurance or to pay toward your deductible. Any balance left at the end of the year can be rolled over and used the following year.

The account goes with you if you change jobs or change your medical coverage. It passes to your spouse or beneficiary upon your death.

flexible spending account (FSA) a plan that allows employees to set aside pretax dollars from their paycheck, to be used during the year for medical expenses not covered by insurance; also called a *cafeteria plan*

Flexible Spending Accounts

A **flexible spending account (FSA)**, sometimes called a *cafeteria plan*, is set up by an employer for its employees. If you choose to participate, you decide how much will be deducted from each paycheck. Your employer puts that amount into your flexible spending account. Because the deduction is made *before* taxes, it reduces your withholding.

You can use the money as needed for deductibles, coinsurance, co-pays, and health care expenses not covered by insurance. Any money left over at the end of a year is generally forfeited, so it is important to estimate your annual out-of-pocket medical expenses as accurately as possible.

Discount Health Plans

Some companies offer discount health plans. These are not insurance policies. They do not pay anything toward your medical bills. Instead, you pay a membership fee and then receive a list of providers who offer discounts on health care. For people who cannot afford health insurance or who cannot get it, these plans provide limited assistance with medical bills. Or, if your insurance has a high deductible, you can buy a membership in a discount health plan to help cover your out-of-pocket expenses until that deducible is met.

One important drawback, however, is that many people pay the fee, thinking they are buying insurance coverage. They are not. These plans are not subject to regulation by a state's insurance commission. The discounts are not always as advertised, and the list of providers might not be current. Access to the providers is not always guaranteed. There are also sometimes hidden administrative fees.

The best advice is to do your homework to be sure the company is legitimate. Call your state's insurance commissioner before you sign up for a discount health plan.

Disability and Long-Term Care Insurance

It is natural to be concerned about the types of insurance you would use most often—auto, home, or health insurance. However, you have to protect yourself against the worst losses. Disability and the need for long-term care fall in that category.

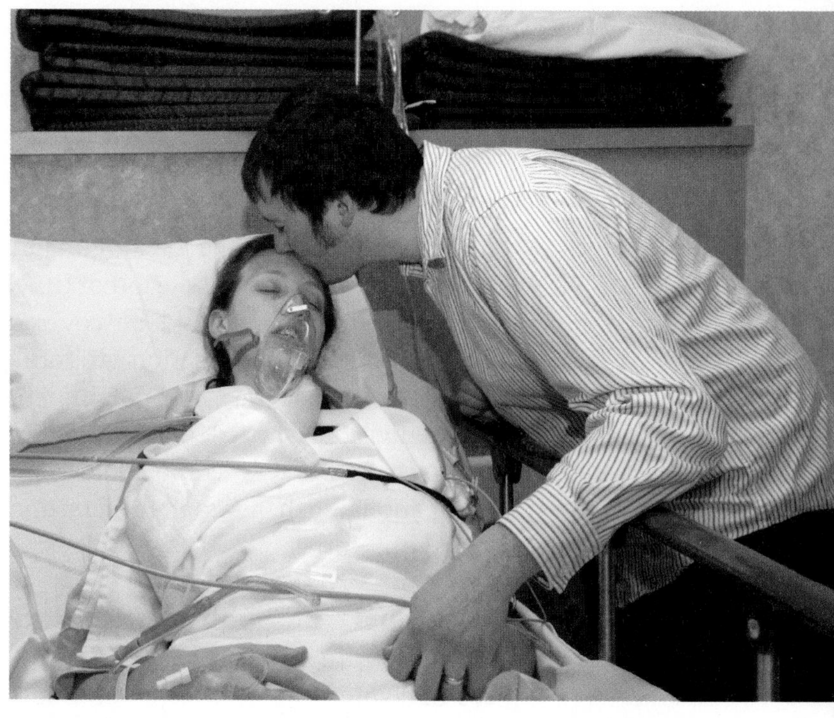

▲ Missing work, and pay, due to an accident is covered by disability insurance, which provides payments to make up for lost income.

Financial Survival During Disability

Lila's older brother, Frank, was 17 and Lila was 15 when their mother became disabled in a car accident—paralyzed from the waist down. Rehabilitation would take a long time. As a single parent, if Lila's mother could not work, the family would have no income. But Lila's mother had protected her family by purchasing **disability insurance**. While she recovered, disability payments filled the gaps from her lost wages. Eventually, Lila's mom was able to return to work part-time. Frank and Lila graduated from high school. They each got part-time jobs and are attending community college. The family's plans were sidetracked, but not abandoned.

Think about what happens to the family if a parent is unable to work for a period of time. Even if you are single—the bills will keep coming if you cannot work due to illness or accident. If you lose your ability to earn income for an extended period of time, the loss in wages might even be more costly than your medical bills. It could jeopardize your ability to pay for housing, your car loan, and other everyday expenses.

Disability insurance can provide some ongoing income. Typically, disability coverage pays 50 percent to 70 percent of your regular pay. Getting disability coverage should be a goal, even if you are just starting out. It can come from several sources, including your employer, the government, or an individual policy you purchase for yourself.

Employer Plans Some employers offer group disability insurance in a package with health insurance or life insurance. In fact, *short-term disability* coverage is required in many states. The length of time covered by short-term disability varies considerably, but two years is usually the maximum.

Employers might also make *long-term disability* coverage available. These benefits would begin after a certain number of weeks or months or when short-term disability coverage runs out. Depending on the policy, benefits might continue for a specified number of years or even for life.

Social Security Disability Coverage If your disability is expected to keep you from working at any job for more than a year, you can apply for Social Security disability benefits. The amount of the payments you can receive depends on your wages and on the

disability insurance insurance coverage that replaces a portion of lost income if the policyholder is unable to work due to illness or injury

number of years you have been paying into the Social Security system. Dependents of workers can also qualify for Social Security benefits.

Workers' Compensation Insurance If you are injured on the job and unable to work for a significant period of time, part of your salary would be covered by the workers' compensation program. The states each have a workers' compensation division. The federal government administers workers' comp for certain occupations such as coal miners and longshore workers.

Individual Disability Insurance Even if you are covered under an employer's disability insurance plan, you might want to supplement that by buying an individual policy for yourself. The coverage offered by employer plans can vary—and might be as little as 50 percent or less. If you became permanently disabled, could you get along on only 50 percent of your salary for ten years or longer? Check the terms of employer coverage carefully. If you do not think it's enough, consider adding an individual policy to provide better protection.

▶ If you are injured on the job, part of any lost wages should be covered by a workers' compensation program.

Do You Need Long-Term Care Insurance?

Long-term care insurance helps pay the costs of health care assistance in the home, in an assisted living facility, or in a nursing home. These services are most often needed by the elderly—but a severe injury or illness at any age can leave you unable to care for yourself. The cost of care can financially drain a family in a short time. Some employers offer long-term care policies at group rates. Individual policies are also available.

Long-term care insurance might not be at the top of your list if you are just starting out, but it is best to apply for coverage well before retirement age. Premiums are generally set at the time you take out a policy, so younger people will pay considerably less. In addition, it is much more difficult to get long-term care insurance after you have developed a significant health problem.

SECTION 1 ASSESSMENT

Factual Recall

1. What is the relationship between your age and the premium you pay for health care insurance?
2. When might a person need COBRA coverage?
3. Who pays for Medicaid programs?
4. What insurance program covers people who are injured or killed on the job?
5. Name three types of managed care plans.

Critical Thinking

1. Why should you have medical coverage, even when you are young and healthy?
2. Compare a flexible spending account (FSA) with a health savings account (HSA).

SECTION 2

Buying Life Insurance

Focus Questions

1. Why should someone in his or her twenties think about getting a life insurance policy?
2. What is an annuity?

Key Terms
beneficiary
term life insurance
whole life insurance
annuity

People of all ages die every day—and they leave behind people who miss them. Many of those who pass away have, up until the time of death, provided an income that their dependents counted on. Life insurance is important for parents and anyone else who provides financial support for another person. Even if you have no children or other dependents, life insurance is worth considering.

Why Buy Life Insurance?

Life insurance protects all of your dependents—spouse and children—or others you name to receive benefits in the case of your death. Life insurance benefits can be used to do the following:

- Pay off debts owed at the time of death
- Provide income to spouse and dependents
- Provide for the education of children
- Make charitable donations

When you take out a life insurance policy, you specify one or more beneficiaries. A **beneficiary** is a person or institution that is named to receive the benefits of an insurance policy. You can name your spouse, children, or other family members. You can name a good friend. You can name a university, hospital, or other charitable institution.

beneficiary a person named to receive the benefits from an insurance policy

term life insurance an insurance policy that pays a stated benefit upon the policyholder's death, if that death occurs within the term of the policy

Types of Life Insurance

There are two major types of life insurance: term and permanent. Permanent insurance policies include whole life, variable life, and universal life. Understanding the differences among these will help you decide which type to purchase.

Term Insurance

Term life insurance pays out benefits *only* if you die during the specific time period when the policy is in force. There is no cash value. Parents might buy term insurance, for example, to make sure there is money for their children to go to college if the parents are not alive.

Answers to Fact or Fiction

1. False—Not all employers offer health insurance plans; **2.** True; **3.** False—Disability coverage typically pays 50 percent to 70 percent of your regular salary; **4.** True; **5.** False—Even if you have no dependents, life insurance benefits can be used to pay off debts you owed or to make charitable donations; **6.** True.

Term life is less expensive than permanent insurance, which is explained below. Some term insurance plans are *renewable*. You can renew the policy when the time period is up—often without a medical exam. The premium usually increases at that time. Other policies are *convertible*. When the term is up, they can be changed to permanent coverage. Again, the premium would increase.

Permanent Insurance

The most common type of permanent insurance is **whole life insurance**. It is considerably more expensive than a term insurance policy. Whole life continues until death, as long as you pay premiums. Most types of permanent life insurance accumulate cash value because the insurance company invests your premiums. When you die, your beneficiaries receive a death benefit usually equal to the sum of the policy's face value plus its cash value. For instance, if the policy is worth $250,000 and the cash value is $10,000, the death benefit would be $260,000.

whole life insurance a permanent insurance policy that protects the policyholder during his or her whole life, paying a death benefit but also building up an additional cash value

Variable life insurance is another form of permanent insurance. Here, you are allowed to determine how to invest a portion of your premiums. If those investments grow, the policy is worth more. If the investments lose money, most variable policies still guarantee a minimum death benefit.

Universal life is a third common form of permanent life insurance. These policies allow you to adjust the amount of coverage to match changes in your life and needs. Growth of the cash value depends on interest rates.

At some point in the future, if you no longer wanted to continue your coverage for any reason, permanent life insurance allows you to "cash out" the policy. In other words, you could stop paying premiums and collect the built-up cash value—although you would forfeit the death benefit. Some permanent life policies allow part of the value of the policy to be paid out before

Maria has been working in the financial aid office at the local college for a year. She's been married for two years. Her husband is an interior designer who works for several home-building companies.

Maria's employer is offering a life insurance plan to its employees. Maria and her husband don't have any kids yet, so she wonders why she should sign up. It will be extra money—$50 a month—to be deducted from each paycheck, and they are trying to save everything they can to build a new house of their own. Besides, she is young and healthy.

But what would happen if she suffered a fatal injury or developed a fatal illness? What about after they have children? What would happen to their dream then if something happened to Maria?

Should she . . .

1. ...skip the life insurance plan for now and concentrate on saving for their house? Give reasons for your answer.
2. ...sign up for the life insurance plan? How would enrolling now benefit Maria and her husband?

Get Good Advice

When Kelly was just 8 years old, her father, Tony, died at work from a massive heart attack. Tony was only 38 years old. Left behind were Kelly's mother, Barbara, 6-year-old brother, Eric, and 1-year-old sister, Veronica. Tony exercised regularly and was careful about what he ate. He seemed to be the picture of health. But nobody can predict the future.

Tony and Barbara's plans were turned upside down. They had planned for Barbara to go back to school and then start a new career after Veronica entered first grade. What would happen now?

Fortunately for Barbara and her children, she and Tony had done their homework. Two years earlier they met with a financial planner. He had stressed the importance of getting adequate life insurance coverage. What would happen if either Barbara or Tony died prematurely? He reminded them that the burden of being a single parent—for either Tony or Barbara—would be significant.

The financial planner talked with them about the cost of child care, lost wages, college savings for the kids, and retirement—issues that are affected by a premature death. "One of the best decisions we ever made was to take the advice of our financial planner and get adequate life insurance coverage for both of us," says Barbara.

Talk with an older family member, an adult mentor, or a financial planner about the importance of having adequate insurance coverage. Here are a few questions to help you get the ball rolling:

1. Why should I care about having the right kind of insurance coverage—auto insurance, health insurance, or life insurance?
2. Do you know anyone who decided not to buy insurance and then suffered the consequences—financially or otherwise—because something happened? What happened?
3. What should I do if I cannot afford adequate insurance coverage for everything—auto, health, and life? Is there a way to prioritize my risk and get only the coverage that is most important and necessary for me now?
4. How should I budget for all the different types of insurance that I need?
5. Did anyone teach you about financial planning, or did you have to teach yourself?

After you have done this short interview exercise, bring your responses back and share them with the class. Making thoughtful decisions about insurance coverage is an essential life skill that might have a significant impact on your short-, medium-, and long-term financial goals.

death if the policyholder has a terminal illness. This can help with expenses such as medical bills.

Sources of Life Insurance Coverage

As with other types of insurance, both group and individual life insurance policies are available. Group life policies are often offered by employers, but many other groups have them as well. For instance, fraternal organizations and labor unions sometimes offer life insurance plans for their members.

Because the purpose of life insurance is to pay a claim at some time in the future, check to be sure the insurance companies you are considering are strong and reputable. Companies such as A. M. Best and Standard & Poor's rate insurance companies' financial strength.

A life expectancy table, a type of actuarial table, tells you how many more years you can expect to live based on your current age. This type of statistical information is used by life insurance providers to determine the risk of insuring people of various ages. The higher the perceived risk, the higher the premium will be. Other factors also influence premium amounts, including preexisting health conditions and smoking.

If you want to find out your life expectancy, or that of people you know, go to the life expectancy table at the Social Security Web site (http://fin.emcp.net/lifeexpectancy).

How Premiums Are Determined

Life insurance premiums are based on the insurance company's predictions about people's life spans. The federal government publishes life expectancy tables that estimate how long a man or woman of a particular age can be expected to live, on average. See the list in Figure 16.2 to find the life expectancy of people at different ages.

The insurance company uses detailed application forms and often medical screening tests to identify other risk factors. For example, if your hobby is skydiving, you might be denied insurance or else might be charged a considerably higher premium. Similarly, smoking, alcohol abuse, or certain medical conditions raise risks.

Evaluating Life Insurance Policies

Figuring out what type of life insurance would be best for you and how much you need can be difficult. Keep these points in mind:

- *Term vs. permanent.* In general, term insurance premiums are less expensive than permanent ones. Just be sure you buy enough coverage for the longest term you need.
- *Look for renewable term policies.* If you have a term life policy, is it renewable at the end of the term? The new premium will be higher, but you might not need another medical exam.
- *How much do you need?* There are quite a few online calculators that can help you figure how much life insurance to buy. One calculator can be found at Bankrate.com (http://fin.emcp.net/bankrate). Another is available from LIFE, the Life and Health Insurance Foundation for Education (http://fin.emcp.net/life). Financial planners, insurance agents, and brokers who sell life insurance can also help determine how much life insurance you should carry and which type of policy best fits your needs.

Figure 16.2 SAMPLE LIFE EXPECTANCY TABLE

Insurance companies gather data about life expectancy from actuarial publications.

Age (in years)	Male life expectancy	Female life expectancy
1	73.97	79.60
20	55.46	60.40
40	36.88	41.11
60	20.00	23.21
80	7.43	9.00

You Can Succeed Financially

Have you ever wondered how insurance companies decide how much to charge for different people's insurance premiums? Insurance actuaries are the people responsible for that. Actuaries assess and determine risk for individuals who want to buy insurance. They use mathematical equations to figure out variables such as life expectancy for different groups, the effects of risky behaviors, and the likelihood of passing on genetic diseases.

Shawn Voight is an insurance actuary. Like most actuaries, Shawn went to college and got a bachelor's degree. (He had a double major, in math and Spanish.) After he graduated from college, Shawn took some extra courses and passed the actuarial exams. He got a job with a major insurance company. Over the years, he has taken additional courses and passed

additional exams, moving up in the company.

In addition to his continuing education, Shawn has honed his computer skills and his people skills. He has learned a lot about the insurance industry and continues to read industry news to stay on top of it all. Shawn's career outlook is good. Actuaries make a good salary, and demand for their skills is expected to rise.

What Would You Do?

1. If you like math, would you consider a career as an insurance actuary? Why or why not?
2. Do you think Shawn's degree in Spanish can also help him in the insurance business? In what way? How does reading industry news help his career?

Annuities

Another insurance program that acts somewhat like an investment is an **annuity**. People purchase annuity contracts from insurance companies. However, instead of paying a benefit to your survivors when you die, an annuity guarantees regular payments *to you*—usually from the time you retire through the remainder of your lifetime or for a fixed number of years. Annuity payments supplement Social Security and payments from other retirement accounts, providing you with a guaranteed source of income after retirement. Annuities are tax-deferred, so you pay no taxes on the earnings until you withdraw the money.

annuity an investment that guarantees regular payments to the holder, usually beginning at retirement and continuing for a fixed number of years or until death

SECTION 2 ASSESSMENT

Factual Recall

1. When someone dies, who receives the person's life insurance benefits?
2. Briefly describe the two major types of life insurance.
3. What is the *cash value* of a life insurance policy?
4. Name three kinds of permanent life insurance.
5. How are life insurance premiums determined?

Critical Thinking

1. Why are life insurance premiums higher for people who smoke or abuse alcohol?
2. If a policyholder has no dependents, who may benefit from his or her life insurance policy?

CHAPTER 16 REVIEW AND ASSESSMENT

Chapter Summary

Section 1 Choosing Health Care Insurance

- Health care coverage includes various types of insurance, such as medical, dental, vision, disability, and long-term care plans.
- The sources of health care insurance include group, individual, and government plans.
- Because group plans insure large numbers of people, premiums are usually lower.
- Individual policies are an option for those who do not have access to group plans. However, individual policies are expensive.
- Government programs help insure senior citizens, people who cannot afford or obtain group or private insurance, and workers who might be injured or killed on the job.
- A health care policy might be a traditional plan or a managed care plan, such as an HMO, PPO, or POS plan.
- When comparing plans, consider what is covered and what is excluded, how your health care providers will be selected, and what your costs will be.
- Health savings accounts, flexible spending accounts, and discount health plans can help reduce the costs of medical care.
- Disability insurance replaces part of your income if you become unable to work.
- Long-term care insurance helps pay the costs of health care assistance in the home, in an assisted living facility, or in a nursing home.

Section 2 Buying Life Insurance

- Life insurance pays benefits to one or more beneficiaries after the policyholder dies.
- Some policies allow withdrawals during the policyholder's lifetime for certain situations.
- The two major types of life insurance are term and permanent. The most common type of permanent insurance is whole life.
- Premiums for life insurance are based on life expectancy. Premiums are lower for people expected to live a long time.
- When comparing life insurance policies, consider the type of policy and your particular insurance needs.

Reviewing Key Terms

For each of the following statements, choose the answer that best completes the sentence.

1. ______ is a federally funded health insurance program for people who are over age 65 or who have certain disabilities.
   a. Medicaid
   b. COBRA
   c. Medicare
   d. Social Security
2. Earnings on a ______ are tax-free.
   a. managed care policy
   b. flexible spending account
   c. health savings account
   d. both b and c
3. ______ typically pays 50 to 75 percent of the policyholder's regular pay.
   a. Whole life insurance
   b. Coinsurance
   c. An annuity
   d. Disability insurance
4. ______ insurance coverage ends at a specified time.
   a. Term life
   b. Whole life
   c. Disability
   d. All of the above
5. A beneficiary is ______.
   a. an investment that guarantees regular payments to the holder
   b. a person named to receive benefits from an insurance policy
   c. an insurance policy that pays a stated death benefit
   d. none of the above
6. Instead of paying benefits to survivors, ______ guarantees regular payments to the policyholder.
   a. an annuity
   b. a co-pay

c. a flexible spending account
d. whole life insurance

7. A(n) ______ is a flat fee that a policyholder pays to a health care provider for each visit, test, treatment, or drug.
   a. FSA
   b. HSA
   c. coinsurance
   d. co-pay
8. ______ plans focus on controlling the cost, use, and quality of the health care system.
   a. Medicare
   b. Managed care
   c. Flexible spending account
   d. COBRA

Understanding the Main Ideas

1. If your employer does not offer group health insurance, what options do you have?
2. Besides the premium, what other out-of-pocket costs might relate to health insurance?
3. List three drawbacks of individual health insurance policies.
4. What three groups of people might be covered by state-run health care programs?
5. Which type of health care policy offers the widest choice of health care providers?
6. What is the key difference between a discount health plan and an insurance plan?
7. Name four sources of disability insurance.
8. Is long-term care coverage needed only by older people? Explain your answer.
9. If you have term life insurance that is convertible, what does that mean?
10. Which type of life insurance policy allows you to adjust the amount of coverage to match changes in your needs?

Practicing Math

1. Kelsy's health insurance has a $500 deductible. Last year, she paid $300 toward the deductible. This year, she filed a claim for $1,000. How much deductible will she have to pay before the insurance coverage begins?
2. Jamahl's bill for a hospital stay came to $16,800. His health insurance plan includes a $500 deductible and a 20 percent coinsurance. How much will his insurance company pay?

Applying Critical Thinking Skills

1. Corporation A offers you a job with group health insurance. Corporation B offers you a job that pays $5,000 more per year, but there is no health insurance. Which offer do you take? Why?
2. If you lose your job and do not want to pay for COBRA coverage, what is another option?
3. What is the difference between Medicare and Medicaid?
4. An annuity that pays a regular, fixed amount of money each month provides a reliable source of retirement income. What might be the drawback in having such an annuity as your *only* source of income?

Working with Real-World Documents

1. Examine a health insurance policy. See if you can find answers to the following questions.
   a. What is covered?
   b. How much freedom does the policyholder have in choosing health care providers?
   c. Is there a deductible?
   d. Is there a coinsurance provision?
   e. Is there an out-of-pocket maximum?
   f. Are there lifetime maximum benefits?
2. Use an online life insurance calculator to figure out how much life insurance is recommended for a 23-year-old single person with no dependents. Two sites with these online calculators are Bankrate.com and the Life and Health Insurance Foundation for Education.

Taking It Home

1. Gather information from ads, mailings, or the Internet about discount health plans. What kinds of plans are offered? What are the costs? What do state insurance commissions or consumer groups say about the companies offering these plans?
2. Find out what a nursing home in your area typically charges per month. Then find out how much a long-term care insurance policy would pay per month toward nursing home costs.

Conclusion: Putting It All Together

You have covered a lot of territory in the sixteen chapters of this book—everything from how to get a job, to the importance of creating your own values-based financial plan, to saving for retirement. You have learned many aspects of what it means to be financially successful. Setting financial goals, talking with family members about the role money plays in their lives, learning investment terminology and strategy, developing and maintaining healthy financial habits—all these activities serve as building blocks to your short-, medium-, and long-term financial success.

You might not know it, but you have a big advantage over adults when it comes to making wise money decisions. That's

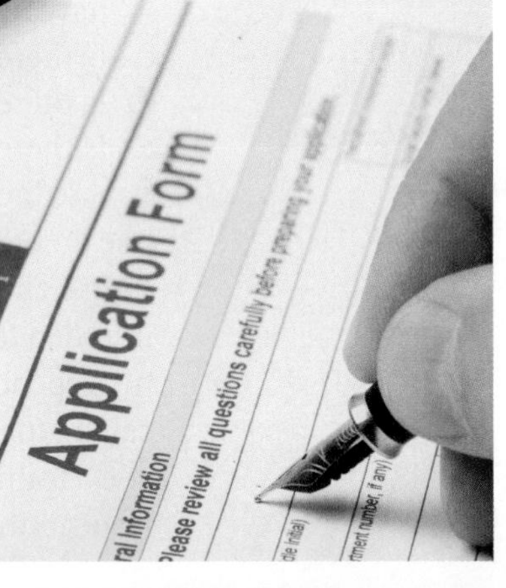

because it's easier to establish healthy money habits when you are young than it is to unravel unhealthy habits at age 30, 40, or 50. The sooner you adapt the core concepts discussed in this book, the better off you will be. You will be ready to make thoughtful money decisions—like saving for a car, contributing to your education fund, carefully using a credit card, saving for your first home, or investing for retirement.

You can be confident that the skills you learned in this class will benefit you for the rest of your life. That might sound like a bold claim, but it's true. Money management and all of the decisions that go with it will be a part of your routine at each stage of life.

As you set out to apply your new knowledge, keep in mind the following Top Ten Money Tips for Teens. These recommendations will help you extend your success beyond this class and into the next phase of your life. Use them as reminders for developing and maintaining healthy money habits.

Top Ten Money Tips for Teens

1. **Let your values guide your money decisions.** The average American is exposed to 5,000 advertising impressions a day—in other words, 5,000 suggestions for how to spend your money. You don't have to give in to those ads if you know what is important to you and if you set your money priorities accordingly. Finding balance in the choices you make with your money can greatly enrich your life as well as the lives of others.

2. **Set and track your financial goals.** People who are financially successful not only take the time to map out their financial goals, but also to measure their progress and revise the goals as necessary to make sure each is met. Setting up a realistic budget and following it are the keys to this process. When you combine tips 1 and 2—linking your financial goals and budget to your values—great things can happen!

3. **Get good advice.** Find family members, friends, financial professionals, and others who will be sounding boards for your financial questions, concerns, and ideas. When it comes to building your money skills, be curious, ask good questions, and learn from others who have more experience. A brief conversation with a money mentor today can yield powerful results in the future.

4. **Learn from your financial mistakes.** It's okay to make money mistakes—just try not to make too many, and do not repeat them. Doing well at managing money is not about perfection. It is about looking at the results of your financial decisions and making improvements when necessary. It is also about avoiding obvious pitfalls like gambling and get-rich-quick schemes.

5. **Learn to earn.** Understanding how to get a job—or, more important, the right job for you—will pay huge dividends down the road. Keep in mind that college graduates earn 62 percent (or about $19,000) more per year than people who have only a high school education. Bottom line: It pays to extend your learning to trade school, college, and beyond. It also pays to look for learning opportunities on the job. Many companies offer training and education for their employees.

6. **Establish wise money habits.** When you get money, what is your immediate thought? Do you want to invest it in a savings account or a mutual fund, share it with your favorite charity, or rush to the mall and spend it on the latest electronic gadget? Spending money is not a bad thing—in fact, it can be a lot of fun and stimulates the economy. But you need to balance your spending habits with other financial responsibilities.

7. **Monitor your spending.** Set up a working budget, and then keep track of your actual spending habits. Do you stay within the limit you have set for impulse purchases? Do you research large purchases? Do you ask questions about service agreements? Spending carefully and thoughtfully helps you get more out of the money you have.

8. **Know how credit works.** When you use a credit card, you are spending money. The same basic rule for using money wisely applies to using credit wisely: Spend only the money you have. If you get in the habit of monitoring your spending, you will be in a much better position to use credit to your advantage. One more benefit: A healthy credit score can improve your chances of getting a good job. Check your credit score and your credit report at least once a year, to be sure they are accurate.

9. **Remember that time is your ally.** Nothing makes money like time. Choosing investments thoughtfully and committing money to them regularly over a long period of time is a recipe for financial success. Albert Einstein said, "The most powerful force in the universe is compound interest." If you establish a healthy routine for saving and investing today, you can reap the rewards tomorrow.

10. **And finally . . . Share Save Spend.** People who focus less on spending and more on sharing and saving tend to be healthier and happier. Benjamin Franklin said, "The more a man has, the more he wants." Instead of just accumulating stuff, concentrate on doing well by doing good. Remember: The choices you make with your money can change the world!

Economic Principles Reference Guide

Managing your personal finances is an important part of your lifelong journey to financial success. In an increasingly global economy, your journey may take you around the world. As you participate more actively in society, you will make all kinds of financial decisions. To help prepare you for the global, economic conversation, the *Economic Principles Reference Guide* defines terms that you are likely to come across in the "real world" of finance. As you learn these terms, you will understand how managing your finances fits into the big picture of global economics and you'll be well on your way to financial freedom!

appreciation—An increase in value; for example, of a particular currency compared to other currencies over a period of time (the opposite of *depreciation*). A currency is said to appreciate if it buys more of another currency. If the exchange rate goes from $1 for €0.60 to $1 for €0.80, the dollar buys more euros and as a result has appreciated in value. Another example is the increase of the market value of an asset (such as a property) over a period of time. If you bought a house in 2005 for $200,000 and in 2007 its market value was $300,000, your house appreciated $100,000, or 50 percent, in value.

capital—A produced good from which other goods may be produced. The term "capital" can refer to just about anything that produces wealth—such as money, machinery, factories, and manpower. We say that a business owner makes a "capital" investment when he buys a factory in which goods are manufactured, or when a farmer buys equipment for plowing his fields. In both cases, the item purchased will allow the owner to produce more goods.

circular flow of economic activity—The interrelationship among different economic forces in an economy. In America, this includes three basic sectors: households, businesses, and the government. The circular flow in Figure EP-01, opposite, illustrates the exchanges in a market economy.

comparative advantage—The ability of one country to produce a particular good or service at a lower cost than another country. For example, if Canada produces lumber at a lower cost than Mexico produces lumber, then we say that Canada has a comparative advantage over Mexico in the lumber industry.

consumer price index (CPI)—The most commonly cited measure of the average prices of goods and services. The average prices may rise or fall, or remain constant. By comparing the CPI from consecutive months or years, we can determine the percentage rate of inflation, or deflation, if any. Economists determine the annual CPI with the following formula:

$$\text{Percentage change in CPI} = \left(\frac{\text{CPI in later year} - \text{CPI in earlier year}}{\text{CPI in earlier year}} \right) \times 100$$

For example, the CPI in 2006 was 117 and the CPI in 2007 was 120, so we would figure out the percentage rate of inflation, or deflation, like this: [(120 – 117) ÷ 117] × 100, which is 2.56%. This means the inflation rate was 2.56%. If the final number had been negative, then the percentage would have indicated a deflation rate. For the latest CPI statistics visit http://fin.emcp.net/cpi.

deflation—A decrease in the average price level of goods and services (the opposite of *inflation*). Deflation usually occurs for one of two reasons. First, the quantity of goods and services may remain steady, but a demand for those goods decreases, which makes the price of the goods fall. In other words, there is a steady level of goods but fewer people who want and can afford them, so their prices drop. This

Figure EP-01 THE CIRCULAR FLOW OF ECONOMIC ACTIVITY IN THE U.S. ECONOMY

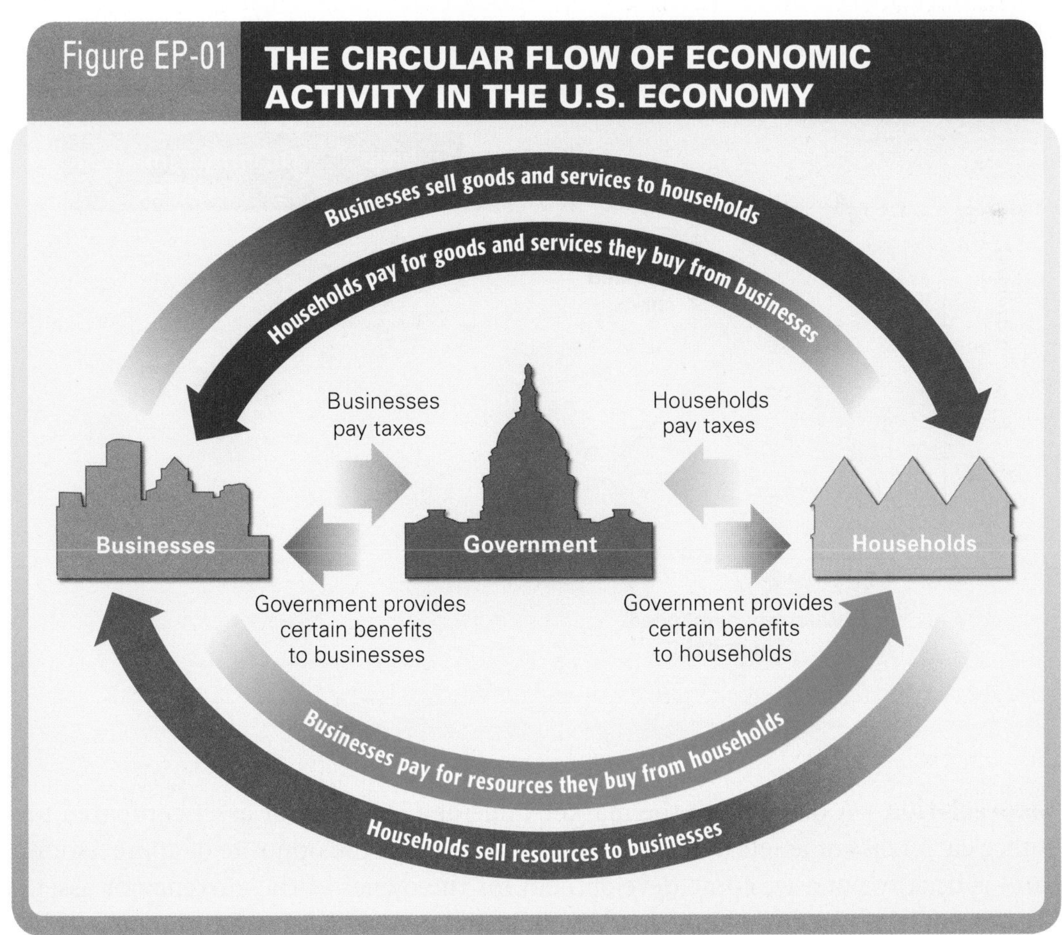
Businesses sell goods and services to households
Households pay for goods and services they buy from businesses
Businesses pay taxes
Households pay taxes
Businesses
Government
Households
Government provides certain benefits to businesses
Government provides certain benefits to households
Businesses pay for resources they buy from households
Households sell resources to businesses

could be caused by a decrease in the money supply, making people unable to afford the goods. Second, the quantity of goods may increase, while the demand for those goods stays the same, which also makes the price of the goods fall. In other words, if more goods are being produced than people want, the price drops. Developments in technology make it possible for large supplies of goods to be mass produced, even if people do not want the goods, which results in lower prices.

demand—The relation between the cost and availability of goods or services and the ability and willingness of consumers to buy those goods or services during a specified time. For example, as the demand for a particular stock increases, the price goes up; as the demand decreases, the price goes down.

demand curve—A graph that represents the quantity of a particular item that consumers are willing and able to buy at a certain price. For example, when the price of a good, such as a candy bar, is at its height—$4 in the figure below—demand is relatively low. As the price drops, demand rises. (See Figure EP-02a, below.)

demand schedule—A numerical chart that shows the law of demand at work for any particular good. A demand schedule is an alternate way to present the same material you would find in a demand curve. (See Figure EP-02b, below.)

Figure EP-02 **DEMAND CURVE AND DEMAND SCHEDULE**

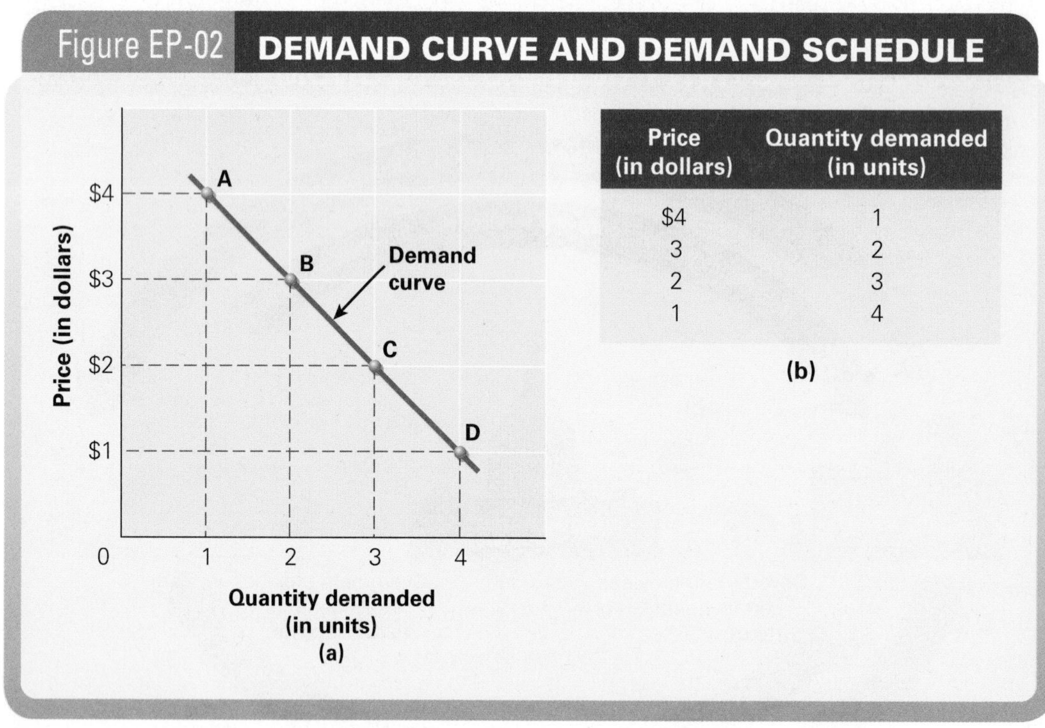

Price (in dollars)	Quantity demanded (in units)
$4	1
3	2
2	3
1	4

(b)

depreciation—A decrease in the market value of a currency or asset compared to other currencies or assets over a period of time. This is the opposite of appreciation and is usually not a welcome development for the owner of the currency or asset. For example, if you buy a home for $250,000, and two years later your home is only worth $200,000, we would say your home depreciated 20 percent in value.

economic system—the organized way in which a given society provides a framework for commerce and industry, allocating resources, and directing the production of goods. An economic system is the way that a society answers the three basic economic questions: (1) What goods will be produced? (2) How will they be produced? and (3) For whom will they be produced? Different countries utilize different kinds of economic systems. For example, the United States has a free market economy, which basically allows market forces to determine the production and allocation of goods. In contrast, China has a command economy, which means the government largely determines the production and distribution of goods. In today's world most economies contain aspects of both market and command systems.

economics—The science that studies how people, companies, and societies use their scarce, or limited, resources to satisfy their unlimited wants. Economists study both individual (microeconomics) and more universal (macroeconomics) behaviors and then draw conclusions and make predictions for society about financial and social matters. For example, in microeconomics an economist might investigate the ways in which individuals pay for drugs, doctor bills, and medical insurance. In macroeconomics an economist would investigate and compare health care systems in different countries.

elasticity of demand—The relationship between the percentage change in the demand for a good or service and a percentage change in its price. The formula for determining the elasticity of demand is to divide the percentage change in the quantity demanded by the percentage change in price:

$$\text{Elasticity of demand} = \frac{\text{Percentage change in quantity demanded}}{\text{Percentage change in price}}$$

If the result is greater than one, demand is said to be elastic—but if it is less than one, it is said to be inelastic. If the percentages are the same, it is called unit-elastic.

elasticity of supply—The proportionate relationship between the percentage change of a quantity supplied of a good or service and the percentage change in its price. The formula for finding out the elasticity of supply is to divide the percent change in quantity supplied by the percent change in price:

$$\text{Elasticity of supply} = \frac{\text{Percentage change in quantity supplied}}{\text{Percentage change in price}}$$

If the result is greater than one, supply is said to be elastic—but if it is less than one, it is said to be inelastic. If the percentages are equal, the result is called unit-elastic.

employment rate—The percentage of the adult civilian labor force that is employed. For example, if the employment rate is 95 percent, then 95 out of every 100 qualified adults are employed. Generally speaking, a high employment rate is a sign that an economy is thriving, that businesses are making profits, and that the members of most households are bringing home paychecks. People who do *not* qualify as part of the "adult civilian labor force" include people under the age of 16, people in the military, people in a mental or correctional facility, and retired persons.

equilibrium—In a market economy, the point of equal relation between the quantity of a good being demanded by consumers and the quantity of that good being supplied by the sellers. In other words, a situation in which demand equals supply. According to economist Adam Smith, a free market economy will tend toward establishing equilibrium via the price mechanism (pricing low when supply is high; pricing high when supply is low).

equilibrium price—The price of goods or services in a market that is experiencing equilibrium. If a surplus of supply occurs, prices usually drop, but if a shortage of supply occurs, prices usually increase.

factors of production—The four basic categories of sources used to produce consumer goods and services. Generally, the four basic categories include land and other natural resources, capital, labor (working force), and entrepreneurs (ideas and new businesses).

Federal Reserve System (the Fed)—The central bank of the United States. Established by Congress in 1913, the Fed is the chief monetary authority in the country. The Fed is responsible for creating and issuing Federal Reserve notes, or dollar bills, as well as supervising banks and determining the money supply. The principal components of the Federal Reserve System are the Board of Governors and the twelve Federal Reserve district banks.

fiscal policy—The federal government's promotion of specific economic goals, achieved through spending and taxation changes. Usually, these goals include increasing employment and decreasing inflation rates. When we speak of fiscal policy, we usually refer to the policy determined by Congress and the President. Once in place, spending and taxation programs stabilize the level of disposable income among consumers.

free enterprise—An economic system in which competitive market forces largely determine who owns and controls the use of resources, and in which the government plays a limited role, primarily a regulatory one. Generally, the means of production are privately owned, and "supply and demand" forces stabilize the economy, allowing people the freedom to find creative solutions to their wants. A free enterprise economy is the opposite of a Marxist economy, in which the government sets fiscal policy, allocates resources, and limits the creative freedom of individuals.

globalization—A situation in which economic realities in one part of the world affect those in another part of the world. The current trend toward globalization seems to suggest worldwide integration and connectedness. Keep in mind that certain dangers exist when the economies of the world are dependent upon each other—a downturn in the market of one country, say the United States, can have a negative ripple effect on the markets of other countries.

goods—In the most strict economic terms, anything that consumers desire and that brings satisfaction (utility). In more general usage, "goods" are distinguished from "services" and include tangible products that are sold in the marketplace, such as cars, cell phones, and jeans for example.

gross domestic product (GDP)—The total market value of all final goods and services produced annually in a country. The GDP varies from year to year, as the quantity produced and the prices of various products increase and decrease. To calculate GDP you would multiply the quantity of each good produced by its price and then add all the resulting totals.

incentive—Anything that motivates or encourages a person to act. In economics, this term refers more specifically to any reward or benefit that motivates an individual's behavior and choices. For example, an employer may offer bonus incentives to employees who sell a certain amount of products in an attempt to increase sales. The concept of incentive is essential to a free market economy.

inelastic demand—The resulting situation in which the percentage change of quantity demanded of a good is less than the percentage change in its price. In this case, a change in the price of a particular good or service has little effect on consumer demand for that good or service. Inelastic demand usually applies to most goods and services for which there is no substitute—such as insulin and antibiotics, or other items considered "necessities." See the formula for determining "elastic demand." A result less than 1.0 is generally considered inelastic demand.

inelastic supply—The resulting situation in which the percentage change of quantity supplied is less than the percentage change in price. The change in price for a particular good or service may have little effect on the quantity supplied—supply is simply not very sensitive to price changes. To figure out if supply is inelastic, see the formula for determining "elastic supply." A result less than 1.0 is generally considered inelastic supply.

inflation—An increase in the average price level of goods and services in an economy (the opposite of deflation). See the formula under "consumer price index (CPI)" to determine inflation rates; in the formula, wherever you see "CPI," insert "the price of a good or service."

law of demand—An economic principle stating that as the price for a good or service decreases, the quantity demanded for that good increases, and as the price for that good increases, the quantity demanded decreases. Generally, the price of a good and its demand are inversely related. For example, when airline ticket prices rise, the demand for vacation flights drops and fewer people fly—but as ticket prices fall, the demand for vacation flights increases as people begin flying again.

law of diminishing marginal utility—The economic law that holds that the more of a particular good a buyer consumes in a given period, the less satisfaction, or utility, each additional unit of that good will bring. This law explains why "all you can eat" buffet restaurants do such great business—they know that with each plate of food comes less pleasure or enjoyment because you are getting full. Because your stomach is only so big, the amount of food you can eat is about the same between a regular meal and a buffet meal. The restaurant makes more money because you pay for the *idea* of getting more food—even though you usually do not take it, and so they serve you about the same amount of food for a higher price.

law of supply—The economic law that holds that the quantity supplied of a good is directly proportionate to the price of that good. In a given time period, as the price of a good increases, the quantity supplied increases; conversely, as the price of a good decreases, the quantity supplied decreases. For example, when the average price of new homes increases because consumers demand new homes, contractors build—or supply—more homes.

macroeconomics—A branch of economics that examines economies as a whole and analyzes aggregate supply, aggregate demand, and monetary and fiscal policies. In other words, macroeconomics studies the "big picture" and develops models to explain the relationship among societal factors such as employment, inflation, taxation, and the gross domestic product. These models are used by both private businesses and the government to guide the development of business strategies and to set effective economic policies.

marginal—A frequently used economic term that means additional. Marginal applies to a variety of fiscal decisions and actions, such as "marginal cost" and "marginal revenue."

microeconomics—A branch of economics that examines individual and localized forces at work in the economy, such as consumer decisions or small business policies. Microeconomics studies how and why individuals, households, and small companies make their financial decisions—and how those decisions affect supply and demand. For example, a microeconomist might analyze how the diminished purchasing power of a particular group—say, senior citizens—is impacting the profitability of the leisure travel industry.

monetary policy—The decisions that the U.S. central bank, the Fed, makes in regards to the money supply and availability of credit, in order to promote full employment and price stability. The tool the Fed uses most frequently to effect such change is the adjustment of the federal funds rate—which in turn affects short-term interest rates, currency exchange rates, long-term interest rates, and the amount of money and credit available in the market. For example, the Fed often cuts the federal funds rate to stimulate the economy—making it easier to borrow, and therefore spend, money.

opportunity cost—The most valuable option that is forfeited when a choice is made. The option you forfeit is the cost of your pursuing the opportunity you do choose.

For instance, if you are trying to decide between investing $1,000 in a mutual fund that has a great track record or buying a new television set, if you buy the mutual fund, the television set is the opportunity cost.

profit—The amount of money remaining after all production costs have been paid. Profit is the opposite of loss. Companies earn a profit when their revenues (money coming in) are greater than costs (money going out). For example, if you own an organic foods store and your annual operating costs (including rental of store space, employee payroll, and product cost) are $550,000 but your total revenues from sales are $850,000, your profit for the year is $300,000.

quantity demanded—The quantity of a particular good or service that consumers are able and willing to buy at a given price. The quantity demanded of a certain item refers to a specific point on a demand curve. The quantity demanded decreases as the price for that good goes up, and the quantity demanded increases as the price goes down. For example, many people demand bottled water during the summer when the weather is hot, but if the price for bottled water gets too high, people will drink from the tap or find another beverage, and buy fewer bottles of water.

quantity supplied— The number of units of a particular good or service that a producer is able and willing to supply at a given price. This number refers to a specific point on the supply curve. The quantity supplied increases as the price goes up, and the quantity supplied decreases as the price goes down. When prices are high, producers supply large quantities of goods in an effort to maximize their revenue. For example, when people demand a lot of bottled water because the weather is hot, suppliers produce more bottles and make them available to consumers.

rationing device—A tool for determining who gets what portion of the available resources and goods. In a free market economy, the principal rationing device is price. In other words, people who can afford the goods get them. In a command economy, the government is the rationing device because it decides who gets what goods.

real GDP—A gross domestic product (GDP) adjusted for price changes from year to year. Economists and others concern themselves with real GDP as opposed to GDP to find out whether an increase in GDP was the result of increased production or higher prices, or both. Real GDP for a particular year is calculated by multiplying base year prices by the quantity produced in that particular year.

recession—An economic period marked by a decline in the real GDP for two consecutive quarters. Recessions usually lead to higher unemployment rates and a general decline in the standard of living since fewer goods are being produced and purchased. Short recessions are a natural part of the contraction phase of the business cycle, as shown in Figure EP-03.

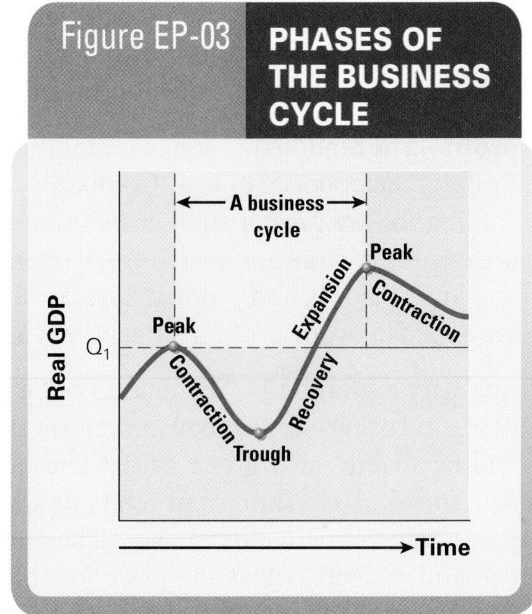

resources—Anything used in the process of creating goods and services. Economists often consider land (and other natural resources), labor, capital, and entrepreneurs as the four basic categories of resources. An example of *land* is water, an example of *labor* is technical expertise, an example of *capital* is a piece of machinery, and an example of an entrepreneur is a person who sees an opportunity to make money by producing and selling a new kind of frozen seafood. Resources are also referred to as factors of production.

scarcity—A situation in which our wants exceed the quantity of resources available to satisfy those wants. Scarcity forces people to make choices, which forms the basis of economics. Without scarcity, the science of economics would likely not exist.

services—The activities performed by individuals, private sector companies, and the government to meet—or satisfy—human wants. For example, you must pay your dry-cleaner in exchange for his or her service of cleaning your clothes. Industries in which people are paid to perform tasks for others are called "service industries." Two examples of this type of industry include the hotel industry and the restaurant industry. Compare service industries to manufacturing industries, for example, that produce material goods.

supply—The ability and willingness of sellers to produce and sell quantities of a good or service at different prices during a given time. As prices of a good or service increase, producers are willing to supply more of those goods and services. For example, if consumers are willing and able to pay a higher price for iPods, and the price increases, Apple will probably produce more iPods.

supply curve—A graph representing the quantity of a particular item that producers are able and willing to sell at different prices. A supply curve Slopes upward from left to right showing that as price rises so does quantity supplied. (See Figure EP-04a, opposite.)

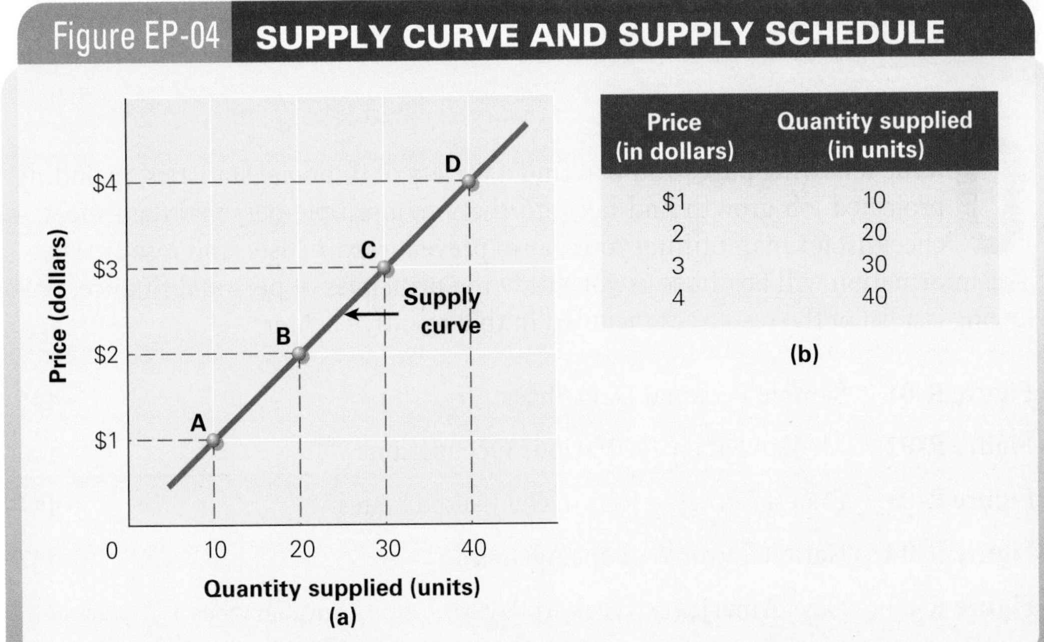

Figure EP-04 **SUPPLY CURVE AND SUPPLY SCHEDULE**

Price (in dollars)	Quantity supplied (in units)
$1	10
2	20
3	30
4	40

(b)

supply schedule—A numerical chart that shows the law of supply and demand. A supply schedule is usually divided into two columns, with the unit price in one column and the quantity supplied in the other. (See Figure EP-04b, above.)

trade-off—The situation in which having more of one good means having less of another good. Talking about trade-offs is another way of talking about opportunity costs. If you are on a diet and decide to eat an ice cream cone, the trade-off for the enjoyment you receive from ice cream is the increased number of calories that negatively impact your desire to lose weight. If our society decides to produce more guns and tanks during a time of war, we will have to sacrifice the items we would have produced instead, if we had not been at war.

unemployment rate—The percentage of people in a civilian labor force who are not working for pay. To determine the percentage, subtract the number of people who are working from the total number of people in the civilian labor force and multiply the answer by 100. A high unemployment rate is generally a sign of a struggling economy. Many of the government's fiscal policies attempt to increase employment in the hopes of decreasing the unemployment rate.

utility—The ability of a good or service to bring about happiness or satisfaction. As consumers, we often purchase goods or services according to the degree of happiness or satisfaction we expect to get from them. We are often willing to pay more for a good or service that we perceive will provide a sense of well-being or of pleasure. For example, people pay more money to eat at gourmet restaurants than at fast food restaurants because they receive more utility from the gourmet meal.

Personal Finance Resource Center

On the following pages you will find a variety of financial statistics, including projected job growth and tax information, a sample personal data sheet, a checklist for maintaining your car to prevent repair costs, and resource lists. The information will be of use as you study the principles of personal finance. Following is a list of the resources included in this resource center:

Figure R-01 SAMPLE PERSONAL DATA SHEET

Once you have taken the time to prepare a personal data sheet, you will have all of the information you need to fill out job application forms. Your personal data sheet is so convenient! Here is one example of a complete personal data sheet:

- **Name:**
  John Gerards
- **Local (current) address:**
  University of Maine
  Memorial Union
  Orono, ME 04469
- **Permanent address:**
  1000 SW Villanova Avenue
  Calais, Maine 04619
- **Home phone:**
  (866) 888-8888
- **Cell:**
  (800) 555-5555
- **Emergency contact info:**
  Mr. and Mrs. Norman and Elizabeth Gerards (parents)
  1000 SW Villanova Avenue
  (866) 888-8888
- **Social Security #:**
  555-55-5555
- **Education history:**
  LaSalle High School
  12345 N. Main Street
  Calais, ME 04619
  Degree: Graduated 2009, 3.9 GPA
- **Work history:**
  Hannah's Lobster House
  9876 SW Forest Drive
  Calais, ME 04619
  (866) 888-8888
  Supervisor: Victor Vincenzo
  Start date: May 2007
  End date: September 2009
  Job title: Busser, waiter, head waiter
  Duties: Organize seating floor to ensure wait staff received equal customers, greet diners pleasantly and share local history, upkeep of dining area, bus tables
  Starting salary: $7.00/hr + tips
  Ending salary: $10.00/hr + tips
  Reason for leaving: Began college at UM

  Mowed lawns for family and neighbors
  $8.00/hr
  Mr. James Peters (866) 888-0000
  Mrs. Vanessa Marion (866) 000-8888
- **Special skills:**
  Languages: French (fluent), Latin (read-only), Greek (read-only), Spanish (fluent)
  Type speed: 65 words per minute
  Computer programs: Vista, Excel, Word, PowerPoint, Quark, BookMaster
- **Honors and awards:**
  First place in state debate club, 2008, 2009; all-state tennis; all-state golf; Boy Scouts of America Eagle scout
- **References:**
  Bernard and Nancy Lovett
  44444 NW Hills Road
  Calais, ME 04619
  (866) 000-1111
  Family friends

  Mr. Dean Jameson
  11100 Native Avenue
  Calais, ME 04619
  (866) 000-2222
  Boy Scout leader

  Drs. Donald and Louise Karamazov
  33333 SW Grigory Lane
  Calais, ME 04619
  (866) 000-3333
  High school teachers

Figure R-02 **MEDIAN SALARY FOR VARIOUS OCCUPATIONS**

Below you will find median salaries for twenty-three randomly selected occupations. This information will give you a general idea of the wide range of salaries you could earn someday, depending on your chosen occupation.

To obtain current salary information for these occupations and others, go to http://fin.emcp.net/handbook.

Annual salary	Occupation
$132,140	Dentist (general dentistry)
$117,240	Air traffic controller
$101,580	Computer/ information systems manager
$ 98,974	College professor
$ 94,520	Pharmacist
$ 68,600	Civil engineer
$ 68,500	Stock broker
$ 64,150	Architect
$ 62,820	Gaming manager
$ 55,000	Power plant operator
$ 53,810	Food scientist
$ 48,290	Surveyor
$ 47,460	Police officer
$ 47,040	Kindergarten teacher
$ 46,670	Video and film editor
$ 39,760	Real estate agent
$ 39,750	Music composer
$ 38,190	Legal secretary
$ 34,370	Chef (or head cook)
$ 40,560	Environmental engineering technician
$ 29,210	Travel agent
$ 27,250	Fisher
$ 25,910	Fitness trainer

Source: U.S. Department of Labor, 2006 salaries

Figure R-03 FASTEST GROWING JOBS IN THE UNITED STATES

This figure shows the numbers (in thousands) of people who hold the jobs listed below as of 2006, as well as the projected numbers of people who will hold the same jobs in 2016. For the most current numbers, see the U.S. Bureau of Labor Statistics at http://fin.emcp.net/handbook.

Expected job growth (%)	Job title	Number of jobs (in thousands)	
		2006	2016
53.4	Network systems/data communications analysts	262	402
50.6	Personal and home care aides	767	1,156
48.7	Home health aides	787	1,171
44.6	Computer software, applications engineers	507	733
41.0	Veterinary technologists and technicians	71	100
41.0	Personal financial advisors	176	248
39.8	Makeup artists, theatrical and performance	2	3
35.4	Medical assistants	417	565
35.0	Veterinarians	62	84
34.3	Substance abuse, behavioral disorder counselors	83	112
34.3	Skin care specialists	38	51
33.8	Financial analysts	221	295
33.6	Social and human service assistants	339	453
33.6	Gaming surveillance officers, gaming investigators	9	12
32.4	Physical therapy assistants	60	80
32.0	Pharmacy technicians	285	376
30.7	Forensic science technicians	13	17
30.1	Dental hygienists	167	217
30.0	Mental health counselors	100	130
29.9	Mental health and substance abuse social workers	122	159

Source: *Monthly Labor Review*, 2007

Figure R-04 NATIONAL EMPLOYMENT AGENCIES

Employment agencies around the country help many people find jobs. Check out the Web site for each of the national agencies listed below to find available jobs in your area when you begin looking for work.

Employment agency	Web site
AppleOne	http://fin.emcp.net/appleone
Career.com	http://fin.emcp.net/career
Kelly Services	http://fin.emcp.net/kellyservices
Craigslist	http://fin.emcp.net/craigslist

Employment agency	Web site
Manpower	http://fin.emcp.net/manpower
Monstertrak	http://fin.emcp.net/monstertrak
Randstad Work Solutions	http://fin.emcp.net/randstad
Select Staffing	http://fin.emcp.net/selectstaffing

Figure R-05 DAYS AMERICANS WORK TO PAY FOR GOODS AND SERVICES

How much money do you make in one day? In a year? How much money do you spend each year on certain goods and services? How many days do you have to work to pay for them? Let's find out.

Let's say you make $30,000 per year and you spend $3,000 on food each year. How many days out of the year must you work to pay for your food?

Divide your yearly salary by the number of days in a year:

$30,000 ÷ 365 days = $82/day

Next, divide $3,000 by $82 to find out how many days it takes you to earn the $3,000 you need for food:

$3,000 ÷ $82 = 37 days

This means that you work 37 days each year to pay for food.

In 2007, the Tax Foundation did a study based on a 365-day year and found out that the average American does work about 30 days in order to pay for food. The pie graph above shows how many days the average American works to pay for other goods and services. Are you surprised at how many days the average American works to pay for taxes?

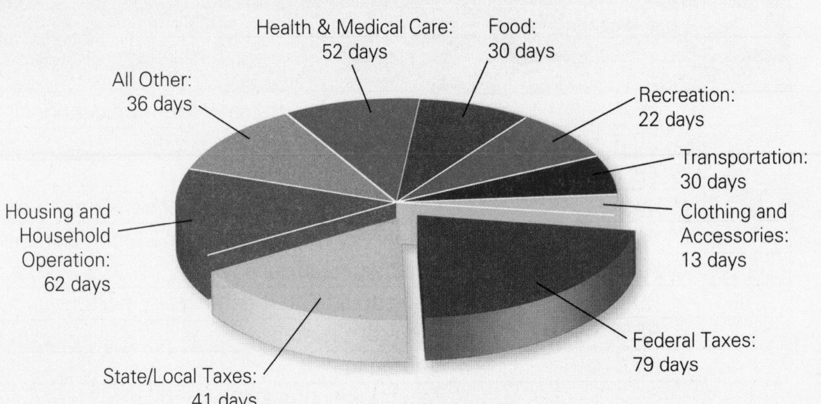

Source: Tax Foundation (www. taxfoundation.org/taxfreedomday)

Figure R-06 PERCENTAGE OF INCOME PAID TO TAXES

Country	Income (%) paid in taxes
Sweden	51.3
Denmark	50.3
Belgium	45.5
Norway	44.3
France	44.0
Finland	43.9
Iceland	42.4
Austria	42.0
Italy	40.6
Germany	38.8
Hungary	38.5
Luxembourg	38.2
Netherlands	38.2

Country	Income (%) paid in taxes
United Kingdom	37.0
New Zealand	36.6
Czech Republic	36.3
Spain	35.6
Malta	35.3
Portugal	35.3
Poland	34.2
Canada	33.5
Turkey	32.3
United States	26.8
South Korea	25.5
Mexico	19.9

Source: NationMaster, 2005

Figure R-07 COMPARING INTEREST RATES

You can earn interest by keeping your money in savings accounts, and some checking accounts. The longer you leave your money in the account, the more money you make! Compare the amount of interest you can earn at 2.0% annual percentage rate (APR) and at 4.5% APR, based on the initial amount of your deposit.

What you can earn at 2.0% APR					
Initial deposit:	**$250**	**$500**	**$1,000**	**$1,500**	**$2,000**
1 month	$ .40	.79	1.59	2.38	3.17
6 months	$2.49	4.98	9.95	14.93	19.90
12 months	$5.00	10.00	20.00	30.00	40.00

What you can earn at 4.5% APR					
Initial deposit:	**$250**	**$500**	**$1,000**	**$1,500**	**$2,000**
1 month	$ .88	1.76	3.53	5.29	7.06
6 months	$ 5.56	11.13	22.25	33.38	44.50
12 months	$11.25	22.50	45.00	67.50	90.00

The chart below compares the different amounts of interest you make at 2.0% APR versus 4.5% APR on an initial deposit of $2,000. A higher APR percentage can mean significantly more money for you! Of course you can also earn more money if you deposit and save more.

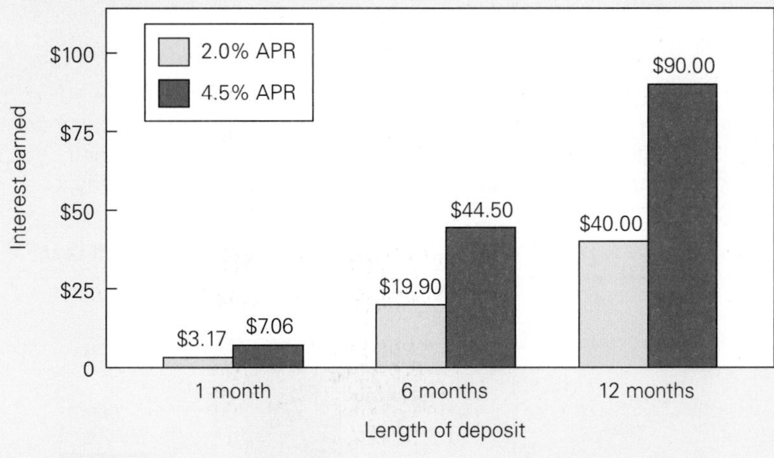

Figure R-08 WHAT YOUR LOAN *REALLY* COSTS YOU

Car Loan
Say you buy a car for $15,000, taking out a loan to finance the full amount at 6 percent interest, paid back over 48 months. Your monthly payment is $352. But what if you add an extra $100 per month to your payment? Take a look at what you save!

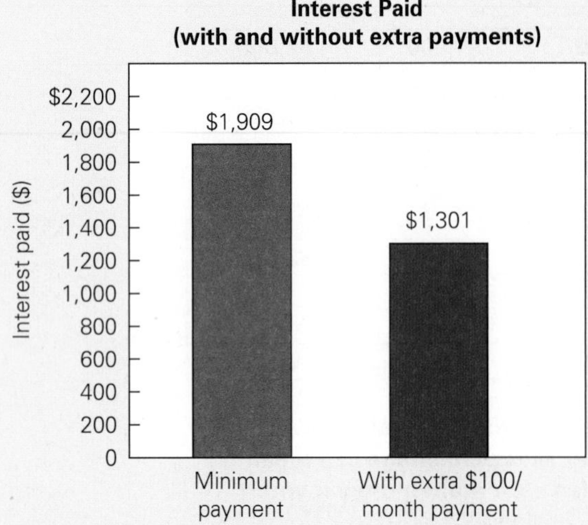

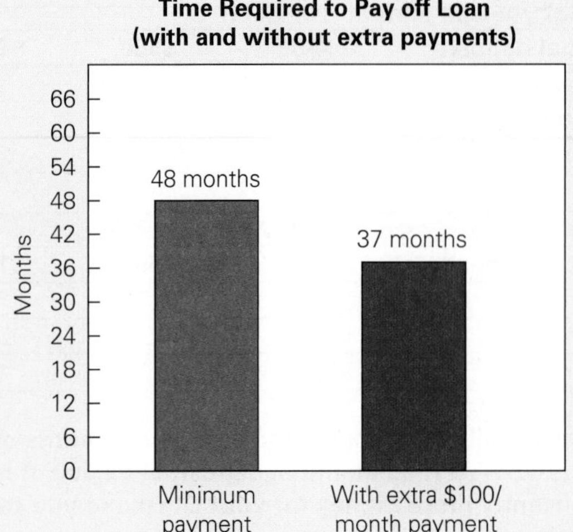

For car loan calculator, check out http://fin.emcp.net/carsdirect.

Student Loan
Say you borrow $40,000 at 8 percent interest to pay for college. The term for paying off the loan is 10 years, and your monthly payment, as billed by the lender, is $486 (this is the minimum payment due). But, if you want to save money in time and interest, you could add $200 to your monthly payment, for a total of $686 a month. You shave years off your loan—and save thousands in interest. Compare the amounts, in both time and money.

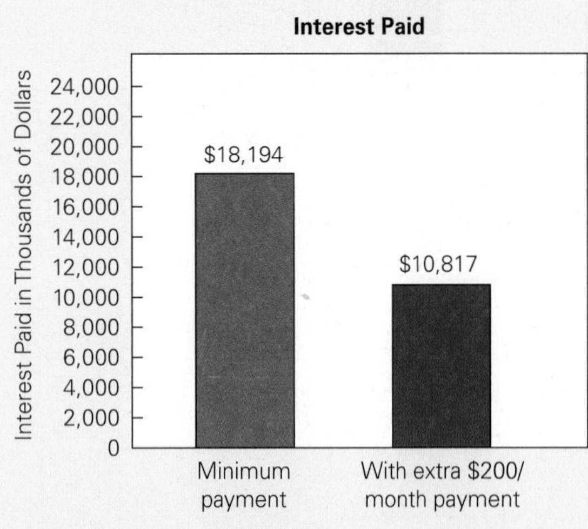

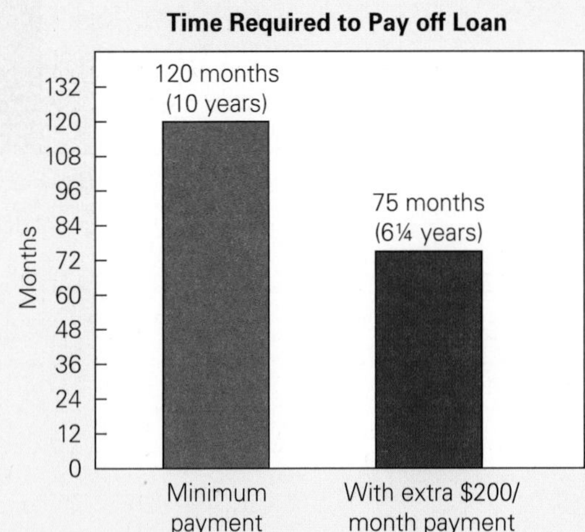

For student loan calculator, check out http://fin.emcp.net/cgi.

Figure R-09 INVESTMENT INCOME COMPARED

Imagine that 15 years ago, your parents bought a $100 EE bond (for $50) and also invested $100 in the S&P Index Fund. The chart below shows $69 interest income from their EE bond—and $251 in interest income from their S&P Index Fund account from one particular 15-year period (1992–2007). How might these results change during other 15-year periods?

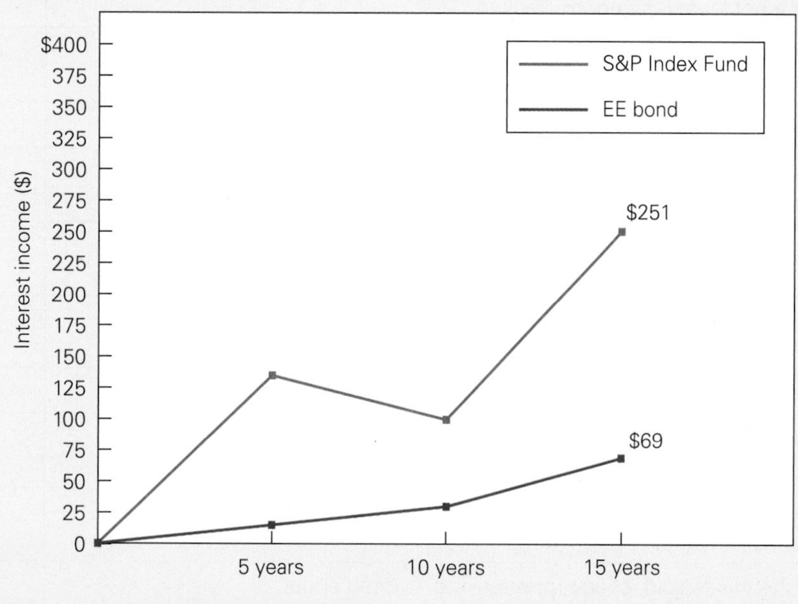

Figure R-10 MONTHLY PAYMENTS ON A $10,000 LOAN

Because the calculation can be complicated, loan officers often use tables such as the one below to quickly determine monthly loan payments.

Yearly interest rate	Length of loan in years					
	1	2	3	4	5	6
3%	$846.94	$429.81	$290.81	$221.34	$179.69	$151.94
4%	$851.50	$434.25	$295.24	$225.79	$184.17	$156.45
5%	$856.08	$438.72	$299.71	$230.30	$188.72	$161.05
6%	$860.67	$443.21	$304.22	$234.86	$193.33	$165.73
7%	$865.27	$447.73	$308.78	$239.47	$198.02	$170.50
8%	$869.89	$452.28	$313.37	$244.13	$202.77	$175.34
9%	$874.52	$456.85	$318.00	$248.86	$207.59	$180.26
10%	$879.16	$461.45	$322.68	$253.63	$212.48	$185.26
11%	$883.82	$466.08	$327.39	$258.46	$217.43	$190.35
12%	$888.49	$470.74	$332.15	$263.34	$222.45	$195.51

Figure R-11 SAVING MONEY ON YOUR CAR COSTS

Here are some helpful hints to care for your four-wheeled investment.

Perform these routine maintenance checks once a month:	
• **Engine oil**—Top off; if you need more, add the same grade that is already in the engine.	✔
• **Belts**—Make sure that they are not loose, frayed, or cracked.	✔
• **Hoses**—Squeeze them (when they are cold), to make sure they are not too soft, which means they might be ready to split.	✔
• **Air filter**—If accessible, replace this when it is dirty and before it becomes clogged.	✔
• **Radiator coolant**—Make sure that there is enough and that it is not rusty. Don't open any cap when the engine is hot.	✔
• **Battery water**—Clean off any corrosion at the posts and check the fluid levels. Don't get corrosion or fluid on your hands or clothing.	✔
• **Other fluids**—Check fluid levels for automatic transmission, power steering, brake master cylinder, and windshield washer.	✔
• **Tires**—Check the inflation pressure of all tires, including the spare, and check for wear.	✔
• **Wheels and shock absorbers**—Check the inside of the wheels for brake fluid leakage. Check the shocks for leaks.	✔
• **Lights**—Check the headlights (low and high beams), turn signals (front and rear), brake lights, and taillights. Replace any burned-out bulbs.	✔
• **Wipers**—With some fluid on the windshield, check for streaking, missed spots, or chattering. Make sure wiper blades are securely fastened.	✔
• **Leaks on the pavement**—Note the colors: black or brown for engine oil or rear axle fluid, usually reddish for automatic transmission fluid, and greenish for antifreeze.	✔

Keep these items in your car to save time, trouble, and money later:
• Good flashlight
• Fire extinguisher
• First-Aid kit
• Spare tire
• Jack and lug wrench for changing tires
• Flares (stored where children can't easily get to them) or reflective day/night devices
• Fire department-approved empty can for carrying gasoline, in case you run out of gas
• Small toolbox containing all the basics
• One or two cans of engine oil
• Container of radiator coolant and windshield washer fluid
• Battery jumper cables
• Plastic sheet for when you are changing a tire in the rain, or for checking the underside of car
• Bottled water and a blanket, in case you're stranded on the side of the road for a while

Figure R-12 WHAT TO DO IF YOU ARE INVOLVED IN AN AUTOMOBILE ACCIDENT

These are general guidelines. Check out http://fin.emcp.net/dmv to find your state's DMV Web site and learn more about what do to in an automobile accident.

- **Check for injuries.** It's important that you check to see if anyone involved in the accident has any injuries. Do not move any injured parties—you could further harm them.
- **Call the police and cooperate with them.** When the police arrive at the scene, cooperate fully, answering their questions and providing factual information.
- **Find out how to get a copy of the police report**. Very often you will need a copy of the police report to give to your insurance company or to use as evidence in a court proceeding.
- **Obtain vital information.** You must be sure to get the names and addresses of all drivers and passengers involved in the accident; the license plate number, make, and model of all cars involved; the insurance identification numbers of other driver(s); the names and phone numbers of any witnesses; and the names of the police officers on site.
- **Take pictures of the accident scene, if possible.** If you have a camera or camera phone handy, take pictures at the accident scene. If you don't have a camera available, then do a quick sketch of the accident scene.
- **Get in touch with your insurance company.** As soon as possible, contact your insurance agent—most companies have an 800 number you need to call to report an accident—and provide him or her with all the details of the accident.
- **Track all accident-related expenses**. Be sure to keep track of all the expenses resulting from the accident, including car rental fees, lost wages due to missing work, and medical expenses.
- **Be sure to keep copies of all accident-related paperwork.** All information regarding the accident must be documented.
- **Leave a note.** If you hit an unattended vehicle, leave a note on the car's windshield so the owner can contact you. Include at least your name and telephone number.

Figure R-13 PRIMARY U.S. LAWS GOVERNING FINANCE*

Law	Brief explanation
Sarbanes-Oxley Act of 2002	Mandates a number of reforms to enhance corporate responsibility, enhance financial disclosures and combat corporate and accounting fraud
Securities Act of 1993	Requires that investors receive financial and other significant information concerning securities being offered for public sale; prohibits deceit, misrepresentations, and other fraud in the sale of securities
Investment Advisers Act of 1940	Requires that firms or sole practitioners compensated for advising others about securities investments must conform to regulations designed to protect investors
Investment Company Act of 1940	Regulates the organization of companies, including mutual funds, that engage primarily in investing, reinvesting, and trading in securities in order to minimize conflicts of interest that arise in these complex operations
Trust Indenture Act of 1939	Stipulates that bonds and notes may not be offered for sale to the public unless a formal agreement between the issuer of bonds and the bondholder conforms to the standards of this Act
Securities Exchange Act of 1934	Establishes the Securities and Exchange Commission, empowering the SEC with broad authority over all aspects of the securities industry

*For more information on these and other financial laws, check out http://fin.emcp.net/sec.

Source: Securities and Exchange Commission Web site

Figure R-14 PRIMARY U.S. LAWS GOVERNING COMMERCE*

Law	Brief explanation
Truth in Lending Act	Requires a lender to tell you how much it will cost to borrow money so that you can compare the terms of credit offered by different lenders
Fair Credit and Charge Card Disclosure Act	Requires a lender offering you a credit card to fully disclose the terms of your credit agreement
Equal Credit Opportunity Act	Prohibits credit lenders from discriminating against you on the basis of race, color, religion, national origin, sex, familial status, or handicap
Fair Housing Act	Prohibits housing lenders from discriminating against you on the basis of race, color, religion, national origin, sex, familial status, or handicap
Fair Credit Reporting Act	Controls how your credit history is kept by credit bureaus and used by lenders
Real Estate Settlement Procedures Act	States that lenders must give purchasers information about the costs required to close a mortgage loan
Truth in Savings Act	Requires lenders to disclose the terms of their deposit accounts in a uniform way
Electronic Fund Transfer Act	Limits an individual's liability if their ATM card is lost or stolen and calls for investigation and correction of errors made to the account

*For more information on these and other consumer laws, check out http://fin.emcp.net/federalreserve.

Source: U. S. Federal Reserve Board Web site

Figure R-15 STEPS IN THE DECISION-MAKING PROCESS

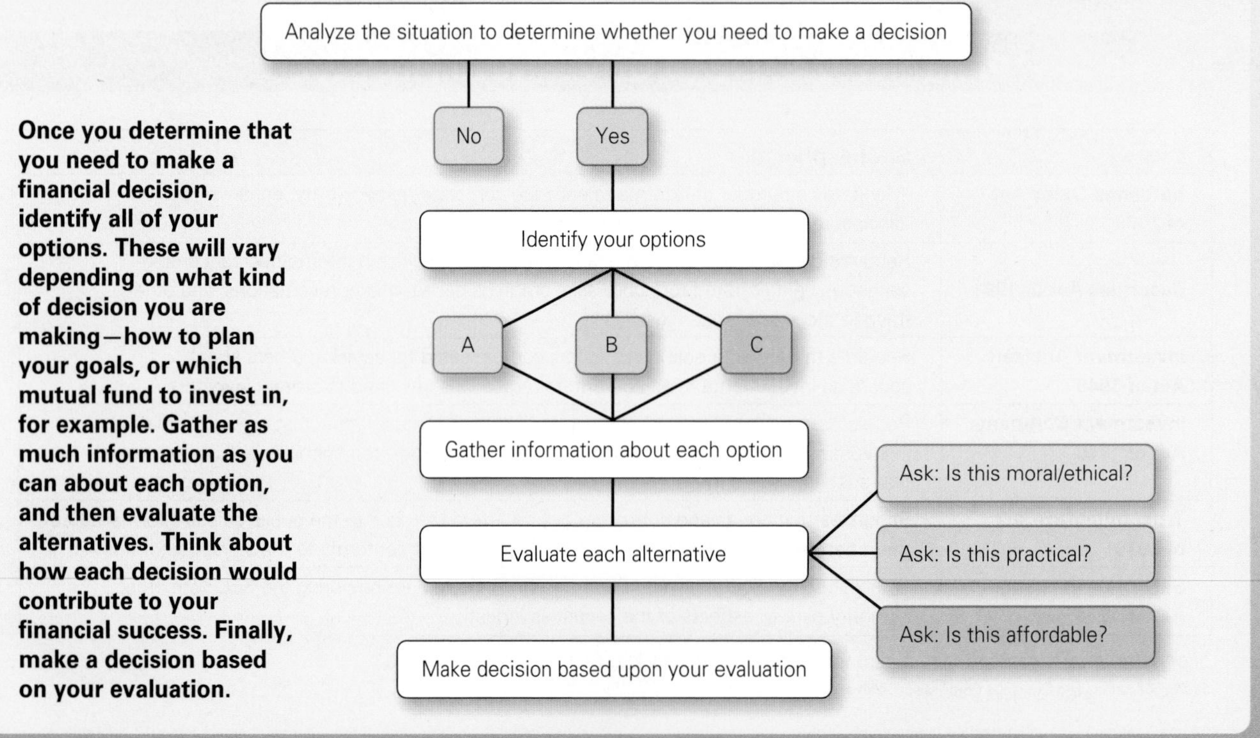

Once you determine that you need to make a financial decision, identify all of your options. These will vary depending on what kind of decision you are making—how to plan your goals, or which mutual fund to invest in, for example. Gather as much information as you can about each option, and then evaluate the alternatives. Think about how each decision would contribute to your financial success. Finally, make a decision based on your evaluation.

Figure R-16 CURRENCY EXCHANGE RATES

If you travel outside the United States or invest in foreign business, you will want to know the exchange rate for your U.S. currency. According to the chart below, it takes 10.73 Mexican pesos to buy one U.S. dollar. These exchange rates are current as of February 2008. Go to http://fin.emcp.net/exchangerate for the most up-to-date currency exchange rates.

Country	Currency	Currency units per U.S. dollar
China	yuan	7.15
European Union	euro	.67
Australia	dollar	1.07
Sweden	krona	6.20
India	rupee	39.77
Mexico	peso	10.73
Japan	yen	107.04
Great Britain	pound	.50

Source: Yahoo.com

Figure R-17 CONSUMER WATCHDOG GROUPS

These consumer watchdog groups exist to help keep you safe. Read the brief explanations to find out the purpose of each one. For links to these and other consumer advocacy organizations, check out http://fin.emcp.net/consumerworld.

Government

- **Federal Trade Commission:** Keeps public informed about competition/consumer issues
- **Federal Reserve Board:** Provides a stable monetary and financial system
- **Securities and Exchange Commission:** Exists to protect investors; maintain fair, orderly, and efficient markets
- **U.S. Consumer Product Safety Commission:** Safeguards the public from unreasonable risks
- **Consumer Action Web site:** Offers assistance with consumer questions and/or problems

Consumer organizations

- **Better Business Bureau:** Provides information to the public to help them identify trustworthy businesses and charities
- **Center for Study of Responsive Law:** Offers reports on a number of public interest issues
- **Consumer Credit Counseling Service:** Offers free credit counseling and debt assistance

Net fraud fighters

- **http://fin.emcp.net/sec:** Reports on financial swindles with lots of information on scams and tips to avoid getting victimized
- **http://fin.emcp.net/scambusters:** Provides information on Internet-based scams

Public service sites

- **Consumer Reports Online:** Provides information on product recalls, shopping guidance, ratings, and the like.
- **Insurance Information Institute:** Offers information, analysis, and referrals on auto, home, and business insurance
- **nolo.com Self-Help Law Center:** Provides online legal assistance for individuals

Glossary

account statement the official monthly list of transactions that the bank has recorded

adjustable-rate mortgage (ARM) a home loan with an interest rate that might increase or decrease during the life of the loan

adjusted gross income total income *minus* certain adjustments and reductions such as contributions to a retirement account, interest on a student loan, and exemptions claimed on Form W-4

advertising agencies agencies whose job is to promote brand names and persuade consumers to buy goods and services

altruism selfless concern for the welfare of others

Amtrak the federally subsidized National Railroad Passenger Corporation that operates trains in the United States

annual percentage rate (APR) the amount of interest expressed as a yearly rate

annual percentage yield (APY) the amount of interest that a deposit would earn after compounding for one year, expressed as a percentage

annual report a detailed report about the financial condition of a company, published each year

annuity an investment that guarantees regular payments to the holder, usually beginning at retirement and continuing for a fixed number of years or until death

application form a questionnaire that helps an employer determine whether or not an applicant is qualified for a job and should come in for an interview

appraisal a professional estimate of the market value of a property

apprenticeship program an education that combines on-the-job training with formal classroom instruction

arbitration a process for settling disputes by allowing an unbiased third party to decide the outcome

articles of incorporation the primary rules governing the management of a corporation

assets money or anything else of value that a person or an organization owns

Automated Clearing House (ACH) an electronic system for transferring money between banks

automated teller machine (ATM) a computerized electronic machine that performs basic banking functions

bankruptcy a legal process in which a person or business declares the inability to repay debts

bear market condition that exists when investors are pessimistic about the economy and the market goes down

beneficiary a person named to receive the benefits from an insurance policy

Better Business Bureau (BBB) a nonprofit organization that tries to resolve disputes between consumers and businesses

Blue Book a widely used guide to used-car values, published by the Kelley Blue Book Company

blue-chip stocks safe investments in the ownership of large, respected, and well-established companies

bodily injury liability coverage auto insurance coverage that pays for expenses related to injuries or deaths caused by the policyholder's car

bond a promise to pay a certain amount on a certain date, issued by a corporation or government for the purpose of borrowing money

boycott to protest a product by refusing to buy it

brand the name that identifies a product or manufacturer

broker a person who works for a brokerage firm and who buys and sells stocks, bonds, and securities for clients

budget a plan for how to use your money during a given time based on expected income

budget deficit a situation in which there is not enough money to cover expenses

budget surplus a situation in which money is left over after all expenses have been paid

bull market condition that exists when investors are optimistic about the economy and the market goes up

capital gain the profit from the sale of assets such as stocks, bonds, or real estate

cash flow the amount of money you take in (income) and give out (expenses)

cash flow statement a summary of receipts and payments for a given period of time; also called an *income and expense statement*

caveat emptor a Latin phrase meaning "Let the buyer beware," warning consumers about a seller's doubtful claims

certificate of deposit (CD) a savings alternative in which money is left on deposit for a stated period of time to earn a specific rate of interest

certification seals labels placed on products certifying that they meet safety or performance standards set by an industry or private organization

check a preprinted form ordering a bank to withdraw money from an account and pay it to someone else

checking account a bank account that allows the account holder to withdraw money, pay a bill, or make a purchase by writing checks

class-action suit a lawsuit filed by one party on behalf of a large group of individuals who all have the same complaint

COBRA a federal law (the Consolidate Omnibus Budget Reconciliation Act) that allows employees, spouses, and dependent children to continue their group insurance coverage for a period of time after they leave the job or lose insurance coverage for some other specified reason

coinsurance the percentage of expenses the policyholder must pay in addition to the deductible amount

collateral a valuable asset that a borrower must give up if the loan is not repaid

collectibles items that appeal to collectors and investors, including stamps, works of art, antiques, and sports memorabilia

collision coverage insurance coverage for accident damage to the policyholder's car

commercial bank the most common type of financial institution—privately owned, offering a wide range of services, and run to make a profit

commission a percentage of the total sale, paid to an employee instead of, or in addition to, salary or wages

commodities bulk items such as grains, metals, and food that are bought and sold on a commodities exchange

common stock a stock whose owner has voting rights and receives dividends based on company profits, paid out after preferred stockholders receive their dividends

community college a two-year college that offers an associate's degree; also called a *junior college* or a *city college*

commuter service public transportation systems that bring people from the suburbs or nearby communities into cities

company policy handbook a booklet outlining a company's rules, policies, and procedures

comparison shopping researching various brands to buy the highest quality item at the lowest price

competent parties the requirement in a contract that all parties understand what they are doing

compounding interest figuring interest earnings on both the original amount *and* any previous interest that has been added to the balance

comprehensive coverage insurance coverage for damage to the policyholder's car resulting from things other than an accident, such as a natural disaster, theft, or vandalism

condominium multifamily housing in which the units are owned by individuals and the common grounds and building structure are owned jointly by the unit owners

consideration the requirement in a contract that money or something of value is exchanged

consumers people who acquire goods and services

consumer action panels (CAPs) groups of people not employed in an industry who try to resolve consumer complaints about the industry

consumer advocates those who support the interests of consumers through activities such as testing products and services, lobbying, and reporting on products and services

Consumers' Bill of Rights a list of consumer rights, including the right to safety, the right to be informed, the right to choose, and the right to be heard

contract a legal agreement between two or more parties

co-pay a flat fee that the policyholder pays directly to the provider for each doctor visit, test, treatment, or prescription drug, with the insurance company paying the balance

corporation a business owned by a group of stockholders

cosign to act as joint signer on a loan or contract, guaranteeing payment if the primary signer does not meet the requirements

cover letter a short letter to accompany a résumé, introducing the applicant to an employer and explaining why the applicant would do a good job for the company

credit any positive addition to an account balance; or, an agreement in which someone purchases something now but promises to pay for it later

credit bureau an agency that collects and sells personal credit information about individuals

credit cards plastic cards issued by banks, retail stores, and other businesses that allow the user to buy products or services on credit, with an interest charge if the balance is not paid in full by the due date

credit counselors individuals who are trained to give advice on handling money and getting out of debt

credit fraud the theft and illegal use of someone else's credit information

credit score a number based on information in a credit report, indicating the person's credit risk

credit slip a document, also called a store credit, stating that a customer is entitled to merchandise from the store equal to a certain dollar amount

credit unions nonprofit financial institutions that are owned by their members and organized for the members' benefit

customer advocate an organization that offers unbiased information about product choices

debit any transaction that removes funds from an account, including cash withdrawals, checks written on the account, and fees charged by the bank

debit card a plastic card used to withdraw cash from a checking account or make payments electronically without having to write a check

debt management plan (DMP) a plan for paying off debt, in which the consumer deposits money each month with the credit counseling service, and the service uses the money to pay the debts

deductible the amount paid out-of-pocket by the policyholder before the insurance company pays benefits on a claim

deductions amounts subtracted from gross pay, such as Social Security tax, federal and state income tax withholding, health insurance, retirement, and so forth; also refers to expenses that are subtracted from income on a tax return

deed a written document transferring ownership of property from one person to another

deposit an addition of funds to an account balance

deposit slip a document that accompanies bank deposits, showing the account holder's name and account number and the amount to be deposited

depreciation the decline in value of a car or other property due to age

deregulation the removal of government regulations on businesses in order to encourage free operation in the marketplace

disability insurance insurance coverage that supplies a portion of lost income if the policyholder is unable to work due to illness or injury

discretionary income income left over after savings and essential expenses have been accounted for

dividends company earnings distributed to shareholders, usually in the form of money or stock

dormitory a college or university building containing living quarters for students

Dow Jones Industrial Average a daily average of the stock prices of thirty of the largest and richest blue-chip companies in the United States, used to measure changes in stock market activity

emergency fund money set aside for unexpected expenses

employment agencies companies and institutions that help people find jobs or that find people to fill jobs

endorsement a modification or addition to an insurance policy; also called a *rider*

entrepreneur someone who organizes, manages, and assumes the risks of owning a business

entrepreneurship the skills related to organizing, managing, and taking on the risks of owning a business

equity the value of a home minus the amount still owed on it

escrow account money, documents, or other valuable items that are held by a third party for safekeeping, until the requirements of a contract are met and the deal is closed

estate tax a tax collected when someone dies and passes wealth along to a family member or other heir

estimate an educated guess or ballpark figure, based on the information you have

exclusions items that an insurance policy does not cover

exemptions another word for *tax allowances*

exempt status a release from paying taxes because of insufficient income

expenses the things people pay for with their money

expiration date a date printed on food packaging that indicates the last day a food is acceptable for its intended use

Fair Access to Insurance Requirements (FAIR) Plan a program to provide property insurance for those whose property is located in areas with high exposure to hazards they cannot control

finance charges the costs of using credit, including interest, late charges, and other fees

financial adviser a person with the knowledge to give financial advice based on the client's goals, income, debts and assets, stage in life, and other personal factors

financial records documents such as bank statements, receipts, contracts, tax records, and bills, containing the history of how someone's money is spent

financial transaction any exchange of money between two or more businesses or individuals

fixed expenses expenses—such as rent or mortgage, health insurance premiums, and student loan payments—that stay the same from month to month and must be paid no matter what

fixed-rate mortgage a home loan with an interest rate that does not change during the life of the loan

flexible spending account (FSA) a plan that allows employees to set aside pretax dollars from their paycheck, to be used during the year for medical expenses not covered by insurance; also called a *cafeteria plan*

flextime a work schedule with flexible hours

foreclosure the legal process that a lender uses to take possession of a house and sell it when a borrower fails to make mortgage payments

Form W-4 an IRS form indicating how much should be withheld from an employee's earnings to pay federal income taxes

Form W-2 an IRS document from an employer showing the total amount of money withheld from an employee's paychecks throughout the year

Fortune 500 a list of the 500 U.S. companies with highest earnings, published yearly by *Fortune* magazine

401(k) plan a tax-deferred retirement plan funded by regular contributions from the employee

403(b) plan a tax-deferred retirement plan for employees of public schools and tax-exempt organizations

franchise a legal contract allowing an individual or group to operate a business in the name of a recognized company

franchisee the person who operates a franchise

franchisor the recognized company under which a franchise operates

futures contracts to buy or sell a specific commodity or financial instrument at a set price on a set date in the future

garnishment a court order allowing all or part of a person's wages to be paid directly to the person's creditors

generic products products that carry no brand name, with packaging that simply describes the contents

grace period a period of time, usually twenty to thirty days, when interest is not charged on current credit card purchases

grants payments or property given to people or institutions, which do not have to be paid back

gross pay the total amount of wages or salary earned before any deductions are subtracted

health savings account (HSA) a tax-free savings account that the owner can use to pay for medical expenses not covered by insurance; available only to people with high deductibles

house brands "private label" product names found only in one chain of supermarkets

housing subsidies grants of money from the U.S. government that help low-income families pay their housing costs

identity theft the act of gathering enough information about a person to assume his or her identity, and then using that identity to commit fraud or other crimes

income money earned in exchange for work, or received from investments, allowance, or gifts

income tax a tax figured as a percentage of someone's earnings

individual retirement account (IRA) a personal retirement plan that permits individuals to set aside money; with the contributions and earnings not taxed until the funds are withdrawn

inheritance an amount of money, property, or an object of value, given by someone who has died

in-service training employee classes for developing skills, providing information, and improving working relationships among employees; also called *professional development seminars*

installment credit a loan repaid with interest in equal amounts over a set period of time

intercity public transportation public transportation connecting cities, usually involving buses, trains, and airplanes

interest the cost of using money—paid by banks to their depositors, and paid by borrowers to the institutions that provide their loan

interview a formal meeting between an employer and a job applicant

investing committing money to an enterprise in order to earn a financial return

invoice price the price the dealer pays the manufacturer for the car

job leads information about possible job openings

job sharing a situation in which two or more employees share the same job

keywords the words and phrases in a résumé that a computer program will search for to determine whether an applicant is qualified for a job

landlord the owner of property that is leased or rented to a tenant

layaway plan a purchase option in which the customer makes a small down payment and the retailer holds the item until the customer pays in full

learning networks online discussions in which participants share skills and knowledge

"lemon" laws laws providing relief for people who buy new cars that do not meet basic standards of quality and performance

liabilities money or other debts that a person or an organization owes

liability in insurance, responsibility for damages caused

liens financial claims against a property

limited liability company (LLC) a relatively new type of corporate arrangement whose owners have limited personal liability for the debts and actions of the company, and with other features more like a partnership

line of credit an approved loan amount that can be used at the borrower's discretion

liquidity the ability of an asset to be quickly and easily converted into cash

load funds mutual funds that charge a commission every time shares are bought or sold

loan a temporary transfer of funds from one person or company to another, to be repaid over time with additional money paid as interest

loan consolidation combining two or more existing loans into a single new loan, usually to reduce monthly payments or obtain a lower interest rate

loan sharks people who loan money illegally and set very high interest rates

long-term goals things to be obtained or achieved in ten or more years

loss leaders sale items deliberately sold at a loss but designed to attract customers into the store

managed care health insurance that focuses on managing the overall cost, use, and quality of the health care system

manufactured homes homes that are built in a factory and towed to the home site, where they are installed

marketing tactics advertising methods that rely on human nature and emotional responses to sell products

mass transit public transportation in an urban area

mediator a person who helps two parties settle a dispute

Medicaid a government-funded medical assistance program for certain low-income individuals and families

medical payments coverage insurance coverage for medical bills of the policyholder and his or her family members involved in an accident

Medicare a federally funded health insurance program for people at least 65 years old and others with certain disabilities

medium-term goals things to be obtained or achieved in five to ten years

mentor a more experienced person who offers advice and support to guide someone's career decisions

miles per gallon (MPG) the average number of miles a car travels on one gallon of gasoline

money market account a type of savings account that invests in securities

money order a financial instrument, purchased at a bank or post office, that orders a specified amount of money to be paid to a specified person or organization

monopoly a market with only one seller or producer

mortgage a long-term loan made on a home or other real estate property

multifamily housing housing that features two or more family dwellings within the same building

mutual assent the requirement in a contract that all parties agree on the terms

mutual fund an investment in which people pool their money to buy stocks, bonds, real estate, or other assets selected by professional managers

NASDAQ the largest U.S. stock market in terms of number of companies listed and number of shares traded per day—all done electronically through a network of computers

national brands heavily advertised product names that are found in stores around the country

net pay the amount received after all deductions have been subtracted from a paycheck; also called *take-home pay*

networking the process of building professional relationships that will assist both parties in reaching their goals

net worth the difference in value between total assets and total liabilities

New York Stock Exchange (NYSE) the world's largest stock market in terms of dollar volume

no-load funds mutual funds that do not require an up-front fee

North American Free Trade Agreement (NAFTA) a treaty signed by the United States, Mexico, and Canada that called for gradual elimination of tariffs and other trade restrictions on goods produced and sold in North America

nutrient density the amount of nutrients in a food, compared with the number of calories

oligopoly a market with a limited number of sellers or producers

opportunity cost the cost of giving up one thing to get something else

options contracts that give the owner the right, but not the obligation, to buy or sell a stock or commodity at a set price on or before a specified date

organic foods healthy foods produced without the use of pesticides, chemical fertilizers, antibiotics, or hormones

origination fee a fee for starting the paperwork on a loan

overdraft fee a penalty payment for having a negative balance in an account

overruns garments or products resulting from excess production

overtime hours worked in addition to the legal limit of forty hours per week

pack date a date printed on food packaging that indicates when the item was manufactured, processed, or packaged

partnership a business with co-owners, in which both parties are legally joined together

payday lenders companies that make small short-term, high-interest loans to tide a person over "until payday"

penny stocks high-risk stocks that typically sell for less than $1 per share when they are first offered

pension a retirement plan that is funded at least in part by an employer

personal data sheet a detailed list of personal information, which you bring to a job interview, that makes filling out the application easier

personal injury protection (PIP) optional insurance that pays expanded benefits for the policyholder's medical care, lost wages, and certain other services

personal property coverage insurance coverage that pays if personal property is stolen, damaged, or destroyed by fire or some other disaster

philanthropy the act of giving away money, goods, services, or time to support a cause

plan of action a list of the steps needed to reach a career goal

portal site a Web site that serves as an entrance to other related sites on the Internet

preapproval the process of obtaining an official commitment for a mortgage loan prior to making an offer to buy a home

preferred stock a stock whose owner has no voting rights, but receives a fixed dividend, paid before common stockholders receive their dividends

premium the rate charged for an insurance policy

preventive maintenance automotive service intended to keep a car running well and to prevent major problems

principal the amount of money originally borrowed or still owed, on which interest is charged; also the amount of money deposited or invested, on which interest is credited

product standards standards, set by government agencies, that specify requirements for particular products

profit-sharing plan a retirement plan that allows employees to share in the company's profits

property damage liability coverage auto insurance coverage for damage caused by the policyholder's car to another person's property

property tax a tax that owners pay on their land or homes; sometimes called *real estate tax*

pull date a date printed on food packaging that indicates the last day a store should sell the item (but not the last day it can be eaten)

pyramid scheme a fraudulent system in which money from new investors is used to pay profits to earlier investors

quotas legal limits on the amount of a good that can be imported

real estate land and any houses or other buildings that are on it

reconciling matching one's personal account records with the bank's records

replacement cost coverage insurance coverage that pays to replace the insured item at today's prices

repossessed taken back because of missed loan payments

résumé a summary of a job applicant's personal information, education, skills, work experience, and special interests

return earnings from a savings account or profit from an investment

revolving account a charge account that has a credit limit but does not have to be paid in full before the borrower can make further purchases

Roth IRA a personal retirement plan in which the original contributions are not tax-deductible, but the earnings are tax-free

royalties a percentage of the sales in dollars paid to an author, songwriter, or inventor when copies of his or her creation are sold

salary pay that is a fixed amount, regardless of the hours worked

sales receipt a document that verifies the purchase of an item from a particular store, including the date of sale and the price paid

sales tax a tax that people pay when they make a purchase

S&P 500 index an indicator of overall stock market performance based on the average stock prices of 500 top U.S. companies, compiled by Standard & Poor's

savings account a bank account in which money is deposited for safekeeping

savings and loan associations (S&Ls) financial institutions that originally provided home loans but now offer most of the same services as a bank

savings bonds nontransferable bonds issued by the U.S. government initially sold at half their face value

secured loans loans that are backed up by collateral combining two or more existing loans into a single new loan, usually to reduce monthly payments or obtain a lower interest rate

securities documents indicating ownership—such as stock certificates, bonds, or Treasury bills—that can be bought and sold in the investment markets

security deposit a sum of money a tenant gives to the landlord before moving in, to cover any damage to the property while the tenant lives there

service-learning a teaching method that combines service to the community with classroom studies

Share Save Spend® system an approach to money management that divides funds into three categories—sharing, saving, and spending—according to the investor's values

short-term goals things to be obtained or achieved in the next five years

signature authorization form a document that leaves the account holder's signature on file with the bank to prevent fraud

Simplified Employee Pension (SEP-IRA) a tax-deferred retirement plan for small businesses and self-employed people, in which the employer makes contributions directly to employee IRA accounts

small-claims courts courts without lawyers, settling disputes over small amounts of money

Social Security the federal program that people pay into while they are working, that pays disability, retirement, and life insurance benefits to eligible recipients

sole proprietorship a business owned by one person

sticker price the retail price that the manufacturer sets for the car

stock an investment in the ownership of a corporation, usually represented by shares of the business

stock-bonus plan a type of profit-sharing plan in which the employer rewards employees with company stock instead of cash

stop-payment order a request that a bank or another financial institution not cash a particular check

structural damage coverage insurance coverage for damage to the physical structure of a home resulting from fire, severe weather, or other disasters listed in the policy

tariffs taxes on goods imported into a country

tax allowances amounts calculated on the Form W-4 that reduce the federal tax withheld from a person's paycheck

tax deductions expenses subtracted from adjusted gross income before figuring a person's taxable income

taxes the money that people pay to their local, state, and federal governments to fund government programs and public services

telecommuting working outside the office, usually from home, using a computer

tenant someone who rents or leases property from a landlord

term life insurance an insurance policy that pays a stated benefit upon the policyholder's death, if that death occurs within the term of the policy

tip a voluntary payment that a customer makes to an employee, often based on the quality of service provided

title a document that indicates the legal owner of a vehicle

trade-ins the cars that new-car buyers turn in as partial payment on their new-car purchases

trade school an institution of higher learning that teaches the skilled trades

transfer a movement of funds from one account to another

unit pricing a method of expressing the price of an item per unit of measure, such as cost per ounce or cost per piece

universal default a provision in some credit card contracts that allows the company to review its customers' credit reports and charge a higher default interest rate if a customer's credit score goes down for any reason

universal product code (UPC) the pattern of black and white lines on a package, forming a bar code that identifies the product

Used-Car Rule a federal trade rule requiring dealers to place an informative sticker on every used car, telling the buyer both whether the car is being sold "as is" or with a warranty, and how much of the repair costs the dealer will pay

variable expenses expenses—such as auto repairs, clothing, and medical costs—that vary from month to month

vehicle identification number (VIN) a unique number assigned to a car at the factory for identification purposes

vested being eligible to receive a pension or other employer-contributed benefits, usually after working at a company for a certain number of years

wages pay that is figured at an hourly rate

warranty an official guarantee to replace or repair a product that does not work properly

whole life insurance a permanent insurance policy that protects the policyholder during his or her whole life, paying a death benefit but also building up an additional cash value

WiFi short for *wireless fidelity*, a high-speed Internet connection

withdrawal the removal of cash from an account, either at the bank or at an ATM

withholding the amount deducted from a person's paycheck to pay for taxes and other items such as health insurance and a pension plan

work permit an official document that verifies an employee's age and usually outlines the duties that he or she is allowed to perform

Credits

t = top, b = bottom, l = left, r = right, m = middle

vi(t), Erik Dreyer/Getty; **vi(b),** Ken Mellott/Shutterstock; **vii(t),** Comstock/Corbis; **vii(b),** David Young-Wolff/PhotoEdit; **viii(t),** Image100/Corbis; **viii(b),** Fred Greaves/Corbis; **xii,** Michael Newman/PhotoEdit; **xiii(t),** L. Nagy/Shutterstock; **xiii(m),** Victor Newman/Shutterstock; **xiii(b),** Tan Wei Ming/Shutterstock; **xiv(t),** William Milner/Shutterstock; **xiv(m),** Archetype/Shutterstock; **xiv(b),** Sofos Design/Shutterstock; **xvii,** Jeff Xiong; **2,** Erik Dreyer/Getty; **4(inset),** Lynn Goldsmith/Corbis; **4–5,** Ed Bock/Corbis; **6,** Grady Kimbrell; **7,** Grady Kimbrell; **8,** Courtesy of TerraCycle; **10,** Yuri Arcurs/Shutterstock; **12,** David Young-Wolff/PhotoEdit; **13,** Grady Kimbrell; **14,** Kharidehal Abhirama Ashwin/Shutterstock; **15,** Kim Kulish/Corbis; **16,** © iagora.net; **17(tl),** Nicole Waring/iStockphoto, **17(tr),** Richard Foreman/iStockphoto, **17(ml),** Jacob Wackerhausen/iStockphoto, **17(mr),** Kristian Sekulic/iStockphoto, **17(bt),** Sean Locke/iStockphoto, **17(b),** Ed Hidden/iStockphoto; **18,** Laser222/Shutterstock; **23,** Myrleen Ferguson/PhotoEdit; **27(l),** David Young-Wolff/PhotoEdit; **27(m),** David Young-Wolff/PhotoEdit; **27(r),** Bill Aron/PhotoEdit; **31;** Michael Newman/PhotoEdit; **32(inset);** Suzanne Tucker/Shutterstock; **32–33,** Zsolt Nyulaszi/istockphoto; **34(l),** Elena Elisseeva/Shutterstock; **34(r),** Gabriel Moisa/Shutterstock; **36,** Spencer Grant/PhotoEdit; **39,** Phil Date/Shutterstock; **42,** David Young-Wolff/PhotoEdit; **44,** Grady Kimbrell; **45,** Grady Kimbrell; **46,** Katrina Brown/Shutterstock; **47,** Grady Kimbrell; **48,** Myrleen Ferguson/PhotoEdit; **49(l),** Grady Kimbrell; **49(r),** Marten Czamanske/Shutterstock; **52,** Ariel Skelley/Corbis; **53(t),** Ed Bock/Corbis; **53(l),** Morgan Lane/Shutterstock; **53(r),** Chuck Savage/Corbis; **55,** Hespenheide Design; **57,** Grady Kimbrell; **60–61,** Ken Mellott/Shutterstock; **62(inset),** Ryasick/Shutterstock; **62–63,** Goncalo Veloso de Figueiredo/Shutterstock; **64,** Thinkstock/Corbis; **66,** Michael Newman/PhotoEdit; **67,** Edyta Pawlowska/Shutterstock; **68(l),** JC Hix/Shutterstock; **68(r),** Suzanne Tucker/Shutterstock; **68(b),** Stavchansky Yakov/Shutterstock; **69,** David Young-Wolff/PhotoEdit; **70,** Penelope Berger/Shutterstock; **72,** Andi Berger/Shutterstock; **73,** Andresr/Shutterstock; **74,** Bobby Deal/Shutterstock; **76,** Naashon Zalk/Corbis; **77,** Bob Daemmrich/PhotoEdit; **78,** Michael Newman/PhotoEdit; **79,** David Young-Wolff/PhotoEdit; **80,** Ariel Skelley/Corbis; **81,** Geir Olav Lyngfjell/Shutterstock; **83,** Carsten Reisinger/Shutterstock; **84,** Frank Herzog/Shutterstock; **85,** Radu Razvan/Shutterstock; **86;** Galina Barskaya/Shutterstock; **92(inset),** Anne Kitzman/Shutterstock; **92–93,** Thinkstock/Corbis; **94,** Clayton Sharrard/PhotoEdit; **95(t),** Nicholas Monu/istockphoto; **95(b),** Digitalskillet/istockphoto; **96,** Gideon Mendel/Corbis; **98,** Gabe Palmer/Corbis; **99,** Jörg Jahn/Shutterstock; **100,** David Young-Wolff/PhotoEdit; **101(l),** DivaNir4a/istockphoto; **101(r),** Pattie Steib/Shutterstock; **102,** Grady Kimbrell; **103,** Asiana/Shutterstock; **105(t),** Gabriela Trojanowska/Shutterstock; **105(l),** Jeff Greenberg/PhotoEdit; **105(r),** Jaimie Duplass/Shutterstock; **106,** Grady Kimbrell; **107,** David N. Madden/Shutterstock; **108,** Timothy R. Nichols/Shutterstock; **110,** David Davis/Shutterstock; **112(t),** Pakhnyushcha/Shutterstock; **112(b),** Tony Freeman/PhotoEdit; **115,** Tom Stewart/Corbis; **117,** Anthony Berenyi/Shutterstock; **118(inset),** Valentyn Volkov/Shutterstock; **118–119,** Chuck Savage/Corbis; **121,** Ryan McVay/GettyImages; **122(l),** Park Street/PhotoEdit; **122(r),** Annette Coolidge/PhotoEdit; **123,** Patrick McCall/Shutterstock; **127,** Ariel Skelley/Corbis; **128,** Elena Elisseeva/Shutterstock; **129,** Grady Kimbrell; **132,** Philip James Corwin/Corbis; **133,** Grady Kimbrell; **140(t),** Comstock/Corbis; **140(b),** Nuno Silva/iStockphoto; **141,** Quavondo Nguyen/iStockphoto; **142,** James Steidl/Shutterstock; **143,** Image Source/Corbis; **146–147(l),** Comstock/Corbis; **146–147(r),** Tom Fewster/istockphoto; **148(inset),** David Frazier/Corbis; **148–149,** Christy Thompson/Shutterstock; **151(t),** Andresr/Shutterstock; **151(b),** Grady Kimbrell; **152(tl),** Igor Terekhov/Shutterstock; **152(bl),** Keellla/Shutterstock; **152(m),** Yuganov Konstantin/Shutterstock; **152(tr),** Ene/Shutterstock; **152(br),** Koksharov Dmitry/Shutterstock; **153,** Robynrg/Shutterstock; **154,** Diego Cervo/Shutterstock; **156,** Kayte M. Deioma/PhotoEdit; **157,** Susan Van Etten/PhotoEdit; **160,** Grady Kimbrell; **161,** Dariusz Urbanczyk/Shutterstock; **162,** Grady Kimbrell; **164(l),** Jennifer Nickert/Shutterstock; **164(r),** Bill Aron/PhotoEdit; **165,** Kayte M. Deioma/PhotoEdit; **166,** Pling/Shutterstock; **167,** Robert Brenner/PhotoEdit; **170(inset),** Dann Tardif/Corbis; **170–171,** Richard Ustinich/GettyImages/The Image Bank; **173,** Charles O'Rear/Corbis; **175,** Michal Mrozek/Shutterstock; **176,** Bernard Bisson/Corbis; **178,** K. Geijer/Shutterstock; **181(l),** Terrance Emerson/Shutterstock; **181(r),** Javier Barbancho/Corbis; **182,** Reuters/Corbis; **185,** Grady Kimbrell; **186(t),** Lisa F. Young/Shutterstock; **186(b),** Steven Pepple/Shutterstock; **187,** Mary Kate Denny/PhotoEdit; **188,** Jerry Arcieri/Corbis; **188,** David Young-Wolff/PhotoEdit; **189,** Ausloeser/Corbis; **190,** Helen King/Corbis; **191,** James Leynse/Corbis; **193,** Leonora Hamill/Getty; **194,** Image Source/Corbis; **195,** Robyn Beck/Getty; **197,** Tetra Images/Corbis; **198,** David Young-Wolff/PhotoEdit; **200(inset),** Zave Smith/Corbis; **200–201,** Yuri Arcurs/Shutterstock; **202,** Jason Stitt/Shutterstock; **203(l),** Randy Faris/Corbis; **203(r),** Edyta Pawlowska/Shutterstock; **204,** Tyler Olson/Shutterstock; **206,** Roy McMahon/Corbis; **207,** Image

100/Corbis; **208,** Spencer Grant/PhotoEdit; **211(b),** Greg Vote/Corbis; **211(t),** Alexander Yakovlev/Shutterstock; **212,** Serge Krouglikoff/Corbis; **213,** George Tiedemann/Corbis; **215,** Dave Cutler/Corbis; **216(t),** Jack Howard/Corbis; **216(b),** Kim Kulish/Corbis; **217,** Mascarucci/Corbis; **218,** Josh Gosfield/Corbis; **220,** Tokyo Space Club/Corbis; **221,** RichVintage/istockphoto; **221,** Copyright 2006 by Consumers Union of U.S., Inc. Yonkers, NY 10703-1057, a nonprofit organization. Reprinted with permission from ConsumerReports.org® for educational purposes only. No commercial use or reproduction permitted. www.ConsumerReports.org.; **222,** James Leynse/Corbis; **223,** Radius Images/Masterfile; **225,** Hespenheide Design; **226(inset),** Gabe Palmer/Corbis; **226–227,** Irina Tischenko/Shutterstock; **228,** Grady Kimbrell; **229,** Grady Kimbrell; **230,** Sn4ke/Shutterstock; **231,** Justin Sullivan/Getty; **232,** David Young-Wolff/PhotoEdit; **233,** Autobytel; **234,** Grady Kimbrell; **235,** Grady Kimbrell; **236,** Michael Newman/PhotoEdit; **238,** Franco Vogt/Corbis; **239,** Grady Kimbrell; **240,** Grady Kimbrell; **242,** Tom Grill/Corbis; **245(all),** Grady Kimbrell; **247,** Thinkstock/Corbis; **250(inset),** Pixland/Corbis; **250(t),** Amy Walters/Shutterstock; **250(b),** CJPhoto/Shutterstock; **251,** Image Werks/Corbis; **252,** Ron Chapple/Corbis; **254,** Lori Howard/Shutterstock; **256,** Gary Conner/PhotoEdit; **258(t),** Grady Kimbrell; **258(b),** Wolfgang Kaehler/Corbis; **259,** Grady Kimbrell; **264,** Robert J. Beyers II/Shutterstock; **266,** Bob Rowan/Corbis; **267,** Tony Freeman/PhotoEdit; **268,** Moodboard/Corbis; **270,** Grady Kimbrell; **271,** Grady Kimbrell; **272,** © Realtor.org; **273,** Tomasz Trojanowski/Shutterstock; **274,** Bartosz Ostrowski/Shutterstock; **275,** Moodboard/Corbis; **277,** Tomasz Pietryszek/Shutterstock; **278(inset),** David Young-Wolff/PhotoEdit; **278(t),** Grady Kimbrell; **278(b),** Steve Prezant/Corbis; **279(t),** Grady Kimbrell; **279(b),** Darren Greenwood/Corbis; **281,** Lucy Schaeffer/Kenny Lao; **281,** Artiga Photo/Corbis; **283,** Bloomimage/Corbis; **284(all),** Grady Kimbrell; **287,** Michael Newman/PhotoEdit; **288,** Leah-Anne Thompson/Shutterstock; **289(all),** Grady Kimbrell; **290(all),** Grady Kimbrell; **293,** Colin Young-Wolff/PhotoEdit; **294,** Grady Kimbrell; **295,** Grady Kimbrell; **297,** Courtesy of BettyRides; **298,** Grady Kimbrell; **302(inset),** Bloomimage/Corbis; **302–303,** Owaki-Kulla/Corbis; **304,** Grady Kimbrell; **306,** Grady Kimbrell; **308,** Grady Kimbrell; **309,** Greg Vote/Corbis; **313(l),** NHTSA; **313(r),** NHTSA; **314(t),** David Young-Wolff/PhotoEdit; **314(bl),** Tony Freeman/PhotoEdit; **314(bm),** Edward Bock/Corbis; **314(br),** Artiga Photo/Corbis; **317,** Galushko Sergey/Shutterstock; **319,** David Young-Wolff/Shutterstock; **320,** Grady Kimbrell; **327,** Alexander Maksimenko/Shutterstock; **328–329,** Image100/Corbis; **330(inset),** Burke/Triolo Productions/Brand X/Corbis; **330–331,** Tim Pannell/Corbis; **333,** Tracy Kahn/Corbis; **334,** Push Pictures/Solus-Veer/Corbis; **335,** Catalin Plesa/Shutterstock; **338,** Tetra Images/Corbis; **340,** Tammy Peluso/istockphoto; **342,** Grady Kimbrell; **343,** Alan Levenson/Corbis; **344,** Feng Yu/Shutterstock; **345,** Alan Schein/Corbis; **346,** Hespenheide Design; **347,** Pippa West/Shutterstock; **348,** Ariel Skelley/Corbis; **349,** Michael Newman/PhotoEdit; **350,** Grady Kimbrell; **351,** Grady Kimbrell; **352,** David Young-Wolff/PhotoEdit; **356(inset),** Grady Kimbrell; **356–357,** Bob Daemmrich/PhotoEdit; **362,** Karen Kasmauski/Corbis; **364,** Susan Van Etten/PhotoEdit; **366,** Randy Faris/Corbis; **367,** Stephen Lovekin/Getty; **368,** Art-Line Productions/Brand X/Corbis; **370,** Image100/Corbis; **373,** Agb/Shutterstock; **374,** Ekaterina Monakhova/istockphoto; **376,** Ariel Skelley/Corbis; **377,** Ramin Talaie/Corbis; **378,** David Young-Wolff/PhotoEdit; **379,** Holger Winkler/Corbis; **382–383,** Fred Greaves/Corbis; **384(inset),** Tobias Machhaus/Shutterstock; **385,** Vuk Vukmirovic/Shutterstock; **387,** Keith Muratori/Shutterstock; **388,** Rachel Epstein/PhotoEdit; **389,** Aaron Whitney/Shutterstock; **390,** Hespenheide Design; **392,** David Young-Wolff/PhotoEdit; **393,** Insurance.com © 2008 All Rights Reserved; **394,** David Young-Wolff/PhotoEdit; **395,** Jim Craigmyle/Corbis; **396,** Peter Steiner/Corbis; **397,** Don Hammond/Design Pics/Corbis; **400,** Stuart Westmorland/Corbis; **401,** Paul Barton/Corbis; **402,** Andrea Rugg/Corbis; **403,** Peter Byron/PhotoEdit; **404(t),** Yenwen Lu/istockphoto; **404(b),** Rudi Tapper/istockphoto; **405,** Raymond Gehman/Corbis; **407,** David Young-Wolff/PhotoEdit; **408(inset),** Grady Kimbrell; **408–409,** Ed Kashi/Corbis; **411,** Michael Newman/PhotoEdit; **412,** Spencer Grant/PhotoEdit; **413,** Sandy Huffaker/Getty; **414,** Iofoto/Shutterstock; **416,** Spencer Grant/PhotoEdit; **418,** Myrleen Ferguson Cate/PhotoEdit; **420,** Curt Ziegler/Shutterstock; **421,** Naomi Bassitt/istockphoto; **422,** Mark William Richardson/Shutterstock; **425,** Myrleen Ferguson Cate/PhotoEdit; **427,** Sean Nel/Shutterstock; **430(l),** Kharidehal Abhirama Ashwin/Shutterstock; **430(tm),** Oktay Ortakcioglu/istockphoto; **430(tr),** Bill Bachmann/PhotoEdit; **430(bm),** Olivier Le Queinec/Shutterstock; **430(br),** Gina Smith/Shutterstock; **431(t),** Jason Stitt/Shutterstock; **431(ml),** Jaimie Duplass/Shutterstock; **431(mc),** Prism_68/Shutterstock; **431(mr),** Laura Stone/Shutterstock; **431(bl),** Cornel Achirei/Shutterstock; **431(br),** Grady Kimbrell; **433(t),** Andresr/Shutterstock; **433(b),** Nathan Dungan; **439,** Peter Baxter/Shutterstock; **441,** Envision/Corbis; **442(t),** Chet Mitchell/Shutterstock; **442(b),** Catherine Karnow/Corbis.

Index

C

D

G

H

I

J

P

T